Cognitive and Emotional Processes in Web-Based Education:
Integrating Human Factors and Personalization

Constantinos Mourlas
National & Kapodistrian University of Athens, Greece

Nikos Tsianos
National & Kapodistrian University of Athens, Greece

Panagiotis Germanakos
National & Kapodistrian University of Athens, Greece

INFORMATION SCIENCE REFERENCE

Hershey · New York

Director of Editorial Content:	Kristin Klinger
Senior Managing Editor:	Jamie Snavely
Managing Editor:	Jeff Ash
Assistant Managing Editor:	Carole Coulson
Typesetter:	Jennifer Johnson, Sean Woznicki
Cover Design:	Lisa Tosheff
Printed at:	Yurchak Printing Inc.

Published in the United States of America by
Information Science Reference (an imprint of IGI Global)
701 E. Chocolate Avenue,
Hershey PA 17033
Tel: 717-533-8845
Fax: 717-533-8661
E-mail: cust@igi-global.com
Web site: http://www.igi-global.com/reference

and in the United Kingdom by
Information Science Reference (an imprint of IGI Global)
3 Henrietta Street
Covent Garden
London WC2E 8LU
Tel: 44 20 7240 0856
Fax: 44 20 7379 0609
Web site: http://www.eurospanbookstore.com

Library of Congress Cataloging-in-Publication Data

Cognitive and emotional processes in Web-based education : integrating human factors and personalization / Constantinos Mourlas, Nikos Tsianos, and Panagiotis Germanakos, editors.

  p. cm.

 Includes bibliographical references and index.
 Summary: "This book presents theories and practical frameworks to assist educators and trainers in developing e-learning applications"-- Provided by publisher.

 ISBN 978-1-60566-392-0 (hardcover) -- ISBN 978-1-60566-393-7 (ebook) 1. Web-based instruction. 2. Individualized instruction. 3. Emotions and cognition. 4. Cognitive styles. I. Mourlas, Constantinos. II. Tsianos, Nikos. III. Germanakos, Panagiotis.
 LB1044.87.C58 2009
 371.33'44678--dc22
                          2009013278

British Cataloguing in Publication Data
A Cataloguing in Publication record for this book is available from the British Library.

All work contributed to this book is new, previously-unpublished material. The views expressed in this book are those of the authors, but not necessarily of the publisher.

Advances in Web-Based Learning (AWBL) Series

Editor-in-Chief: Nikos Karacapilidis, University of Patras, Greece
ISBN: 1935-3669

Cognitive and Emotional Processes in Web-Based Education: Integrating Human Factors and Personalization
Edited By: Constantinos Mourlas, National & Kapodistrian University of Athens, Greece; Nikos Tsianos, National & Kapodistrian University of Athens, Greece; Panagiotis Germanakos, National & Kapodistrian University of Athens, Greece

Information Science Reference ~ 2009 Copyright ~ H/C (ISBN: 978-1-60566-392-0) ~ Pages: 328
Our Price: $195.00

Cognitive and Emotional Processes in Web-Based Education: Integrating Human Factors and Personalization enhances the effectiveness of Web-based learning by incorporating cognitive and emotional human factors into adaptive hypermedia applications. This book covers a large number of topics in the area of human individuality that will be of importance to researchers, academicians, and practitioners in the areas of e-learning and education.

Solutions and Innovations in Web-Based Technologies for Augmented Learning: Improved Platforms, Tools, and Applications
Edited By: Nikos Karacapilidis, University of Patras, Greece

Information Science Reference ~ 2008 Copyright ~ H/C (ISBN: 978-1-60566-238-1) Pages: 402
Our Price: $195.00

Solutions and Innovations in Web-Based Technologies for Augmented Learning: Improved Platforms, Tools, and Applications provides cutting-edge research on a series of related topics and discusses implications in the modern era's broad learning concept. Addressing diverse conceptual, social, and technical issues, this book provides professionals, researchers, and practitioners in the field with up-to-date research in developing innovative and more effective learning systems by using Web-based technologies.

Web-Based Education and Pedagogical Technologies: Solutions for Learning Applications
Edited By: Liliane Esnault, EM Lyon, France

IGI Publishing ~ 2008 Copyright ~ H/C (ISBN: 978-1-59904-525-2) ~ Pages: 364 ~ Our Price: $150.00

Web-Based Education and Pedagogical Technologies: Solutions for Learning Applications provides cutting-edge research on such topics as network learning, e-learning, managing Web-based learning and teaching technologies, and building Web-based learning communities. This innovative book provides researchers, practitioners, and decision makers in the field of education with essential, up-to-date research in designing more effective learning systems and scenarios using Web-based technologies.

The *Advances in Web-based Learning (AWBL) Book Series* endeavors to broaden the overall body of knowledge regarding the above issues, thus assisting researchers, educators and practitioners to devise innovative Web-based Learning solutions. Much attention will be also given to the identification and thorough exploration of good practices in developing, integrating, delivering and evaluating the impact of Web-based Learning solutions. The series intends to supply a stage for emerging research in the critical areas of web-based learning to further expand to importance of comprehensive publications on these topics of global importance.

Table of Contents

Detailed Table of Contents

Section I
Cognition and Learning

Section I places in the centre of interest the cognitive aspects of learning, focusing on how learners assimilate information in relation to cognitive processes. Specifically, emphasis is placed upon individual differences and cognitive parameters, cognitive/learning style, and working memory.

The first chapter of the book summarizes the whole concept of incorporating individual differences in e-learning. Human factors such as style, gender, working memory, prior knowledge and anxiety are taken into consideration as variables that have a significant impact. Furthermore, these concepts are not only described and discussed, but actually placed within the context of Web-based learning, in order to propose ways of adapting the learning environment on each individual. It is also very important that these factors are not only discussed separately, but their interactions are also taken into account.

The need to personalize Web-based learning environments on individuals is the main argument of the chapter by Steve Rayner. The activation of a "differential pedagogy" is proposed, by taking advantage of personalization technologies, in contrast to uniform traditional instructional practices. From the perspective of an educationist, the issue of learner diversity is addressed and discussed, substantiating the notion of individualization in learning. In particular, style is considered as a basic parameter of a new e-pedagogy, in order to applicably reform future educational practices.

Martin Graff focuses on the role of cognitive style in learning hypermedia environments and hypertext systems, elucidating the relation between style and behavior of users. Concept maps, navigational strategies, hypertext segmentation, and overview provision are also related to patterns of behavior, while cognitive style is shown to have an additional impact. Previous research work is presented, exploring the efficiency of Web-based learning, and a method for optimizing e-learning design is suggested.

The controversy over the efficiency of e-learning is discussed by Michael Workman, in parallel to the effect of the medium on the quality of learning. Style is also considered as a significant factor, both from the instructor and the learner perspective. An integration of the theory of style in Web-based learning, but within the limitations of the medium, is considered as beneficiary, along with methods of reducing cognitive load and facilitating the acquisition and application of problem solving skills. In sum, the author underpins the importance of increased flexibility and the provision of multiple modes of delivery of information.

George Spanoudis and Eleni A. Kyza adopt a deeper cognitive approach in their chapter, by relating findings from cognitive and developmental psychology with the design of e-learning applications. The basic mechanisms of cognition and their development are firstly presented, while the concept of learning and how one could utilize theory and research results from cognitive psychology is discussed afterwards. The notion of individual differences is placed within the context of cognitive, metacognitive and problem solving skills. The chapter concludes with a synopsis of essential parameters that should be taken into account when designing the content, representations and interactional features for a computer-based learning environment.

Chapter VI

In this chapter, the construct of working memory is comprehensively described, by analyzing the major models of this key process of the human cognitive system. This analysis aims to clarify which model suits better the needs of Web-based education, and to render possible for designers and educationists to deeply understand the concept of working memory. The conclusion is that e-learning should be flexible and incorporate adaptive techniques, placing working memory in the backbone of cognitive processes within Web-based interactions.

Section II
Affection and Learning

Section II addresses the role of affect in Web-based learning environments, raising relevant concerns and methodological issues in a rather new and innovative area of research. To that end, affective computing, emotion recognition and measurements of different forms of anxiety are thoroughly discussed.

Chapter VII

Makis Leontidis, University of Athens, Greece
Constantin Halatsis, University of Athens, Greece

Makis Leontidis and Constantin Halatsis place emphasis on affective issues and the role of emotions in Web-based learning processes. They suggest that the omission of these human factors in adaptive learning hypermedia would result in reduced efficiency of these applications, thus underlining the importance of affective computing. Their chapter presents basic concepts of affecting computing and corresponding theories and models, methods of formal representation of affective knowledge and emotions elicitation, and applications related to the field of affective education. Finally, having discussed the problems of identifying affective mechanisms, suggestions for future research conclude this chapter.

Chapter VIII

Elena C. Papanastasiou, University of Nicosia, Cyprus
Aimilia Tzanavari, University of Nicosia, Cyprus
Patricia Lowe, University of Kansas-Lawrence, USA

The identification of affective mechanisms and their impact is the main concept of the chapter by Elena C. Papanastasiou, Aimilia Tzanavari, and Patricia A. Lowe. Particularly, different concepts of anxiety are experimentally evaluated in order to explore their effect on learning performance. Learner trait, test, and computer anxiety were measured, while gender differences were also taken into consideration. According to their findings, computer anxiety has the most significant impact on learning performance, thus introducing an additional parameter in designing educational hypermedia. Moreover, the same consideration applies on the notion of widely using computer testing, since not all individuals are equally familiar with Web-based interactions.

Section III
Cognition-Aware and Affective Hypermedia

Section III presents developed learning environments that bridge the theory with the design and realization of personalized applications. This section aims to provide a clear insight on how it would be feasible to integrate individual differences and pedagogical theories into Web applications design and development.

Chapter IX

Nikos Tsianos, National & Kapodistrian University of Athens, Greece
Panagiotis Germanakos, National & Kapodistrian University of Athens, Greece
Zacharias Lekkas, National & Kapodistrian University of Athens, Greece
Costas Mourlas, National & Kapodistrian University of Athens, Greece

Nikos Tsianos, Panagiotis Germanakos, Zacharias Lekkas, and Costas Mourlas present empirical results on the effectiveness of personalization on cognitive style and visual working memory. According to this experimental approach, personalization of these factors improves learner performance, while the proposed adaptive mechanisms seem to reflect the implications of the psychological theories that were opted for.

Chapter X

Christian Gütl, Graz University of Technology, Austria; Infodelio Information Systems
    and GÜTL IT Research & Consulting, Austria
Victor Manuel García-Barrios, Graz University of Technology, Austria

Christian Gütl and Victor Garcia describe a system of guided access to open repositories, providing learners with increased flexibility in relation to their characteristics. The main idea is to offer tailored learning and teaching activities, in contrast to close-ended non adaptive systems, focusing on the notion of concepts. The progress of their work through subsequent dynamic prototypes is described, and according to their evaluation, it is feasible to build a system that integrates various information services and correspondingly guides learners with concept and context sensitivity.

Chapter XI

    Elvira Popescu, University of Craiova, Romania

Elvira Popescu addresses the issue of modeling learners in Web-based environments, and suggests a complex typology that is derived from multiple style theories. Instead of traditional psychometrical testing and style dichotomies, the author describes an implicit, constantly dynamic method of measuring different dimensions of learners' style, based on their interactions with a Web-based environment. The mapping process is thoroughly described and experimentally evaluated in terms of accuracy, addressing the issue of learner diagnosis through Web-based techniques.

Ray Adams and Andrina Granic explore the possibility of pedagogically enriching accessible e-learning platforms. They present a framework for effective e-learning that includes numerous aspects of human factors and contextual parameters such as cognitive user modeling, user sensitive design, and usability and accessibility issues to name a few. This results in relating types of human learning to different forms of e-learning solutions, offering a practical taxonomy. Their work follows a cognitive learning approach, in order to identify which e-learning practices are the most appropriate based on human requirements.

William Billingsley and Peter Robinson discuss issues concerning the design of Intelligent Books, which are Web-based textbooks with adaptive content and computer-supported exercises. They describe the optimal characteristics of the specific e-learning method and present existing research and actualizations of Intelligent Books, while some economical factors are also addressed. The authors focus on design considerations such as content, structure, separation and narrative continuity, and student modeling/adaptation, in order to exemplify the key factors in this Web-based learning approach. They conclude that Intelligent Books are valuable in a practical way, and should be developed in a collaborative way.

Web-based technologies, virtual reality, information visualization/computer graphics techniques, and low cost multimedia tools are employed in the research presented in this chapter, for the purpose of sharing Web-based knowledge in the context of primary education. They support their multi-level approach with empirical data, and suggest that passive education should be transformed into an active learner centered experience. The authors also take into consideration the issue of digital divide, since their work in schools also aimed to improve computer literacy, and propose an educational policy with the use of the abovementioned technologies.

Section IV
Collaborative Learning and Pedagogical Approaches in Web-Based Environments

Section IV covers the field of social and collaborative learning approaches in Web-based environments, since this area of research is becoming increasingly popular. A number of these approaches and corresponding applications are presented, along with the discussion of the underlying theories of social pedagogy.

Chapter XV
    Robert Z. Zheng, University of Utah, USA
    Jill A. Flygare, University of Utah, USA
    Laura B. Dahl, University of Utah, USA
    Richard R. Hoffman, University of Utah, USA

Robert Z. Zheng, Jill A. Flygare, Laura B. Dahl, and Richard R. Hoffman bridge social communication patterns with the construct of cognitive style in the context of on-line learning. According to their empirical findings, individual differences in cognitive style have an effect on the formation of on-line social communication. With the use of the method of social network analysis it is demonstrated that learners exhibit different consistent patterns of behavior according to their cognitive style; thus, learning support should be adapted on the different types of learners. Additionally, according to the authors, a set of additional factors (ranging from complementary personality to online chat experience) is also significant in Web-based collaborative learning.

Chapter XVI
    Yin Zhang, Kent State University, USA

Yin Zhang reports a comparison study over the effectiveness of collaborative learning. Since collaborative learning has been proven useful in a traditional classroom, this evaluative approach aims to investigate whether the same applies in Web-based learning. The author first presents the benefits of collaborative learning, and subsequently describes methods for incorporating this form of instruction in on-line distance education. As it concerns the empirical findings, distance learning students are found to be more positive in adopting collaborative learning techniques than their on-campus counterparts, and that they can achieve the same learning goals with the latter.

The relation of collaborative learning, communication styles (as a personality factor) and social networks is explored by Hichang Cho and Richard Gay by adding a personality theory to structural analysis. Their main finding is that pre-existing friendship networks and communication styles have an impact in developing collaborative learning networks. Therefore, it is supported that an appropriate social infrastructure that would trigger the desired interactions is necessary in order to built collaborative e-learning systems, prompting designers not to merely implement new technologies.

Jan-Willem Strijbos, Theresa A. Ochoa, Dominique M. A. Sluijsmans, Mien S. R. Segers, and Harm H. Tillema argue that formative peer assessment perfectly fits the purpose of collaborative learning. They firstly review both the shortcomings (such as students' ability and interpersonal variables) and benefits of peer assessment practice, while also addressing the issue of directionality, frequency and constellation of interactivity. What is more important is that the authors propose a set of guidelines for peer assessment in Web-based collaborative learning contexts, systematizing their approach.

Supporting collaborative learning in Web-based environments from the perspective of the tutor is the main theme of the chapter by Francesca Pozzi. The author proposes a flexible monitoring model that allows the tutor to control the learning process in different aspects and levels. This model consists of four dimensions: participative, cognitive, social and teaching, which are described and analyzed. The evaluation of this approach is conducted through three case studies, in order to ground the importance of individualizing the collaborative learning process with the use of appropriate monitoring techniques.

Andrina Granić, Maja Ćukušić, Aimilia Tzanavari, and George A. Papadopoulos present an extensive incorporation of pedagogical approaches and assessment techniques into an e-learning platform. A number of learning theories and strategies is reviewed, with the presentation of relevant classifications, and a pedagogically enriched e-learning platform is described. Issues concerning the requirements of e-learning are discussed, along with mobile learning considerations. The authors also present and compare learning scenarios that were applied in schools, evaluating the implementation of different pedagogical approaches.

Paula Peres and Pedro Pimenta, focus on providing high quality e-learning standards by including learning theories in the design of Web-based applications. The authors propose a model of instruction that consists of five phases (analysis, design, development, implementation, and evaluation). Each phase is described, emphasizing upon the learning approaches that have a pedagogical impact on the design process (ranging from learning styles to socio-constructivism). This five-step procedure aims to aid the selection of the appropriate learning strategies, from a very wide range of theories, resulting in a useful combined learning process.

Preface

Web-based interactions are becoming more prominent in every aspect of a person's activities, transforming both individuals' lives and society as a whole. In this context, learning as an integral part of personal and social development should not be excluded from this phenomenal proliferation of Web-based activities. The availability of vast Web technologies and resources could potentially be turned to advantage in favor of better learning environments, available to all individuals regardless of demographic limitations.

This notion of e-learning environments and applications that are accessible to anyone, anywhere, and anytime has indeed generated academic research and applicable realizations. All these efforts are quite differentiated from traditional instructional methods, due to the very different nature of the context and the medium. However, the extent of the success of these efforts is yet to be established, since it remains unresolved whether e-learning could offer an equal or even optimized learning outcome, compared to traditional instruction.

To that direction, there are indeed some possibilities in Web-based instruction that may as well be proven beneficiary for learners, apart off course from the ubiquitous accessibility, with individualization being one of the most promising aspects of e-learning. This is actually the main subject of the book: the incorporation of cognitive, affectional and pedagogical theories into the domain of Web-based education, in order to provide individuals tailored-suited learning environments. Instead of a uniform approach that, at its best, would simply replicate traditional classroom instructional methods, the aim of this book is to propose a meaningful integration of human factors in Web-based learning processes, providing added value to the use of Web technologies in education.

This approach is related to personalization, by placing emphasis on individual differences, which have been proven to have a significant impact on how individuals learn. Therefore, the research that is presented in this book is focused upon understanding cognitive, emotional and social processes of learners, in order to propose and construct Web-based learning environments that adapt on these characteristics, or at least provide a considerable degree of flexibility. Such an approach would essentially lead to the augmentation of the potential of Web-based education, by addressing learner needs and abilities that are out of the scope of traditional instruction, which in general employs a uniform methodology.

As implied above, the book covers three main axes of learning: cognitive characteristics, emotional/affectional processes, and social pedagogical approaches. It should also be mentioned that in the short history of developing adaptive educational applications, the construct of style was proven quite popular. Both cognitive and learning style, and the corresponding theories that propose typologies of learners, provided a basis for personalized learning environments. On the other hand, a solid theoretical and ex-perimentally evaluated approach has not been adopted by the educational community, underpinning the importance of further elucidating the possible uses of style in e-learning. This is the main reason why research on style is presented on all sections of the book.

Additionally, while research on individual differences and Web-based learning progresses into greater depth, the importance of cognitive constructs, such as working memory, is brought into the foreground. Therefore, the first axis of the book addresses issues that are related to how each learner assimilates information according to individual cognitive characteristics.

In parallel, the affective aspect of learning and the effect of emotional parameters are lately concentrating the attention of the research community. Learning cannot be considered merely the outcome of cognitive processes, regardless of the affective state or traits of the learner. The effect of emotion may be more elusive in terms of measuring and manipulating, but affect is a significant part of human behavior that Web-based learning environments should be adapted upon. This rather new direction of research is also addressed by the book, raising concerns and methodological issues on a field that may as well be of significant importance in future applications, especially if e-learning becomes a predominant rather than a complementary method of instruction.

The social dimension of Web-based learning on the other hand is probably becoming one of the main directions of relevant research. The so-called social Web is increasingly popular, and it inevitably leads to the incorporation of social parameters in Web-based learning and training environments. Besides the differences in the cognitive and affective characteristics of learners, which can be considered as an individualistic approach, learning also involves social interactions, or at least occurs in a social environment (e.g., in a classroom). Terms such as social pedagogy and collaborative learning are becoming more common in the theoretical basis of e-learning applications, substantiating a new approach on the issue. Therefore, a corresponding section in this book widely covers the social and collaborative approach in Web-based learning.

On the basis of the aforementioned axes, there have been quite a few actualized learning environments or platforms for development of applications, which can be considered as interdisciplinary, bridging the theory with the design and development of personalized environments. It is considered that the presentation of these endeavors would provide a clear insight on how it would be feasible to integrate individual differences and social theories into Web applications design. Therefore, a number of authors propose ways of building Web-based environments based on cognitive, affective, and pedagogical parameters.

The basic aim of this book is not to merely present theories that would potentially be useful for an educationist, but to also provide a practical framework for further developing e-learning applications. It is expected that the coverage of a wide array of issues involved in learning processes will motivate educationists and Web developers to include human factors in their instructional approach in a necessarily interdisciplinary way. The overall objective is to bring into effect a more coherent design and development procedure for Web-based environments, by providing insights over a number of human characteristics. The argument for the equivalence or even prevalence of e-learning in relation to traditional methods of instruction could mainly be strengthened by increasing the efficiency of Web instruction; each chapter of this book is oriented towards the realization of optimized interactions between the learner and the Web environment.

Therefore, it is anticipated that both educationists and Web designers will find this book useful, since a new approach could be adopted by bridging two distinct fields of research. This is also in line with the notion of human-centered design that is often mentioned in the area of human computer interaction as a main trend. It could also be supported that a potential conclusion for the reader of this book would be that it is highly important to place the learner and his characteristics in the centre of research and development, the same way that every product or service seems to be designed today.

Additionally, the fact that e-learning is in the center of future educational policies generates extensive academic research; the numerous theoretical perspectives included in this book are expected to provide academic researchers with a comprehensive Web-based educational background, and to trigger the emergence of innovative and efficient combined approaches. The field of Web-based learning at an academic level is quite diversified, and it could be supported that there is a need for grounding the proposed theories and conducting extensive empirical evaluation. To that end, this book also aims to provide a basis for integrating various learning approaches into a broad theoretical framework, as a common ground among diverse directions of research on e-learning.

The book consists of four sections. **Section I** places in the centre of interest the cognitive aspects of learning, with emphasis on individual differences, cognitive/learning style, and working memory. **Section II** addresses emotional and affective issues, while **Section III** presents personalized environments that are based on theories and issues discussed in the previous sections. Finally, **Section IV** is focused on the social and collaborative aspect of learning.

In **Section I**, the first chapter of the book, written by Michael Grimley and Richard Riding, summarizes the whole concept of incorporating individual differences in e-learning. Human factors such as style, gender, working memory, prior knowledge and anxiety are taken into consideration as variables that have a significant impact. Furthermore, these concepts are not only described and discussed, but actually placed within the context of Web-based learning, in order to propose ways of adapting the learning environment on each individual. It is also very important that these factors are not only discussed separately, but their interactions are also taken into account.

The need to personalize Web-based learning environments to individuals is the main argument of the second chapter by Steve Rayner. To that end, the activation of a "differential pedagogy" is proposed, by taking advantage of personalization technologies, in contrast to uniform traditional instructional practices. From the perspective of an educationist, the issue of learner diversity is addressed and discussed, substantiating the notion of individualization in learning. In particular, style is considered as a basic parameter of a new e-pedagogy, in order to applicably reform future educational practices.

Martin Graff, in the next chapter, focuses on the role of cognitive style in learning hypermedia environments and hypertext systems, elucidating the relation between style and behavior of users. Concept maps, navigational strategies, hypertext segmentation, and overview provision are also related to patterns of behavior, while cognitive style is shown to have an additional impact. Previous research work is presented, exploring the efficiency of Web-based learning, and a method for optimizing e-learning design is suggested.

The controversy over the efficiency of e-learning is discussed in the fourth chapter of the book by Michael Workman, in parallel to the effect of the medium on the quality of learning. Style is also considered as a significant factor, both from the instructor and the learner perspective. An integration of the theory of style in Web-based learning, but within the limitations of the medium, is considered as beneficiary, along with methods of reducing cognitive load and facilitating the acquisition and application of problem solving skills. In sum, the author underpins the importance of increased flexibility and the provision of multiple modes of delivery of information.

George Spanoudis and Eleni A. Kyza adopt a deeper cognitive approach in their chapter, by relating findings from cognitive and developmental psychology with the design of e-learning applications. The basic mechanisms of cognition and their development are first presented, while the concept of learning and how one could utilize theory and research results from cognitive psychology is discussed afterwards. The notion of individual differences is placed within the context of cognitive, metacognitive and problem solving skills. The chapter concludes with a synopsis of essential parameters that should be taken into account when designing the content, representations and interactional features for a computer-based learning environment.

An analogous cognitive approach is presented in the final chapter of the first section by Zoe Bablekou. The construct of working memory is comprehensively described, by analyzing the major models of this key process of the human cognitive system. This analysis aims to clarify which model suits better the needs of Web-based education, and to render possible for designers and educationists to deeply understand the concept of working memory. The conclusion is that e-learning should be flexible and incorporate adaptive techniques, placing working memory in the backbone of cognitive processes within Web-based interactions.

In **Section II**, Makis Leontidis and Constantin Halatsis place emphasis on affective issues and the role of emotions in Web-based learning processes. They suggest that the omission of these human factors in adaptive learning hypermedia would result in reduced efficiency of these applications, thus underlining the importance of affective computing. Their chapter presents basic concepts of affecting computing and corresponding theories and models, methods of formal representation of affective knowledge and emotions elicitation, and applications related to the field of affective education. Finally, having discussed the problems of identifying affective mechanisms, suggestions for future research conclude this chapter.

The identification of affective mechanisms and their impact is the main concept of the following chapter by Elena C. Papanastasiou, Aimilia Tzanavari, and Patricia A. Lowe. Particularly, different concepts of anxiety are experimentally evaluated in order to explore their effect on learning performance. Learner trait, test, and computer anxiety were measured, while gender differences were also taken into consideration. According to their findings, computer anxiety has the most significant impact on learning performance, thus introducing an additional parameter in designing educational hypermedia. Moreover, the same consideration applies on the notion of widely using computer testing, since not all individuals are equally familiar with Web-based interactions.

In the area of fully developed and existing or experimental Web-based educational applications that incorporate cognitive, affective and pedagogical theories, which is the main axis of **Section III**, Nikos Tsianos, Panagiotis Germanakos, Zacharias Lekkas, and Costas Mourlas present empirical results on the effectiveness of personalization on cognitive style and visual working memory. According to this experimental approach, personalization on these factors improves learner performance, while the proposed adaptive mechanisms seem to reflect the implications of the psychological theories that were opted for.

Chapter X

Christian Gütl and Victor Garcia describe in the following chapter a system of guided access to open repositories, providing learners with increased flexibility in relation to their characteristics. The main idea is to offer tailored learning and teaching activities, in contrast to close-ended non adaptive systems, focusing on the notion of concepts. The progress of their work through subsequent dynamic prototypes is described, and according to their evaluation it is feasible to build a system that integrates various information services and correspondingly guides learners with concept and context sensitivity.

Elvira Popescu addresses the issue of modeling learners in Web-based environments, and suggests a complex typology that is derived from multiple style theories. Instead of traditional psychometrical testing and style dichotomies, the author describes an implicit, constantly dynamic method of measuring different dimensions of learners' style, based on their interactions with a Web-based environment. The mapping process is thoroughly described and experimentally evaluated in terms of accuracy, addressing the issue of learner diagnosis through Web-based techniques.

The next chapter of the book, written by Ray Adams and Andrina Granic, explores the possibility of pedagogically enriching accessible e-learning platforms. They present a framework for effective e-learning that includes numerous aspects of human factors and contextual parameters such as cognitive user modeling, user sensitive design, and usability and accessibility issues to name a few. This results in relating types of human learning to different forms of e-learning solutions, offering a practical taxonomy. Their work follows a cognitive learning approach, in order to identify which are the most appropriate e-learning practices based on human requirements.

William Billingsley and Peter Robinson discuss issues concerning the design of Intelligent Books, which are Web-based textbooks with adaptive content and computer-supported exercises. They describe the optimal characteristics of the specific e-learning method and present existing research on Intelligent Books, while some economical factors are also addressed. The authors focus on design considerations such as content, structure, separation and narrative continuity, and student modeling/adaptation, in order to exemplify the key factors in this Web-based learning approach. They conclude that Intelligent Books are valuable in a practical way, and should be developed in a collaborative way.

Chapter XIV

Jorge Ferreira Franco, Irene Karaguilla Ficheman, Marcelo Knörich Zuffo, Valkiria Venâncio, and Roseli de Deus Lopes employ Web-based technologies, virtual reality, information visualization/computer graphics techniques, and low cost multimedia tools for the purpose of sharing Web-based knowledge in the context of primary education. They support their multi-level approach with empirical data, and suggest that passive education should be transformed into an active learner centered experience. The authors also take into consideration the issue of digital divide, since their work in schools also aimed to improve computer literacy, and propose an educational policy with the use of the abovementioned technologies.

The final section of the book emphasizes on social and collaborative aspects of Web-based learning. Robert Z. Zheng, Jill A. Flygare, Laura B. Dahl, and Richard R. Hoffman bridge social communication patterns with the construct of cognitive style in the context of online learning. According to their empirical findings, individual differences in cognitive style have an effect on the formation of online social communication. With the use of the method of social network analysis, it is demonstrated that learners exhibit different consistent patterns of behavior according to their cognitive style; thus, learning support should be adapted on the different types of learners. Additionally, according to the authors, a set of additional factors (ranging from complementary personality to online chat experience) is also significant in Web-based collaborative learning.

Yin Zhang in the next chapter reports a comparison study over the effectiveness of collaborative learning. Since collaborative learning has been proven useful in a traditional classroom, this evaluative approach aims to investigate whether the same applies in Web-based learning. The author first presents the benefits of collaborative learning, and subsequently describes methods for incorporating this form of instruction in online distance education. As it concerns the empirical findings, distance learning students are found to be more positive in adopting collaborative learning techniques than their on-campus counterparts, and can achieve the same learning goals as the latter.

The relation of collaborative learning, communication styles (as a personality factor) and social networks is explored by Hichang Cho and Richard Gay by adding a personality theory to structural analysis. Their main finding is that pre-existing friendship networks and communication styles have an impact in developing collaborative learning networks. Therefore, it is supported that an appropriate social infrastructure that would trigger the desired interactions is necessary in order to built collaborative e-learning systems, prompting designers not to merely implement new technologies.

Jan-Willem Strijbos, Theresa A. Ochoa, Dominique M. A. Sluijsmans, Mien S. R. Segers, and Harm H. Tillema argue that formative peer assessment perfectly fits the purpose of collaborative learning. They first review both the shortcomings (such as students' ability and interpersonal variables) and benefits of peer assessment practice, while also addressing the issue of directionality, frequency and constellation of interactivity. What is more important is that the authors propose a set of guidelines for peer assessment in Web-based collaborative learning contexts, systematizing their approach.

Supporting collaborative learning in Web-based environments from the perspective of the tutor is the main theme of the next chapter by Francesca Pozzi. The author proposes a flexible monitoring model that allows the tutor to control the learning process in different aspects and levels. This model consists of four dimensions: participative, cognitive, social and teaching, which are described and analyzed. The evaluation of this approach is conducted through three case studies, in order to ground the importance of individualizing the collaborative learning process with the use of appropriate monitoring techniques.

Andrina Granić, Maja Ćukušić, Aimilia Tzanavari, and George A. Papadopoulos present an extensive incorporation of pedagogical approaches and assessment techniques into an e-learning platform. A number of learning theories and strategies are reviewed, with the presentation of relevant classifications, and a pedagogically enriched e-learning platform is described. Issues concerning the requirements of e-learning are discussed, along with mobile learning considerations. The authors also present and compare learning scenarios that were applied in schools, evaluating the implementation of different pedagogical approaches.

In the last chapter of the book, Paula Peres focuses on providing high quality e-learning standards by including learning theories in the design of Web-based applications. The author proposes a model of instruction that consists of five phases (analysis, design, development, implementation, and evaluation). Each phase is described, with emphasis placed upon the learning approaches that have a pedagogical impact on the design process (ranging from learning styles to socio-constructivism). This five-step procedure aims to aid the selection of the appropriate learning strategies, from a very wide range of theories, resulting in a useful combined learning process.

Conclusively, all of the above chapters contribute to a better understanding of the role of human factors in Web-based learning. Having read this book, a shift in the perspective of Web designers, educationists and academic researchers, from technological determinism and simplified approaches towards combined efforts in satisfying the needs of learners, is anticipated. The cognitive, affective and pedagogical aspects of e-learning are shown to be equally significant and, knowing that, it would be highly surprising to omit these parameters in the design and development of future applications.

Academic knowledge that can be put into practice is perhaps the most important contribution of this work, and the gathering of a vast number of different perspectives in a book is perhaps an unprecedented endeavor, especially in terms of bridging human factors with the design of Web-based learning environments. The wide coverage of human parameters that have an impact in the context of the Web was, from the very beginning, at the core of this book project as a response to the lack of an interdisciplinary corpus of relevant research.

Furthermore, the diversity of the work that is included in this book clearly demonstrates that there is much potential in optimizing Web-based learning environments and providing far more effective applications. Still, this requires a multi-level methodology that has not yet been put into practice, but could be extracted from the contents of this book. The inclusion of research work from various and quite differentiated areas should not be considered as an indication of an isolated segmentation in the field; on the contrary, it contributes to the understanding of the complex nature of human learning processes and hopefully to the emergence of innovative human-centered instructional methodologies. Web-based learning could then be significantly improved and satisfy the expectations of educational policy makers.

Constantinos Mourlas
Nikos Tsianos
Panagiotis Germanakos

Editors

Section I
Cognition and Learning

Chapter I
Individual Differences and Web–Based Learning

Michael Grimley
University of Canterbury, New Zealand

Richard Riding
University of Birmingham, UK

ABSTRACT

This chapter considers a range of individual difference variables that have potential relevance to specifically designed Web-based learning packages. These include: cognitive style, working memory efficiency, anxiety, gender, and current knowledge. It discusses, in general terms, the conditions under which the variables are important, and the potential interaction between them in affecting learning performance. The roles of the variables within the context of Web-based learning are then examined. It is argued that technical developments in computer technology that allow materials that can accommodate learning preferences by responding to the student's choices and learning performance combined with a better psychological understanding of individual differences in learning should result in improved educational effectiveness.

INTRODUCTION

Web-based learning can range from putting topics into a search engine and then selecting from those found, on the one hand, to on the other, using specifically designed learning materials for, say, a university course. In the former, the search is likely to bring up much that is either ir-relevant, out of date, or items that are not directly accessible such as some journal articles or books. The focus here will be limited to the design of specifically designed learning materials for a particular course.

The chapter is in two sections: the first will consider the individual difference variables, the second their relative importance and interaction, and the practical application to the particular characteristics of web-based learning. The sections will be as follows:

- **Section 1: Individual difference variables**. The variables of cognitive style, working memory efficiency, anxiety, gender, and current knowledge are examined in terms of their nature, assessment and effect on learning performance.
- **Section 2: Variables that affect learning and their relevance to web-based learning**. The individual differences are considered to see under which conditions they are related to learning performance and contrast these with those conditions when they have little or no effect. The variables are then examined in combinations to see how they may interact with one another in affecting learning outcomes. Finally, strategies developed by individuals to overcome or compensate for missing facilities in their learning repertoire of natural abilities are considered.

Web-based learning offers a special learning environment, which has characteristics that differ from traditional learning modes and materials. These characteristics include, for example, the mode of presentation in terms of verbal and pictorial and diagrammatic format, the choice between spoken and textual format, the rate of presentation, the opportunity for on-going assessment of learning performance and the provisions of feedback on progress, etc.

Each of these will be examined in the context of individual difference constructs to evaluate the relevance of individual difference assessments to the range of features available with web-based learning. Recommendations will then be made of the application of individual differences research to practical web-based learning.

SECTION 1: INDIVIDUAL DIFFERENCE VARIABLES

The variables of cognitive style, working memory efficiency, anxiety, gender, and current knowledge are examined in terms of their definition, nature, assessment and effect on learning performance.

Cognitive Style

Nature

Cognitive style, in the context of this chapter, is seen as the default approach that an individual takes when processing information. Two fundamental dimensions of style will be considered – the Verbal-Imagery and the Wholist-Analytic:

- Verbal-Imagery style is seen as an individual's preference in terms of how information is represented during thinking – verbally or in terms of images. On this basis an individual may be categorised as either a Verbaliser or an Imager.
- Wholist-Analytic style is the inclination of an individual to prefer to integrate information into a whole versus separating information into its constituent parts – the wholist approach or the analytic. Here an individual may be seen as either a Wholist or an Analytic.

When the two dimensions are taken together, one individual may be labelled, for example, as a Wholist-Verbaliser, while another may be an Analytic-Imager. Each dimension is seen as a continuum such that an individual may be at any point from one extreme to the other on either dimension.

An important point to note is that style represents a preference (the default), but this does not preclude representing information in a different mode if necessary. Thus, for instance, Verbalisers can generate images and Imagers can code information verbally. Analogy may be drawn with handedness where an individual prefers to use one hand rather than the other as the main one for particular tasks such as to hold a pencil while writing, or holding scissors while cutting. The point is that, for instance, a left-handed person can use their right hand for tasks if they wish although they may not be as proficient with it as they are with their left. The same type of choice applies to style.

Assessment

The Context of the Assessment of Style

The Verbal-Imagery dimension is an extension of the tradition of earlier psychological research related to the representation of information during processing going back to Betts' (1909) work on the vividness of mental imagery, Bartlett's (1932) studies of imagery, and Pavio's (1971) 'dual-coding theory' approach to verbal and visual representation. The Wholist-Analytic dimension may be traced back to the Gestalt psychology of the first half of the 20th century with the work on perception. Witkin used the Gottstat figures as the basis for the Embedded Figures Test (EFT), which he used to assess what he termed 'field dependence' and 'field independence'. In the present approach, 'field dependence' corresponds to the Wholist approach and 'field independence' to the Analytic style. A limitation of Witkin's approach was that the EFT did not positively assess 'field dependence' and was confounded with intelligence (see, for example, Flexer & Roberge, 1980).

The Cognitive Styles Analysis

These two approaches were refined and included in a single assessment – the *Cognitive Styles Analysis* (CSA) (Riding 1991). The background to the development of the Cognitive Styles Analysis is given in Riding and Cheema (1991).

The CSA directly assesses both ends of the Wholist-Analytic and Verbal-Imagery dimen-

sions, and comprises three sub-tests. The first assesses the Verbal-Imagery dimension by presenting statements one at a time to be judged true or false. Half of the statements contain information about conceptual categories while the rest describe the appearance of items. Half of the statements of each type are true. It was assumed that imagers would respond more quickly to the appearance statements, because the objects could be readily represented as mental pictures and the information for the comparison could be obtained directly and rapidly from these images. In the case of the conceptual category items, it was assumed that verbalisers would have a shorter response time because the semantic conceptual category membership is verbally abstract in nature and is difficult to represent in visual form. A computer is used to record the response time to each statement and calculate the Verbal-Imagery Ratio. A low ratio corresponds to a Verbaliser and a high to an Imager, with the intermediate position being described as Bimodal. It may be noted that in this approach individuals have to read both the verbal and the imagery items so that it is not a test of reading ability or of reading speed.

The second two sub-tests assess the Wholist-Analytic dimension. The first of these presents items containing pairs of complex geometrical figures which the individual is required to judge either the same or different. Since this task involves judgements about the overall similarity of the two figures, it was assumed that a relatively fast response to this task would be possible by wholists. The second presents items each comprising a simple geometrical shape (e.g., a square or a triangle) and a complex geometrical figure, and the individual is asked to indicate whether or not the simple shape is contained in the complex one by pressing one of the two marked response keys. This task requires a degree of disembedding of the simple shape within the complex geometrical figure in order to establish that it is the same as the stimulus simple shape displayed, and it was assumed that Analytics would be relatively quicker at this. Again a computer is used to record the latency of the responses, and calculate the Wholist-Analytic Ratio. A low ratio corresponds to a Wholist and a high ratio to an Analytic. Ratios between these positions are labelled Intermediate.

The Action of Style
It is useful to commence a consideration of the effects of style with a general model of the ways in which the two style dimensions may act.

Wholist-Analytic Dimension
This dimension influences the structural way in which individuals think about, view and respond to information and situations. This affects the manner in which they organise information during learning, perceive their environment and relate to other people.

Wholists tend to see a situation as a whole, are able to have an overall perspective, and to appreciate its total context. By contrast, Analytics see a situation as a collection of parts and often focus on one or two aspects of the situation at a time to the exclusion of the others.

The positive strength of the Wholists is that when considering information or a situation they see the whole 'picture'. They are 'big picture people'. Consequently, they can have a balanced view, and can see situations in their overall context. This makes it less likely that they have extreme views or attitudes. The negative aspect of the style is that they find difficulty in separating out a situation into its parts. For the Analytics, their positive ability is that they can analyse a situation into the parts, and this allows them to come quickly to the heart of any problem. They are good at seeing similarities and detecting differences. However, their negative aspect is that they may not be able to get a balanced view of the whole, and they may focus on one aspect of a situation to the exclusion of the others and enlarge it out of its proper proportion.

Verbal-Imagery Dimension
This style affects the way information is represented. It influences the characteristic mode in which people represent information during thinking; verbally or in images. For instance, when a person reads a novel they can represent the actions, happenings and scenes in terms of word associations or by constructing a mental picture of what they read. Just as it is possible to set down thoughts on paper in two possible ways - in words or in sketches - so they may also be represented during thinking in those two modes. People can think in words, or they can think in terms of mental pictures or images. On this dimension people may be categorised as; Verbalisers or Imagers. *Verbalisers* consider the information they read, see, or listen to, in words or verbal associations. When *Imagers* consider information, they experience fluent, spontaneous and frequent mental pictures either of representations of the information itself or of associations with it.

The style thus affects the processing of information and the mode of representation and presentation that an individual prefers, and this is likely to affect the types of task they find easy or difficult. However, it is important to note that both groups can use either mode of representation if they make the conscious choice, e.g., Verbalisers can form images if they try, but it is not their normal, habitual mode.

Style, Ability and Learning Strategies

In considering the action of style, it is necessary to be aware that the two style dimensions in combination will affect how an individual processes information. Further, the distinctions between style and ability, and between style and strategy, are important.

Complementary-Unitary Styles
The use of their style characteristics by a person may either complement or duplicate one another, depending on the characteristics. It is possible to

order the style grouping on the basis of a combination of styles offering complementary facilities. For example, consider an Analytic-Imager. Since the analytic aspect of their style will not provide an overview of a situation, they could attempt to use the whole-view aspect of imagery to supply it. If another person were a Wholist-Verbaliser, then since the wholist facility does not support analysis, they might use the 'analytic' property of verbalisation as a substitute. By contrast, a Wholist-Imager only has a whole facility available, with no style that may be pressed into service to provide an analytic function. The style groups may be approximately ordered from Complementary to Unitary as follows:

COMPLEMENTARY							UNITARY	
WV	AI	IV	II	WB	AB	IB	AV	WI

Style and Ability

For both style dimensions, it is the relative ability to process in a particular mode that is assessed, since it measures speed of processing for each pair of task types, and this indicates the default mode for each dimension.

The distinction between style and ability is important. Both style and ability will affect performance on a given task. The basic difference between them is that performance on all tasks will improve as ability increases, whereas the effect of style on performance for an individual will either be positive or negative depending on the nature of the task. It follows from this that for an individual at one end of a style dimension, a task of a type they find difficult will be found easier by someone at the other end of the dimension, and *vice versa*. For instance, if the dimension were the Verbal-Imagery style, then Verbalisers would find pictorial tasks more difficult than would Imagers, but they would find highly verbal tasks easier than would Imagers. In other words, in terms of style a person is *both* good *and* poor at tasks depending on the nature of the task, while for intelligence, they are *either* good *or* poor.

Style and Strategies

The difference between *style* and *strategy* should be noted. Style probably has a physiological basis and is fairly fixed for the individual. By contrast, strategies are ways that may be learned and developed to cope with situations and tasks, and particularly methods of utilising styles to make the best of situations for which they are not ideally suited. Within the literature the term 'learning style' is sometimes used to refer to what here is considered to be a strategy.

Cognitive Styles and Learning

This section will summarise the effect on learning performance of the interaction between style and the way the instructional material is structured, its mode of presentation, its type of content, and representational preference.

The Structure of Instructional Material

Studies have found that an individual's position on the Wholist-Analytic dimension interacts with the structure of the learning material to affect performance. There is evidence that the structure of the material to be learned interacts particularly with the Wholist-Analytic style dimension. Basically, the findings appear to be as follows:

- *Window Size.* Analytics need a large 'viewing window' compared to Wholists, when dealing with information, (Riding & Grimley, 1999).
- *The use of a section title as an organiser.* When presented with material Wholists learn best when the title of the section is given before it is presented, rather than at the end, although this has little effect for Analytics. This is probably because Wholists are less good at structuring material and are helped by a title at the beginning to give some organisation to the material, (Douglas & Riding, 1993).

5

- *Step Size.* Individuals of complementary style (Wholist-Verbalisers and Analytic-Imagers) are affected by the step size of the learning material and improve from large to small steps, while those of unitary style are not affected, (Riding & Sadler-Smith, 1992)
- *Headings.* There is an interaction between gender and Wholist-Analytic style in the facilitating effect of structure in the form of both headings and overviews, such that these most help male Analytics and female Wholists, (Riding & Al-Sanabani, 1998; Riding & Read, 1996).

Mode of Presentation: Pictorial Versus Verbal
With learning from computer presented instructional materials, there are varieties of possible mode of presentation:

- *Picture versus Text.* Generally, Imagers learn best from pictorial presentations of information, while Verbalisers do better with verbal presentations, (Riding & Ashmore, 1980).
- *Text-plus-Picture versus Text–plus-Text.* The presentation of material in a Text-plus-Picture format facilitates the learning by Imagers compared to the same content in a Text-plus-Text version. (Riding & Douglas, 1993).
- *Picture-plus-Sound, versus Picture-plus-Text versus Picture-plus-Text-plus-Sound.* With learning from computer presented instructional materials, there are varieties of possible mode of presentation such as picture-plus-sound (PS), picture-plus-text (PT), and picture-plus-text-plus-sound (PTS). Overall, PTS is superior to PS and PT. The most likely reason for this is that with PTS the wider range of methods of presentation mean that there are more options for the individual learner to choose from, and consequently this meets the needs of a wider variety of styles, and results in better learning. With PTS the non-complementary groups did best in the males (Analytic-Verbalisers and Wholist-Imagers), and in the females the Analytics (Verbalisers and Imagers), (Riding & Grimley, 1999).

Type of Content of the Instructional Material
In terms of content type, individuals appear to learn best when information can be readily translated into their preferred Verbal-Imagery mode of representation, (Riding & Calvey, 1981; Riding & Dyer, 1980).

Representational Preference
Various modes of representing material are possible:

- *Use of Diagrams.* Imagers were more likely than Verbalisers to use diagrams in answering questions about the material, (Riding & Douglas, 1993).
- *Written versus Pictorial Representation.* With respect to mode of working, with higher ability students, Imagers, particularly if they are Wholists, report that they use less writing and more pictures than Verbalisers, especially where the subject matter allows, as in science. The tendency by Imagers to use pictures, and Verbalisers writing, increases with ability. Lower ability students were more constrained by the usual format of the subject than were those of higher ability, (Riding & Read, 1996).
- *Verbal versus Illustrated Materials.* Given a free choice between verbal presentation and verbal plus pictorial versions, Verbalisers prefer the Verbal version and the Imagers the Pictorial plus verbal. On the Wholist-Analytic dimension the Pictorial plus verbal version was preferred by the Wholists, perhaps because it looked more 'lively', while the Analytics had a preference for the more 'neat and tidy' Verbal format. Students are attracted to, and prefer to select, materials

that appear to suit their own style, (Riding & Watts, 1997).

Locus of Control

Although more work needs to be done on the extent to which the learner is able to control and manage their learning there is some evidence that this could be important:

- *Locus of Control.* Sadler-Smith and Riding (1999) In terms of locus of control the Analytics preferred to have control themselves rather than to be controlled, while the Wholists had no preference.

Working Memory Efficiency

Nature

Working memory is seen as a system for temporarily holding and manipulating information when a person is engaged in thought processes such as reasoning or learning. This is in contrast to long-term memory that is a more stable large capacity store. The model has been developed through a number of iterations from the original concept of 'Short-Term-Memory' (Atkinson & Shiffrin, 1971; Hebb, 1949; Brown, 1958) to 'Working-Memory' (Baddeley & Hitch, 1974) that places an emphasis on active memory, which was lacking in the original short-term memory concept. Therefore working memory can be seen as a complete information processing system rather than a passive store that only stores information until it passes into long-term memory.

The architecture involved in working memory constitutes the central executive that has control over the whole information processing system; the phonological loop that is capable of holding speech based information and the visuo-spatial sketch pad that holds visual and spatial information. These components work together as a short-term processing system with the visuo-spatial sketchpad and articulatory loop working as slave systems to the central executive. Baddeley (2000) proposed a further addition to working memory in the form of the episodic buffer. The episodic buffer is a limited capacity store holding information that is multimodal (unlike the phonological loop and visuo-spatial sketchpad that are mono modal) and explains a number of inconsistencies of the original model. The episodic buffer allows information from long-term memory and other stores to be synthesised and stored as episodic representations (an episode integrated across space).

From a learning design standpoint it is important to note that the elements of working memory, individually and collectively, have limited processing capacity which can be overloaded and therefore are vulnerable to the loss of information from displacement by further incoming information.

Assessment

The determination of an individual's working memory capacity/efficiency may be ascertained by increasing the amount of information presented until a point is reached where some information is lost by displacement. Daneman and Carpenter (1980) devised the Working Memory Span test (WMS) to measure working memory capacity. In this task, subjects are asked to read aloud or listen to a series of unrelated sentences of moderate complexity and then to do two things: (a) to comprehend each sentence; (b) to remember the last word of each sentence. The task typically starts with two sentences and increases to a point at which subjects are no longer able to recall all the terminal words. Memory span is then measured by the number of sentences in the largest set of sentences for which a subject is able to remember the last word of each sentence.

As part of their research into the relationship between working memory and educational achievement Gathercole and Pickering (2000) developed a battery of tests to measure different aspects of working memory in children. Subtests included tests to measure central executive, phonological loop and visual spatial sketchpad performance. These tests were subsequently developed as an automated version entitled the Automated Working Memory Assessment (Alloway, Pickering & Gathercole, 2006).

Riding (2000) developed a computer presented displacement test, the Information Processing Index, showing railway trains comprising carriages of different colours entering the left side of a station into which the whole train disappears from view and then reappears on the right side with some carriage colours changed. The task is to indicate whether or not each carriage colour has changed, when it emerges in to view from the station. While this is being done, the information about the remaining carriages that are still obscured has to be retained in working memory. As the test progresses the lengths of the trains increases. Since both the amount to be retained and the quantity of processing increases with the length of the train, the total number of carriages correctly identified is taken as the indication of working memory efficiency.

Effects on Learning Performance

Since working memory has a limited capacity and is crucial in information processing, individual differences in memory capacity are likely to be reflected in performance. There is evidence that working memory capacity differs among individuals, and that this difference affects a wide range of cognitive tasks such as problem solving, reasoning, acquiring new vocabulary, and reading comprehension, (e. g. Cantor & Engle, 1993; Conway & Engle, 1994; Daneman & Carpenter, 1980, 1983; Engle, Cantor & Carullo, 1992).

Investigations, mostly with school-aged students, have shown a relationship between working memory performance and comprehension (see, for instance, Mackintosh, 1999), and with educational achievement (Gathercole & Pickering, 2000). The complex processing required in mathematics and science constrain the educational attainment for students with low working memory (Gathercole, Pickering, Knight & Stegmann, 2004). Riding, Grimley, Dahraei and Banner (2003) found that attainments by students in science, music, technology, art and geography were particularly sensitive to working memory differences.

Working Memory and Models of Learning

Models have been developed that build upon contemporary working memory theories. Two such models that describe how learning scenarios can be designed in light of working memory architecture that are relevant to web-based learning will be described.

Cognitive Load Theory (Sweller, 1988) was developed to take into account working-memory capacity limitation when designing instructional material. Cognitive Load Theory states that information when processed in working memory is split into two streams differentiated by modality, thus utilising the capacity of both the visuo-spatial scratch pad and the phonological loop. In essence, this means that more cognitive capacity should be available when information is split between auditory and the visual systems. Sweller and Chandler (1994) argue that two important considerations when designing learning materials are: whether the materials are presented in such a way as to cause split attention effects, and whether they are presented so as to cause redundancy effects. Split attention effects are those caused by the material being split into a number of elements that require active integration before the material makes sense. Quite often learning materials require learners to attend to both text and diagrammatic information in order to understand a particular concept, and in this case the learner's attention is split between the two elements that require integration. A consequence of this split is an increase in the cognitive load for the learner. An effective method of ameliorating the split attention effect is to present the text as narration simultaneously with the picture or diagrammatic information (Kalyuga, Chandler, & Sweller, 1999). The redundancy effect is found when extra material is included that is not relevant to the concept being presented forcing the learner to pay attention to extra material not necessary for the particular element being learned. When redundant information interferes with relevant information, a higher cognitive load is placed on the learner. Clearly, web-based materials can take account of such effects to enhance learning.

Multimedia Learning Theory (Mayer 1999, 2001) extends cognitive load theory and presents a theory that applies to learning from any materials combining more than one mode of delivery (e.g. pictorial and textual). This model is depicted in Figure 1.

The ears or eyes allow words to enter as sound (spoken) or visual (written) stimuli. Pictures, however, can only enter as visual stimuli. Information enters sensory memory and, if selected, is transferred to working memory where sound or visual information is organised to create a model in a form that makes sense to the learner. The subsequent model (pictorial or verbal) is further integrated using prior knowledge. Words and pictures can be translated into different forms once selected in working memory; however, this happens at a cost. Pictures can be verbalised and textual information can be represented in pictorial form (shown by the arrows going between sounds and images in Figure 1). In terms of Baddeley's

working memory model we see that the visual pathway corresponds to the visual-spatial sketch pad, the auditory pathway represents the articulatory loop and the integrating module represents the episodic buffer. Mayer (1999, 2001) outlines seven guiding principles for presenting information in a multimedia format, each predicted by the model:

- *Multimedia principle*: there is better learning when learners receive words and corresponding pictures rather than words alone. The benefit of using both channels is that the capacity is increased and the learner receives the benefit of two representations (visual and auditory).

- *Spatial contiguity principle*: there is better learning when words and corresponding pictures are near rather than far from each other. The benefit of having words and pictures near to one another is that both representations can be held in working memory simultaneously and cognitive resources are reserved because the learner does not have to search for relevant material.

- *Coherence principle*: there is better learning when extraneous words and pictures are excluded rather than included. Extraneous words and pictures tend to compete with

Figure 1. Mayer's multi-media model. Adapted from Mayer, Heiser & Lonn (2001)

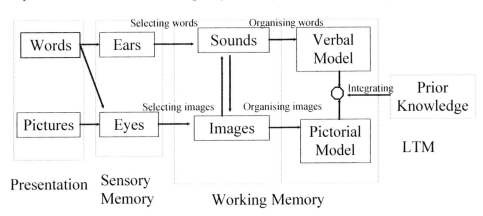

more relevant information for limited resources.

- *Modality principle*: there is better learning when words are presented as narration rather than in visual form. This is predicted by the model because if words are narrated then both channels are used, one for the text and one for the picture.
- *Redundancy principle*: there is better learning from animation and narration than from animation, narration, and on-screen text as on-screen text would compete with animation for resources.
- *Temporal contiguity principle*: there is better learning when corresponding words and pictures are presented simultaneously rather than successively. If words and pictures are processed in parallel they will be integrated into a more coherent model.
- *Individual difference principle*: there are stronger effects in low rather than high prior knowledge learners and high rather than low spatial learners. This principle suggests that it is particularly important to implement good multimedia design for low knowledge and high spatial ability learners.

Web-based learning allows models such as cognitive-load and multimedia theory to be implemented as part of the learning design to enhance individual learning.

Anxiety

Nature

In general, anxiety is a feeling of fear, dread, nervousness and worry. The feeling has associated physiological symptoms including increased blood pressure, rapid heartbeat, sweating, dryness of mouth and weakness, (see, for instance, Spielberger & Rickman, 1991, p69). Trait anxiety is seen as a relatively stable individual difference in anxiety proneness (Spielberger, Ritterband,

Sydeman, Reheiser & Unger, 1995, p44), while state anxiety fluctuates over time with the external conditions, (M.W Eysenck, 1992, p38). Some workers distinguish between anxiety and neuroticism, (see Gray & McNaughton, 2000, p337).

Trait anxiety is generally seen as largely genetically determined. Both trait and state anxiety are important when considering academic work as the two are additive. In addition, it has been suggested that some academic subjects elicit specific anxiety, the more common of these being maths anxiety and computer anxiety (King, Bond & Blandford, 2002; Miller & Bichsel, 2004). In addition, increased anxiety is thought to provoke hypervigilance for the detection of threatening stimuli and an analytic mode of processing, presumably to aid the analysis of threatening stimuli (Baroun, 2005).

Assessment

Due to the fact that anxiety produces distinct physiological changes we can use these to measure the presence of anxiety. For instance a simple measure is whether finger temperature changes occur which reflect increased sympathetic activity associated with increased anxiety levels (Sorg & Whitney, 1992). In addition, and more commonly, self-report questionnaires can be utilised to record perceived feelings. A number of these self-report tests have been developed to measure maths and computer anxiety (for example see King, et al, 2002; Miller & Bichsel, 2004).

Effects on Learning Performance

Increased levels of both state and trait anxiety are thought to produce negative effects on a number of cognitive tasks and this is thought to be associated with decreases in working memory capacity (MacLeod & Donnellan, 1993; Sorg & Whitney, 1992). Individuals with high state anxiety conditions are thought to utilise more working memory capacity when completing tasks. Similarly, individuals with high trait anxiety are thought to utilise more working memory resources to complete a task than individuals with low trait anxiety. A number of researchers have suggested that verbal tasks are most affected by high anxiety (Rapee, 1993). However, when considering maths anxiety Miller and Bichsel (2004) reported that the type of anxiety specifically related to maths disrupts visual working memory rather than verbal and that outcome is moderated by gender. Of particular importance for web based learning is computer anxiety with participants that demonstrate computer anxiety being vulnerable to reduced working memory capacity and consequently reduced performance on more complex tasks.

Gender

Nature

The sex of an individual generally refers to the biological distinction made between males and females, whilst gender refers to masculinity or femininity, which is thought to be constructed through interactions between biological factors and socio-cultural factors. In considering how to modify learning materials to suit all individuals there should be consideration of both biological and socio-cultural influences. Thus, we prefer to use the term gender throughout this section.

Gender Bias

Traditional learning environments have been fraught with gender bias issues and these are only recently being redressed to make them equitable (Burger, 2007). It is important that web-based learning takes these issues seriously to avoid gender bias and inequity and an informed view of gender bias is needed by any web-based team implementing instruction.

There has been some research around gender equity in the use of educational technology with evidence suggesting an equal use of computers and the internet across genders (Abbott & Bievenue,

2007). In addition, elementary and middle school pupils have been found to be equally computer literate but at secondary school age they display gender differences in what they tend to use computers for with girls using computers more as a tool and boys beginning to get more interested in computer science (Abbott & Bievenue, 2007) Also females have lower confidence in the use of technology (Abbott & Bievenue, 2007). Differences have emerged in self-efficacy for women in maths and science with males attributing failure to external factors and women to internal factors (Lufkin & Wiberg, 2007). Adult and adolescent anxiety studies show marginally higher anxiety in females than males and greater computer self efficacy in males.

Effects on Learning Performance

Lack of Overall Differences in Performance
Gender differences are not evident in overall cognitive ability and overall intelligence (eg, Halpern, 1992). Even when specific abilities, such as mathematics and verbal ability are examined, only very small differences have been found, (Hedges & Nowell, 1995; Hyde, Fennema & Lamon, 1990; Hyde & Linn, 1988). Spatial ability studies show small differences for spatial visualisation, small to medium gender differences for spatial perception and medium gender differences for mental rotation all favouring males (Linn & Petersen, 1986). Hyde (2005) argues that generally males and females show similar abilities on most psychological variables but it is important to take contextual factors into account when making this judgment. In addition, Spelke (2005) states that men and women have equal intrinsic aptitudes for Mathematics and Science despite the imbalance of men and women in the higher levels of these disciplines and despite the arguments for this imbalance.

Thus, studies indicate that abilities between males and females are probably more alike than they are dissimilar. Differences within genders are much more striking and perhaps more relevant. However, there is evidence from neurological studies that males and females process information in different ways.

Neuropsychological Gender Differences

There is evidence that males and females process information in different ways, and this may reflect male-female brain differences (Bradshaw and Nettleton 1983; Udry 1994). The main findings may be summarised as follows:

- Males and females differ in terms of functional cortical geometry (Goldberg, Harner, Lovell, Podell, & Riggio, 1994; Levy and Heller 1987) due to hormonal influences in-utero (Halpern 1997; Kimura 1996;Udry 1994).
- Female brains have been shown to have larger language associated areas than males and increased verbal processing capacity in the right hemisphere compared to males (Harasty, Double, Halliday, Kril & McRitchie, 1997).
- Degree of lateralisation is less in females than in males, in, for example, phonological tasks (Levy & Gur, 1980; McGlone, 1980; Shaywitz et al, 1995).
- Male brains show a predominantly left-brained response but female brains show a much more diffuse neural pattern. In women there are between-hemisphere (inter-hemispheric) functional interactions, with strong within-hemisphere (intra-hemispheric) functional interactions in men (Azari et al, 1995; Corsi-Cabrera, Arce, Ramos, Guevara, 1997; Kocel; 1980; Wood, Flowers & Naylor, 1991). These differences may enable women to excel on tasks that require co-operation of both hemispheres but this may precipitate poor performance for tasks requiring intra-hemispheric co-operation such as spatial tasks or uni-hemispheric co-operation tasks. Men are more likely to perform well for tasks that rely on intra-hemispheric co-operation.
- Patterns of neuro-psychological asymmetry for men and women tend to be reversed for a number of neuro-psychological tasks. These results indicate that men and women show sex differences in right relative to left hemisphere function (Azari et al, 1995).

The important point here is that males and females process information in a different manner, which will show itself in gender differences in performance on specific tasks.

Gender and Technology Preferences

The notion of different genders having different preferences in the learning environment is an important issue and is described by many as a particular cognitive style in itself. It should be emphasised that the important factor being considered here is not a difference in ability between the sexes but, as Head (1996) remarked: "…men and women tend (ed) to use their abilities in different ways." These differences in cognitive style between the genders may well be the reason for a number of long debated gender differences in abilities and would explain why these so called ability differences are so small and sometimes ambiguous. Additionally, these gender-style differences are probably evident both between the genders and within the genders. In fact it maybe incorrect to talk of these cognitive style differences as being gender style differences as they are most probably distributed along a continuum within the sexes but with a slight bias for each sex towards a particular cognitive style.

Gender and Reversal Effects

These neurological differences between males and females may underlie reversal effects seen in style by sex by task interactions in the cognitive styles literature. These effects show a tendency for males of a particular style to react to a task in quite the opposite manner to females of a similar style (See for example: Riding & Armstrong, 1982; Riding & Borg, 1987; Riding & Cowley, 1986; Riding & Dyer, 1983; Riding & Egelstaff, 1983; Riding & Rigby-Smith, 1984).

Gender Differences in Interaction with Repetition and Speed of Presentation of Learning Material

Riding and Smith (1981) found that females improved in recall when a passage was repeated as opposed to males whose recall declined slightly. This improvement in recall for girls was enhanced for slow speech rates. Riding (1998) explained this as a fundamental difference in information processing between males and females. Specifically males process to a superficial level whereas females process to a much deeper level, taking their time when processing. Consequently, males perform better than females when processing time is short, but females surpass males when processing time is sufficiently long for their more elaborate processing style. Consequently, females use their slower processing abilities to consolidate information when the passage is repeated. However, males process on a superficial level and fail to consolidate the information, which may lead to some interference. Alternatively, males may fail to synthesise material effectively therefore leading to interference effects. Females may use elaborate processing in order to match and consolidate information more effectively. Persinger and Richards (1995) suggested that verbal memory for men is poorer than that of women and this effect is enhanced when the processing load is increased.

Gender Differences in Interaction with Material Format

Some verbal recall effects have been seen across genders and appear to be related to information-processing mode. Riding and Vincent (1980) found that females were poorer at recalling prose passages with details positioned distantly when speech rate was increased.

Within a computer assisted learning environment clear preferences are found between boys' interface preferences and girls' interface preferences. Boys emphasise their preference for being in control of the computing environment preferring sharp image changes and lots of on screen movement. However, girls showed a preference for writing, drawing, calm-moderate games, the physical aspects of the environment such as the colours and on-line help facilities (Passig & Levin, 2000).

Current Knowledge

Information processing models described earlier in this chapter reflect an important influence of Long-Term-Memory on the learning process. Prior knowledge is all knowledge that is contained within such a store. It is generally accepted that such knowledge is in the form of organised sets of facts or concepts called schemata. As learners we tend to assimilate new knowledge by trying to accommodate it into already developed schemata. As a consequence of this process existing schemata or prior knowledge facilitates the retention and understanding of new knowledge. Researchers tend to distinguish between prior knowledge and domain knowledge (Alexander, 1992) with the latter referring to knowledge of a particular field of study rather than the more generic term prior knowledge that defines a more general knowledge. Much of the research in this area has been conducted by considering domain knowledge.

Nature

Prior knowledge is an extremely important determinant of learning. In other words it is much easier to learn something new if you already have prior knowledge in that area of study. In fact prior knowledge is one of the main predictors of how well a learner will assimilate new information. Research makes clear distinctions between expert learning and novice learning showing that experts can easily identify meaningful patterns, perform tasks within the domain quickly and without error, have good long-term and short term memories, take more time to work through a given problem within the domain and have a better feel for when they make mistakes (Chi, Glaser & Farr, 1988).

Another important element within the area of prior knowledge is the nature and occurrence of misconceptions. Everyone appears to have misconceptions whether expert or novice and these misconceptions are extremely hard to dispel. In addition, misconceptions tend not to be just isolated facts but networks of knowledge that need considerable disruption and re assimilation to rectify, consequently, if the misconception is central to the domain being studied the misconception becomes more debilitating for the individual. However, it should also be noted that misconceptions are a natural bi-product of conceptual change, thus, they are inevitable if learning is to occur.

Assessment

It is clearly advantageous to know more about learners' prior knowledge so that current prior knowledge can be built upon and moved in a positive direction. It is however important to emphasise that the concept of learning is not about transmitting information to the learner or 'filling the empty vessels'. Learning is so much more complicated than that and might be seen better as moving the learner through conceptual changes. Consequently, in order to get a useful picture of where a learner currently is with their thinking within a particular domain it is important to build a complex picture of their current thinking. In essence, this means that it is not sufficient to administer a quick multi-choice test to ascertain what the person knows. It is important when assessing prior knowledge that the assessment is dynamic and detailed to uncover misconceptions, interests and current views within the domain. In the context of Web-based learning this

may mean that the program needs to respond to learner-material interactions as it proceeds rather than being an add-on at the beginning or end of a learning module. Assessment of prior knowledge must be approached from the learners' perspective rather than being tested from an experts' point of view. Learning opportunities are built through paying attention to the learners' experiences and knowledge and these cannot be ascertained by simple tests of knowledge.

SECTION 2: CONDITIONS AND INTERACTION BETWEEN VARIABLES AND WEB-BASED LEARNING

The individual differences will be considered to see under which conditions they are related to learning performance and contrasted with those conditions where they have little or no effect. The variables will then be examined in combinations to see how they may interact with one another in affecting learning outcomes. Finally, strategies developed by individuals to overcome or compensate for missing facilities in their learning repertoire of natural abilities will be examined.

Effects of the Variables in Combination

Critical States

There is the problem of deciding which variables matter and which have little effect for most tasks. Studies of individual differences often find little or no effect of individual difference variables, and there are simple reasons for this.

When the task is very easy or very difficult then there will be no individual difference effects. Consider, for example, the effect of coaching in high jump performance on a group of fit 18-year-olds. A control group receive no coaching while a treatment group have ten sessions of instruction on jumping techniques. If the final assessment is too easy, say with a bar height of one metre then this will probably be cleared by all and show no effect of the coaching. Similarly, if the bar is set at three metres then this will be impossible for all, and again no effect will be observed. To demonstrate any effect, an intermediate range of heights will need to be used to detect whether there was any effect. In general the major individual effects will be at the intermediate level of task difficulty. There will be an inverted 'U' shaped relationship between the degree of effect and the relative difficulty of the task for the individual.

A similar effect will be apparent with individual characteristics and educational performance. The effect of a particular individual difference variable will be dependent on the level of other variables, and the relative difficulty of the task. For instance, if intelligence is very high or very low then style and gender will have little effect. However, when it is moderate then style and gender are worth considering as variables that may have an effect.

Gender by Cognitive Style Interactions

Although there are no main gender differences for style gender and cognitive style have been shown to interact to mediate task outcome (Riding & Armstrong, 1982; Riding & Boardman, 1983; Riding & Borg, 1987; Riding & Cowley, 1986; Riding et al., 2001; Riding & Egelstaff, 1983; Riding & Rigby-Smith, 1984). These interactions tend to involve gender and the verbal–imagery dimension, with outcome varying according to the type of task performed. As previously discussed in the section on gender this reinforces the notion that males use different processing mechanisms. When the task is verbal, males perform as they would be expected to according to their verbal–imagery style characteristics with verbalisers doing well but females performing poorly (Riding & Armstrong, 1982; Riding & Cowley, 1986; Riding, Dahraei, Grimley & Banner, 2001; Riding

& Rigby-Smith, 1984). For visuo-spatial tasks female imagers and male verbalisers perform well. This is the reverse of the pattern seen for verbal tasks (Riding & Boardman, 1983; Riding & Egelstaff, 1983). Quantitative tasks show a different gender by verbal–imagery interaction pattern, with bimodal males, female verbalisers and female imagers performing well (Riding & Armstrong, 1982; Riding & Borg, 1987).

Turning our attention to mode preferences for individuals in learning situations Riding and Grimley (1999) compared learning in computer-presented multimedia materials of picture and speech (P-S) and of picture and text (P-T). They found gender by style differences for P-S and P-T presentations. P-S involves two modes and two senses ("look and listen", i.e., two channels), while P-T involves two modes but only a single sense ("look" only, i.e., a single channel). For the wholist-verbalisers and analytic-imagers (the complementary groups), males did better on P-S than on P-T, while this was reversed for females. For the unitary groups, the wholist-imagers and analytic-verbalisers, the tendency was the other way around, with the male wholist-imagers doing better on P-T and females better on P-S. Thus, for the complementary groups males perform best when there are separate channels of pictures and words, while females perform best when there is a single channel of picture and words. With the unitary groups, males perform best with a single channel, while females' performance is superior with separate channels.

Working Memory by Style Interactions

Studies (Riding et al, 2001; Riding et al, 2003) indicate an interaction between working memory and the wholist analytic style dimension with better learning outcomes for analytics if working memory capacity is high. However, outcomes for wholists appear to be independent of working memory capacity. Similarly, outcomes for verbalisers are also affected by working memory capacity with verbalisers improving their outcome measures with increased working memory capacity. The reason for this dependence on high memory capacity for analytics and verbalisers could be due to the elaborate method of information processing used for these two style groupings compared to wholists and imagers.

Anxiety-Stability and Working Memory Interactions

A relationship between anxiety level and memory capacity has been observed by several researchers, (e.g., Calvo & Eysenck, 1996; Elliman, Green, Rogers & Finch, 1997; Eysenck, 1992; Hopko, Ashcraft & Gute, 1998). The general view is that some of the capacity of working memory is devoted to the objects of anxiety, and this reduces the resources available for general processing. Studies indicate that individuals with higher working memory will benefit in high anxiety situations (Miller & Bichsel, 2004).

Memory by Style by Gender Interactions

Riding et al. (2001) observed, for maths and English attainment, an interaction between gender, verbal–imagery style, and working memory efficiency. Results indicated reversal patterns between males and females of the same verbal–imagery styles. In maths, male verbalisers with low working memory scores performed poorly but high memory male verbalisers performed well. However, female imagers performed best for both high and low memory. In English, for females low memory imagers performed better than verbalisers, but the reverse was true for high memory students. Male verbalisers, however, showed a superior performance for both memory types. In males the English results (verbal in nature) were typically strong for verbalisers at both working memory levels. However, in females, working memory seemed to mediate the verbal–imagery

effect, with low working memory suited to imagers but high working memory suited to verbalisers.

Style by Anxiety Interactions

Grimley, Dahraei and Riding (2008) conducted a study to explore the interaction of style, working memory, gender and anxiety in school children where anxiety was the outcome measure. Firstly, it was clear that students with a higher working memory capacity showed higher stability measures reflecting previous work in this area, (e.g., Calvo & Eysenck, 1996; Elliman et al, 1997; Eysenck, 1992; Hopko et al, 1998). Secondly analytics were observed to be more stable than wholists supporting the idea that induced anxiety requires an analytic approach to effectively deal with threats in the environment (Baroun, 2005). Thirdly, complementary styles with high working memory tended to show lower anxiety scores than those with low working memory and vice versa for the unitary style groupings. Finally, female Wholist-Imagers were more stable than males and male Wholist-Verbalisers were more stable than the females. This study indicated that working memory, cognitive style and gender interacted in their effect on overall anxiety-stability levels for children in the classroom situation. More specifically, females or low working memory children with a complementary cognitive style show increased anxiety in the classroom.

It is evident that style, working memory, gender and anxiety are inextricably linked. For females or low working memory children with a complementary cognitive style classroom anxiety may be a major problem because this combination may give rise to increasing levels of instability due to a cyclical affect of decreasing working memory capacity and increasing levels of anxiety. If stress increases anxiety, which reduces the effective working memory capacity, then there is the problem that this reduction causes misunderstanding, confusion and uncertainty when processing information. This may in turn cause further stress and hence increase anxiety. This effect combined with gender and style effects may be particularly problematic for some children.

Significance of Individual Differences to Web-Based Learning

Accommodating versus Coping Strategies

With respect to taking account of individual differences, two basic approaches are possible in instruction. One is to accommodate the material and the mode of teaching to the individual characteristics of the student. Accommodation could, for instance, involve matching the material content, structure and mode to the cognitive style of the student. There could be a revision of a student's present knowledge of information necessary for the understanding of new learning, since learning is somewhat similar to building a wall where to be successful each course must have the bricks beneath it already in place. The presentation rate of material could be adjusted to maximise working memory efficiency. Reducing the stress of the learning environment in the case of anxious students could relieve pressure on the student.

The other approach would be to teach coping strategies (e.g. Carver, Scheier & Weintrab, 1989) to enable students to process material that they naturally find difficult. With respect to cognitive style and mode of presentation this could involve teaching students how to translate material into the mode of presentation to suit their preferred mode. Pupils could be made aware of the need to review past related material before embarking on a new topic. Strategy development should increase success in learning and build confidence.

The difference between these two approaches lies with the locus of control that in the former is with the teacher and in the latter with the student. A progressive shift from the former to the latter is desirable over time, such that the student is in charge of the layout, format and presentation of the learning materials. The choice of method chosen may depend on the ability of the students.

Unique Features of Web-Based Learning

Web-based learning offers a special learning environment, which has characteristics that differ from traditional learning modes and materials. These characteristics related to, for example, the mode of presentation in terms of verbal and pictorial and diagrammatic format, the choice between spoken and textual format, the rate of presentation, the opportunity for on-going assessment of learning performance and the provisions of feedback on progress, etc.

Each of these will be examined in the context of individual difference constructs to evaluate the relevance of individual difference assessments to the range of features available with web-based learning. Recommendations will then be made of the application of individual differences research to practical web-based learning.

The advent of web-based learning has given instructors much more flexibility in terms of how they design learning materials and more specifically how instructors tailor learning experiences to suit our generic view of how people learn and their individual nuances. Probably the greatest advantage of web-based learning is that it allows the learner to actively interact with the learning content rather than being passive, a common feature of more traditional learning environments. Some of the features of web-based learning that allow active participation are methodologies such as game-based learning, simulations, tutorials, hypermedia and collaborative learning. Web-based learning can allow more meaningful and authentic learning activities to be implemented thus negating the commonly cited criticism of learners being taught in the abstract allowing little or no transfer to the real world. It is now possible thanks to web technology to allow more experiential learning. In addition, web-based learning has now transformed learning from classroom based to learning that is anytime and any place. The web allows people to have access to vast amounts of information at their fingertips and can connect effortlessly with people from around the world. Further, web-based learning allows the learner to work within structures that replicate the real world without it being overly complex and to allow learners to observe and control things that may not normally be observable or controllable. Some instances that are usually dangerous can be explored safely and the learner can undergo experiences normally out of their reach (e.g. manipulating atoms at a sub molecular level) by scalability. Computerised learning is beneficial when costs would normally preclude exploration, safety is a concern, complexity requires simplification, extensive practice is necessary, motivation is low and learners have special needs (Allessi & Trollop, 2001).

A number of factors within the learning situation can be adjusted to suit individual learners. These factors are many but include visual characteristics of the task, organisation of the material, rate of presentation of material, types and amount of interactivity, feedback characteristics, route through the learning materials (linear, non-linear), guidance characteristics (computer control vs learner control), content choices (computer controlled vs learner controlled), navigation and orientation characteristics and human interface characteristics.

Clearly a key element of web-based learning when considering individual differences is the ability to be able to dynamically gather information about the learner and their performance on the learning tasks and to be able to instantly modify any key factors. Learning suddenly becomes individualised and customised to the learner.

Characteristics of Web-Based Learning Compared to Book Learning

A comparison of the features of Web-based learning, in contrast to book-based learning, is relevant. With book-based learning, for a given book on a topic, there are limits in the choices that can be economically made to the learner in terms of presentation mode (verbal versus diagrammatic/pictorial), subject matter order (use of organisers/no organisers), step size, layout and structure, the use of headings. A similar set of restrictions also apply to lecture versus web-based learning.

Individual Differences and Web-Based Learning: A Cafeteria Approach

The CSA was originally developed in the late 1980's with support from the Learning Technologies unit of the Department of Employment in the UK. The intention at the time was to design an assessment of cognitive style that could 'front end' computer-based training (CBT) materials such that the format of the CBT presented would match the cognitive style of the student. This approach tried to match the presentation to the student's style.

An alternative and preferable approach is to use knowledge of the individual difference variables to design material that combines a number of structural and format features. This provides a 'cafeteria' approach to choice of presentation, such that rather than matching the student to the presentation, the student is presented with choices and selects those that most suit their style of learning.

Alternatively, a hybrid approach could be taken where the learner initially chooses options that suit their style of learning but the computer monitors other factors that need to be dynamically altered as the learning episode(s) develop. For instance, an individual may choose a textual format preference with a particular organisational structure but the program would gather information dynamically about success criteria (e.g. difficulty of material) and misconceptions.

The range of options in a cafeteria approach could include (some of these may be chosen by the learner others automatically adjusted via feedback through the computer and others built into the learning task):

- **For the Verbal-Imagery dimension:**
  o *Verbal:* Text or spoken or both
  o *Imager:* Verbal or pictorial/diagrammatic or both
- **For the Wholist-Analytic dimensions:**
  o *Organisers:* Initial Summary or Concluding Summary or both
  o *Step size:* Choice of material step size small or large
  o *Structural format:* Paragraphs without headings or with headings
  o *Screen format:* Busy unstructured versus uncluttered
  o *Screen viewing window size/screen size:* Small or large
  o Navigation and orientation tools/guides
- **For Working Memory:**
  o Rate of presentation
  o Amount of information on each screen
  o The ability to dynamically record and review important information (e.g. a scratchpad facility)
  o Efficient multi-media design
  o Good organisational design to reduce cognitive load
- **For Gender:**
  o Rate of presentation/pace modification
  o *Repetition:* Ability to reply/repeat
  o Cooperation versus competition
  o *Interface:* Ability to modify the user interface
  o *Verbal (text or Spoken or both):* Visual (pictorial or diagrammatic or both)

- **For Prior Knowledge:**
  o Ongoing assessment to match the learning material with prior knowledge
  o Assessment of interests
  o Assessment of current views of the domain
  o Tracking of ongoing experiences and knowledge
  o Identification of misconceptions
- **For Anxiety:**
  o Verbal-visual characteristics to suit anxiety level
  o *Success rate:* Ability to adjust difficulty level
  o Reduction of threat characteristics
  o Interface characteristics
  o Working memory factors
  o Type and frequency of feedback

The management of the options would require a presentational framework into which the options slot.

The list above indicates that learning preferences represent a complex range of variables which need to be taken in combination for learning to be made more efficient.

CONCLUSION

Technical developments in computer technology provide new ways of presenting learning materials and of enabling individual students to adapt the learning materials to suit their individual characteristics and to make learning more efficient and effective.

In parallel with technical computer and web developments has been an increasing psychological understanding of the range of individual differences that occur in students that may affect their understanding and learning. What has become clear is that individual differences are not limited to two or three variables that affect performance, but to many. Consequently allowing adaptation to just, two, variables is not sufficient to really influence learning to a large extent. In practice, individual variation can work in many ways depending on the nature, format and difficulty of the learning task.

The challenge to Web-learning designers is to combine both technical development and psychological understanding to produce instructional materials that are flexible and allow the student to mix and match the content, formats and instructional methods in a way which maximises the individual's performance. The aim is to produce materials that can accommodate learning preferences by responding to the student's choices and learning performance. This will not happen overnight, but the continuing technical developments of the media together with further psychological understanding of individual differences in learning should result in improved educational effectiveness.

REFERENCES

Abbott, G., & Bievenue, L. (2007). Gender equity in the use of Educational technology. In Klein (Ed.), *Handbook for achieving gender equity through education* (pp. 191-214). Lawrence Erlbaum Associates.

Alexander, P. A. (1992). Domain knowledge: Evolving themes and emerging concerns. *Educational Psychologist, 27*(1), 33-51.

Allessi, S. M., & Trollop, S. R. (2001). *Multimedia for learning: Methods and development.* Boston, Allyn and Bacon.

Alloway, T. P., Pickering, S. J., & Gathercole, S.E. (2006). Verbal and visuospatial short-term and working memory in children: Are they separable? *Child Development, 77*(6), 1698-1716.

Atkinson, R.C., & Shiffrin, R.M. (1971). The control of short-term memory. *Scientific American, 224*, 82-90.

Azari, N. P., Pettigrew, K. D., Pietrini, P., Murphy, D. G., Horwitz, B., & Schapiro, M. B. (1995). Sex differences in patterns of hemispheric cerebral metabolism: A multiple regression/discriminant analysis of positron emission tomographic data. *International Journal of Neuroscience, 81*, 1-20.

Baddeley, A., & Hitch, G. J. (1974). Working memory. In G. Bower (Ed.), *Recent advances in learning and motivation* (Vol. 8) (pp. 47-49). New York: Academic Press.

Baddeley, A.D. (2000). The episodic buffer: A new component of working memory. *Trends in Cognitive Sciences, 4*, 417-423.

Baroun, K. A., & Al-Ansari, B. M. (2005). Impact of anxiety and gender on perceiving the Mueller-Lyer illusion. *Social Behaviour and Personality, 33*(1), 33-42.

Bartlett, F. C. (1932). *Remembering: A study in experimental and social psychology.* Cambridge: Cambridge University Press.

Betts, G. H. (1909). *The distributions and functions of mental imagery.* New York: New York Teacher's College.

Bradshaw, J. L., & Nettleton, N. C. (1983). *Human cerebral asymmetry.* New Jersey: Prentice-Hall.

Brown, J. (1958). Some tests of the decay theory of immediate memory. *Quarterly Journal of Experimental Psychology, 10*, 12-21.

Burger, C. (2007). Gender equity in science, engineering and technology. In Klein (Ed.), *Handbook for achieving gender equity through education* (pp. 255-280). Lawrence Erlbaum Associates.

Calvo, M. G., & Eysenck, M. W. (1996). Phonological working memory and reading in test anxiety. *Memory, 4*, 289-305.

Cantor, J., & Engle, R. W. (1993). Working memory capacity as a long-term memory activation: An individual differences approach. *Journal of Experimental Psychology: Learning, Memory, and Cognition*, 19, 1101-1114.

Carver, C. S., Scheier, M. F., & Weintraub, J. K. (1989). Assessing coping strategies: A theoretically based approach. *Journal of Personality and Social Psychology,* 56(2), 267-283.

Chi, M. T. H., Glaser, R., & Farr, M. J. (Eds.). (1988). *The nature of expertise.* London: Lawrence Erlbaum Associates.

Conway, A. R. A., & Engle, R. W. (1994). Working memory and retrieval: A resource-dependent inhibition model. *Journal of Experimental Psychology: General,* 123, 354-373.

Corsi-Cabrera, M., Arce, C., Ramos, J., & Guevara, M. A. (1997). Effect of spatial ability and sex on inter- and intrahemispheric correlation of EEG activity. *Electroencephalography and Clinical Neurophysiology,* 102, 5-11.

Daneman, M., & Carpenter, P. A. (1980). Individual differences in working memory and reading. *Journal of Verbal Learning and Verbal Behavior,* 19, 450-466.

Douglas, G., & Riding, R. J. (1993). The effect of pupil cognitive style and position of prose passage title on recall. *Educational Psychology,* 13, 385-393.

Elliman, N. A., Green, M. W., Rogers, P. J., & Finch, G. M. (1997). Processing efficiency theory and the working memory system: Impairments associated with sub-clinical anxiety. *Personality and Individual Differences,* 23, 31-35.

Engle, R. W., Cantor, J., & Carullo, J. J. (1992). Individual differences in working memory and comprehension: A test of four hypotheses. *Journal of Experimental Psychology: Learning, Memory, and Cognition,* 18, 976-992.

Eysenck, M. W. (1992). *Anxiety: The cognitive perspective.* Hove: Lawrence Erlbaum Associates.

Flexer, B. K., & Roberge, J. J. (1980). IQ, field-dependence-independence, and the development of formal operational thought. *Journal of General Psychology,* 103, 191-201.

Gathercole, S.E., & Pickering, S.J. (2000). Working memory deficits in children with low achievements in the national curriculum at 7 years of age. *British Journal of Educational Psychology,* 70, 177-194.

Gathercole, S.E., Pickering, S.J., Knight, C., & Stegmann, Z. (2004). Working memory skills and educational attainment: Evidence from national curriculum assessments at 7 and 14 years of age. *Applied Cognitive Psychology,* 18, 1-16.

Goldberg, E., Harner, R., Lovell, M., Podell, K., & Riggio, S. (1994). Cognitive bias, functional cortical geometry, and the frontal lobes: Laterality, sex, and handedness. *Journal of Cognitive Neuroscience,* 6, 276-296.

Gray, J. A., & McNaughton, N. (2000). *The neuropsychology of anxiety: an enquiry into the functions of the septo-hippocampal system.* (2nd ed.) Oxford: Oxford University Press.

Grimley, M., Dahraei, H., & Riding, R. J. (2008) The relationship between anxiety stability, working memory and cognitive style. Educational Studies, 34(3) 213-223.

Halpern, D. F. (1997). Sex differences in intelligence: Implications for education. *American Psychologist,* 52(10), 1091-1102.

Halpern, D., F (1992). *Sex differences in cognitive abilities.* New Jersey: Lawrence Erlbaum Associates.

Harasty, J., Double, K. L., Halliday, G. M., Kril, J. J., & McRitchie, D. A. (1997). Language associated cortical regions are proportionally larger in the female brain. *Archives of* Neurology, 54, 171-175.

Head, J. (1996). Gender identity and cognitive style. In P. Murphy and C. Gipps (Eds.), *Equity in the classroom:Towards effective pedagogy for girls and boys* (pp. 59-69). London, UNESCO Publishing:.

Hebb, D. O. (1949). *Organization of behaviour.* New York: Wiley.

Hedges, L. V. & Nowell, A. (1995). Sex differences in mental test scores, variability, and numbers of high-scoring individuals. *Science, 269,* 41-45.

Hopko, D. R., Ashcraft, M. H., & Gute, J. (1998). Mathematics anxiety and working memory: Support for the existence of a deficient inhibition mechanism. *Journal of Anxiety Disorders, 12,* 343-355.

Hyde, J. S., & Linn, M. C. (1988). Gender differences in verbal ability: A meta-analysis. *Psychological Bulletin, 104*(1), 53-69.

Hyde, J. S. (2005). The gender similarities hypothesis. *American Psychologist, 60*(6), 581-592.

Hyde, J. S., Fennema, E., & Lamon, S. J. (1990). Gender differences in mathematics performance: A meta-analysis. *Psychological Bulletin, 107*(2), 139-155.

Kalyuga, S., Chandler, P., & Sweller, J. (2000). Incorporating learner experience into the design of multimedia instruction. *Journal of Educational Psychology, 92,* 126-136.

Kimura, D. (1996). Sex, sexual orientation and sex hormones influence human cognitive function. *Current Opinion in Neurobiology, 6,* 259-263.

King, J., Bond, T., & Blandford, S. (2002). An investigation of computer anxiety by gender and grade. *Computers in Human Behavior, 18,* 69-84.

Kocel, K. M. (1980). Age-related changes in cognitive abilities and hemispheric specialization. In J. Herron (Ed.), *Neuropsychology of left-handedness.* London: Academic Press.

Levy, J., & Gur, R. (1980). Individual differences in psychoneurological organization. In J. Herron (Ed.), *Neuropsychology of left-handedness.* London: Academic Press.

Levy, J., & Heller, W. (1987). Diversities in right-handers in left-hemisphere processing. In D. Ottoson (Ed.), *Duality and unity of the brain.* Basingstoke: Macmillan.

Linn, M. C., & Petersen, A. C. (1986). A meta-analysis of gender differences in spatial ability: Implications for maths and science achievement. In J. S. Hyde and M. C. Linn (Eds). *The psychology of gender: Advances through meta-analysis* (pp. 67-101). Baltimore: The Johns Hopkins University Press.

Lufkin, M. E. & Wiberg, M. (2007). Gender equity in career and technical education.. In Klein (Ed.), *Handbook for achieving gender equity through education* (pp. 421-444). Lawrence Erlbaum Associates.

MacLeod, C. & Donnellan, A. M. (1993). Individual differences in anxiety and the restriction of working memory capacity. *Personality and Individual Differences, 15*(2), 163-173.

Mayer, R. E. (1999). Research-based principles for the design of instructional messages: The case of multimedia explanations. *Document Design, 2,* 7-20.

Mayer, R. E. (2001). *Multimedia learning.* New York: Cambridge University Press.

Mayer, R.E., Heiser, J., & Lonn, S. (2001): Cognitive constraints on multimedia learning: When presenting more material results in less understanding. *Journal of Educational Psychology, 93*(1),187-198.

McGlone, J. (1980). Sex differences in human brain asymmetry: A critical survey. *Behavioral and Brain Sciences, 3,* 215-263.

Miller, H. & Bichsel, J. (2004). Anxiety, working memory, gender, and math performance. *Personality and Individual Differences, 37,* 591-606.

Paivio, A. (1971). *Imagery and verbal processes.* New York: Holt, Rinehart and Winston.

Passig, D., & Levin, H. (2000). Gender preferences for multimedia interfaces. *Journal of Computer Assisted Learning, 16,* 64-71.

Persinger, M. A., & Richards, P. M. (1995). Women reconstruct more detail than men for a complex five-minute narrative: Implications for right-hemispheric factors in the serial memory effect. *Perceptual and Motor Skills, 80,* 403-410.

Rapee, R.M. (1993). The utilisation of working memory by worry. *Behavior Research and Therapy, 31*(6), 617-620.

Riding R. J, & Ashmore, J. (1980). Verbaliser-imager learning style and children's recall of information presented in pictorial versus written form. *Educational Psychology, 6,* 141-145.

Riding, R. J. (2000). *Information processing index.* Birmingham: Learning and Training Technology.

Riding, R. J., & Al-Sanabani, S. (1998). The effect of cognitive style, age, gender and structure on recall of prose passages. *International journal of Educational Research, 29,* 173-185.

Riding, R. J., & Armstrong, J. M. (1982). Sex and personality differences in performance on mathematics tests in 11-year-old children. *Educational Studies, 8,* 217-225.

Riding, R. J., & Armstrong, J.M. (1982). Sex and personality differences in mathematics tests in 11-year-old children. *Educational Studies, 8,* 217-225.

Riding, R. J., & Boardman, D. J. (1983). The relationship between sex and learning style and graphicacy in 14-year old children. *Educational Review, 35,* 69-79.

Riding, R. J., & Borg, M. G. (1987). Sex and personality differences in performance on number computation in 11-year-old children. *Educational Review, 39*(1), 41-46.

Riding, R. J., & Cheema, I. (1991). Cognitive styles: An overview and integration. *Educational Psychology, 11,* 193-215.

Riding, R. J., & Cowley, J. (1986). Extroversion and sex differences in reading performance in eight-year-old children. *British Journal of Educational Psychology, 56,* 88-94.

Riding, R. J., & Douglas, G. (1993). The effect of cognitive style and mode of presentation on learning performance. *British Journal of Educational Psychology, 63,* 297-307.

Riding, R. J., & Dyer, V. A. (1983). The nature of learning styles and their relationship to cognitive performance in children. *Educational Psychology, 3,* 275-287.

Riding, R. J., & Egelstaff, D. W. (1983). Sex and personality differences in children's detection of changes in prose passages. *Educational Studies, 9,* 159-168.

Riding, R. J. & Read, G. (1996). Cognitive style and pupil learning preferences. *Educational Psychology, 16,* 81-106.

Riding, R. J., & Rigby Smith, E. M. (1984). Reading accuracy as a function of teaching strategy, personality and word complexity in seven-year-old children. *Educational Studies, 3,* 263-272.

Riding, R. J., & Sadler-Smith, E. (1992). Type of instructional material, cognitive style and learning performance. *Educational Studies, 18,* 323-340.

Riding, R. J., & Smith, D. M. (1981). Sex differences in the effects of speech rate and repetition on the recall of prose in children. *Educational Psychology, 3,* 253-260.

Riding, R. J., & Vincent, D. J. T. (1980). Listening comprehension: The effects of sex, age, passage structure and speech rate. *Educational Review,* 32, 259-266.

Riding, R. J., & Watts, M. (1997). The effect of cognitive style on the preferred format of instructional material. *Educational Psychology,* 17, 179-183.

Riding, R. J. (1991). *Cognitive styles analysis.* Birmingham: Learning and Training Technology.

Riding, R. J. (1998). The nature of cognitive style. *Educational Psychology, 17*(1-2), 29-49.

Riding, R. J., & Grimley, M. (1999). Cognitive style and learning from multi-media materials in 11-year-old children. *British Journal of Educational Technology,* 30, 45-56.

Riding, R. J., Dahraei, H., Grimley, M., & Banner, G. (2001). Working memory, cognitive style and academic attainment. In R. Nata (Ed.), *Progress in education* (Vol. 5) (pp. 1-19). New York: Nova Science Publishers Inc.

Riding, R. J., Grimley, M., Dahraei, H., & Banner, G. (2003). Cognitive style, working memory and learning behaviour and attainment in school subjects. *British Journal of Educational Psychology, 73*(2), 149-169.

Riding, R.J., & Calvey, I. (1981). The assessment of verbal-imagery learning styles and their effect on the recall of concrete and abstract prose passages by eleven-year-old children. *British Journal of Psychology,* 72, 59-64.

Riding, R.J., & Dyer, V.A. (1980). The relationship between extraversion and verbal-imagery learning styles in 12 year old children. *Personality and Individual Differences,* 1, 273-279.

Sadler-Smith, E., & Riding, R.J. (1999). Cognitive style and instructional preferences. *Instructional Science,* 27, 355-371.

Shaywitz, B. A., Shaywitz, S. E., Pugh, K. R., Constable, R. T., Skudlarski, P., Fulbright, R. K., Bronen, R. A., Fletcher, J. M., Shankweiler, D. P., Katz, L., & Gore, J. C. (1995). Sex differences in the functional organization of the brain for language. *Nature 373*(16), 607-609.

Sorg, A. B., & Whitney, P. (1992). The effect of trait anxiety and situational stress on working memory capacity. *Journal of Research in Personality,* 26, 235-241.

Spelke, E. S. (2005). Sex differences in intrinsic aptitude for mathematics and science. *American Psychologist, 60*(9), 950-958.

Spielberger, C. D, Ritterband, L. M., Sydeman, S. J., Reheiser, E. C., & Unger, K. K. (1995). Assessment of emotional states and personality traits: Measuring psychological vital signs. In J. N. Butcher (Ed.), *Clinical personality assessment: Practical approaches* (pp42–58). New York: Oxford University Press.

Spielberger, C.D., & Rickman, R.L. (1991). Assessment of state and trait anxiety. In *Psychobiological and clinical perspectives* (pp. 69-83). Washington: Hemisphere/Taylor & Francis.

Sweller, J. (1988). Cognitive load during problem solving: Effects on learning. *Cognitive Science,* 12, 257-285.

Sweller, J., & Chandler, P. (1994). Why some material is difficult to learn. *Cognition and Instruction,* 12, 185-233.

Udry, R. J. (1994). The nature of gender. *Demography, 31*(4), 561-573.

Wood, F. B., Flowers, D. L., & Naylor, C. E. (1991). Cerebral laterality in functional neuroimaging. In F. L. Kitterle (Ed.), *Cerebral laterality: Theory and research.* New Jersey: Lawrence Erlbaum.

Chapter II
Personalizing Style in Learning:
Activating a Differential Pedagogy

Steve Rayner
University of Gloucestershire, UK

ABSTRACT

The need to personalize Web-based learning environments on individuals is the main argument of this chapter. The activation of a "differential pedagogy" is proposed, by taking advantage of personalization technologies, in contrast to uniform traditional instructional practices. From the perspective of an educationist, the issue of learner diversity is addressed and discussed, substantiating the notion of individualization in learning. In particular, style is considered as a basic parameter of a new e-pedagogy, in order to applicably reform future educational practices.

INTRODUCTION

A theme running through-out this chapter is the idea of personalizing learning. In the UK, recent Government policy has seen a remodelling of the school workforce and national curriculum. It has in large part taken on what has been described as the transforming reform of an educational system that is now deeply implicated with *personalized education* and e-technology *(*Rayner, 2007a; Ritchie & Deakin Crick, 2007). What the UK policy does not consider in any detail is the kind of learning and pedagogy required for personalized education. There is much to do to make best use of emerging new technology and opportunities for using e-learning to support diversity in the classroom. Researchers in the field of e-technology, for example, have increasingly been drawn to the design of adaptive learning systems centring upon the learner, firstly as an individual (Shi, Revithis & Chen, 2002), and secondly when learning in a social context (Naismith, 2005).

Much of the modernizing direction in the research of e-technology, in respect to learning design, echoes previous work in educational psychology (Riding & Rayner, 1995), associated with the advent of an information superhighway and the idea of an individualized learning system (ILS). More recent developments, both in advancing the idea of the ILS, as well as other applications for learning design, focus upon the learner, and re-working theories of differential psychology. For example, developments in web-based learning (Graf, 2003; Fiorina et al., 2007), adaptive hypermedia (Brusilovsky & Peylo, 2003; Brusilovsky & Nejdl, 2004), web-based personalization (Germanakos et al., 2007), tutoring systems configured around artificial intelligence (Haykin, 1998, Curilem et al., 2007), learner responses to multi-media and blended e-learning (Ghinea & Chen, 2003; Derntl & Motschnig-Pitrik, 2005; Kimberly, 2007). It is this work which again raises the questions of learner performance and pedagogy: that is, how the learner best learns and most prefers to learn; and how a teacher develops their teaching craft to accommodate the learner.

The intention in this chapter is to examine a relationship between learning styles, individual differences and pedagogy by addressing several particular questions about personal or individual differences in the learner and learning. These questions include firstly asking how teachers can more successfully work in 1) dealing with learning diversity and individual difference – that is – operationalizing the concept of a personalized education; and 2) establishing *learning* and *involving the learner* in a pedagogy that seeks the goal of learning mastery – while managing differences in the challenge of developing pedagogic practice.

In considering each of these questions, an account of how the theory of cognitive style and a differential pedagogy can impact upon performance in learning and teaching will be examined. This chapter ends by asking what is likely, by the year 2020, to be the preferred or accepted pedagogic face of instructional design, teaching and learning in a formal educational setting. A response to this last question requires considering the place of an individual learner as a student in a '*boundedless space for learning and teaching*', as well as the utilization of technologies and media available

for developing a '*post-modern pedagogy for Personalized Education*'. This development, in turn, arguably requires work aimed at advancing and re-activating the concepts of personalized learning, e-learning and a differential pedagogy.

INDIVIDUALS LEARNING: THEORY AND PRACTICE

Diversity in the learning community is a very real challenge in any educational context (Rayner, 2007a). It is, however, not only a social phenomenon. McInerney (2005), for example, while pointing to the increasing importance of social psychology and the study of cross-cultural contexts in this area, states that there is less variation between groups than within groups and diversity is a multi-faceted phenomenon. Individual differences, and in particular the psychology of self associated with cognitive style and self reference (Riding and Rayner, 2000; Riding and Rayner, 2001), are acknowledged aspects of personal performance in effective learning and teaching (Prashnig, 1998; Reid, 2005; Rayner, 2007b). The focus in this chapter is *personal diversity*, and the term is used to refer to a traditional knowledge domain of individual differences and an underpinning theory of differential psychology (Jonassen & Grabowski, 1983; Messick, 1984; Furnham, 2001; Collis & Messick, 2001; Rayner, 2001, 2007b).

A practical beginning for researcher and teacher alike in managing educational diversity is to focus upon individual differences and personal diversity. The following actions provide a basis for better understanding the interaction between learner, learning and teaching and how this might contribute to informing an educational approach to personal diversity in the learning and teaching context:

1. **Understanding the Psychology:** Learner and learning performance

In terms of dealing with diversity, style differences and learning technologies, '*the teacher*' as mediator is central to enabling effective learning (Weber, 1993), and 'pedagogy' is the 'key' to successfully mediating the *learning needs* of the student (Rayner, 1998). This should not, however be seen to contradict the goal of learning mastery or independent learning. It is important, furthermore, that the impact of information technology is recognized in this process, not only as a driver for change but also as an opportunity. It is, in fact, an invaluable tool for further developing professional understanding of personal diversity (Laurillard, 2007; Ritchie & Deakin Crick, 2007). Advances too in the field of educational technology will continue to enable alternative research methodologies (De Freitas & Yapp, 2005), as well as reveal new insights into the psychology and construction of personal diversity for the teacher, learner and learning performance.

Understanding the Psychology: Learner and Learning Performance

An individual's performance in learning is influenced by several key constructs in a personal psychology interacting with the learning context (Riding & Rayner, 1998). These include, for example, variables such as personality, intelligence, motivation, self-concept, and cognitive style. This interaction or set of processes is the 'real stuff of teaching and learning'. It reflects an inter-section of the personal and the social worlds – involving and impacting upon an individual's state of affect, cognition and ultimately behaviour. Interestingly, a teacher can only ever really be sure of any of this learning process by observing and respond-

ing to behaviour. Nonetheless, as teachers or educators work directly with the surface features of performance, reflecting motivation, skills, attitudes and knowledge; they intuitively and continuously work with a 'beneath the surface' psychology of self, including a cognitive style, personality, learning preferences, an orientation to study and learning strategies, as well as the key psychological functioning of self reference or regulation as a learner (see Vermunt, 1996; Dunn & Dunn, 1999; Riding & Rayner, 1998; Rayner, 2001; Rayner, 2007b; Zimmerman, 2008;). The implications of all of this for education are that a greater awareness of differential psychology in an approach to instruction will yield improved performance for individuals engaged in the formal event of learning and teaching.

Life, teaching and learning, however, is not actually that straight-forward. What is also important at this juncture, consequently, is to acknowledge a deeply contested basis to some of the theory in differential psychology. This is, for example, reflected in a continuing debate around research theory, with recent re-defining and use of constructs such as intelligence (Neisser et al., 1996), abilities (Gardner, 1993) or style differences in cognition and learning (Messick, 1994; Furnham, 2001; Kozhevnikov, 2007). Differential Psychology is by tradition a study of the ways in which individual people differ in their behavior. It is, to date, theory largely reflecting a positivist epistemology and grounded in a 'classical' form of empiricism. This intellectual tradition has dominated the field. Research, consequently, has been reliant upon a use of psychometric testing, and statistical controls that are applied to data generated in groups of people. An excellent example of this approach is seen in the early work of Thurstone (1944), who identified stylistic factors across individual perceptual performance. Indeed, Messick (1994:126) describes this research as the first succinct, working formulation of 'the cognitive-style thesis' in the field of differential psychology.

Many psychologists, in spite of this controversy, have continued working in a positivist empirical tradition that is claimed to be scientific, in which an interest in the individual's psychology is pursued by studying groups to identify dimensions or factors shared by all individuals but upon which individuals differ by comparison. For educational researchers, this continuing approach points to a need for cautious and consistent use of psychological tests and theory. For the practicing educationist, it stresses a need to be tentative and deliberate in a choice of psychological model, use of any related measure and an understanding of the theory. What this continuing debate does not justify, however, is an abandonment of differential psychology in the domain of education or psychology. The theory of a differential psychology is undoubtedly work in progress. Indeed, research in the field of e-technology offers a rich opportunity for inter-disciplinary and applied research and a path-way toward a deeper understanding of these constructs with obvious implications for pedagogy, learning and education (see for example Sabry & Baldwin, 2003; Laurillard, 2007).

Assessing the Learner Learning: Controversy, Differentiation and Diversity

Models, measures and meaning in the field of individual differences are inextricably linked and to date, are dominated by the development and application of psychometric assessment. To a great extent this reflects the work of proving test validity and reliability using a quantitative methodology. A need to focus upon assessment, however, is also central to learning and teaching as well as any application of differential psychology. Assessment then may have several purposes and take many forms but nonetheless it is an essential ingredient in all learning and teaching. Interest in specifically knowing more about how the learner learns usefully involves developing forms of assessment that profile a learner's approach to

learning (Rayner, 2000). There are, however, dangers in the normative idea of differentiation, including the negative effects of labeling and a pronounced individualism in a general approach to learning. These are reflected in a debate questioning the educational desirability of attempting to develop individualized learning systems or a differentiated curriculum.

Critics of individualization or differentiation have over time re-stated a definition of learning as a social phenonemon, and therefore by implication, argue the need for a social basis to any construction of learning and teaching (Beetham, 2005). Other critics have identified a number of dangers invoked by differential assessment including:

- Its mis-use to predict individual performance causing a constriction of opportunity for the learner, learning and teaching
- Its use as a means of organizing fixed groups of learners according to learner traits.
- Specialization and a restrictive structuring of the curriculum
- The perpetration of social injustice with elitist labelling and regenerating forms of an institutional self-fulfilling prophecy.

Finally, some educationists have completely rejected as perverse the epistemology and ontology underpinning differential psychology. A charge of reductionism, as identified by Ritter (2007), is seen to discredit any attempt at explaining learning and teaching in terms of individual differences. This view perceives such an approach as educationally counter-productive. Ritter (p. 570) argues that research methods and educational practices associated with differential psychology actively '*subvert discourses of diversity and promote commonality*'. An epistemological gap is said to exist between pedagogy and psychology. It is described as a philosophical divide, which by inference should not be mediated or indeed cannot be bridged. This means that psychology is, at the least, seen to be an irrelevance for the educationist or yet more seriously, as a dangerous and illusory distraction facilitating and accommodating authentic diversity in the classroom.

Ritter goes on to identify a conceptual paradox in the psychometric conceptualization of diversity (individual differences), and argues that as a consequence of differential assessment, a dangerous and perverse irony is generated in the use of inventories, measures and tests, facilitating a reductionism and a social control of diversity in the educational setting. A similar critique is presented by Reynolds (1997, p. 122), targeting the research tradition underpinning the development of learning styles. It is criticized for producing an individualized, de-contextualized concept of learning. This epistemology is roundly rejected by Reynolds for producing a 'depoliticized treatment' of the learner's differences, reflecting identity and perhaps more important differences such as social class, race and gender. He argues that psychometric assessment forms a process of reductionist labeling that is not impartial or disinterested as the very idea of types of personal learning style *'obscures the social bases of difference expressed in the way people approach learning'.*

Again, this argument demonstrates the need to be clear as to why and how any form of assessment focusing upon either the learner or learning is used in the design of instruction or construction of a learning system. It is also worth stating, however, that organizing information into categories or sets for making sense of our world is as necessary a part of the human condition– both in terms of a social or personal context – as is establishing commonality in a moral compact when seeking social justice, cultural cohesion, personal accommodation and educational inclusion. The differential perspective, however, is not exclusive nor should it be used to conversely reject the importance of social psychology or sociology, with for example, key constructs such as the learning community, social cognition, identity and mythos, in turn, contributing to our understanding and knowledge of educational

diversity. I am, however, at this point, arguing for the necessary place of differential psychology in learning and teaching, reflecting the benefits of awareness in both learner and teacher, as well as the contribution of a personal psychology in an individual's learning performance. As previously stated, the focus here is with the personal dimension of diversity as it is expressed in the notion of individual differences when it occurs in the learning context.

Personalizing Learning: Pedagogy, Learning Theory and ICT

Concern for the learner is part of an approach to using differential psychology and developing a form of 'best-fit pedagogy'. It is not straight-forward, simple nor an exact science. The DEMOS Working Group, in a useful response to the question what is learning advises us that:

. . . learning theory does not provide a simple recipe for designing effective learning environments, but there are implications about the design of learning environments. These are characterized as learner-centered, knowledge centered, assessment-centered and community-centered. (DEMOS, 2005, p. 12)

This is exactly the kind of approach to learning and the learner previously described as a basis for personalizing education. The extent to which an awareness of learning style or the self as a learner is focused upon in learning design raises the following priorities in developing pedagogy, including a continuing challenge:

- For the school in an assessment-based approach to learning and teaching
- For subject knowledge leaders managing differentiation within the learning process of the curriculum
- For the teachers engaging with the development and application of a differential pedagogy

- For the learner in activity on 'learning how to learn' (developing strategies and routines – within and across the curriculum)
- For the whole school workforce when planning continuing professional development in the area of individual differences and an inclusive pedagogy

Exploiting learning styles as a teaching device and utilizing differential psychology therefore requires developing a broad-based approach to the ideas of a process curriculum, person-centered learning and an inclusive education. A great deal of theory in a psychology of the self as a learner, regardless of whether it is drawn from the differential, cognitive or humanistic domain, can and should be used to help inform the design of learning and instruction. It is important to locate this theory within a coherent and consistent pedagogic framework that is deliberately linked to the practice of formative assessment (Black & Wiliams, 2001). This means developing a pedagogic framework that is assessment-led and grounded in process. Assessment, in the form of profiling the learner and the learning process, particularly when using new forms of e-technology, opens up access to meta-levels of cognition and learning in the instructional context (Rayner, 2000).

Differentiation in the curriculum is both about designing and developing new ways of accommodating individual differences in learning as well as facilitating choice-making, decision-taking, adaptivity or flexibility in the learner and the learning environment. This demands a pedagogy that can enable a teacher in meeting the diverse needs of individuals and the group. It requires a 'proactive approach' from the school workforce, that is, forming part of an attitude to education predicated upon a person-centered notion of learning (Tomlinson, 1999; Ritchie & Deakin Crick, 2007). The planning and implementation of a differentiated curriculum is not simply a commitment to an individualized learning system (ILS). While e-technology affords considerable advances

in developing an ILS, as for example, is reflected in the development of adaptive hypermedia as an alternative to the traditional "one-size-fits-all" approach in learning design, there are also blended learning approaches to group as well as individualized learning systems in the e-learning context (De Freitas & Yapp, 2005). Adaptive hypermedia (AH) systems build a model of the goals, preferences, and knowledge of each individual user, and use of this model for adaptive navigation within an e-learning programme. Personalizing learning and developing a differential pedagogy, however, also involves increasing awareness of 'learning spaces' and 'knowledge communities' providing an opportunity for collaborative and independent learning (Milner, 2006). This management of the learning group invokes personalizing learning within a social space and place, and in turn can lead to other forms of group-based learning blending with a person-centered and inclusive approach to instruction.

Personalizing Education: Personal Diversity and E-Learning

The modernizing agenda for personalizing education is deeply implicated in notions of individual difference and the concept of learning styles. West-Burnham & Coates (2005) link this policy in the UK to a need for re-defining the school curriculum. Their argument is that personalizing learning must encompass a process that is both individual and social, and a curriculum that reflects an integrated consideration for social justice with individual growth and learning. As part of this argument, the authors see the need to 'take learning styles further', in the sense of seeking a consensual theory that in a worthwhile way can be safely and securely applied to the learning context. The call for research that will offer a more coherent and consensual theory is not new and it is hoped might be successfully advanced in the contemporary effort to develop e-learning, with new forms of pedagogy suitable for personalizing education. It is this intention that reflects recent attempts at defining a 'differential pedagogy' as one such new contribution to the practical knowledge of teaching (Rayner, 2007b).

In terms of personal diversity, and in spite of recent criticism (Yates, 2000; Coffield et al, 2004; Ritter, 2007), the intuitive appeal of style differences (cognitive, intellectual and learning) is very popular amongst educational practitioners. It offers a way of explaining and meaningfully understanding individual differences in the classroom (regardless of place or space or virtual reality). It points at potential too for enhancing self-awareness, self-regulation and fostering independence in the learner, as well as providing the educator with a tool for increasing their reference to the individual in the design of instruction and an enhancement of pedagogic knowledge and expertise (Reid, 2005; West-Burnham & Coates, 2005; Ritchie and Deakin-Crick, 2007). The advancements of design in e-learning infrastructure and operation reinforce this exciting potential but at the same time can easily create a technology dazzle obfuscating or even displacing a meaningful pedagogic and educational function (De Freitas & Yapp, 2005).

It is useful nonetheless to turn again to the educational potential of ICT and e-technology as a tool when thinking through the implications of managing personal diversity in the educational setting. Smeets and Mooij (2001, p. 416), in a project for the EU Directorate of General Education and Culture, identified the following key features in pupil-centred learning and curriculum differentiation:

- Teachers act as coaches.
- Learning environments are adapted to the needs, abilities, and interests of individual pupils.
- Pupils are encouraged to be active, co-operate and take more responsibility for the learning processes.

- Teachers pay attention to the potential of ICT to facilitate curriculum differentiation.

Villaverde (2006:197) argues that in order to be effective, e-learning systems should be capable of adapting the content of courses to learner characteristics such as style. In research aimed at improving levels of adaptivity, the potential for modeling of neural networks is demonstrated, offering a system that will automatically recognize the learning preferences of individual students according to the actions that he or she has performed in an e-learning environment. This builds upon earlier development of educational systems exploiting a theory of neural networking and artificial intelligence summarized by Haykin (1998). It is yet a further example of developing forms of an ILS and how differentiated approaches to learning and teaching can be achieved using e-technology. It is, however, not presented as a single approach to learning, or can it nor does it reject the importance of the social dimension and the notion of a learning community.

RE-APPRISING THE USE OF STYLE: A DIFFERENTIAL PEDAGOGY?

Pedagogy is the act and discourse of teaching, and is variously described as a science, a craft and an art form (Mortimore, 1999). Indeed, Galton et al., (1999) follow William James' original assertion in a series of seminal lectures in 1892 *(Talks to Teachers on Psychology and Life)*, inaugurating the field of educational psychology at Harvard, when claiming that pedagogy is actually a *'science of art'*. Alexander (2001) unfavourably contrasts a contemporary status of pedagogy in English education to a more fully developed 'science of teaching' in continental Europe. The latter tradition brings together within the one term, the act of teaching and the body of knowledge, argument and evidence in which it is embedded and by which particular classroom practices are justified. This means pedagogy is characterized as an integration of distinctive conceptual foci including:

- *Children*: Their characteristics, development and upbringing.
- *Learning*: How it can best be motivated, achieved, identified, assessed and developed.
- *Teaching/ instruction*: Its planning, execution and evaluation
- *Curriculum*: The various ways of knowing, understanding, doing, creating, investigating and making sense desirable for children to encounter, and how these are most appropriately translated and structured for teaching.

Further, Alexander's argument in developing a greater reference to and understanding of pedagogy is apposite in dealing with educational diversity, as is his suggestion that pedagogy generally might also be conceived as comprising several distinctive pedagogies, and how these might contribute to a teacher's professional development. He uses the example of 'dialogic teaching' aimed at:

... incorporating evidence about the nature and advancement of human learning, and to the conditions for education in a democracy, in which the values of individualism, community and collectivism stand in a complex and sometimes tense contrapuntal relationship. (Alexander, 2004b, p. 13).

The implications are that there exist or might be constructed different forms of pedagogy, a combination of which educationists will need to acquire as they develop their own professional pedagogic expertise. Is there, for example, when managing educational diversity and working with individual differences in the learner such a thing as a distinctive pedagogy?

Norwich and Lewis (2001), drawing upon a systematic review to address this question in relation to educational provision for children with special educational needs (SEN), found evidence that teachers attempt to differentiate their teaching according to broad perceptions of pupil ability. They found little evidence to support the idea of teachers adapting or developing an SEN specific pedagogy. They suggested, however, the existence of a 'high density' teaching approach that is comprised of a sliding rule or continuum of common 'pedagogic strategies'. Their review found a trend in research accounts signaling a movement away from ideas of a special needs-specific pedagogy toward an understanding of pedagogy in terms of a 'general differences' composition. The import for all of this, Norwich and Lewis argue, is the proposition of further focusing upon individual differences when managing educational diversity, and developing a differential rather than SEN specific pedagogy for inclusive education. They state, for example, that:

More pedagogically relevant groups may be identified in terms of learning process, such as learning styles ... than in terms of the general definitions (for example, MLD, SpLD). (Norwich & Lewis, 2001, p. 325)

Their argument is that learners with different styles of cognition and learning may benefit from specialized or personalized pedagogic strategies that form part of a generalized pedagogy. This is of considerable significance for the application of both a differential and inclusive pedagogy.

This also leads us to another question – what is the scope for developing a differential pedagogy? There are several examples of a deep commitment to the idea of a differential pedagogy linked to the field of learning styles and individual differences (Jonassen & Grabowski, 1993; Riding & Rayner, 1998; Dunn & Dunn, 1999; Reid, 2005). The extent, however, to which the idea of an individualized approach to education has been explored, debated and passed over during the past fifty years or more points to the paramount importance of a social and pragmatic dimension in learning and education (Coffield et al., 2004). It is also an indication that teachers will invariably resist a prescriptive catch-all in developing modes of pedagogy. Tomlinson makes the very important point that:

Differentiating instruction is not an instructional strategy or a teaching model. It's a way of thinking about teaching and learning that advocates beginning where individuals are rather than with a prescribed plan of action, which ignores student readiness, interest, and learning profile. It is a way of thinking that challenges how educators typically envision assessment, teaching, learning, classroom roles, use of time, and curriculum. (Tomlinson, 1999, p. 108)

If we wish to take the notion of a differential pedagogy further, it is helpful to begin assembling a working description of such an approach.

The extent to which an awareness of learning style or the self as a learner is currently considered and managed within the educational context raises key issues for the design of instruction and pedagogic practice, including implications for:

- *The school*: Designing an assessment-based approach focusing upon the inter-relationship between the learner, learning and teaching.
- *The subject and pastoral leaders*: Creating differentiation within the learning process of the curriculum.
- *The teachers*: Development of a differential pedagogy building upon the concept of the 'matching hypothesis' and 'style-flexing' for personal growth.
- *The learner*: Activity on 'learning how to learn' method and strategies and routines – within subject knowledge areas and across the curriculum.

- *The use of e-technology and learning theory*: in the development of all aspects of a differential pedagogy.
- *The school workforce*: continuing professional development in the area of extending and developing new and inclusive forms of pedagogy for an increasingly diverse school population.

A practical and useful example of this type of person-centred approach in the classroom is reflected in the work of McCoombs & Miller (2006). It is an integration of humanistic approaches with style-led practices that may very well contribute to developing a differential pedagogy suited to enabling a personalized education. Reid (2005), Mortimore (2003) and Prashnig (1998) amongst others, offer useful summaries of additional practical approaches to developing learning strategies and teaching tactics associated with a style-led approach. Their work provides guidance in the use of some of the building blocks to be applied in constructing a differential pedagogy.

As Luarilliard (2007) has suggested, research in education and computer science is now contributing massively to interdisciplinary innovation in teaching and learning. She suggests there is a tipping point in constant motion at the heart of this work. It is framed in the work of developing new forms of learning design and pedagogy. This also reflects a pivotal area in educational research, and as described by Laurilliard, it is also set upon a balance tilting from time to time towards technology, offering new flexibilities with a freedom from formality, and then towards education, with its formal organization, reflected in structuring forces of assessment, knowledge, categorization and accreditation. While knowledge and content remain key aspects of instruction, processes of learning, learner differences and formative assessment are the lead foci for a developing model of differential pedagogy, aimed at better managing personal diversity in learning and teaching.

ACTIVATING AN E-PEDAGOGY: ENABLING THE LEARNER

The more recent research and development in web-based learning (WBL) represents only one of several major innovations in the application of information and communication technology (ICT) for learning and teaching (Laurilliard, 2007). The focus here, however, is not on a consideration of the design of individualized instruction, which has always interested researchers working with theories of differential psychology (Riding & Rayner, 1995). It is, rather, on how approaches to personalizing learning can build upon this earlier work, say for example, with regard to ILS and WBL. Assessment and profiling the learner's interests and motivation form a basis for this approach, but should also be integrated with other related social and experiential aspects of the learning process - that is - interaction between the learner and learning (Cox et al., 2003; Germanakos et al., 2007). An ideal scenario for the future is one in which e-technology increasingly provides the means with which to shape an e-pedagogy associated with enabling as well as complementing an emerging differential pedagogy.

Advances in e-technology during the past decade have been quite staggering, opening up opportunities for developing adaptive forms for a personalized learning. This, however, should be seen as a part of and not apart from an inclusive model of learning (Rayner, 2007a). Recent inventions in the technology of WBL support this development, with for example the construction of *semantic learning webs,* claimed by Sheth et al. (2005), to be a breakthrough for incorporating *human perception and pervasive computing* in the educational task. A second example of innovative advancement is the more widely established research on adaptive hypermedia, which Brusilovsky and Peylo describes as:

... an alternative to the traditional "one-size-fits-all" approach in the development of hypermedia systems. Adaptive hypermedia (AH) systems build a model of the goals, preferences, and knowledge of each individual user, and use this model throughout the interaction with the user, in order to adapt to the needs of that user. (Brusilovsky and Peylo, 2003, p. 487)

The development of systems and design of ICT architecture aimed at facilitating adaptive and responsive inter-action between user, structural system, inter-face and content in a virtual learning context, generally mirrors other more traditional forms of activity in learning and teaching (see Smeets, 2001; Calcaterra, 2005).

It is, perhaps, important to stress at this point that while these approaches build systems that are conspicuously individualized, a social aspect to learning and the support of social communication and exchange is also an equally conspicuous and recurring feature in emerging e-pedagogy (Moss, 2005; Bilham, 2005; Prinsen et al., 2007). One example of developing a dynamic interactive model for an e-pedagogy was presented in the Palm project (Somekh & Davies, 1991, pp. 156–157). The researchers identified pedagogic change captured in teachers moving from a view of teaching and learning as:

- Discrete, complementary activities to an understanding that teaching and learning are independent aspects of a single activity.
- A sequential to an organic structuring of learning experiences.
- A focus shifting from solely targeting individualized to communicative learning.
- A view of the teacher's role as an organizer of learning activities to one as a shaper of quality learning experiences.
- A preoccupation with fitting teaching to a group, to a knowledge that teaching needs to be suited to individuals, which calls for continual self-monitoring to manage unintended forms of bias and discrimination.

- The learning context as confined to the classroom and controlled by the teacher to one of the learning context as a supportive, interactive, whole school culture.
- Technology as either a tutor or a tool to one where it is part of a complex of interactions with learners, sometimes providing ideas, sometimes providing a resource for enquiry, and sometimes supporting creativity.

The pedagogic approaches utilizing ICT adopted by teachers in traditional classrooms can range from only small enhancements of practices using what are essentially traditional methods, to more fundamental changes in their approach to teaching. In any attempt at personalizing learning, implications for a pedagogic framework are that teaching, tutoring, and training must all be primarily concerned with the learning process and the individual learner.

Similarly, the development of learning and tutoring systems in a range of e-technology must be linked to these pedagogic considerations. The '*conversational framework*' developed by Laurillard et al. (2000) is a helpful example of a template for building such an approach. This framework focuses upon method reflecting the learning process as an interaction between teacher and student(s). It attempts to capture the iterative interactions that must take place for conceptual learning to occur. The framework can be applied at any level of the learning process. These interactions might involve a short dialogue with the teacher explaining something, suggesting a practical example, and commenting on the pupil's performance, or a much more involved event covering several encounters, class sessions, assignments and debriefing. This, in turn, can be linked to the concept of a multidimensional e-pedagogy as described by Cox et al. (2003), in a research report for the UK Government. The report is emerging as one useful starting point for defining a pedagogic approach to e-learning. This model, capturing a range of issues and features,

such as: a realization that teachers' knowledge, beliefs and values will affect their pedagogical reasoning; and that their view on the power and scope of ICT, its new modes of knowledge representation and therefore the different ways in which pupils may learn, as well as a commitment to the social as well as personalized dimensions of any model of learning, will actually shape the design of learning.

The implications of research and development in e-technology for further developing both an e-pedagogy and a differential pedagogy are illustrated in the following cases: the first is work looking at hypermedia navigation in computerized learning systems; the second work developing a personalization of web-based learning; the third is a study researching the semantic dimension of e-learning; the last is work on pedagogic practice linked to a system of tutoring driven by artificial intelligence.

Case 1: Hypermedia & Cognitive Style

This study (Calcaterra, 2005) explored the effects of learners (N=306), interacting with a hypermedia presentation. The research attempted to measure the impact of learner characteristics (cognitive style, spatial orientation and computer expertise) upon hypertext navigation patterns and learning outcomes. The researchers found that hypermedia navigation behaviour was linked to computer skills rather than to cognitive style and that learning outcomes were unaffected by cognitive style or by computer skills. The study showed, however, that learning outcomes were positively affected by structuring searches to allow for the re-visiting of hypermedia sections and use of overview sections in the early stages of hypermedia browsing. The researchers concluded that the study indicated how individual differences can affect cognitive processing in hypermedia navigation, even though their role is more complex than initially predicted.

Case 2: Personalizing Web-Based Learning

This study (Germanakos et al., 2007) presents a model of web adaptation and a process of personalization that implements a comprehensive user profile. The learning system is therefore built around a model of the learner and an assessment-led pedagogy, in which key learning techniques are identified such as the extraction of user profiles and generation of a comprehensive user profile. These aspects of the learner include visual, cognitive, and emotional processing, which when combined together are found to give an *optimized, adapted and personalized outcome'*. The value for this and other related systems are arguably foremost in their contribution to multi-channel delivery of web-based content for learning in the educational context and the work-place. A second example is provided by the work reported in a study looking at sequential and global learning style dimensions as they affect the progress of understanding in the learning process (Sabry et al., 2003). These researchers identify three categories of web-based interaction: learner tutor, learner-learner, and learner-information. They explore the way in which the learning preferences of a group of learners are evidenced in these three categories of interaction. Sabry et al. conclude by asserting that an awareness of the pedagogical needs of different learning styles can result in a more effective integrated learning system. Importantly, they also suggest that such improvements to this kind of instructional system will help learners respond more effectively to different learning tasks and support developing a more flexible and autonomous learner.

Case 3: Developing the Semantic Web

This study (Dzbor et al., 2007) offers an alternative but complementary perspective on integrating e-technology, learning and instruction. It focuses upon the idea of a structural fabric in e-technology, and in particular, the *'semantic web'*, to develop an approach that is in effect a service-led, open learning system or e-community, which can incorporate and extend the use of semantic technologies as a means of providing services that are owned and created by learning communities. For example, the researchers show how it is possible to develop a range of educational Semantic Web services, such as interpretation, structure-visualization, support for argumentation, novel forms of content customization, novel mechanisms for aggregating learning material and citation services. This approach provides an example of how an inclusive e-pedagogy should eventually accommodate social as well as personal diversity, in its emergence as a distinct and enabling pedagogic practice. Related work which reflects a broader field of traditional and more recent developments in the field of a semantic web is described by Naeve et al. (2006), in which networking semantic content and engineering ontological frameworks has provided a basis for an integration of both personal and social aspects of educational diversity in a developing model of e-pedagogy. The widening field of semantic design in e-technology is important because of its potential as a basis for ensuring structures and content that capture expression of meaning, ontologies, concepts, levels of inter-operability with information exchange, and finally, the networking of social dimensions in the learning object and the community.

Case 4: Artificial Intelligent Tutor Systems

Curilem et al. (2007), report upon an attempt to identify ways forward in the use of artificial intelligence (AI) for the construction of Intelligent Tutoring Systems (ITS). The work is based on observations of the behaviours of systems in a range of AI applications for an intelligent learning environment. The researchers identify a need for carefully defining e-pedagogy to establish a common language between knowledge areas made up from pedagogical, computing and subject-based domains. A mathematical model provides a structural framework for an AI-based system development while integrating these different areas, so that it identifies the elements that constitute the system itself and defines the technological tools to implement it.

This builds upon a new generation of tutoring systems and owes its development to the advances of AI and related cognitive theories on learning, thereby locating the place of pedagogic strategies in a range of simulations modeling knowledge. An interesting example is given by demonstrating how formalization was used to design the adaptive mechanism in an ITS, enabling the adapting of its interface module to pre-selected student characteristics operating in the system. The system is shaped by earlier developments of the *'didactic ergonomy'* concept (Curilem & De Azevedo, 2003). This model requires that that pedagogic software must be configured so that the interface between user and environment is structured as two axes, the first is an apprentice (learner), and the second is a pedagogic (tutor), axis. The system generates an adaptive and interactive exchange between the apprentice and the learning object being studied.

A second exciting project (Villaverd et al., 2006), looks more closely at the assessment of an individual's learning style as part of the challenge of personalizing individualized learning systems, so that these are capable of adapting the content of courses to the individual characteristics of students. The method used by these researchers is based on artificial neural networks (ANNs). These are computational models for classification following a theory of the neural structure of the brain. In the proposed approach, feed-forward neural networks are used to recognize students' learning styles based upon the actions they have performed in an e-learning system. The authors claim that their model is effective and can be used in an adaptive e-learning environment to help in the assessment of students' learning styles. They also suggest that the same mechanism can be introduced to consider further input actions available in other e-learning systems.

These four cases represent only a small selected sample of a widening field of study. Further research, focusing upon an integration of e-learning, pedagogy and personalized learning, reported by JISC (2007), and De Freitas & Yapp, (2005) respectively, reinforces the argument presented in this chapter, of an emerging model of a multi-dimensional e-pedagogy as described by Cox et al (2003). As Laurilliard argues, however:

We are still in the early stages of understanding the relationships between technology, pedagogy and education. The technology moves fast, and although the underlying theories of pedagogy are reasonably stable, their instantiation within the context of a formal education system is a complex process. (Laurilliard, 2007, p. 360)

These relationships, in turn, will continue to more broadly affect the pedagogic approaches to design and interpretation of the curriculum and control of learning activity in the classroom. Importantly, in the task of personalizing education, it is also an e-pedagogy that not only can complement but may actually be used to re-activate an emergent model of differential pedagogy.

A WAY FORWARD: PERSONALIZING A 2020 EDUCATION?

The approach to personalizing education in this chapter is about designing a new school experience for the individual learner. It is also about using technological innovation to support systemic renewal in the curriculum. Its aim is to transform learning and teaching. It is, as argued by West-Burnham & Coates (2005), an attempt to re-contextualize education in the modern world of an information society. In a recent review of style differences research Coffield et al., (2004) vehemently argued for a much greater emphasis upon the study of pedagogy across the field of education. They identified a communication impasse, amounting to a knowledge block existing in all educational research. This situation was strongly criticized for preventing 'joined-up' thinking and acting as a barrier to enabling interdisciplinary contributions in an applied domain. They argued that,

What is needed in the UK now is a theory (or set of theories) of pedagogy for post-16 learning, but this does not exist. What we have instead is a number of different research schools, each with its own language, theories, methods, literature, journals, conferences and advice to practitioners; and these traditions do not so much argue with as ignore each other...... (Coffield et al., 2004, pp. 142-3)

The field of cognitive and learning styles was identified in this review as a worse case scenario, clearly revealing these difficulties for research in an applied discipline. Coffield et al., saw a fundamental contribution to this impasse as the continuing conflict between two key underpinning disciplines in the study of Education, namely psychology and sociology.

The practical consequence of this divide is two separate literatures on pedagogy which rarely interact with each other. Typically, sociologists and psychologists pass each other by in silence, for all the world like two sets of engineers drilling two parallel tunnels towards the same objective in total ignorance of each other. Coffield et al. (2004, p. 143)

The need for an inclusive approach to applied research is similarly demonstrated in the cases of e-learning and managing educational diversity. Again, a way forward should reflect distinct advances in research methodology and epistemology

for each key constituency, as applied to the field of personalizing education. It will also, however, crucially require the construction of an inter-disciplinary and integrative paradigm to inform and support this same work. For applied research to be effective, it must encompass theoretical and practical contexts in the creation, capture and transfer of relevant knowledge. In the same way, there is a need to ensure that the development of pedagogy combines the key contexts of learning, teaching and the curriculum.

A deepening challenge for practitioners and educationists in responding to this way forward is activating a differential pedagogy. To do this involves: 1) dealing with learning differences and personal diversity – that is – exploiting the concept of a personalized education; and 2) establishing deeper understandings of *learning process* and how ways of *engaging the learner* can be embedded in a *participatory pedagogy* when developing pedagogic practice.

The main direction taken here is to call for a more integrated form of research in support of particular professional development. Researchers in the fields of style differences and e-learning are in a good position to lead the way. They should aim to encourage teachers to construct, enable and activate pedagogies that will further support personalizing learning. If this is to impact upon educational practice, there must be a continuing generation and exchange of new knowledge, both academic and applied, across a number of domains relevant to the practical contexts of learning and teaching.

A movement toward creating a consensual theory of learning, teaching and assessment is an underlying premise to the argument in this chapter. This does not mean, as previously stated, that there is one simple menu for learning design, or a single model of psychology to explain the performance of the learner. It is much more likely that none of these approaches will produce easy or simple models of learning, curriculum, instruction and pedagogy. What is necessary, however, is research that can provide a more clearly established framework or script with which to contextualize the ideas, concepts and knowledge used to help understand and improve upon the work of personalizing learning. This should take the form of an inclusive framework, integrating a number of underlying disciplines combining the constituent fields of research and practice in a focused effort to realize pedagogic development.

An agenda for realizing this goal might usefully include reciprocal action in the following three constituent domains: differential psychology, learning theory and e-technology. These domains of knowledge represent a theoretical underpinning for the construction of a dedicated programme of research. The intention is to realize a coherent theory as a framework for supporting and extending the development of personalized learning and a differential pedagogy.

Differential Psychology and the Learner

A recurring set of problems identified in this chapter reflect a controversy surrounding definition, structure and validity of a number of core constructs in differential psychology. One example is the debate surrounding ability and intelligence. Attempts to create a more coherent and unified theory of individual differences should build upon the work carried out by an American Association of Psychology task force field which tackled the question of unifying theories of intelligence (Neisser et al., 1996). In terms of style differences and differential psychology, following a similar argument mounted by Messick (1994), work is needed in the re-framing of cognitive styles with-in a broader personality system. Kozhevnikov (2007) has also argued for theoretically re-integrating the style construct in the traditional model of individual differences. She claimed that this will problematize methodology, stimulating greater understanding of the 'dynamic systems' that make up an individual's cognitive functioning.

The desire for a strategic movement in the field is also reflected in an argument that paradigm shift across this domain should be deliberately targeted (Rayner, 2007c). A combination of research in e-technology and differential psychology is arguably one opportunity for triggering this kind of shift, beginning with evidence-based knowledge exchange, and creating new points of reference for theory building (for example, see Graf et al, 2008). A second opportunity lies with researchers in e-technology and computer sciences following a similar direction as identified by Laurilliard (2007) in her elaboration of a conversational framework for the development of e-learning.

Cognition, Learning Theory and Instruction

Mosely and colleagues have identified a great number of theoretical frameworks for thinking and learning that have been used in schooling (Mosley et al., 2005). Their conclusion is that human learning is a complex and multidimensional phenomenon. This is perhaps stating the obvious, but it is useful to take this point as a reference when focusing on any particular aspect of learning theory. It is also a reminder that effective teaching and learning will seek to foster for the learner both individual and social activity. What is perhaps most important for professional development is an opportunity for educationists to further explore and investigate ways of integrating some of these fundamental structures of learning, in actual life, as a scenario that will always involve aspects of the individual interacting with an external world to learn. This re-emphasizes the importance of contextualized research and evidence-based activity located in the real world of applied practice (Rayner, 2007b, c). Similarly, conflicting models of learning theory that are social or personal in origin need to be mediated in an account of the learner learning. This work should be directed to constructing new models of pedagogy as a proper product of educational research (see Alexander 2004a; Coffield et al., 2004).

Learning, E-Technology and Pedagogy

Advances in e-technology remain both a key driver and an end-game in the work of personalizing education. A desire to develop an e-pedagogy is a third and equally important constituent in the work of supporting learning and managing educational diversity. The JISC Newsletter (JISC, 2007) identifies several key actions that are deemed essential in further advancement of an e-pedagogy. These include a consideration of the basic purpose of technology in the learning context and require thinking about:

- **Usability:** Ease of application and efficiency of design.
- **Contextualisation:** Relevance and appropriateness of the technology.
- **Professional learning:** Support for developing expertise, re-conceptualizing learning theories and forming an e-pedagogy.
- **Communities and networking:** Links to issues of social and contextual aspects of learning as well as authenticity and ownership in the work of research and development.
- **Adaptability:** Sustainable and relevant application within context.

The question of purpose, utility and relevance remains the first and final issue for researchers (academic and professional) collaborating in education and computer science.

It is with this purpose in mind that researchers and educationists need to remain aware that technology can create an aura of innovation. It is easy to be dazzled by the enhanced flexibilities and opportunities offered by new sleek and shiny machines for the virtual environments and digital natives of an 'emailing, browsing ipod generation'. It is this vulnerability for 'technological tautology' in the work of computer science that perhaps leads Luarilliard to argue that if we are to discover how to optimize our use of learning technologies, then,

.... the focus has to be on pedagogy—what does it take to learn, and how do we help learners in the process? Technology offers a range of different ways of engaging learners in the development of knowledge and skills. Precisely because of the richness of possibilities, we have to be careful not to focus simply on what the technology offers, but rather on what the pedagogy requires. (Luarilliard, 2007, p. 359)

The purpose here then is to construct, extend and continue to refine an e-pedagogy. This is a distinct and particular endeavour but we would argue here that it is best attempted in unison with a similar development of a differential pedagogy.

CONCLUSION

It is always important to be clear about the place of research in developing professional knowledge and to be careful in deciding just which theory or perspective shapes working practice. I argue here that a differential pedagogy is not a theory which is a simple, uniform, one-size solution for effective learning and teaching. It offers the idea of a framework for developing approaches to diversity and individual needs in the classroom. In this respect, it is part of an opportunity to build a 'better-fit' rather than a 'perfect pedagogy'. I am, in fact, arguing at this point for retaining the place of differential psychology in an integrated framework of learning theory, teaching and pedagogy. It is vital that teachers are aware of and have a concern for the psychology of an individual's learning performance. In turn, the forming of an e-pedagogy is an integral contribution to a differential pedagogy and each set of practices will ideally inform the other in mutual exchange and a reciprocating development.

The over-arching concept that provides a basis for moving toward a consensus model of learning theory as demanded by Coffield et al. (2004) and in turn a re-construction of pedagogy, is personalized education. Fink stated that:

I think personalised learning is an idea for our time. It's a recognition of human uniqueness – we are not just trying to turn out assembly-line children. It means redesigning our schools to fit the pupils rather than what we do now, which is to take the kids and force them to fit into the existing structures. It means a focus on learning, deep learning, learning for understanding, learning for meaning and giving people time. (Fink, 2005, p. 21)

Fink's assertion is a challenging call to better manage personal diversity in the educational system. It perhaps raises more questions than it actually answers by correctly inferring a resource dilemma posed in the recognition of 'uniqueness'. Yet, the desire to re-focus upon the process of an individual learner(s), engaging in learning, is a core aspect to a working differential pedagogy.

This chapter began by asking the question, what is likely by the year 2020, to be the preferred pedagogic face of instructional design, teaching and learning in a formal educational setting? The learning endeavour will increasingly be construed as a life-long process. It will more frequently feature the scenario of a '*boundedless space for learning and teaching*', as well as technologies or media for developing a '*post-modern pedagogy for Personalized Education*'. To further realize this approach in the form of personalized learning, a re-grouping of sets of domain knowledge, and a blending of differential psychology, assessment of the learner and learning, as well as e-technology, are all required. Developing distinctive pedagogies for e-learning and personal diversity in the learning process form a major purpose for this

endeavour. Activating and integrating these pedagogies will in turn create new areas of research and an opportunity for improvements to pedagogic knowledge, with a greater chance for realizing positive impacts on young people's learning and therefore their future.

REFERENCES

Alexander, R. J. (2001). Border crossings: Towards a comparative pedagogy. *Comparative Education, 37*(4), 507-523.

Alexander, R. J. (2004a). Still no pedagogy? Principle, pragmatism and compliance in primary education. *Cambridge Journal of Education, 34*(1), 7-33.

Alexander, R. J. (2004b). *Towards dialogic teaching: Rethinking classroom talk.* York: Dialogos.

Beetham, H. (2005). Personalization in the curriculum: A view from learning theory. In S. De Freitas & C. Yapp (Eds.), *Personalizing learning in the 21st century* (pp. 17-24). Stafford: Network Educational Press.

Bilham, T. (2005). Online learning: Can communities of practice deliver personalization in learning? In S. De Freitas & C. Yapp (Eds.), *Personalizing learning in the 21st century* (pp. 73-76). Stafford: Network Educational Press.

Black, P., & Wiliams, D. (2001). *Assessment and classroom learning.* London: School of Education, King's College London.

Brusilovsky, P., & Nejdl W. (2004). *Adaptive hypermedia and adaptive Web.* CSC Press LLC.

Brusilovsky, P., & Peylo C. (2003). Adaptive and intelligent Web-based educational systems. *International Journal of Artificial Intelligence in Education, 13,* 156-169.

Calcaterra, A., Antonietti A., & Underwood, J. (2005). Cognitive style, hypermedia navigation and learning. *Computers & Education,* 44, 441-457.

Coffield, F. C., Moseley, D. V. M., Hall, E., & Ecclestone, K. (2004). *Learning styles and pedagogy in post-16 Learning: Findings of a systematic and critical review of learning styles models.* London: Learning and Skills Research Centre.

Collis J. M., & Messick, S. (Eds.), (2001). *Intelligence and Personality: Bridging the gap in theory and measurement.* Mahwah S., NJ: Lawrence Erlbaum Associates.

Cox, M., Webb, M., Abbott, C., Blakeley, B., Beauchamp, T., & Rhodes, V. (2003). ICT and pedagogy: A review of the research literature. *ICT in schools research and evaluation series – No.18.* Nottingham: DfES & BECTA.

Curilem, G. M. J., & De Azevedo, F. M. (2003). Didactic ergonomy for the interface of intelligent tutoring systems. In *Computers and education: Toward a lifelong learning society* (pp. 75-88). Dordrecht: Kluwer Academic Publishers.

Curilem, S. G., Barbosa, A. R., & de Azevedo, F. M. (2007). Intelligent tutoring systems: Formalization as automata and interface design using neural networks. *Computers & Education,* 49, 545-561.

De Freitas, S., & Yapp, C. (Eds.) (2005). *Personalizing learning in the 21st century.* Stafford: Network Educational Press.

DEMOS (2005). About learning: The report of the Working Group. *DEMOS Report.* London: DEMOS. Retrieved May, 13, 2006, from http://www.demos.co.uk.

Derntl, M., & Motschnig-Pitrik, R. (2005). The role of structure, patterns, and people in blended learning. *The Internet and Higher Education,* 8(2), 111-130.

DfES (2006). 2020 vision. *Report of the Teaching and Learning in 2020 Review Group.* Nottingham: DfES.

Dunn, R., & Dunn, K. (1999). *The complete guide to the learning styles inservice system.* Boston, MA: Allyn & Bacon.

Dzbor, M., Stutt, A., Motta, E., & Collins, T. (2007). Representations for semantic learning Webs: Semantic Web technology in learning support. *Journal of Computer Assisted Learning,* 23, 69-82.

Fink, D. (2005). Growing into it. In NCSL (Ed.), *Leading personalised learning in schools* (pp. 13-22). Nottingham: National College of School Leadership.

Fiorina, L., Antonietti, A., Colombo, B., & Bartolomeo A. (2007). Thinking style, browsing primes and hypermedia navigation. *Computers & Education,* 49, 916-941.

Furnham, A. (2001). Test-taking style, personality traits and psychometric validity. In J. M. Collis & S. Messick (Eds.), *Intelligence and personality: Bridging the gap in theory and measurement* (pp. 289-304). Mahwah, NJ: Lawrence Erlbaum Associates.

Galton, M., Hargreaves, L., Comber, C., Wall, D. & Pell, A. (1999). *Inside the primary classroom: 20 years on.* London: Routledge.

Gardner, H. (1993). *Multiple intelligences: The theory in practice.* New York: Basic Books.

Germanakos, P., Tsianos, N., Lekkas, Z., Mourlas, C., & Samaras. G. (2007). Realizing comprehensive user profile as the core element of adaptive and personalized communication environments and systems. *Oxford Computer Journal,* 1-29.

Ghinea, G., & Chen, S. H. (2003). The impact of cognitive styles on perceptual distributed multimedia quality. *British Journal of Educational Technology,* 34(4), 393-406.

Graff, M. (2003). Learning from Web-based instructional systems and cognitive style. *British Journal of Educational Technology,* 34(4), 407-418.

Graf, S., Lin, T., & Kinshuk. (2008). The relationship between learning styles environments with feed-forward neural networks and cognitive traits – Getting additional information for improving student modeling. *Computers in Human Behavior*, 24, 122-137.

Haykin, S. (1998). *Neural networks: A comprehensive foundation* (2nd ed.). Upper Saddle River, NJ: Prentice Hall.

JISC (2007). Designing for learning. *An update on the pedagogy strand of the JISC e-learning programme*. Retrieved 15 March, 2007, from http://www.jisc.ac.uk/elearning_pedagogy

Jonassen, D. H., & Grabowski, B. L. (1993). *Handbook of individual difference, learning and instruction*. Hillsdale, NJ: Lawrence Erlbaum Associates.

Kimberly, B. W. (2007). Blended learning and online tutoring: A good practice guide - A Book Review. *Internet & Higher Education*, *10*(4), 283-286.

Kozhevnikov, M. (2007). Cognitive styles in the context of modern psychology: Toward an integrated framework of cognitive style. *Psychological Bulletin, 133*(3), 464-481.

Laurillard, D., Stratfold, M., Luckin, R., Plowman, L., & Taylor, J. (2000). Affordances for learning in a non-linear narrative medium. *Journal of Interactive Media in Education*, 62.

Laurilliard, D. (2007). Technology, pedagogy and education: Concluding comments. *Technology, Pedagogy and Education, 16*(3), 357-360.

McInerney, D. M. (2005). Educational psychology – Theory, research, and teaching: A 25-year retrospective. *Educational Psychology, 25*(6), 585-599.

McCombs, B., & Miller, M. (2006). *Learner-centred classrooms practices and assessments*. Thousand Oaks, CA: Corwin Press.

Messick, S. (1984). The nature of cognitive styles: Problems and promise in educational practice. *Educational Psychologist*, 19, 59-74.

Messick, S. (1994). The matter of style: Manifestations of personality in cognition, learning, and teaching. *Educational Psychologist, 29*(3), 121-136.

Milner, Z. (2006). *Learning by accident: A report for a personalized learning project for disaffected learners*. Bristol: ViTaL Partnerships.

Mortimore, P (Ed.), (1999). *Understanding pedagogy and its impact on learning*. London: Paul Chapman Pubs.

Mortimore, T. (2003). *Dyslexia and learning style*. London: Whurr Pubs.

Mosely, D., Baumfield, V., Elliot, J., Gregson, M., Higgins, S., Miller, J., & Newton, D. (2005). *Frameworks for thinking: A handbook for teaching and learning*. Cambridge: Cambridge University Press.

Moss, M. (2005). Personalized lLearning: A failure to collaborate. In S. De Freitas, & C. Yapp (Eds.), *Personalizing learning in the 21ˢᵗ century*. Stafford: Network Educational Press.

Naeve, A., Lytras, M., Nejdl, W., Balacheff, N., & Hardin, J. (2006). Editorial: Advances of the Semantic Web for e-learning: Expanding learning frontiers. *British Journal of Educational Technology, 37*(3) 321-330.

Naismith, E. (2005). Enabling personalization through context awareness. In S. De Freitas & C. Yapp (Eds.), *Personalizing learning in the 21ˢᵗ century* (pp. 103-108). Stafford: Network Educational Press.

Neisser, U., Boodoo, G., Bouchard, Jr., T. J., Boykin, A W., Brody, B., Ceci, S. J., Halpern, D. E., Loehlin, J. C., Perloff, R., Sternberg, R. J., & Urbina, S. (1996). Intelligence: Knowns and unknowns. *American Psychologist, 51*(2), 77-101.

Norwich, B., & Lewis, A. (2001). Mapping a pedagogy for special educational needs. *British Educational Research Journal, 27*(3), 313-329.

Prashnig, B. (1998). *The power of diversity: New ways of learning and teaching.* Auckland, NZ: David Bateman.

Prinsen, F., Volman, M.L.L., & Terwel, J. (2007). The influence of learner characteristics on degree and type of participation in a CSCL environment. *British Journal of Educational Technology, 38*(6), 1037-1055.

Rayner, S.G. (1998). Educating pupils with emotional and behavioural difficulties: Pedagogy is the key! *Emotional and Behavioural Difficulties, 3*(2), 39-47.

Rayner, S. G. (2000). Re-constructing style differences in thinking and learning: Profiling learning performance. In R. J. Riding & S. Rayner (Eds.), *International Perspectives in Individual Differences.* (pp. 115-180). Stamford, CT: Ablex Press.

Rayner, S.G. (2001). Aspects of the self as learner: perception, concept and esteem. In R.J. Riding & S.G. Rayner (Eds.), *International perspectives on individual differences* (pp. 25- 52). Westport, CT: Ablex Pubs.

Rayner, S. (2007a). *Managing special and inclusive education.* London: Sage.

Rayner, S. G. (2007b). A teaching elixir, learning chimera or just fool's gold? Do learning styles matter? *Support for Learning, 22*(1), 24-31.

Rayner, S. (2007c). Whither styles? In T. Redmond, A. Parkinson, C. Moore & A. Stenson (Eds.), *Exploring style: Enhancing the capacity to learn. Proceedings of the 11ᵗʰ Annual Conference of the European Learning Styles Information Network* (pp. 293-296). Dublin: University of Dublin.

Reid, G. (2005). *Learning styles and inclusion.* London: Sage.

Reynolds, M. (1997). Learning styles: a critique. *Management Learning, 28*(2), 115-133.

Riding, R., & Rayner, S.G. (1995). The information superhighway and individualised learning. *Educational Psychology, 15*(4), 365-378.

Riding, R.J., & Rayner, S.G. (1998). *Cognitive styles and learning strategies.* London: David Fulton Pubs.

Riding, R. J., & Rayner, S. G. (2000). (Eds.) *International perspectives in individual differences.* Stamford, CT: Ablex Press.

Ritchie, R., & Deakin Crick, R. (2007). *Distributing leadership for personalizing education.* London: Continuum Network Pubs.

Ritter, L. (2007). Unfulfilled promises: How inventories, instruments and institutions subvert discourses of diversity and promote commonality. *Teaching in Higher Education, 12*(5 & 6), 569-579.

Sabry, K., & Baldwin, L. (2003). Web-based learning interaction and learning styles. *British Journal of Educational Technology, 34*(4), 443-454.

Sheth, A., Ramakrishnan, C., & Thomas, C. (2005). Semantics for the Semantic Web: The implicit, the formal and the powerful. *International Journal of Semantic Web and Information Systems, 1*(1), 1-18.

Shi, H., Revithis, S., & Chen, S. (2002). An agent enabling personalized learning in e-learning environments. *International Conference on Autonomous Agents: Proceedings of the first international joint conference on Autonomous agents and multi-agent systems, Part 2* (pp. 847-848).

Smeets, E., & Mooij, T. (2001). Pupil-centred learning, ICT, and teacher behaviour: Observations in educational practice. *British Journal of Educational Technology, 32*(4), 403-417.

Somekh, B., & Davies, R. (1991). Towards a pedagogy for information technology. *The Curriculum Journal, 2*(2), 153-170.

Thurstone, L. L. (1944). A factorial study of perception. *Psychometric Monograph, Number 4*. Chicago: Chicago University of Press.

Tomlinson, C. A. (1999). *The differentiated classroom: Responding to the needs of all learners.* Alexandria, VA: ASCD Press.

Vermunt J. D. (1996). Metacognitive, cognitive and affective aspects of learning styles and strategies: a phenomenographic analysis. *Higher Education*, 31, 25-50.

Villaverde, J. E., Godoy, D., & Amandi, A. (2006). Learning styles' recognition in e-learning. *Journal of Computer Assisted Learning*, 22, 197-206.

Weber, K. (1982). *The teacher is the key.* Milton Keynes: The Open University Press.

West-Burnham, J., & Coates, M. (2005). *Personalizing learning.* Stafford: Network Educational Press.

Yates, G. C. R. (2000). Applying learning styles research in the classroom: Some cautions and the way ahead. In R. J. Riding & S. G. Rayner (Eds), *International perspectives on individual differences. Cognitive styles* (pp. 347-364). Stamford, CT: Ablex.

Zimmerman, (2008). Investigating self-regulation and motivation: historical background, methodological developments, and future prospects. *American Educational Research Journal, 45*(1), 166-183.

Chapter III
Can Cognitive Style Predict How Individuals Use Web–Based Learning Environments?

Martin Graff
University of Glamorgan, UK

ABSTRACT

This chapter considers the question of whether Web-based learning environments can be employed to effectively facilitative learning. Several questions are considered around this issue, principally whether variations in hypertext architecture, and individual differences in information processing are salient factors for consideration. Furthermore, whether the effectiveness of learning depends precisely upon how learning is defined. Finally, differences in hypertext navigational strategies are assessed in terms of whether these can be predicted by individual differences in cognitive style. The chapter ends by concluding that the research on Web-based instructional systems is to some extent promising, although the field of cognitive style is diverse, and realistic predictions regarding the use of this construct in instructional design is, as yet, tenuous.

INTRODUCTION

One of the salient features of web-based learning environments is that they can provide an explicit structure to instructional material, which should ultimately facilitate the learning process. For example, such structures can be designed to explicitly indicate the conceptual links between related information. The following chapter as-sesses the degree to which this theoretical position can be supported by the extant literature. More precisely, this chapter reviews the literature on how web-based or hypertext-learning systems have been employed in an educational context. We will consider issues such as the most facilitative hypertext architecture for assisting the learning process. Later in the chapter the evidence on the extent to which cognitive style mediates the effects of architecture are reviewed. Finally, evidence will be assessed regarding the way in which users navigate hypertext and how this may influence their comprehending of its structure.

BACKGROUND

Web-based learning environments are structured around hypertext systems, which allow conceptually related pieces of information to be connected or linked. Information on one page in the system can be linked to a related piece of information contained in a separate page. Such systems are user driven, in as much as individuals can choose to be 'transported' or moved within the system to pages containing related information. Furthermore, web-based or hypertext systems can by structured in a variety of ways, and the way in which the system is structured is referred to as the system architecture. Typical architectures found in the literature are 'linear', where pages of information are linked sequentially, rather like they are in a book; 'hierarchical' where superordinate information is contained in pages higher up the system, and linked to more detailed information further down in the structure and 'relational', which is similar to the hierarchical architecture, although this structure also contains lateral links between conceptually related information at the more detailed level.

This chapter considers the effectiveness of learning from web-based systems, and it is appropriate at this stage to consider the term 'learning', and the way in which it has been applied in the literature. Perhaps one of the most expedient notions of learning to consider in this respect is that offered by Bloom's Taxonomy of levels of learning (Bloom, 1968). In essence, Bloom advocated that learning could be arranged at different levels ranging from basic knowledge or recall, up to a more sophisticated type of learning manifest in evaluation or synthesis of material. The notion that learning can be applied at different levels is

important to consider as we review the extent to which learning may be facilitated by web-based learning environments.

WEB-BASED LEARNING AND HYPERTEXT ARCHITECTURE

A useful starting point would be to question whether using different hypertext structures differentially affect learning performance. The earlier studies considering this question seem to suggest that mixed or relational web-based or hypertext systems appear to be the most facilitative.

For instance in a study by Mohageg (1982) the issue of whether question answering performance would vary following delivery of learning materials via three different web structures or architectures was considered. The architectures used in this study were hierarchical, where the learning material was constructed such that more general information was contained higher up the structure, and more specific information lower down; network, where the information was structured in a complex system of links; and mixed which was a combination of the other two structures. The findings indicated that learning performance was poorest in the network architecture condition. However, there were no differences in learning performance in the other conditions. The interpretation of this finding was that as the mixed condition featured more links than the other conditions, this may have increased the learners' facility for learning.

McDonald and Stevenson (1998) employed 30 undergraduate and postgraduate students in their study of web-based learning. They also used three hypertext architectures, which were hierarchical (as described above), non-linear (in which the information was constructed in a type of network) and mixed (hierarchical with lateral links). After using one of the three systems, participants answered ten questions on information they had read in the learning system. The findings revealed that those student participants who had used the mixed system found information quicker than participants in the other conditions, which is possibly due to the fact that the mixed architecture made it easier for the users to understand the overall structure.

The above studies sought to measure learning using tests of recall, which is synonymous with basic knowledge or recall at the lower level of Bloom's Taxonomy of Learning (Bloom, 1968). However, as outlined earlier, learning also takes place at a deeper level, which could be said to involve an appreciation of the interrelationships between the various concepts and procedures in a particular subject domain. This more sophisticated approach to learning might necessitate comprehending how related concepts within a subject domain, may be arranged or constructed into a unified whole. This issue is considered with respect to web-based learning, in the following section.

Learning at a Deeper Level

In one study, Shapiro (1998) used an essay question to investigate how effectively learners showed an appreciation of the overall structure of the information contained within a web-based learning system. Three different architectures were employed in this study, which were hierarchical with some lateral links, unstructured, which had the same links as the hierarchical, but with no specific information about the structure, and linear where the material was presented sequentially, one step at a time. Seventy-two participants were asked to write an essay which required them to integrate the material they had learned from reading information from one of the web architectures. Essays were rated on four criteria which were integration of material in the essay, how well the participant understood the topic about which they were writing, the clarity of the essay and the overall quality of the essay. On all of these criteria, it was found

that participants in the unstructured hypertext condition scored higher than those in the other conditions. The interpretation of this finding was that the lack of any explicit information in this condition required a deeper level of processing of the information in order for participants to understand it, and this resulted in a higher level of performance.

Concept Maps

Concept maps provide a visual representation of the interrelationships among concepts or pieces of knowledge relating to a particular subject domain. This idea was pioneered by Joseph Novak in the 1960s, and it is suggested that the technique may facilitate an individual's learning of how the finer details contributing to a wider body of knowledge are integrated. It is also conceivable that concept maps may also be employed to facilitate a user's understanding of the interrelationships between smaller, more detailed pieces of information presented in web-based learning environments.

Shapiro (1998) in the study outlined above, compared also the concept mapping performance of participants, assigned to one of the three hypertext learning environments outlined. Participants were required to recall the structure of the hypertext web by producing drawings, one measure of which was amount of detail present. Participants in the linear condition included less detail in their concept maps than participants in the hierarchical and unstructured conditions. This finding was explained in terms of participants in the hierarchical and unstructured conditions visiting the same pages in the structure more times than the participants in the linear condition, thus the amount of exposure to the information, led to differences in the amount of detail recalled. Shapiro also found that participants in the hierarchical and unstructured conditions produced concept maps which reflected the actual links in these structures, and it therefore seems that the links reflect the participants' internal representations of the hypertext.

A slight variation to this finding was reported by McNamara, Hardy and Hirtle (1989). They found that despite using non hierarchical hypertext environments, their participants still produced map representations which tended to be hierarchical. They explain this finding in terms of certain types of information being mentally organised in a hierarchical manner. Such a mental organisation facilitates effective recall of the information.

We now move on to consider the different ways in which individuals navigate or move around hypertext environments, and assess how this may be used to provide information on the affect it has on an individual's ability to apprehend its structure. The reasoning behind this notion is that the route an individual takes through an environment is likely to influence their representation of that space. Indeed Maglio and Matlock (1999) found that the way in which individuals move around in hypertext affects the ways in which they think about it. From their interview data, they suggest that people view hypertext as a type of physical space in which they move around. Their participants remembered landmarks and routes, and also the key information they found while navigating. In addition to this they found that participants relied on personal routines, similar to the types of routines individuals employ when travelling from one point to another. The suggestion is that the way in which an individual navigates will affect their mental representation of the hypertext. In the next section the types of navigational strategies which have been identified in the literature are examined. In the literature, the terms 'navigation' and 'browsing' are sometimes used interchangeably with regard to moving around in hypertext. The broad distinction would appear to be that browsing is considered to be a more casual non-goal related task, whereas navigating is more purposely directed towards some final end. Nevertheless, both terms refer to how we move around a hypertext system.

Navigational Strategies

Batra, Bishu and Donohue (1993) identified differences in navigational behaviour according to the hypertext architecture to which users were assigned. The two architectures they employed in their study were hierarchical and hypertorus (pages arranged in a rectangular pattern). They also looked at the effect of each type of architecture on participants' ability to answer ten questions, the answers to which could be found in the hypertext. Their results suggested that the hypertorus structure generated more exploratory browsing behaviour, but despite this the hierarchical structure made it easier for participants to locate information. However, it is easy to interpret the findings as being attributable to the number of links in each architecture.

In their study Canter, Rivers and Storrs (1985) categorised navigational strategies as being related to the function each strategy serves for the user of the hypertext. These strategies included pathiness, where users follow long linear paths; loopiness, where users navigate around the hypertext in circles; ringiness, which are small loops or circles and spikeiness, where users follow paths to dead ends. The researchers also examined the number of pages within the hypertext users visited, and number of different pages visited, and the ratio of different pages visited to the total number of pages visited. From this information, they devised five distinct navigational strategies, which were scanning (covering a large area without depth), browsing (following a path until a goal is reached), searching (striving to find an explicit goal), exploring (finding out the extent of the information system) and wandering (purposeless and unstructured globe-trotting). The authors also concluded that these navigational strategies apart from wandering, have a function in navigating hypertext. Scanning and exploring are used to get an overview of the hypertext, whereas browsing is following a train of thought through the hypertext. All in all, this study provides a useful way of categorising navigational behaviour.

Despite the fact that the above studies provide comprehensive information regarding the relative effectiveness of different hypertext architectures on learning, none of the studies reviewed so far has considered individual differences in the ways in which various users engage with hypertext. Because it specifically refers to individual differences in information processing the construct of cognitive style is pertinent to consider in assessing how effectively individuals learn from hypertext.

COGNITIVE STYLE, HYPERTEXT AND LEARNING

Cognitive style can be defined as a variation in the ways in which individuals process information, in terms of differences in perceiving, remembering, recalling and applying this information. Various cognitive style constructs have been proposed by various researchers, for example reflective-impulsive (Kagan, Rosman, Day, Albert and Phillips, 1964), convergent-divergent (Guildford, 1959), leveller-sharpener (Holzman and Klein, 1954) and serialist-holist (Pask, 1972). All these style constructs are based on the notion that different style types exist at opposite ends of a continuum. The style type field dependent-independent which developed from the work of Herman Witkin is one of the most extensively used models of cognitive style. Field dependence-independence is defined in terms of whether individuals perceive entities as separate units, (field independent) or as complete wholes (field dependent). There is also evidence to suggest that there are differences in the ways in which field dependent and field independent individuals learn (Witkin, Moore, Goodenough and Cox, 1977). Field independent learners are able to see a degree of structure in what they learn, whereas field dependent learners rely more upon being provided with a structure externally.

Theoretically, a highly structured hypertext instructional architecture will be of greater benefit to field dependent learners, because this will provide an organisational aid to their learning. Conversely, a poorly structured learning environment where a degree of organisation would need to be provided by the learner would be less beneficial to field dependent learners, although in such an unstructured environment, field independent learners would suffer no debilitation in learning, because of their superior capacity for imposing structure on the material they are attempting to learn. However, the empirical evidence reviewed in the following does not necessarily support this reasoning.

For example, Lin and Davidson-Shivers (1996) assessed verbal recall in a group of 139 undergraduate students, following a period of time using one of five hypertext architectures. The architectures corresponded to linear, hierarchical, hierarchical-associative, associative and random, and all of the architectures contained the same information. The participants were also assessed using the Group Embedded Figures Test (GEFT) designed to measure field dependence-independence (Witkin, Oltman, Raskin, and Karp, 1971). The results of this study revealed that participants who were more field independent as indicated by their higher GEFT scores, outperformed participants who were assessed by the GEFT as being more field dependent. In addition to this, field independent users displayed more favourable attitudes to using the hypertext than field dependent participants. The researchers explained the results by suggesting that field independent learners are more self motivated and have greater expectations of achievement.

Consistent with the previous study, a further investigation assessing the differences between field dependent and field independent learners' ability to answer questions following a period of time browsing a hypertext architecture, again revealed that field dependent participants performed less well than field dependents (Korthauer and Koubek, 1994). In this study the learners were experienced with the hypertext document they used. The findings are explained by the fact that the existing knowledge of the field dependent learners and the way in which these learners attempted to represent the information, conflicted with the more explicitly structured hypertext, thus affecting their learning.

However, one possible drawback with the above studies, is that the GEFT has been found to correlate with standard tests of spatial intelligence (McKenna, 1984, 1990). Accordingly, another possible interpretation of the above studies is that field independent learners possessed greater intelligence, and this accounted for their superior performance rather than any differences in the strategies they employ in organising the information they learn.

Accordingly, there is s a need to consider potential differences in learning from hypertext employing a cognitive style measure independent of spatial intelligence. Melara (1996) employed forty participants who were students of computer science, maths or engineering and required them to complete Kolb's Learning Style Inventory. This instrument identified participants as possessing either a reflective or active style. Following this participants were assigned to one of two hypertext architecture conditions, which were either hierarchical or network in structure. The design of the network structure was such that it linked together related concepts in order to form a web, and the task of the participants was to answer ten questions on the information featured in the hypertext. The results revealed no differences between the participants of different learning styles in each condition, however the results were approaching significance with superior performance from participants in the hierarchical condition. Furthermore, individuals with active and reflective styles displayed superior performance when using the hierarchical architecture. In essence the results merely show that a difference exists between the two hypertext structures, although style seemed to have no effect. One further difference was that

the participants in the hierarchical architecture condition took significantly longer to complete the task, than participants in the network condition, which seems to be a more likely explanation for the superior performance of participants in this condition.

Learning Measured by Essay Questions

In an extension to the studies described above, Graff (2003a) looked at whether the way in which learning was assessed made a difference to the effect of matching different hypertext architecture conditions to the cognitive style of the learner. This study employed three hypertext architectures, which were linear, hierarchical and relational, with each representing a way in which the information to be learned was arranged. Cognitive style was measured using the Cognitive Styles Analysis (Riding, 1991), which identifies cognitive style in a way similar to the Group Embedded Figures Test (Witkin et al, 1971), but uses the label wholist for field dependent and analytic for field independent. Essay scores were measured by length and amount of detail included. The results indicated that in the relational architecture condition, intermediates (i.e. individuals between wholist and analytic styles) achieved superior scores.

The findings reviewed so far appear to indicate that cognitive style does have an impact on the degree to which individuals learn from hypertext, and therefore need to be considered in the design of web-based instructional systems. However, the findings from the above studies are somewhat perplexing as they derive from an array of style measures, and therefore more research is required, with a view to unifying and consolidating different measures of style.

We now move on to analyse how the application of style research can be applied to slightly more complex cognitive tasks performed within the parameters of hypertext.

Graff (2002a, 2005a) assessed differences in the types of concept maps produced by learners, and whether the types of maps could be predicted from measures of cognitive style. In one study 55 participants were assigned to one of three hypertext architecture conditions which were linear, hierarchical or relational, and were instructed to recall information and produce maps of the hypertext used (Graff, 2005a). In this study cognitive style was measured with the analysis-intuition measure of cognitive style (Allinson and Hayes, 1996), and the results revealed that analysts scored highest in the hierarchical condition, intermediates scored highest in the relational condition and intuitives scored highest in the linear condition. In terms of assessment of the concept map density (the degree to which users were able to integrate the concepts in the hypertext), participants using the hierarchical condition produced the least dense maps, with little difference between the relational and linear architectures. The higher density scores which users in the relational architecture condition produced was explained by the fact that the intricate relational architecture encouraged participants to produce dense maps purely because of the impression that this architecture gave them. The finding differs from that of Shapiro (1998) as here no differences in density scores were found between participants performing in different architectures. However, in the study by Graff (2005a), no differences in maps were found between individuals possessing different cognitive styles. In terms of assessment of map complexity, (how representative the map was of the architecture) the results revealed that participants performing in the relational architecture condition produced the most complex maps, with participants in the hierarchical condition producing the least complex maps. These results were explained by the fact that there were differences in perceived ease of use by participants in each architecture condition. The rather complex array of findings presented here provide no real

evidence that cognitive style is a factor in predicting differences in concept map production.

Hypertext Segmentation and Overview Provision

When considering hypertext design, two further considerations need to be addressed. Firstly, the degree to which the hypertext should be segmented, in other words whether it should be designed with long scrolling pages, or whether the pages should be segmented and topics which are conceptually related be connected via hyperlinks. Secondly, whether the provision of an overview of the hypertext provides any advantage in guiding the user through the structure. Indeed, Dee-Lucas and Larkin (1995) discovered that the provision of a diagrammatic overview of the hypertext system made it easier for users by directing them to significant information within the system. Similarly, Hsu and Schwen (2003) compared the effects of structural cues derived from single and multiple metaphors in the design of hypermedia documents. Fifty-four undergraduate students were required to perform selected information searching tasks, and the findings indicated that the provision of metaphorical cues helped participants to find a greater number of accurate answers and do so in a shorter period of time.

However, it is entirely possible that an individual's cognitive style could influence the degree to which segmentation and provision of an overview is useful. An investigation of this issue, Graff (2003b) employed 50 participants who browsed one of two hypertext architectures containing information on psychological ethics, and also completed the Cognitive Styles Analysis (Riding, 1991). The differences between the architectures was in terms of the degree of segmentation, with one being more segmented (required less scrolling of pages) than the other. Furthermore, half the participants were provided with an overview of the architecture, and the other half received no overview. After spending a period of time browsing one of the two hypertext systems, participants were requested to answer questions regarding their understanding of the material featured in the hypertext. Both cognitive style and degree of segmentation influenced the degree to which participants learned from each architecture. More specifically, analytics displayed superior learning performance in the less segmented architecture, whereas wholists showed superior performance in the more segmented architecture. However, the provision of an overview of the system had no effect here.

Cognitive Style and Hypertext Navigation

The final question to be considered in this chapter is whether cognitive style can predict differences in the ways in which individuals navigate hypertext, and several studies on this issue are considered here. Firstly, Ellis Ford and Wood (1992) investigated this issue employing postgraduate student participants and who completed a Study Preferences Questionnaire (SPQ) which was a non standardised test developed by the authors of the study, and which measured holist and serialist study strategies, presumably conceptually similar to field dependent and field independent respectively. Participants were provided with navigation tools for using the hypertext, which were: a self-orientating global concept map, keyword index menus and a backtracking facility, and the subject matter of the hypertext was the European Single Market. The 40 participants used the hypertext, and were then required to answer several questions which required both factual recall and also integration of information from different parts of the hypertext. Their findings revealed that participants with a holist approach tended to make more use of the maps provided, whereas participants with a serialist strategy used the index menu.

In a further study, Chen and Ford (1998) employed 20 postgraduate students who used a hypertext system in order to attempt to learn about artificial intelligence. Using the Cognitive Styles Analysis to test style they discovered that wholists made greater use of a menu system for navigation, whereas analytics were more likely to use the backward and forward buttons on the browser software they were using. It must be said that the sample size in this study was small, and accordingly, it is unlikely that the results can be generalised from the findings.

The above studies however, tell us more about the user's typical selection of hypertext navigational aids, and it is also relevant to examine navigation of hypertext in terms of the routes users take to move through the system.

In a study employing 60 participants, who used a structured hypertext and completed the Embedded Figures Test, Stanton and Stammers (1990) found that field dependent participants used bottom-up navigational strategies, progressing from the more basic information upwards, whereas field independent users tended to use top down strategies, which was viewing the most important information first. This finding is rather perplexing and seems contrary to the reasoning that field dependent users would be able to apprehend the structure of the whole hypertext, and therefore use a top-down strategy, whereas the opposite would be the case for field independent users. What was also contrary to what might have been predicted was the fact that field independent individuals viewed fewer pages than field dependent individuals, whereas the more likely finding would have been that as field dependent learners should have been able to gain an overview more easily, they would have viewed fewer pages.

Verheiji, Stoutjesdijk and Beishuizen (1996), performed a study where navigation was assessed by requesting participants to search for information in a hypertext. They identified style by using the Dutch Inventory of Learning Styles which identifies individuals as deep or surface processors (Vermunt and Van Rijswijk, 1987). The findings revealed that different strategies were employed by individuals with different styles, more precisely that those identified as deep processors used a more global approach to navigate the text, whereas surface processors adopted a more step by step approach.

The final study considered (Graff, 2005b) employed two groups of participants, who were assigned to either a hierarchical or a relational hypertext architecture and allowed ten minutes to read information contained in the hypertext. Participants were told in advance that they would be expected to answer questions on the information they read, and hypertext navigational patterns were measured by using various indices, including the number of pages visited and the proportion of pages visited to pages revisited. Cognitive style was measured using the Cognitive Styles Analysis (Riding, 1991) which also reveals the extent to which individuals display imager or verbaliser styles. Variations were found between imagers and verbalisers, with the latter visiting more pages in the hierarchical architecture, and the former visiting more pages in the relational architecture. This preliminary evidence is somewhat encouraging in as much as it would appear to suggest that individuals with different cognitive styles do exhibit different navigational strategies.

CONCLUSION

This chapter has examined much of the evidence on the effectiveness of using hypertext or web-based learning systems as a medium of instruction. The general conclusion which can be drawn here is that the most facilitative hypertext architecture for

Figure 1. Model of performance in using hypertext, determined by cognitive style mediated by architecture design

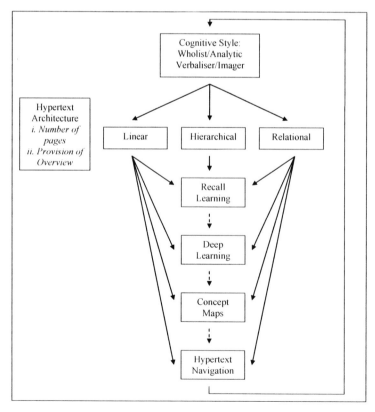

effective learning is hierarchical in structure with lateral links, although to some extent it appears that cognitive style also influences the effectiveness of the hypertext architecture employed, and this is illustrated in the model shown in Figure 1. For example, cognitive style may to some extent determine how effective a particular architecture is to an individual for learning. Furthermore, the manner in which an individual navigates hypertext also influences his/her ability to understand its structure, and this is because the route followed has an effect on the individual's mental representation of the hypertext. It is possible then that the route followed by an individual browsing hypertext could have an influence on the effectiveness with which they learn.

From the literature, it is clear, that numerous research questions regarding use of hypertext and cognitive style remain. More precisely, further research should pursue an attempt to investigate learning at a deeper level. As mentioned learning in many previous studies has been measured in a relatively simplistic way, and studies should now focus on attempts to assess learning in more realistic situations. While a few studies have sought to investigate the navigational strategies of users, further research should attempt to investigate this in relation to users' cognitive style. Finally, in the literature, definitions of the term cognitive style appear fragmented, with little agreement on how the term may be properly operationalised. Accordingly, attempts to consolidate the construct under a single definition are now well overdue. Regardless of the pressing need for further work in the area, the initial conclusion indicates cognitive style to be a pertinent factor for consideration in the design and implementation of instructional systems. The evidence presented here, although mixed and rather unsettled at present, is nevertheless promising, and cognitive style ultimately has implications for the design of hypertext instructional systems.

REFERENCES

Allinson, C. W., & Hayes, J. (1996). The cognitive styles index: A measure of intuition-analysis for organisational research. *Journal of Management Studies, 33*(1), 119-135.

Batra, S., Bishu, R. R., & Donohue, B. (1993). Effects of hypertext typology on navigational performance. *Advances in Human Factors and Ergonomics, 19*, 175-180.

Bloom, B. S. (1968). Learning for mastery. *Evaluation Comment, 1*, 1-12.

Canter, D. Rivers, R., & Storrs, G. (1985). Characterising user navigation through complex data structures. *Behaviour and Information Technology, 4*(2), 93-102.

Chen, S. Y., & Ford, N. (1998). Modelling user navigation behaviours in a hypermedia-based learning system: An individual differences approach. *Knowledge Organisation, 25* (3), 67-78.

Dee-Lucas, D., & Larkin, J. H. (1995). Learning from electronic texts: Effects of interactive overviews for information access. *Cognition and instruction, 13*, 431-468.

Ellis, D., Ford, N., & Wood, F (1992). Hypertext and learning styles. *Final Report of a Project funded by the Learning Technology Unit*. Sheffield: Employment Department.

Graff, M. G. (2002a). Learning from hypertext and the analyst-intuition dimension of cognitive style. In *Proceedings of E-Learn., Montreal, Canada, 1* (pp. 361-368).

Graff, M. G. (2002b). Hypertext navigation and cognitive style. In M. Valcke (Ed.), *Proceedings of the Seventh European Learning Styles Conference* (pp. 185-192). University of Gent, Belgium.

Graff, M. G. (2003a). Assessing learning from hypertext: An individual differences perspective. *Journal of Interactive Learning Research, 14*(4), 425-438.

Graff, M. G. (2003b). Learning from Web-based instructional systems and cognitive style. *British Journal of Educational Technology, 34*(4), 407-418.

Graff, M. G. (2005a). Information recall, concept mapping, hypertext usability and the analyst-intuitive dimension of cognitive style. *Educational Psychology, 25*(4), 409-422.

Graff, M. G. (2005b). Individual differences in hypertext browsing strategies. *Behaviour* and Information Technology, 24(2), 93-100.

Guildford, J. P. (1959). *Personality.* New York: McGraw-Hill.

Holzman, P. S., & Klein, G. S. (1954). Cognitive system principles of levelling and sharpening: individual differences in visual time error assimilation effects. *Journal of Psychology, 37,* 105-122.

Hsu, Y. & Schwen, T. (2003). The effects of structural cues from multiple metaphors on computer users information search performance. *International Journal of Human Computer Studies, 58*(1), 39-55.

Kagan, J., Rosman B., Day, D., Albert, J., & Phillips, W. (1964). Information processing and the child: Significance of analytic and reflective attitudes. *Psychological Monographs, 78.*

Korthauer, R. D., & Koubek, R. J. (1994). An empirical evaluation of knowledge, cognitive style and structure upon the performance of a hypertext task. *International Journal of Human Computer Interaction, 6*(4), 373-390.

Lin, C. H., & Davidson-Shivers, G. V. (1996). Effects of linking structure and cognitive style on students' performance and attitude in a computer-based hypertext environment. *Journal of Educational Computing Research, 15*(4), 317-329.

Maglio, P. P., & Matlock, T. (1999). The conceptual structure of information space. In A. J. Munro, K. Hook & D. Benyon (Eds.), *Social navigation of information space* (pp. 155-173). London: Springer.

McDonald, S., & Stevenson, R. J. (1998). Effects of text structure and prior knowledge of the learner on navigation in hypertext. *Human Factors, 40*(1), 18-27.

McKenna, F. P. (1984). Measures of field dependence: Cognitive style or cognitive ability. *Journal of Personality and Social Psychology, 47*(3), 593-603.

McKenna, F. P. (1990). Learning implications of field dependence-independence: cognitive styles versus cognitive ability. *Applied Cognitive Psychology, 4,* 425-437.

McNamara, T. P., Hardy, J. K., & Hirtle, S. C. (1989). Subjective hierarchies in spatial memory. *Journal of Experimental Psychology: Learning Memory and Cognition, 15,* 211-227.

Melara, G. E. (1996). Investigating learning styles on different hypertext environments: Hierarchical-like and network-like structures. *Journal of Educational Computing Research, 14*(4), 313-328.

Mohageg, M. F. (1992). The influence of hypertext linking structures on the efficiency of information retrieval. *Human Factors, 34,* 351-367.

Pask, G. (1972). A fresh look at cognition and the individual. *International Journal of Man Machine Studies, 4,* 211-216.

Riding, R. J. (1991). *Cognitive styles analysis user manual.* Birmingham: Learning and Training Technology.

Shapiro, A. M. (1998). Promoting active learning: The role of system structure in learning from hypertext. *Human Computer Interaction, 13*(1), 1-35.

Stanton, N. A., & Stammers, R. B. (1990). Learning styles in a non-linear training environment. In R. MCaleese & C. Green (Eds.), *Hypertext: State of the art* (pp. 114-120). Norwood, NJ: Ablex.

Verheoj, J., Stoutjesduk, E., & Beishuizen, J. (1996). Search and study strategies in hypertext. *Computers in Human Behaviour, 12*(1), 1-15.

Vermunt, J. D. H., & Van Rijswijk, F. A. W. M. (1987). *Inventaris leerstijlen voor het hoger onderwijs* (Inventory of Learning Styles for Higher Education). Tilburg. Netherlands: Katholieke Universiteit Brabant.

Witkin, H. A., Moore, C. A., Goodenough, D. R., & Cox, P. W. (1977). Field-dependent and field-independent cognitive styles and their educational implications. *Review of Education Research, 47*, 1-64.

Witkin, H. A., Oltman, R., Raskin, E., & Karp, S. (1971). *A manual for embedded figures test*. Palo Alto, CA: Consulting Psychologists Press.

Chapter IV
Cognitive Styles and Design Interactions in Web–Based Education

Michael Workman
Florida Institute of Technology, USA

ABSTRACT

Online education has experienced phenomenal growth, but some researchers and practitioners, as well as some students, have raised serious questions about the efficacy of online education. The research literature shows a clear division between those who maintain that the quality of online education is at least on par with traditional classroom education, while another body is more dubious about that conclusion. In this chapter, we will examine some of the personal and situational variables that confound these findings –both positive and negative, and suggest that media and their interactions with individual learning styles and instructor educational philosophies need to be taken into account in the design and delivery of online education.

INTRODUCTION

The ease with which information can be distributed over the Internet to a large number of recipients has vastly expanded the reach of education and information access (Giannakoulopoulos, & Kodellas, 2005). Consequently, there has been an explosion of online educational programs as well as in the proportion of students who are studying online (Harasim, 2001). A significant body of research, over the years, has asserted the notion that student performance is equivalent between those enrolled in online education compared to students taught in a traditional classroom (c.f. Arbaugh, 2000; Blackley & Curran-Smith, 1998; Freeman & Capper, 1999; Johnson, Aragon, Shaik & Palma-Rivas, 2000; Maki, Maki, Patterson & Whittaker, 2000). However, the difficulty found in studies such as these is the extrapolation of performance across student populations, who in most of these cases are not randomly selected or assigned to study groups. This presents a variety of research design and control issues including variations in subject matter, student abilities and other important factors that would affect the conclusions. As an example, students who attend traditional classrooms are usually younger and have less "world knowledge" and experience than those who take online courses (Harasim, 2001; Lake, 2008).

Not only do student demographics and maturation characteristics tend to vary between student populations, but also there are differential characteristics among instructors and instructional styles, teaching philosophies, and designs. For instance, Maki, et al. (2000) conducted a two-year quasi-experimental study of undergraduate students and concluded that students in the online sections of an introductory psychology course assimilated more information as measured by content questions and performed better on examinations than those in the classroom. However, this study, as with most of the others, along with the lack of randomization, failed to account for important instructor and instructional differences.

Some studies have attempted to control for these instructor and instructional differences by having the same instructor teach both the online and proximal groups, yet at same time, the instructor has also been the researcher –raising issues of bias, or used an instructor who applied dissimilar instructional designs between the two modes, making a valid comparison impossible.

In addition to the contamination from the research design problems, there are also a number of personal and situational variables that impact the findings and yet are rarely if ever controlled in the research designs or analyses, such as class sizes, types of technologies used in the instruction, student learning styles, the degree of student involvement, and the type of subject matter taught such as whether the materials require domain specific or domain general skills and knowledge (Bailey & Iqbal, 2007; Bangert, 2008; Martinez-

Torres, Marin, Garcia, Vazquez, Oliva, & Torres, 2008; Oliver, & Moore, 2008; Workman, 2004).

Furthermore, the motivations of students taking classes online versus in the more traditional classroom may differ. While both online and traditional students are primarily concerned with subsequent employment opportunities and in the educational experience (Lake, 2008), one of the most significant attractions for students studying online is, first, convenience, followed by flexibility, beyond that of educational quality or learning outcomes (Kariya, 2003).

On the other hand, studies (e.g. Broadbent & Shane, 2008) have shown for example that students who enroll in traditional classroom programs tend to be more interested in the social learning experience, prefer observational modeling in the learning process, and feel that social interaction with peers, which develops spontaneously in proximal settings, lends to the learning transfer. Traditional students are also more attracted to the prestige or reputation of an academic institute, followed by desires for a campus experience such as attending sports events, social-friendship opportunities and interactions, or belonging to an academic or Greek society (Lake, 2008). It is within the interacting variables where disparities in student performance between online and traditional learning are found.

This is not to say the online education is certainly less effective than classroom learning, or vice versa, but rather that they are not simply interchangeable. The extant research findings touting equality are suspect. Online instructors need to be mindful of important differences and many situational and individual variables in play in order to create a rich and effective online learning environment and experience for students (Roca & Gagne, 2008). In this chapter, we will focus specifically on a set of key interactions among technology mediation, student learning styles, and instructional philosophies and design approaches that can affect online learning outcomes.

MEDIA MATTERS!

Clark (1983) argued that media used for instructional delivery were incidental to the learning process, amounting to little more than the analogy of delivery trucks delivering packages. But research over the years has suggested otherwise (c.f. Moos & Azevedo, 2008; Workman, 2004). When media intervenes in communication and collaboration, varying amounts of the information context is constricted depending on the type of media used. As an example, the telephone is capable of transmitting only about 37% of the sound frequency that the human voice can emit, and only 5% of the sound frequency that the human ear can perceive (Workman, Bommer, & Kahnweiler, 2003). If instruction is delivered through teleconferences, this constraint can make it difficult to detect subtle emotive nuances such as the difference between excitement and agitation, or boredom and relaxation, particularly without a visual component (Raghuram, 1996).

To help overcome these constraints, many online programs have begun to incorporate video teleconferencing, or at the least, video-recorded lectures. Nevertheless, these have mediation effects on students as well. One example is that differences in the sizes and resolution of computer screens obscure (to varying degrees) some of the visual content, and latency in video delivery from limitations on network bandwidths and computer system configurations can cause distracting visual and sound "jitter" (Chiu, Chiu, & Chang, 2007; Kozma, 1991; Wieland, 1999).

Other revealing ways that show a video medium is not the same as face-to-face interaction involves the *salience phenomenon*. In studies of this phenomenon (Fussell & Benimoff, 1995) researchers ask people who have adjourned from a proximal brainstorming session what ideas the participants remembered most from the meeting. Participants consistently remember ideas from individuals who were "most distinctive" in terms of some manner or physical characteristic –such as the person who became the most emotional, or the one with the most peculiar dress or mannerisms. When participants of a virtual brainstorming session are queried about ideas, those ideas most remembered come from the person seated in the center of the videoconference window (or in the center window if there are multiple video windows). This has important implications for learning, because ideas must first be remembered before someone can decide whether or not to agree with the ideas –or to be influenced by them.

While some programs have tried to utilize media that have more robust information carrying properties such using visual and audio channels for content delivery (Daft & Lengel, 1986), in many if not most online-focused programs have to date relied primarily on asynchronous discussion board interaction or on linear synchronous chat forms of textual content delivery using Blackboard or other content management systems. On the other hand, the Open University in the United Kingdom has been among the leaders in combining rich media and simulations with the more conventional text-based instruction. This situational flexibility is an important mediator in student learning outcomes (Workman, 2004).

When a purely textual medium is used, such as discussion threads or emails, readers are left to fill in significant amounts of missing context. In cases where only instructions need to be communicated, a lean medium can be perfectly appropriate; but if the information is complex or involves an affective element, issues arise. With a lean medium, one's writing style becomes particularly influential in how someone interprets what is written. By-and-large, even with substantial close-distance writing styles, written texts leave people with feelings of information loss (Konradt & Schmook, 1999; Turban, et al., 1996; Wieland, 1999).

In some cases this can lead to people fantasizing and expressing unqualified and unbridled intimacy with those whom they have never met in person (Workman, 2006). In other cases, it leads people to feeling isolated, detached, and even alienated, and causing some to respond with unusual hostility (Fussell & Benimoff, 1995; Jehng, 1997; Wellman, et al., 1996) –a phenomenon sometimes called *flaming effects* (Straus & McGrath, 1994). Studies (Workman, 2006) consistently show that people will sometimes write in an email, either strongly positive or strongly negative, that which they would not dare say to someone face-to-face.

Perhaps one of the most significant impediments in an online learning setting is the lack of spontaneity that blooms from interactive conversations that seems only possible in a proximal setting (Bailey & Iqbal, 2007; Mason, 2004). Because of the amount of time it takes to type out course content or respond to queries and questions, there are characteristically reduced informal interactions in a virtual environment that otherwise normally take place face-to-face (Ellison, 1999; Raghuram, 1996). And the interactions that do take place are altered compared to proximal exchanges because of the constraining factors as mentioned (Fritz, et al., 1996).

Beyond having the potential to elevate ambiguity and increase isolation, online learning is also less externally structured. Since online learning is done remotely, and communication is constrained to varying degrees by the *richness* or *leanness* of electronic media, there are fewer opportunities for students to share or model others' approaches to tasks. This necessitates individual approaches to doing things (Baruch & Nicholson, 1997; Erben & Dafler, 1998; Hill, et al., 1998; Jehng, 1997; Wieland, 1999). Baruch and Nicholson (1997) found, for example, that people who have high needs for certainty may feel disoriented when confronted with the high discretionary environment of being online.

After all the mounting evidence, it is difficult to continue to argue in this day and age the point that Clark (1982) tried to maintain over two decades ago, that media is of no consequence to the online learning process or outcomes. Such a simplistic view of media effects has led to some disastrous online learning programs and experiences presented in the literature. In the least, time lags that are involved in synchronous communications and the constriction of shared understanding deriving from limitations of various media (Fussell & Benimoff, 1995; Jehng, 1997) reduce people's ability to acquire tacit, if not explicit, knowledge (Raghuram, 1996). These conditions have inescapable impacts on learning outcomes (Bailey & Iqbal, 2007).

TECHNOLOGY MEDIATION AND HUMAN PERCEPTS AND CONCEPTS

As indicated, there are some aspects of media that universally affect people. For instance, people more reliably detect changes in technologically rendered visual cues when they are consistent (e.g., constant interval or color) than when they are intermittent, ambiguous, and inconsistent (Kraut, et al., 1998; Montgomery, 1999; Wieland, 1999). This indicates that the interaction between technology media and people have some generalized effects, especially when people are working on problems that do not consist of a single correct solution, but rather involve judgments about a solution in which there are multiple subjective points of view (Daft & Lengel, 1986). We understand from the research on group interaction (c.f. Workman, 2005) that when subjective judgment is exercised in determining a course of action for a problem, the perspectives are enriched when diverse viewpoints are infused into the dialog.

When a lean medium (Daft & Lengel, 1986) such as discussion boards, chat sessions, email, or other linear textual forms of communications are used, there are attenuations of meaning partly as an artifact of delays in responding to the "stream of consciousness" that occurs when ideas are being formulated (Bailey & Iqbal, 2007; Wieland, 1999). But also, lean media lacks immediate feedback, it uses a single channel for its conveyance, and it is limited in the number of cues it can support (Kraut, et al., 1998; Webster, 1998). Consequently, leanness of media serves to increase ambiguity about tasks and interpersonal situations (Fussell & Benimoff, 1995; Raghuram, 1996).

The results of these media affects are such that the leaner the medium used in learning and collaboration, the greater the concomitant ambiguity about both the problem and the expectations of the instructor concerning the solution, particularly when combined with subjective (equivocal) learning problems or tasks (Daft & Lengel, 1986). In terms of learning then, the consequence of media leanness is that it requires more cognitive effort to figure out "what is wanted," which tends to siphon off some of the cognitive resources required and available for formulating ideas and developing the solution to the problem, particularly as a socially interactive process (Jehng, 1997; Mason, 2004).

Although there are some generalized effects from media as indicated, especially in terms of the interactions between the richness or leanness of the medium and the type of learning tasks that students perform, there are also significant individual differences in that effect. For example, people exhibit differences in perceptual judgments (Levin, et al., 1998-99; Shrum, 1997) and differences in sensitivity to visual display cues and graphical display information (Kozma, 1991; Montgomery, 1999; Pillay, 1998; Wieland, 1999). These differences demonstrate variances in personal characteristics interacting with media and the suitability of some individuals over others in a technologically mediated situation.

Another particularly interesting aspect of this phenomenon is that online learning outcomes are also mode sensitive (Bangert, 2008). In one study, Workman (2004) found that depending on how students formulated concepts combined with the types of content they were learning (e.g. domain general versus domain specific learning), the delivery mode affected performance outcomes differently. In that study on *learning how to write computer programs*, it was found that depending

on how students conceived information – either as concrete or abstract concepts—their performance depended on whether they were learning from a computer-based educational (CBE) system delivered from CD-ROM that was more structured, was more repetitive, and was geared more toward individualized learning, or whether they learned with computer-aided education (CAE) delivered over the World Wide Web that was less structured and more interactive.

The study found further that those students who were able to work more easily with abstract information and could blend information between cognitive categories performed better with the Web-based CAE. Students who preferred more concrete detail and conceived information more discretely, those students performed better using self-paced CBE delivered on CD-ROM. Furthermore, the study found that students who preferred more collaborative interaction for ideational generation performed better in the Web-based CAE than did their counterparts who preferred more introspective and deliberative concentration for ideational generation. These present significant issues to consider. Not everyone learns one way – or put another way, one size does not fit all. We cannot say that online learning is as effective as traditional classroom, or vice versa. The results are individual, situational, and context sensitive (Bangert, 2008).

COGNITIVE STYLES AND ONLINE LEARNING

One key individual element in online learning success involves how a student gathers, processes, and evaluates information (Hayes & Allinson, 1998; Pillay, 1998). These tendencies affect how students solve problems and make decisions (Ferraro & Sternberg, 1998; Messick, 1994; Sternberg, 1997). The rubric under which these facilities or preferences are classified has been called *cognitive* or *learning styles*.

For a period of time, the study of cognitive styles was "out of style" (Flavell, 1992; Sternberg & Grigorenko, 1997), but over the years, cognitive styles research has shown fairly high validity and reliability (Grigorenko & Sternberg, 1995; Workman, 2004) in terms of learning. Where many of the difficulties have been found in cognitive styles research have been in cases where the research subjects were required to perform some form of laboratory experiment such as a rod-and-frame test (RFT), which lacks ecological validity (not to mention that only the occipital lobe is focalized in these perceptual tasks), and then trying to extrapolate those findings into classroom performance.

For example, with a visual test such as the RFT, there are different structures involved in the transformation of perceptual information from the eyes through the optic nerve and into visual cortex in the occipital lobe in the back of the brain. In other words, visual perception involves very different cognitive processes than what are involved in other forms of conceptualization and learning (Bagozzi, Davis, & Warshaw, 1992; Jacoby, 1991). Nevertheless, researchers have concluded that there is clearly something about the ways that human brains work that leads to how people learn and conceive information (Rehder & Hoffman, 2005), and there have been some areas of resurgent interest.

One derivation of cognitive or learning styles that has been informative in the online learning literature has been Sternberg's (1997) theory of mental self-government, assessed with the *thinking styles inventory*. The theory is complex and multidimensional, and at times, difficult to operationalize. However, three dimensions of the model (scope, leaning and level) have received strong support in the research literature on virtual work and online education (c.f. Workman, et al., 2003).

The theory of mental self-government suggests that students organize and govern their tasks in ways that are consistent with how they cogni-

tively formulate concepts and process information (Sternberg, 1997). These thinking styles guide the manner in which mental representations of objects or symbols are encoded into cognitive concepts, such as whether they are created by means of individual deliberation or as a process of group interaction. The effects of this can be observed in differences between students who need quiet solitude and concentration for ideational generation, and those who find group processes (such as group brainstorming) an important means of priming ideas.

The implication from this aspect of learning style is that students who are forced to learn with lean media, such as discussion boards or written lectures, or even a richer medium if it is "canned" such as in a taped lecture, will likely find this a particularly savage impediment for those who require spontaneous group interaction for cognitive priming. On the other hand, those who are more deliberative and introspective usually find no such impediment (Moos & Azevedo, 2008; Roca & Gagne, 2008).

In a related way, some students prefer to learn through observational modeling (Bandura, 1978). For these people, seeing similar others succeed by perseverant effort raises the student's beliefs that he or she will be able to successfully perform comparable behavior, which enhances his/her cognitive appraisal and self-efficacy towards performing the observed behavior. Successful performance of that behavior in turn enhances the student's attitude and raises expectancies about the successful performance of the behavior in the future.

Alternatively, other students prefer novelty, change, uncertainty, and minimally structured environments. These students prefer to transcend existing boundaries and procedures and do things their own way, and tend not to do much by way of observational modeling. Since mediated communications have limitations on the capabilities to support observational modeling (Fussell & Benimoff, 1995; Jehng, 1997), those students who prefer individualized approaches to doing things have a performance advantage in online learning settings over students who use observational modeling. One way this is mitigated is by using simulations and demonstrations, which can be created with software such as Captivate, but simulations apply mainly to skills-based learning tasks and are more difficult to employ in less applied learning.

Next, learning styles determine the amount of information that students need for formulating concepts and the degree to which the concepts are "fuzzy" or "discrete" (conceptual boundary thinness or thickness). Students' metacognitive processes are used to evaluate the problems they face in a learning task and coordinate constituent cognitive processes involved in acquiring information, providing mental feedback, and monitoring progress toward solving the problem (Hayes & Allinson, 1998). Students who formulate thin cognitive boundaries can be easily abstract information between different cognitive categories depending on the context of a situation or task (Levin et al., 1998–1999). For them, ambiguous information corresponds naturally with the ways in which they categorize, compare, and process their mental structures (Ferrari & Sternberg, 1998).

Conversely, other students derive thick cognitive boundaries between concepts, and these concepts are more rigidly formulated (Levin et al., 1998–1999). They need concrete detail to construct or compare mental representations, and their metacognitive processes are such that they tend to have difficulties perceiving progress toward task solution from ambiguous information (Ferrari & Sternberg, 1998). Since online learning elevates ambiguity in terms of both tasks and expectations, students who are more comfortable with abstractions have a performance advantage online, although richer media such as video conferencing serves to level this effect to some degree (Stout, Cannon-Bowers, et al., 1999).

SITUATIONS BEYOND INSTRUCTORS' CONTROL

The reality is that there are many situational variables that are outside the control of the online instructor, which may lead an instructor to make compromises in his or her preferred pedagogical approach. One example of such a case is the growing trend toward increasing online class sizes –driven often by financial considerations. In the College of Information at the Florida State University for example, online classes can have 50 students or more, taught with Blackboard as the content management system. Since the content delivery depends largely on typed linear discourse, the ability to evaluate and respond in a timely manner to student questions and issues can become a significant problem unless a particular instructional approach is used, which may not be compatible with an instructional style.

Understanding the issues with linear discourse, Bangert (2008) argued that using computer-mediated conferencing (CMC) could boost meaningful interactions in accordance with social constructivist learning theory. Yet even with this consideration, CMC may not be effective with large online classes because of interactive collisions (Lake, 2008). To appreciate why, it is important to consider how collective understanding is achieved (Moos & Azevedo, 2008; Roca & Gagne, 2008). In discourse, people communicate by means of channels. The linguistic channel is that of the verbal aspects of communication. Paralinguistic channels include verbal intonations, patterns, and pauses, and are used for signally turn-taking in a communications protocol. Non-linguistic channels include eye gaze, posture, gestures and signs such as blushing. Collectively, these channels of information provide a shared context by which communicative partners exchange expressed and tacit information, and formulate shared understanding. For example, a shift in eye gaze may be used for turn taking, or it may signal boredom or indicate disinterest in an idea –the surrounding

Table 1. Instructional philosophies

Design Philosophy	Approach and Assumptions	Basis and Techniques
Exogenous Mechanistic Content Delivery	Delivered instruction ✓ Learner as "receiver" ✓ Knowledge is hierarchically structured with parts logically separated into categories ✓ Learning from the environment and assimilation of information	Information processing theory ✓ Lecture ✓ Rote skills acquisition ✓ Repetition and testing ✓ Individual-focused learning
Dialectical-Contextual Social Constructivism	Negotiated instruction ✓ Knowledge is learned best when socially structured ✓ Cognitive apprenticeships ✓ Learning from interactions with peers and facilitator who help one to assimilate and accommodate new information through situated, real-world contexts and problems	General systems theory ✓ Situated and social cognition ✓ Socratic dialog ✓ Collaborative learning, reciprocal teaching ✓ Metacognitive cues, hints, prompts
Endogenous-Organismic Development	Personal instruction ✓ Knowledge is learned best when individually directed ✓ Learning from one's self and the use of prior knowledge to reflect on and accommodate new information	Adaptive structuration theory ✓ Self-initiated research activity ✓ Independent study ✓ Knowledge scaffolding

context from other channels are what people use to draw the proper conclusion.

Communication success also depends on how well a communicator is able to articulate his or her ideas and information. People negotiate meaning through the communication dialog, which depends on how well each other are understood. To the extent that there is fairly good congruence between what a speaker or writer articulates and what the hearer or reader interprets, people then consolidate their ideas into shared conceptions. This process is labor intensive, and may be illustrated by an analogy to the "inverse square law" for communicative behavior, where the communications capacity is inversely proportional to the square of the number of participants. Hence even with computer-medicated-communications, CMC, there are practical limitations in acquiring

shared context when the numbers of participants grow. Moreover, adding CMC into the mix, there are technological considerations; for instance, computer screen sizes and phone subscriptions create physical limitations on the number of participants.

INSTRUCTIONAL PHILOSOPHY AND DESIGN

To this point, this chapter has presented individual and situational factors that influence online instructional processes and outcomes. In this last section of this chapter, we will discuss some important factors concerning instructional philosophy and instructional fit relative to online learning. The purpose of this section is to draw the connection between educational and instructional philosophy and the design of the materials for given learning and teaching styles, considering the situational variables presented.

Each instructor whether cognizant or not brings to his or her classroom a philosophy about education. Sometimes philosophies are molded into the fabric of a culture, and other times, they are fashioned out of one's own experience. The educational philosophy frame of reference from which an instructor designs and teaches his or her courses tends to divide along the lines of whether the instructor believes that the primary purpose of education is to develop a skilled workforce, or to create knowledge for its own sake. These two positions dissolve slightly into whether the approach taken is for the primary benefit of the learner or to benefit society (Dewey, 1963; Kincheloe, 1993; Kohli, 1995). We will first briefly review some basic educational assumptions and philosophies that are held by teachers, and then contemplate how these philosophies might translate into approaches in online learning.

Most educators at some point are introduced to classic idealism. Idealism derived from Plato's renowned thesis of "Ideas" in which the highest "form" of reality was spiritual –an Ideal which only human intelligence can conceive (Brown, 1966). An educational philosophy that derives from this is characterized by the basic beliefs that there is a real and independent order, universal tenets, ultimate forms and higher laws. From this philosophy comes the perspective that reason and faith can coexist and are mutually supportive. Educators who work from this philosophy strive to inculcate both moral and intellectual ideals, where the same set of universal standards can be applied to each student. They believe that the tragedies of unemployment and stultified lives can be ameliorated through education by teaching principles of excellence as they apply to ordinary life, for example with the liberal arts, or the role of technology in shaping a "good" society (Brubacher, 1962).

Pragmatism (Dewey, 1963, 1966; Noddings, 1995) views education as an instrument for developing ideas and experiential learning, but it is seen as a tool for achieving practical results (Steinhouse, 1985). The key to pragmatism is in the development of the form of education that is consistent with a democratic process, a form that provides the student with the maximum number of career options at any given point in the learning experience.

Educational designs that evolve from both the philosophies of idealism and pragmatism consists of dialectical and contextual social constructivism; the former utilizing techniques such as Socratic dialog that allows learners to perpetually explore, and the latter to experience, construct and develop.

An educational philosophy of essentialism (McKeon, 1995) is grounded in the roots in realism, and it attempts to preserve extant customs and cultural values. Education under essentialism is based upon the needs of the individual within a society. It prepares students by giving the skills, knowledge and competencies required for a successful life. It focuses on the development of applied skills necessary for international competition, and strives to prepare future workers with skills, competencies and knowledge that are salable on the labor market (Wingo, 1997).

Behaviorism is the view that education's most basic form is scientific (McKeon, 1995). Behaviorism advances the notion that education should seek to set goals for students by modifying and conditioning students with reinforcements. The learners are shaped to seek or model behaviors that result in rewards and avoid negative sanctions. In this philosophy, competency based education is mandatory for classroom success, and so all goals must be measurable. Training tasks and learning materials are directly related for specific task requirements. Educational designs that evolve from the philosophies of essentialism and behaviorism are exogenous and mechanistic, and depend on explicit instruction and competency-based skills training.

The philosophy of reconstructionism asserts that education is central to changing the nature of work and mitigating conditions in employment. Starting from what exists in current societies, reconstructionism is actively involved in promoting what work should be done in the future (Kincheloe, 1993; Kohli, 1995). Work can be planned and improved, and the basis for these improvements derives from what has been previously learned or experienced. It asserts that education ought to lead in the development of clear-cut goals for the humanization of work and take an active part in the reconstruction of societies for the common good through co-adaptation and adaptive structuration, and organismic approaches (Noddings, 1995).

These basic assumptions about the purpose and nature of education translate into the approaches that teachers take in their instructional designs, for example whether to utilize lectures or experiential techniques (Kincheloe, 1993). A brief survey of educational programs (Lake, 2008) has revealed that online education has had a significant trajectory toward "producing skilled workers." This view was reflected in the words of Kohli (1995, p. 176) who wrote: "we must reject aesthetics in favor of a more practical education." This view has not always been present, for example Brubacher (1962, p. 93) had insisted that: "schools should be for learning for the sake of learning, not for the sake of earning."

In a traditional classroom, teachers can negotiate and adapt their delivery based on the needs and abilities of the students in ways that are difficult to do with online instruction. In some cases, teachers have to adapt their approaches in spite their philosophies around the online learning environment in order to "make it work." In other cases, an instructional philosophy may be very compatible with online education. This may account for why there are such diverse perspectives and little consensus about the efficacy of online education by both students and instructors.

As indicated, an instructor who operates from a behaviorism or essentialism philosophy will likely find online learning very compatible with his or her teaching style. To illustrate this point, behaviorism has led to an exogenous-mechanistic approach to mechanical content delivery, which is based on the view of "delivered instruction." It presupposes that a learner is a receiver of information, and that lectures are provided in which rewards follow for good performance. It structures information such that students acquire skills in a hierarchical manner where the parts are logically separated, and content is delivered as a set of learning objectives for student assimilation.

A philosophy that lends itself to endogenous organism-centric approaches to radical constructivism is consistent with personal instruction, reflection, and individually directed exploration, where learners use of prior knowledge to reflect on and accommodate new information they discover. The self-initiated activity accommodates the lower structure and greater autonomy found in online education.

It is from the position of a dialectical contextual perspective on social constructivism to learning, where negotiated instruction and dynamic social interaction is crucial to knowledge development, is most impinged online. Constructivism assumes primacy in the notion that knowledge is learned best when socially structured, and it relies on learning from interactions with peers and facilitators who help one to assimilate and accommodate new information through situated, real-world contexts and problems encountered and that emerge from the reciprocal teaching and collaborative processes. It is working from this philosophy where the greatest accommodation by instructors is needed for online education.

CONCLUDING THOUGHTS

In this chapter, we have reviewed a number of important factors that impact learning online. At this point, we will conclude with some implications for future design and development of online educational systems. Some of the limitations in media, though they may vary depending on type, have universal effects that must be considered as has been discussed. There are also significant interactions with individual learning styles, and situational variables to consider. All of these factors collide with the philosophies and approaches that instructors take with their designs and delivery approaches. An important point to consider relative to cognitive styles is that as currently implemented in most programs, learning online is primarily a visual process (Lake, 2008).

In this manner, many of the online instructional designs are geared for the delivery of content as "data availability" versus a "data extraction" as evidenced by the pervasive use of discussion threads and typed lecture materials employed. A data-availability design focuses on rending as much information as possible, and generally relies on linear forms of rendering owing to the massive amounts of information that must be rendered. A design for data extraction approach instead tends to focus on summarization and often uses graphical representations of information.

These design approaches are important considerations because performance on a learning task is inversely related to the amount cognitive load required to carry out that task. When cognitive load increases there are deteriorations in performance as observed in lower response times and increased errors because performance crucially depends on the relationship between cognitive resources and cognitive load in a task (Hazeltine, et al., 2006). The deteriorations often appear as a gradual decline in task performance rather than a calamitous breakdown, but the decline is measurable (Richardson-Klavehn, et al., 2002).

However, as discussed earlier, not all cognitive styles are compatible with symbolic or graphical information representation, or with the ambiguity created by information summarization. Students who need concrete detail or who cannot easily

abstract information between cognitive categories will most likely have difficulties with data extraction designs. Hence, mixed mode designs of rendering are important to support information visualization in ways that exploit cognitive assimilation most compatible with an individual's cognitive style, and an important goal should be to reduce cognitive load so that higher-level problem-solving skills can be acquired and used more effectively. In summary, designs of online instruction in the future should concentrate on augmenting the range of delivery modes, providing greater student flexibility in choosing an appropriate or more compatible mode for learning, and should introduce more ways to satisfy the information extraction aspects of content delivery (Sung, Chang, & Haung, 2008).

REFERENCES

Arbaugh, J. B. (2000). Virtual classroom versus physical classroom: An exploratory study of class discussion patterns and student learning in an asynchronous Internet-based MBA course. *Journal of Management Education, 24*, 213-233.

Bagozzi, R. P., Davis, F. D., & Warshaw, P. R. (1992). Development and test of a theory of technology learning and usage. *Human Relations, 45*, 659-686.

Bailey, B.P., & Iqbal. S.T. (2007). Understanding changes in mental workload during execution of goal-directed tasks and its application for interruption management. *ACM Transactions on Computer-Human Interaction, 14*(4), 1-21.

Bandura, A. (1978). The self-system in reciprocal determinism. *American Psychologist, 33*, 344-358.

Bangert, A. (2008). The influence of social presence and teaching presence on the quality of online critical inquiry. *Journal of Computing in Higher Education, 20*, 34-61.

Blackley, J. A., & Curran-Smith, J. (1998). Teaching community health nursing by distance methods: Development, process, and evaluation. *Journal of Continuing Education for Nurses, 29,* 148-153.

Broadbent, W. H., & Shane, T. R. (2008). Learning and training: They are not the same. *Training and Transfer, 3,* 211-233.

Brown, L. M. (1966). *General philosophy in education.* New York: McGraw Hill.

Brubacher, J. (1962). *Eclectic philosophy of education.* Englewood Cliffs, New Jersey: Prentice Hall.

Bullen, M. (1998). Participation and critical thinking in online university distance education. *The Journal of Distance Education, 13,* 1-32

Chiu, C-M., Chiu, C-S., & Chang, H-C. (2007). Examining the integrated influence of fairness and quality on learning's satisfaction and Web-based learning continuance intention. *Information Systems Journal, 17,* 271-287.

Clark, R. E. (1983). Reconsidering research on learning from media. *Review of Educational Research, 53,* 445-459.

Daft, R. L., & Lengel, R. H. (1986). Organizational information requirements. Media richness and structural design. *Management Science, 32,* 554-570.

Dewey, J. (1959). *Dewey on education.* New York: Bureau of Publications, Teachers College, Columbia University Press.

Dewey, J. (1963). *Experience and education.* New York: Collier

Dewey, J. (1966). *Democracy and education.* New York: Free Press.

Ferrari, M., & Sternberg, J. J. (1998). The development of mental abilities and styles. In W. Damon, D. Kuhn, & R. S. Siegler (Eds.), *Handbook of child psychology* (Vol. 2) (pp. 899-946). New York: John Wiley & Sons.

Flavell, J. H. (1992). Cognitive development: past, present, and future. *Developmental Psychology, 28,* 998-1005.

Freeman, M. A., & Capper, J. M. (1999). Exploiting the Web for education: An anonymous asynchronous role simulation. *Australian Journal of Educational Technology, 15,* 95-116.

Fussell, S. R., & Benimoff, I. (1995). Social and cognitive processes in interpersonal communication: Implications for advanced telecommunications technologies. *Human Factors, 37,* 228-250.

Giannakoulopoulos, A., P., & Kodellas, S. N. (2005). The impact of Web information availability in Journalism: The case of Greek journalists. In P. Masip & J. Rom (Eds), *Digital utopia in the media: From discourses to facts. A Balance, Tripodos* (Vol. 2, pp. 547-560). Barcelona, Spain.

Grigorenko, E. L., & Sternberg, R. J. (1995). Thinking styles. In D. H. Saklogske & M. Zeidner (Eds.), *International handbook of personality and intelligence* (pp. 205-229). UK: Plenum Press.

Harasim, L. (2001) Shift happens: Online education as a new paradigm in learning. *Internet and Higher Education, 3,* 41-61.

Hayes, J. & Allinson, C. W. (1998). Cognitive style and the theory and practice of individual and collective learning in organizations. *Human Relations, 51,* 847-871.

Hazeltine, E., Ruthruff, E. & Remington, R. W. (2006). The role of input and output modality parings in dual-task performance: Evidence for content-dependent central interference. *Cognitive Psychology, 52,* 291-345.

Jacoby, L. L. (1991). A process discrimination framework: Separating automatic from intentional uses of memory. *Journal of Memory and Language, 30*, 531-541

Johnson, S. D., Aragon, S. R. Shaik, N., & Palma-Rivas, N. (2000). Comparative analysis of learner satisfaction and learning outcomes in online and fact-to-face learning environments. *Journal of Interactive Learning Research, 11*(1) 29-49.

Kariya, S. (2003). Online education expands and evolves. *IEEE Spectrum, 40*, 49- 51.

Kimbrough, R. & Nunnery, M. (1988). *Educational administration*. New York: Macmillian Publishing.

Kincheloe, J. L. (1993). *Toward a critical politics of teacher thinking*. Westport CT: Bergin & Garvey.

Kohli, W. (1995). *Critical conversations in philosophy of education*. Routledge, New York: Miller Publishing.

Konradt, U., & Schmook, R. (1999). Telework: Stress and strain in a longitudinal study. *Zeitschrift Fur Arbeits-Und Organisationspsychologie, 43*, 142-150.

Kraut, R. E., Rice, R. E., Cool, C., & Fish, R. S. (1998). Varieties of social influence: The role of utility and norms in the success of a new communication medium. *Organization Science, 9*, 437-453.

Lake, M. (2008). Learning perspectives and pedagogical challenges in distance education. *Phukett Thailand: The 3rd Symposium on Distance and Virtual Learning, 4* (pp.122-143).

Martinez-Torres, M. R., Marin, S. L. T, Garcia, F. B., Vazquez, S. G., Oliva, M. A., & Torres, T. (2008). A technological acceptance of e-learning tools used in practical and laboratory teaching, according to the European higher education area. *Behaviour & Information Technology, 27*, 495-505.

Maki, R. H., Maki, W. S., Patterson, M., & Whittaker, P. D. (2000). Evaluation of a Web-based introductory psychology course. *Behavior Research Methods, Instruments, & Computers, 32*, 230-239.

Mason, R. (2004). Online education using learning objects. *British Journal of Educational Technology, 35*, 752-754

Messick, S. (1994). The mater of style: Manifestations of personality in cognition, learning and teaching. *Educational Psychologist, 29*, 121-136.

Montgomery, D. A. (1999). Human sensitivity to variability information in detection decisions. *Human Factors, 41*, 90-105.

Moos, D. C., & Azevedo, R. (2008). Monitoring, planning, and self-efficacy learning with hypermedia: The impact of conceptual scaffolds. *Journal of Computers in Human Behavior, 24*, 1686-1706.

Noddings, N. (1995). *Philosophy of education*. Boulder, CO: Westview Press.

Oliver, K., & Moore, J. (2008). Faculty recommendations for Web tools: Implications for course management systems. *Journal of Computing in Higher Education, 19*, 3-24.

Pillay, H. (1998). An investigation of the effect of individual cognitive preferences on learning through computer-based instruction. *Educational Psychology, 18*, 171-182.

Rehder, B, Hoffman, A. B. (2005). Eye tracking and selective attention in category learning. *Cognitive Psychology, 51*, 1-41.

Richardson-Klavehn, A., Gardiner, J.M., & Ramponi, C. (2002). Level of processing and the process-dissociation procedure: Elusiveness of null effects on estimates of automatic retrieval. *Memory, 10*, 349-364.

Roca, J. C., & Gagne, M. (2008). Understanding e-learning continuance intention in the workplace: A self-determination theory perspective. *Journal of Computers in Human Behavior, 24,* 1585-1604.

Schulman, A. H., & Sims, R. L. (1999). Learning in an online format versus an in-class format: An experimental study. *THE Journal (Technological Horizons in Education), 26,* 63-72.

Steinhouse, D. (1985). *Active philosophy in education and science.* Englewood Cliffs, New Jersey: Prentice Hall.

Sternberg, R.J. (1997). *Thinking styles.* NY: Cambridge University Press.

Sternberg, R. J., & Grigorenko, E. L. (1997). Are cognitive styles still in style. *American Psychologist, 52,* 700-712.

Straus, S., & McGrath, J. E. (1994). Does the medium matter? The interaction of task type and technology on group performance and member reactions. *Journal of Applied Psychology, 79,* 87-97.

Sung, Y-T., Chang, K-E, & Haung, J-S. (2008). Improving children's reading comprehension and use of strategies through computer-based strategy training. *Journal of Computers in Human Behavior, 24,* 1552-1571.

Wieland, R. (1999). Mental workload in VDU-assisted office work: Consequences for the design of telework. *Zeitschrift Fur Arbeits-Und Organisationaspsychologie, 43,* 153-158.

Wingo, G. M. (1997). *Philosophies of education: An introduction.* Boston, MA: Houghton Mifflin.

Workman, M. (2004). Performance in computer-based and computer-aided education: Do cognitive styles make a difference? *Journal of Computers in Human Behavior, 20,* 517-534.

Workman, M. (2005). Virtual team culture and the amplification of team boundary permeability on performance. *Human Resource Development Quarterly, 16,* 435-458.

Workman, M. (2006). Virtual communities and imaginary friends: Affiliation and affection from afar. *Proceedings from the Annual Conference on Technology and Innovation, CTI'06* (pp. 122-131), Stowe, VT.

Workman, M. (2007). Virtual team performance and the proximal-virtual team continuum. *Journal of the American Society for Information Science and Technology, 58,* 794-801.

Workman, M., Kahnweiler, W., & Bommer, W. H. (2003). The effects of cognitive style and technology media on commitment to telework and virtual teams. *Journal of Vocational Behavior, 63,* 199-219.

Chapter V
Integrating Knowledge of Cognitive System and E–Learning Applications

George Spanoudis
University of Cyprus, Cyprus

Eleni A. Kyza
Cyprus University of Technology, Cyprus

ABSTRACT

This chapter outlines key findings of cognitive and developmental psychology which could be used as a theoretical framework to guide the design and research of e-learning applications. The chapter consists of two main sections. The first section presents the basic cognitive mechanisms and their development, while the second part discusses how our knowledge of the cognitive system can guide the design of computer-based learning environments. It is proposed that the human mind is organized in three levels: two of them are general-purpose mechanisms and processes and one consists of domain-specific structures of knowledge representation and problem solving processes. These three levels are associated with an effective learning framework. The suggested framework describes the basic points that any designer of e-learning environments must consider. The second section of the chapter discusses e-learning, connecting it to knowledge about the human cognitive system. In this section, we first present the conceptual bounds of the e-learning construct and discuss how cognitive theories of learning should guide the design of technologically-enhanced learning environments. It is proposed that a synergy between the study of human cognition and the design of e-learning applications is required for effectively understanding both fields.

INTRODUCTION

In the last decades the world has witnessed an 'electronic revolution'. It is widely argued that the transition from the 'industrial' to the so-called 'information' society has been made possible by the development of novel information and communication technologies (Castells, 2000). New technologies, and especially computers, have dramatically altered both thinking and acting in almost all fields of human activity (Gentile & Walsh, 2002). Hence, it is critical to understand the changes which are being brought about by the introduction of communication and information technologies in order to maximize their benefits and minimize their shortcomings.

Nowadays, we use computers for learning (e.g. educational software), entertainment (e.g. animations, cartoons), communicating (e.g. electronic mail), or performing complex tasks, such as calculations and graphing, storing multi-layer information, text reading and writing, special scientific tasks, etc. (Gentile & Walsh, 2002). It is estimated that nearly half (48%) of all children six and under have used computers and that more than one in four (30%) have played video games (Rideout, Vanderwater, & Wartella, 2003). The impact of computers on modern societies is so vast and multifarious that our age has arguably been called the 'electronic age'.

Education is one of the fields of human endeavor most affected by the electronic revolution. The impact of computer technologies on children's cognitive, social and emotional development has been the subject of systematic research in the last decades. This research produced a number of myths and debates concerning the possibilities and dangers resulting from the introduction and extensive use of computers and its related applications in education. Some scholars even go to the extreme by arguing that the use of computers is linked to numerous disadvantages like low self-esteem, low intelligence, exposure to undesirable material, aggression, and obesity (Rocheleau, 1995; Roe & Muijs, 1998), whereas others suggest the exact opposite and stress the importance of outcomes, such as higher academic achievement and cognitive skills (Healy, 1998). Some could attribute such apparent inconsistencies and contradictory findings to the complexity and novelty of the field. However, most researchers would entirely agree on the need for the development of a theoretical framework for understanding the effects of computers on human mind and society.

The present chapter aims to outline key findings of cognitive and developmental psychology which could be used as a theoretical framework to guide the design and research of e-learning applications. The chapter proceeds as follows. First, we describe the basic mechanisms of cognition and their development. Then we explore the concept of learning and how one could utilize theory and research results from cognitive psychology, in order to design and implement e-learning environments. The chapter will conclude with a synopsis of essential parameters that a designer of web-based environments must take into account when s/he plans the content, representations and interactional features for a computer-based learning environment.

THEORETICAL FRAMEWORK

Cognition, Metacognition and Problem Solving Skills

Cognition refers to the ability of human mind to acquire and manage information. The concept of cognition encompasses mental processes such as attention, perception, memory, learning and problem solving (Solso, MacLin & MacLin, 2005). The term also refers to the concept of cognitive architecture as it is used in the frame of cognitive science. According to Ritter and Young (2001) a cognitive architecture is an embodiment of a scientific hypothesis about those aspects of human cognition that are relatively constant over time and relatively independent of task. This architecture is a product of systematic interaction between a biologically predetermined neurological development and experience gained by the actions of the architecture upon its environment. Cognition is usually analyzed at two levels: at a fundamental level which involves basic mechanisms or abilities, like perception, attention, and memory, and at a higher level which concerns cognitive functions and processes like comprehension, reasoning, decision-making, planning, problem-solving and learning.

Human cognition is a dynamic system whose architecture is to a great extent predisposed biologically but its functioning is greatly determined by experience. This implies that the cognitive system can reach its final potential after a period of development. The term cognitive development refers to changes in cognitive architecture (structure) over time. After a rapid period of development the cognitive system is molded and operates in an adult-like fashion. In addition, it should be noted that recent approaches of cognitive development also emphasize individual differences in cognitive processes and its life-span character (Bjorklund, 2005).

However, three different paradigms regarding cognitive development have been put forth: empiricism, rationalism and socio-historic tradition (Case, 1998). Regardless of the particular research tradition there are some basic principles which crosscut and tie together the study of cognition and its development. These basic principles could constitute, and as such we will discuss them in this chapter, the needed theoretical base for the advancement of a cognitive learning theory of e-learning. First, the cognitive system becomes increasingly able to manage and comprehend successively and/or simultaneously more complex relationships of external or internal reality due to structural or functional reasons. In other words, the cognitive system becomes more flexible and efficient in using, storing and retrieving

information in order to make sense and master its environment. Second, we progressively develop and apply self-regulatory processes which act upon our behaviour and cognition. Simply put, a metacognitive system gradually emerges, operating as a general manager of our cognitive and behavioural processes.

More specifically, our mind is organized in three levels, two of them comprising general-purpose mechanisms and processes -the information processing system and metacognitition- and one comprising domain-specific structures of knowledge representation and processes of problem solving (Demetriou, Christou, Spanoudis, & Platsidou, 2002). These levels could be distinguished from each other on the basis of functional criteria. Each of the levels is itself a complex network of structures and processes organized across multiple dimensions and tiers. The most basic of these levels involves general cognitive processes and mechanisms that define the processing potential available at a given time. Therefore, the condition of the processes comprising this level constrains the condition and functioning of the systems included in the other two levels. The other two are *knowing levels* (Demetriou et al., 2002), in that they involve systems and functions underlying knowledge representation and problem solving. The duty of one of these two knowing levels is to process and represent the different aspects of the physical and social environments. The other knowing level is intended for monitoring, managing or regulating and storing knowledge concerning the self. That is, it pertains to all strategic processes underlying self-monitoring, self-representation, and self-regulation. Metacognitive skills emerge during the preschool period and fully mature during adolescence, playing an important role in many types of high-level cognitive processes like learning, reasoning and problem solving. Understanding, learning, or performing any task, at a particular point in developmental time, is a mixture of the processes involved at all three levels. In the section below we will briefly outline this architecture and present supporting empirical evidence.

Cognitive (Baddeley, 2007; Engle, 2002), and developmental psychologists (Case, 1998; Flavell, Miller, & Miller, 2004) agree that working memory is a core system of our cognition that has limited resources for representing and processing information concerning the environment and the self. The capacity of working memory to simultaneously process information defines the processing potential of our cognition. Three parameters have mainly been identified by cognitive and developmental research as primary indexes of processing potential: *speed of processing, control of processing*, and *representational capacity*.

The term *speed of processing* basically refers to the maximum speed at which a given mental act may be efficiently carried out. Usually, we measure speed of processing by asking individuals to recognize or choose a very simple stimulus as quickly as possible, such as locating or identifying a geometrical figure, a letter, or a word. Under these conditions, speed of processing indicates the time needed by the system to process the stimulus giving meaning to information. Traditionally, the faster an individual can recognize a stimulus, the more efficient information processor s/he is thought to be (MacLeod, 1991). It is deemed that these behavioral measures of speed of processing correspond to the attributes of our neural substrate. That is, the neural traces of stimuli encountered at a given moment tend to decay rapidly or to be overwritten by the traces of information encountered at the next moment (Nelson, de Haan, & Thomas, 2006). Therefore, fast processing ensures that the goals of a particular step of processing will be met before the initiation of a new step, which will, in turn, impose its own competing demands on the system (Salthouse, 1996).

The term control of processing pertains to the decision processes which allow human cognition to focus on specific aspects of a stimulus at all times. Given that our cognitive system is flooded by complex stimuli, our ability to process any

stimulus would be widely restricted without the existence of decision processes. These processes are assigned with the work of, at a first step, discriminating the relevant features of stimuli being processed against non-relevant and, at a second step, directing attention to relevant ones. Efficient processing requires a mechanism that would allow cognition to keep control of processing, filtering out interfering and goal-irrelevant information and shifting focus to the selected information, if this is required (MacLeod, 1991). Control of processing is usually tested under conditions which include competing dimensions that force cognition into selecting one dimension over another, such as the well-known Stroop phenomenon. In this test, words denoting color are written with a different ink color (e.g., the word "red" written with blue ink), and the individual is asked to name the ink color as quickly as possible. These conditions accurately test control of processing, because the individual is required to inhibit a dominant but irrelevant response (to read the word) in order to select and express a weaker but relevant response (name the ink color) (Demetriou, et al., 2002; Dempster & Brainerd, 1995).

Representational capacity is defined as the maximum amount of information and mental acts that our cognition can efficiently activate and process simultaneously at a given moment. In current psychological literature, working memory capacity is regarded as the functional manifestation of representational capacity. According to Baddeley (2003) the working memory system is a multifaceted structure which consists of two kinds of systems, i.e., fluid and crystallized. In turn, the fluid systems consist of three discrete mechanisms, i.e., a central executive mechanism, a phonological loop, and a visuo-spatial sketchpad. The central executive is a limited capacity attentional mechanism which has a supervising role on storing and processing incoming information, and coordinates the interaction of fluid and crystallized systems through phonological and visuo-spatial subsystems. The phonological loop specializes in the temporary storage of phonological-verbal material and is divided into two subsystems, one for storing and one for subvocally rehearsing the phonological information. The subvocal subsystem emerges during the first school years and serves the transportation of visual information to the phonological loop for storing and refreshing decaying phonological representations within the phonological store. The visuo-spatial system maintains temporary visual or spatial information. Further, the crystallized systems are constituted by three components: visual semantics, episodic long-term memory and language. The capacity of the working memory systems develops steadily until late adolescence.

The second general-purpose system pertains to metacognitive knowledge and processes. To understand the necessity of such a supervisory system, we have to bear in mind the complexity of environment, the multilevel functioning of cognition and, especially, the need for deliberate action of our mind on its environment. Our cognitive system must be able to record its own cognitive experiences (self-mapping) and keep knowledge of them that can be used in the future (self-regulation), if the need arises (Demetriou, 2000). Metacognition can be thought of as a second-order level of knowing and acting. The input to this system is information coming from the action of cognition and can roughly encompass knowledge about persons, tasks and strategies (Flavell et al., 2004). This information is organized by the mind into categories or models of mental activity and is used to guide the monitoring and controlling of cognitive processes. Thus, the metacognitive system consists of two sub-systems, one responsible for monitoring and regulating the functioning of cognitive system (*working metacognition),* as it operates, and one for storing and retrieving the knowledge which is produced by the action of working metacognition (*long-term metacognition).*

Working metacognition revolves around a strong monitoring, planning and executing func-

tion responsible for setting mental and behavioral goals, and pursuing them until they are attained. Specifically, working metacognition includes processes enabling the person to (i) monitor the current situation and compare it with the mind's current goal, (ii) plan the steps needed to attain the goal, and, finally, (iii) execute the planned actions, constantly monitoring them and taking corrective actions, if and when these are required (Demetriou, 2000).

Long-term metacognition pertains to knowledge or models relative to past cognitive experiences resulting from the functioning of working metacognition. These models are broad descriptions of the general functional characteristics of the mind, suggesting the existence of different cognitive functions, such as perception, attention, and memory. Moreover, these models include a wide range of information about the efficient use of the psychological functions by the person itself, for instance, that detailed information requires organization to be retained in memory, or knowledge about the level of one's own mathematical skills. In other words, our long-term metacognition encompasses general knowledge about psychological functions common to all human beings, and specific knowledge about the psychological functions relative to the individual experiences of the person.

Working metacognition could be part of, and use, the resources of fluid systems, while long-term metacognition could be part of crystallized systems as they are respectively described in Baddeley's (2007) model. It is worth noting that the incorporation of metacognitive sub-components in corresponding fluid and crystallized systems creates a parsimonious architecture which offers a simple solution to the issue of self-regulation. Specifically, in the context of that architecture the metacognitive system can efficiently cooperate with and supervise the cognitive system, so that the former can be the general manager and the latter the accurate executive tool. Having in mind the form and function of the metacognitive system, metacognition becomes a tool of wide application for solving many practical and theoretical problems.

The *third domain-specific level of mind* comprises of specialized processes oriented to aspects of the environment and of domain knowledge. These specialized processes are problem solving skills suitable for managing different types of information and kinds of problems. These processes allow the mind to choose and process particular *types of representations* between environmental stimuli. Additionally, they involve *specialized operations* that are appropriate for the specific type of representation and relations. In a sense, the operations and processes of a specific domain of thought are the mental analogues of the type of relations concerned. Moreover, they are *biased to a particular symbol system* that is better appropriate than other symbol systems to represent the type of relations concerned and facilitate the execution of the operations.

Each of the specialized domains involves two types of processes: core processes and mental operations and processing skills. The functioning of these processes produces domain-specific knowledge and skills. Core processes are fundamental processes that ground each of the domains into its respective environmental realm. During development, core processes are the first manifestations of the systems, and they are predominantly action and perception bound. If a minimum set of conditions is present in the input, they are activated and provide an interpretation of the input, which is consistent with their organization. In other words, core processes are inferential traps within each of the systems that respond to informational structures with core-specific interpretations that have adaptive value and "meaning" for the organism.

Operations and processing skills are systems of mental (or, frequently, physical) actions that are used to deliberately deal with information and relations in each of the domains. From the point of view of development, core processes constitute the starting points for the construction of operations and skills included in each of the domains. That is, at the initial phases of development, operations, skills, and knowledge arise through interactions between domain-specific core processes, the environment, and the executive and self-monitoring and self-regulation processes of the metacognitive system. That is, the systems of operations and processes within each domain emerge as a process of differentiation and expansion of the core processes when these do not suffice to meet the understanding and problem solving needs of the moment. In other words, the initial inferential traps are gradually transformed into inference that is increasingly self-guided and reflected upon.

Learning

Clearly, the way that we view learning has changed dramatically in the last fifty years due to the 'cognitive revolution', the intellectual movement that led to the birth of cognitive science by integrating psychology, linguistics, philosophy and anthropology against behaviorism. For the first half of the 20th century, psychology was dominated by behaviorism that attempted hard to reveal the general laws of learning. Learning was viewed as a primarily passive activity, concerning the formation of simple associations governed by reinforcements. Learning of complex behaviors was explained as cases of extension, generalization or combination of simple associations. After the cognitive revolution the way of viewing the concept of learning was, to a great extent, transformed. This transformation revolved around two issues: learners' cognitive characteristics and the context of learning. The first issue was introduced by Piaget's theory of cognitive development and information processing theories (Flavell et al., 2004), while the second by Vygotsky's theory of social cognition (Rogoff, 1998). In this sense, learners are now viewed as active constructors of their knowledge, while learning is seen as a multi-component dynamic procedure rather than simply a state. Important components of the learning procedure are deemed to be the *learning environment, features of cognitive architecture, prior knowledge* and *motivation*. We examine each of these four components next.

The ideal learning environment for effective learning is one that stimulates individuals to engage in active learning and provides several opportunities to make sense of the various aspects of the concepts being learned. Such environments are learner-centered as they emphasize the learner's ability to interpret and construct meaning based on their own experiences and interactions. Learners are actively engaged in meaningful projects and activities that promote exploration, experimentation, construction, collaboration, and reflection of what these learners are studying (Marton & Booth, 1997). The learner's engagement and active involvement in the learning procedure are achieved when the context is characterized by specific properties. First, the context should allow for a structured interaction between learners with the same or different levels of understanding. The term structured refers to the presence of a mediator, for instance, teacher, software or peers, or a combination of these. The mediator facilitates interaction and engagement in meaningful activities. In the case of learners with different levels of understanding, the work of the mediator is to scaffold the knowledge transfer from the more competent to the less competent learner. Second, the context should enable learners to control the flow of information and rate of learning, and experience the learning procedure as an enjoyable and meaningful experience.

Concerning the features of the learners' cognitive architecture, as mentioned before, there are two levels of cognition that play an important role in learning: information processing system and metacognition. During learning the learner's mind has to handle a cognitive load effectively (Kirschner, 2002). The extent to which the mind manages the cognitive load efficiently depends on

its features, more specifically, on the speed, control, and the representational processing capacity. Given that working memory is a limited capacity system, it is apparent that speed and control of processing could define the quantity and quality of stored representations. We could imagine our working memory as a workbench continuously receiving information coming from our senses (sensory), or our specialized knowledge domains (mental). This information must be processed very quickly because other information is waiting for processing. At the same time, processing must be targeted to a specific object and not be spread out. Simply put, the ability to learn is dependent on our working memory capacity.

On the other hand, our cognitive system as we grow older is supervised by metacognitive processes. This implies that effective learning could be achieved through acting upon or 'instructing' metacognition. A learner who has learned to manage her cognitive load effectively could be a better learner. Also, a learner who has learned to organize material into easily accessible chunks, or work strategically in problem solving, could acquire deeper understanding of the learning material, or perform better on problem solving tasks.

Research has shown that a learner's prior knowledge plays a crucial role in learning. A large body of findings demonstrates that prior knowledge acts as a framework through which the learner filters new information and attempts to make sense of what is learned. We tend to organize and understand new information in terms of what we already know. As mentioned before our mind has specialized processes which strive to package information into coherent domains of knowledge utilizing core processes and mental operations and skills. This well-connected domain knowledge allows our cognitive and metacognitive system to understand, retrieve and apply new knowledge very efficiently. Without a basis of prior knowledge characterized by these properties, learning new material would be very laborious and time-consuming (Van Merriënboer & Sweller, 2005).

Based on what we have presented thus far, one can conclude that the prerequisites of learning are the ability of the cognitive system to quickly select and focus on the incoming information, to make sense and organize it aided by prior knowledge and to integrate it into the domain-specific representational systems. Additionally, our metacognitive processes supervise and, if necessary, redirect a part or the whole process of learning. But who should be responsible for activating metacognitive thinking? Given that research has shown that many learners are not particularly metacognitively aware (Collins, Brown, & Newman, 1989) pedagogical design needs to raise student awareness of themselves as learners and adopt strategies for training to engage in metacognitive thinking. In other words, it is necessary to motivate learners to the extent that her or his metacognition can effectively manage the learning process.

Scientific fields like cognitive and developmental science have grown up rapidly and matured to the point where they can definitely contribute to learning theory and its application in educational settings and practice. Nowadays, cognitive psychology is developing and suggesting models of cognition, challenging human-computer interaction and investigating expert performance, in an attempt to illuminate cognitive processes of competence.

Our review of cognition and learning, thus far, outlines the basic points that any designer of e-learning environments must take into consideration. In recent years, designers of e-learning environments started incorporating ideas, findings and methods originating from the area of cognitive and developmental psychology. The convergence of theory and research regarding both e-learning and cognitive and developmental psychology is necessary. The latter will be helpful for both, as e-learning will acquire the needed theoretical framework, while cognitive and developmental

psychology will have a new scientific field for applying ideas and models.

E-LEARNING

Historically, e-learning has developed concurrently with information and communication technologies (ICTs), which have shattered conventional ideas about the limitations on human communication imposed by physical location and geographic proximity and re-defined learning. The inception of the first network technologies in the early 1960's was related to the Cold War, in an attempt to re-establish the United States' technological lead and as a response to the USSR's launching of Sputnik. It was not until a few decades later that the internet had reached a maturity level that would allow exploring its possibilities in educational settings.

The construct of e-learning includes any electronic means that facilitates learning. According to Wentling et al. (2000):

E-learning is the acquisition and use of knowledge distributed and facilitated primarily by electronic means. This form of learning currently depends on networks and computers but will likely evolve into systems consisting of a variety of channels (e.g., wireless, satellite), and technologies (e.g., cellular phones, PDA's) as they are developed and adopted. (p.5)

It is frequently observed that media outlets, lay people, and many academics do not consistently differentiate between different e-learning categories, putting the emphasis rather on the medium of delivery as the most important common denominator amongst e-learning applications. Thus, often, e-learning is reserved solely for online, distance applications (e.g. Huffaker & Calvert, 2003), even though the definition by Wentling et al. allows for a variety of delivery media, which do not all require network access. The lack of ontological clarity propagates the confusion as to what exactly constitutes e-learning (Ally, 2008); in turn, this holds the field back, since it complicates the development of a sound theoretical basis that would distinguish the field from others, could promote community building, and would enhance knowledge sharing about principles that should be guiding the development and instructional delivery of e-learning environments.

It is true however, that web-based e-learning applications share important benefits as compared to stand-alone computer applications (Kyza, 2005). Web-based environments are accessible from anywhere and anytime thus offering opportunities for learning at a distance and enhancing lifelong learning opportunities and just-in-time training. Such web-based learning environments share many innovative features that offer multimodal experiences to learners: for example, they feature synchronous and asynchronous communication capabilities, embed technologies for customizing and personalizing learning, and employ multiple tools for facilitating online collaboration. These features, whether used only online or as part of a blended learning model, have expanded educational horizons to specifically include informal learning settings.

Harasim (2006) identified three educational models in e-learning applications: a) online collaborative learning, which emphasizes collaboration and group work, b) online distance education, which most often refers to a new way of delivering distance learning while still relying on similar conventional pedagogical methods such as the ones employed in traditional distance learning, and c) online computer-based training, which relies on human-computer interaction through software tutoring programs. Anderson (2008) further distinguishes e-learning as intending to cater to two types of learning settings: collaborative or independent.

COGNITIVE MODELS UNDERLYING E-LEARNING

The development of learning materials is influenced by the specific tradition about human learning that their developers subscribe to, whether these beliefs are made explicit or not. Even though the three main schools of thoughts about learning (rationalist, empiricist, and sociohistorical) have influenced educational design (Greeno, Collins & Resnick, 1996), they have not systematically touched educational technology design, with most e-learning discussions being driven by practice rather than by theory (Ravenscroft, 2001). It is, perhaps, no exaggeration to say that many of the online environments described as e-learning do not reflect any truly transformative practices, such as those denoted by Harasim's first educational model cited earlier. Furthermore, in spite of discussions about e-learning practices abounding in the literature, the theoretical basis of these discussions, and most notably the theory driving e-learning development and application, seems weak and murky, to say the least.

In an attempt to contribute towards a theory of e-learning, Anderson (2008) discusses the similarities and differences between face to face learning (f2f) and online (distance) learning. Accepting that e-learning is a subset of learning, Anderson goes on to argue that as long as one develops rich learning experiences and as long as some basic presuppositions are met, learning can be experienced in both f2f and online environments; he goes on to identify the presuppositions as building learning environments that support interaction between students, teachers, and content (student-to-student, student-to-teacher, and student-content) and which are learner-centered, content-centered, community-centered, and assessment-centered (Bransford, Cocking & Brown, 1999).

In this chapter, we argue that there is a strong need to use learning theories in designing e-learning environments; however, we need to look no further than existing theories of cognition. Theories about individual cognition and collaborative learning can guide the design of such environments according to the goals of each design effort; we discuss this topic next.

COGNITIVE THEORIES OF LEARNING AND THE DESIGN PROCESS

At the onset of each principled design effort, designers have to answer questions about the target audience, the learning goals and expected learning outcomes, and the learning context. The answers to these questions will provide the design framework. For example, the age of the learners will help the designers examine research and experience, in order to provide the initial postulations about what could be cognitively feasible and accessible by this audience, and will suggest what a common baseline of knowledge might be. Setting learning goals will help focus the design while describing the expected learning outcomes will bootstrap the design activity. The design of efficient e-learning environments requires knowledge about human cognitive architecture, the learners' prior knowledge and motivation, and the learning environment. We examine each one of these next.

HUMAN COGNITIVE ARCHITECTURE

Design efforts need to take into account the architecture of the human cognitive system and existing knowledge about how people learn and how the mind develops. One of the most important contributions of cognitive science is the constructivist framing of learning. Even though e-learning environments have the capacity to allow active engagement with ideas, this is not an inherent property of this type of learning, as

it is often, quite optimistically, being portrayed. Rather, designers need to make concerted efforts and build upon knowledge about human cognition, motivation, and social interaction in order to produce environments that afford, but do not guarantee, active learner engagement.

Two other important findings from cognitive science research is the importance of attending to cognitive load during the design process and of creating opportunities for metacognitive engagement. Several strategies have been proposed to help overcome the cognitive load that can result from the well-established processing and storing limitations of human working memory. Applying strategies to overcome these memory limitations becomes increasingly important, as pedagogical designs of domain-specific educational technology applications increasingly place emphasis on problem-based learning and making sense of complex data (Hmelo-Silver, 2004; van Merriënboer & Ayres, 2005). Chandler and Sweller's theory of cognitive load (1996) suggests that instructional design is most critical in situations of high interactivity between intrinsic cognitive load, which is content-related, and extraneous cognitive load, which is dependent on the instructional representation method. High extraneous cognitive load and, especially, high interaction between the two types of cognitive load increase the demand on working memory and may negatively influence the learning outcomes. Thus, designers of complex, information-rich e-learning environments should strive to reduce extraneous cognitive load and increase germane cognitive load, which can lead to the integration of new information into the long-term memory which does not share the limitations of working memory.

Intentional learning requires the deployment of metacognition. In the case of personalized, self-paced e-learning environments, metacognition is crucial in supporting the learner in planning and monitoring their learning activity, as well as in understanding their strengths and weaknesses as learners and engaging in appropriate and effective help-seeking. According to Lin (2001) researchers have used the following two approaches to support metacognition in instructional interventions: a) strategy teaching, to facilitate the working metacognition and self-regulated learning, and b) creating a supporting social environment to facilitate long-term metacognition.

As a construct, self-regulation is important in that it regulates cognitive, motivational, and behavioral states of the learner (Azevedo, 2005).

Metacognitive engagement in e-learning environments can be supported through either software or human mediation (e.g. the teacher as a facilitator of learning). Software mediation can take a variety of forms, such as being embedded in the representations of the learning environment or constructed on the fly from computational agents who monitor the user actions and provide advice as needed. However, technological solutions for dynamic metacognitive support, tracing the learners' process and providing on-demand support have only been possible in very constrained problem-solving situations, such as intelligent tutoring systems (e.g. Cognitive Tutors, Koedinger, Anderson, Hadley, & Mark, 1997), while even in these environments there have been reports of ineffective use of the software. Because of the lack of adaptive, technology-based scaffolding, non-adaptive scaffolds (e.g. metacognitive prompts) have been used to support ongoing metacognition (Azevedo, 2005).

LEARNERS' PRIOR KNOWLEDGE AND MOTIVATION

As mentioned earlier, learners' prior knowledge frames and constrains any new learning that takes place. Increasingly, e-learning environments have the capacity for customizing and personalizing the learning experience, allowing the learners to draw from their own experience, set their pace of learning according to their background, and seek additional information to complement what

they already know. For example, an e-learning environment may be easily customized for different age learners, or learners from different cultural contexts, thus making the material to be learned more accessible by the target users of the e-learning application.

Learner motivation to actively participate can be detrimental to the successful outcomes of any e-learning approach. When learning is completely self-paced and online, managing to capture and sustain the learners' motivation is what will eventually support the learner's cognitive engagement. Keeping learners motivated at a distance is difficult to achieve (Keller & Suzuki, 2004); some strategies to increase learner motivation include building learning environments that involve authentic learning, drawing from problems that connect to the learners' experiences and real-life issues, inviting active participation, and providing systematic feedback and customization. Keller & Suzuki (2004) have proposed a model for achieving learner motivation. According to this model, the following criteria have to be met for an environment to support motivation: a) the learning environment needs to attract and sustain the learner's attention; this can be achieved by a variety of techniques, such as personalization to address personally meaningful learning opportunities, building upon natural curiosity, placing the learner in a problem-solving situation, varying the approach to avoid boredom, etc.; b) the learning environment needs to be relevant to the learners' lives. Learners need to understand why they are engaging in this e-learning task and share the goals of the designers, transforming them into their own personal goals; c) tasks have to be designed at an appropriate level of difficulty, so that the learners gradually build confidence in what they are doing and increase their self-efficacy about engaging in the task; d) the environment needs to evoke positive affective reactions, balancing intrinsic and extrinsic motivation. Learner motivation and self-efficacy beliefs can then, in turn, impact upon their self-regulation strategies and interact with metacognitive engagement (Pintrich, 1999).

THE LEARNING ENVIRONMENT

The design of the learning environment is another very influential factor contributing to the effectiveness of e-learning. Psychological research has indicated that contextual factors can influence the impact of e-learning applications. The context of learning can be defined as consisting of all factors contributing to the learning activity, which are external to the learner. Examples of these are interactions between the learner, the teacher and other peers. Knowledge about peer interaction processes and the role of tools and inscriptions as extending the individual cognition capabilities can greatly enhance the design of electronic learning environments. Exactly because interaction is key to learning, e-learning applications need to maximize possibilities for interaction, while structuring them to avoid unnecessary cognitive load.

While in the previous section we discussed the principles for supporting cognitive and motivational engagement, the focal point in considering the learning environment is on capitalizing on the interactional elements. New technologies can support this interaction, both in asynchronous and synchronous modes. For example, forums, an example of an asynchronous technology and a component of many web-based environments, can help sustain the dialogue between members of a learning community, even when these learners are not physically or temporally co-located.

CONCLUSION

In this chapter we have described how cognitive theory is prerequisite to integrating theory, data, and knowledge concerning human and computer interaction. Current psychological research provides a clear image of how and under which conditions we could achieve efficient learning. Learners are seen as cognitive and socio-emotional creatures able to learn effectively when are granted specific conditions. The learners' cognitive and motivational characteristics, in combination with an appropriate learning context, are deemed as necessary conditions to achieve learning (Huffaker, & Calvert, 2003). Models of learners' cognitive and motivational features, as well as learning theories, would constitute a sound and well-elaborated framework which can be utilized in improving the usability of e-learning applications and user interfaces. Designers of e-learning applications should be aware of current learning and cognitive theories, as such knowledge would allow them to take into consideration basic psychological principles about learning and apply them into e-learning environments. If the inherent features of e-learning as a flexible, enjoyable and creative medium are coupled with the cognitive and learning principles that were mentioned before, the future of e-learning would be very promising. In addition, adopting a cognitive and developmental psychology framework to e-learning research would benefit both fields, as e-learning applications provide a creative and flexible applied area for testing the theories and data produced from cognitive and developmental studies.

REFERENCES

Ally, M. (2008). Foundations of educational theory for online learning. In T. Anderson (Ed.), *The theory and practice of online learning* (pp. 15-44). AU Press.

Anderson, T. (2008). Towards a theory of online learning. In T. Anderson (Ed.), *The theory and practice of online learning* (pp. 45-74). AU Press.

Anderson, T. (Ed.). (2008). *The theory and practice of online learning*. AU Press.

Azevedo, R. (2005). Using hypermedia as a meta-cognitive tool for enhancing student learning? The role of self-regulated learning. *Educational Psychologist, 40*(4), 199-209.

Baddeley, A. D. (2007). *Working memory, thought, and action.* Oxford: Oxford University Press.

Baddeley, A. (2003). Working memory and language: An overview. *Journal of Communication Disorders, 36,* 189-208.

Bjorklund, D. F. (2005). *Children's thinking: Cognitive development and individual differences* (4th ed.). Belmont, CA: Wadsworth.

Bransford, J., Brown, A. L., & Cocking, R. R. (1999). *How people learn: Brain, mind, experience, and school.* Washington, D.C.: National Academy Press.

Case, R. (1998). The development of conceptual structures. In D. Kuhn & R. S. Siegler (Eds.), *Handbook of child psychology: Vol. 2. Cognition, perception, and language.* (5th ed., pp. 745-796). New York: Wiley.

Castells, M. (2000). *The Rise of the Network Society* (2nd ed.): Wiley-Blackwell.

Collins, A., Brown, J. S., and Newman, S. E. (1989). Cognitive apprenticeship: Teaching the crafts of reading, writing, and mathematics. In L. Resnick (Ed.), *Knowing, learning, and instruction: Essays in honor of Robert Glaser.* (pp. 453-494). Hillsdale, NJ: Lawrence Erlbaum Associates.

Demetriou, A., (2000). Organization and development of self-understanding and self-regulation: Toward a general theory. In M. Boekaerts, P. R. Pintrich, & M. Zeidner (Eds.), *Handbook of self-regulation* (pp. 209-251). Academic Press.

Demetriou, A., Christou, C., Spanoudis, G., & Platsidou, M. (2002). The development of mental processing: Efficiency, working memory, and thinking. *Monographs of the Society of Research in Child Development, 67,* Serial Number 268.

Dempster, F. N., & Brainerd, C. J. (Eds) (1995). *Interference and inhibition in cognition.* New York: Academic Press.

Engle, R. W. (2002). Working memory capacity as executive attention. *Current Directions in Psychological Science, 11,* 19-23.

Flavell, J. H., Miller, P. H., & Miller, S. A. (2004). *Cognitive development.* (4th Ed.). NJ: Prentice Hall.

Gentile, D. A. & Welsh, D. A. (2002). A normative study of family media habits. *Applied Developmental Psychology, 23,* 157-178.

Greeno, J. G., Collins, A. M., & Resnick, L. (1996). Cognition and learning. In D. B. a. R. Calfee (Ed.), *Handbook of educational psychology* (pp. 15-46). New York: MacMillan.

Harasim, L. (2006). A History of e-learning: Shift happened. In J. N. Joel Weiss, Jeremy Hunsinger and Peter Trifonas (Ed.), *The international handbook of virtual learning environments* (pp. 59-94). The Netherlands: Springer.

Healy, J. M. (1998). *Failure to connect: How computers affect our children's minds – For better or for worse.* New York: Simon & Schuster.

Hmelo-Silver, C. (2004). Problem-based learning: What and how do students learn? *Educational Psychology Review, 16*(3), 235-266.

Huffaker, D. A., & Calvert, S. L. (2003). The new science of learning: Active learning, metacognition, and transfer of knowledge in e-learning applications. *Journal of Educational Computing Research, 29*(3), 325-334.

Keller, J. M., & Suzuki, K. (2004). Learner motivation and e-learning design: A multinationally validated process. *Journal of Educational Media, 29*(3), 229-239.

Kirschner, P. (2002). Cognitive load theory: implications of cognitive load theory on the design of learning. *Learning and Instruction, 12,* 1-10.

Koedinger, K. R., Anderson, J. R., Hadley, W. H., & Mark, M. (1997). Intelligent tutoring goes to school in the big city. *International Journal of Artificial Intelligence in Education, 8*, 30-43.

Kyza, E. (2005.) Supporting data-rich inquiries on the Web. In Zacharia, Z. C. & Constantinou, C. P., (Eds.) *Proceedings of the 7ᵗʰ International Conference on Computer-based learning in Science*. Zilina, Slovakia.

Marton, F., & Booth, S. (1997). *Learning and awareness*. Mahwah, New Jersey: Lawrence Erlbaum Associates.

McLeod, C. M. (1991). Half a century of research on the Stroop effect: An integrative review. *Psychological Bulletin, 109*, 163-203.

Nelson, C. A., de Haan, M., & Thomas, M. M. (2006). *Neuroscience of cognitive development: The role of experience and the developing brain*. New Jersey, NY. Wiley & Sons.

O'Donnell, A. M. (2006). The role of peers and group learning. In P. Alexander & P. Winne (Eds.), *Handbook of educational psychology* (2ⁿᵈ Ed., pp. 781-802). Mahwah, NJ: Lawrence Erlbaum.

Pintrich, P. R. (1999). The role of motivation in promoting and sustaining self-regulated learning. *International Journal of Educational Research, 31*, 459-470.

Ravenscroft, A. (2001). Designing e-learning interactions in the 21st century: Revisiting and rethinking the role of theory. *European Journal of Education, 36*(2), 133-156.

Rideout, V. J., Vandewater, E. A., & Wartella, E. A. (2003). *Zero to six: Electronic media in the lives of infants, toddlers and preschoolers*. Menlo Park: The Henry J. Kaiser Family Foundation. Retrieved July 27, 2008, from http://www.kaiser-network.org/health_cast/uploaded_files/102803_kff_kids_report.pdf

Ritter, F. E., & Young, R. M. (2001). Embodied models as simulated users: Introduction to this special issue on using cognitive models to improve interface design. *International Journal of Human-Computer Studies, 55*, 1-14.

Rocheleau, B. (1995). Computer use by school-age children: trends, patterns and predictors. *Journal of Educational Computing Research, 1*, 1-17.

Roe, K., & Muijs, D. (1998). Children and computer games: A profile of the heavy user. *European Journal of Communication, 13*, 181-200.

Rogoff, B. (1998). Cognition as a collaborative process. In D. Kuhn & R.S. Siegler (Eds.), *Cognition, perception and language* (pp. 679-744). New York: Wiley.

Salthouse, T. A. (1996). The processing-speed theory of adult age differences in cognition. *Psychological Review, 103*, 403-428.

Solso, R. L., MacLin, M. K., & MacLin, O. H. (2005). *Cognitive Psychology* (7ᵗʰ Ed). Upper Saddle River: Prentice Hall.

van Merriënboer, J. J. G., & Ayres, P. (2005). Research on cognitive load theory and its design implications for e-learning. *ETR&D, 53*, 5-13.

Van Merriënboer, J. J. G., & Sweller, J. (2005). Cognitive load theory and complex learning: Recent developments and future directions. *Educational Psychology Review, 17*(2), 147-177.

Chapter VI
Nous:
Cognitive Models of Working Memory

Zoe Bablekou
Aristotle University of Thessaloniki, Greece

ABSTRACT

The path to the study of cognition has to take into account working memory, as it is a key process of thinking operations in the human cognitive system. Naturally, this also holds for cognitive operations in the Web. The chapter introduces readers to current trends regarding models of working memory. The major models proposed in the literature are discussed here: Baddeley and Hitch's multi-component model, Daneman and Carpenter's account, Cowan's embedded-process model, Kane and Engle's executive attention model and long-term working memory model by Ericsson and Kintsch. The chapter focuses on the Baddeley and Hitch model, and the author argues that this specific model offers a more theoretically sound account of working memory operations. Unresolved issues and inefficiencies are also discussed and research directions are proposed.

INTRODUCTION

In order to explain how learning occurs, we have to thoroughly investigate phenomena like memory, language and thinking. Learning and memory provide the theoretical substratum for the study of education. Therefore, research in cognition, from perception to memory and from problem solving to higher-order interactions, is of great importance. That evidently applies to learning in the Web because, as Wolfe (2001) stresses, the web is basically based on cognitive technology. Recent advances in the psychology of learning point towards four dimensions of importance in web learning: a) individual differences that are provided for in a web environment, b) learning as a social process, c) the learning context, which web learners seem to be very sensitive to, and d) fundamental cognitive processes, such as perception, memory and metacognition.

In order to introduce memory structures and operations, we should at this point refer to the most basic distinction proposed in the literature, the distinction between short-term memory (STM) and long-term memory (LTM) (see Atkinson & Shiffrin, 1968). Short-term memory is the part of memory that deals with our "psychological present"; it receives and retains stimuli for very short periods of time. It is a fragile system of very limited capacity (typically 7 ± 2 items of information at any given time) and duration (information is retained there for approximately 20 seconds). When short-term memory capacity becomes overloaded, information is very susceptible to loss, because it either decays or is replaced by new items. Loss of information also occurs when stimuli remain in the system longer than approximately 20 seconds. After 20 seconds elapse, items must either be transferred to a permanent memory system, long-term memory, or they are cleared from short-term memory. Long-term memory deals with our "psychological past". It is viewed as a huge store of practically unlimited capacity and duration. Information from short-term memory is transferred there and can remain for long periods up to a lifetime. Everything we know about ourselves and the world is stored in this system.

In the past 30 years, the concept of working memory has appeared to challenge the traditional view of short-term memory. Working memory is, no doubt, one of the "hottest" and most exciting areas in cognitive psychology and cognitive neuroscience. It also is one of the most researched areas, as it serves as a backbone to cognitive processes. Various working memory models have been developed, quite diverse in their scope and emphasis. As Miyake and Shah (1999, p. xiii) rightly point, existing models account for certain aspects of processes and functions in a sophisticated manner, nevertheless they tend to omit specifying in detail some other aspects.

This chapter is concerned with the ways working memory plays a major role in information processing. The objective set is to present the main theoretical frames of working memory and to describe its structure and organization.

The chapter also aims at demonstrating how the system is intertwined to learning and academic performance. It introduces working memory accounts by Daneman and Carpenter (1980), Cowan (1995; 2005), Kane and Engle (2000), Ericsson and Kintsch (1995) and focuses on the multi-component model by Baddeley and Hitch (1974; Baddeley, 2000). I will argue that the Baddeley and Hitch model is better equipped to offer a theoretical explanation of how working memory operates and how it is connected to higher-order cognitive functions.

BACKGROUND

The working memory (WM) framework was proposed to replace the traditional STM concept. Since the new framework was introduced, about 30 years ago, research has exploded. However, the bridging has not been achieved to a significant extent. Although the concept of WM has invaded cognition research, in everyday life much uncertainty is related to its nature and functions. Among this voluminous research, the chapter will inevitably present selective work in the area, based on the author's theoretical views. However, an effort has been made to include the main approaches to the WM concept.

Elaborating on the distinction mentioned in the Introduction, between STM and LTM, let us point that memory was initially conceptualized as a tri-partite structure (see Figure 1). This structure comprises a sensory register (receiving and identifying all environmental stimuli), a limited capacity short-term store (holding information temporarily and at the same time processing that information for the needs of the task to be executed) and an essentially unlimited capacity long-term store, which is fed by the elements that remained long enough in the short-term store (Atkinson & Shiffrin, 1968). Keeping memory traces active in STM (mainly by using rehearsal) was considered to achieve transfer to LTM and,

Figure 1. The multi- modal model by Atkinson & Shiffrin (1968)[1]

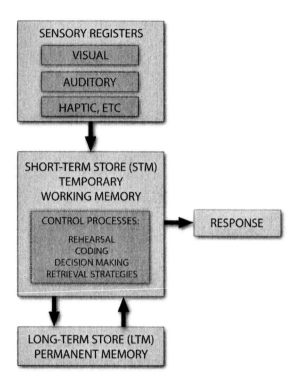

thus, to secure learning. The main coding mode is sensory in the sensory register (i.e., an auditory stimulus is registered on the basis of its sound properties, a color as a color, a smell by registering the smell properties, and so on), verbal in the STM store (e.g. a color arriving in the system becomes encoded on the basis of its *name)* and semantic in the LTM store (i.e., the *meaning* of information is stored in LTM, even if the material is a movie par example).

Although this tri-partite model of memory explains well a wide range of, verbal in particular, data and argues clearly for the separation between STM and LTM systems, the shortcomings of this account gave rise to different explanations. As Craik and Lockhart (1972) have shown in their approach, various levels of information processing lead to different types of learning. The emphasis is shifted, from memory stores to coding strategies. Mere retention of information in STM does

not guarantee transfer to LTM (Bjork & Whitten, 1974). More elaborate ways of coding (e.g. semantic) result in more durable learning, whereas more superficial coding (e.g. rehearsal) results in less sustained learning. This concept of processing "depth" proved to be a valuable idea for the explanation of learning mechanisms and has also been extremely useful in terms of educational applications. In other words, deeper, meaningful understanding of verbal material leads to better memory than rehearsal or memorization based on the physical features of the same material.

The modal concept of memory has another serious shortcoming, and it lies with neuropsychological evidence. If STM is the necessary path, which information must pass through in order to end in LTM, then a STM deficit should result in a deficit in LTM as well. Clearly, this is not the case (Shallice & Warrington, 1970). Besides, if STM served as a general WM, as Atkinson and Shiffrin (1968) assume, STM patients should exhibit handicaps in many different cognitive areas. Again, this is not the case. Such patients' problems appear to be of a limited extent.

BADDELEY AND HITCH'S MULTICOMPONENT MODEL

The working memory concept was developed on the basis of the inefficiencies of the modal model. One popular account of WM is that of a memory system, which is involved in the temporary retention and in the concurrent processing of incoming information, until the task or the tasks at hand are completed (Baddeley & Hitch, 1974; Baddeley, 2000). The model formulates a separate-resources WM hypothesis and assumes four components: (a) a core system, which is the central executive, and three temporary storage systems, (b) the phonological loop, (c) the visuo-spatial sketchpad and, (d) the episodic buffer. The central executive was initially conceived as a limited resources pool of general processing capacity that controls attention and is involved in temporary storage as well as in higher-order mental processes (Baddeley, 1996). The "heart" of WM, it is implicated in all mental activities that call for coordination between storage and deliberate information processing (e.g., mental arithmetic, text comprehension, driving a car while listening to the radio). Very recently, Baddeley (2007, p. 139) attributed three attentional features to the central executive: the capacity to focus, to divide and to shift attention. As Baddeley admits, the concept of a general resource processor was not effective in the frame that it is unable to shed light into the specific processes implicated in executive control. Thus, he currently visualizes the executive as an attentional control system, probably bearing specific subcomponents. As it will be further explained below, a forth characteristic is that the central executive is considered to operate as an interface between WM and LTM.

The phonological loop is specialized in temporary storage and manipulation of oral language material, like words, sentences or numbers. The main mechanism via which the loop operates is articulatory rehearsal; that is, subvocal articulation of incoming material and formation of a phonological code to be retained. The loop can also function as a distinct offline system that stores and manipulates language-based input (Vallar & Papagno, 2002). The visuo-spatial sketchpad handles images, information involving space movement and direction, as well as pictures. When given instructions at the super-market reception as to how we can find pet food three aisles to the left, it is the sketchpad's job to draw a sketch of the directions. Finally, the episodic buffer was proposed by Baddeley in 2000. It is the fourth component and is visualized as an interface between the other three components and LTM. The buffer binds the information coming from the loop, the sketchpad, the executive, perception and LTM into coherent episodes, albeit limited in their number. It functions as a workspace and is supposed to be accessible via conscious aware-

ness. Following this introductory presentation, let us give a more detailed account of each of the modal model components.

Phonological Loop

The phonological loop (PL) is assumed to be speech-based. It is of limited capacity, as all four WM components are. Information remains there temporarily, based on its duration length rather than on time elapsed. While STM store in the modal model by Atkinson and Shiffrin (1968) is assumed to retain information for about 20 seconds, the loop resembles an audio tape, with duration of approximately 2 seconds: the longer the time it takes for the loop to articulate the stimuli, the fewer the words it can maintain. It consists of at least two elements: a passive phonological input store and an active, subvocal articulatory rehearsal process. Auditory information gains direct access to the loop, with no need for prior phonological coding (Hitch, 1990). On the contrary, visual language must be converted to a phonological code in order to gain access (Bablekou, 1989). In one of our experiments, we presented children 5-12 years of age with the very same stimuli (pseudowords) in both modalities, visual and aural. More items were recalled in the aural than in the visual mode, as if children had different spans for the same material presented

Figure 2. The multi-component working memory model proposed by Baddeley (2000)[2]

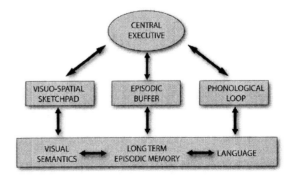

in the two modalities. We interpreted this strange at first look finding in terms of diverse coding prerequisites set at input. Visual stimuli do not gain access to the loop unless converted to and retained briefly in an appropriate phonological code. Auditory stimuli, on the other hand, gain automatic access to the loop and are readily retained briefly, in the same form they entered the system. This hypothesis explains children's capability of recalling more spoken stimuli, which did not need any rehearsal, than visual stimuli, which needed conversion into a speech-based code. The storage-rehearsal distinction above is also supported by neuropsychological evidence (Vallar & Papagno, 2002).

A point of interest is whether the PL of WM is a language system, having evolved from speech perception and speech production systems. Evidence so far shows that the loop can function as an offline component for the storage and manipulation of verbal material (see Chrysochoou & Bablekou, submitted), going beyond the fundamentals of speech perception and production (Vallar & Papagno, 2002). It is responsible for transforming perceptual stimuli into phonological codes that retain the acoustic, temporal and sequential properties of the material (Gilliam & van Kleeck, 1996). The codes are then compared against pre-existing ones in LTM and also against meaning representations, and the right match is selected. However, higher level comprehension is not executed by the loop, as it demands the involvement of the central executive.

Visuo-Spatial Sketchpad

The visuo-spatial component (VSSP) of WM has been almost totally neglected for many years. Although it embarks from the privileged, rich field of vision research, limited data have been gathered so far. Lately, this pattern seems to be changing. It has been proposed that no more than one and the same system handles both kinds of data, visual and verbal (Farrand & Jones, 1996). However, data

reveal the existence of two separate systems, one holding visual objects and a second one responsible for spatial location (Klauer & Zhao, 2004). In a similar line, neuropsychological evidence has pointed to the direction of separate visual and verbal systems (DeRenzi & Nichelli, 1975; Hanley, Young, & Pearson, 1991). The VSSP is thought to operate as an interface between vision, attention and action. The idea brought forward is that of a storage system having the capacity to integrate visual and spatial information, arriving from vision, touch, language or LTM, into a single representation (Baddeley, 2007).

It seems that we are able to maintain up to four items in visual memory, each of them perhaps consisting of multiple features (Irwin & Andrews, 1996). There appears to be no typical short-term forgetting in visual search tasks (Vogel, Woodman, & Luck, 2001), whereas the opposite is the case for spatial STM. Both visual and spatial STM appear to hold serial order with simple tasks. Some initial evidence suggests the existence of a third subsystem that can store actions. The tasks testing the above hypotheses call for simply holding and recalling small amounts of information. However, the WM concept entails some type of manipulation and processing of the items to be remembered. In this frame, more complex tasks are to be involved. The mechanisms underlying visuo-spatial rehearsal are far from evident and it is difficult to untangle the visual and the spatial part experimentally. On the other hand, Garden, Cornoldi and Logie (2002) have shown that sketchpad use is not mandatory. They asked their participants to learn a route through the streets of an unfamiliar city under two conditions: a spatial tapping task on a hidden keyboard or suppressed articulation. Subjects who had the habit of using a mental map deteriorated when using the visuo-spatial task, whereas subjects who reported using landmarks deteriorated when given the articulatory suppression task.

The theoretical implications of the data gathered in this area, could be shaped in two different forms: is VSSP a kind of "attentionally enhanced perception" or a "post-LTM workspace"? These two hypotheses are not necessarily competitive. They rather investigate the field from different angles. Visual attention researchers place emphasis on attentional and encoding processes (see Woodman, Vogel, & Luck, 2001), whereas WM researchers stress manipulation and executive control (see Della Salla & Logie, 2002). The two traditions seem to be able to merge data in the future and interact on the road to the formation of a unitary theoretical frame, drawing from neuroimaging and animal research (Goldman-Rakic, 1996). In conclusion, current approaches to VSSP see it as a workspace that unifies information deriving from various sources: tactile, visual, kinaesthetic, LTM. Along these lines emerges the similarity to the episodic buffer. Baddeley (2007) suggests that VSSP can be accessed from both perception and LTM and assumes a bridge between VSSP and episodic buffer.

Central Executive

The central executive (CE) is the most significant and the least investigated WM component. Two core specifications are its limited capacity and attentional features. Researchers like Baddeley place a strong emphasis on capacity, whereas others, like Cowan (2005), stress attentional and developmental aspects. Baddeley's work in the area, epitomized recently (2007), concerns four main executive processes; focus, division and switching of attention, as well as interfacing WM and LTM. Evidence shows that localization of the CE lies in the frontal lobes of the brain (Kane & Engle, 2002). Case studies of patients suffering from a bilateral frontal lobe damage serve as the strongest supporters of the frontal lobe hypothesis (see Baddeley & Wilson, 1988).

- *Focus of attention.* Overwhelming evidence exists in favor of system limited capacity, in directing and focusing attention. In fact,

this attribute probably is the most crucial feature of WM. Still, when absolutely needed, two demanding tasks can be carried out concurrently (Allport, Antonis, & Reynolds, 1972). Practice and automaticity play a major role. Tasks that were executed with a detrimental effect of one onto the other were conducted with no effect after practice (Teasdale, Dritschel, Taylor, Proctor, Lloyd, Nimmo-Smith, & Baddeley, 1995).

- *Attention switch.* Influential research has brought forward the question whether task switching is based on attentionally demanding processes and implicates a limited capacity executive system or not (Allport, Styles, & Hsieh, 1994; Rodgers & Monsell, 1995). The data seem to point to the conclusion that, at least under certain circumstances, switching may be attentionally demanding. Very active experimentation efforts have proved fruitful, leading to the suggestion that task executive switching does not seem to be dependent on some unitary executive function (see Monsell, 2005). Nevertheless, no solid evidence exists for a subcomponent of the CE devoted to this operation. It appears that attention switching is not a general function. Rather, pros and cons of switching between tasks seem to vary depending on the specific circumstances (Rubenstein, Meyer, & Evans, 2001). Again, task switching proves to be much easier when direct cues are given (Baddeley, Chincotta, & Adlam, 2001).

- *Attention division.* Many times people have to divide attention between tasks. Writing a report and also listening to music is an example, as is cooking, watching a favorite TV program and keeping an eye on the little one playing on the floor at the same time. Divided attention implies certain limited capacity to be allocated in tasks. However, this is not a one-and-only interpretation. Performance decrement could, for instance, be attributed to varying degrees of difficulty between the tasks or variations in processing speed (see Baddeley, 2007). Unlike task switching, divided attention seems to be directed by a specific CE subcomponent (Baddeley, Bressi, Della Sala, Logie, & Spinler, 1991).

Summing up, the CE is considered to be an attentionally limited control system. The CE notion was primarily based on neuropsychological evidence, from patients with frontal lobe damage in particular. Three executive component processes have been proposed: the capacity to focus system resources, the capacity to switch attention and the capacity to divide attention.

Episodic Buffer

The fourth feature attributed to the CE is different and refers to connecting WM with LTM. The original model by Baddeley and Hitch fell short of accounting for certain important issues. One of them was short-term storage of information that could not readily be explained by the PL or the VSSP, the second one referred to the ways the visuo-spatial and the phonological systems interact and, last and most important, how WM and LTM interact and communicate. Thus, the question to be answered was how WM systems can act as a workspace, as manipulators and information processors and as a connection with LTM. For instance, where are phonological and semantic codes stored, if the CE has no storage capacity? How are they combined?

In order to account for these problems, Baddeley (2000) proposed a new component, named the episodic buffer (EB). The component integrates information into coherent episodes and this information may be arriving from the loop, the sketchpad, LTM, or even perception. Its connection to episodic and also semantic memory is obvious. It is of limited storage capacity. Capacity in the buffer is defined in terms of chunks of items and its main responsibility is to bind

information from various sources into chunks. Contrary to retrieval from LTM, the buffering process may be demanding in terms of attention. There appear to be two types of binding: a rather passive one, like automatically applying the "same color" principle to organize parts of an object into the same chunk; and an active one, attentionally demanding, like unifying fragments of a picture into a chunk. Based on its binding capacity, Baddeley considers the EB to form the foundations of conscious awareness.

ALTERNATIVE MODELS OF WORKING MEMORY

The Baddeley and Hitch proposal is not the only WM model. Some popular alternative accounts view WM as a general resource, limited capacity system, operating as a kind of mental workspace in which material can be processed and maintained at the same time (e.g., Daneman & Carpenter, 1980). To this hypothesis, other researchers add that WM is either the activated part of LTM and not a functionally distinct system, or a system very closely connected to LTM (e.g., Engle, Cantor, & Carullo, 1992; Ericsson & Kintsch, 1995; Cowan, 2005).

Daneman and Carpenter's Account

Daneman and Carpenter's work (1980) has expanded the WM construct with reference to language processing. On the basis of their data, the two researchers have developed a complex WM measure that has become a reliable and very popular tool among other researchers in the area. They argued that simple spans, like digit spans, are not able to pinpoint complex operations as reading comprehension is. Daneman and Carpenter devised a complex measure, called *reading span*, demanding simultaneous processing and storage operations. This new measure obtained high correlations with complex cognitive performance, like reading comprehension. Daneman and Carpenter stress the processing aspect of WM and they argue in favor of a "trade-off" between processing and storage. They point that what seems to be limited storage capacity may in fact be the outcome of inefficient processing mechanisms, thus reducing resources available for information maintenance. Activities that tax too much either processing or storage functions will probably overload the system and result in task failure. The more efficient the processing, the more capacity is available for temporary storage.

In essence, this is a *processing efficiency hypothesis;* processing efficiency and not storage capacity is the factor differentiating WM performance (Daneman & Tardiff, 1987). This is the domain people vary. Individual differences in performance are due to more or less efficient manipulation between processing and storage operations. According to this approach, WM essentially corresponds to the CE of the Baddeley and Hitch Model. However, this is an argument challenged by data showing that an important determinant of WM complex span performance is storage capacity (Bayliss, Jarrold, Gunn, & Baddeley, 2003). Nevertheless, it should be stressed that reading span predicts cognitive operations much more efficiently than measures of simple word span or episodic LTM.

Cowan's Embedded-Process Model

Nelson Cowan, a leading figure in memory research, has expanded the WM construct significantly. His work has connected WM to LTM and has modified our view of WM capacity. His *embedded-process model* (1995, 1999, 2005) uses focus of attention, activation levels and expertise as key concepts. He views memory as a single memory storage system that functions depending on various activation levels. Since the single memory storage system is LTM, Cowan in essence embeds WM within LTM. He acknowledges the need for the two different constructs, however he

posits that long-term retrieval precedes short-term processing. In this frame, long-term structures enhance WM performance. Working memory refers to information held in LTM and activated above a certain threshold level.

One main distinction in the model is between the activated part of LTM and the focus of attention. The model can be conceived in terms of three concentric circles, the smallest one being embedded in the second, and the two of them being embedded in the outer circle. The outer circle contains a vast pool of long-term memories in an inactive state, which are available for activation and retrieval. The middle circle consists of LTM items, recently activated through automatic or conscious effort. Finally, the inner circle contains only a few items that are highly activated and are found in the focus of attention every single time. Items in the middle, activated circle move in and out of the inner, focus-of-attention circle, depending on the cognitive task to be executed. Thus, activation spreads automatically among related information and, on reaching a critical threshold level, enters the inner circle, which is the easy accessibility circle. Thus, the focus-of-attention pool is embedded within the activated memory pool.

The focus-of-attention concept replaces the CE and the separate storage subsystems in the Baddeley model. The focus-of-attention idea restricts WM retention and processing, but not storage capacity. Storage in the focus-of-attention pool is limited to 3-5 items or units of information. On the other hand, the activated items pool can hold a much larger number of items. This rationale explains the ability we have to handle much more information than is accounted for by experimental measures of WM. Information processing demands constant shift of attention to necessary items only. Relevant findings support Cowan's hypothesis. McElree (1998) has shown that items expected to be in the focus of attention are retrieved more quickly than recently activated ones that are no longer within the focus. Besides, activated items being outside the focus of attention need more time to be accessed (Verhaeaghen, Cerella, & Basak, 2004).

According to Cowan (2005), WM interacts with LTM by forming new episodic links between items activated in LTM and items being processed on the spot. A high activation level refers to current WM elements, the focus of attention, whereas a moderate activation level refers to information that has been in the focus very recently, being connected with the current WM elements but no longer belonging there. Because of this moderate activation, contents are readily available upon WM request. When they are called into WM, they form new episodes for long-term storage. In this frame, Cowan's formulation of new episodes in LTM is consistent with Baddeley's (2000) EB operations.

Cowan also presents strong evidence in favor of 4 items defining WM capacity (2001). He posits that the limit of 4 is universal, across modalities and irrespective of expertise. The differentiating factor is the size of the chunks people form, not their number. In his view, 4 is the limit found in people under normal circumstances in which processing is automatic. If rehearsal or another memory strategy is used, capacity can be extended to 6 or 7 items. Although Cowan offers strong evidence in support of his view, recent studies indicate that the focus of attention capacity may actually be just one chunk (Oberauer, 2002; Verhaeaghen et al, 2004).

Kane and Engle's Executive Attention Model

In these researchers' view, WM is an executive attention system, distinct from STM. The main function of WM does not have to do with short-term capacity, but with attention control. Attention control is related to the maintenance of information in an active and easily accessible state. Kane and Engle state that executive (or controlled) attention is "an executive control capability; that is, an ability to effectively maintain stimulus, goal, or context information in an active, easily accessible state in the face of interference, to effectively inhibit goal-irrelevant stimuli or responses or both" (Kane, Bleckley, Conway, & Engle, 2001). Controlled attention focuses on targeted information while inhibiting irrelevant stimuli. Thus, WM capacity depends on the effectiveness of attention: on the extent to which executive attention is directed to relevant information. It does not depend on short-term storage or interval lengths between stimuli.

Kane and colleagues (2001) base their proposal on observations, according to which high span individuals are also better in controlling attention and resisting interference. By focusing on selected material and by paying attention to it, they are able to process more information. Thus, WM efficiency does not have to do with capacity. It has to do with the ability to block distracting stimuli and remain focused on processing the relevant ones (Hester & Garavan, 2005).

Kane and Engle (2000) also stress WM involvement in retrieving and maintaining information from LTM. Individuals achieve that by attaching appropriate cues to stimuli in the beginning of the retrieval phase. Besides, cues are used to bring back stimuli just lost from STM due to various distractions. Their research shows that low WM capacity individuals are less capable of selecting the right retrieval cues for effective LTM search. This results in too many irrelevant items interfering with the desired ones and retrieval failure occurs. Thus, WM differences are not just related to attention control, but also to the ability to block irrelevant items and employ appropriate cues to retrieve relevant information from LTM (Unsworth & Engle, 2007). In the 2007 paper, it is proposed that WM consists of activated memory units, some of which are at a high activation level and correspond, so to speak, to STM storage while some other units are at a lower activation level and remain in a larger pool for longer times. Focus of attention allows for maintenance of a few representations for ongoing processing, and this is a notion consistent with Cowan's model above.

Kane and Engle (2000) study the relationship between WM and cognition, too. They believe that controlled attention is the factor uniting all higher-level processes and functions. In this respect, executive attention binds WM to fluid intelligence (Engle, 2002). The reader may detect that the present and Baddeley's model share certain views. Baddeley (2007) also stresses the importance of attentional and executive processes in the CE. They divert in terms of WM capacity. Baddeley places emphasis on PL span. Kane and Engle do not consider this parameter to be of great significance, for they attribute span differences to more or less efficient inhibition of distracting stimuli. Miyake and Friedman (2008) hold a different view in relation to this issue. They demonstrate that complex WM span tasks, demanding both processing and storage operations are good predictors of general intelligence, a finding well established in the literature. The complex span tasks they used were a reading span, an operation span (equation verification plus digit span) and a rotation span task (mental rotation plus orientation).

In conclusion, the model views WM as a domain-general controlled attention system, which maintains activation of relevant information in LTM and retrieves desired stimuli. Individual differences are attributed to the degree of efficiency of inhibiting undesired items and retrieving desired ones. Thus, inhibitory control and concurrent selection of appropriate stimuli are features of primary significance and capacity is closely related to them.

Long-Term Working Memory

Long-term and WM are so interconnected that certain researchers advocate a *long-term working memory* (LT-WM) (Ericsson & Kintsch, 1995). In this frame, LTM and WM are not distinct. Rather than arguing in support of a separate WM system, LTM advocates argue in favor of the currently activated part of LTM which functions as a WM. This is to say, it processes input and encodes new information into LTM. Such a notion alters our perspective on storage capacity. Instead of examining how many items or chunks can be maintained in short-term storage, capacity is now defined in terms of number of nodes or representations in a highly active state at any given time (Richardson, 1996a, 1996b). If Cowan's suggestion regarding a capacity of 4 items is correct, then an individual can manipulate that amount of information concurrently. This assumption means that activated parts of LTM must return to an inactive state fast, thus giving space to new long-term representations to become activated. In this frame, WM span can never be strictly identified. It is also possible that the currently activated material is retrieved from LTM and not WM. One recognizes in this frame of reference the ideas of Anderson (1983), one of the very first to conceive WM as the currently activated LTM knowledge.

According to Ericsson & Kintsch (1995), effective use of LTM information depends on the person's expertise and the use of memory strategies, both of which enable the person to employ LTM as an extension of WM. Strategies allow the individual to encode incoming stimuli fast into LTM and at the same time to attach retrieval cues to them in STM. The cues activate relevant long-term information during recall, thus giving the impression of an extremely high WM capacity. An example of that is chess masters' performance, seemingly having tremendous WM capacity. Long-term WM theorists argue that what seems to be WM capacity is in fact LTM storage. Extended WM is based on chunking information and creating associations with familiar schemas already stored in LTM. Encoding in LTM needs to happen rapidly. On the other hand, the schema the new information is associated with must be quickly accessible on demand, via retrieval cues that are well practiced and deliberately attached.

When successful cueing takes place, then LTM retrieval is as fast as STM retrieval. Deliberate retrieval from LTM takes 1-2 seconds on average; however, experts' LTM retrieval can reduce time to an impressive 400 milliseconds, because STM limitations are bypassed (McNamara & Kintsch, 1996).

Another example of application of the LT-WM hypothesis seems to be text comprehension. Comprehension makes significant, ongoing demands on WM. Besides, it could not be carried out effectively without LTM participation. Text representations are constructed in LTM as the reader proceeds with the text. These representations expand more and more, as new information is arriving and needs to be integrated while it remains continually accessible. In essence, the accessible parts in question constitute an extended WM. As Dehn (2008) points out, Ericsson and Kintsch's (1995) argument seems to hold well in view of the individuals' dramatic increase in the ability to comprehend text, while their short-term and WM capacity remain the same. The increase in performance is attributed to the greater skill of encoding information in LTM.

Although comprehension data fit nicely with a LT-WM explanation, some data deriving from experiments in new word and pseudoword learn-ing offer evidence against the LT-WM hypothesis. In a study by Masoura, Gathercole and Bablekou (2004), a group of Greek children 5-7 years were assessed for their nonverbal intelligence, vocabulary knowledge and PL capacity using three different means: digit span, repetition of Greek pseudowords and repetition of English pseudowords. As it can be observed in Table 1, a strong correlation was observed between the measures of phonological memory and the vocabulary test. The correlation remained strong even when non-verbal ability and chronological age were partialled out. These results allow for the following conclusion: since the children in the study did not have any knowledge whatsoever or habituation with English, it seems highly unlikely they were based on a LT-WM system or long-term knowledge in order to repeat the English pesudowords. The pseudowords, being totally new material, were not related to any LTM representations. Thus, their nonword repetition ability was based on the quality of PL entries rather than on long-term knowledge.

In fact, most theorists adopt a separate WM concept (Gobet, 2000). Even if this system is fed by LTM information that becomes activated, it still is considered to be a separate cognitive entity. On the other hand, exceptional WM performance

Table 1. Correlations among nonword repetition, digit memory, vocabulary, non-verbal intelligence and chronological age

Measure	1	2	3	4	5
1. Greek nonword repetition	-				
2. English nonword repetition	**.43**	-			
3. Digit memory	**.53**	**.47**	-		
4. Vocabulary	**.44**	**.48**	**.45**	-	
5. Non-verbal intelligence	.29	.13	**.30**	**.42**	-
6. Chronological age (months)	.15	.26	**.32**	**.34**	.26

Numbers in bold indicate a significant difference at the 5% level.
df= 46

seems to apply only to individuals who have developed specialized memory strategies to achieve it. Besides, their exceptionally broad WM span is limited to their area of expertise, (e.g. chess). Nevertheless, even if WM is different from LTM, their interaction is extremely close. It is probable that incoming stimuli activate relevant LTM representations before being processed in WM (Logie, 1996). This assumption is also shared by Conway and Engle (1994). On the other hand, Baddeley (2007) criticizes LT-WM models on the grounds that they offer no clear explanation of how WM is connected to LTM. Undoubtedly, there is a very close interaction and the evidence shows that WM depends on LTM. That does not equate WM and LTM though. Exploration of LTM operations does not guarantee understanding of WM functions. Similarities between WM and LTM should not be interpreted as identity of the two.

WORKING MEMORY MODELS: HOW DO THEY FARE?

In the above section, I tried to present the distinctive ideas related to the most popular WM accounts found in the literature. In this part, I will attempt to evaluate the models presented so far. Most of the section will refer to the multicomponent model, which holds a prominent position. The model has fared with several advantages and also disadvantages. Let us discuss certain representative issues.

We are all aware of the golden rule of scientific research: between a simple and a complex account, in order to explain a phenomenon equally well, we always opt for the simple account. Researchers can comprehend and apply a simple model. A major advantage of the Baddeley and Hitch WM account lies in its *simplicity*. This simple model is tested with a very wide range of well designed and elegant experiments. In the case of the CE, simplicity may be a drawback, because it appears that the executive is a very sophisticated

system that needs a more complex explanation than the one offered so far. However, as Andrade rightly points out (2001), the introduction of a CE concept to an essentially STM model has been highly successful, for it has enabled research on the relationship between WM and attention using dual-task methodology (i.e. concurrent execution of two competing tasks). In the case of STM operations, on the other hand, it does offer an excellent description of short-term functions.

The *breadth* of the model is a noteworthy parameter. It provides for the analysis of verbal, auditory, visuo-spatial information, as well as for the temporary storage and concurrent manipulation of material. Such an attribute is valuable when attempting to transfer cognitive processes research to applied settings and real world situations. As its formulations have stayed close to the data, it may not be very exciting theoretically. However, this "boring" feature turns out to be strength, for it has allowed the model to remain in the focus of WM literature for 35 years now. As we have seen, some significant research connects WM to cognitive functions and has managed to show the central place that WM holds in human cognition

As opposed to the North American notion of WM, the Baddeley and Hitch multi-modal proposal allows for the formulation of specific hypotheses and predictions in relation to how verbal, aural and visuo-spatial material becomes temporarily stored and manipulated. This model exhibits *specificity*. Adams and Willis (2001) stress that various WM measures are not equally good predictors of language ability. Therefore, a general resource WM model is not of significant help, as compared to a fractionated model that allows specific predictions to be made as to how each part contributes to cognitive functions. As Phillips and Hamilton (2001) point out, the fractionation facilitates research, because we can move from correlational to causality studies, by manipulating experimentally different functions (e.g. verbal rehearsal, visuo-spatial WM) and observing how they affect cognitive performance. Even brain structures underlying WM operations cannot be pinpointed by a general resource model.

Entering the "shortcomings area", the strongest shortcoming of the model appears to be the *vagueness* in the specification of its components, as well as of the interrelationships among them. The CE, in particular, is the system that has received the strongest criticism so far. The years that have elapsed have brought the importance of the CE into light. Nevertheless, what turned out to be the major asset of the multi-component model is also a drawback. The absence of clear formulations regarding the system and how it fares in several fields inevitably led to the phenomenon all unexplained findings, all questions, all problems with various WM approaches to be attributed to the executive. Data show moderate correlations amongst assumed executive functions. Besides, deficits in one function and preservation in another is a sign that CE may not be a unitary entity, but a multiple system (see Andrade, 2001). Although Baddeley's recent work (2007) advances our knowledge in this area, theoretical fractionation of the CE is still not in sight. The experimental fractionation is therefore impossible, since no theoretical account exists to guide researchers to the type of tasks they should design, in order to tap particular executive functions. The "chaotic" nature of the concept led it to end up being used as "rag-bag" and there appeared the tendency to explain all kinds of cognitive data, which cannot be accounted by the slave-systems, using the CE as a resource tool.

A related point is the observation that the simplicity of a model can reach a critical value, where simplicity can develop into *lack of precision*. Cognition is too complex a phenomenon, several researchers argue (May, 2001), to be explained by simple accounts of memory. What embarked as a simple and clear-cut WM model may need to include further subcomponents. As discussed, the CE in particular is nowadays an unsatisfactory account of executive functions, especially as long as it remains unspecified. Besides, a

point we made above with reference to our own studies (see Masoura, Gathercole, & Bablekou, 2004; Masoura, Gathercole, & Bablekou, 2006), the vast majority of data are correlational and have no capacity to shed further light into the relationship between cognitive performance and WM. Thus, although we theorize about that, we have been unable so far to prove experimentally that WM causes cognitive changes.

Having introduced the causality issue, let us elaborate further. No clear data exists to point to the *direction of causality*: that is, to indicate if WM affects other cognitive functions or vice versa. However, some evidence is available. Several years ago, we conducted research attempting to address this issue of causality (Bablekou, 1989) in the University of Leeds, U.K. Among other cognitive functions, we investigated WM processes in typical children aged 5-13 and in children with specific language difficulties. In order to explore the direction of causality, we used three groups of participants: an experimental group (children with specific language difficulties), a control group matched for chronological age and a control group matched for language age. It has been stressed that children with specific language difficulties (that is, language difficulties that cannot be attributed to any apparent cognitive, emotional, social, neurological or other dysfunction) may have less exposure to certain cognitive operations connected to language and, thus, the assumed limited exposure could in turn affect memory operations. This rational leads to the suggestion that memory difficulties may derive from language problems, instead of memory difficulties causing language problems. The introduction of a second control group, of younger *chronological* but of the same *language* age, could allow us to draw some conclusions in relation to whether it is poor WM that causes poor language (in this case, we would expect children with language difficulties to perform worse than younger children of the same language age) or poor language that results in poor memory (in this case we would expect children with language difficulties to perform similarly to or better than younger children of the same language age). Four experiments provided data defending the hypothesis of a specific WM deficit being causally linked to specific language difficulties in children. For the types of stimuli we employed (letters, digits, words, pictures, colors, pseudowords, geometric shapes and abstract shapes), the deficit was pinpointed in the PL component. The comparison of the two experimental groups revealed a very interesting tendency. Overall, the children with language difficulties exhibited similar or worse recall levels to their language age control group. This pattern challenges the view that the memory deficit should be treated as the outcome of limited written language exposure (e.g., Bryant & Bradley, 1995), providing evidence that makes us able to infer (albeit not to prove directly) that it should in fact be memory operations that affected language functions. Even rather typical STM tasks, like the tasks we used involving strings of items, tapped the underlying WM deficit. Similar findings have been provided by other researchers (e.g. Jorm, Share, MacLean, & Matthews, 1984).

It is a hard task to establish the direction of causality experimentally; among other variables, time consuming longitudinal designs covering a very wide age span are needed for that. Methods similar to ours have been used in other studies as well, in an effort to infer the relationship between memory and language functions. Gathercole and Baddeley (1989) used a longitudinal study to examine children's phonological WM and vocabulary acquisition. They demonstrated that WM scores at four years predicted vocabulary knowledge at five years, even when vocabulary knowledge at four had been partialled out. Such data indicate that language development follows WM development. We also explored the relationship between WM and certain language functions in two studies. We already referred to the first one (see Table 1), which investigated contributions of phonological STM to vocabulary acquisition in

Greek children aged 6.5 years (Masoura, Gathercole, & Bablekou, 2004). Children were assessed on non-verbal intelligence, vocabulary knowledge and PL capacity, using three different measures (digit span, repetition of Greek nonwords and repetition of English nonwords). A strong link was found between the phonological memory measures and the vocabulary test. Crucially, the link remained strong even when the non-verbal ability and the chronological age factors were partialled out. The findings are in harmony to those reported for the English language (Michas & Henry, 1994; Gathercole, Hitch, Service, & Martin, 1997). The fact that children did not have any contact with English makes the possibility of them being based on LTM knowledge to repeat stimuli highly unlikely. Our assumption is that the task was executed on the basis of phonological WM traces rather than previous language knowledge. Thus, phonological WM capacity, as examined by the nonword repetition test, seemed to contribute to vocabulary acquisition rather than the opposite. Children also exhibited much higher repetition rates for Greek than English nonwords. It seems that repetition in the mother tongue was facilitated by exposure to familiar language speech patterns, but repetition of nonwords in an unfamiliar language could only be based on the phonological memory strength.

We also evaluated how children's phonological WM and vocabulary knowledge are involved in new-word learning tasks (Masoura, Gathercole, & Bablekou, 2006). Six-year-old Greek children were assessed using measures of phonological WM (Greek nonword repetition, English nonword repetition, digit span), vocabulary knowledge and nonverbal ability. They also participated in a learning simulation task, in which they learned Greek nonwords, which followed the phonotactic rules of Greek language. Learning of the sound structure of nonwords was associated with children's vocabulary knowledge. Very strong correlations were observed between phonological memory and new nonword learning and weaker between vocabulary knowledge and nonword learning. When age and nonverbal ability were partialled out, Greek and English nonword repetition remained significantly correlated with vocabulary knowledge. Our findings suggest that learning of new words was supported by phonological WM. Again, we infer that it is WM that has an effect on language functions and not the opposite. However, the possibility of a third factor having an effect on both WM and language cannot be dismissed.

Working memory as activated long-term memory. The idea of WM being the currently activated part of LTM has derived from North American researchers in the 1960's (Melton, 1963) and has been reintroduced recently in different variations (e.g. Cowan, 1995, 2005; Ericsson & Kintsch, 1995; Kane & Engle, 2000; Nairne, 2002). Supporters of a unitary memory system base their argument on demonstrating experimental analogies between the two systems, WM and LTM. Baddeley (2007) notices that the tasks employed involve both WM and LTM operations, thus it is not surprising to observe similarities. On the contrary, a rich volume of WM data derives from treating it as a separate memory system. It seems to involve various subsystems and mechanisms. The point of interest here is how WM and LTM interact. The PL, for instance, makes use of LTM knowledge, when it comes to remembering words, digits, and so forth. In this respect, LTM becomes activated in relation to PL operations. Nevertheless, most cognition involves LTM activation. That does not necessarily mean cognition is the activated part of LTM.

A general resource versus a separate resource working memory. Some researchers (Kyllonen & Christal, 1990; Engle, Cantor, & Carullo, 1992) advocate the hypothesis of a memory system that is unitary in architecture. Processing and storage compete for the same pool of resources. Others take the opposite stand (Daneman & Tardiff, 1987; Sha & Miyake, 1999; Baddeley, 2007), proposing a fractionated WM system with domain-specific subsystems specialized in different types of material. Some of the differentiations concern the information code (e.g., phonological, propositional, spatial), the modality via which it is coded (e.g., visual, aural, haptic), the brain parts involved, the processing domain (e.g., oral language, arithmetic, object recognition). The various models focus on different aspects of WM operations and use different methodology, probably resulting in diversions appearing larger than they may in fact be. The general conclusion so far is that there is limited support for the unitary view of WM (Kintsch, Healy, Hegarty, Pennington, & Salthouse, 1999; Baddeley, 2007). However, the number and nature of components postulated should only be established after been tested with different methodologies and clear evidence for system dissociations is observed.

FUTURE TRENDS

Where do we go from here? A good way to try and answer this question would be to summarize the consensus points across WM models. First, and very important, is the recognition that all current models do not postulate a structurally distinct system, located in a specific place in the mind or in the brain. Working memory descriptions refer to functional or content dimensions rather than structural ones, namely the "position" of the system, its "place" in the mind. The closest to a structural separation may be the slave systems proposal by Baddeley and Hitch (1974). Similarly, WM seems to be a separate-resource construct and not a general domain one, as was summarizes in the previous section.

The WM system does not serve to strictly memorize things. Instead, it is involved in supporting complex cognition, like language comprehension, problem solving or visuo-spatial thinking. Such a link is valuable, for it constitutes the driving force of WM research. The heart of the system does not of course beat with the recall of strings of digits or words. Rather, it beats with much more complex cognitive functions. Executive control is an integral part of WM operations. In fact, WM deals with control and regulation of cognitive performance. All current models provide for an executive system within WM, a system that allocates resources to the execution of cognitive tasks and supervises the operations.

The role of LTM is of central importance to WM functions. The core idea is that WM cannot be understood without the contributions from long-term knowledge. This conclusion does not refer to higher order cognitive tasks exclusively; interestingly enough, mundane laboratory tasks, as immediate recall of words is, are affected by LTM. Even models that do not attribute a major role to LTM involvement (e.g., Engle, Kane, & Tuholski, 1999) acknowledge that LTM factors play a role in executing WM tasks.

What is next? Which directions should future WM research follow?

- A main inadequacy is pointed by Miyake and Shah (1999), serving as editors of a very comprehensive book. An unresolved question, still, concerns the basic mechanisms and representations in WM. More investigation is needed as to how exactly encoding, maintenance and retrieval mechanisms function. We also need to know more about the format of information representations in the system. The gap appears to have been created because most work in this area refers to STM tasks. It has not addressed memory processes supporting complex cognitive operations so far. Some steps are being taken by researchers like Engle and collaborators (e.g., Rosen & Engle, 1997) and Ericsson and Kintsch (1995) in the LT-WM framework.

- Obviously, discovery of the precise mechanisms underlying executive control and regulation will remain one of the most challenging WM areas. The clarification of the relationships between the various control

processes and of how they are regulated will advance WM theorizing significantly. We think that the same argument holds for the fractionation of the CE in the multicomponent model.

- Although the domain-general versus domain-specific WM system question has been answered to a significant extent, more research would enlighten us as to precisely how domain-specific operations take place, what kind of subsystems are involved and which factors affect domain-specific processing.

- Our knowledge of the biological substratum of WM is still rather limited, although impressive progress has taken place in the past years. Functional neuroimaging studies will offer a powerful tool for mapping WM in the brain and possibly implicating its framework in the mind. We should exercise research cautiously though. No "technical" studies can advance knowledge if they are not supported by a good theory.

- In relation to the multicomponent model, since we believe it proposes the most convincing frame in the literature, more research is due regarding the model subcomponents. The loop has sustained much laboratory work. This has enabled the PL concept to go beyond laboratory, to developmental, educational and neuropsychological applications. However, areas like how exactly serial order is stored and recalled, or how exactly the loop breaks down as length and difficulty of incoming material increase, remain to be investigated. More research is also due in relation to the buffer. Does the EB connect direct to the PL and the VSSP? We have no conclusive evidence yet. Besides, the buffer introduces a separation between the attentional and the storage capacities of the WM model and this is suggested to be a theoretical advancement (Baddeley, 2007). Future research will either prove or disprove the validity of the separation. In conclusion, the VSSP is currently viewed as a unification workspace; it unifies information from various sources: tactile, visual, kinaesthetic, LTM. It has been suggested that VSSP can be reached from both perception and LTM and is assumed to operate as a bridge between VSSP and the episodic buffer (Baddeley, 2007). This emerges as a theoretical challenge. Data seem to have established the existence of a WM system that integrates visuo-spatial information. It is still unknown whether this system is a subordinate to some other, higher-order system.

- The links and relationships between WM and LTM remain unclear, as equally (or even more so) unclear are the relationships between WM, attention and consciousness. How long-term knowledge is differentiated, but still contributes to WM functioning is yet unknown. Current frames that include an explanation (e.g., Cowan's, Ericsson and Kintsch's) seem to account experimentally for particular types of information only, under specific conditions, as Ericsson and Kintsch's account for comprehension par example. On the other hand, although attention has been in the center of certain analyses in the past few years, in fact it has not received so much "attention" from WM models, as Miyake and Shah (1999) rightly point out. It is possible that both attention and consciousness are not unitary constructs and this implicates different properties and operations.

- Finally, where exactly do we draw the line between WM and other cognitive systems in explaining cognition? In order to answer this, we have to delineate WM responsibilities and also illustrate its limitations. To achieve such an ambitious goal, we need to demonstrate how WM subcomponents cooperate as a system. We have acquired knowledge regarding single component functions in particular domains, but we have not gained satisfactory insight into subsystems' cooperation or the various types of codes and representations demanded when complex cognitive processes are executed.

CONCLUSION

When talking about the psychology of the learner, we must consider all fundamental cognitive processes. Cognitive studies are increasingly concerned with how cognition and interaction co-work (Anderson, 2001). Learning, on the other hand, acquires a new dimension in a media environment:based upon the flexibility of navigation, the said environment allows for the learning path each user selects to follow to be individual and ultimately determined by her/ him. Compared to the structured school setting, a media environment can become more "custom-made" according to the user's personal needs and preferences. In the words of Schroeder and Grabowsky (1995, p. 313, in Riva, 2001), "in a highly learner controlled hypermedia environment, learners navigate through the information creating a personal interpretative representation of that information. Each individual can take a different path encountering different amounts and types of information".

An impressive volume of research shows that WM is heavily involved in all kinds of cognitive activities: from attention (Cornish, Wilding, & Grant, 2006), mathematics (Bull & Andrews-Espy, 2006), written (Cain, Oakhill, & Bryant, 2004) and oral comprehension (Chrysochoou & Bablekou, submitted) to reasoning (Kyllonen & Christal, 1990), reading (Dufva, Niemi, & Voeten, 2001; Cain, 2006), learning a computer language and playing bridge (Baddeley & Hitch, 2000), to name but a few. On the other hand, poor WM skills can impede learning and academic achievement.

What has been discussed so far in this chapter should enable the reader to conceive the basic implications WM functions bear for learning activities and knowledge acquisition. Even the less familiar with memory research could infer certain applications when learning in a web environment. The aim of the present chapter is to introduce readers to WM concept, properties and ways of operating in the frame of cognition. Thus, a discussion of web learning applications is beyond our scope; besides, this is an intact research area. To the best of our knowledge, no studies on precise WM functions in web environments exist yet. Nevertheless, based on the general principles, let us illustrate the link between WM and web learning with an example. Kozma (1991) reviewed the relevant literature on the effect of presentation mode on learning in a media environment. He concluded that simultaneous presentation in more one than codes (f.i., visual, aural) results in better recall of material. On the contrary, visual-only or aural-only presentation of information leads to inferior recall levels. Anderson (2001), however, argues that findings are inconclusive, in relation to whether students get benefited from dual coding conditions (Paivio, 1971, 1991) when exposed to a multimedia environment. Certain other research shows that individuals are not influenced in a similar manner by multimodal presentations. Anderson proceeds suggesting that coding and subsequent recall depends on type of material and type of media employed.

In relation to this argument, we think that recall depends mainly on the type of cognitive systems involved in the processing of specific material and on the different processes implicated on every occasion, not simply on material or media types. Let us use the WM paradigm: the way visual information is processed depends on the subsystems involved. If the information is in a verbal code (e.g. a word or a sentence), it is processed by the PL, whereas information containing spatial elements (e.g. a maze route on the computer screen or the solution to a visuo-spatial task) is processed by the VSSP. In this case, tasks can be processed relatively unobstructed. On the other hand, tasks competing for resources within the executive system (as is, for example, concurrent processing of written directions in relation to a screen map and of navigation instructions given over headphones) will be executed less effectively that those competing for different subsystems' resources. The overall picture is significantly more complicated than learning dependent on dual coding, visual and/ or aural.

The present chapter attempted to discuss basic research in working memory, as a backbone to cognition and learning. In this frame, learning environments should be highly adaptive and memory strategies not predetermined, but flexible. A major feature in this complex, higher-order interaction is metamemory, the individual's ability to evaluate the quality and the processes of his/ her memory functions and to plan his/ her mental operations accordingly. Metamemory research clearly indicates that high metamemory abilities are closely related to academic performance, in children (Kurtz & Weinert, 1989) as well as in young adults (Everson & Tobias, 1998).

In conclusion, applied research on the effects of working memory functions in web education appears to be a prominent new and exciting area and such research is long due. We have, hopefully, shown that there is no general consensus regarding one theory of WM and many theoretical and experimental issues remain unresolved. Nevertheless, the knowledge provided by cognitive psychologists in the memory field so far offers stable grounds in order to embark on combined studies, exploring WM operations in the web and influences on web learning. Of the prestigious WM proposals outlined in the chapter, we think that the multicomponent model of WM is the most theoretically sound account and will serve as a valuable tool in this direction. In our view, however, selection of one particular model does not exclude all other accounts that can be used in combination and in fruitful interaction.

REFERENCES

Adams, A.M. & Willis, C. (2001). Language processing and working memory: A developmental perspective. In J. Andrade (Ed.), *Working memory in perspective* (pp. 79-100). Hove: Psychology Press.

Allport, A., Styles, E.A., & Hsieh, S. (1994). Shifting attentional set: Exploring the dynamic control of tasks. In C. Umilta & M. Moscovitch (Eds.), *Attention and performance XV* (pp. 421-62). Cambridge, MA: MIT Press.

Allport, D.A., Antonis, B., & Reynolds, P. (1972). On the division of attention: A disproof of the single channel hypothesis. *Quarterly Journal of Experimental Psychology, 24,* 225-35.

Anderson, J.R. (1983). *The architecture of cognition.* Cambridge, MA: Harvard Univeristy Press.

Anderson, M.D. (2001). Individual characteristics and Web-based courses. In C.R. Wolfe (Ed.), *Learning and teaching on the world wide Web* (pp. 45-72). San Diego, CA: Elsevier.

Andrade, J. (2001). *Working memory in perspective.* Hove: Psychology Press.

Atkinson, R.C. & Shiffrin, R.M. (1968). Human memory: A proposed system and its control processes. In K.W. Spence & J.T. Spence (Eds.), *The psychology of learning and motivation: Advances in research and theory: Vol. 2* (pp. 89-195). New York: Academic Press.

Bablekou, Z. (1989). *Memory processes in children with specific language difficulties.* Unpublished Doctoral Thesis. The University of Leeds, Psychology Department.

Baddeley, A.D. (1996). Exploring the central executive. *Quarterly Journal of Experimental Psychology, 49A*(1), 5-28.

Baddeley, A.D. (2000). The episodic buffer: A new component of WM? *Trends in Cognitive Sciences, 4*(11), 417-423.

Baddeley, A.D. (2007). *Working memory, thought, and action.* Oxford Psychology Series 45. New York: Oxford University Press.

Baddeley, A.D. & Hitch, G.J. (1974). Working memory. In G.A. Bower (Ed.), *The psychology of learning and motivation: Vol. 8* (pp. 47-90). New York: Academic Press.

Baddeleley, A.D. & Hitch G.J. (2000). Development of working memory: Should the Pascual-Leone and the Baddeley and Hitch models be merged? *Journal of Experimental Child Psychology, 77,* 128-37.

Baddeley, A.D. & Wilson, B. (1988). Frontal amnesia and the dysexecutive syndrome. *Brain and Cognition, 7*(2), 212-230.

Baddeley, A.D., Bressi, S., Della Sala, S., Logie, R., & Spinler, H. (1991). The decline of working memory in Alzheimer's disease: A longitudinal study. *Brain, 114,* 2521-42.

Baddeley, A.D., Chincotta, D., & Adlam, A. (2001). Working memory and the control of action: evidence from task switching. *Journal of Experimental Psychology: General, 130,* 641-57.

Bayliss, D.M., Jarrold, C., Gunn, D.M., & Baddeley, A.D. (2003). The complexities of complex span: explaining individual differences in working memory in children and adults. *Journal of Experimental Psychology: General, 132*(1), 71-92.

Bjork, R.A. & Whitten, W.B. (1974). Recency-sensitive retrieval processes. *Cognitive Psychology, 6,* 173-89.

Bryant, P. E. & Bradley, L. (1985). *Children's reading problems.* Oxford: Blackwell.

Bull, R. & Andrews-Espy, K.A. (2006). Working memory, executive functioning, and children's mathematics. In S.J. Pickering (Ed.), *Working memory and education* (pp. 93-123). Burlington, MA: Academic Press.

Cain, K. (2006). Children's reading comprehension: The role of working memory in normal and impaired development. In S.J. Pickering (Ed.), *Working memory and education* (pp. 62-91). Burlington, MA: Academic Press.

Cain, K., Oakhill, J., & Bryant, P. (2004). Children's reading comprehension ability: Concurrent prediction by working memory, verbal ability, and component skills. *Journal of Educational Psychology, 96*, 31-42.

Chrysochoou, E. & Bablekou, Z. (submitted). Phonological loop and central executive contributions to oral comprehension skills of 5.5 to 9.5 years old children.

Conway, A.R.A. & Engle, R.W. (1994). Working memory and retrieval: A resource-dependent inhibition model. *Journal of Experimental Psychology: General, 123*, 354-73.

Cornish, K., Wilding, J., & Grant, C. (2006). Deconstructing working memory in developmental disorders of attention. In S.J. Pickering (Ed.), *Working memory and education* (pp. 157-88). Burlington, MA: Academic Press.

Cowan, N. (1995). *Attention and memory: An integrated framework.* Oxford Psychology Series 26. New York: Oxford University Press.

Cowan, N. (1999). An embedded-process model of working memory. In A. Miyake & P. Shah (Eds.), *Models of working memory: Mechanisms of active maintenance and executive control* (pp. 62-101). Cambridge, UK: Cambridge University Press.

Cowan, N. (2001). The magical number 4 in short-term memory: A reconsideration of mental storage capacity. *Behavioral and Brain Sciences, 24*, 87-185.

Cowan, N. (2005). *Working memory capacity.* New York: Lawrence Erlbaum.

Craik, F.I.M. & Lockhart, R.S. (1972). Levels of processing: A framework for memory research. *Journal of Verbal Learning and Verbal Behavior, 11*, 671-684.

Daneman, M. & Carpenter, P.A. (1980). Individual differences in working memory and reading. *Journal of Verbal Learning and Verbal Behavior, 19*, 450-66.

Daneman, M. & Tardif, T. (1987). Working memory and reading skills reexamined. In M. Coltheart (Ed.), *Attention and performance XII: The psychology of reading.* Hillsdale, NJ: Erlbaum.

Dehn, M.J. (2008). *Working memory and academic learning: Assessment and intervention.* Hoboken, NJ: Wiley.

Della Salla, S. & Logie, R.H. (2002). Neuropsychological impairments of visual and spatial working memory. In A.D. Baddeley, M.D. Kopelman & B.A. Wilson (Eds.), *Handbook of memory disorders* (pp. 271-92). Chichester: Wiley.

De Renzi, E. & Nichelli, P. (1975). Verbal and nonverbal short-term memory impairment following hemispheric damage. *Cortex, 11*, 341-53.

Dufva, M., Niemi, P., & Voeten, M. J.M. (2001). The role of phonological memory, word recognition, and comprehension skills in reading development: From preschool to grade 2. *Reading and Writing, 14* (1-2), 91-117.

Engle, R.W. (2002). Working memory capacity as executive attention. *Current Directions in Psychological Science, 11*(1), 19-23.

Engle, R.W., Cantor, J., & Carullo, J.J. (1992). Individual differences in working memory and comprehension: A test of four hypotheses. *Journal of Experimental Psychology: Learning, Memory and Cognition, 18*, 972-92.

Engle, R.W., Kane, M.J., & Tuholski, S.W. (1999). Individual differences in working memory capacity and what they tell us about controlled attention, general fluid intelligence and functions of the prefrontal cortex. In A. Miyake & P. Shah (Eds.), *Models of working memory: Mechanisms of active maintenance and executive control* (pp. 102-34). Cambridge, UK: Cambridge University Press.

Ericsson, K.A. & Kintsch, W. (1995). Long-term working memory. *Psychological Review, 102,* 211-45.

Everson, H.T. & Tobias, S. (1998). The ability to estimate knowledge and performance in college. *Instructional Science, 26,* 65-79.

Farrand, P. & Jones, D.M. (1996). Direction of report in spatial and verbal short-term memory. *Quarterly Journal of Experimental Psychology, 49A,* 140-58.

Garden, S., Cornoldi, C., & Logie, R.H. (2002). Visuo-spatial working memory in navigation. *Applied Cognitive Psychology, 16*(1), 35-50.

Gathercole, S.E., & Baddeley, A.D. (1989). Evaluation of the role of phonological STM in the development of vocabulary in children: A longitudinal study. *Journal of Memory and Language, 28,* 200-13.

Gathercole, S.E, Hitch, G.J., Service, S., & Martin, A.J. (1997). Phonological short-term memory and new word learning in children. *Developmental Psychology, 33*(6), 966-79.

Gilliam, R.B. & van Kleeck, A. (1996). Phonological awareness training and short-term working memory: Clinical Implications. *Topics in Language Disorders, 17,* 72-81.

Gobet, F. (2000). Some shortcomings of long-term working memory. *Brisish Journal of Psychology, 91,* 551-570.

Goldman-Rakic, P.S. (1996). The prefrontal landscape: Implications of functional architecture for understanding human mentation and the central executive. *Philosophical Transactions of the Royal Society (Biological Sciences), 351,* 1445-53.

Hanley, J.R., Young, A.W., & Pearson, N.A. (1991). Impairment of the visuospatial sketchpad. *Quarterly Journal of Experimental Psychology, 43*(1), 101-25.

Hester, R. & Garavan, H. (2005). Working memory and executive function: The influence of content and load on the control of attention. *Memory and Cognition, 33,* 221-233.

Hitch, G.J. (1990). Developmental fractionation of working memory. In G. Vallar & J. Shallice (Eds.), *Neuropsychological impairments of short-term memory* (pp. 221-246). New York: Cambridge University Press.

Irwin, D.E. & Andrews, R.V. (1996). Integration and accumulation of information across saccadic eye movements. In T. Innui & J.L. McClelland (Eds.), *Attention and performance XVI: Information integration in perception and communication* (pp. 125-55). Cambridge, MA: MIT Press.

Jorm A.F., Share D.L., Maclean R., & Matthews, R. (1984). Phonological recoding skills and learning to read: A longitudinal study. *Applied Psycholinguistics, 5,* 201-07.

Kane, M.J. & Engle, R.W. (2000). Working memory capacity, proactive interference, and divided attention: Limits on long-term memory retrieval. *Journal of Experimental Psychology: Learning, Memory and Cognition, 26,* 336-358.

Kane, M.J. & Engle, R.W. (2002). The role of prefrontal cortex in working memory capacity, executive attention, and general fluid intelligence: An individual-differences perspective. *Psychonomic Bulletin and Review, 9,* 637-671.

Kane, M.J., Bleckley, M.K., Conway, A.R.A., & Engle, R.W. (2001). A controlled-attention view of working memory capacity. *Journal of Experimental Psychology: General, 130,* 169-83.

Kintsch, W., Healy, A.F., Hegarty, M., Pennington, B.F., & Salthouse, T.A. (1999). Models of working memory: Eight questions and some general issues. In A. Miyake & P. Shah (Eds.), *Models of working memory: Mechanisms of active maintenance and executive control* (pp. 412-41). Cambridge, UK: Cambridge University Press.

Klauer, K.C., & Zhao, Z. (2004). Double dissociations in visual and spatial short-term memory. *Journal of Experimental Psychology: General, 133*, 355-81.

Kozma, R.B. (1991). Learning with media. *Review of Educational Research, 61*, 179-211.

Kurtz, B.E., & Weinert, F.E. (1989). Metamemory, metaperformance, and causal attributions in gifted and average childern. *Journal of Experimental Child Psychology, 48*, 45-61.

Kyllonen, P.C. & Christal, R.E. (1990). Reasoning ability is (little more than) working memory capacity. *Intelligence, 14*, 389-433.

Logie, R.H. (1996). The seven ages of working memory. In J.T.A. Richardson, R.W. Engle, L. Hasher, R.H. Logie, E.R. Stoltzfus, & R.T. Zacks (Eds.), *Working memory and human cognition* (pp. 31-65). New York: Oxford University Press.

Masoura, E.V., Gathercole, S.E., & Bablekou, Z. (2004). Contributions of phonological short-term memory to vocabulary acquisition. *Psychology, 11*(3), 341-55 [in Greek].

Masoura, E.V., Gathercole, S.E., & Bablekou, Z. (2006). Phonological working memory involvement in new-word learning tasks: An investigation among young children. *Annals of the Psychological Society of Northern Greece, 4*, 43-65 [in Greek].

May, J. (2001). Specifying the central executive may require complexity. In J. Andrade (Eds.), *Working memory in perspective* (pp. 261-77). Hove: Psychology Press.

McElree, B. (1998). Attended and non-attended states in working memory: Accessing categorized structures. *Journal of Memory and Language, 38*, 225-252.

McNamara, D.S., & Kintsch, W. (1996). Working memory in text comprehension: Interrupting difficult text. In G.W. Cottrell (Ed.), *Proceedings of the Eighteenth Annual Meeting of the Cognitive Science Society* (pp. 104-109). Hillsdale, NJ: Lawrence Erlbaum.

Melton, A.W. (1963). Implications of short-term memory for a general theory of memory. *Journal of Verbal Learning and Verbal Behavior, 2*, 1-21.

Michas, I.C., & Henry, L.A. (1994). The link between phonological memory and vocabulary acquisition. *British Journal of Developmental Psychology, 12*, 147-63.

Miyake, A., & Friedman, N. (2008, September). *How are working memory capacity, updating ability, and general intelligence related? A behavioral genetic analysis.* Paper presented at the Fourth European Working Memory Symposium, Bristol, UK.

Miyake, A., & Shah, P. (1999). Preface. In A. Miyake & P. Shah (Eds.), *Models of working memory: Mechanisms of active maintenance and executive control* (pp. xiii-xvii). Cambridge, UK: Cambridge University Press.

Miyake, A., & Shah, P. (1999). Toward unified theories of working memory: Emerging general consensus, unresolved theoretical issues, and future research directions. In A. Miyake & P. Shah (Eds.), *Models of working memory: Mechanisms of active maintenance and executive control* (pp. 442-81). Cambridge, UK: Cambridge University Press.

Monsell, S. (2005). The chronometrics of task-set control. In J. Duncan, L. Phillips, & P. Mcleod (Eds.), *Measuring the mind: Speed, control and age* (pp. 161-90). Oxford: Oxford University Press.

Nairne, J.S. (2002). Remembering over the short-term: The case against the standard model. *Annual Review of Psychology, 53*, 53-81.

Oberauer, K. (2002). Access to information in working memory: Exploring the focus of attention. *Journal of Experimental Psychology: Learning, Memory and Cognition, 28*, 411-421.

Paivio, A. (1971). *Imagery and verbal processes.* New York: Holt, Rinehart & Winston.

Paivio, A. (1991). Dual coding theory: Retrospect and current status. *Canadian Journal of Psychology, 45*, 255-87.

Phillips, L.H., & Hamilton, C. (2001). The working memory model in adult aging research. In J. Andrade, (Ed.). *Working memory in perspective* (pp. 101-25). Hove: Psychology Press.

Richardson, J.T.E. (1996a). Evolving concepts of working memory. In J.T.E. Richardson, R.W. Engle, L. Hasher, R.H. Logie, E.R. Stoltzfus, & R.T. Zacks. *Working memory and human cognition* (pp. 3-30). New York: Oxford University Press.

Richardson, J.T.E. (1996b). Evolving issues in working memory. In J.T.E. Richardson, R.W. Engle, L. Hasher, R.H. Logie, E.R. Stoltzfus, & R.T. Zacks. *Working memory and human cognition* (pp. 120-54). New York: Oxford University Press.

Rodgers, R.D. & Monsell, S. (1995). Costs of a predictable shift between simple cognitive tasks. *Journal of Experimental Psychology: General, 124*, 207-31.

Riva, G. (2001). From real to virtual communities: Cognition, knowledge, and intention in the world wide Web. In C.R. Wolfe (Ed.), *Learning and teaching on the world wide Web* (pp. 131-51). San Diego, CA: Elsevier.

Rosen, V.M., & Engle, R.W. (1997). The role of working memory capacity in retrieval. *Journal of Experimental Psychology: General, 126*, 211-27.

Rubenstein, J., Meyer, D.E., & Evans, J.E. (2001). Executive control of cognitive processes in task switching. *Journal of Experimental Psychology: Human Perception and Performance, 27*, 763-97.

Schroeder, H., & Grabowsky, B. (1995). Patterns of exploration and learning with hypermedia. *Journal of Educational Computing Research, 13*, 313-35.

Shah, P., & Miyake, A. (1999). Models of working memory: An introduction. In A. Miyake & P. Shah (Eds.), *Models of Working Memory: Mechanisms of active maintenance and executive control* (pp. 1-27). Cambridge, UK: Cambridge University Press.

Shallice, T., & Warrington, E.K. (1970). Independent functioning of verbal memory stores: A neuropsychological study. *Quarterly Journal of Experimental Psychology, 22*, 261-73.

Teasdale, J.D., Dritschel, B.H., Taylor, M.J., Proctor, L., Lloyd, C.A., Nimmo-Smith, I., & Baddeley, A.D. (1995). Stimulus-independent thought depends on central executive resources. *Memory & Cognition, 23*, 417-33.

Unsworth, N., & Engle, R.W. (2007). The nature of individual differences in working memory capacity: Active maintenance in primary memory and controlled search for secondary memory. *Psychological Review, 114*, 104-132.

Vallar, G. & Papagno, C. (2002). Neuropsychological impairments of verbal short-term memory. In A.D. Baddeley, M.D. Kopelman & B.A. Wilson (Eds.), *Handbook of memory disorders* (pp. 249-70). Chichester: Wiley.

Verhaeghen, P., Cerella, J., & Basak, C. (2004). A working-memory workout: How to expand the focus of serial attention from one to four items, in ten hours or less. *Journal of Experimental Psychology: Learning, Memory & Cognition, 30*, 1322-37.

Vogel, E.K., Woodman, G.F., & Luck, S.J. (2001). Storage of features, conjunctions and objects in visual working memory. *Journal of Experimental Psychology: Human Perception and Performance, 27,* 92-114.

Wolfe, C.R. (2001). Learning and teaching on the world wide Web. In C.R. Wolfe (Ed.), *Learning and teaching on the world wide Web* (pp. 1-22). San Diego, CA: Elsevier.

Woodman, G.F., Vogel, E.K., & Luck, S.J. (2001). Visual search remains efficient when visual working memory is full. *Psychological Science, 12,* 219-24.

ENDNOTES

[1] Reprinted from *The psychology of learning and motivation: Advances in research and theory,* Vol.2, R. C. Atkinson & R. M. Shiffrin, "Human memory: A proposed system and its control processes," pp. 89-195, © 1968 with permission from Elsevier.

[2] Reprinted from *Trends in Cognitive Sciences*, Volume 4, Issue 11, A. D. Baddeley, "This episodic buffer: A new component of WM?" pp. 417-423, © 2000 with permission from Elsevier.

Section II
Affection and Learning

Chapter VII
Affective Issues in Adaptive Educational Environments

Makis Leontidis
University of Athens, Greece

Constantin Halatsis
University of Athens, Greece

ABSTRACT

Research in computer science recently began to take emotions into account because their influence in perception, reasoning, decision-making and learning is considered catalytic. In learning the appropriate sentimental background constitutes a significant requirement in order to be effective. However, many designers of adaptive learning systems develop their systems without taking into consideration the emotional factors that are related to the mood and the personality of the student. This omission deprives the learning process from a very important pedagogical dimension. In this chapter, the focus is on affective factors that are involved in the learning process and can be considered in designing adaptive learning environments. We present first the basic theories and models for affective computer. We deal with methods of affective elicitation and representation of affective knowledge. We then present affective educational applications. Finally, we discuss issues and future trends of affective computing in relation to the learning.

INTRODUCTION

From one point of view, human beings are intelligent information systems whose everyday activities are characterized by social, cognitive and affective attributes. Especially the affective attribute is the most critical one in order for some person to interact effectually with other people and communicate with clarity his ideas. Regardless of the fact that emotions are a determined and discriminated factor for the human relations, almost until recently the emotional dimension was absent from artificial intelligent information systems which are constructed as a mirror image of human beings.

A new field, that is located in the scientific area in the intersection of artificial intelligence, cognitive psychology and physiology, has come to surface with the promise to cover this deficiency and offers a wide range of methods, techniques and applications which take into account affectivity. This field is called affective computing and owes its name to Rosalind Picard who studied and developed in her book "Affective Computing" (Picard, 1997) methods and techniques related to the computer's capability to recognize, model, respond, and express emotions in order to interact effectively with users. These features which are basic components of human emotional intelligence (Goleman, 1995), remain today major concerns of the designers of affective machines.

Affective computing is a hopeful and fertile domain that promises to contribute to the integration of emotional and rational aspects of the human's behavior in machines. Its main purpose is the association of computers with the human beings' abilities such as the observation, interpretation and generation of emotions and the further improvement on the intelligence of computer systems and the human-computer interaction. While the effort to investigate emotional processes and to implement affective models is not new, the availability of accurate methods and advanced techniques in computer science contributed decisively to the implementation of powerful tools in order to support, refine and evaluate psychological theories of emotion.

Despite the importance of the affective aspect, in most educational systems this crucial parameter seems to have been ignored, since the significant process of learning is supported by methods which are mainly concentrating on the cognitive abilities of the student. Indeed, these systems in their majority develop their educational dimension, based only on cognitive parameters such as learning styles, without taking into consideration

the emotional factors that are related to the mood and the personality of the student. Many Web learning designers realize that this omission deprives the learning process from a very important pedagogical dimension. Thus, web designers are at the forefront of shifting attention to affective subjects that influence learning.

As a result, a notable few contemporary educational systems designers began to consider their operation under an affective perspective with the aim of modeling the emotional processes which are taking place during the educational session (Andre, 1999; Conati & Zhou 2002; Lester et al., 1999). Work conducted by Keller (1999), Oren and Ghasem-Aghaee (2003) and Martinho (2000), correspond to affective techniques are being incorporated more frequently in educational systems with the aim of recognizing student's emotions, mood and personality. These educational researchers have begun to examine how traditional student model can be modified in order to be capable of storing affective information.

At this time affective computing is one of the most active research areas in instructional systems and it appears to have increasingly serious attention. Innovative technologies such as speech recognition, text-to-speech, video processing and virtual reality are driving this interest and are providing sufficient tools to construct powerful affective systems. In spite of this ultimate progress, according to Picard there are two major concerns in this field. The first one is how to provide a computer system with a reliable inference engine for the detection of user's affective state and the second is how to devise an efficient mechanism to generate believable emotions and behaviour in human-like artifacts such as animated agents and robots.

The aim of this chapter is to deal with issues, which involve the field of affective computing. For this reason it concerns theories, methods, techniques, trends and applications in the aforementioned field. The structure of this chapter is articulated in order to comprise the following topics: (a) Basic Concepts of Affecting Computing, (b) Theories and Models for Affective Computing. (c) Methods of formal representation of affective knowledge, (d) Methods of emotions elicitation, (e) Applications related to the field of Affective Education, and (f) Discussion and Future Trends.

More analytically, according to the first topic, the reader is going to be provided with the relative definitions on the field of the Affective Computing and is going to be familiar with the most well-known and influential researchers of this field.

In the second topic, affective theories are going to be presented in an extensive way, while being exemplified by appropriately selected examples and cases. For instance, theories such as the Five Factor Model (FFM) which results from the study of Costa and McCrae (1992) are going to be examined. In addition, distinctive models which played a crucial role in the development of the field, such as the cognitive theory of emotions, known as OCC model, which was formulated by Ortony, Clore and Collins (1988) is going to be included.

The third topic concerns the important and demanding subject of the formal representation of personality, mood and emotions. There are many different ways in order for knowledge to be represented formally and flexibly and the most accurate are going to be presented, commented and evaluated. Moreover, in relation to this topic, the cutting-edge methodology of ontology is going to be mentioned particularly, along with the Semantic Web technology.

In the next topic, the methods which are used for emotion recognition, accompanied by an extensive bibliographical support are going to be cited. The variety of these methods points out the ingenuity of interdisciplinary researchers and their significant efforts pay tribute to the ongoing developing field of Affective Computing.

At this point, applications related to the field of Affective Education are going to be presented, in order to epitomize all the above analysis and to demonstrate some of the most innovative attempts of the researchers. Educational environments such as the Prime Climb Educational Game (Conati & Zhou, 2002) and pedagogical agents (Faivre et al., 2002) are scheduled to be presented in this topic.

Finally, this chapter concludes with an extensive discussion with the aim of providing remarks, insights and future trends. According to the topics of the chapter and the following discussion, a wide range of conclusions will be drawn and the reader will be given hints and opportunities for further research.

BASIC CONCEPTS OF AFFECTIVE COMPUTING

The term Affective Computing involves the intention of Artificial Intelligence researchers to model and incorporate emotions in intelligent systems. It is a novel and important topic for the field of human computer interaction in order to improve quality of communication and transaction intelligence between human and computer. It is Picard (1997), who coined the term affective computing. She defines affective as the "computing that relates to, arises from or deliberately influences emotions". Based on this definition, an affective system must be capable of recognizing emotions, respond to them and react "emotionally". It adopts an interdisciplinary aspect, takes advantage of the knowledge background of different sciences such as cognitive psychology, physiology and computer science. The objective goal of affecting computing is the observation and interpretation of human capabilities in order to integrate affective attributes in computers. It is the key idea and a very challenging task, to develop computer systems which would be genuinely intelligent, provide them with the ability to recognise, understand and express emotions in order to interact naturally with us; that is "behave" in a human-like way in relation to our needs.

In the conceptual map of affective computing, emotions play a predominant role. Although many efforts have been made, there is not an explicit definition for emotion. It is easy to feel, but it is hard to describe it. There are still basic questions in the emotion theory such as what are emotions, why do we have emotions, what exactly causes them, how could we control them effectively, but satisfactory answers are forthcoming. According to Ortony, Clore and Collins, who formulated the so called OCC[1] theory (1988), emotions are valenced reactions to events, agents, or objects. Their nature is determined by the way in which a particular situation is perceived. For Scherer (2000) emotion is the synchronized response for all or most organic systems to the evaluation of an external or internal event. Dipert (1998) considers that emotions are intentional and are caused by certain beliefs towards a primarily conceptual and not perceptual target. He maintains the view that "the emotion is an intentional mental state, because it is directed toward an object, its intentional object and produces some physiological, behavioral, or cognitive effects. Parkinson and Coleman have introduced the aspect of a relatively short – term evaluative mental state. Their explanation about the term emotion is focused on a particular intentional object (a person, an event, or a state of affairs).

Love, hate, joy, sadness, fear, hope and anger are some representative emotions. From the literature it appears that there are contradictory views according to whether emotions could be categorized into a set of basic emotions such as joy, sadness, love and hate or should be considered in relation to some intrinsic attributes such as their valence (positive – negative), attention (external – internal) and arousal (excited – calm).

Another important concept in the terminology of affective computing is the term "mood". While emotion is analogous to a state of mind that is only momentary, mood is a prolonged state of mind, resulting from a cumulative effect of emotions (Fridja, 1994). Mood differs from the emotion because it has lower intensity and longer duration. It can be consequently considered that mood is an emotional situation more stable than emotions and more volatile than personality. Dipert (1998) supports the view that emotion differs from mood primarily because the latter lacks of an intentional object and its causes are mostly evaluative. For instance, a particular situation is evaluated either as desirable or not. According to this rationale, mood can be upbeat, optimistic, cheerful, unhappy, depressed, ill-tempered. Scherer (2000) mentions that mood is an affective state of low intensity but long duration, which is incurred without evident reason and is formulated and varied in relation to person's subjective sensitivity.

In affective computing the particular occurrence of emotions and the consequent expression of mood are assigned to some extent to the individual characteristics that distinguish one human being from another. These characteristics determine the personality of a person. This is related to the person's behavior and mental processes and has a permanent character. It would be considered that personality refers to the determinant and predictable attributes and behaviors by which people are identified and categorised. Emotions and moods are connected with the term of personality by the name of traits or factors. Scherer (2000) defines the personality factors as the specific characteristics which consists in one person's typical inclination of his behaviour and comprise the certain dispositions of his personality. For instance, optimist, imaginative, moderate, nervous, envious, rational, conservative are some personality traits which personify a person.

Motivation is another important term in affective computing. It implies the impetus and the encouragement of a person's predisposition to perform activities in a certain way. According to Weiner (1992), motivation explains how and why a specific behavior is initiated, retained and terminated in relation to particular decisions and preferences. Motivation is related straightforwardly with emotions as it can be considered that consists of the appropriate actions which can be taken in order to engage someone in an activity while positive emotions are concurrently preserved and promoted. From this point of view motivation is a crucial factor of thought, belief and action and can trigger a set of definite emotions.

Taking into account the above descriptive frame of the affective computing it is evident that the main research topics of affective computing are focused on three areas, which are examined in more detail in the next session of this chapter. These are: (1) Emotion detection and understanding (2) Emotion synthesis / simulation and (3) Generation of artificial emotions.

Main Areas of Affective Computing

As it has been already mentioned in the previous section, the main aim of the research which is being conducted in the field of affective computing is concentrated mainly on the emotion's recognition /understanding, simulation and generation. In the first one, the objective is the elicitation and detection of the user's emotions with the aim of adapting the system to his preferences. In effect, the recognition of the user's emotions aims at improving the interaction between user and system by achieving the system's appropriate emotional response to the user's affective state. In the second, the basic concern of most researchers is to develop devices with the ability to express emotions. To achieve this, they work on the implementation of believable entities, like emotionally artificial agents or robots which make use of techniques in order to simulate emotional processes. The final sector of affective research is considered rather the more ambitious and controversial debate in affective computing the autonomous productive synthesis of emotional processes by the machine. Researchers who advocate affective machines believe that machines will be capable in the near future of demonstrating the capacity of possessing emotions as well as developing their own emotions. A typical example is the ability of a machine to empathise a human being. The following summarizes the key issues of the three areas.

Emotion Detection and Understanding

Emotion detection and understanding is the most expedient area among the three where the main burden of researchers' efforts has been focused. It concerns the way to predict, recognise and interpret the emotional states of the user. The main reason for this is the belief that the interaction between the computer and the user could be improved effectively if the machine was capable of recognising the emotions of the person and responding adequately to them. There are four main methods of emotion recognition: (1) emotional speech processing (Delaert et al., 1996), (2), facial expression (Ekman, 1999), (3) physiological signs such as skin conductivity, breathing (Picard et al., 2001) and (4) observable behavior such as eye tracking, mouse movement (Martinho et al., 2000). A wide range of information sources can be used for the evaluation of monitoring changes in emotional states which is captured by speech analysis, face, gesture and posture observation and physiological signal processing, which machines can detect. These sources can prove to be extremely useful to provide researchers with tangible evidence of the intrinsic emotional tasks. The natural data which are collected by the novel interaction devices (such as a touch-sensitive mouse, an eye-tracking camera, a wired seat), in combination with the AI-based processing of them, contribute to building the suitably affective user models that describe user's emotional states. Picard (1997) bears the view that the most efficient way for the emotion detection is possibly to come up from the harmonic interoperation of low-level signal recognition devices and higher-level reasoning artificial data which help to the construction of reliably multi-modal affective models.

Despite the inaccuracies of the proposed methods for the emotion recognition some of the researchers managed to achieve reliable results measuring physiological signs. For example, Picard et al. (2001) analyzed measures of skin conductivity, blood volume pulse, breathing and muscle tension of a person for five weeks recognized with a success rate of about 81% eight emotional states (neutral, anger, hate, grief, platonic love, romantic love, joy and reverence), while Kaiser and Wehrle (2000) analyzing the muscular activity of the face by appropriate apparatus detected emotions related to the facial expression. In a similar way Wilson and Sasse (2000) achieved the adaptation of a multimedia conferencing system according to the level of user's stress. Measuring and exploiting physiological signs during an interaction between the computer and the user they provided the system with real-time indicators such as the heart rate and the blood pressure, gathering sufficient information in order for the system to respond adequately to the user's anxiety. Regardless of the medium used to elicit emotions, the affective information could be accumulated from any of these sensory devices channels, or even more ideally, by a combination of all of them together with reasoning about user's emotional states to detect his current emotions.

As the next logical step to the sequence of emotion recognition, and fully interrelated with it, is the affective understanding that follows in the chain of emotion appraisal. It concerns the process of the perceived emotions in order to classify them according to their particular nature. In this direction, the OCC theory of emotions, which will be described in a following section in more detail, provide a catalytic model for the comprehension of emotions. The affective understanding comprise tasks such as the information gathering, absorption and storage, the building, maintaining and updating of accurate users affect models, the modeling of user's current mood and the appropriate handling of the affective information (Picard, 2003). Overall, the understanding of emotions plays an important role in exploring their complicated nature, in conceiving their sophisti-

cated operation, in clarifying their structure and finally in categorizing them accordingly.

Emotion Synthesis / Simulation

Research in the area of motion synthesis focuses almost exclusively on the methods, models and architectures that allow machines to synthesize and represent believable emotions. This feature is crucial for an effective interaction between a human and a machine (or between machines), because machines, which are capable of demonstrating an emotional behavior, even though delusive, have better chances to be more acceptable to human beings. The researchers of this area direct their efforts to obtain machines which are able to have and express emotions. This ability acts complementary to emotion detection in order for the computer systems to exhibit sentimental behavior in a convincing manner. There is considerable argument concerning whether machines must have emotions or whether they can demonstrate ultimately emotional behavior (Picard, 1997). Despite questions whether machines can demonstrate emotional behavior (Picard, 1997), researchers (e.g., Clore & Ortony, 1999) continue to develop theories, exploring methodologies and designing architectures with the aim of constructing emotion models for the integration of motivational, cognitive and mental components which enhanced the ability of machines to express emotions.

Emotion simulation can be also helpful in making more interesting and attractive the delivery of information, the acceptance of decision making and the approval of reasoning process in a reliable and more realistic way. For this purpose many researchers concentrated on the development of believable emotional entities such as lifelike agents (Reilly & Bates, 1992; Bates, 1994). Consistent to this view is the Elliot's Affective Reasoner Framework (1992), which is an effort to obtain human-like emotional software agents with rational and credible behavior. Elliot, taking advantage of the existent emotional theories, focused on developing a multi-agent world populated by several agents who can make inferences on the affective states of other agents. To achieve this, he made use of a formal representation of twenty-four emotion types. The major benefit of this framework is the possibility to reason and make inferences about emotions while in parallel test the beliefs and theories of emotions.

The Generation of Artificial Emotions

This controversial and to some extent science-fiction issue concerns the capability of a computational system to produce new emotions. This aspect implies the existence of mechanisms and methods capable of creating believable emotions either from scratch or in relation to existing emotions emitted by others (Picard, 1997, 2003). The objective of the researchers in this area is to construct working affective models or human-like agents based on a psychological theory and to obtain an adequate and flexible mechanism in order to create new emotions from the already developed emotions. In addition to the Picard's perspective, Bercht (2001) claims that it is possible to develop a mechanism and to be incorporated into an affective system in order to generate new emotions from the emotions that it has already had. For example, an affective agent could be trained to learn or to produce new emotions making use of an affective model that will allow the extension of the existent one. The current operation of the affective systems relies on a specific computational affective model, so the developed emotions are restrictive to this model. In the whole world scientific literature until now, no affective model has ever been presented, that would account for such an agent or any computational system that has the capacity of generating new emotions.

On balance research in the three areas of affective computing fall under four major perspectives: (1) methods for the automatic recognition of the affective state of a person or mechanism in order for a computerised system to express emotional behavior in human-computer interaction; (2) studies of the relationship between cognitive and affective factors which characterize processes such as learning; (3) use of the affective information in order for the system's adaptation to be achieved; (4) affective computing relates to the designing and simulation of lifelike agents which are software entities capable to exhibit believably emotional behaviour optimizing in this way the effectiveness of human-computer interactions.

THEORIES AND MODELS OF AFFECTIVE COMPUTING

In both the Psychology and the Computer Science literatures many valuable theories of emotions have been formulated and used to model emotions and support affective systems. These theories describe emotion either with a multi-dimensional point of view in relation to an individual's affective current state (Russell, 2003; Scherer, 2005), or considering that a number of basic emotions' categorization exist (e.g., Ekman, 1999; Izard, 1977). For instance, the circumplex theory of emotion (Russell, 2003), which belongs to the first perspective, proposed that there are two essential dimensions (axes) of emotions, activation versus deactivation and pleasantness versus unpleasantness. The names of various emotions could then be arranged in a circular fashion around these axes. The researchers of the second perspective suggested that an emotional typology is appropriate and there is a consensus on what of these basic emotions might be. In most typology models, emotions such as happiness, sadness, anger, and anxiety are essential. Nevertheless, they hold divergent opinions on some issues such as the number of basic emotions. For example, Ekman's model (1999) describe six, Plutchic's (1980) eight and Izard's (1977) ten. Another important theory is the Lazarus theory (1991), which emphasizes the cognitive aspect. This theory considered that an emotion - provoking stimulus triggers a cognitive appraisal, which is followed by the emotion and physiological arousal.

Despite the significant theories that have been proposed for affective computing, the two major theories, where the majority of affective systems are relied on, are the *cognitive theory of emotions (OCC)* which is related to the origination and the appraisal of emotions and the *Five Factor Model* which is connected to the explanation and the prediction of a person's behavior according to his personality.

In order to explain the origins of emotions and to describe the cognitive processes that elicit them, Ortony et al. (1998) formulated the cognitive theory of emotions known also as the OCC model. Regardless of the various attempts that have been made in order to define and explain sufficiently the emotional processes, this theory keeps a distinctive position among them. According to this theory, in connection to a person's perception of the world, his emotions can be elicited. This process is named appraisal and the OCC model assumes that the emotions can be triggered by the assessment of three perception aspects of the world. These aspects are events, objects and agents. The OCC model provides a classification scheme for 22 in total emotions based on a valence reaction in relation to them. That is, all emotions engage a kind of positive or negative reaction to the way the world is conceived. The intensity of the affective reactions determines whether or not they will be experienced as emotions.

Events are situations which are interpreted by people in a certain way. Consequently, events result to emotional reactions which are provoked by pleasant or unpleasant situations. The emotions of the OCC model that are attributed to events are grouped into three sets. The first set includes the happy-for, resentment, gloating, and pity emotions and is characterized as fortunes-of-others set. The second set includes the hope, fear, satisfaction, disappointment, fear-confirmed, and relief emotions and is characterized as prospect-based

set. The third set includes the joy and distress emotions and is characterized as well-being set. Objects are material or abstract constructions. This aspect of the world includes emotional reactions with objects which are related to the emotions of attraction such as liking and disliking. Agents can be human beings, animals, artificial entities which represent humans or animals and software components which act in a specific way. This aspect of the world includes emotional reactions which are related to the emotions of attribution such as pride, shame, reproach, and admiration. There are also compound emotions due to agents' interactions. These include gratification, remorse, gratitude, and anger emotions.

The origin of emotions relate to the subject's perspective against Goals, Standards, and Attitudes. The events are evaluated in terms of their desirability, according to the goals of the subject. For example, one may be pleased if the event is desirable and displeased in the opposite case. The particular emotion emitted depends on whether the consequences of the event are for oneself or for another person. Standards are used to evaluate actions of a subject arising emotional reactions of approval or disapproval kind. Objects are evaluated as appealing depending on the compatibility of their attributes with subject's attitudes.

Nonetheless, the authors of the OCC model admit that their model is oversimplified, since in a real situation a person experiences usually a mixture of emotions, however they consider that it could be computationally implemented and help explain the emotions that human beings feel, and under which conditions emotions are exhibited. Furthermore, they believe that relying on this model, human reactions to the events and objects are predictable and explained. According to this point of view, the OCC model has been integrated in many affective computational systems with the aim of recognizing the user's affective state and implementing emotions in machines.

The second significant theory that is used for the integration of affective systems is the Five

Factor Model (FFM; McCrae & John, 1992). This is the most known model of personality and results from the study of Costa and McCrae (1992). It is a descriptive model with five dimensions (Openness, Conscientiousness, Extraversion, Agreeableness, and Neuroticism) and views the personality as the set of all those characteristics that distinguish one human being from another. Due to these dimensions the model is also called OCEAN model. This model describes an Openness person as accessible to new experiences, creative, imaginative, intellectual, interested in culture, social, emotionally aware, with a significant sense of freedom and exploration. According to the intensity of these characteristics a person who belongs to the Openness category is characterized either as Explorer, or as Moderate or as Preserver. Conscientiousness refers to a person who is well-organized, dutiful, responsible, persistent in achieving goals, thoughtful and in detail before acting, controlling his impulses, with consolidated points of view. According to the intensity of these characteristics, a person who belongs to the Conscientiousness category is characterized either as Focused, Balanced or as Flexible. Extroversion refers to a social, energetic, talkative person who is liable to make new acquaintances easily and to demonstrate positive emotional behavior. According to the intensity of these characteristics a person who belongs to the Extroversion category is characterized either as Extrovert, or as Ambivalent or as Introvert. Agreeableness refers to a person who is cooperative, modest, friendly, accommodating, trusting, positive motivated in his interactions with other people and lacks antagonistic intentions. According to the intensity of these characteristics a person who belongs to the Agreeableness category is characterized either as Adapter, or as Negotiator or as Challenger. Finally, a negative emotionality is predominant in a Neuroticism person, thus this person usually feels nervous, anxious, in pressure, insecure, emotionally unstable and prone to pessimist thoughts. According to the intensity of these characteristics a person who belongs to the Neuroticism category is characterized either as Reactive, or as Responsive or as Resilient.

The FFM provides a reliable way to connect a user's personality with his mood and emotions that he possibly develops during his interaction with an affective system. The descriptive character of FFM and the particular characteristics that accompany each type of personality (traits) allow us to model effectively the user's personality (Oren & Ghasem-Aghaee, 2003) and use this information in a wide range of applications (commercial, educational, etc.) (Conati & Zhou, 2002).

METHODS OF FORMAL REPRESENTATION OF AFFECTIVE KNOWLEDGE

The recognition of the user's emotions or the detection of his emotional state would be invaluable without the subsequent storing, processing and reasoning of this information. In order to take advantage of these features the integration of the emotional information is demanding. In affective computing the various affective-captured data are integrated in user affective models. In this way the adaptation of a computer system to the human feelings is achieved via a well-structured model with the capability of maintaining the sensitively acquired data. After the emotions detection and representation the system is required to infer the origins of these emotions. This necessity indicates imperatively the use of a dynamically updated rational user model enhanced with the emotional dimension which is named affective model. The affective models have to deal with emotional and subconscious factors which affect our behavior and to handle user personalized information in dynamic situations in order to promote and support sustainable information of the real world. In general, dynamic situations are characterised by increasing complexity and for that reason their representation is difficult to be restricted to explicit declarations. Our senses perceive selectively the knowledge of the real world, our mental models are however simplified and our reasoning mechanisms are also imperfect. As a result, the anticipated knowledge is incomplete and with nuggets of uncertainty. This intrinsic deficiency is underlined in case of the computer systems, the "intelligent potential" of which is limited further due to the low degree of the emotions' recognition accuracy and by the interrelation of affective and rational factors.

For the above reasons the representation of emotions is an extremely complicated and challenging process. Despite these difficulties computational models of emotions have been proposed since the early sixties. For example, Abelson's model of hot cognition (1963), Colby's model of neurotic defence (1963) and Gullahorns' model of a homonculus (1963) are some of the theories which have been applied. Psychologists suggest three kinds of emotions' modelling. Dimensional models with three dimensions (valence, arousal, and stance) (Russell, 1997), discrete models which regard emotions as basic universal adaptive mechanisms, that evolved during the evolution in order to ensure survival (Ekman, 1992), and cognitive models which consider that emotions are triggered by inner cognitive process (Ortony, et al., 1988).

The formulation of the OCC theory as a cognitive model of emotions changed the scientific view and led the appraisal theory of emotions to renegotiation. The OCC model provided us with a useful framework for the modelling and representation of emotions. The vast majority of the contemporary affective systems are based on the OCC cognitive model of emotions. This model has a great contribution to the appropriate representation of emotions in the affective models. For instance, after a user is identified either as surprised or happy, the application ought to represent his emotional state. This representation is conducted ideally via the OCC model leading to the suitable adaptation of the computer system

to the user's affective state. Based on the OCC model more sophisticated models of emotions have been proposed by Conati and McLaren (2005) and Marsella and Gratch (2006). Despite the indisputable usefulness of these advanced models, most of them are highly dependent on the context, user's prior knowledge and individual traits such as user's personality.

Recently, some researchers focused on alternative ways of emotions' representation. Meyer (2004) developed KARO a logical formalization framework which comprises of actions, beliefs and choices under a specific logical perspective. He used this framework to describe happy, sadness, fear and anger and to associate these emotions with complex production rules. On the other hand, Ochs et al. (2005) concentrated on the emotional facial expression for embodied agents. Based on the OCC model and a rational interaction theory Sadek et al. (1997) developed a logical formalization for the representation of joy, sadness, hope and fear. They assigned to these four emotions attributes such as intensity degree and tried to handle uncertainty factors. Moreover, they applied logics of belief, intention and uncertainty for the spatial mixing of emotional facial expressions.

Another modern approach in relation to emotions' representation is the use of ontologies. Ontological knowledge representation contributes to the building of consistent user models and obtains the basis for interoperability support to authors and system developers especially in the complex knowledge domains of the Web-based educational systems (Dicheva & Aroyo, 2002). The use of ontologies to the representation of emotions in Web-based educational systems has the benefit that allows the student model to handle explicitly information related to the student's goals, his prior knowledge, his individual cognitive abilities, his emotional states and his interaction with the system (Mizoguchi et al., 1996). In the usage of ontologies in Web-based educational systems significant attention must be paid to the design, maintenance, integration, sharing, re-using, and evaluation of the ontology (Mizoguchi et al., 2000). Leontidis et al. (2008) make use of the ontological methodology in order to achieve the formal representation of emotions in MENTOR a Web-Based Affective Educational Module for the student's affective and learning support in distance learning. Using an XML ontological structure managed to represent an overlay student's affective model open for inspection by him in case that he wishes to make comparisons with his own model.

Furthermore, many researchers in order for building intelligent educational systems and integrating flexible, reliable, consistent and robust affective student models into them, engaged a wide range of knowledge representation methods such as neural networks, fuzzy logic, symbolic rules, Bayesian networks, case-based reasoning (Alani et al., 2004; Conati & Zhou 2002; Oren & Ghasem-Aghaee, 2003; Kinshuk et al., 2001; Horvitz et al., 1998). Any of these methods aims to ground a strong theoretical basis in combination with intelligent techniques to model student's affectivity while concurrently adding a human-like sense to the represented knowledge.

Of late, some other researchers (e.g., Picard, 2003) took an interest in the area of affective databases and employed a novel methodology to achieve efficient interrelation between the knowledge that is represented and the interactions of the students. The benefits from this method are focused on the tacit background knowledge, change of emotional states, personality traits, and situations with increasing complexity. Besides, well-designed affective databases operate as part of an overall model for web-based affective educational systems where the domain and the student model, the learner interactions and goals and the teaching methods are being integrated effectively. Despite the innovative character of this methodology the lack of significant amount of affective databases is a major cause of the stall of affective computing. Motion captured data, speech recognition and expression, and facial expression recognition demand an important database storing and handling of multi-model affective data. Because of the shortage of related affective theories and experiments this method is not enough mature to be used credibly in the area of affective computing.

METHODS OF EMOTIONS ELICITATION

The process of capturing the affective information comprises of a certain range of methods such as the emotional speech recognition and processing, the facial recognition and expression, physiological signals such as skin conductivity, heart rate and observable behaviour such as eye tracking. In this section the main methods of emotion elicitation is analysed furthermore.

Emotional Speech Recognition and Processing

The field of emotional speech recognition involves methods which can deal with the bulk of enormous real-time speech data, extracting the speech characteristics that convey emotion and attitude in a systematic manner (Mozziconacci & Hermes, 2000). The task of recognising emotions in speech is difficult even for humans, who can in generally recognize one of about six different emotional states from speech with about 60% accuracy (Scherer, 1981). This task in a computer is performed by a speech recognition component that receives speech signals via an input device (e.g. microphone), recognizes the speech as a path through its grammar, and outputs a semantic token representing the speech. Research results on human vocal (prosody), led to the implementation of emotional speech models which have been integrated into computers with the aim of recognising emotions. For instance a person who is talking loud and fast in a specific moment might be recognised with high accuracy as angry

(Murray & Arnott, 1993). In emotion recognition the methods are focused on extraction of voice features (Mansoorizadeh & Charkari, 2008). The most important features are the pitch signal, the shape of the vocal tract and the short-term energy. The pitch signal, also known as the glottal waveform is produced from the vibration of the vocal folds and has information about emotion (Pierre-Yves, 2003). The emotional states modified the shape of the vocal tract and this feature is a significant factor in the speech processing (Zhou et al., 2001). Related to the arousal level of emotions is the short-term speech energy from which useful information can be extracted for emotion recognition (Ververidis & Kotropoulos, 2006). For instance, fear is an emotion with with a high pitch level and a raised energy level, though anger is the emotion of the highest energy and pitch level (Iida et al., 2000).

Usually, the systems of speech emotion recognition make use of pattern recognition methods and algorithms to perform emotion classification and prediction. The output of an emotion classification method is a prediction value about the emotional state of an utterance, which is a segment of speech that corresponds to a phrase or a word. The most significant emotion classification methods are the (ANNs) (Womack & Hansen, 1996), which is based on artificial neural networks, the multi-channel hidden Markov Model (Womack & Hansen, 1999) and the mixture of hidden Markov models (Fernandez & Picard, 2003). There are also, other valuable prediction algorithms in emotion recognition for sadness, anger, happiness and fear such as the maximum likelihood Bayes classification, kernel regression, and k-nearest neighbor in emotion recognition for sadness, anger, happiness and fear (Dellaert, 1996). Although these algorithms perform its prediction using restrictive assumptions, such as when the sentence content is known, the systems manage to achieve automated speech recognition with 60% accuracy (Hansen, 1999).

Currently, researchers are concentrated on finding adequate combinations of classifiers to improve the classification efficiency in real-life applications. The research findings are used in dialogue systems to enhance the expressive ability of computer systems. For example, in a ticket reservation system or a call-centre application that use speech recognition algorithms to recognize the annoyance or frustration of a user and to change its response accordingly (Schiel et al., 2002, Lee & Narayanan, 2005), or in the case of giving commands to a robot (Batliner et al., 2004). Despite the great progress that it has been done in the speech recognition area, the lack on the capture and the process of more reliable physiological data restricts the expected advance in this field. It is expected in the near future, that the enhancement of the theoretical models in relation to the vocal communication of emotion and the ability to acquire and process large-scale speech data, to make a great contribution to the emotional speech research. More detailed information for readers who interested in emotional speech recognition and processing can be found in the overview of Ververidis and Kotropoulos (2006).

Facial Expression Recognition

Researchers in the facial expression recognition field examine approaches with the aim of recognising specific muscle movements, such as eye lids, eye brows, nose, lips and skin texture, often revealed by wrinkles and bulges that can be used to recognise emotions or to construct any facial emotional expression (Tian et al., 2001). To deal with this use appropriate apparatus such as cameras, sensors to observe one person's behaviour and to match it into patterns (Lisetti & Rumelhart, 1998; Yacoob & Davis, 1996). In the facial expression recognition the main purpose of the computer system is to assess a set of measures according to such patterns and relate them to the user's emotional state. Sophisticated pattern recognition software in combination with the corresponding equipment are used with the intention to detect facial muscle movements such as wrinkled brows, wide opened eyes, smiled face and assign them with emotions like anger, surprise, happiness (Chibelushi & Bourel, 2003). Also important is the intensity of facial actions which may be measured by determining either the geometric deformation of facial features or the density of wrinkles appearing in certain face regions (Fasel & Luettin, 2003). Visually trained information data processed under certain restricted conditions produce automated models capable of recognizing a wide range of facial expressions (Chen et al., 1998). Although a specific expression doesn't always mean the existence of the corresponding emotion, facial expression recognition has demonstrated high rates of accuracy (approximate 95%). For example, Essa and Pentland (1997) relied on the Facial Action Coding system (FACS) theory of Ekman and Rosenberg (1997) who developed a system that can recognize from video six deliberately made facial expressions for a group of eight people with an accuracy of 98%. FACS uses 44 action units (AUs) for the description of facial actions with regard to their location and their intensity. Another, similar method which proposed by Pantic and Rothkrantz (2000) described facial expressions as combinations of Facial Action Units (FAUs). Based on this method, Kotsia and Pitas (2005) developed two novel real-time techniques for facial expression recognition in image sequences, which achieved a facial expression recognition accuracy of 95% for six basic facial expressions (anger, disgust, fear, happiness, sadness and surprise).

Other methods for facial expression recognition are Hidden Markov Models (HMM), neural network, Point Distribute Model (PDM), optical flow, geometrical tracking method, electromyograms (EMG) method, Gabor wavelets (Yamamoto et al., 1992; Lyons et al., 1998; Kobayashi & Hara, 1992). Due to its good performance and low restriction in relation to the sensitivity of face posture and the lighting background, the Gabor wavelets method is the primary choice by many researchers. Finally, the MPEG-4-SNHC (Koenen, 2000) is another sophisticated standard that encompasses analysis, coding and animation of faces (Tsapatsoulis et al., 2000). For readers who require more detailed information Fasel and Luettin (2003) have conducted a seminal survey.

Physiological Pattern Recognition

Physiological Pattern Recognition relies on the point of view that emotion recognition is more accurate when engages multiple types of low-level signals which are provided by monitoring physiological variables such as blood volume pulse, muscle tension, galvanic skin conductivity, respiration and heart rate. Physiologists have invented appropriate laboratory apparatus and tests in order for the user's emotional state to be reliably measured. The main idea is to relate a person with particular patterns of his behavior using sensors and to input these patterns into a computer system in order to associate them with affective information that had been stored in user's affective model. In this way the computer assesses measurable external changes and makes inferences about the user's emotions.

The methods that the psychologists make of use are electromyograms (EMG) to detect electrical activity in muscles (Wiederhold et al., 2003), eye tracking devices to measure pupil responses to emotional stimulations (Partala & Surakka 2003), electroencephalograms (EEG) to monitor users' brain activity for the detection of task engagement and user attention (Pope et al., 1995), Galvanic Skin Response (GSR) to sense user affective states, such as stress (Healey, 2000), or cognitive load (Verwey & Veltman 1996) and heart rate measurements to determine user's affect (Prendinger et al., 2005). Although a significant number of experimental methods are available, existing empirical results suggest that the most reliably assessed affective measures are arousal and valence. The most accurate practical signal for arousal detection is heart rate (Cacioppo et al., 1993). Other measures of arousal, such as galvanic skin response, or blood volume pressure do not supply readily assessed data (Orr & Abowd, 1998).

Picard et al. (2001) made use some of the above methods to recognise eight different emotional states (happiness, sadness, anger, fear, disgust, surprise, neutrality, platonic love, and romantic love), when a user intentionally expresses these, by showing emotion specific pictures to elicit them. The measured signals were further analysed by specific algorithms and pattern recognition tools. As a result an important classification accuracy of 81% had been achieved.

Observable Behaviour

There is a significant amount of research based on methods which aim at recognising user's affect from the observation of his interactions with the system (Paiva, 2005; Vicente & Pain, 2002). Such interactions might be the engagement with the system's user interface, the execution time, how frequently a specific tool is used etc. The system is provided with such actions and in the next step these actions are further analysed by suitable algorithms. In this way it makes inferences about user's emotions. According to Picard (1997) the recognition of emotions can be achieved by a multi-modal approach which combines a low-level signal recognition and a sophisticated software inference mechanism. Paiva (2000) adopts the view of a multi-modal affective sensory system and considers the different means of emotions recognition complementary. Related to this approach, the user's affective model is a major factor and assists the affective system to respond properly after the user's emotional state has been detected. It is a debatable issue on how to analyze the dynamic characteristics of the user's affect and how to make the computer react properly according to the identification result of affective information. Some work on this field has been

conducted by using different techniques. Among them are Conati and Zhou (2002), who made use of Dynamic Decision Networks (DNNs) to model affective characteristics of a student during his interaction with an educational game, Vicente and Pain (2002), who model the student's motivational states based on factors which are obtained by the student's observable behavior in order to motivate him appropriately, and Martinho et al. (2000), who defined a dynamic affective model for the collaborative game Teatrix. The affective information that is produced by the observable behavior is related to personal, cognitive, social and cultural factors to extract inferences about the current emotions and mood.

AFFECTIVE ADAPTIVE EDUCATIONAL SYSTEMS

During the last years, in the list of the affective computing bibliography, an ongoing number of affective educational systems have been recorded. Among them the work of Martinho et al. (2000), Conati and Zhou (2002), Faivre et al. (2002), Leontidis et al. (2008) seems to exploit efficiently features of affective computing in order to implement educational systems.

Martinho et al. (2000) integrated an affective student model in an educational game named Teatrix. Based on foundations of collaborative learning Teatrix motivates collaborative students for creating a story. Using a list of available actions, Teatrix encourages students to pick up the most suitable of them in order to manipulate an animation character. Evaluating these actions Teatrix appraises student's emotions making use of predefined rules which map emotions to student's actions. In addition to the description of inferring rules the system relies on student's preferences and goals, which were detected in a previous session, in combination with the OCC model to elicit student's emotions. According to this approach that is best known as Cognitive-Based Affective User

Modeling the student's observable behavior is a way to forecast, detect and interpret his emotional state. The dynamic student model that contains the affective information is constituted of two parts. In the first one the detected student's emotions are stored. In the second is stored the student's affective profile which holds information about the likelihood of a user to experience a particular emotion and the usual duration of this emotion. The Teatrix's affective student model is based also on the BDI (Belief-Desire-Intention) model, which perceives an affective system as a rational agent (Rao & Georgeff, 1991; Woldridge, 1999) which has certain mental attitudes of belief, desire and intention. This theory describes the exact way for the representation of the motivational and deliberative states of an agent.

The Prime Climb is an educational game designed by the EGEMS (Electronic Games for Education in Math and Science) at the University of British Columbia and is designed with the aim of supporting students to learn number factorization. The operation of this game is relied on a probabilistic model which proposed by Conati and Zhou (2002) in order to infer student's emotions. The model was based on the OCC model and was built using Dynamic Decision Networks (DNNs), represents the goals of the student, the satisfying status of these goals, the educational events and their desirability and the action's of an agent. The use of Dynamic Decision Networks allows the explicit definition of the student's emotions especially in cases that he experiences mixed emotions. Furthermore, Prime Climb enables the explicit representation of the probabilistic dependencies between student's emotions and the causes which trigger them. Prime Climb takes into account six emotions of the student (joy, distress, pride, shame, admiration and reproach) and divides them into two categories, the positive and the negative according to the desirability of the educational events and the agent's actions. That is, events which are evaluated as desirable in relation to the student's goals are considered to provoke positive emotions (joy, pride, admiration) while undesirable events provoke negative emotions (distress, shame, reproach). Correspondingly, the emotions which are triggered by the actions of the agent are categorized in the same way. The students' goals are defined in two phases. In the first, before playing with Prime Climb, they are given a pretest and a questionnaire in order to evaluate their prior knowledge on the number factorization and to measure their exact goals according to the game. In the second, log files with the interactions of the students are collected with the aim of analyzing how the students play the game. The FFM theory is used in this phase in order for the students' goals to be identified. For instance, a person who is conscientious is more likely to have the goal Avoid-Falling, that is to perform careful movements during the play of the game, while a disagreeable person is more likely to have the goal of Succeed-by-Myself, without external help.

Having considered the relations among cognition, emotion and action in contextual learning, Faivre et al. (2002) proposed a multi-agent architecture in which two emotional agents were integrated in an Intelligent Tutoring System, ITS. The first is designed with the aim of recognising and analyzing student's emotions by his interactions with the user, while the second displays the tutor's emotional expressions and gestures. The system uses an affective model which is divided into two units. The first is the Short Term Mood Memory and is in charge of storing the emotions which has been recognised. The second is the Long Term Mood Memory and contains information about the student's mood profile. This information is the result of the average of measures which are taken during various learning sessions. The Tutor is implemented as a 3D embodied agent and makes use of non-verbal facial expressions and body gestures to interact with the student. It controls the learning process by selecting the educational content and resources, and tutorial strategies in order for the system adaptation to be achieved suitably according to student needs. The selection of the appropriate tutorial strategies is determined by the affective state of the student and is performed by the use of "if – then" rules. The Tutor uses also "if – then" rules in relation to the OCC model for the emotion modelling.

MENTOR (Leontidis et al., 2008) is another Web-based affective adaptive educational module for distance learning that has been designed with the aim of providing the student with a more personalized and friendly environment for learning according to his personality, moods and emotions. The basic concern of MENTOR is to promote and maintain a positive emotional state in the student during the learning process. To achieve this, MENTOR recognizes the emotions of the learners and takes them under consideration to provide the students with the suitable learning strategy. This kind of strategy is based both on the cognitive abilities and the affective preferences of the student and is stored in the student's model. The operation of MENTOR is based on the FFM and the OCC model. The module is attached to an Educational System providing the system with the essential "emotional" information in order to determine the strategy of learning in collaboration with the cognitive information. MENTOR has three main components: The Emotional Component (EC), the Teacher Component (TC) and the Visualization Component (VC), which are respectively responsible for: a) the recognition of student's personality, mood and emotions during the learning process, b) the selection of the suitable teaching and pedagogical strategy and c) the appropriate visualization of the educational environment. The combined function of these components "feeds" the Adaptive Educational System with the affective dimension optimizing the effectiveness of the learning process and enhancing the personalized teaching. The affective model of MENTOR uses an ontology of emotions for their formal representation. It is a proper way to represent the specific knowledge of a domain, providing an explicit and extensive

framework to describe it. This ontology has been built to represent 10 emotions which are: joy, satisfaction, pride, hope, gratification, distress, disappointment, shame, fear, reproach. The former five emotions compose the classification of positive emotions and are related to the positive student's emotional state. The latter five emotions compose the classification of negative emotions and are related to the negative student's emotional state. The construction of the ontology was based on the OCC cognitive theory of emotions. The affective module uses the DL-OWL (Description Logic – Ontology Web Language), a reasoning and inference mechanism to acquire the essential production rules, as well as to analyse the domain knowledge and interaction data. An AI technique (decision tree approach) is adopted to extract information from the proposed "emotional" ontology and to make inferences about the emotions of the student. This approach, which is used for carrying off the representation and the inference of emotions, is based on the OCC model which combines the appraisal of an Event with the Intentions and Desires of a subject. Thus, taking advantage of this model, MENTOR infers about the student's emotions after the occurrence of an educational event which is related to his learning goal. After the recognition of student's emotion, MENTOR has sufficient information to provide the student with the appropriate affective tactic. Its structural characteristics enable MENTOR to be independent from the specific domain model of educational systems, so that it has the capability to be used by a wide range of users.

DISCUSSION AND FUTURE TRENDS

Affective computing is a relatively new area of interdisciplinary research interest. The coordinated efforts of psychologists, computer scientists and physiologists promise a breakthrough in this field. However, at this moment affective computing is still in its infancy. The shortage of a sufficient amount of adequate affective theories, namely, psychological studies which can be exploited effectively by AI scientists in order to reason unambiguously about the emotions, limit progress in affective computing. As a result, computer systems capable of adapting appropriately to the emotional state and the sentimental needs of a human being have a long way to go before coming to fruition.

Furthermore, another weak point is the current inadequacy to integrate affective information into affective models. In most cases the nature of this information is dynamic and for this reason demands suitably real-time processing algorithms to deal properly with them. On the other hand, the impotence of existing representation methods to define and describe satisfactory this dynamic information and the partial relations between the different formats of the affective data remains a restricting factor to the development of completely affective models. Accordingly, the adaptation of the affective system to the user's affective states and personalized requirements cannot be considered persuasive especially in real scenarios.

Moreover, the methodological problems of affective computing occur in Web-based educational systems and believable pedagogical agents. Here, the objective of research is focused on how emotions and affective states can be recognized in the educational environment during the learning process. Which are the mental and emotional processes and the interrelations between them? Which are the basic emotions that must be selected for modeling? Which are the teaching and pedagogical methods that are more appropriate in relation to the student's affectivity? The emotional and cognitive processes which take place during learning are not neither fully understood, nor easily observable. The use of today's specialized affective apparatus does not enhance the accuracy of the observable measurements. We are still far from the point of appraising the subtle fluctuation in a person's affective state.

Despite the promising evidence that is brought by the emergence of affective computing, some ethical and sociological questions have been also raised. The modern societies "face" with skepticism the new era that comes into view and the potential prevalence of intelligent machines which will be not only be intellectual but also sentimental and more "human" than ever. Some authors (e.g., Whitby, 1996; Warwick, 1998) have alarmed the public about the social effects and dangers that possibly would be brought about by the progress of this AI's branch.

Apart from these debatable points, there are practical dimension of affective computing which have been already stated implicitly in the previous sections. For instance, the detection of a person's affective state from the perceived data is an extremely complex process; the existing developed methods and techniques need significant improvement. Even for a human being the recognition of another's emotions is a difficult and questionable task and its success depends on individual factors and abilities such as the personality and the instinct. Whereas some researchers according to their experiments claim that a computer system is able to detect user's emotion with about 80% accuracy (Picard et al., 2001), major assumptions and simplifications had been made such as the specific selection among eight kinds of emotions. Matters are worse in case of emotional states where we have of mixture emotions. In this case instead of recognizing discrete emotions, a much more complicated identification of mixing emotions is required. Despite some progress, significant work remains to be conducted to advance research in the elicitation of emotions.

Besides, when the recognition of emotions has been accomplished, a forthcoming step will be the appropriate classification and regulation of them in order to reinforce positive emotions and avoid possibly negative impact during the system's response to the user's affective state. The main purpose for an affective application is to support effectively the user to his goals achievement such as demonstrating motivation and interest in educational environments, empathy in persuasive dialogues and compassion or enthusiasm in computer games.

However, the emotional expressiveness by computer system is restricted by the lack of physical body. Facial movements, gestures, postures, eye movements cannot be performed in a natural and persuasive way by computers. Due to the absence of anthropomorphic appearance the existing computer systems are not able to express realistic or at least convincing behavior. The designers of embodied agents and mechanical robots have a long distance to cover before building believable, human-like artifacts that respond humanly to human beings.

Having considered all the above issues the question is how close enough are we for building a realistic affective system? An emotional machine which could be recognize in great accuracy user's emotions and to respond appropriately to his affective states by adapting itself suitably? Our sense is that we have a long way to go before such a system comes a reality.

Suggestions for Future Research

Future research must concentrate on the discovery of new methods or improvement the existing ones in order an affective system to be able to recognize accurately the user's motivational states. New methods of emotion detection should be adequately assessed and validated as well. A significant drawback of most affective systems is the shortage of evaluative reports which test the reliability and the validity of their affective adaptive mechanisms. Although, in the field of affective educational systems some proposed models (Vicente & Pain, 2002; Martinho et al., 2000; Leontidis et al., 2008) point to the possible direction, there is still a need for further refinement of their quality and applicability in various educational situations.

In addition there is also a need for the emotional information to be formally represented and stored in a consistent affective model. There are three critical questions to be answered. Firstly, which are the basic emotions and the affective states that it would be better to represent? Especially, in educational environments, where there are specific interactions between the student and the system during the learning process, the affective and cognitive information should be formalized and validated in an appropriate way. Secondly, how the perceived dynamic affective information can be adequately represented and handled? That is, h, how this information can be exploited efficiently and how the adaptation algorithms can be improved in order to achieve better response to the user's affective states in real scenarios? Finally, because of the dynamic nature of affective information how often and under which circumstances should an affective system be adapted to the user's affective state? Change of the mood over the time is different from the corresponding emotions. Also additional factors related to a person's individual traits and personality must be taken into account. Currently the existing affective models make use of clichéd emotional cues and personality traits. As a consequence their flexibility and efficiency in natural interactions with a user is today questionable. The answer to these questions in a satisfactory way would be unquestionably a catalytic factor in order to produce better affective educational systems in the near future.

Despite of the above remarks the progress that has been made in the field of affective computing is remarkable, and many past problems have been overcome. The number of affective systems is increasing and this makes promising the future advancement of emotional machines and their application.

REFERENCES

Abelson, R. P. (1963). Computer simulation of "hot" cognition. In S. Tomkins & S. Messick

(Eds.), *Computer simulation of personality* (pp. 277-298). New York: Wiley.

Alani, H., Kim, S., Millard, D. E., Weal, M. J., Hall, W., Lewis, P. H., & Shadbolt, N. (2004). Using Protégé for automatic ontology instantiation. In *Proceedings of the 7th International Protégé Conference.* Bethesda, Maryland, USA

Andre, E., Klesen, M., Gebhard, P., Allen, S., & Rist T. (1999). Integrating models of personality and emotions into lifelike characters. In *Proceedings International Workshop on Affect in Interactions - Towards a New Generation of Interfaces* (pp. 136-149).

Bates, J. (1994). The role of emotion in believable agents. *Communications of ACM, 37*(7), 122-125.

Batliner, A., Hacker, C., & Wong, M. (2004). "You stupid tin box" – Children interacting with the AIBO robot: A cross-linguistic emotional speech corpus. In *Proc. Language Resources and Evaluation (LREC '04).* Lisbon.

Cacioppo, J. T., Klein, D. J., Berntson, G. G., & Hatfield, E. (1993). The psychophysiology of emotion. In M. Lewis & J. M. Haviland (Eds.), *Handbook of emotions* (pp. 119-142). New York: Guilford Press.

Chen, L. S., Huang, T. S., Miyasato, T., & Nakatsu, R. (1998). Multimodal human emotion / expression recognition. In *Proceedings of International Conference on Automatic Face and Gesture Recognition.* Nara, Japan: IEEE Computer Society

Chibelushi, C.C., & Bourel, F. (2003). Facial expression recognition: A brief tutorial overview. In *CVonline: Online compendium of computer vision.*

Clore, G. & Ortony, A. (1999). Cognition in emotion: Always, sometimes, or never? In L. Nadel, R. Lane & G.L. Ahern (Eds.), *The cognitive neuroscience of emotion.* New York: Oxford University Press.

Colby, K. M. (1963). Computer simulation of a neurotic process. In S. Tomkins S. & S. Messick (Eds.), *Computer simulation of personality* (pp. 165-179). New York: Wiley.

Conati, C., & McLaren, H. (2005). Data-driven refinement of a probabilistic model of user affect. In *Proceedings of the Tenth International Conference on User Modeling* (pp. 40-49). Edinburgh, Scotland

Conati, C., & Zhou., X. (2002). Modeling students' emotions from cognitive appraisal in educational games. In *Proceedings of the 6th International Conference on ITS.* Biarritz, France.

Costa, P. T., & McCrae, R. R. (1992). Four ways five factors are basic. *Personality and Individual Differences, 1*(13), 653-665

Dellaert, F., Polzin, T., & Waibel, A. (1996). Recognizing emotion in speech. In *Proceedings of ICSLP 1996* (pp. 1970-1973). Philadelphia, PA.

Dicheva, D., & Aroyo, L. (2002). Concept-based course-ware authoring: An engineering perspective. In *ICALT'2002.*

Dipert, R. (1998). *The nature and structure of emotions* (draft). US Military Academy.

Douglas-Cowie, E., Cowie, R., & Schroder, M. (2000). *A new emotion database Considerations, sources and scope.* Paper presented at the ISCA-Workshop on Speech and Emotion: A conceptual framework for research.

Ekman, P. (1992). An argument for basic emotions. *Cognition and Emotion, 6,* 169-200.

Ekman, P. (1999). Facial expressions. In T. Dalgleish & T. Power (Eds.), *The handbook of cognition and emotion* (pp. 301-320). Sussex, UK: John Wiley & Sons.

Ekman, P., & Rosenberg, E. L. (1997). *What the face reveals: Basic and applied studies of spontaneous expression using the facial action* coding system (FACS). New York: Oxford University Press.

Elliot, C., Rickel, J., & Lester, J. (1999). Lifelike pedagogical agents and affective computing: an exploratory synthesis. In M. Wooldridge & M. Veloso (Eds.) (LNAI 1600, pp. 195-212).

Elliott, C. D. (1992). *The affective reasoner: A process model of emotions in a multiagent system.* PhD thesis, Northwestern University, Evanston, Illinois

Essa, I. & Pentland, A. (1997). Coding, analysis, interpretation and recognition of facial expressions. *IEEE Transactions on Pattern Analysis and Machine Intelligence, 19*(7), 757-763.

Faivre, J., Nkambou, R., & Frasson, C. (2002) Integrating adaptive emotional agents in ITS. In *Workshop of Architectures and Methodologies for Building Agent-Based Learning Environments* (In conjunction with ITS 2002 Conference) (pp. 1-7).

Fasel, B. & Luettin, J. (2003). Automatic facial expression analysis: A survey. *Pattern Recognition, 36*, 259-275.

Fernandez, R., & Picard, R. (2003). Modeling drivers' speech under stress. *Speech Comm., 40*, 145-159.

Frijda, N. (1994). Varieties of affect: Emotions and episodes, moods, and sentiments. In P. Ekman & R.J. Davidson (Ed.), *The nature of emotion.* New York: Oxford University Press.

Goleman, D. (1995). *Emotional intelligence.* New York: Bantam Books.

Gullahorn, J. T., & Gullahorn J. E. (1963). A computer model of elementary social behavior. In E.A. Feigenbaum & J. Feldman (Eds.), *Computers and thought* (pp. 375-386). New York: McGraw-Hill.

Hansen, J., (1999). *Speech under stress.* Paper presented at ICASSP'99. Phoenix, Arizona.

Healey, J. (2000). *Wearable and automotive systems for affect recognition from physiology.* PhD thesis, Massachusetts Institute of Technology.

Horvitz, E. Breese,J. Heckerman, D. Hovel, D., & Rommelse, K. (1998). The Lumiere Project: Bayesian user modeling for inferring the goals and needs of software users. In *Proceedings of the Fourteenth Conference on Uncertainty in Artificial Intelligence* (pp. 256-265). Madison, WI.

Iida, A., Campbell, N., Iga, S., Higuchi, F., & Yasumura, M. (2000). A speech synthesis system with emotion for assisting communication. In *Proceedings of the ISCA Workshop on Speech and Emotion* (Vol. 1, pp. 167-172). Belfast.

Izard, C. E. (1977). *Human emotions.* New York: Plenum Press.

Keller, J. M. (1999). Using the ARCS motivational process in computer-based instruction and distance education. In M. Theall (Ed.), *Motivation in teaching and learning: New directions for teaching and learning.* San Francisco: Jossey-Bass.

Kinshuk, N.A., & Patel, A. (2001). Adaptive tutoring in business education using fuzzy backpropagation approach. In M. J. Smith, G. Salvendy, D. Harris & R. J. Koubek (Eds.) *Usability evaluation and interface design: Cognitive engineering, intelligent agents and virtual reality: Proceedings of The 9th International Conference on Human-Computer Interaction.* New Orleans, USA.

Kobayashi, H., & Hara, F. (1992). Recognition of six basic facial expressions and their strength by neural network. In *Proceedings of the Int'l Workshop Robot and Human Comm.* (pp. 381-386).

Koenen, R. (2000). Mpeg-4 Project Overview, International Organisation for Standardization, ISO/IEC/JTC1/SC29/WG11, La Baule.

Kotsia, I., & Pitas, I. (2005). Real time facial expression recognition from image sequences using Support Vector Machines. In *IEEE Inter-*

national Conference on Image Processing (ICIP 2005) (pp. 11-14).

Leontidis, M., Halatsis, C., & Grigoriadou, M. (2008). E-learning issues under an affective perspective. In F. Li, et al. (Eds.), *ICWL 2008* (LNCS 5145, pp. 27-38).

Lazarus, R.S. (1991). *Emotion and adaptation.* New York: Oxford University Press

Lee, C.M., & Narayanan, S.S. (2005). Toward detecting emotions in spoken dialogs. *IEEE Trans. Speech Audio Process. 13*(2), 293-303.

Lester, J., Towns, S., & Fitzgerald, P. (1999). Achieving affective impact: Visual emotive communication in lifelike pedagogical agents. *International Journal of Artificial Intelligence in Education, 10,* 278-291.

Lisetti, C., & Rumelhart, D. (1998). An environment to acknowledge the interface between affect and cognition. In *Proceedings of AAAI Spring Symposium, Stanford University.* Menlo Park, CA: AAAI Press.

Lyons, M., Akamatsu, S., Kamachi, M., & Gyoba, J. (1998). Coding facial expressions with Gabor wavelets. In *Proceedings of the Third IEEE International Conference on Automatic Face and Gesture Recognition, IEEE Computer Society* (pp. 200-205). Nara Japan.

Magali O., Niewiadomski, R., Pelachaud, C., & Sadek, D. (2005). Intelligent expressions of emotions. In *1st International Conference on Affective Computing and Intelligent Interaction ACII,* China.

Mansoorizadeh M., & Charkari. (2008). Bimodal person-dependent emotion recognition comparison of feature level and decision level information fusion. In *PETRA 2008.*

Marsella, S., & Gratch, J. (2006). EMA: A computational model of appraisal dynamics. In J. Gratch, S. Marsella, & P. Petta (Eds.), *Agent construction*

and emotions, (pp. 601-606). Austrian Society for Cybernetic Studies, Vienna

Martinho, C., Machado, I., & Paiva, A. (2000). A cognitive approach to affective user modeling. In A. Paiva (Ed.), *Affective interactions - Towards a new generation of computer interfaces.* (LNCS 1814, pp. 64-75).

McCrae, R. R., & John, O. P. (1992). An introduction to the five factor model and its applications. Special Issue: The five factor model: Issues and applications. *Journal of Personality, 60,* 175-215.

Meyer, J. J. (2004). Reasoning about emotional agents. In R. L'opez de M'antaras and L. Saitta (Eds.), *16th European Conf. on Artif. Intell. (ECAI)* (pp. 129-133).

Mizoguchi, R., Sinitsa, K., & Ikeda, M. (1996). Task ontology design for intelligent educational/ training systems. In *Proc. of Workshop on Architectures and Methods for Designing Cost-Effective and Reusable ITSs* (ITS'96) (pp. 1-21). Montreal.

Mizoguchi, R., & Bourdeau, J. (2000). Using ontological engineering to overcome common AI-ED Problems. *Int. J. AI in Education, 11,* 1-12.

Mozziconacci, S.J.L., & Hermes, D.J., (2000). Expression of emotion and attitude through temporal speech variations. In *Proceedings of the Internat. Conf. on Spoken Language Processing (ICSLP '00), Beijing* (Vol. 2, pp. 373-378).

Murray, I. R., & Arnott, J. L. (1993). Toward the simulation of emotion in synthetic speech: A review of the literature on human vocal emotion. *Journal Acoustical Society of America, 93*(2), 1097-1108.

Oren T.I., & Ghasem-Aghaee N. (2003). Personality representation processable in fuzzy logic for human behavior simulation. In *Proceedings of the 2003 Summer Computer Simulation Conference, Montreal, PQ, Canada, July 20-24* (pp. 11-18).

Orr, R.J., & Abowd, G.D. (2000). The smart floor: A mechanism for natural user identification and tracking. In *CHI '00: CHI '00 Extended Abstracts on Human Factors in Computing Systems* (pp. 275-276). New York: ACM Press.

Ortony, A., Clore, G. L., & Collins, A. (1988). *The cognitive structure of emotions.* Cambridge: Cambridge University Press

Paiva, A. (2000). Affective interactions: Toward a new generation of computer interfaces? In A. Paiva (Ed.), *Affective interactions - Towards a new generation of computer interfaces.* (LNCS 1814).

Paiva, A., Dias, J., Sobral, D., Aylett, R.,Woods, S., Hall, L., & Zoll, C. (2005). Learning by feeling: Evoking empathy with synthetic characters. *Applied Artificial Intelligence 19,* 235-266.

Pantic, M. & Rothkrantz, L. J. M. (2000). Expert system for automatic analysis of facial expressions. In B. Parkinson & A.M. Coleman (Eds.), *Image and vision computing. Emotion and Motivation.* London: Longman.

Partala, T., & Surakka, V. (2003). Pupil size variation as an indication of affective processing. *Int. J. Human–Comput. Stud. 59,* 185-198.

Picard, R.W. (1997). *Affective computing.* Cambridge, MA: MIT Press.

Picard, R.W. (2003). Affective computing: Challenges. *Int. Journal of Human-Computer Studies, 59*(1-2), 55-64.

Picard, R.W., Vyzas, E., & Healey, J. (2001). Toward machine emotional intelligence: Analysis of affective physiological state. *IEEE Trans. Pattern Anal. Mach. Intell., 23*(10), 1175-1191.

Pierre-Yves O. (2003). The production and recognition of emotions in speech: Features and algorithms. *Int. J. Human-Computer Studies, 59,* 157-183.

Plutchik, R. (1980). *Emotion: A psychoevolutionary synthesis.* New York: Harper & Row.

Pope, A., Bogart, E., & Bartolome, D. (1995). Biocybernetic system evaluates indices of operator engagement in automated task. *Biol. Psychol. 40,* 187-195

Prendinger, H., Mori, J., & Ishizuka, M. (2005). Using human physiology to evaluate subtle expressivity of a virtual quizmaster in a mathematical game. *International Journal Human–Computer Studies. 62,* 231-245.

Rao, A., & Georgeff M. (1991). Modeling rational agent within a BDI-architecture. In *Proceedings of the 2nd Int. Conf. on Principle of Knowledge Representation and Reasoning, KR91.* San Mateo, CA.

Reilly, W. S., & Bates, J. (1992) *Building emotional agents.* Pittsburgh: School of Computer Science, Carnegie Mellon University.

Russell, J.A. (1997). How shall an emotion be called? In R. Plutchik & H. Conte (Eds.), *Circumplex models of personality and emotions* (pp. 205-220). Washington, DC: APA.

Russell, J.A. (2003). Core affect and the psychological construction of emotion. *Psychological Review, 110,* 145-172.

Sadek, D., Bretier, P., & Panaget, F. (1997). Artimis: Natural dialogue meets rational agency. In *Proceedings of 15th International Joint Conference on Artificial Intelligence (IJCAI'97),* (pp. 1030-1035). Nagoya, Japon.

Scherer, K. R. (1981). Speech and emotional states. In J. K. Darby (Ed.), *Speech evaluation in psychiatry* (pp. 189-220). Grune and Stratton, Inc.

Scherer, K. (2000). *Psychological models of emotion.* In J. Borod (Ed.), *The neuropsychology of emotion* (pp. 137-162). Oxford/New York: Oxford University Press.

Scherer, K. R. (2005). What are emotions? And how can they be measured? *Social Science Information, 44*(4), 693-727.

Schiel, F., Steininger, S., & Turk, U. (2002). The Smartkom multimodal corpus at BAS. In *Proceedings of Language Resources and Evaluation* (LREC '02).

Tian, Y., Kanade, T., & Cohn, J. F. (2001). Recognising action units for facial expression analysis. *IEEE Trans Pattern Analysis and Machine Intelligence, 23*(2).

Tsapatsoulis, N., Karpouzis, K., & Stamou, G. (2000). A fuzzy system for emotion classification based on the MPEG-4 facial definition parameter. In *European Association on Signal Processing EUSIPCO.*

Ververidis, D., & Kotropoulos C. (2006). Emotional speech recognition: Resources, features, and methods. *Speech Communication, 48,* 1162-1181.

Verwey, W., Veltman, H. (1996). Detecting short periods of elevated workload: A comparison of nine workload assessment techniques. *Journal of Experimental Psychological Applications 2*(3), 270–285.

Warwick, K. (1998). *March of the machines. In the mind of the machine: The breakthrough in artificial intelligence.* London: Arrow.

Wehrle, T., & Kaiser, S. (2000). Emotion and facial expression. In A. Paiva (Ed.), *Affect in interactions: Towards a new generation of interfaces,* (pp. 49-64). Heidelberg: Springer.

Weiner, B. (1992). *Human motivation.* Sage Publications, Inc.

Whitby, B. (1996). *Reflections on artificial intelligence. The legal, moral and ethical dimensions.* Exeter, UK: Intellect Books.

Wiederhold, B., Jang, D., Kaneda, M., Cabral, I., Lurie, Y., May, T., Wiederhold, M., & Kim, S. (2003). An investigation into physiological responses in virtual environments: An objective measurement of presence. In G. Riva & C. Galimberti (Eds.), *Towards cyberpsychology: Minds, cognitions and society in the Internet age* (pp. 175-184). Amsterdam: IOS Press.

Wilson, G., & Sasse, A. (2002). Listen to you heart rate: Counting the cost of media quality. In *Proceedings of the International Conference on Intelligent Tutoring Systems,* 6. Biarritz, France.

Woldridge, M. (1999). Intelligent agents. In G. Weiss (Ed.), *Multi-Agent system* (pp. 27-28). Cambridge, MA: The MIT Press.

Womack, B.D., & Hansen, J.H.L. (1996). Classification of speech under stress using target driven features. *Speech Comm. 20,* 131-150.

Womack, B.D., & Hansen, J.H.L. (1999). N-channel hidden Markov models for combined stressed speech classification and recognition. *IEEE Trans. Speech Audio Processing 7*(6), 668-677.

Yacoob, Y., & Davis, L. S. (1996). Recognizing human facial expressions from log image sequences using optical flow. *IEEE Transactions on Pattern Analysis and Machine Intelligence, 18*(6), 636-642.

Yamamoto E., Nakamura, S., & Shikano, K. (1998). Lip movement synthesis from speech based on Hidden Markov Models. *Speech Communication, 26,* 105-115.

Zhou, G., Hansen, J.H.L., & Kaiser, J.F. (2001). Nonlinear feature based classification of speech under stress. *IEEE Trans. Speech Audio Processing, 9*(3), 201-216.

ENDNOTE

[1] OCC comes after the initials of the three authors Ortony, Clore and Collins

Chapter VIII
Understanding Learner Trait, Test and Computer Anxiety in the Context of Computer-Based Testing

Elena C. Papanastasiou
University of Nicosia, Cyprus

Aimilia Tzanavari
University of Nicosia, Cyprus

Patricia Lowe
University of Kansas-Lawrence, USA

ABSTRACT

Testing is an integral part of the learning process that aims to estimate the learner's abilities as accurately and efficiently as possible. This estimation frequently is influenced by factors such as the learner's emotional state and traits. This chapter looks into the area of Computer-based Testing (CBT), visiting the relevant literature on the subject, and then investigates the particular emotional states of learner trait, test and computer anxiety in that context. A study was carried out and revealed that although both trait and test anxiety as variables do not significantly affect learner performance, computer anxiety does. Finally, future research trends in this area are outlined.

INTRODUCTION

The goal of tests in general, as well as of computer-based tests is to be able to estimate the examinee's abilities as accurately and efficiently as possible, by removing as many extraneous effects (such as the computer itself) as possible. However, in many cases the computer itself might become an obstacle to the learning and testing process. The medium of computer technology might even be a reason that can explain a portion of the differences in the performance of students on computer administered tests compared to paper-and-pencil tests. For example, many examinees might be unfamiliar with the use of computers for learning purposes, or for taking tests on the computer. More specifically, they might be unfamiliar with the computer-testing mode, or with the fact that they have to read the test items on a computer screen and enter their answers through the keyboard. Therefore, taking tests on the computer might create anxiety for such examinees, and even more so for test anxious examinees (Wise, Roos, Plake & Nebelsick-Gullett, 1994). However, the literature seems to be lacking in this area, since relatively few studies have examined examinee characteristics and their levels of trait, test and computer anxiety in relation to computer administered tests. This is even more so when considering examinees of lower socioeconomic status (SES) that do not have frequent access to computer technology. Such students might not be as familiar with the use of computers, and more specifically with taking tests on a computer, which in turn could interfere with their test performance.

Examinees with high levels of computer or test anxiety might end up responding to computer administered tests in ways that are different compared to the examinees that are familiar with the use of the computer and with taking tests on them. Individual differences like these can provide a framework for explaining significant divergences in test performance and be used to improve the way computer-based tests are designed. Therefore, it is essential for researchers to also understand the examinee characteristics, and on how they can be simulated appropriately in simulation studies, and how that can affect the creation of e-learning content and their corresponding tests (Harwell, Stone, Hsu & Kirisci, 1996; Stocking, Steffen & Eignor, 2001).

This chapter examines the level of test anxiety and computer anxiety that is held by students in Cyprus, in relation to their performance on a computer-based test. More specifically, this chapter attempts to provide answers to the following research questions:

- Can the variables of overall anxiety, computer anxiety, and test anxiety predict a significant portion of an examinee's score on a computer-based abstract reasoning test?
- What are the variables that affect the levels of test and computer anxiety for undergraduate students in Cyprus?

BACKGROUND

Computer-Based Testing

There is no doubt that the new trend in assessment worldwide, is that of computer-based and/or web-based testing. Computer-based tests (CBT) could be defined as any type of assessment that is administered through the computer. However, computer-based testing can encompass many forms, depending on how adaptable the test is on the item level (The College Board, 2000). For example, some CBT, which are also called computerized fixed tests, are purely linear (Parshall, Spray, Kalohn & Davey, 2002). These are the tests that most closely resemble paper and pencil tests, since they are fixed form, fixed length, and the test items are organized in advance and placed in a predetermined order. In contrast to computerized fixed tests, computer adaptive tests (CAT) are the computer-based tests that have the maximum degree of adaptivity since they can be adapted for each examinee, based on the amount, difficulty and order in which the items are administered to each examinee. Web-based tests are computer-based tests delivered through the internet or an intranet. The tests themselves reside on the examiner's web server and examinees can access them through their web browsers. One of the main strengths of this type is that the tests can be taken anytime, from anywhere.

So overall, computer-based tests in general, as well as web-based tests represent the next generation in educational testing because of their many advantages over paper and pencil tests. One of the advantages of computer-based tests in general is that they can be comprised of more creative and interactive item types than regular paper and pencil tests. Tests today no longer have to be confined to pure text items that might include a few two dimensional pictures. Items used for computer-based tests can include colorful high resolution pictures, movies with motion and sound, voice synthesizers, and oral comprehension of spoken language (Parshall, Spray, Kalohn & Davey, 2002; Wainer, 2000), which all make the testing process more interesting and appealing to the students. In addition, when combined with computer-based learning, computer-based tests could also include test items obtained from examples or experiments used during the computer-based learning process. These types of items, when combined with their multimedia properties could make the testing situation a bit more realistic and more similar to the actual learning process. In addition to making the testing situation more realistic, such items have the advantage of eliciting positive attitudes from the students who take such tests on the computer. Consequently, the students end up being more motivated to do their best, which in turn increases the reliability of the student's test scores.

Administering tests on the computer also has the advantage of being able to accommodate students with different special needs. More specifically, because of the advanced multimedia properties of technology today, computers have the capability of easily enabling educators to teach, as well as test students with disabilities such as visual or hearing impairments. For example, CBTs could easily assign longer testing times to students with disabilities, as well as use sound, motion or text to assist these students appropriately, based

on their impairments. These types of accommodations could alleviate some of the frustration that is typically faced by students with special needs, which in turn could assist them in demonstrating their actual knowledge more accurately.

Another advantage of computer-based tests is that they can provide direct and immediate feedback to students as well as to teachers. With typical paper and pencil tests, there always tends to be a lag of time between the administration of the test and of its scoring. As a result, most of these tests end up being used only summatively in an attempt to assign grades to students. Educationally this is not a very sound practice since it does not allow the use of formative feedback that could supplement the learning process. With computer-based testing however, test results could be provided to students immediately after they finish responding to their test. In addition, a list of the content areas and objectives that have been met by each student can also be produced by such tests.

Finally, computer-based tests also include some additional advantages that will not be discussed in length. These include the fact that CBTs enhance test security, since test sheets or booklets can no longer be stolen or passed around from student to student. In addition, through CBTs, other collateral types of data can be collected that can provide additional pieces of information for educators and parents. Such information can include response times, which is the amount of time needed to answer each question), and the number of changes that the students made to their answers on the test. Response times are useful because they also tend to provide an indication on the amount of effort that has been placed by each student on each test item. For example items with minimal response times at the beginning of the test might indicate that the student did not give any effort to those items overall. However, items with minimal response times at the end of the test might indicate that a student might not have had enough time to answer the item and has randomly guessed the answer. Examining patterns of answer changing might also provide information on the quality of certain items (Papanastasiou & Reckase, 2008). For example items to which many examinees tend to change their answers might be an indicator of a flawed item.

Computer Adaptive Tests

In addition to the advantages that are associated with the general use of computer technologies to administer tests, there are some additional advantages that are associated specifically with computer adaptive tests. In order to comprehend the advantages associated with CATs, it is necessary to comprehend the way in which these tests are compiled. Typically, computer adaptive tests start by administering an item of about average difficulty to the examinees. This is done because the ability of most examinees lies in the middle of the ability continuum. Consequently, the majority of the students or examinees are able to respond to such average difficulty items, because they will not be too easy or too difficult for them. After the first item is answered, and based on if it is correct or incorrect, the second item is administered. If for example an examinee A, has responded to the first item on a science computer adaptive test correctly, that indicates to the adaptive test that this examinee has above average ability in science. Consequently, the computer will administer a second, more difficult item to that examinee. If this examinee also answers the second item correctly, then the third item administered will be even more difficult that the first two items. The goal is to be able to administer a test whose difficulty matches the achievement level of the examinee. When this is achieved, the ability of the examinee can be estimated with small margins of error.

If another examinee B had responded incorrectly to the first item, that indicates to the adaptive test that the science ability of this student is below average. So in an attempt to find out where the ability level of this examinee really is, the next item that will be administered will be easier than the first one. If examinee B also responds incorrectly to the second item, the third item that will be administered will be even easier. This process will continue to take place until an accurate estimate of the examinee's science ability is obtained. Therefore, by administering more items that are matched to each student's ability, the examinees are least likely to despair about their performance, particularly if s/he already suffers from anxiety about the test (Linacre, 2000).

The main advantage of computer adaptive testing however, is based on the fact that it can estimate examinees' abilities with better accuracy compared to other types of tests (e.g. computerized fixed tests that are not adaptable). Moreover, this accuracy can be achieved by administering fewer items, which in turn reduces the testing time needed for examinees to complete the test and also their fatigue, a factor that can significantly affect an examinee's test results. Another benefit is that examinees are less likely to be led to unwanted behavior such as guessing, carelessness or response patterns (Linacre, 2000), since the items they receive are matched to their ability, and are therefore neither too easy nor too difficult for them.

Computers and Anxiety

In order to be able to properly develop and implement a web-based test, a lot of attention needs to be paid to the educational context within which it will be implemented. In order to ensure that students' true ability or trait is being measured by a web-based test with a small amount of measurement error, students need to be familiar with the use of computers. Although in most developed countries computers are easily available for most students to use, this is not always the case worldwide. For example, the impact of computers familiarity on achievement in the Republic of Korea, where 98 percent of the students own computers, cannot be directly compared to Indonesia where only 17 percent of students own computers. Nor could one compare the Islamic Republic of Iran, where only 2 percent of students use computers both at home and at school, with Hong Kong, where 89 percent of students use a computer in both locations (Papanastasiou & Paparistodemou, 2007).

Consequently, if certain students do not know how to use computers and are asked to take a test on a computer, most likely these students' test scores will actually represent their amount of computer knowledge rather than their true abilities. Such results would be similar to asking very bright students who do not speak English to take a geography test in English. Although the students might know a lot about geography, the language factor will be a barrier to them in demonstrating their actual geography knowledge. The same is the case with computer skills. Students who are not familiar with the use of computers might have to struggle to understand how to enter their test results on the computer, which would prevent them from actually demonstrating what they really know. For example, a study based on data from the PISA database, found that the students in the United States of America who felt least comfortable with using computers to write papers, and who did not have easy access to use a computer at home or in the library, and who rarely used word processing software were more likely to have lower science scores (Papanastasiou, Zembylas & Vrasidas, 2003).

Consequently, it is possible that computer-based tests could disadvantage students from lower socioeconomic backgrounds since they tend to have limited access to computers. In these cases, it is possible that the computer itself might become an obstacle to the testing process for the students. The medium of computer technology might even be a reason that can explain a portion of the differences in the performance of students on computer administered tests from paper-and-pencil tests. More specifically, many examinees might be unfamiliar with the use of computers or with taking tests on computers, which could hurt their performance on such tests. A study by

Stricker and Wilder (2001) found that "computer liking" and "computer confidence" were positively related to the performance of students on a computer adaptive version of the Test of English as a Foreign Language (TOEFL) test. So the students who were most familiar with the use of computers and who liked computers had higher scores on the TOEFL compared to other students with less confidence and more negative attitudes towards computers.

The existence of a negative relationship between test anxiety and test performance is nothing new in the psychometric and educational psychology literature. In a meta-analysis of 562 studies, Hembree (1988) found that an inverse relationship existed between test anxiety and performance on tests, starting from grade 3. Similar results have also been found in more recent research studies. In a study performed by Powers (1999), the worry component of anxiety was negatively related to test performance on the GRE quantitative, analytical and verbal test scores combined. However, the emotionality component of anxiety was not significantly related to the performance on the GRE. The results of a different study performed by Hancock (2001), also found that students with high levels of test anxiety tend to perform more poorly on tests, especially when the tests count towards their evaluation in the classroom.

Other studies claim that computer-based tests cause increased levels of anxiety to students, beyond the regular test anxiety that students typically feel. In a study by Stricker and Wilder (2001), a negative relationship was found between computer anxiety and performance on the computer-based version of the TOEFL . However, Wise, Barnes, Harvey and Plake (1989) found no negative effects of computer anxiety on the performance of students on a computer-based test in a study was much smaller in scale and was not as high stakes as the test used in the Stricker and Wilder (2001) study.

In a single study that examined the effects of computer adaptive testing on anxiety, the results that were found indicated that the test anxiety levels of examinees who took computer adaptive tests were lower that their counterparts who took a paper-and-pencil test (Powers, 2001). According to the author however, the design of the study was not able to demonstrate whether this difference was due to the mode of testing, or whether there were other preexisting differences between the two groups of students.

Overall, based on the extant literature, it can be concluded that issues of computer experience, computer anxiety, test anxiety, and state and trait anxiety are all variables that add additional sources of error in students' test scores on computer-based tests. What is also likely is that these sources of error might be even larger for students who are not as familiar with the use of computer technology. Therefore, it is imperative that researchers and educators should determine what extraneous variables possibly mask or interfere with the performance of students on computer and web-based tests. Knowledge of these factors is essential to be able to prepare students for the specific testing situation. This would ensure that measurement error in students' test scores would be minimized, which in turn would lead to more accurate test results.

METHODS

For the purpose of this study, the students who were enrolled in a research methods course at the University of Cyprus were asked to participate in this study. The majority of the sample consisted of sophomore students, who were all training to become elementary school teachers in Cyprus. The average age of the students in the sample was 19.96 years, with a standard deviation of 2.42 years. Of the 381 students who were in the sample, 15.2% were male and 84.8% were female. The disproportionate amount of males to females in the sample reflects the fact that elementary school teaching is a predominantly female oriented field

in the Greek culture, as in many other Western cultures.

The students that participated in the study were asked to respond to a background survey, a computer anxiety measure, an abstract reasoning test as well as to two anxiety surveys. All of these measures and surveys were web-based. The software used for the administration of the computer administered portion of this study was CATGlobal. In addition, the students were also asked to respond to the Adult Manifest Anxiety Scale-College Version (AMAS-C; Reynolds, Richmond, & Lowe, 2003a) that was administered on paper. On average, the students spent a total of one hour in this study.

Computer Anxiety Measure

The computer anxiety measure, which was created by the researchers, is a 7-item self-report measure used to assess the student's anxiety in relation to the use of computers. The items included in this measure assess the student's self perceived anxiety and unfamiliarity and fear of computers. Cronbach's alpha reliability estimate for this measure was 0.83.

Adult Manifest Anxiety Scale-College Version (AMAS-C)

The Adult Manifest Anxiety Scale-College Version (AMAS-C; Reynolds, Richmond, & Lowe, 2003a) is a 49-item self-report measure used to assess chronic, manifest anxiety in the college student population. The AMAS-C consists of four anxiety subscales (Worry/Oversensitivity, Physiological Anxiety, Social Concerns/Stress, and Test Anxiety) and a Lie scale. The Lie scale is a measure of social desirability. In addition to the four anxiety subscales and Lie scale, the AMAS-C has a Total Anxiety scale. The Total Anxiety scale provides a global measure of chronic, manifest anxiety (Lowe, Papanastasiou, DeRuyck & Reynolds, 2005). Raters rate their responses to the

49 items on a dichotomous scale, using a yes/no format. A "yes" response to an item is indicative of how a student generally thinks, feels, or acts, whereas a "no" response to an item is not indicative of how an individual generally thinks, feels, or acts. Scores are derived from a student's "yes" responses, with higher scores suggesting higher levels of anxiety (Reynolds et al., 2003b).

The AMAS-C has adequate psychometric properties. Internal consistency reliability estimates for the Total Anxiety scale, four anxiety subscales, and Lie scale scores ranged from .72 to .95. Temporal stability of the AMAS Total Anxiety scale and four anxiety subscales scores ranged from .76 to .87 over a 1-week test-retest interval. Evidence supporting the construct validity of the AMAS-C test scores has been reported (see Reynolds et al., 2003b). The convergent validity of the AMAS-C test scores has also been examined. Lowe, Peyton, and Reynolds (2007) found moderate correlation coefficients between the AMAS-C Total Anxiety scale scores and four anxiety subscale scores and the Trait scale scores of the State-Trait Anxiety Inventory (Spielberger, Gorsuch, & Lushene, Vagg, & Jacobs, 1977). These findings provide support for the convergent validity of the AMAS-C test scores.

Test Anxiety Inventory (TAI)

The Test Anxiety Inventory (TAI; Spielberger, 1980a) is a 20-item self-report measure designed to assess test anxiety in high school and college students. The TAI consists of a Total scale and two subscales (Worry and Emotionality). Respondents rate their responses to the 20 different statements on a 4-point Likert scale.

The TAI has good psychometric properties. Coefficient alphas of .92 and above were found for the TAI Total scale scores. Internal consistency reliability estimates for the Worry and Emotionality subscales scores were .88 and .90, respectively. Test-retest reliability coefficients for the TAI Total scale scores ranged from .80 to .81 over a two- to four-week test-retest interval. Evidence supporting the construct validity of the TAI test scores has been found (see Spielberger, 1980b).

Abstract Reasoning Test

The only timed section of the study was the abstract reasoning test (Embretson, 1998), in which the students had 35 minutes to respond to 30 multiple-choice abstract reasoning items. The items were presented in a 3x3 matrix format, with the bottom left corner intentionally left blank. A series of 8 response options were provided and the students had to choose a single correct answer for each matrix. An example of such a problem is presented in Figure 1. In this example, the student would have to examine the 3x3 matrix that is presented on the left of Figure 1, and try to determine which figure should be included where the question mark is located. The eight response options are located in the left of the figure.

After the test was completed, the total score of each student was converted to t-scores for the analyses that were performed for this study.

RESULTS

A primary purpose of this study was to try to explain a portion of the variance of student's scores on a web-based test. Possible variables

Figure 1. Abstract reasoning item example

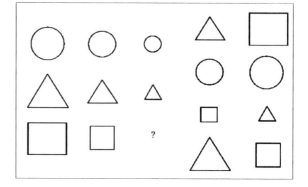

that were hypothesized to influence the performance of the students on computer-based tests were issues of test anxiety and computer anxiety. These analyses were performed through a series of regression models.

Predicting Computer-Based Testing Test Scores

The first regression model that was performed, examined whether the performance of the students on the computer-based test of abstract reasoning could be explained in part by their trait anxiety, by their test anxiety, as well as by their levels of computer anxiety. As presented in Table 1, the overall model was statistically significant ($F_{3,204}$=8.205, p=0.000), which explained 10.9% of the variance of the student's abstract reasoning score. However, of the three variables that were entered into the regression, only the variable of computer anxiety was statistically significant in predicting the student's test score (β=-0.241, t=-4.185, p=0.000). So students with lower levels of computer anxiety performed better on the CAT than students with higher levels of computer anxiety. The student's trait and test anxiety though, did not significantly predict the dependent variable of the student's total score on abstract reasoning.

Test Anxiety

The second regression that was performed tried to determine the variables that could predict a student's test anxiety. The overall regression whose results are presented in Table 2 was statistically significant ($F_{3,286}$=19.413, p=0.000), which explained 16.9% of the variance of the student's test anxiety level. This analysis included three independent variables. Two of those were demographic (age and gender), while the third variable was that of the student's computer anxiety. The variables of gender and computer anxiety were significant in predicting test anxiety in students, while age was not. More specifically, the results of this analysis showed that females tended to have higher levels of test anxiety than males (β=-0.723, t=-4.557, p=0.00), and that students with a higher level of computer anxiety also had a higher level of test anxiety (β=0.031, t=5.802, p=0.00).

Computer Anxiety

There was 31.8% of the sample that indicated that they were afraid of computers, 30.5% who indicated that they usually feel nervous when they use computers, and 27.3% who found it difficult to use a computer. In terms of computer anxiety, 6.5% of the students responded that they have a lot of computer anxiety, 60.8% responded that they have some anxiety, while only 32.7% of the sample indicated that they have no computer anxiety.

When asked about their familiarity with the use of computers, 1.2% of the sample indicated that they were very unfamiliar and 13.2% were unfamiliar with the use of computers. Seventy

Table 1. Predicting student's scores on a computer-based tests

	Unstandardized Coefficients		Standardized Coefficients	t	Sig.
	B	S.E.	Beta		
(Constant)	63.507	2.896		21.927	0.000
Trait anxiety (AMAS-C)	0.478	0.620	0.057	0.771	0.442
Test anxiety (TAI)	-0.866	0.637	-0.105	-1.359	0.176
Computer anxiety	-0.241	0.058	-0.293	-4.185	0.000

six percent of the sample indicated that they were familiar and only 9.2% responded that they were very familiar with the use of computers. When asked about how comfortable they felt with the use of computers, 7.7% indicated that they were not at all comfortable, 34.8% were somewhat comfortable and only 12.0% were very comfortable with the use of computers.

In terms of taking tests on the computer, the students from Cyprus tended to have higher levels of anxiety. More specifically, only 36.5% of the students had no anxiety, while 53.5% had some anxiety and 10.0% had a lot of anxiety. It should be noted however, that these responses are in light of the fact that this test was not high stakes.

The third regression that was performed examined whether students' computer anxiety was influenced by the variables of owning a computer, number of years of using computers, hours per week of using computers, and gender. This regression model was also statistically significant ($F_{4,313}$=39.523, p=0.000), and it explained 33.8% of the variance of the student's computer anxiety.

All but one of the variables used in this regression were statistically significant. More specifically, students who owned a computer at their home had lower levels of computer anxiety (β=4.712, t=2.906, p=0.004). Students who had been using computers for many years also had lower levels of computer anxiety (β=-1.552, t=-7.452, p=0.000). Finally, students who used the computer for many hours per week also had lower levels of computer anxiety (β=-0.577, t=6.154, p=0.000). However, gender was not significant in predicting the computer anxiety score of the sample. These results are presented in Table 3.

CONCLUSION

The results of the study presented in this chapter show that trait anxiety and test anxiety are not variables that can significantly affect performance of students on computer administered tests. However, computer anxiety is a variable that significantly affects the performance of students.

Table 2. Predicting test anxiety

	Unstandardized Coefficients		Standardized Coefficients	t	Sig.
	B	S.E.	Beta		
(Constant)	-0.782	0.566		-1.382	0.168
Gender	-0.723	0.159	-0.255	-4.557	0.000
Age	0.002	0.025	0.005	0.082	0.935
Computer anxiety	0.031	0.005	0.314	5.812	0.000

Table 3. Predicting computer anxiety

	Unstandardized Coefficients		Standardized Coefficients	t	Sig.
	B	S.E.	Beta		
(Constant)	57.547	2.618		21.985	0.000
Home computer	4.712	1.622	0.141	2.906	0.004
Years of computer use	-1.552	0.208	-0.361	-7.452	0.000
Hours per week of computer use	-0.577	0.094	-0.301	-6.154	0.000
Gender	-1.648	1.289	-0.060	-1.278	0.202

In turn, this anxiety is affected by whether the student has a computer available to use at home, by the number of years each students has been using computers, as well as by the number of hours of computer use per week. The results of this study indicate that since the exposure that students have to computers can be manipulated by intentionally increasing their use of computers in their educational settings, the possible disadvantages associated with computer-based tests (such as the student's computer anxiety) can be reduced dramatically. This is especially important when taking into account students with a lower socioeconomic status that might be disadvantaged from such technology if they cannot afford to own a computer at home. Therefore, it is important to ensure that all students have equal access to such technologies before trying to implement computer-based tests on a broad basis.

An encouraging result of this study is that gender does not play a role on students' computer anxiety although males typically experienced lower levels of test anxiety compared to females. Although the gender composition of the present sample appears to reflect that of most educational courses (Onwuegbuzie, Bailey & Daley, 1999), the fact that participants were predominantly female is a limitation of the present study (see also, Onwuegbuzie, 2000). Certainly, the inclusion of more male students would facilitate the generalizability of the findings. The generalizability of the findings would also be strengthened with the inclusion of high school students in the sample, in addition to graduate students at the University level.

In sum, a conclusion that is very clear from this study is that the attempt to reach the goal of removing as many extraneous effects of testing from computer-based tests has not been completely successful yet. Although computer-based and adaptive tests might be able to estimate the examinee's abilities with high levels of accuracy and efficiency, they have not managed to meet this objective yet. It is possible that in the future, when the use of computers becomes even more widespread than it is today, many such problems will be alleviated. However, until that time comes, we need to be more considerate to those students who are not privileged enough to have access to computer technology. In addition, future research should also determine whether the anxiety levels of examinees on computer adaptive tests are comparable to those expressed on traditional computer-based tests or not, and if not, try to examine how they can be dealt with.

ACKNOWLEDGMENT

We would like to sincerely thank CATGlobal for permitting us to use their software and services through the Computer Adaptive Technologies (CAT) Software System research grant. We would also like to acknowledge the invaluable help of John Stahl at Promissor for his assistance to us while we were using the CATGlobal software throughout this process.

REFERENCES

The College Board. (2000, April). *An overview of computer-based testing.* RN-09.

Embretson, S. E. (1998). A cognitive design system approach to generating valid tests: Application to abstract reasoning. *Psychological Methods, 3,* 380-396.

Hancock, D. R. (2001). Effects of test anxiety and evaluative threat on student's achievement and motivation. *The Journal of Educational Research, 94*(5), 284-290.

Harwell, M., Stone, C. A., Hsu, T. & Kirisci, L. (1996). Monte Carlo studies in item response theory. *Applied psychological measurement, 20*(2), 101-125.

Hembree, R. (1988). Correlates, causes, effects and treatment of test anxiety. *Review of Educational Research, 58*(1), 47-77.

Linacre, J.M. (2000). Computer-adaptive testing: A methodology whose time has come. In S. Chae, U. Kang, E. Jeon & J. M. Linacre (Eds.), *Development of computerized middle school achievement test*. Seoul, South Korea: Komesa Press.

Lowe, P. A., Papanastasiou, E. C., DeRuyck, K. A., & Reynolds, C. R. (2005). Test score stability and construct validity of the Adult Manifest Anxiety Scale-College Version (AMAS-C) scores among college students: A brief report. *Measurement and Evaluation in Counseling and Development, 37*(4), 220-227.

Lowe, P. A., Peyton, V., & Reynolds, C. R. (2007). Test score stability and the relationship of Adult Manifest Anxiety Scale-College Version scores to external variables among college students. *Journal of Psychoeducational Assessment, 25,* 69-81.

Onwuegbuzie, A. J. (2000). Statistics anxiety and the role of self-perceptions. *Journal of Educational Research, 93,* 323-330.

Onwuegbuzie, A., Bailey, P., & Daley, C. (1999). Factors associated with foreign language anxiety. *Applied Socio Linguistics 20,* 218-239.

Papanastasiou, E. C. & Paparistodemou, E. (2007). Examining educational technology and achievement through latent variable modeling. In T. Loveless (Ed.), *Lessons learned. What international assessments tell us about math achievement* (pp. 205-225). Washington D.C.: Brookings Institution Press.

Papanastasiou, E. C. & Reckase, M. D. (2008, June). *Item review as a non-traditional method of item analysis*. Paper presented at the Annual conference of the Psychometric Society, Durham, NH.

Papanastasiou, E. C., Zembylas, M., & Vrasidas, C. (2003). Can computer use hurt science achievement? The USA results from PISA. *Journal of Science Education and Technology, 12*(3), 325-332.

Parshall, C. G., Spray, J. A., Kalohn, J. C. & Davey, T. (2002). *Practical considerations in computer-based testing*. New York: Springer.

Powers, D. E. (1999). *Test anxiety and test performance: Comparing paper based and computer-adaptive versions of the GRE general test*. (Research Report 99-15). Princeton, NJ: Educational Testing Service

Powers, D. E. (2001). Test anxiety and test performance: Comparing paper based and computer-adaptive versions of the Graduate Record Examinations (GRE) general test. *Journal of Educational Computing Research, 24*(3), 249-273.

Reynolds, C. R., Richmond, B. O., & Lowe, P. A. (2003a). *The Adult Manifest Anxiety Scale-College Version*. Los Angeles, CA: Western Psychological Services.

Reynolds, C. R., Richmond, B. O., & Lowe, P. A. (2003b). *The Adult Manifest Anxiety Scale Manual*. Los Angeles, CA: Western Psychological Services.

Spielberger, C. D. (1980a). *Test Anxiety Inventory (TAI)*. Palo Alto, CA: Consulting Psychologists Press.

Spielberger, C. D. (1980b). *Test Anxiety Inventory (TAI): Manual*. Palo Alto, CA: Consulting Psychologists Press.

Spielberger, C.D., Gorsuch, R.L., Lushene, R., Vagg, P.R., & Jacobs, G.A. (1977). *State-Trait Anxiety Inventory*. Palo Alto, CA: Consulting Psychologists Press.

Stricker, L. J. & Wilde, G. Z. (2001). *Examinee's attitudes about the TOEFL-CBT, possible determinants, and relationships with test performance* (Research Report 01-01). Princeton, NJ: Educational Testing Service.

Stocking, M. L., Steffen, M. S. & Eignor, D. R. (2001). *A method for building a realistic model of test taker behavior for computerized adaptive testing* (RR-01-22). Princeton, NJ: Educational Testing Service.

Wainer, H. (2000). CATs: Whither and whence. *Psicologica, 21*(1-2), 121-133.

Wise, S. L., Barnes, L. B., Harvey, A. L. & Plakes, B. S. (1989). Effects of computer anxiety and computer experience on the computer-based achievement test performance of college students. *Applied Measurement in Education, 2*(3), 235-24.

Wise, S. L., Roos, L. R., Plake, B. S., & Nebelsick-Gullett, L. J. (1994). The relationship between examinee anxiety and preference for self-adapted testing. *Applied measurement in education, 7*(1), 81-91.

Section III
Cognition–Aware and Affective Hypermedia

Chapter IX
Individual Differences in Adaptive Educational Hypermedia:
The Effect of Cognitive Style and Visual Working Memory

Nikos Tsianos
National & Kapodistrian University of Athens, Greece

Panagiotis Germanakos
National & Kapodistrian University of Athens, Greece

Zacharias Lekkas
National & Kapodistrian University of Athens, Greece

Costas Mourlas
National & Kapodistrian University of Athens, Greece

ABSTRACT

The purpose of this chapter is to experimentally explore the effect of individual differences in an adaptive educational hypermedia application. To that direction, the constructs of cognitive style (Cognitive Style Analysis) and visual working memory (visuo-spatial subsystem of Baddeley's model) were employed as personalization parameters, thus rendering possible the provision of personalized learning environments according to users' intrinsic characteristics. Two distinct experiments were conducted, with a total sample of 347 university students, seeking out to ground the hypothesis that matching the instructional style to learners' preferences would increase their performance. Both experiments demonstrated that users in the personalized condition generally outperformed those that were instructed in a condition mismatched to their cognitive style or visual working memory ability.

INTRODUCTION

Web-based educational applications have proliferated throughout the extensive development of the internet, in parallel with a significant research interest on this channel of instruction. Individual differences in e-learning constitute an interdisciplinary research area, and most approaches derive from the fields of Computer Science and/or Psychology, as a result of combined efforts to improve the effectiveness of web-based education.

In any case, it is a fact that web information resources are numerous, and the internet has become extremely vague (De Bra, Aroyo & Chepegin, 2004), making information processing very difficult for users. This has provided a good basis for the notion of personalization and for the development of adaptive hypermedia systems (Eklund & Sinclair, 2000; Brusilovsky & Nejdl, 2004;), that take into account users' (or learners') individual characteristics, aiming to provide tailor-suited information.

The integration of human factors or traits in web-based education is also under the scope of many researchers, and in accordance to the aims of this paper we consider that this research is being carried out in two distinct ways: (a) computer scientists have developed systems that usually adapt on users' learning or cognitive styles (Papanikolaou et al, 2002; Carver, Howard & Lane, 1999; Gilbert & Han, 2002) or respond to their current affective state (Picard, 1997), whereas (b) researchers mainly from the field of Psychology have examined the role of different cognitive traits in computer-mediated learning (De Stefano & Lefevre, 2007; Graff, 2003; Graff 2005, Bilda, 2007; Parkinson & Redmond, 2002; Federico, 2000; Workman, 2004). It is evident that the constructs of learning and cognitive styles have proven to be quite popular in this area, whilst the concept of the Working Memory (WM) has also gained some popularity in terms of examining interaction of WM span with different hypertext levels of complexity (De Stefano, 2007; Lee &

Tender, 2003). Moreover, there have been efforts to build more complex models of human factors that may be proven useful in e-learning applications (Germanakos et al, 2007a; Lin, Kinshuk & Patel, 2003).

The main idea behind these approaches is to improve the effectiveness of web-based instruction by not ignoring individuals' top-down processes (Eysenck & Keane, 2005), and to determine which factors (mainly cognitive) have a dominant role in web-based information processing. These efforts could be characterized as the first steps of introducing the notion of individual differences into web-based education, even if there are severe limitations imposed by the structure of the web.

On the basis of the aforementioned research directions in e-learning, we are in the process of developing and evaluating both a theoretical model of information processing in the web (Germanakos et al, 2007a), and a corresponding Adaptive Hypermedia system that implements our theoretical approach and assumptions (Germanakos et al, 2007b). Our experimental model is comprised of three dimensions: Cognitive Style, Cognitive Processing Efficiency and Emotional Processing. The first dimension is unitary, whereas Cognitive Processing Efficiency is comprised of (a) Working Memory Span (WMS) (Baddeley, 1992) and (b) speed and control of information processing (Demetriou, 1993). The emotional aspect of the model focuses on different aspects of anxiety (Cassady & Johnson, 2002; Cassady, 2004; Spielberger, 1983) and self-regulation.

Existing hypermedia systems mostly focus on a single cognitive construct, usually learning style, and both evaluation and assessment of the system in terms of benefit for the learners are often neglected or methodologically less elaborated. In our research we make efforts to theoretically introduce new concepts into web-based education and to experimentally assess the value of the proposed human factors. This process is continuous and revisions of the theoretical framework are driven by experimental results. In that sense, we differentiate our system from previous rather rigorous and not extensively evaluated system realizations.

Whilst the experiments we have conducted were focused consecutively on all three dimensions, we consider that the first level of evaluating our approach would be the assessment of the personalizing process on the basis of cognitive style and working memory. These two factors are somehow more supported in literature, in the sense that hypermedia design implications and guidelines are more easily extracted from the theoretical framework.

It should be mentioned though that building a web-based system that can automatically adapt the educational content to learners' preferences or abilities is a difficult and challenging problem. It requires an automated mechanism that is not possible to include all aspects of a cognitive psychological theory; the web structure can be altered but not without limitations, web objects are of a specific form (pre-determined images, text, video and audio), and the "intelligent" functions of an application are in fact rule-based. Therefore, while a tutor in a traditional classroom can interpret and apply a theory in a flexible and intuitive way, in the case of an online educational system designers have to experimentally conclude to an implementation suitable for most learners.

This paper addresses two main issues respectively: (a) to examine how can a web-based system incorporate cognitive traits such as cognitive style and working memory in consistence to theory that has not been grounded in the context of the web and (b) to evaluate whether personalizing an e-learning procedure on the basis of such traits can increase learners' levels of comprehension (or performance). It is clear of course that the former is a prerequisite for the latter.

The next section presents the rationale behind incorporating specific theories into our approach, with regards to the nature of the web. Section 3 presents the way our system provides personalization that is consistent to our theoretical assumptions. The experimental methodology and results/discussion are presented at sections 4 and 5 respectively, while the last section focuses on conclusions, further research considerations and limitations of the study.

THEORETICAL BACKGROUND

As mentioned above, the factors that we focused upon at this phase of our research were cognitive style and visual working memory span (VWMS). Both these constructs are related to information processing, and the actual effect of these parameters in the context of the web is yet to be elucidated. As it will be discussed later, what is more important is the interaction of these two parameters that has yielded interesting results.

Cognitive Style

Cognitive style has been defined by Messick as consistent individual differences in preferred ways of organizing and processing information and experience, a construct that is different than learning style (Sadler-Smith, 2001). Cognitive styles represent an individual's typical or habitual mode of problem solving, thinking, perceiving or remembering, and "are considered to be trait-like, relatively stable characteristics of individuals, whereas learning strategies are more state-driven…" (McKay, Fischler & Dunn, 2003). The use of cognitive style has also been supported by Sternberg and Grigorenko (1997) as "…an important interface at the border of personality and cognition".

According to Curry's onion model (Curry, 1983), cognitive style theories fall into the innermost layer of "cognitive personality style", which is the most stable and relatively permanent; the factor of stability is quite important in user profiling considerations that will be discussed later.

A study by Lee et al (2005) suggests that style is essential in order to accommodate for different user needs. Indeed, this idea has been explored in systems such as the INSPIRE (Papanikolaou et al, 2003), CS383 (Carver, Howard & Lane, 1999), Arthur (Gilbert & Han, 2002) and AES-CS (Triantafillou, Pomportsis and Demetriadis, 2003) to name a few.

Amongst an impressive number of cognitive and learning style theories (Cassidy, 2004; Rayner & Riding, 97), we have used the concept of cognitive rather than learning style for a number of reasons:

- Cognitive style is not restricted to the context of strictly educational settings, since the focus is on information processing in general. This seems to be better aligned with the generic structure of the web, where learning can be widely differentiated from traditional classroom environments and strategies.
- Learning styles are "a construct that by definition is not stable- it was grounded in process and therefore susceptible to rapid change" (Rayner, 01).
- Most learning style theories, such as Kolb's (2005), Honey and Mumford's (1986) or Dunn's (1989), have a social dimension in the proposed typologies; some types are more socially oriented in learning than others. However, web-based education is often an individual process, usually asynchronous. Therefore, since we are also interested in building a generic model of information processing in the web, this family of typologies includes parameters that are not found in web-based environments.

More specifically, Riding and Cheema's Cognitive Style Analysis (CSA) has been used for quite relevant reasons. The CSA is actually derived from a factor analytic approach on previous cognitive style theories, summarizing a number of different yet highly correlated constructs into two distinct independent dimensions (Riding and Cheema, 1991). This covers a wide array of the former cognition based style typologies, without going into unnecessary depth- for the needs of web education that is.

Most importantly, the two independent scales of the CSA (verbal/imager and wholist/analyst) correspond ideally to the structure of web environments. A personalized environment that is supported by an automated mechanism can be altered mainly at the levels of content selection and hypermedia structure; the content is essentially either visual or verbal (or auditory), while the manipulation of links can lead to a more analytic and segmented structure, or to a more holistic and cohesive environment. These are actually the differences in the preferences of learners that belong to each dimension of the CSA scales (Sadler-Smith & Riding, 1999).

Subsequently, the mapping of personalized educational material on learners' preferences (or profiles) can take an actual form of well defined rules and it does not rely on heavily hypothesizing or is susceptible to designers' subjective reasoning (e.g. what is considered to fit better an accommodator or an assimilator according to Kolb's theory?).

An interesting point of view over the physiological basis of cognitive style and the use of the CSA as a psychometric tool of classification is the correlation with hemispherical preference and EEG measurements that has been reported (Glass & Riding, 1997; McKay, Fischler & Dunn, 2003). This seems to strengthen the relationship between cognitive style and actual mode of information processing.

Finally, the CSA has been also applied in other multimedia applications with significant results (Ghinea & Chen, 2003), while the test has been developed electronically; therefore we didn't have to worry about how to construct an electronic version of a psychometric tool.

At this point we must clarify that we are not unaware of reports that question the reliability of the CSA (Rezai & Katz, 2004; Peterson, Deary & Austin, 2003). The assessment of style is still an issue, and definitely practical reasons such as the ones described above should not become the sole criterion of adopting a theory. However, judging from our results that will be presented later, research-wise the CSA has been shown to support its underlying theoretical basis, at least within the boundaries of a web-based environment.

Conclusively, our rationale behind using the construct of cognitive style as a personalization factor in educational hypermedia is to provide learning environments that are matched to learners' preferences, in order to increase their level of comprehension and performance. Consequently, our research hypothesis is that those who are taught in the supposedly ideal condition of matched teaching and learning style will outperform other learners.

Working Memory

The concept of working memory (Baddeley, 1981) also fits very well into our rationale of personalizing the educational web-content on the basis of learners' cognitive abilities and preferences. "The term working memory refers to a brain system that provides temporary storage and manipulation of the information necessary for such complex cognitive tasks as language comprehension, learning, and reasoning" (Baddeley, 1992); Baddeley also refers to individual differences in the working memory (digit) span of the population, thus providing a very good argument for using this concept as a personalization factor.

A brief description of the working memory system is that is consisted of the central executive that controls the two slave systems (visuo-spatial sketchpad and phonological loop), plus the episodic buffer that provides a temporary interface between the slave systems and the Long Term Memory (Baddeley, 2000). We are mainly inter-

ested in the notion of the working memory span, since it can be measured and the implications on information processing are rather clear. Due to the visual form of presentation in the web, we have focused especially on the measurement of visual working memory (Logie, Zucco & Baddeley, 1990) in terms of psychometrics- this will be discussed further in the methodology section.

The idea of exploring the role of working memory in hypertext environments has indeed generated research. DeStefano and LeFevre (2007) reviewed 38 studies that address mainly the issue of cognitive load in hypertext reading, and working memory is often considered as an individual factor of significant importance, even at the level of explaining differences in performance. Lee and Tedder (2003) examine the role of working memory in different computer texts, and their results show that low working memory span learners do not perform equally well in hypertext environments. The term Cognitive Load Theory is often used when referring to guidelines for designing hypermedia applications, and it is often correlated with working memory span (Kirchsner, 2002).

As depicted in the previous section, the role of working memory will not been examined separately, but in parallel with cognitive style. Our proposed web-based environment provides personalization on the basis of both these two parameters, and their combined effect is expected to support the argument for personalization on cognitive traits. This somehow differentiates our approach from the ones mentioned above, in the sense that in our case the hypermedia structure is mainly affected by cognitive style rather than working memory span, while the latter concept affects the amount of information provided (as to decrease cognitive load).

The interaction of working memory and cognitive style has also been explored by Riding, Grimley, Dahrai and Banner (2003). In sum, their results show that in a traditional classroom setting analytics and verbalizers are more susceptible to working memory span deficiencies, since both these methods of processing information are more demanding in resources. Though this is probably true, our rationale is to alleviate such differences in performance by personalizing the online educational environment to each learner's preferences.

Therefore, the approach we describe in this paper leads to an educational adaptive hypermedia architecture that may be separated into subsequent phases (Figure 1).

Firstly, according to learner's visual or verbal preference, the appropriate content is selected; this of course requires adequate learning objects or resources (both visual and verbal), but it's rather a technical than a theoretical issue. Next, the structure of the environment is built upon learner's way of organizing information (holistically or analytically). This includes the organization of links, the navigational tools and the amount of learner control (framed/holistic or free/analytic navigation). Finally, the segmentation of simultaneously presented information is affected by individual's visual memory digit span. The aggregation of the aforementioned personalization factors leads to a personalized educational environment. The whole process is supported by existing Information Technologies (IT).

The theoretical approach we have described has necessary lead us to the following research questions:

- Is it possible to map learners' cognitive style and working memory span on an adaptive educational environment in a coherent and meaningful way?
- Are these parameters actually important in the context of web-based education, in terms of increasing comprehension and performance?

Before presenting the methodology and the results of the experiment we have conducted, we should briefly describe how our system maps learners' cognitive preferences on the information space.

THE ADAPTIVE WEB INTERFACE

The reasons for this brief description of the educational platform that has been used to conduct our experiments are: (a) to illustrate an instructional approach that in our opinion "translates" the cognitive theories that we have adopted into web-design implications and (b) to provide the reader with a more specific and comprehensive insight of the overall methodology we have used.

At the level of e-learning instruction, we should point that the issue of general approved design guidelines is not yet resolved, and we consider that this happens also with the use of learning/cognitive styles by previous efforts in adaptive hypermedia systems. The working memory span implications, on the other hand, seem to be better elaborated.

The system and a "guided" tour can be accessed in the following url: http://www3.cs.ucy.ac.cy/ adaptiveweb/.

Figure 1. Personalization architecture

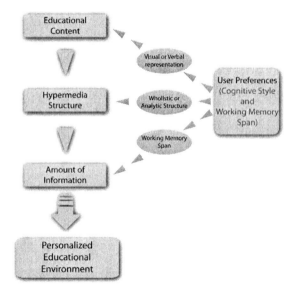

Nevertheless, in our system these cognitive factors are translated in a coherent way into actual learning personalization parameters, remaining as consistent as possible to the theories described in the previous section (Riding, 91; Baddeley, 1992), as follows:

- **Imager (cognitive style):** Images, diagrams and schemes are used, when possible, for the representation of information. Specifically, instead of lengthy verbal descriptions, a schematic approach has been adopted as an equally important mean of instruction. Text is also used, but is reduced by app. 40% in comparison to verbal learners.
- **Verbal (cognitive style):** The prominent representation of information is textual, and images are used when required, accompanying and not replacing texts.
- **Analyst (cognitive style):** In the analytic condition, learners are free to navigate through the educational environment. They are not guided externally, though they may choose to follow a linear suggested path. They also have access to a separate index of concepts in order to follow an analytic path in accessing information and forming knowledge. The information is extensively interconnected since hypertext is used at a greater extent, and users can access at the same time different parts of the educational content.
- **Wholist (cognitive style):** In the wholist condition learners navigate through the environment in an externally guided way, which provides prefixed linkage and descriptions of the sequentially interconnected information. The organization of the distinct parts of the course is strict and outlined in a clear way. Users have access to previously acquired information, but they do not have access to links that lead to information of chapters not visited. Additional guiding information is constantly given.

Figure 2 illustrates the differences between the imager/wholist and the verbal/analytic version of the same webpage:

- **Intermediate (cognitive style):** Intermediate users are provided with an environment which combines characteristics of all dimensions of cognitive style, in order to maintain a balance; moreover, they serve as a control group in our experiments.

Figure 2. An imager/wholist (left) and a verbal analytic environment (right)

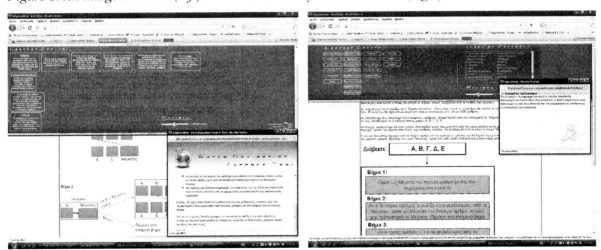

- **Low Visual Working Memory Span:** Since a large amount of information, especially when presented in the form of hypertext, may impair learners' comprehension, the system presents web-objects in a consecutive way, allowing users to devote more reading time to each resource. Learning objects do not disappear when the next ones are provided; on the contrary, each lesson "unfolds" gradually.
- **Medium/High Visual Working Memory Span:** Users with medium and high WMS are treated the same, since we are interested in alleviating difficulties and not boosting efficient learners.

It is evident that the instructional value of such an approach can be evaluated only experimentally, in the absence of well defined grounded guidelines for the purposes of web-based education.

METHOD

Our results were gathered from two subsequent experiments. In both cases, the experimental design was a between participants memory posttest, in order to assess the differences in performance between learners who were taught in a personalized, matched to their preferences way, and those who were taught in a way that was not consistent to their cognitive preferences. Those that were classified as intermediates (no cognitive style preference) received a non-personalized balanced environment.

The three conditions (matched, mismatched and "intermediate" way of teaching) were expected to provide statistically significantly different results only if the factors involved are indeed important for web-based learning.

The first experiment was conducted at the University of Cyprus, while the second was conducted at the University of Athens. The aim of the first experiment was to clarify whether

matching (or mismatching) instructional style to users' cognitive style improves performance. The second experiment focused on the importance of matching instructional style to VWMS.

Sample and Procedure

All participants were students from the Universities of Cyprus and Athens; experiment I was conducted with a sample of 138 students, whilst experiment II with 209 individuals. Approximately 30% of the participants were male and 70% were female, and their age varied from 17 to 22 with a mean age of 19. Participating in the experiment was voluntary, though most students were willing to take the course, as an additional help on a difficult academic subject that is part of their academic curriculum. We should clarify that there was not any pretesting, or restrictions to participation, other than lack of previous knowledge. Both experiments were conducted in July of 2007.

The environment in which the procedure took place was an e-learning introductory course on algorithms. The specific subject was chosen due to the fact that students of the social sciences departments where the experiment took place had absolutely no experience of programming and computer science and traditionally perform poorly. By controlling the factor of experience in that way, we divided our sample in two groups: almost half of the participants were provided with information matched to their cognitive preferences, while the other half were taught in a mismatched way. We expected that users in the matched condition, both in experiments I and II, would outperform those in the mismatched condition. The two groups were divided randomly, in the sense that each user that logged into the system received the opposite to the previous user condition.

In order to evaluate the effect of matched and mismatched conditions, participants took an online memory test on the subject they were taught (algorithms). This exam was taken as soon as the e-learning procedure ended, in order to control for long-term memory decay effects. The dependent variable that was used to assess the effect of adaptation to users' preferences was participants' score at the posttest.

Learners accessed the environment through a web browser, using personal computers located at the laboratories of both universities. Participants took the tests and built their profiles before participating at the online course. Users' profiles were kept at the system database. The assignment of participants in the matched or mismatched condition was quasi random- the first user that logged in received a matched environment, the second a mismatched, and the condition was consecutively alternated. The system provided a matched or mismatched environment for each user by accessing his/her profile from the database. The actualization of each environment was based on a simple algorithm; according to each user characteristic, a visible aspect of the environment was personalized on the basis of the aforementioned rules presented in section 3.

The profiling procedure lasted for about 20 minutes; after that, users' were encouraged to take a 5-10 min break. The course lasted for approximately 40 minutes, and the memory test for about 15 minutes.

Materials

In this specific e-learning setting, cognitive style and VWMS were the main parameters consisting each user profile, since demographics and traditional profiling characteristics were controlled for by the homogeneity of the sample (although we also gathered information concerning these parameters).

The tools we used were:

- **Cognitive Style:** Riding's Cognitive Style Analysis, standardized in Greek and implemented in the .NET platform. The test is separated in three parts: the first part as-

sesses the imager/verbalizer dimension by calculating the time required for participants to construct mental representations of 24 given sentences. In the following two phases, the time that users devote to integrate or disambiguate two sets of figures indicates their position on the analyst/wholist axis. The latter phases are based on Witkin's et al Group Embedded Figures Test (1971).

- **Visual Working Memory Span:** Visuospatial working memory test (Demetriou, A., Christou, C., Spanoudis, G., & Platsidou, M., 2002), firstly developed at the E-prime platform, afterwards implemented in the .NET platform. This visual memory test examines participants' ability to temporarily store visual figures. Each figure that has to be remembered is shown for two seconds, and afterwards a set of five figures is presented, including the one that had to be stored. Users are asked to identify the figure that was shown before. Complexity and resemblance of the stimuli increases gradually. There are a total of 21 figures, divided in three broad categories: low VWMS learners should to be able to answer the first group of seven, medium VWMS learners are expected to progress to the next seven, while the remaining seven require high visual working memory span.

The reasons we used the CSA were presented at the theoretical framework section of the paper. Regarding the use of the specific working memory span measurement tool, we adopted the specific approach because it can be easily presented visually in a computer screen, and most importantly all information presented in the experimental procedure is actually visual and not auditory; therefore we considered that measuring this aspect of the working memory span can provide an adequate indication of learners' WM span in the web environment.

The e-learning course, the profiling building procedure and the psychometric tools can be accessed at http://www3.cs.ucy.ac.cy/adaptiveweb/.

RESULTS AND DISCUSSION

Experiment I

As hypothesized, the mean score of those that received matched to their cognitive style environments is higher than the mean score achieved by those that learned within the mismatched condition (see table 1). Since the variance of participants' scores was homogeneous (Levene's statistic=0.20, p=0.980) one way analysis of variance was performed on the data. The difference in score between the three groups (matched, mismatched and intermediates) is statistically significant: $F_{(2,137)}$=3.479, p=0.034 (see table 2).

Post hoc analysis has shown that the difference is significant only between groups in the matched and the mismatched condition (8.741 percentage points in the memory posttest), whilst intermediates do not differ from any of the other two categories (see table 3).

As depicted in the theoretical framework section, intermediate users have no specific cognitive style preference. Consequently, they received a non-personalized (though balanced) environment; this may explain the fact that their mean score does not differ significantly from those that learned in the matched condition, since any environment could be proven as matched for them.

Still, the fact that their score also does not differ from the mismatched condition participants', could perhaps be attributed to some other variable that may be of significant importance in performance, as long as there are not cognitive style preferences to be satisfied.

We should note that a closer inspection of the means for all categories of learners placed in both axes of cognitive style (Imager/Intermediate/Verbalizer and Wholist/Intermediate/Analyst) shows that the differences in score are often very high

Table 1. Descriptives of differences in mean score of matched and mismatched condition

Score %

	N	Mean	Std. Deviation	Std. Error	95% Confidence Interval for Mean		Minimum	Maximum
					Lower Bound	Upper Bound		
Matched	53	66.53	18.901	2.596	61.32	71.74	13	100
Mismatched	61	57.79	18.149	2.324	53.14	62.44	9	93
Intermediate	24	58.58	18.429	3.762	50.80	66.37	22	93
Total	138	61.28	18.821	1.602	58.11	64.45	9	100

Table 2. ANOVA for differences in mean score of matched and mismatched condition

Score %

	Sum of Squares	df	Mean Square	F	Sig.
Between Groups	2378.708	2	1189.354	3.479	**.034**
Within Groups	46153.270	135	341.876		
Total	48531.978	137			

between the two conditions, with the exception of the Verbalizer-Wholist learners, who do not seem to benefit from the personalization of the web-content. This can be explained by the fact that the specific cognitive style preference is considered to be complementary (Riding & Wigley, 1997) and more adaptive to mismatched situations.

Though learners' VWMS was not a factor of personalization in this experiment, this measurement was also available. This independent variable had no effect of its own, nor interaction with each experimental condition (matched/ mismatched/ intermediate environment) on participants' scores. Also, in the mismatched and intermediate condition, VWMS is insignificant.

However, in the matched condition VWMS becomes significant, since a 3X3 ANOVA has shown interaction between WMS and the Wholist/Analytic dimension on participants' scores ($F_{(4,52)}=3.506$, p=0.014) . According to theory, analysts are in further need of working memory span in order to use their analytic mode of processing; thus, analysts with low working memory span should perform worse- which is the case with this experiment. Besides that, wholists also benefit from high levels of VWMS (though not from medium levels), whilst intermediates demonstrate a rather reverse behaviour (see table 4). This latter finding is somehow puzzling, and it should be further experimentally investigated.

Table 3. Post hoc analysis of differences in mean scores
Dependent Variable: Score %
Tukey HSD

(I) Matched Environment	(J) Matched Environment	Mean Difference (I-J)	Sig.
Matched	Mismatched	8.741(*)	**.034**
	Intermediate	7.945	.192
Mismatched	Matched	-8.741(*)	**.034**
	Intermediate	-.796	.983

* The mean difference is significant at the .05 level.

Table 4. Estimated marginal means of Wholist/Analyst dimension interaction with VWMS
Dependent Variable: Score %

Wholist/Analyst	W.M.S.	Mean	Std. Error	95% Confidence Interval	
				Lower Bound	Upper Bound
Analyst	Low	63.000	8.818	45.228	80.772
	Medium	100.000	10.800	78.234	121.766
	High	87.000	10.800	65.234	108.766
Intermediate	Low	85.500	7.637	70.109	100.891
	Medium	66.400	6.831	52.634	80.166
	High	74.833	6.235	62.267	87.400
Wholist	Low	56.917	4.409	48.031	65.803
	Medium	55.357	4.082	47.130	63.584
	High	76.400	6.831	62.634	90.166

The findings of this experiment may support the notion that applying a cognitive style theory in the context of the web could be proven useful for learners, or at least that mismatching the web-environment to their preferences may hamper their performance. The mean difference of app. 9% is not striking of course, but taking under consideration the little variance of participants' scores, it could be supported that organizing information in the web-space according to learners' preferences can provide added value to an e-learning application.

Experiment II

In this experiment, only learners with low VWMS are involved in the two conditions (match/mismatch); those with medium/high VWMS are considered as a control group that do not require any manipulation of the web-content in order to learn efficiently.

The results are quite similar to the first experiment. Segmentation of the web-content for low VWMS learners (matched condition) increases their performance, while users that receive the same with the control group content perform worse (see table 5). Since the variance of participants' scores was homogeneous (Levene's statistic=1.038, p=0.356), one way ANOVA has shown that this difference is statistically significant: $F=5.623_{(2,208)}$, p=0.004 (see table 6).

Post hoc analysis of the data has shown that mismatched (low VWMS) learners differ significantly from the control group (minus 10.086 percentage points), while matched (low VWMS) learners do not. Even so, since matched learners have scored between the two other categories, they also do not differ significantly from the mismatched learners (see table 7).

Subsequently, since cognitive style preference is controlled for, it seems that VWMS is significant in achieving higher performance. Nevertheless,

Table 5. Descriptives of differences in mean score of matched and mismatched condition
Score %

	N	Mean	Std. Deviation	Std. Error	95% Confidence Interval for Mean		Minimum	Maximum
					Lower Bound	Upper Bound		
match	42	56.10	18.404	2.840	50.36	61.83	26	93
mismatch	41	50.05	15.735	2.457	45.08	55.02	20	82
control	126	60.13	16.817	1.498	57.17	63.10	19	93
Total	209	57.34	17.317	1.198	54.98	59.71	19	93

Table 6. ANOVA for differences in mean score of matched and mismatched condition
Score %

	Sum of Squares	df	Mean Square	F	Sig.
Between Groups	3228.968	2	1614.484	5.623	**.004**
Within Groups	59144.228	206	287.108		
Total	62373.196	208			

personalizing the web-content according to users' working memory span seems to moderate the negative effect of low VWMS on learning. This is actually the idea that supports the notion of personalization in adaptive web-environments: to incorporate into the system functional components that address users' needs in a way that their differences are not hampering their information processing of the web-content in an equally efficient way.

Nonetheless, it must be clearly stated that this interaction needs to be elaborated in a more complex process of personalization, by addressing more aspects of individual differences in working memory span. These results can be considered as rather indicative of the role of working memory in web-based indication, which of course is not really a novel finding, and most importantly provide a basis for investigating ways to alleviate difficulties that individual differences may impose on e-learning processes.

CONCLUSION

The notion of integrating individual differences approaches from the field of social sciences, predominantly derived from psychological research, has a great appeal to developers of information and learning multimedia/hypermedia systems.

The fact that the technologies that such systems are based on often have an adaptive and/or semantic nature enhances the role and importance of individual user profiling. Since it is now possible to develop systems that adapt to each unique user, processes such as learning can be highly personalized.

Nevertheless, these technologies and the predefined at some extend structure of hypermedia/multimedia systems impose certain constraints on the individual characteristics that can be included in users' profile in order to comprise personalization factors. More specifically, in the case of e-learning, though there are many educational and pedagogical theories of undisputable value, the structure of the web limits the range of possible implementations.

Our approach focuses on matching some aspects of web-based learning to learners' corresponding characteristics, with regards to the organization, presentation and segmentation of information. Constructs such as cognitive style (especially based on the axis of field dependence/field independence) and working memory seem to address these issues at a satisfying extent.

The experiments presented in this paper also seem to validate such an approach, though not at a conclusive level, since there are limitations in our study that should be also taken into account. First of all, building web-environments that

Table 7. Post hoc analysis of differences in mean scores
Dependent Variable: Score %
Tukey HSD

(I) Matched WM	(J) Matched WM	Mean Difference (I-J)	Sig.
match	mismatch	6.046	.237
mismatch	control	-10.086(*)	**.003**
control	match	4.040	.376
	mismatch	10.086(*)	**.003**

* *The mean difference is significant at the .05 level.*

respond to learners' preferences has been a trial and error procedure, since there is no comprehensive theory of web-design with regards to these issues. The translation of theory into practice is by itself a challenge, which has been carried out in a conservative way. Experimentally, our web environment has provided us with rather clear indications, but in terms of a comprehensive learning system there is more research to be conducted. Moreover, even if the role of VWMS has been experimentally underlined, the personalization process should be more elaborated than simply segmenting the web-content, although this has been proven somehow useful.

We also did not take into account the social aspect of web-learning and the implications of collaborative learning, which are certainly of importance, but instead we have focused exclusively on individuals' processing of web-information. Perhaps in a collaborative environment these factors could interact with socializing processes in an interesting way. Finally, we used the specific psychometric tools not only because of the theories underlying them, but also for convenience reasons (suitable and optimized for the web).

Besides further experimental evaluation of the role of working memory (and not merely visual working memory span), a major part of our future work is the role of the emotional state of the user and possible interactions with the cognitive constructs that this paper addresses. We have already constructed a computer mouse that has Galvanic Skin Response and heart rate sensors integrated, and we are in the process of seeking out personalization rules for learners with high levels of academic anxiety. The utter aim is to gradually develop a comprehensive user model for educational adaptive hypermedia. Still, for the time being, experiments are conducted in the direction of an in-depth exploration of Baddeley's working memory model not only in educational but also in e-services web-environments.

Even so, in the specific context of web-learning, learners that are being taught in an environment

that is personalized on the basis of their cognitive style and VWMS outperform those that do not have their preferences satisfied. The latter may be the case with non-personalized e-learning courses, where the designers' style predominates, allowing random matching or mismatching of teaching and learning style. Though we do not claim that an event like that would undoubtedly be heavily influencing learners in a negative way, there could possibly be a difference in performance, mainly attributed to such a random matching/mismatching.

Personalization, on the other hand, aims to the resolution of these issues, and in our opinion the constructs of cognitive style and working memory seem to offer an insight with regards to the ways people interact with a web-based learning environment; thus, optimization of performance may be significantly correlated with satisfying learners' preferences.

REFERENCES

Baddeley, A. (2000). The episodic buffer: A new component of working memory? *Trends in Cognitive Sciences, 11*(4), 417-423.

Baddeley, A. (1992). Working memory. *Science, 255*, 556-559.

Baddeley, A. (1981). The concept of working memory: A view of its current state and probable future development. *Cognition, 10*(1-3), 17-23.

Bilda, Z., & Gero, J. S. (2007). The impact of working memory limitations on the design process during conceptualization. *Design Studies, 28*(4), 343-367.

Brusilovsky, P., & Nejd, W. (2004). Adaptive hypermedia and adaptive Web. In M. P. Singh (Ed.), *The practical handbook of Internet computing* (pp. 1.1-1.14). USA: Chapman & Hall/CRC.

Carver, C. A., Jr., Howard, R. A., & Lane, W. D. (1999). Enhancing student learning through hypermedia courseware and incorporation of student learning styles. *IEEE Transactions on Education, 42*(1), 33-38.

Cassady, J. C., & Jonhson, R. E. (2002). Cognitive test anxiety and academic performance. *Contemporary Educational Psychology, 27*(2), 270-295.

Cassady, J. C. (2004). The influence of cognitive test anxiety across the learning–testing cycle. *Learning and Instruction, 14*(6), 569-592.

Cassidy, S. (2004). Learning styles: An overview of theories, models, and measures. *Educational Psychology, 24*(4), 419-444.

Curry, L. (1983). *An organization of learning styles theory and constructs.* Paper presented at the Annual Meeting of the American Educational Research Association, 67th, Montreal, Quebec.

De Bra, P., Aroyo, L., & Chepegin, V. (2004). The next big thing: Adaptive Web-based systems. *Journal of Digital Information, 5*(1).

De Bra, P., & Calvi, L. (1998). AHA: A generic adaptive hypermedia system. In *Proceedings of the 2nd Workshop on Adaptive Hypertext and Hypermedia, HYPERTEXT'98*, Pittsburgh, USA.

Demetriou, A., Christou, C., Spanoudis, G., & Platsidou, M. (2002). The development of mental processing: Efficiency, working memory, and thinking. *Monographs of the Society for Research in Child Development, 67*(1), 1-155.

Demetriou, A., Efklides, A., & Platsidou, M. (1993). *The architecture and dynamics of developing mind: Experiential structuralism as a frame for unifying cognitive development theories* (Monographs of the Society for Research in Child Development). Chicago, IL: University of Chicago Press.

DeStefano, D., & Lefevre, J. (2007). Cognitive load in hypertext reading: A review. *Computers in Human Behavior, 23*(3), 1616-1641.

Dunn, R., & Dunn, K. (1989). *Learning style inventory.* Lawrence, KS: Price Systems.

Eklund, J., & Sinclair, K. (2000). An empirical appraisal of the effectiveness of adaptive interfaces of instructional systems. *Educational Technology and Society, 3*(4), 165-177.

Eysenck, M. W., & Keane, M. T. (2005). *Cognitive psychology.* (5th ed.). New York: Psychology Press.

Federico, P. (2000). Learning styles and student attitudes toward various aspects of network-based instruction. *Computers in Human Behavior, 16*(4), 359-379.

Germanakos, P., Tsianos, N., Lekkas, Z., Mourlas, C., & Samaras, G. (2007a). Capturing essential intrinsic user behaviour values for the design of comprehensive Web-based personalized environments. *Computers in Human Behavior (2007).* doi:10.1016/j.chb.2007.07.010

Germanakos, P., Tsianos, N., Lekkas, Z., Mourlas, C., Belk, M., & Samaras G. (2007b). An adaptive Web system for integrating human factors in personalization of Web content. In *Proceedings of the 11th International Conference on User Modeling (UM 2007)*, Corfu, Greece.

Ghinea, G., & Chen, S. Y. (2003). The impact of cognitive styles on perceptual distributed multimedia quality. *British Journal of Educational Technology, 34*(4), 393-406.

Gilbert, J. E., & Han, C. Y. (2002). Arthur: A personalized instructional system. *Journal of Computing in Higher Education, 14*(1), 113-129.

Glass, A., & Riding, R. J. (1999). EEG differences and cognitive style. *Biological Psychology, 51*(1), 23-41.

Graff, M. G. (2003). Learning from Web-based instructional systems and cognitive style. *British Journal of Educational Technology, 34*(4), 407-418.

Graff, M. G. (2005). Differences in concept mapping, hypertext architecture, and the analyst–intuition dimension of cognitive style. *Educational Psychology, 25*(4), 409-422.

Honey, P., & Mumford, A. (1986). *A manual of learning styles.* Maidenhead, UK: Peter Honey Publications.

Kirschner, P. A. (2002). Cognitive load theory: Implications of cognitive load theory on the design of learning. *Learning and Instruction, 12*(1), 1-10.

Kolb, A. Y., & Kolb, D. A. (2005). *The Kolb learning style inventory – version 3.1 2005 technical specifications.* Boston, MA: Haygroup Experience Based Learning Systems Inc.

Lee, C. H. M., Cheng, Y. W., Rai, S., & Depickere, A. (2005). What affect student cognitive style in the development of hypermedia learning system. *Computers & Education, 45*(2005), 1-19.

Lee, M. J., & Tedder, M. C. (2003). The effects of three different computer texts on readers' recall: Based on working memory capacity. *Computers in Human Behavior, 19*(6), 767-783.

Lin, T., Kinshuk, & Patel, A. (2003). Cognitive trait model for persistent student modelling. In D. Lassner & C. McNaught (Eds.), *EdMedia 2003 Conference Proceedings*, Norfolk, USA.

Loggie, R. H., Zucco, G. N., & Baddeley, A. D. (1990). Interference with visual short-term memory. *Acta Psychologica, 75*(1), 55-74.

McKay, M. T., Fischler, I., & Dunn, B. R. (2003). Cognitive style and recall of text: An EEG analysis. *Learning and Individual Differences, 14*(1), 1-21.

Papanikolaou, K. A., Grigoriadou, M., Kornilakis, H., & Magoulas, G. D. (2003). Personalizing the interaction in a Web-based educational hypermedia system: The case of INSPIRE. *User-Modelling and User-Adapted Interaction, 13*(3), 213-267.

Parkinson, A., & Redmond, J. A. (2002). Do cognitive styles affect learning performance in different computer media? In *Proceedings of the Annual Joint Conference Integrating Technology into Computer Science Education, Proceedings of the 7th annual conference on Innovation and technology in computer science education*, Aarhus, Denmark (pp. 39-43).

Peterson, E. R., Deary, I. J., & Austin, E. J. (2003). The reliability of Riding's cognitive style analysis test. *Personality and Individual Differences, 34*(5), 881-891.

Picard, R. W. (1997). *Affective computing.* Cambridge, MA: MIT Press.

Rayner, S. (2001). Cognitive styles and learning styles. In N. J. Smelser & P. B. Baltes (Eds.), *International encyclopedia of social & behavioral Sciences.* UK: Elsevier Science Ltd.

Rayner, S. & Riding, R. (1997). Towards a categorisation of cognitive styles and learning styles. *Educational Psychology, 17*(1/2), 5-27.

Rezaei, A. R., & Katz, R. (2004). Evaluation of the reliability and validity of the cognitive styles analysis. *Personality and Individual Differences, 36*(6), 1317-1327.

Riding, R. J., Grimley, M., Dahraei, H., & Banner, G. (2003). Cognitive style, working memory and learning behaviour and attainment in school subjects. *British Journal of Educational Psychology, 73*(2), 149-169.

Riding, R. J., & Cheema, I. (1991). Cognitive styles – an overview and integration. *Educational Psychology, 11*(3/4), 193-215.

Riding, R. J., & Wigley, S., (1997). The relationship between cognitive style and personality in further education students. *Personality and Individual Differences, 23*(3), 379-389.

Sadler-Smith, E. (2001). The relationship between learning style and cognitive style. *Personality and Individual Differences, 30*(4), 609-616.

Sadler-Smith, E., & Riding, R. J. (1999). Cognitive style and instructional preferences. *Instructional Science, 27*(5), 355-371.

Spielberger, C. D. (1983). *Manual for the state-trait anxiety inventory (STAI)*. Palo Alto, CA: Consulting Psychologists Press.

Sternberg, R. J., & Grigorenko, E. L. (1997). Are cognitive styles still in style? *American Psychologist, 52*(7), 700-712.

Triantafillou, E., Pomportsis, A., & Demetriadis, S. (2003). The design and the formative evaluation of an adaptive educational system based on cognitive styles. *Computers & Education, 41*(2003), 87-103.

Witkin, H. A., Oltman, P. K., Raskin, E., & Karp, S. A. (1971). *Group embedded figures test manual*. Palo Alto, CA: Consulting Psychology Press.

Workman, M. (2004). Performance and perceived effectiveness in computer-based and computer-aided education: Do cognitive styles make a difference? *Computers in Human Behavior, 20*(4), 517-534.

Chapter X
The DEKOR System:
Personalization of Guided Access to Open Repositories

Christian Gütl

Graz University of Technology, Austria; Curtin University of Technology, Austria; Infodelio Information Systems and GÜTL IT Research & Consulting, Austria

Victor Manuel García-Barrios

Graz University of Technology, Austria

ABSTRACT

Due to the wide diversity of learning styles and learner characteristics, delivering learning material from modern ICT-based learning must also be conducted in a diverse manner rather than with a "one-fits-all" approach. By focusing on content aspects, the majority of adaptive Web-based educational systems are only able to deal with closed repositories and therefore only pre-defined content alternatives for limited learner characteristics are manageable. One possible solution is to enable and technologically support students' freedom to select appropriate learning content of their own choice. The WWW as an extensive repository of diverse content has gained considerable interest as an open-ended learning environment, but most students cannot cope well with such open accessibility. To overcome this, the authors have started research towards a system of personalized access to open repositories. In this book chapter, they introduce the evolution of their linked approaches and discuss the findings in the context of learner characteristics.

INTRODUCTION

Modern society has become significantly more globalized and knowledge-driven in recent decades. Consequently, modern citizens have high expectations for their ever-changing society. Keeping pace with changes and effectively dealing with knowledge is vital for the success in this modern environment, and continued learning and training are therefore also fundamental for today's human beings. According to Bransford et al. (2000), the objectives of and expectations for the learning process have changed dramatically from repetitive learning to learning with understanding to move towards being independent in the learning process, strengthen meta-cognitive skills and link knowledge acquired in cultural context. In order to meet the requirements of educational goals for the 21st century, several aspects of learner-centered, knowledge-centered and assessment-centered environments must be considered. In this context, information and communication technology (ICT) can be very useful in educational setting such as in general schools, universities and in vocational education centers.

By further focusing on the knowledge aspects or more precisely on the learning content within the learning process, it is commonly agreed that from modern ICT-based learning settings much more is expected than simply delivering learning material to students in a "one-fits-all" approach. Learning activities and learning content must be well-tailored to (1) the *individual needs* of the students including the knowledge or competence state, preferred learning style, motivation, problem-specific and cultural context, (2) *group aspects* such as student-student and teacher-student interactions and collaborations, (3) *teaching objectives* including didactic concepts and (4) *environmental aspects* such as physical learning environment and front-end devices. (Germanakos et al., 2007; Gütl, 2007b; Hodges, 2004) There is no doubt, however, that it is time consuming and expensive to prepare such personalized learning activities or to focus specifically on the learning content. To overcome this problem, some approaches have been developed such as reusable learning content (Conlan et al., 2002) and collaborative content creation (Kortemeyer, 1999). Despite the existence of such interesting approaches, the great variety of individual needs can hardly be met and the ever-changing knowledge in the

subject domain will lead to a Sisyphean task in keeping pace with this situation. (Thyagharajan & Nayak, 2007).

To overcome the situation stated so far, we have developed the Dynamic E-learning Knowledge Repository System (*DEKOR System*). The initial idea was motivated by the goal to supplement e-learning systems lacking personalization features with a background repository of resources that are automatically compiled for different knowledge levels by means of an information retrieval system. The first proof of concept was described in (Dietinger et al., 1998) and developed into a first prototype called *E-Help System* (García-Barrios et al., 2004). The findings from implementation and evaluation of E-Help led to a second prototype called Concept-based Context-Modeling System (*CO2 System*) which provides students with content from different types of information sources based on the learning context (Safran et al., 2006). Further enhancements led to our DEKOR system, which delivers personalized content from different sources based on user and group information (Gütl, 2007).

In this book chapter we want to outline the three systems mentioned above and explore the extent to which they can support different cognitive and learning styles.

BACKGROUND

Tailored learning and teaching activities can hardly be considered as new concepts developed in our modern knowledge society. Such concepts can be traced back to at least 4th century BC. In those days, adapted instructions were seen as a primary success factor. To give another example, tutoring given by adaptive instructions was a common method of education until the mid-1800s (Park & Lee, 2003). In the 20th century, instructional design and technology emerged, enabling the analysis of learning and performance problems to improve the learning process in diverse learning settings (Reiser, 2001). According to Bransford et al. (2000), the development of the science of learning itself began in the later part of the 19th century, when systematic attempts were made to study the human mind through scientific methods. Since that time, different theories and notions have emerged (Bransford et al., 2000; Sampson et al., 2002; Santally & Senteni, 2005). Active research in this area has shown that students' individual learning is strongly influenced by numerous dimensions.

Consequently, research on learner characteristics and their influence on the learning process has been an active research topic for a long time. It is out of the scope of this work to discuss this aspect in detail; however, to illustrate the complex situation, a selection of important characteristics and aspects are given in this section. The selected categorization of *learner characteristics* was strongly influenced by Schulmeister (2006) and Jonassen & Grabowski (1993). Many other categorization approaches exist in literature, however, and some of the characteristics in one category may address or include aspects of characteristics in other categories.

Learner Characteristics

The category of *cognitive styles* addresses variables describing the ways in which learners organize stimuli and construct meaning. They include: (1) perception by sensing (observation and gathering of data through senses) or intuition (unconscious perception, e.g. speculation, imagination, hunch), (2) modality input for effective perception (e.g. visual, auditory, kinesthetic), (3) organization of information preferred by learners, which can be either inductive (facts and observations are given, underlying principles are inferred) or deductive (principles are given, consequences and applications are deduced), (4) processing of information by either active experimentation (activities in the real world e.g. experimenting, discussing, testing) or reflective

observation (e.g. introspectively examining and manipulating information), (5) understanding built either by sequential learning (following a linear reasoning process) or holistic learning (following a more global or conceptual way), and (6) selective attention by field independence (analytical, competitive, individualistic or task-oriented) and field dependence (group-oriented, sensitive to social interactions and extrinsically motivated). (Blochl et al., 2003; Felder & Silverman, 1988; Hall, 2000)

The category of *cognitive control* addresses how an individual coordinates himself within his environment by variables that describe motor skills, perception, memory and other basic quantitative forms of cognitive functioning. Variables include: (1) field dependence vs. independence, (2) cognitive flexibility (constricted vs. flexible control expresses the ability to ignore distractions of the environment), (3) cognitive tempo (impulsivity vs. reflectivity), (4) focal attention (scanning vs. focusing), (5) category width (breadth of categorizing), (6) cognitive complexity vs. cognitive simplicity, and (7) automation (strong vs. weak automation). (Jonassen & Grabowski, 1993)

Personality is a category with more general aspects: (1) anxiety (negative and positive effects, which motivate and facilitate as well as disrupt and inhibit cognitive actions as learning), (2) ambiguity tolerance (willingness to accommodate or adapt to handle ambiguous situations or ideas), (3) frustration tolerance (quality of a person's performance in a task after frustration occurs), (4) extroversion vs. introversion (thinking and behavior that are directed either outwardly or inwardly), (5) locus of control (individual's feelings about the placement of control over his or hers life's events), (6) achievement motivation (individual's willingness to achieve), and (7) risky vs. cautious behavior (individual's preference to choose high-payoff/low-probability or low-payoff/high-probability alternatives). (Jonassen & Grabowski, 1993)

Prior knowledge addresses the knowledge, skills or abilities that students bring to the learning process. This category includes the following characteristics: (1) knowledge and skills in domain (the knowledge and skills the students already know related to the contents and which are necessary to understand new information), and (2) general knowledge and skills (domain-independent knowledge and skills, such as language skills, technology skills, social skills as well as cognitive strategies and meta-cognitive strategies). (Jonassen & Grabowski, 1993; Blochl et al., 2003; Bransford et al., 2000)

Further, Schulmeister (2006) has also outlined the category *mental abilities*, which addresses aspects of psychology of intelligence analysis. Mödritscher (2007) highlights the category *constitutional attributes and states*, which addresses physical properties of the body (e.g. age, special needs) and short-term states (e.g. emotion, tiredness, concentration).

From the aforementioned great number of learning characteristics, it can be concluded that learning is a very complex and highly individualized process. Therefore, a *learning style model* helps to classify students according to the way they receive and process information. Such models also support obtaining a better understanding about diverse learning processes. Efficient and effective knowledge transfer requires well-tailored instructional methods which must correspond to the individual's preferred learning style. Further, *teaching style models* help to classify instructional methods with respect to those learning style components that an instructional method addresses (Felder & Silverman, 1988).

(Un-)Successfulness of General Solutions

Knowledge about the great diversity of learning methods has led to the concept of personalized instructions. Since the beginning of the 20th century, various approaches and methods of adaptive instructions have been developed and attempted. Three highly relevant approaches that have strongly influenced computer-based systems for personalized learning are: (1) *macro-adaptive approach* (supports the selection of alternatives for main components of the instruction such as instructional goal, depths of curriculum content and delivery system), (2) *aptitude-treatment interaction (ATI) approach* (adapts instructional methods and strategies to specific student characteristics), and (3) *micro-level approach* (adapts to instructional prescriptions based on learners' needs during instructions). Since the early days of the computer era, computer media have been used for didactic purposes. Even computer-based personalized systems were already available at that time. Some worth mentioning are *Computer-Managed Instructional* (CMI) systems, *Intelligent Tutoring Systems* (ITS), and *Adaptive Educational Hypermedia* (AEH) systems (Brusilovsky, 2000; Park & Lee, 2003; Reiser, 2001b). Web-based AEH systems (based on concepts of link, content and presentation adaptation by using appropriate models) have gained increased interest since the mid 1990s (Brusilovsky, 2000; De Bra et al., 1999; Koch & Rossi, 2002).

In spite of the substantial interest in e-learning from diverse research and industrial sectors that has been evident for decades, just a few systems and projects can truly be seen as real success stories. The reasons can be found in both the high complexity of the subject domain itself and also in failures in the project management domain (Romiszowski, 2004; Wopereis et al., 2005). Given the great number and diversity of learner characteristics, it is virtually impossible to consider all of them in concrete implementations in terms of waging system functionality, capturing appropriate information about the users, and providing a useful set of content alternatives. Nevertheless, some evaluated successful adaptive e-learning systems exist, but they have concentrated only on very specific learner characteristics or adaptation methods for specific student groups (e.g. Papanikolaou et al., 2002; Brusilovsky, 2004; Kelly & Tangney, 2006). Furthermore, Brusilovsky and Peylo (2003) have conducted a review of modern adaptive and intelligent Web-based educational systems (AIWBES) and found potential benefits for teachers and students of five classes of adaptive technologies: (1) *Adaptive Hypermedia* (AHM), (2) *Intelligent Tutoring* (IT), (3) *Adaptive Information Filtering* (AIF), (4) *Intelligent Student and Class Monitoring* (ISCM), and (5) *Intelligent Collaborative Learning* (ICL).

Content-Based Aspects

Regarding the content delivered by adaptive e-learning systems, the majority of these systems are only capable to deal with *closed content repositories*. This closed content has to be designed especially for such a specific system and covers usually an entire learning unit. The adaptability of such a learning unit is embedded directly into the content or is computed at run-time by the system. Furthermore, although adaptive techniques may support the achievement of specific educational goals, these goals are restricted for the majority of existing systems to the domain scope of the available content (Brusilovsky et al., 2007; Meccawy et al., 2007). In addition, authoring tools help to create specific content alternatives (Sasakura & Yamasaki, 2007), but it is practically impossible to take the aforementioned complex situation of learner characteristics into consideration.

To reduce the efforts of the course compiling process and to prevent multiple creations of the same content assets, Courseware Reuse Systems (CRS) have emerged to provide access to *open content repositories*, e.g. ARIADNE and PROMETEUS. Indeed, reusing content or educational objectives would help to reduce these efforts, but most of the systems are not designed as flexible as to support such a reuse and support only a limited content integration from open content repositories. (Brusilovsky et al., 2007). To overcome this problem, adaptive systems' design has made progress

regarding the integration of static content or simple interactive content, e.g. questions. (Meccawy et al., 2007) Further, to manage rich interactive content in adaptive e-learning environments, the approach of adaptive services for e-learning has emerged, e.g. Adaptive Personalized e-Learning Service (APeLS), Knowledge Tree Architecture (Brusilovsky et al., 2007).

Thus, although there is a significant development towards reusability and reduction of effort in the content creation process, there are still at least three serious problems: (1) content alternatives are pre-defined by the content author or teacher, and hereby, students are not adequately involved to improve their self-directed and life-long learning skills; (2) the rapid and ever-changing knowledge of our modern society requires a conscious update of learning content, which in turn causes a continuously hard-to-manage effort to create appropriate content alternatives and to ensure their quality; and (3) due to the limited number of content alternatives and of user characteristics in practical use, such approaches can only focus on very specific learning style options and motivational aspects.

Open-Ended Learning Environments

To overcome the aforementioned problems, one solution approach is to enable and technologically support students' freedom to select appropriate learning content. Stary & Totter (2006) emphasize that students should be able to take *learning control* according to their needs, learning styles and other preferences. Web-based teaching enables to pass this control from the teacher or program designer to the student, which implies a higher flexibility regarding information exploration and access (Lin & Hsieh, 2001). On a more general level, learner control in computer-supported learning includes control over object type (e.g. exercises or questions), content, sequence, presentation, learning pace (speed and time), and learning context (Schulmeister, 1997; Sims & Hedberg, 1995).

The importance of learner control is stressed by various motivational theories, e.g. the effect of learning outcomes and the possibility to take choices makes students feel more competent and increase intrinsic interest (Lin & Hsieh, 2001). In this context, the results of many studies conducted over decades have shown that learner control can incur benefits, but that it can also cause a variety of problems, and all this depends on factors such as experiences and cognitive skills of students (for details see Lin & Hsieh, 2001; Schulmeister, 1997; Sims & Hedberg, 1995).

Web-based learning environments can provide a great variety of material for students, and further, the range of support can address both novice and experienced learners. Lin & Hsieh (2001; pp. 380-381) emphasize that the wealth of the Web *"provides an experiential space for learners to follow their own thoughts and insights. The web also provides access to experts and cases that can provide virtual hands-on experiences"*. As a concrete example, consider that Simkins (1999) proposed to use the Web as a repository of additional learning content in economics education to actively support the students' engagement in the learning process and to generate a broader interest in the subject domain. The World Wide Web (WWW) as the most prominent and widespread hypermedia information system, provides an extensive repository of diverse content in various media types to students and information retrieval systems support the access to relevant ones. Therefore, we consider the WWW to be an *Open-Ended Learning Environment* (OELE).

Hill & Hannafin (1997) conducted a study about cognitive strategies and learning from the WWW and showed that five key factors affect open-ended learning strategies: (1) meta-cognitive knowledge (awareness of student's cognitive processes), (2) perceived orientation (awareness of strategies and actions needed), (3) perceived self-efficacy (student's judgment of one's capability to perform actions), (4) system knowledge (prior knowledge and skills with information systems),

and (5) prior subject knowledge (existing knowledge and expertise in the subject). According to the study, meta-cognitive knowledge seems to be the most influencing factor, and weaknesses herein result in disorientation, discomfort and confusion. Further, the lower levels of perceived self-efficacy, system and subject knowledge affect the strategies applied to find and deal with information. Shapiro & Niederhauser (2003) also found out that learning from hypertext requires meta-cognitive functions, e.g. choosing the content to read or the reading path. Regarding navigational strategies, students with less prior knowledge are comfortable with well-defined structures, but they face the "lost in hyperspace" problem at more complex structures. If increased meta-cognitive activities take place, however, these activities can contribute positively to hypertext-based learning results.

For the purpose of at least partly solving the aforementioned problems of an OELE (defined by the WWW as open content repository and by the available information retrieval services as selectors and finders of relevant learning content), we have developed a solution approach which we call *Dynamic E-learning Knowledge Repository* (DEKOR). Based on the background knowledge given in this section and that which will be described in the next sections, this solution approach goes along with the current trends regarding personalized e-learning systems, and thus, it represents a contribution to the modern requirements of technology-enhanced teaching and learning.

THE INITIAL APPROACH: E-HELP

The idea of developing a dynamic e-learning knowledge repository for personalized learning activities was born from the identified need to solve some problems of closed-content, non-adaptive instructional systems. The encountered solution integrates the OELE principle and aims at supporting personalized learning activities through an automatic assignment of query-based hyperlinks (pointing to relevant content in the OELE) to the closed-content resources. The search keywords behind each hyperlink are directly related to the domain concepts of the resource. Thus, each concept points to topical and context-relevant resources enables an OELE approach, e.g. a Web content-based one. This section outlines the evolution of this idea and the evaluation results of the first developed prototype solution, the *E-HELP* system. For the purpose of developing E-HELP, a concept-based approach was chosen to describe the semantic associations between the content of a course resource and a (dynamically generated) set of resources relying outside the closed course repository. To clarify the fundaments of the proposed solution, the next two sub-sections focus on two critical aspects: *dealing with closed-content* and *dealing with concepts*.

Dealing with Closed-Content

Regarding the overall scope of knowledge provisioning, e-learning systems often provide the capability to store and administer courseware through so-called *learning repositories*. Such a repository is usually a static entity in these systems, e.g. previously uploaded content is stored there as long-term static data. Further, these repositories may allow teachers to structure their materials for example in chapters, sub-chapters and other sub-divisions. Even more, some systems provide the possibility to store additional materials in background repositories, such as libraries or glossaries. Considering then the point of view of learners and teachers, such additional background repositories might be seen as static background knowledge because the resources are considered not to change over a learning journey (or even over several years). Therefore, it is up to the teachers and the course authors to ensure the topicality and domain-relevance of these resources.

Regarding this circumstance, many problems may arise, as already depicted in the previous sec-

tion. So why not take advantage of the increasing amount of relevant knowledge resources on the Web and dynamically integrate them as an additional background library? For the retrieval of such resources, a smart search engine could help. Knowledge acquisition and learning processes can be supported by *information retrieval* techniques, as stated for example in Baeza & Ribeiro (1999) and Liaw et al. (2003). Furthermore, some problems related with the *freedom* in and *chaotic growth* of the Web (e.g. censorship of information as well as reliability, accuracy and topicality of resources) can be solved through methods such as a white list of servers (Lennon & Maurer, 1994) and the Quality Metadata Schema approach discussed in (Gütl et al., 2002).

Dealing with Concepts

In general terms of adaptation, biological and artificial life-forms tend to build their own internal representations of their environment by means of the inputs from their sensory components. This internal view is well modeled by neuronal networks in human beings on the one hand, but on the other hand, it can be modeled in software systems by artificial intelligence methods such as connectionist or logic-based knowledge bases. Taking a closer look at human beings, they tend to simplify, unify and cluster traits in phenomena (e.g. observations from environment, or complex systems and processes) as well as to inter-relate them into semantic structures for their thoughts and notions. Considering this latter aspect and analyzing research work in the fields of cognitive science and social science, the idea of dealing with concepts can be identified (see e.g. Gütl & García-Barrios, 2005b). Concepts and their relations may describe statements and assertions for particular situations or knowledge domains. While learning, new concepts and relations are either built or integrated into prior knowledge (i.e. existing concepts and relations can be adapted). This might be induced by stimuli and information in everyday life as well as initiated by an active knowledge transfer process applying different styles such as declarative and constructivist approaches (Gärdenfors, 2001; Chieu et al., 2004).

From the teaching perspective, the use of concepts supports the identification and description of syllabi, topics and main subjects within courses and lectures. In addition, course content itself can be modeled through concepts and relations which in turn can help to identify or define learning paths. From the learning perspective, concept relations have the power to structure perceptions and insights, to allow expressing knowledge about a specific situation, and to make it possible to detect and explain dependences to and influences by other concepts. Thus, concept relations provide the means to develop applications, for example to codify prior knowledge and to modify or adapt knowledge through concept map tools. Concept relations also provide the means to discover or generate knowledge from unknown or hidden relations by using co-occurrence analysis. Further

details for this context can be found in (Gütl & García-Barrios, 2005b).

The First Prototype

In order to give learners the freedom to discover new knowledge in open (but domain-relevant) information spaces, we implemented a first prototype solution called *E-HELP* (García-Barrios et al., 2002). The E-HELP system presents a set of domain-relevant hyperlinks to learners, and these links are attached to used learning materials and might be followed in order to explore additional materials residing outside the mandatory (closed and static) learning repository. These hyperlinks are defined in advance by teachers through concepts, but these concepts are not directly connected to specific Web resources; rather they are used as keyword definitions for queries of search engines. E-HELP provides a communication layer to the information retrieval systems *xFIND* (http://xfind.iicm.edu) or *Google*

Figure 1. E-HELP viewing mode "In File"

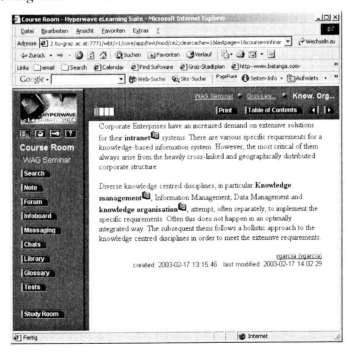

171

(http://www.google.com). Thus, each hyperlink (as a specialized search query) brings learners to relevant, topical and context-relevant resources. Within the E-HELP system, the data structure to internally represent and compute such a hyperlink is called a *Concept*, which is also the term used by learners for the E-HELP hyperlinks in their front-end user interfaces.

For learners, E-HELP provides the possibility of choosing (a) the personal *level of expertise* regarding the knowledge domain of a given course, and (b) one of four available *viewing modes* for displaying E-HELP concepts while navigating through the course contents. Specifically, these four viewing modes are: *In File* (whereby the concepts are displayed within the text of a course page, as shown for the term "intranet" in Figure 1); *After File* (the E-HELP concepts corresponding to the page are appended at the end of the page); *After Chapter* (the concepts are listed at the end of each chapter); and *After Content* (a new page is generated at the end of the course with a list of all concepts).

The general architecture of the E-HELP system is presented in Figure 2. The background knowledge accessible through the *Information Retrieval System* (IRS) is abstracted as a set of *Concepts*, which are basically defined within ex-

pertise level groups (novice, regular and expert). Furthermore, each concept is assigned to one or more course sections each of which is said to define its *Context*. Therefore, this set of contextualized concepts represents the core of the *E-HELP System*. Depending on the chosen viewing mode, a course page requested from the *Web Client* side is dynamically adapted by E-HELP for the *Learning Management System*. Clicking on a delivered E-HELP hyperlink will trigger a search request to the IRS using the pre-stored and concept-specific *Query*. This process is symbolized by the long arrow on the top of Figure 2.

Evaluation Results

An extended evaluation of E-HELP conducted in 2004 focused on the examination of the following aspects: (a) functionality of the system from the authoring and teaching points of view; (b) usefulness of the system from the learners' point of view; (c) knowledge acquisition improvement; and (d) comprehension improvement regarding distinct types of learners (students, research staff, and project employees). The main findings of the evaluation regarding the learner type *students* are described in this sub-section.

Figure 2. Overall architecture and functionality of the E-HELP system

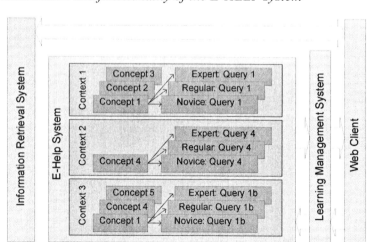

The evaluation was conducted as an observed online lesson within the lecture *Information Retrieval* at Graz University of Technology (summer course, 2004). Attendees of this lecture represented the test subject group. Details about this evaluation can be found in García-Barrios et al. (2004a). Participants of the experiment (in the following, *subjects*) were requested to take the online lessons using their own laptops and Web browsers (the IRS *Google* was chosen to be used in E-HELP). The subject group consisted of 14 males. Furthermore, 28 distinct concepts were prepared whereby each course chapter was assigned a certain number of these concepts. The experiment included the following steps (the time period for each step, in minutes, is given in parentheses): introduction into the learning platform and E-HELP (15), pre-questionnaire (15), online lesson (120), post-questionnaire (15), and short written exam (15). Within the context of this book, the most relevant general findings of this evaluation can be summarized as follows.

At that time, the subjects expressed their preference to learn from lecture notes and books on paper, but they were very interested in acquiring additional (relevant and up-to-date) background knowledge and using these additional resources for their learning activities. Regarding the usefulness of E-HELP, it could be extracted from the analysis of the post-questionnaire that the system was rated with an average of 1.9 points, where 43% of the subjects gave it the grade of '1' (1 best, 6 worst). A positive feedback could be also gained from the post-questionnaire, for example when asking for the efficiency of the information retrieval process through the system. The subjects stated (among others) in the *free-text section* the following:

- *I particularly liked*: cross references directly embedded in text; idea of graded information behind entries according to user's expertise; ease of use.
- *I did not like*: the hyperlinks within the text are intrusive; I had to modify queries manually to find more useful information.

- *For improvement, I recommend*: reducing hyperlinks because a large number of embedded hyperlinks is confusing; modifications in the index of the search engine may represent a risk, because one may get wrong documents in the future; delivering search results in user's language; providing other relevant resources from online-lexica (e.g. Wikipedia or dict.leo.org) and separating them from the results of Google.

In addition, the students were asked for their opinion about the benefit of using E-HELP. A positive tendency may be concluded from the personal estimation about the improvement of learning activities through the system: the average rate was 2.6 (from 1: good, to 6: bad). Regarding user interaction preferences, the evaluation showed that it is highly important for E-HELP users to keep control over individual settings. In the special case of E-HELP, users wanted to explicitly choose and change the settings for their expertise level and viewing modi by themselves. Furthermore, when requested for the *personal benefits* of using E-HELP, subjects stated in a free-opinion manner that the system gives user-tailored and up-to-date hints about relevant and additional literature, provides up-to-date information and other perspectives on the subject, enables corrections of individual knowledge gaps (e.g. expertise knowledge, foreign words), supports autonomous investigation activities, enables a rapid retrieval of specific terminology, and that it refreshes the forgotten. Finally, referring to the *overall functionality* of E-HELP, the subjects stated (among others) that:

- *I particularly liked*: that explanations appear in the place where they are needed; the possibility to change personal settings; that E-HELP works as an activator, deviating from the reading monotony.
- *I did not like*: that E-HELP hyperlinks appear in the text; irrelevant documents were

also found in the search results; the search results are too global.

- *For improvement, I recommend*: improving the design of E-HELP links in the text; using tool-tips; moving concepts without an influence on topicality to a static glossary; restructuring concepts if too many concepts defined (e.g. in *End of Chapter* viewing mode).

As stated in García-Barrios (2007), the use of such a system should represent a guided motivation and controlled starting point to leave the mandatory repository and discover new knowledge at one's own pace.

THE CO2 APPROACH

The last section presented the results from an evaluation of E-HELP. Based on these findings, an improved second prototype has been developed. This section focuses on this second solution approach.

The Need for Improvements

The main problems and most relevant recommendations from the evaluation of E-HELP motivated us to start a new project for the development of an enhanced version of the system (see also García-Barrios, 2006a or 2006c). Some of the conclusions from this evaluation can be summarized as follows.

Too many concepts displayed within the text of a course page represent a usability problem because overwriting content with too many added-on styles leads to subjective acceptance troubles and was evaluated as too obtrusive. The problem is the noisy redundancy of concepts if appearing often in a page. Furthermore, adapting the content of a long page may be time-consuming for the server side of a system, and thus, unacceptable waiting time periods for the user may be the re-

sult. In addition, using only the global interface of a search engine (as done during the evaluation) may lead to the appearance of irrelevant (i.e. not context-relevant) search results, which in turn leads to the necessity of time-consuming query refinement.

Essentially, the efficiency of utilizing E-HELP concepts is dependent on the didactical goal of a teacher and on the learner's expectation at the moment the *recommended concept* is detected. Consequently, the pragmatic value of concepts is much higher than the semantic value (i.e. intention before meaning). For example, from the teacher's perspective, a concept is created because it is considered to be relevant within specific course segments and thus, it will be assigned accordingly (through keywords) to some search results considered to be useful. In the teacher's mind, learners should follow the hyperlinked concept when they have a knowledge gap, i.e. when they need an explanation. And at this exact point, the problem from the learner's perspective appears because the *current intention of a learner* (just before following the hyperlink) may be distinct from the *defined didactical need* (the expectation of the teacher). This means that when learners depend on the current situation, they expect distinct explanations behind the hyperlinks, for example a translation, definition, graph, or a statistic table, etc.

Second Prototype

The improved version of E-HELP, called *Concept-based Context Modeling System* (CO2), was developed within the AdeLE research project (Adaptive e-Learning with Eye-tracking; http://adele.fh-joanneum.at, http://adeledemo.iicm.edu). As E-HELP, the CO2 system aims to provide accurate background knowledge and thus, it assists users in their teaching or learning activities. Within the AdeLE system, in contrast to the E-HELP solution, the CO2 concepts are provided solely through one viewing mode, namely as additional navigational elements. As depicted in Figure 3, the CO2 concepts are visualized under the area *Background Knowledge* (bottom left-hand side of the figure). One of the concepts for the current learning page is visualized as *Service-Oriented*; for this concept, three *information retrieval services* (IRS) are registered, one of them being *Wikipedia (Castellano)*. Clicking on the hyperlink leads to the additional window in Figure 3 for which the keyword *SOA* was added to the search query of the Spanish version of *Wikipedia*.

Concerning improvements and within the scope of this chapter, the major distinctions between E-HELP and CO2 can be explained as follows. The E-HELP system delivered each concept as a hyperlink to one IRS. Analyzing the outcome of the system evaluation, it becomes clear that distinct learners expected distinct results behind one concept (e.g. a translation, a textual explanation, or even images). It is highly relevant to mention at this point that this problem cannot be accurately predicted and thus, it can hardly be solved through fully adaptive techniques. To overcome this problem, a teacher may register more IRSs in CO2, and in turn define distinct specialized queries for each concept. Through this way, solving the problem of predicting the

distinct (momentary) clarification needs of the learners was expected.

Hence, instead of trying to personalize towards a single helpful hyperlink, we decided to place a variety of information services at the disposal of the learners, information services from which learners can choose the more suitable one. In other words, the solution principle was shifted to somewhat of an instantaneous *just-in-time customization* because the intention of an individual learner before following a hyperlink appears instantaneously and is dependent on the current state of the learner's mental model and thus, it is meant to be unpredictable. The main problem here is that a need for clarification can have different reasons which depend on the learning journey within the already delivered page. In other words, the learner switches among different contexts within the elements and domain granularity of the page rather than simply being in a known context. Therefore, the decision of selecting a certain hyperlink is transferred to the learner, whereby the variety of selectable hyperlinks is given by the teacher (e.g. depending on didactical goals or expectations). According to the example shown in Figure 3, (a) if the learner needs an explanation in Spanish, "Wikipedia (Castellano)" could lead

Figure 3. Web-based user interface of the AdeLE system

to the corresponding solution, (b) if the learner needs results from a specific information space (i.e. needs a smart search service that works on a white list of relevant servers), "xFIND (smart search)" may help, or (c) if the learner needs more graphical hints related to the concept, "Google (images)" could lead to accurate results from the Google Images search service.

From the architectural point of view on the CO2 system, as shown in Figure 4, the main distinction to E-HELP relies on the additional internal management of various *Information Services*. In this way we generalized the E-HELP notion of *Information Retrieval System* to break the limitations of dealing only with traditional query-based search services. CO2 is a fully service-oriented solution and is capable of communicating with other information services through distinct Web-based interfaces (e.g. Web Services, REST, native SOAP, etc).

The CO2 system has been also evaluated to corroborate the usefulness of the improvements of and differences to its first approach, the E-HELP system. The next sub-section summarizes some relevant aspects of this evaluation.

Evaluating Cognitive Styles

The evaluation of CO2 was conducted within the course *Software Development in Distributed Systems* (IICM; winter semester 2005/2006; sixty students participated). The time schedule for this evaluation consisted of three phases for four different groups of learners (two of them were assigned a common time slot). The learning part of the evaluation (i.e. the lesson) had the title *Adaptive E-Learning Technologies*. During this lesson, for which we provided one hour of time, the learners had to consume 3 main lesson sections with a total of 14 pages, including 3 assessment pages for each main section. For these pages, 32 concepts were defined, and for each concept at least 3 information services were included. For each page, 2 different *versions* of content have been created, one with more *textual* information and another with more *images*. Within the AdeLE project, we were also interested in the possibilities of personalization with respect to the cognitive styles of *Riding's WAVI model*. This model considers the cognitive styles *Wholist, Analyst, Verbaliser and Imager* (Riding & Cheema, 1991; Riding & Watts, 1997). Due to this research interest, the main focus of attention in this evaluation was set on eye-tracking technology and personalization. For the sake of simplicity, the following paragraphs just summarize the relevant findings in the scope of this book.

Regarding the WAVI model for cognitive styles, we could corroborate that there is *no difference on learning performance* for verbalizers

Figure 4. General architecture of the CO2 modeling system

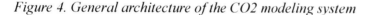
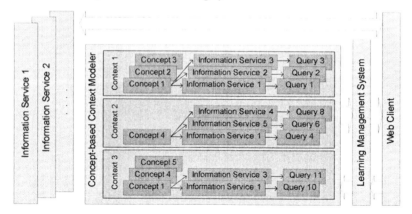

or imagers if they consume textual or illustrative information; see also Bajraktarevic et al. (2003). On the one hand, the subjects were requested at the beginning of the evaluation to give feedback about their styles through indirect questions. On the other hand, as a last step of the evaluation, the students completed the *VICS v2.2b* to measure the real individual WAVI factors. This is a recognized psychological test to retrieve WAVI parameters (Peterson et al., 2003). It is worth mentioning at this point that according to Phillips (2005), students are bad judges of their own styles: assessing the WAVI factors of two different psychological tests (VVSR, CSA) and of a questionnaire for self-assessing these values, Phillips (2005) found out that all three results did not correlate, whereby the self-assessment differed particularly strongly from the calculated values of the two tests. Please refer to Mödritscher (2007) for more details about the overall evaluation of the AdeLE system.

Against this background, it can be stated that the usage of CO2 concepts for the distinct cognitive styles (in terms of quantity of hyperlinks followed) has not shown significant differences. Over the whole usage of the system (i.e. the total of clicks of all students on CO2 concepts) an average of almost 4.66 clicks on each CO2 hyperlink could be calculated from the log files. From the available set of information services, the online dictionary *dict.leo.org* was used most frequently (36.25% of total usage), followed by *Google* (20.8%). This is comprehensible when clarifying that the original course language is German, but the evaluation's content was in English. The third group of subjects (15 students) showed to be more *wholist* than *analyst*, meaning that it preferred getting an overview of the whole content (e.g. *navigation trees*) rather than learning sequentially (step by step over the given learning path, e.g. just using the *previous* and *next buttons*). Taking these latter aspects into account and considering that the CO2 concepts have been provided in the navigational frame, this group has answered the question "Did the

background knowledge mechanism help for or improve your understanding?" with a resulting average rating of 2.8 (1 very good; 6 very bad). In comparison, the overall rating from all the participating students was 3.4 in average. Further, the question "Do you think the position of the background knowledge mechanism is suitable in the navigation frame?" was rated with an average of 4.3 (1 very good; 6 very bad).

Summarizing, independent of the cognitive style, the subjects have left the given closed-content and used the hyperlinked CO2 concepts to explore additional information on the Web. Although the situation *"I need a translation"* appeared more often, all CO2 concepts for the other information services have been used as well.

Regarding the usefulness of the CO2 system, some of the subjects stated in the post-questionnaire phase of the evaluation that:

- **Positive feedback (PF):**
    1. The idea of automatically providing background knowledge is great (8 subjects)
    2. Interesting, relevant and helpful information from external sources (5)
    3. An extensive offer of help (5)
    4. Pre-defined queries are helpful; no refinement was needed (3)
- **Negative feedback (NF):**
    1. I use search systems as background source of information anyway (6)
    2. Please, not in navigation frame (3)
    3. Not enough links for all topics (3)

Let us mention at this point that an unexpected failure in the system led to performance problems for the first group of students (system's cache was disabled; long delays in response time). Based on the explicit feedback of this first group, most of those students admitted having tried to get benefit out of the waiting time during the load of a page; thus, they followed the CO2 hyperlinks in the meantime and found relevant additional resources outside the mandatory content. The fact is that none of them arbitrarily left the closed-content to explore the Web. This behavior could be explained if we assume that they knew that the concepts on the CO2 system had a tight relation to the context of the closed-content pages. In addition, some of these students confirmed having gained a previously non-existing pre-knowledge for new pages, which in turn has compensated the loss of time. The first three PF statements (see the first list above) come from this group of students which also shows their satisfaction with the idea. Essentially we assume that the fact of having problems with the system combined with the stress situation of having limited time to pass the assessment tests has led the students to develop a new strategy for learning, i.e. they took advantage of the CO2 mechanisms to acquire the needed knowledge. In other words, they have preferred the possibility of a guided exit from the closed repository. A positive acceptance of the CO2 system is underlined by the PF statements 3 and 4. Furthermore, the general assumption that wholists tend to preferably jump from one navigational element to another at one's own pace is enforced by the first NF statement, which was given by six wholists. Even more, three of them expressed wanting more CO2 concepts (NF statement 3).

In the other direction, analysts (see NF statement 2) showed displeasure with the position of CO2 concepts in the navigation frame. Nonetheless, from all analysts, these three subjects have used each CO2 concept at least once. Within this evaluation, the system proactively hid the navigation tree (shown in upper left side of Figure 3) if the user was considered to be an analyst. The hyperlinks of the Background Knowledge segment, however, were always shown. Thus, as found out in (Bajraktarevic et al., 2003) and stated in (Mödritscher, 2007), the statement NF2 of analysts can be the result of a cognitive overload for analysts while being shown too many navigational elements.

Enhanced Exploratory Learning

As a key finding from the CO2 evaluation, it can be stated that the CO2 system can be successfully used for *exploratory learning*. According to diSessa et al. (1995), the theory of exploratory learning is related to adaptive e-learning through the following three premises:

- Learning can and should be done at one's own pace.
- Learners may approach a learning task in very diverse ways.
- Learning does not have to be forced.

On the one hand, explorative learning enforces creativity. On the other hand, if the corpus of learning materials is too open (as in an open Web-based environment), problems may arise such as *cognitive overload* or the *lost-in-hyperspace* phenomenon (García-Barrios, 2007). Hence, the application of the CO2 principle can be seen as a practical example of exploratory learning because it gives learners the freedom to discover new knowledge in open (but topic-relevant) information spaces at their own pace and through various ways. The third premise is not absolutely comparable, however. Through CO2 concepts, an analyst may feel forced to leave the close-content. But as stated in García-Barrios (2007), the CO principle minimizes the lost-in-hyperspace problem through *the combination of exploratory learning with guided learning*. This means that students may leave the closed-content through pre-defined starting points, in this case, through didactically prepared concepts. Within this particular context, a personalization-pertinent e-learning system aims at overcoming these difficulties of comprehension and disorientation by reducing and optimizing the material repertory of an open environment (García-Barrios, 2007). This was the main motivation to enhance the CO2 principle by a new personalized approach, as depicted in the following section.

THE DEKOR APPROACH

In the light of our experiences and of the findings discussed in the previous sections, the motivation arose to develop a *Dynamic E-learning Knowledge Repository System* with "personalization capabilities", called *DEKOR*. This approach and its implementation enable personalized concept-based information access applicable for knowledge transfer and learning activities. But moreover, as various information needs are caused by situations or activities given by very specific contexts, the DEKOR system can cope with this requirement as well, what we call *context sensitiveness* (Gütl & Safran (2006); Gütl (2007).

A Context-Sensitive Solution

In general, DEKOR enables to manage various *contexts*, such as courses (in a learning environment) or projects (in a working environment). For the purpose of a more fine-grained structure, a specific context can be composed by various sub-contexts that are modeled by different *context items*. In order to assign sub-contexts to a given information structure, context items can be linked to one or more content pages, such as learning objects, knowledge assets or workflow tasks. A flexible support of various information services is ensured in the DEKOR system by the use of query templates, whereby pre-defined queries can be created through a *placeholder* mechanism. Placeholders are used to replace parts of queries or to extend them, e.g. to fill a query with certain concept keywords or to enrich the query with user group or user information. Each DEKOR concept can be initialized with the default set of information services and pre-defined query templates, and some of them can also be deselected or rewritten. If appropriate, the template-generated query for an information service can be partly adapted or completely rewritten. For example, the keywords "creativity training,", "brainstorming" and "think tank" could be assigned to the concept "idea stage",

whereby a default set of information services (e.g. Wikipedia, Answers.com and Scholar Google) can be chosen to be available. Furthermore, to get more relevant results, the basic search query "think tank" for Scholar Google can be refined to *"think tank" AND "project management"*. For representation purposes, keywords and query instances for specific concepts can be logically clustered by structure elements and displayed by proper titles.

The system described so far addresses a *generic*, non-personalized level, as known from the CO2 system. To enable personalization capabilities, DEKOR can also deal with concept modeling on the *group* and *user* level. All functions from the generic level are also applicable on these two levels, i.e. specific information services, query templates and concepts can be managed for groups and for individual users. In addition, data from the generic level can be wholly or partly inherited and overwritten to the group and further to the user level. To illustrate the added value of this part of the system, consider a group of students that are members of a community "MyCommunity," and thus interested in receiving background knowledge from the MyCommunity Digital Library. Thus, they can specify the portal and use query templates on the group level to easily get access to additional background knowledge without any further effort. On the individual user level, for example, a student may also need additional concepts from another Web-based information service which can easily be added and semantically linked to the course resources during the learning journey.

Figure 5 depicts the conceptual architecture of DEKOR, which consists of the *Personalized Concept-based Context Modeler* (PCo2) and the other surrounding systems. Information consumer services, such as a *Learning Management System*, send requests to PCo2, which include information about the context, the specific context item, the user ID and the result representation. The PCo2 returns a set of concepts and corresponding queries

Figure 5. Dynamic e-learning knowledge repository system with personalization capabilities

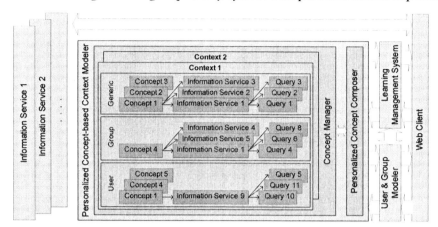

either in XML or XHTML for further processing and presentation. Concepts as well as logically linked information services and their queries are managed on the generic, group and user level by the *Concept Manager Unit* (CMU). The *Personalized Concept Composer* (PCC) is basically responsible for merging concepts, information services and queries for each context. For the purpose of personalized merging and replacing place-holder with group and personalized information, the PCC communicates with the *User & Group Modeling System*.

Beyond Traditional E-Learning: Applicability of DEKOR

The DEKOR system can be incorporated into the context of learning-on-the-job in order to place background information (e.g. from a meeting corpora) at the disposal of company workers during their learning or working activities. Note that in this case, the Learning Management System shown in Figure 5 represents just an instance of many possible *Information Consumer Systems*, e.g. a content management system, a workflow system, or a knowledge management system.

To give an example of this versatility of the DEKOR solution approach, the focus is brought

back to e-learning in terms of learning-on-the-job (see Figure 6). According to Rosenberg (2001), e-learning includes three different focuses: training, knowledge management and performance support. Within the scope of this book, the last issue should be underlined. Rosenberg argues that performance support may indirectly assist humans to enhance their work by means of speed, efficiency and cost reduction. It is provided in different forms, such as books, mentoring, software tools, or checklists. The integrative usage of software solutions for this purpose combines hypermedia systems, expert systems, adaptive systems, real-time support systems and help of real experts.

Furthermore, a critical aspect of personalization systems in the scope of learning activities is given by the possibility that these activities may change continuously over time. Thus, the *User & Group Modelers* in such systems must be continuously aware of situational changes and require advanced and long-term tracking mechanisms to ensure or boost the confidence of inferences. Therefore, the innovative value of the DEKOR approach relies on the integrative character of its components, and therefore it represents a set of goal-oriented and configurable tools (or software modules) being able of supporting company

Figure 6. Personalized concept-based hyperlinks to background knowledge embedded in e-learning content and meeting recording search results for the pre-defined query 'find speaker segments' about the topic 'speech recognition.

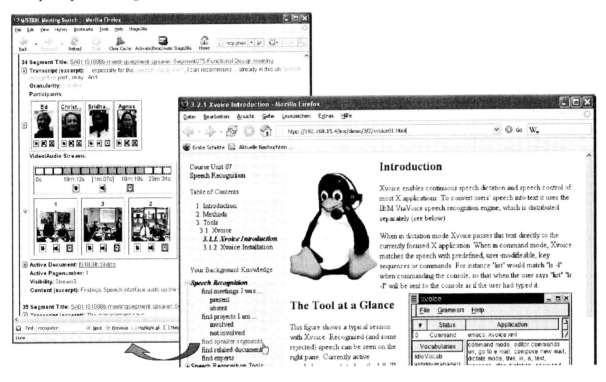

members in their learning and working activities. This *versatility of the DEKOR system* was firstly proven within the MISTRAL research project (see García-Barrios, 2007).

According to García-Barrios (2007), the experiences gained from the E-HELP, CO2 and DEKOR prototypes showed that: (a) such systems can *hide the complexity of accessing information services* and *enable novice users to perform powerful information requests* on a semantic level; (b) the *configurability* of such systems to adapt to the interfaces of Web-based information services *allows to easily build queries, which can be initialized and rewritten for each concept in a flexible and efficient manner*; and (c) the *integration of a smart user modeling component* in the DEKOR system *seems to be a promising approach for efficient personalized access to background knowledge*.

SUMMARY AND FUTURE WORK

This chapter has outlined the evolution of the idea of developing a dynamic e-learning knowledge repository for personalized learning activities (the DEKOR system) by means of the evaluation results and respective enhancements of two previously developed prototype solutions (E-HELP and CO2).

In general, evaluation results and findings have shown that our DEKOR approach is technologically applicable for knowledge transfer and learning activities in various settings, such as in higher education, organizational learning and life-long learning. Moreover, students or employees (1) need access to content alternatives and additional background knowledge, (2) appreciate guidance to open repositories, and (3) require even personalized access to open repositories. The introduced approach can support users in dealing with problems of open ended learning environments but they can also access to a broad range of topical content alternatives.

Towards a system of personalized, guided access to open repositories, the DEKOR approach (1) allows the flexible integration of the system with different information consumer services (such as knowledge management and learning management systems), (2) enables a personalized and guided access on the logical level of concepts and contexts to content alternatives from different information services, and (3) supports a simple way to define concept instances causing less effort because of the template mechanism.

Our intended future work will mainly follow three lines. Firstly, we want to explore the applicability of the DEKOR system by further experiments and by its implementation in real-life applications. Secondly, further research work should be conducted to find solutions on how to combine our approach with e-assessment to improve the user model of our system. Finally, an improved user interface based on Web 2.0 technology will be developed to simplify the creation and modification of concept instances for and through communities of learners.

ACKNOWLEDGMENT

The results presented were partly developed within the AdeLE and MISTRAL research projects. AdeLE was funded by the Austrian ministries BM-VIT and BMBWK (FHplus program). MISTRAL was financed by the Austrian Research Promotion Agency (strategic objective FIT-IT). The support of all individuals involved in both projects is gratefully acknowledged. Special thanks to Helmut Mader, Felix Mödritscher, Martin Ruhmer and Christian Safran for the support.

REFERENCES

Baeza-Yates, R., & Ribeiro-Neto, B. (1999). *Modern information retrieval.* ACM Press.

Bajraktarevic, N., Hall, W., & Fullick, P. (2003). Incorporating learning styles in hypermedia environment: Empirical evaluation. In *Proceedings of the International Conference on Adaptive Hypermedia and Adaptive Web-Based Systems (AH2003)* (pp. 41-52).

Blochl, M., Rumetshofer, H., & Wob, W. (2003). Individualized e-learning systems enabled by a semantically determined adaptation of learning fragments. In *Proceedings of the 14th International Workshop of Database and Expert Systems Applications* (pp. 640-645).

Bransford, J. D., Brown, A. L., & Cocking R. R. (Eds.). (2000). How people learn: Brain, mind, experience, and school. Washington, DC: National Academies Press.

Brusilovsk, P. (2000). *Adaptive hypermedia: From intelligent tutoring systems to Web-based education* (LNCS 1839, pp. 1-7). London: Springer-Verlag.

Brusilovsky, P., & Peylo, C. (2003). Adaptive and intelligent Web-based educational systems. *International Journal of Artificial Intelligence in Education, 13*(2003), 156-169.

Brusilovsky, P. (2004). Adaptive educational hypermedia: From generation to generation. In *Proceedings of the 4th Hellenic Conference on Information and Communication Technologies in Education*, Athens, Greece (pp. 19-33).

Brusilovsk, P., Wade, V. P., & Conlan, O. (2007). From learning objects to adaptive content service for e-learning. In C. Pahl (Ed.), *Architecture solutions for e-learning systems* (pp. 243-261). Hershey, PA: Idea Group Publishing.

Chieu, V. M., Milgrom, E., & Frenay, M. (2004). Constructivist learning: Operational criteria for cognitive flexibility. In *Proceedings of the IEEE International Conference on Advanced Learning Technologies (ICALT-04)* (pp. 221-225).

Conlan, C., Dagger, D., & Wade V. (2002). Towards a standards-based approach to e-learning personalization using reusable learning objects. In *Proceedings of E-Learn 2002*.

De Bra, P., Houben, G.-J., & Wu, H. (1999). AHAM: A dexter-based reference model for adaptive hypermedia. In *Proceedings of the 10th ACM conference on Hypertext and Hypermedia* (pp. 147-156), Darmstadt.

Dietinger, T., Gütl, C., Maurer, H., Pivec, M., & Schmaranz, K. (1998). Intelligent knowledge gathering and management as new ways of an improved learning process. In *Proceedings of the WebNet 98 - World Conference of the WWW* (pp. 244-249). Charlottesville, USA: AACE.

diSessa, A. A., Hoyles, C., Noss, R., & Edwards, L. D. (1995). Computers and exploratory learning: Setting the scene. In A. A. diSessa, C. Hoyles, R. Noss, & L. D. Edwards (Eds.), Computers and exploratory learning (pp. 1-12). New York: Springer.

Felder, R. M., & Silverman, L. K. (1988). Learning and teaching styles in engineering education. *Engineering Education, 78*, 674-681.

Fischer, G., & Scharff, E. (1998). Learning technologies in support of self-directed learning. *Journal of Interactive Media in Education*, 98(4) Retrieved April 8, 2008, from http://www-jime. open.ac.uk/98/4

Gärdenfors, P. (2001). Concept learning: A geometrical model. In *Proceedings of the Aristotelian Society* (Vol. 101, pp. 163-183).

García-Barrios, V. M., Gütl, C., & Pivec, M. (2002). Semantic knowledge factory: A new way of cognition improvement for the knowledge management process. In *Proceedings of Society for Information Technology and Teacher Education,* Nashville, USA.

García-Barrios, V. M., Gütl, C., & Mödritscher, F. (2004). EHELP - enhanced e-learning repository: The use of a dynamic background library for a better knowledge transfer process. In M. Auer & U. Auer (Eds.), *Proceedings of the International Conference on Interactive Computer Aided Learning (ICL 2004)*. Villach, Austria: Carinthia Tech Institute.

García-Barrios, V. M. (2006a). A concept-based enhancement of didactical goals and learning needs with a dynamic background library: Semantics vs. pragmatics. In *Proceedings of the IEEE International Conference on Advanced Learning Technologies (ICALT 2006)* (pp. 1-3). IEEE Computer Society Press.

García-Barrios, V. M. (2006c). Finding the missing link: Enhancement of semantic representations through a pragmatic model. In K. Tochtermann & H. Maurer (Eds.), *Proceedings of the 6th International Conference on Knowledge Management (I-KNOW 06)* (pp. 296-303), Graz, Austria. Springer.

García-Barrios, V. M. (2007). *Personalisation in adaptive e-learning systems - a service-oriented solution approach for multi-purpose user modelling systems*. Unpublished doctoral dissertation, Institute for Information Systems and Computer Media, Graz University of Technology.

García-Barrios, V. M., Gütl, C., & Mödritscher, F. (2004). EHELP - enhanced e-learning repository: The use of a dynamic background library for a better knowledge transfer process. In M. Auer & U. Auer (Eds.), *Proceedings of the International Conference on Interactive Computer Aided Learning (ICL 2004)*.

Germanakos, P., Tsianos, N., Lekkas, Z., Mourlas, C., Belk, M., & Samaras, G. (2007). Embracing cognitive aspects in Web personalization environments – the adaptive Web architecture. In *Proceedings of ICALT 2007.*

Gütl, C., & García-Barrios, V. M. (2005). The application of concepts for learning and teaching. In M. Auer & U. Auer (Eds.), *Proceedings of the International Conference on Interactive Computer Aided Learning (ICL 2005)*. Villach, Austria: Carinthia Tech Institute.

Gütl, C. (2002). *Ansätze zur modernen wissensauffindung im Internet: Eine annäherung an das information gathering and organizing system xFIND (extended framework for information discovery)* (pp. 84-97). Unpublished doctoral dissertation, Graz University of Technology, Austria.

Gütl, C., & Pivec, M. (2003). A multimedia knowledge module virtual tutor fosters interactive learning. *Journal of Interactive Learning Research, 14*(2), 231-258.

Gütl, C., Pivec, M., & García-Barrios, V. M. (2002). Quality metadata scheme xQMS for an improved information discovery process for scholar work within the xFIND environment. In *Proceedings of the Society for Information Technology and Teacher Education*, Nashville, USA.

Gütl, C., Dreher, H., & Williams, R. (2005). E-TESTER: A computer-based tool for auto-generated question and answer assessment. In G. Richards (Ed.), *Proceedings of the World Conference on E-Learning in Corporate, Government, Healthcare, and Higher Education (E-Learn 2005)* (pp. 2929-2936). AACE.

Gütl, C., García-Barrios, V. M. (2005). The application of concepts for learning and teaching. In M. Auer (Ed.), *Proceedings of the International Conference of Interactive Computer Aided Learning (ICL) 2004*, Villach, Austria.

Gütl, C., & Safran, C. (2006). Personalized access to meeting recordings for knowledge transfer and learning purposes in companies. In *Proceedings of the 4th International Conference on Multimedia and Information and Communication Technologies in Education (m-ICTE 2006)*, Seville, Spain.

Gütl, C. (2007). Context-sensitive and personalized concept-based access to knowledge for learning and training purposes. In *Proceedings of the ED-MEDIA 2007*, Vancouver, Canada.

Gütl, C. (2007b). Moving towards a generic, service-based architecture for flexible teaching and learning activities. In C. Pahl (Ed.), *Architecture solutions for e-learning systems* (pp. 1-24). Hershey, PA: Idea Group Publishing.

Hall, J. K. (2000). *Field dependence-independence and computer-based instruction in geography.* Unpublished doctoral dissertation, Faculty of the Virginia Polytechnic Institute and State University. Retrieved Nov 20, 2007, from http://scholar.lib.vt.edu/theses/available/etd-05022000-19260058/unrestricted/JudithHallDissertation.pdf

Hill, J. R., & Hannafin, M. J. (1997). Cognitive strategies and learning from the World Wide Web. *Educational Technology Research and Development, 45*(4), 37-64.

Hodges, C. B. (2004). Designing to motivate: Motivational techniques to incorporate in e-learning experiences. *Journal of Interactive Online Learning, 2*(3). Retrieved March 17, 2008, from http://www.vcolr.org/jiol/issues/getfile.cfm?volID=2&IssueID=8&ArticleID=31

Jonassen, D. H., & Grabowski, B. L. (1993). *Handbook of individual differences, learning and instruction.* Hillsdale, NJ: Lawrence Erlbaum Associates. Retrieved November 20, 2007, from http://www.questia.com/PM.qst?a=o&d=28564357

Kelly, D., & Tangney, B. (2006). Adapting to intelligence profile in an adaptive educational system. *Journal Interacting with Computers, 18*(3), 385-409.

Koch, N., & Rossi, G. (2002). Patterns for adaptive Web applications. In *Proceedings of the Seventh*

European Conference on Pattern Languages of Programs (pp. 179-194). Universitätsverlag Konstanz.

Kortemeyer, G. (1999) Multimedia collaborative content creation (mc3) - the MSU lectureonline system. *Journal of Engineering Education, 88*, 421.

Lennon, J., & Maurer, H. (1994). *Applications and impact of hypermedia systems: An overview. Journal of Universal Computer Science, 0*(0), 54-107.

Liaw, S. S., Ting, I. H., & Tsai, Y. C. (2003). Developing a conceptual model for designing a Web assisted information retrieval system. In *Proceedings of the 2003 International Conference on Computer-Assisted Instruction (ICCAI2003)*.

Lin, B., & Hsieh, C.-T. (2001). *Web-based teaching and learner control: A research review. Computers & Education, 37*(2001), 377-386.

Meccawy, M., Brusilovsky, P., Ashman, H., Yudelson, M., & Scherbinina, O. (2007). Integrating interactive learning content into an adaptive e-learning system: Lessons learned. In G. Richards (Ed.), *Proceedings of the World Conference on E-Learning in Corporate, Government, Healthcare, and Higher Education 2007* (pp. 6314-6319). Chesapeake, VA: AACE.

Mödritscher, F. (2007). *Implementation and evaluation of pedagogical strategies in adaptive e-learning environments.* Unpublished doctoral dissertation, Institute for Information Systems and Computer Media, Graz University of Technology.

Mödritscher, F., García-Barrios, V. M., & Maurer, H. (2005). The use of a dynamic background library within the scope of adaptive e-learning. In G. Richards (Ed.), *Proceedings of the World Conference on E-Learning in Corporate, Government, Healthcare, and Higher Education (E-Learn 2005)* (pp. 3045-3052). Chesapeake, VA, USA: AACE.

Papanikolaou, K. A., Grigoriadou, M., Magoulas, G. D., & Kornilakis, H. (2002). Towards new forms of knowledge communication: The adaptive dimension of a web-based learning environment. *Computers & Education, 39*, 333-360.

Park, O., & Lee, J. (2003). Adaptive instructional systems. *Educational Technology Research and Development, 2003*(25), 651-684.

Peterson, E. R., Deary, I. J., & Austin, E. J. (2003). On the assessment of cognitive style: Four red herrings. *Personality and Individual Differences, 34*(5), 899-904.

Phillips, M. (2005). Cognitive style's influence on media preference: Does it matter or do they know? In *Proceedings of the World Conference on Educational Multimedia, Hypermedia & Telecommunications (ED-MEDIA)* (pp. 1023-1028).

Reiser, R. A. (2001). A history of instructional design and technology: Part II: A history of instructional design. *ETR&D, 49*(2), 57-67.

Reiser, R. A. (2001b). A history of instructional design and technology: Part I: A history of instructional design. *ETR&D, 49*(1) 53-64.

Riding, R. J., & Cheema, I. (1991). Cognitive styles - an overview and integration. *Educational Psychology, 11*(3/4), 193-215.

Riding, R. J., & Watts, M. (1997). *The effect of cognitive style on the preferred format of instructional material. Educational Psychology, 17*(1/2), 179-183.

Romiszowski, A. (2004). How's the e-learning baby? Factors leading to success or failure of an educational technology innovation. *Educational Technology, 44*(1), 5-27.

Safran, S., García-Barrios, V. M., & Gütl, C. (2006). A concept-based context modelling system for the support of teaching and learning activities. In C. M. Crawford, R. Carlsen, K. McFerrin, J. Price, R. Weber, & D. A. Willis (Eds.), Proceedings of the International Conference on Society for Information Technology and Teacher Education (SITE 2006) (pp. 2395-2402). Chesapeake, VA, USA: AACE.

Sampson, D., Karagiannidis, C., & Kinshuk. (2002). Personalised learning: Educational, technological and standardisation perspective. *Interactive Educational Multimedia, 4,* 24-39.

Santally, M. I., & Senteni, A. (2005). A learning object approach to personalized Web-based instruction. *EURODL*. Retrieved March 18, 2008, from http://www.eurodl.org/materials/contrib/2005/Santally.htm

Sasakura, M., & Yamasaki, S. (2007). A framework for adaptive e-learning systems in higher education with information visualization. In *Proceedings of the 11th International Conference of Information Visualization (IV)* (pp. 819-824). Washington, DC: IEEE Computer Society.

Schulmeister, R. (1997). *Hypermedia learning systems. Theory – dedactics – design* (2nd ed.) (T.Flügel, Trans.). München: Oldenbourg. Retrieved April 8, 2008, from http://www.izhd.uni-hamburg.de/paginae/Book/Ch5/Control.html

Schulmeister, R. (2006). *eLearning: Einsichten und aussichten.* München: Oldenburg Verlag.

Shapiro, A., & Niederhauser, D. (2003). Learning from hypertext: Research issues and findings.

In D. H. Jonassen (Ed.), *Handbook of research for education communications and technology* (2nd ed.). Mahwah, NJ: Lawrence Erlbaum Associates.

Simkins, S. P. (1999). promoting active-student learning using the World Wide Web in economics courses. *Journal of Economic Education, 30*(3), 278-291.

Sims, R., & Hedberg, J. (1995). Dimensions of learner control. A reappraisal for interactive multimedia instruction. In J. M. Pearce & A. Ellis (Eds.), *Proceedings of the Twelfth Annual Conference of the Australian Society for Computers in Learning in Tertiary Education* (pp. 468-475).

Stary, C., & Totter, A. (2006). On learner control in e-learning. In *Proceedings of the 13th European Conference on Cognitive Ergonomics: Trust and Control in Complex Socio-Technical Systems* (pp. 41-48). New York: ACM.

Thyagharajan, K., & Nayak, R. (2007). Adaptive content creation for personalized e-learning using Web service. *Journal of Applied Sciences Research, 3*(9), 828-836.

Wopereis, I. G. J. H., Kirschner, P. A., Paas, F., Stoyanov, S., & Hendriks, M. (2005). Failure and success factors of educational ICT projects: A group concept mapping approach. *British Journal of Educational Technology, 36,* 681-684.

Chapter XI
Diagnosing Students' Learning Style in an Educational Hypermedia System

Elvira Popescu
University of Craiova, Romania

ABSTRACT

Individualizing the learning experience for each student is an important goal for educational systems and accurately modeling the learner is the first step towards attaining this goal. This chapter addresses learner modeling from the point of view of learning styles, an important factor for the efficiency and effectiveness of the learning process. A critical review of existing modeling methods is provided, outlining the specificities and limitations of current learning style based adaptive educational systems (LSAES). The controversy regarding the multitude of partially overlapping learning style models proposed in the literature is addressed, by suggesting the use of a complex of features, each with its own importance and influence (the so called Unified Learning Style Model). An implicit modeling method is introduced, based on analyzing students' behavioral patterns. The approach is validated experimentally and good precision rates are reported.

INTRODUCTION

Accommodating the individual needs of the learner is an important goal of today's e-learning, whether it implies disabilities, a different knowledge level, technical experience, cultural background or learning style. This is also one of the advantages of web-based education versus traditional, face-to-face learning: the increased potential of providing individualized learning experiences.

In order to be able to optimize and facilitate students' interaction with a web-based educational system, one must first decide on the human factors that should be taken into consideration and identify the real needs of the students.

The focus of this chapter is on learning style as the human factor, since it is one of the individual differences that play an important role in learning, according to educational psychologists. Learning style refers to the individual manner in which a person approaches a learning task. For example, some learners prefer graphical representations and remember best what they see, others prefer audio materials and remember best what they hear, while others prefer text and remember best what they read. There are students who like to be presented first with the definitions followed by examples, while others prefer abstract concepts to be first illustrated by a concrete, practical case study. Similarly, some students learn easier when confronted with hands-on experiences, while others prefer traditional lectures and need time to think things through. Some students prefer to work in groups, others learn better alone. These are just a few examples of the many different preferences related to perception modality, processing and organizing information, reasoning, social aspects etc, all of which can be included in the learning style concept.

Research on the integration of learning styles in educational hypermedia began relatively recently and only a few systems that attempt to adapt to learning styles have been developed. Consequently, "it still is unclear which aspects of learning styles are worth modeling and what can be done differently for users with different learning styles" (Paredes & Rodríguez, 2004, pp.211). However scientists agree that taking these student characteristics into account can lead to an increased learning performance, greater enjoyment, enhanced motivation and reduced learning time (Kelly & Tangney, 2006). We therefore believe that accommodating learning styles in adaptive educational hypermedia is a worthwhile endeavor.

The first step towards providing adaptivity is selecting a good taxonomy of learning styles. Most of the educational systems developed so far rely on a single learning style model, such as those proposed by (Felder & Silverman, 1988), (Honey & Mumford, 2000), (Biggs, 1987) or (Witkin, 1962). In this chapter we advocate the use of a unified learning style model (ULSM), which integrates characteristics from several models proposed in the literature.

The second step is suggesting a method for identifying the learning style of the student. The traditional diagnosing approach implies having the students fill in a dedicated psychological questionnaire. What we propose in this chapter is an implicit modeling method, which is based on the analysis and interpretation of student behavior in the educational system.

Furthermore we address questions such as: What learning style characteristics should be diagnosed and adapted to? How can we create a quantitative model of complex psychological constructs? What type of information is needed from students' behavior to identify their learning preferences?

Our approach was applied in a dedicated e-learning platform called WELSA (**W**eb-based **E**ducational system with **L**earning **S**tyle Adaptation). The analysis of the student behavior, together with the diagnosing rules, are implemented in a built-in "Analysis tool".

We start this chapter by briefly introducing the concept of learning styles. The background section also includes a short review of the methods that have been proposed in the literature for learning style diagnosis: while the majority of the current learning style based adaptive educational systems (LSAES) use dedicated psychological questionnaires for identifying the learning preferences of the students, there are some systems that also use an implicit modeling method, based on analyzing the behavior of the students in the system.

The third section deals with our own approach for implicitly diagnosing student learning preferences included in ULSM. First the ULSM model is succinctly described, next relevant patterns of behavior are associated to each learning preference and finally the learning preferences are identified using a rule-based modeling method.

The approach is validated empirically, with the help of a 71 undergraduate student sample who interacted with our WELSA system. The results of the experiment are evaluated and discussed in section 4.

The last section of this chapter includes some concluding remarks and points towards future research directions.

BACKGROUND

A distinct feature of an adaptive system is the user model it employs, i.e. a representation of information about an individual user. User modeling is the process of creating and maintaining an up-to-date user model, by collecting data from various sources, which may include: i) implicitly observing user interaction and ii) explicitly requesting direct input from the user (Brusilovsky & Millan, 2007). User modeling and adaptation are strongly correlated, in the sense that the amount and nature of the information represented in the user model depend largely on the kind of adaptation effect that the system aims to deliver. Regarding the information contained in the user model, there are identified six features: knowledge, interests, goals, background, individual traits and context of work. In case of adaptive educational hypermedia systems, the learner's knowledge of the subject being taught is the most widely used student feature. More recently, the learning style of the student also started to be taken into account, as being one of the individual traits that play an important role in learning.

Learning style designates everything that is characteristic to an individual when she/he is learning, i.e. a specific manner of approaching a learning task, the learning strategies activated in order to fulfill the task. According to a widely accepted definition given by (Keefe, 1979), learning styles represent a combination of characteristic cognitive, affective and psychological factors that serve as relatively stable indicators of how a learner perceives, interacts with, and responds to the learning environment.

There has been a great interest in the field over the past 30 years which led to the proliferation of proposed approaches. (Coffield et al., 2004) iden-

tified 71 models of learning styles, among which 13 were categorized as major models, according to their theoretical importance, their widespread use and their influence on other learning styles models. Some of these models have started to be used also in a special case of adaptive educational systems, called LSAES, which focus on students' learning preferences as the adaptation criterion. LSAES present several particularities, related to the large variety of learning style models that can be adopted and the inherent difficulty and subjectivity of the categorization. These systems differ in several aspects: underlying learning style model, diagnosing method (implicit or explicit), modeling techniques (rule-based approach, data mining, machine learning techniques), number of modeled student characteristics besides learning preferences (knowledge level, goals) and the type, size and conclusions of the reported experiments.

In what follows we will focus on the methods used for learner modeling and we classify the systems in two categories: i) those that use questionnaires for identifying the learning style and ii) those that use students' observable behavior.

Explicit Modeling Method

The first adaptive educational systems that dealt with learning styles as adaptation criterion relied on the measuring instruments associated to the learning style models for diagnosing purposes. The main advantage of this method is its simplicity: the teacher / researcher only has to apply a dedicated psychological questionnaire, proposed by the learning style model creators. Based on the students' answers to the questions, a preference towards one or more of the learning style dimensions can be inferred. The main disadvantages of this questionnaire-based approach are:

- some of the measuring instruments used could not demonstrate internal consistency, test–retest reliability or construct and predictive validity, so they may not be totally reflective of the way a particular student learns (Coffield et al., 2004)

- it implies a supplementary amount of work from the part of the student, who has to fill in questionnaires at the beginning of the course (which sometimes may include over 100 questions, as in case of the Hermmann's Whole Brain Model (Herrmann, 1996))
- it can be easily "cheated" by the students, who may choose to skip questions or give wrong answers on purpose
- there can be non-intentional influences in the way the questions are formulated, which may lead the students to give answers perceived as "more appropriate"
- it is difficult to motivate the students to fill out the questionnaires; especially if they are too long and the students are not aware of the importance or the future uses of the questionnaires, they may tend to choose answers arbitrarily instead of thinking carefully about them
- it is static, so the student model is created at the beginning of the course and stored once and for all, without the possibility to be updated.

A method of improving this approach is to give the student the possibility to modify her/his own profile, if she/he considers that the one inferred from the questionnaire results is not appropriate (does not correspond to the reality). This is called an "open model" (scrutable and modifiable) approach and it is used either in conjunction with the questionnaires or instead of them. This direct access of students to their own learner model has several advantages: it provides an increased learner control, it helps the learners develop their metacognitive skills and it also offers an evaluation of the quality of the model created by the system (Kay, 2001). The main disadvantages of this approach are that it increases the cognitive load of the student and that it must rely on the self-evaluation of a student who might not be aware of her/his learning style.

Examples of systems that use this explicit modeling method are:

- CS383 (Carver et al., 1999) – uses the Index of Learning Styles dedicated questionnaire (Soloman & Felder, 1998) in order to assess 3 constructs of the Felder-Silverman model (FSLSM): sensing/intuitive, visual/verbal, sequential/global (Felder & Silverman, 1988)
- AES-CS (Triantafillou et al., 2003) – uses a Group Embedded Figures Test questionnaire at the beginning of the course, in order to assess the field dependence/field independence characteristic of the learner (Witkin, 1962).
- (Bajraktarevic et al., 2003) – uses the Index of Learning Styles questionnaire in order to assess the sequential/global dimension of the Felder-Silverman learning style model.
- INSPIRE (Papanikolaou et al., 2003) – is based on Honey and Mumford (2000) learning style model. The prevalence of the Activist, Pragmatist, Reflector or Theorist dimension is identified either by applying a dedicated questionnaire or by student's self-diagnosis, since students can directly manipulate and modify the learner model.
- Feijoo.net (Paule et al., 2003) - uses the CHAEA Test (Alonso et al., 2002) for classifying the students in one of the four learning styles it proposes: Active, Reflective, Theoretical, and Pragmatic (inspired by the Honey and Mumford learning style model)
- SACS (Style-based Ant colony system) (Wang et al., 2007) - is based on the VARK style (Flemming, 1995), which is identified by means of a dedicated questionnaire or input by the student.

Implicit Modeling Method

There is also a second category of systems, which use an implicit and/or dynamic modeling method. Three different approaches have been identified in this respect:

- analyze the performance of the students at evaluation tests - a good performance is interpreted as an indication of a style that corresponds to the one currently estimated and employed by the system, while a bad performance is interpreted as a mismatched learning style and triggers a change in the current learner model
- ask the students to provide feedback on the learning process experienced so far and adjust the learner model accordingly
- analyze the interaction of the students with the system (browsing pattern, time spent on various resources, frequency of accessing a particular type of resource etc) and consequently infer a corresponding learning style.

Sometimes, these systems use a mixed modeling approach: they first use the explicit modeling method for the initialization of the learner model and then the implicit modeling method for updating and improving the learner model.

Some examples of systems in this implicit modeling category include:

- Arthur system (Gilbert & Han, 1999) uses Auditory, Visual and Tactile learning preferences (basically a VAK learning style model). It divides the courses in concepts; when the user has finished with the first concept which was presented using a learning style that was chosen at random, the system assesses the student's success, and if this is not higher than 80%, the system changes her/his learning style.

- iWeaver (Wolf, 2002) – is based on the Dunn and Dunn learning style model (1992), including five perceptual (Auditory, Visual – Pictures, Visual – Text, Tactile Kinesthetic, Internal Kinesthetic) and four psychological learner preferences (Impulsive, Reflective, Global, Analytical). When the learner first enters the environment, they fill in the Building Excellence Survey. Then the learner is given an explanation of their assessed learning style and recommendations on a media representation for the first content module and also the option to choose another media representation than the one that was recommended for their style. Also, after each module, the learner is asked for feedback on the media representations they encountered and for a ranked rating, which is used to adjust the learner model.
- TANGOW (Paredes & Rodriguez, 2004) – is based on two dimensions of FSLSM: sensing/intuitive and sequential/global. Learners are asked to fill in the ILS questionnaire when they log into the system for the first time and the student model is initialized correspondingly. Subsequently the student actions are monitored by the system and if they are contrary to the behavior expected for that learning preference, then the model is updated. The student observed behavior is restricted to four patterns, each corresponding to one of the four possible FSLSM preferences.
- Heritage Alive Learning System (Cha et al, 2006) – is based on Felder-Silverman learning style model. Learning preferences are diagnosed implicitly, by analyzing behavior patterns on the interface of the learning system using Decision Tree and Hidden Markov Model approaches.
- EDUCE (Kelly & Tangney, 2006) - is based not on a learning style model but on Gardner's theory of multiple intelligences (MI), using 4 types: logical/mathematical, verbal/

linguistic, visual/spatial, musical/rhythmic (Gardner, 1993). The student diagnosis is done both dynamically (by analyzing the student's interaction with MI differentiated material and using a naïve Bayes classification algorithm) and statically (by applying a Shearer's MI inventory (Shearer, 1996)).

- The system presented in (Stathacopoulou et al., 2007) - is based on Biggs' surface vs. deep student approach to learning and studying (Biggs, 1987). The student diagnosis is done by means of a neural network implementation for a fuzzy logic-based model. The system learns from a teacher's diagnostic knowledge, which can be available either in the form of rules or examples. The neuro-fuzzy approach successfully manages the inherent uncertainty of the diagnostic process, dealing with both structured and non-structured teachers' knowledge.

- AHA! (version 3.0) (Stash, 2007) – uses the notion of "instructional meta-strategies" (inference or monitoring strategies), which are applied in order to infer the learner's preferences during her/his interaction with the system. A meta-strategy can track student's learning preferences by observing her/his behavior in the system: repetitive patterns such as accessing particular types of information – e.g. textual vs. visual form or navigation patterns such as breadth-first versus depth-first order of browsing through the course. These meta-strategies are defined by the authors, who can therefore choose the learning styles that are to be used as well as the adaptation strategy. However, there is a limitation in the types of strategies that can be defined and consequently in the set of learning preferences that can be used, so these strategies cannot completely replace existing psychological questionnaires.

- (Garcia et al., 2007) – is based on three dimensions of the FSLSM (active/reflective, sensing/intuitive, and sequential/global). The behavior of students in an educational system (called SAVER) is observed and the recorded patterns of behavior are analyzed using Bayesian Networks.

- (Graf, 2007) – is based on the FSLSM. The actions of the students interacting with Moodle learning management system (Moodle, 2008) are recorded and then analyzed using a Bayesian Network approach as well as a rule-based approach. Since the accuracy of the diagnosis was better in the latter case, the rule-based approach was implemented into a dedicated tool called DeLeS, which can be used to identify the learning style of the students in any LMS.

- The system presented in (Sangineto et al., 2008) - is based on Felder-Silverman learning style model, and uses fuzzy values to estimate the preference of the student towards one of the four categories (Sensing-Intuitive, Visual-Verbal, Active-Reflective, Sequential-Global). Initially, the system offers to the learner the possibility to use the Soloman and Felder's psychological test or to directly set the values of the category types, choosing an estimated value for each category (using a slider-based interface). Also, for those people who do not want or are not able to estimate their own learning styles, the system sets the initial values of all the category types to 0.5, which means that the student is initially evaluated as indifferent with respect to any learning style preference. Next the learning style is automatically updated by the system taking into account the results obtained by the students at the multiple-choice tests presented at the end of each learning phase.

AN AUTOMATIC IDENTIFICATION METHOD FOR STUDENTS' LEARNING STYLE

Towards a Different Approach

The novelty of our approach consists in the proposal of a *Unified Learning Style Model (ULSM)*, specifically adapted for e-learning use. This model was conceived to include learner characteristics from various traditional learning styles models, which meet three conditions:

- have a significant influence on the learning process (according to the educational psychology literature)
- can be used for adaptivity purposes in an educational hypermedia system (i.e. the implications they have for pedagogy can be put into practice in a technology enhanced environment)
- can be identified from student observable behavior in an educational hypermedia system: i) navigational indicators (number of hits on educational resources, navigation pattern); ii) temporal indicators (time spent on different types of educational resources proposed); iii) performance indicators (total learner attempts on exercises, assessment tests) (Papanikolaou & Grigoriadou, 2004). Indeed, not all of the characteristics included in a classic learning style model can be identified through an educational hypermedia system, nor can they be used for adaptation.

In this context, our intention is to offer a basis for an integrative learning style model, by gathering characteristics from the main learning styles proposed in the literature. We can thus summarize learning preferences related to:

- perception modality: visual vs. verbal

- processing information (abstract concepts and generalizations vs. concrete, practical examples; serial vs. holistic; active experimentation vs. reflective observation, careful vs. not careful with details)
- field dependence vs. field independence
- reasoning (deductive vs. inductive)
- organizing information (synthesis vs. analysis)
- motivation (intrinsic vs. extrinsic; deep vs. surface vs. strategic vs. resistant approach)
- persistence (high vs. low)
- pacing (concentrate on one task at a time vs. alternate tasks and subjects)
- social aspects (individual work vs. team work; introversion vs. extraversion; competitive vs. collaborative)
- coordinating instance: affectivity vs. thinking

The above learning preferences were included in ULSM based on a systematic examination of the constructs that appear in the main learning style models and their intensional definitions. In case of similar constructs present under various names in different models, we included the concept only once, aiming for independence between the learning preferences and the least possible overlap. A detailed description of this model together with the justification of its use can be found in (Popescu et al., 2007; Popescu, 2008b) and are outside the scope of this chapter.

Of course, learning is so complex that it cannot be completely expressed by any set of learning style dichotomies (Roberts & Newton, 2001). Therefore we do not claim that our model is exhaustive; we argue however that the above set of characteristics is a first step towards building an integrative model and establishing a unified core vocabulary.

Furthermore, the modeling method that we propose based on this integrator model has several advantages:

- it is an implicit modeling method, based on the direct observation and analysis of learner behavior, thus avoiding the psychometric flaws of the measuring instruments
- it is a dynamic modeling method, based on continuous monitoring and analysis of learner behavioral patterns
- it is a feature-based modeling method (at the level of basic learning preferences) rather than a stereotype-based modeling (at the level of traditional learning style models). In turn, this offers the possibility of finer grained and more effective adaptation actions.

The systems that are closest to our approach among those presented in the previous section are those that identify the learning styles by analyzing the interaction of the students with the educational system, in the form of behavioral patterns, namely (Cha et al., 2006), (Garcia et al., 2007) and (Graf, 2007). The main advantages of our approach versus these related works are:

- All three related systems use the Felder-Silverman learning style model, while we use a combination of learning styles (i.e. ULSM)
- The number of patterns of behavior that are taken into account in our WELSA system is larger (i.e. 11 patterns in (Garcia et al., 2007), 39 in (Graf, 2007) and 58 in (Cha et al., 2006) versus over 100 in WELSA) which should imply a higher precision of the learning style diagnosis (as we will see in section 4). This large number of patterns is due to the fine granularity of the learning objects composing the WELSA courses, which allows for a rich and precise annotation, as detailed in (Popescu et al., 2008).

The methods used for learning style identification are also different: Decision Trees and Hidden Markov Models in case of (Cha et al.,

2006), Bayesian networks in case of (Garcia et al., 2007) and a rule-based approach in case of (Graf, 2007). It should be also noted that (Graf, 2007) deals with an existing learning management system (Moodle) that was enhanced with modeling and adaptation capabilities, while our work is based on our own adaptive educational hypermedia system (WELSA), that we have built from scratch.

This implicit modeling method presents a challenge, in that it is difficult to determine what are the learner actions that are indicative for each of the learning preferences included in ULSM. This is why we performed two experimental studies, trying to identify correlations between students' patterns of behavior and their learning preferences. The results were reported in (Popescu, 2008; Popescu et al., 2009).

More specifically, the behavioral patterns that we took into account in our analysis refer to:

- Educational resources (i.e. learning objects - LOs) that compose the course: time spent on each LO, number of accesses to an LO, number of skipped LOs, results obtained to evaluation tests, order of visiting the LOs. For each LO we have access to its metadata file, including information regarding the instructional role (e.g. *'Definition'*, *'Example'*, *'Exercise'*, *'Interactivity'*, *'Illustration'* etc), the media type (e.g. *'Text'*, *'Sound'*, *'Image'*, *'Video'*), the level of abstractness and formality etc.
- Navigation choices: either linear, by means of the "Next" and "Previous" buttons or non-linear, by means of the course Outline
- Communication tools: a synchronous one (chat) and an asynchronous one (forum) – time, number of visits, number of messages.

Based on the results obtained, as well as similar findings from the literature, we conceived a set of rules for learner modeling and used them to actually diagnose students' ULSM preferences, as detailed in the next subsections.

Definitions and Notations

Please note that in order to illustrate the generality of our approach, we will consider only a subset of ULSM (let's call it ULSM'), in which we included only those learning preferences that could be identified from widely available patterns of behavior (i.e. patterns that can be derived from any educational hypermedia system):

- Visual preference / Verbal preference
- Abstract concepts and generalizations / Concrete, practical examples
- Serial / Holistic
- Active experimentation / Reflective observation
- Careful with details / Not careful with details
- Individual work / Team work

Formally, let L be a learner and let $Pref(L)$ be the set of learning preferences that characterize learner L. In the context of our work, $Pref(L) \subset Pref\_ULSM'$, where $Pref\_ULSM'$ is the set of learning preferences included in ULSM'. Specifically, $Pref\_ULSM' = \{p\_visual, p\_verbal, p\_abstract, p\_concrete, p\_serial, p\_holistic, p\_activeExperimentation, p\_reflectiveObservation, p\_carefulDetails, p\_notCarefulDetails, p\_individual, p\_team\}$ (meaning of each preference obviously results from its name). It should be noted that the preferences in $Pref\_ULSM'$ are grouped on several dimensions, each with two opposite axes: $p\_visual \leftrightarrow p\_verbal; p\_abstract \leftrightarrow p\_concrete$ etc. Let $Dim\_ULSM' = \{p\_visual / p\_verbal, p\_abstract / p\_concrete, p\_serial / p\_holistic, p\_activeExperimentation / p\_reflectiveObservation, p\_carefulDetails / p\_notCarefulDetails, p\_individual / p\_team \}$. Thus a student can only exhibit one of the two

opposite preferences, e.g. if $p\_visual \in Pref(L)$ then $p\_verbal \notin Pref(L)$.

Furthermore, the student can have a level of intensity associated to each preference (either mild, moderate or strong preference). Let C be one of the characteristics in ULSM'. Let us denote by $\tilde{C}$ the opposite characteristic in ULSM'. Thus for each dimension $C/\tilde{C} \in Dim\_ULSM'$ we can have $Val_{C/\tilde{C}} \in \{-3, -2, -1, 1, 2, 3\}$, where positive values imply a preference towards the C axis and negative values imply a preference towards the $\tilde{C}$ axis; the greater the absolute value, the more intense the preference (i.e. ±3 represents a strong preference, ± 2 represents a moderate preference and ± 1 represents a mild preference).

The objective of this section is to conceive an implicit method for diagnosing this set of learning preferences as accurately as possible. The first step is to associate relevant behavioral patterns to each of the ULSM' preferences, as detailed in the next subsection.

Associating Relevant Patterns to ULSM' Dimensions

The correspondence between the patterns and the learning preferences that they are indicative of are usually expressed in an informal manner, e.g. "A high amount of time spent on contents with graphics, images, video is an indication of a *Visual* learning preference", "A high performance in questions related to graphics can be associated to a *Visual* preference" etc. On the other hand, the data collected from the system logs are in a precise quantitative form, e.g. $t\_Image = 2350s$ (the amount of time, in seconds, spent on LOs of type "*Image*") or $t\_Image\_rel = 12.5\%$ (the percentage of time spent on images versus the whole study time); $grade\_image = 8.5$ (the average grade obtained on questions related to graphics). We therefore encode the values that can be taken by the patterns in three categories: *High (H), Medium (M), Low (L)*. Consequently, for each of the patterns we need to establish a mapping from the set of values that can be taken by the pattern to the set *{H, M, L}*. One way to specify this mapping is by means of the thresholds $L \leftrightarrow M$ and $M \leftrightarrow H$. Table 1 includes some common values for these thresholds, based on the recommendations in the literature (Graf, 2007; Garcia et al., 2007; Rovai and Barnum, 2003), as well as our experience.

It should be noted that the values of these thresholds depend to a certain extent on the structure and the subject of the course. The values in Table 1 are some general indications that are based on our experience as well as similar research findings. However, the teacher should have the possibility to adjust these values to correspond to the particularities of her/his course. This is why our WELSA Analysis tool has a Configuration option, which allows the teacher to modify the threshold values.

We can now associate the values of the patterns with the ULSM' characteristics that they are indicative of. Since the ULSM' characteristics come in opposite pairs, if an *H* value for a pattern *P* can be associated with a characteristic *C*, then an *L* value of pattern *P* can be associated with characteristic $\tilde{C}$ (for all dimensions $C/\tilde{C} \in Dim\_ULSM'$). Therefore in Table 2 we only include the values of the patterns that are characteristic for the left hand side axis of each ULSM' dimension. Furthermore, for each pattern we can associate a weight, indicating the relevance (the level of influence) it has on identifying a learning preference. The weight of each pattern is also included in Table 2, denoted by *hW* (high weight), *mW* (medium weight) and *lW* (low weight).

A few notes should be made regarding Table 2: the number of visits (hits) to an educational resource was found to be less indicative of the student's preference than the time spent on that particular resource (Popescu, 2009); consequently, *t_LO* was assigned a higher weight than *h_LO*. The grades obtained by students were generally allocated lower weights in defining their learning preferences since it can be argued that students'

performance depends largely on other factors, such as their motivation; thus a student may obtain a good grade on an item that doesn't correspond to her preferences, in case the student was motivated enough to prepare her for that task. It can also be noted that there are some patterns which are associated to several ULSM' preferences; an example is the level of activity students have in communication channels (chat and forum), which is mainly indicative of a *Team work* preference but could also be associated, to a certain extent, with a *Verbal* preference.

As in the case of thresholds, the above associations and weights are merely general recommendations; the importance of each of the patterns may change with the specificities of the course. For example, in case of a course which contains a very small number of group assignments that the students may choose from, the *n_individualAssignment* pattern is not very relevant anymore and should be assigned a lower weight. Also, some patterns may not be applicable for some courses, in case the course does not include that particular feature. In this case, the teacher should have the possibility to eliminate some of the patterns, which are not relevant for her/his course. Our WELSA Analysis tool has been conceived to accommodate all these requirements, offering the teacher the possibility to adjust the patterns' weights as well as eliminate some patterns.

The values for the patterns are computed from the student actions, as recorded by the system. Obviously, the larger the number of available actions, the more reliable the resulting pattern. Therefore our method (and consequently our Analysis tool) weights the value of each pattern with a reliability coefficient, which is computed from the number of corresponding actions in the system log. Hence a pattern can have a high reliability degree (*hR*), a medium reliability degree (*mR*) or a low reliability degree (*lR*). Thus the particularities of the course are reflected in the patterns' weights, while the particularities of the

Table 1. Description and values for pattern thresholds (note the meaning of prefixes in the pattern names: "n" stands for "number", "t" stands for "time" and "h" stands for "hits")

Pattern	Description	L ↔ M	M ↔ H
t_mediaType t_instrType	the relative time spent by the student on LOs of type *mediaType / instructionalType* versus the relative average time spent on LOs of type *mediaType / instructionalType* (the average time is computed based on an average study time indicated by the course creator for each component LO) $t\_mediaType\_rel /(\dfrac{t\_average\_mediaType}{t\_average\_total\_LO})*100$ $t\_instrType\_rel /(\dfrac{t\_average\_instrType}{t\_average\_total\_LO})*100$	<75%	>125%
h_mediaType h_instrType	the relative number of visits of LOs of type *mediaType / instructionalType* versus the total relative number of LOs of type *mediaType / instructionalType* available in the course $h\_mediaType\_rel /(\dfrac{n\_LO\_mediaType}{n\_LO\_total})*100$ $h\_instrType\_rel /(\dfrac{n\_LO\_instrType}{n\_LO\_total})*100$	<75%	>125%
grade_X	the grade obtained by the student on items of type *X* versus the total average grade of the student $\dfrac{grade\_X}{grade\_average}*100$	<75%	>125%
t_test	the time spent on a test versus the maximum time allowed for that test $\dfrac{t\_test}{t\_test\_max}*100$	<70%	>90%
n_revisions_ test	the number of revisions made before submitting a test versus the total number of answers $\dfrac{n\_revisions\_test}{n\_total\_answers}*100$	<20%	>50%
sequence_X_ before_Y	the number of accesses of LOs in the order *X − Y* versus the number of accesses of LOs in the order *Y − X*. $\dfrac{sequence\_X\_before\_Y}{sequence\_Y\_before\_X}*100$	<80%	>120%

continued on following page

Table 1. Continued

n_nextButton	the number of "Next" button clicks versus the total number of navigation actions $$\frac{n\_nextButton}{n\_nextButton + n\_prevButton + n\_jump} * 100$$	<30%	>70%
n_prevButton	the number of "Previous" button clicks versus the total number of navigation actions $$\frac{n\_prevButton}{n\_nextButton + n\_prevButton + n\_jump} * 100$$	<30%	>70%
n_jump	the number of jump actions versus the total number of navigation actions $$\frac{n\_jump}{n\_nextButton + n\_prevButton + n\_jump} * 100$$	<30%	>70%
n_outline	the number of visits to "Outline" versus the total number of visited LOs $$\frac{n\_outline}{n\_LO} * 100$$	<5%	>15%
t_outline	the time spent on "Outline" versus the total time spent on the course $$\frac{t\_outline}{t\_total} * 100$$	<1%	>5%
n_skippedLO_temp	the number of LOs skipped on a temporary basis versus the total number of visited LOs $$\frac{n\_skippedLO\_temp}{n\_LO} * 100$$	<5%	>15%
n_skippedLO_perm	the number of LOs skipped on a permanent basis versus the total number of visited LOs $$\frac{n\_skippedLO\_perm}{n\_LO} * 100$$	<5%	>15%
n_returns_LO	the number of returns to LOs versus the total number of visited LOs $$\frac{n\_returns\_LO}{n\_LO} * 100$$	<5%	>15%
t_chat	the time spent on chat versus the total time spent on the course $$\frac{t\_chat}{t\_total} * 100$$	<5%	>15%

continued on following page

Table 1. Continued

n_chat_msg	the number of messages sent on chat per course session $\dfrac{n\_chat\_msg}{n\_sessions}$	<10	>30
t_forum	the time spent on forum versus the total time spent on the course $\dfrac{t\_forum}{t\_total}*100$	<5%	>15%
n_forum_msg	the number of messages posted on forum per course session $\dfrac{n\_forum\_msg}{n\_sessions}$	<1	>5
n_forum_read	the number of messages read on forum per course session $\dfrac{n\_forum\_read}{n\_sessions}$	<2	>10
n_askPeerHelp n_offerPeer-Help	the number of times a student asks for / offers peer help per course session $\dfrac{n\_askPeerHelp}{n\_sessions}$ $\dfrac{n\_offerPeerHelp}{n\_sessions}$	<2	>4
n_individu-alAssignment	the relative number of individual assignments chosen versus the relative number of group assignments chosen $\dfrac{n\_individualAssignments}{n\_total\_individualAssignments} / \dfrac{n\_groupAssignments}{n\_total\_groupAssignments}*100$	<80%	>120%

student's interaction with the system are reflected in the patterns' reliability values.

Computing the Learning Preferences

For each characteristic $C \in ULSM'$, we have a set of relevant patterns with values P_1, P_2, ... P_n, each with its weight W_1, W_2, ... W_n, $P_i \in \{H, L\}$, $W_i \in \{hW, mW, lW\}$ (as in Table 2). As already mentioned, if an H value for a pattern P_i can be associated with a characteristic C, then an L value of pattern P_i can be associated with the opposite characteristic $\tilde{C}$.

For each student, we can determine the values corresponding to all the patterns for each of the characteristics in ULSM', together with the reliability levels of these values. Thus for characteristic C and for student j we have: the pattern values P_i^j with the weights W_i (the weights are the same for all students) and the reliability levels R_i^j, with $P_i^j \in \{H, M, L\}$, $W_i \in \{hW, mW, lW\}$, $R_i^j \in \{hR, mR, lR\}$, where the weights and reliability levels are subunitary values (i.e. $hW, mW, lW, hR, mR, lR \in [0,1]$). We can now compute the value of student j's preference for characteristic C with the following formula:

$$V_j(C) = \frac{\sum_{i=1}^{n} p_i^j * R_i^j * W_i}{n}, \text{ where}$$

$$p_i^j = \begin{cases} 1 & \text{if } P_i^j = P_i \\ 0 & \text{if } P_i^j = M \\ -1 & \text{otherwise} \end{cases}$$

The value obtained for $V_j(C)$ can be interpreted as follows: if $V_j(C) > 0$ then we can say that stu-

Table 2. Relevant patterns for each ULSM' dimension, together with associated weights (L / H – low / high value of the pattern; hW, mW, lW – high / medium / low weight of the pattern)

ULSM' dimension	Patterns
p_visual / p_verbal	t_Image (H) - hW
	t_Video (H) - hW
	t_Text (L) - hW
	t_Sound (L) - hW
	h_Image (H) - mW
	h_Video (H) - mW
	h_Text (L) - mW
	h_Sound (L) - mW
	grade_Image (H) - mW
	n_chat_msg (L) - lW
	t_chat (L) - lW
	n_forum_msg (L) - lW
	n_forum_reads (L) - lW
	t_forum (L) - lW
p_abstract / p_concrete	sequence_fundamental_before_illustration (H) – hW
	sequence_abstract_first (H) – hW
	t_Fundamental (H) - hW
	t_abstract (H) – hW
	t_Illustration (L) – hW
	t_concrete (L) – hW
	h_Fundamental (H) – lW
	h_Illustration (L) - lW
	h_abstract (H) – lW
	h_concrete (L) - lW
	grade_abstract (H) – lW
	grade_concrete (L) - lW

continued on following page

Table 2. Continued

p_serial / p_holistic	*n_nextButton (H) – hW* *n_prevButton (L) – hW* *n_outline (L) – hW* *t_outline (L) – mW* *n_jump (L) - hW* *t_Introduction (L) – lW* *t_Objectives (L) – lW* *t_AdditionalInfo (L) - lW* *h_Introduction (L) – mW* *h_Objectives (L) – mW* *h_AdditionalInfo (L) – mW* *n_skippedLO_temp (L) – hW* *n_skippedLO_perm (L) – mW* *n_returns_LO (L) - mW* *grade_details (H) – lW* *grade_overview (L) – lW* *grade_connections (L) – lW* *sequence_exercise_last (L) - lW*
p_activeExperimentation / p_reflectiveObservation	*sequence_interactivity_before_fundamental (H) - hW* *sequence_interactivity_before_illustration (H) – hW* *t_Exercise (H) - mW* *t_Exploration (H) - hW* *h_Exercise (H) - lW* *h_Exploration (H) - lW*
p_carefulDetails / p_notCarefulDetails	*t_test (H) - hW* *n_revisions_test (H) - hW* *grade_details (H) - mW* *t_Details (t_Remark + t_Demonstration + t_AdditionalInfo) (H) – mW* *h_Details (h_Remark + h_Demonstration + h_AdditionalInfo) (H) - lW*
p_individual / p_team	*n_chat_msg (L) – hW* *t_chat (L) – hW* *n_forum_msg (L) – hW* *n_forum_reads (L) – hW* *t_forum (L) – hW* *n_individualAssignment (H) – hW* *n_askPeerHelp (L) – mW* *n_offerPeerHelp (L) - mW*

dent *j* has a preference towards characteristic *C*; if $V_j(C) < 0$ then we can say that student *j* has a preference towards the opposite characteristic, $\tilde{C}$.

Furthermore, the absolute value of $V_j(C)$ gives an indication on the strength of the preference: a value close to 0 implies a mild preference (a rather balanced learning style), while greater values imply stronger preferences.

A few more comments on this formula are in order. First it should be noted that for $\forall j$:

$$V_j(C) \in [-\frac{\sum_{i=1}^{n} W_i}{n}, \frac{\sum_{i=1}^{n} W_i}{n}] \subseteq [-1,1].$$

The maximum value for $V_j(C)$ is obtained when all the patterns have values indicating towards the characteristic C (i.e. $p_i^j = 1, \forall i = 1..n$) and there is enough data available for student j to reliably compute all the patterns P_i^j (i.e. $R_i^j = 1, \forall i = 1..n$). Similarly, the minimum value for $V_j(C)$ is obtained when all the patterns have values indicating towards the characteristic $\tilde{C}$ (i.e. $p_i^j = -1, \forall i = 1..n$) and there is enough data available for student j to reliably compute all the patterns P_i^j (i.e. $R_i^j = 1, \forall i = 1..n$). When we don't have enough information to compute a reliable value for pattern P_i^j, we want that value to contribute less to the final diagnosis; when we have very few data on a student, most R_i^j will be very small and consequently $V_j(C)$ will be close to 0, indicating a balanced learning style. Indeed, when lacking data to make an informed diagnosis, a balanced preference is the safest assumption one can make.

We can also compute a confidence value associated to each $V_j(C)$, reflecting the degree of trust that we can have in the value of the student j's preference for characteristic C (based on the availability of data for student j):

$$Conf_j(C) = \frac{\sum_{i=1}^{n} R_i^j}{n}$$

It should be noted that $Conf_j(C) \in [0, 1]$. A small value implies a low degree of confidence in the value $V_j(C)$, while a large value implies a high degree of confidence.

EXPERIMENTAL VALIDATION OF THE MODELING METHOD

Experiment Settings

In order to validate the proposed rule-based modeling method, we applied it on the data collected from 71 undergraduate students in the field of Computer Science that participated in our study. As test platform we used WELSA educational system and a course module in the area of Artificial Intelligence. The course module deals with search strategies and solving problems by search and is based on the fourth chapter of Poole, Mackworth and Goebel's AI textbook (Poole et al., 1998). The course consists of 4 sections and 9 subsections, including a total of 46 learning objects (LOs). From the point of view of the media type, the course includes both *'Text'* LOs (35), as well as *'Image'*, *'Video'* and *'Animation'* LOs (11). From the point of view of the instructional role of the LO, the course consists of 12 *'Fundamental'* LOs (5 *'Definition'* and 7 *'Algorithm'*) and 34 *'Auxiliary'* LOs (4 *'Additional Info'*, 1 *'Demonstration'*, 14 *'Example'*, 5 *'Exercise'*, 3 *'Exploration'*, 5 *'Introduction'*, 1 *'Objectives'* and 1 *'Remark'*). The course also includes access to two communication tools, one synchronous (*chat*) and one asynchronous (*forum*) and offers two navigation choices – either by means of the *Next* and *Previous* buttons, or by means of the *Outline*.

The experiment lasted for 4 hours: 2 hours were reserved for course studying, and 2 hours for discussions and filling-in some questionnaires. For the first part of the experiment, the students accessed WELSA and all of their interactions with the system were recorded. Afterwards, the students were asked to self-diagnose their learning preferences and characterize them as mild, moderate or strong by filling in the ULSM questionnaire. They were also given the chance to comment on their learning preferences, the structure and presentation of the course and their experience in interacting with WELSA.

In order to analyze the data, we first modified some of the default pattern weights (i.e. the values from Table 2), as well as eliminate some of the patterns which were not relevant in the context of our experiment. Thus we excluded the patterns *t_Sound* and *h_Sound*, since the course did not include any audio resources. Furthermore, although WELSA provides a forum, due to the temporal constraints of the experiment, the learners had neither the time nor the incentive to use this forum. We have therefore excluded the patterns related to it from our analysis (*n_forum_msg, n_forum_reads, t_forum*). Moreover, the course did not include any online evaluation tests, so the two related patterns were also left out (*t_test, n_revisions_test*). Finally, there were no group/individual assignments that the students could choose from, so the patterns *n_individualAssignment, n_askPeerHelp*, as well as *n_offerPeerHelp* were excluded from our analysis. The default pattern thresholds from Table 1 were used, since there were no inconsistencies between these values and the course structure.

Next we computed the pattern values and then, based on them, the learning preferences and the associated confidence degrees. All the configurations and computations were done by means of the WELSA Analysis tool.

Evaluation Method

In order to evaluate the quality of our method, we compared the results obtained using the rule-based modeling approach (LP_{Rule}), with the results obtained by student self-diagnosis, using the ULSM questionnaire (LP_{Quest}). We considered three possible values for each dimension $C/\tilde{C} \in Dim\_ULSM$: strong/medium preference towards C (denoted P_C), strong/medium preference towards $\tilde{C}$ (denoted $P_{\tilde{C}}$) or balanced preference (denoted P_B).

In case of the preferences obtained by means of the rule-based method (i.e. $V_j(C)$), values in $[-w, w]$, with $w = \dfrac{\sum_{i=1}^{n} W_i}{n}$ had to be mapped to the 3-item

scale. The range was divided in 3 equal parts: P_C corresponds to the values greater than $\frac{1}{3} * w$, $P_{\tilde{C}}$ corresponds to the values smaller than $-\frac{1}{3} * w$, while P_B corresponds to the values in $[-\frac{1}{3} * w, \frac{1}{3} * w]$. The precision of our method can be obtained with the formula in Box 1.

M is the number of students in the sample for which we compute the precision.

The above formula is based on the similarity between the results obtained using our rule-based method and the reference results (obtained by means of the ULSM questionnaire).

Results and Discussion

Table 3 presents the results that we obtained using the rule-based modeling method, for each of the ULSM' dimensions.

As can be seen, we obtained very good results for two ULSM dimensions (*p_abstract / p_concrete* and *p_activeExperimentation / p_reflectiveObservation*), good results for three ULSM dimensions (*p_visual / p_verbal, p_serial / p_holistic, p_carefulDetails / p_notCarefulDetails*) and moderate results for one ULSM dimension (*p_individual / p_team*).

The less accurate results obtained for the *p_individual / p_team* dimension can be explained by the very small number of behavioral patterns used (just two patterns were relevant in the current conditions of the experiment). Furthermore, the students' use of chat was very limited, as resulted from the analysis of available data. When questioned about this aspect, the arguments given by students who declared having a preference towards team work fell in two main categories: some of them prefer "face-to-face" interaction, others said that the course did not necessitate large amount of collaboration since no group assignments existed. Further experiments including team assignments and more sophisticated collaborative tools should be performed in order to obtain better outcomes.

Box 1.

$$\text{Precision} = \frac{\sum_{j=1}^{M} Sim(LP_{Rule}^{j}, LP_{Quest}^{j})}{M},$$

where

$$Sim(LP_{Rule}^{j}, LP_{Quest}^{j}) = \begin{cases} 1 & if LP_{Rule}^{j} = LP_{Quest}^{j} \\ 0.5 & if LP_{Rule}^{j} \neq LP_{Quest}^{j} \ and \ (LP_{Rule}^{j} = P_{B} \ or \ LP_{Quest}^{j} = P_{B}) \\ 0 & otherwise \end{cases}$$

Table 3. Precision of the rule-based modeling method

ULSM' dimension	Precision
p_visual / p_verbal	73.94%
p_abstract / p_concrete	82.39%
p_serial / p_holistic	78.17%
p_activeExperimentation / p_reflectiveObservation	84.51%
p_carefulDetails / p_notCarefulDetails	71.13%
p_individual / p_team	64.08%

The very good results obtained in case of *p_abstract/p_concrete* and *p_activeExperimentation /p_reflectiveObservation* can be attributed to the relatively large number of relevant patterns, as well as to the course composition, which included plenty of related educational resources (*Examples, Exercises, Explorations* etc) and consequently led to the availability of the relevant student data. As expected, the efficiency of our method depends on the amount of data available, which is based both on the amount of time spent by students interacting with the platform and on the nature of the course and the variety of resources it is made up of.

For comparison, we include in Table 4 the results obtained with the approaches used in the papers (Cha et al., 2006), (Garcia et al., 2007) and (Graf, 2007), that we introduced in section 2. It can be observed that our rule-based modeling method yielded above average results.

It should be noted that in the three analyzed papers the learning style model used is Felder-Silverman and the approaches are various, ranging from rule-based modeling to Bayesian networks, Decision trees and Hidden Markov models. The formula used for computing precision in case of (Garcia et al., 2007) and (Graf, 2007) is similar with the one defined above. In case of (Cha et al., 2006), only students with moderate to strong FSLSM preferences (i.e. ILS score >= 5) are considered.

CONCLUSION

Attempting to represent knowledge regarding complex psychological characteristics of the learner is a challenging research goal. In this chapter we tried to address the modeling process of the students' learning style, one of the factors that play an important role in learning. We started

Table 4. Precision of learner modeling methods according to FSLSM model in (Cha et al., 2006), (Garcia et al., 2007) and (Graf, 2007)

FSLSM dimension / Modeling Approach	Active / Reflective	Sensing / Intuitive	Visual / Verbal	Sequential / Global
(Cha et al., 2006) – Decision Trees	66.67%	77.78%	100%	71.43%
(Cha et al., 2006) – Hidden Markov Models	66.67%	77.78%	85.72%	85.72%
(Garcia et al., 2007) – Bayesian Networks	58%	77 %	N/A	63%
(Graf, 2007) - Bayesian Networks	62.50%	65.00%	68.75%	66.25%
(Graf, 2007) – Rule based approach	79.33%	77.33%	76.67%	73.33%

with a critical review of existing approaches, succinctly presenting the educational systems that attempt to model the students' learning style.

However this is a controversial issue, especially due to the multitude of partially overlapping learning style models proposed in the literature. We argue that instead of debating over the most appropriate learning style model, it is better to take the best of each model and use a complex of features, each with its own importance and influence. In this respect, we proposed a Unified Learning Style Model approach and outlined its advantages.

As far as the modeling method is concerned, we introduced an implicit approach, based on analyzing student behavior in the educational system. The rule-based approach was validated through experimental research, obtaining good precision results.

A limitation of our work is represented by the relatively restricted student sample that was used in our experiments – in order to allow for generalization, the modeling method should be tested on a wider scale, with learners of variable age, field of study, background knowledge and technical experience. We therefore plan to repeat the experiment for longer periods of time and with a larger and more diverse student sample.

Modeling is just the first step in the adaptation process – providing a learning experience that is individualized to the particular needs of the learner, as identified in the modeling stage, is the ultimate goal. In this context, an adaptation component was conceived and implemented in our WELSA system, with the aim of adapting the course so as to best suit the ULSM characteristics diagnosed in this chapter.

As future work, the modeling component could also be extended to take into account the perturbations introduced by the adaptation on students' actions. Students' behavior in the adapted version could then be used as a valuable feedback on the effect of adaptation. Furthermore, the modeling method could be improved by automatically fine tuning the behavioral patterns' thresholds and weights to conform to the specificities of each course. In this context, our research can be seen as the basis for a truly dynamic learner modeling approach.

FUTURE TRENDS

The accommodation of individual differences in general and learning styles in particular seems to win ground in current educational hypermedia research. However, most of the existing systems treat learning styles in isolation of the rest of the features in the student profile (knowledge, interests, goals). The ideal would be to integrate all these features in a more comprehensive and representative learner profile. The "context of work" feature should start being taken into consideration also, given the recent advent of mobile and ubiquitous learning. In the same integrative context, implicit modeling methods should be used in conjunction with explicit ones, in order to address the cold start problem and improve the accuracy of the diagnosis.

An important concern of educational systems that record the learning style of the students is to ensure the necessary privacy of their users. In case of an automatic diagnosing method, the learning preferences shouldn't necessarily be revealed to either the student or the teacher, but could only be used by the system for adaptation purposes. This would ensure a complete privacy of the learner and avoid the danger of stereotyping. However, an even better approach would be to educate both the students and the teachers to correctly understand and deal with learning styles. Metacognition and learning style awareness can help students understand their strengths and weaknesses in the learning process and use them to their advantage.

Perhaps the most important desideratum of the LSAES in general is that they surpass their current status of research systems and get to be used in practice, gaining a popularity similar to that of the learning management systems.

REFERENCES

Alonso, C. M., Gallego, D. J., & Honey, P. (2002). *The Learning Styles.* Ediciones Mensajero.

Bajraktarevic, N., Hall, W., & Fullick, P. (2003). Incorporating learning styles in hypermedia environment: Empirical evaluation, *Procs. Workshop on Adaptive Hypermedia and Adaptive Web-Based Systems* (pp. 41-52).

Biggs, J. (1987). *Student Approaches to Learning and Studying,* Australian Council for Educational Research, Hawthorn.

Brusilovsky, P., & Millan, E. (2007). User Models for Adaptive Hypermedia and Adaptive Educational Systems. In: P. Brusilovsky, A. Kobsa and W. Neidl (eds.), *The Adaptive Web: Methods and Strategies of Web Personalization* (pp. 3-53). Lecture Notes in Computer Science, Vol. 4321, Springer.

Carver, C. A., Howard, R. A., & Lane, W. D. (1999). Enhancing student learning through hypermedia courseware and incorporation of student learning styles. *IEEE Transactions on Education*, 42, 33-38.

Cha, H. J., Kim, Y. S., Park, S. H., Yoon, T. B., Jung, Y. M., & Lee J. H. (2006). Learning styles diagnosis based on user interface behaviors for the customization of learning interfaces in an intelligent tutoring system. *Procs. ITS 06* (pp. 513-524). Lecture Notes in Computer Science, Vol. 4053, Springer.

Coffield, F., Moseley, D., Hall, E., & Ecclestone, K. (2004). *Learning styles and pedagogy in post-16 learning. A systematic and critical review.* Learning and Skills Research Centre, UK.

Dunn, R., & Dunn, K. (1992). *Teaching secondary students through their individual learning styles.* Needham Heights, MA: Allyn and Bacon.

Felder, R. M., & Silverman, L. K. (1988). Learning and teaching styles in engineering education. *Engineering Education*, 78(7), 674-681. Preceded by a preface in 2002. Retrieved May 23, 2008, from http://www4.ncsu.edu/unity/lockers/users/f/felder/public/Papers/LS-1988.pdf

Flemming, N.D. (1995). I am different; not dumb. Modes of presentation (V.A.R.K.) in the tertiary classroom. In A. Zelmer (Ed.): *Research and development in higher education. Proceedings of the 1995 annual conference of the higher education and research development society of Australia (HERDSA)*, Vol. 18 (pp. 308–313).

Garcia, P., Amandi, A., Schiaffino, S., & Campo, M. (2007). Evaluating Bayesian Networks' Precision for Detecting Students' Learning Styles. *Computers & Education,* 49(3), 794-808.

Gardner, H. (1993). *Multiple Intelligences: The Theory in Practice.* Basic Books, New York.

Gilbert, J.E., & Han, C.Y. (1999). Adapting instruction in search of 'a significant difference'. *Journal of Network and Computer Applications,* 22(3), 149-160.

Graf, S. (2007). *Adaptivity in Learning Management Systems Focussing on Learning Styles.* Unpublished doctoral dissertation, Vienna University of Technology, Austria.

Herrmann, N. (1996). *The Whole Brain Business Book.* McGraw-Hill.

Honey, P., & Mumford, A. (2000). *The learning styles helper's guide.* Maidenhead: Peter Honey Publications Ltd.

Kay, J. (2001). Learner Control. *User Modeling and User-Adapted Interaction,* 11, 111-127.

Keefe, J. (1979). Learning style: an overview. *NASSP's Student Learning Styles: Diagnosing and Prescribing Programs,* 1-17.

Kelly, D., & Tangney, B. (2006). Adapting to intelligence profile in an adaptive educational system. *Interacting with Computers,* 18, 385-409.

Moodle (2008). Available at: http://moodle.org.

Papanikolaou, K. A., Grigoriadou, M., Kornilakis, H., & Magoulas, G.D. (2003). Personalizing the interaction in a Web-based educational hypermedia system: the case of INSPIRE. *User Modeling and User-Adapted Interaction,* 13, 213-267.

Papanikolaou, K. A., & Grigoriadou, M. (2004). Accommodating learning style characteristics in Adaptive Educational Hypermedia Systems. *Procs. Workshop on Individual Differences in Adaptive Hypermedia,* The University of Technology, Netherlands, August 23–26, 2004.

Paredes, P., & Rodriguez, P. (2004). A Mixed Approach to Modelling Learning Styles in Adaptive Educational Hypermedia. *Advanced Technology for Learning,* 1(4), 210-215.

Paule, M. P., Pérez, J. R., & González, M. (2003). Feijoo.net. An Approach to Personalized e-Learning Using Learning Styles. *Procs. ICWE* (pp. 112-115). Lecture Notes in Computer Science, Vol. 2722, Springer.

Poole, D., Mackworth, A., & Goebel, R. (1998). *Computational Intelligence: A Logical Approach,* Oxford University Press.

Popescu, E., Trigano, P., & Badica, C. (2007). Towards a unified learning style model in adaptive educational systems. *Procs. ICALT 2007* (pp. 804-808). IEEE Computer Society Press.

Popescu, E. (2008a). An Artificial Intelligence Course Used to Investigate Students' Learning Style. *Procs. ICWL 2008* (pp. 122-131). Lecture Notes in Computer Science, Vol. 5145, Springer.

Popescu, E. (2008b). *Dynamic adaptive hypermedia systems for e-learning.* Unpublished doctoral dissertation, University of Craiova, Romania.

Popescu, E. Badica, C., & Trigano, P. (2008). Learning Objects' Architecture and Indexing in WELSA Adaptive Educational System. *Scalable Computing: Practice and Experience,* 9(1), 11-20.

Popescu, E. (2009). Learning Styles and Behavioral Differences in Web-based Learning Settings. *Procs. ICALT 2009.* IEEE Computer Society Press (in press).

Roberts, M. J., & Newton, E. J. (2001). Understanding strategy selection. *International Journal of Computer Studies,* 54, 137-154.

Rovai, A. P., & Barnum, K.T. (2003). On-Line Course Effectiveness: An Analysis of Student Interactions and Perceptions of Learning. *Journal of Distance Education,* 18(1), 57-73.

Sangineto, E., Capuano, N., Gaeta, M., & Micarelli, A. (2008). Adaptive course generation through learning styles representation. *Journal of Universal Access in the Information Society,* 7(1), 1-23.

Shearer, B. (1996). *The MIDAS Handbook of Multiple Intelligences in the Classroom,* Greyden Press, Ohio.

Soloman, B., & Felder, R. M. (1998). *Index of learning styles questionnaire.* Retrieved May 23, 2008, from http://www.engr.ncsu.edu/learning-styles/ilsweb.html.

Stash, N. (2007). *Incorporating Cognitive/Learning Styles in a General-Purpose Adaptive Hypermedia System.* Unpublished doctoral dissertation, Eindhoven University of Technology, Netherlands.

Stathacopoulou, R., Grigoriadou, M., Samarakou, M., & Mitropoulos, D. (2007). Monitoring students' actions and using teachers' expertise in implementing and evaluating the neural network-based fuzzy diagnostic model. *Expert Systems with Applications,* 32, 955-975.

Triantafillou, E., Pomportsis, A., & Demetriadis, S. (2003). The design and the formative evaluation of an adaptive educational system based on cognitive styles. *Computers & Education,* 41, 87-103.

Wang, T., Wang, K., & Huang, Y. (2008). Using a style-based ant colony system for adaptive learning. *Expert Systems with Applications,* 34 (4), 2449-2464.

Wolf, C. (2002). iWeaver: Towards an Interactive Web-Based Adaptive Learning Environment to Address Individual Learning Styles. *European Journal of Open, Distance and E-Learning.* Retrieved May 23, 2008, from http://www.eurodl.org/materials/contrib/2002/2HTML/iWeaver.htm

Witkin, H. A. (1962). *Psychological differentiation: studies of development.* New York: Wiley.

Chapter XII
Cognitive Learning Approaches to the Design of Accessible E-Learning Systems

Ray Adams
Middlesex University, UK

Andrina Granić
University of Split, Croatia

ABSTRACT

The creation of exciting, new, powerful and accessible e-learning systems depends upon innovations in cognitive science, human learning, e-learning implementation principles and derivative, technological e-learning solutions. The issues of user sensitive design and user diversity are central to such developments and so must be one of the focuses of any effective e-learning system. This chapter shows how a unique characterization of the interaction between e-learning requirements, accessibility and cognitive user modeling generates an inimitable set of solutions to current e-learning problems, through a simple and supportive conceptual framework. In so doing, the authors show how evidence and insights from diverse subjects such as cognitive science, computing science and social sciences can be integrated to provide a robust platform for the next generations of pedagogically enriched e-learning systems.

INTRODUCTION

In the emerging inclusive Information Society (Savidis & Stephanidis, 2004), the intended users of e-learning systems are becoming much more demanding, expecting systems that are fast and powerful, customized and accessible, intelligent and adaptive, effective and efficient for human learning (Adams & Granić, 2007; Granić, 2008).

Focusing on e-learning, i.e. an instructional content or learning experience delivered or enabled by electronic technology (Pantazis, 2001), it is the case that, despite so much publicity and activity, progress in the field has been unexpectedly slow. In order to improve the learning experience and effectiveness and increase an e-learning system's intelligent behaviour, interactive mechanisms merit additional consideration and enhancement.

There should be a synergy between the learning process and a user's/learner's interaction with the e-learning application (Squires & Preece, 1996), additionally taking into account the different ways users learn, so supporting their natural and flexible interactions with the host system. Most current e-learning applications are static and inflexible, designed with little or no consideration of users' preferences and abilities. It is vital to overcome this one-size-fits-all approach and provide users with individual learning experiences through e-learning systems with intelligent and adaptive user interface.

BACKGROUND

In this background section, we provide broad definitions of helpful concepts that form the basis of 21st century e-learning. They include, but are not limited to, such concepts as: learning environments, e-learning, accessibility, adaptability, adaptivity, ambient intelligence, system smartness and user modeling (Adams, 2008).

A *learning environment* is a setting that is arranged to enhance the learning experience. In order for learning to take place, according to Pulkinen and Peltonen (1998) there are three essential components of any learning environment: pedagogical and psychological functions (learning activities, teaching situations, learning materials, assessment, etc.), appropriate technologies (how the selected tools are connected with the pedagogical model) and social organization of education (time, place and community). From another perspective a learning environment can be defined as constructivist in nature, enabling the learners to engage in "sense-making" about extensive information. On this view, the learning environment comprises four components: an enabling context, resources, a set of tools and scaffolds (Hannafin, Land, & Oliver, 1999). In addition, realistic contexts motivate learners, and involve them in complex, real-world tasks.

Piccoli, Ahmad and Ives *(*2001) argue that learning environments are defined in terms of time, place and space. According to them, it is also possible to expand the traditional definition of learning environment to include three further dimensions: technology, interaction and control. However, their definition did not include the consideration of learning the system usage and the corresponding skills required. A simple definition of e-learning is instructional contents or learning experiences that are delivered or enabled by electronic technology (Pantazis, 2001). One of the most technically advanced form of e-learning can be seen as the virtual learning environment. In early versions (Pimentel, 1999) students learn through an interactive environment that deploys text, images, voice, video, touch and graphics. In later versions (Little, 2008) virtual reality applications such as Second Life™ can proffer virtual realities than can become almost totally immersive and offer enhanced learning opportunities, including social or inter-personal skills.

Accessibility is another of our key concepts. It can be defined as the absence of barriers that would stop or impede user exploitation of a learning system. Adams (2007) has identified at least six types of accessibility problem. The barriers identified are summarized as:

a. hardware barriers,
b. communications barriers,
c. sensory / perceptual problems,
d. cognitive barriers, particularly in navigational demands and comprehension of contents,
e. barriers to learning and performance objectives and
f. unrealistic response requirements (see further ahead in this chapter for more details).

Accessibility is an increasingly noteworthy concept and is more and more supported by punitive legislation. For example, in the UK the Special

Educational Needs and Disability Act (SENDA) was implemented in 2002 and means that UK educational institutions are no longer exempt from the Disability Discrimination Act (1995) and must provide equal access to resources and information in general and website accessibility in particular to people with disabilities. Equally, the USA has the Americans with Disabilities Act of 1990 (ADA). Whilst web accessibility is often defined to mean that "that people with disabilities can use the Web," it is important to point out that web accessibility can also benefit others, as discussed in http://www.w3.org/WAI/intro/accessibility.php (accessed May 15, 2008). In fact, in the context of the emerging inclusive Information Society, the aspiration of universal accessibility is to provide access to everyone who wants it (Savidis & Stephanidis, 2004).

Intelligent User Interfaces (IUIs), bringing the concepts of adaptability and adaptivity, have been recommended as means for making systems individualized or personalized, thus enhancing its flexibility and attractiveness. They facilitate a more natural interaction between users and computers, not attempting to imitate human-human communication, but instead aiding the human-computer interaction process (Hook, 2000). The intelligence in interface can for example make the system adapt to the needs of different users, take initiative and make suggestions to the user, learn new concepts and techniques or provide explanation of its actions *cf.* (Hook, 2000; Lieberman, 1997). A satisfactory framework for taking into account users' heterogeneity has provided (Schneider-Hufschmidt, Kühme & Malinowski, 1993):

- *adaptable systems* along with the concept of *adaptability*, by allowing the user to control the interface customization and
- *adaptive systems* with the concept of *adaptivity*, by adapting the interface behaviour

to user's individual characteristics; adaptive interface generally relies upon the use of user models (UMs), a collection of information and assumptions about particular users which is needed in the adaptation process of the system to an individual (Kobsa, 1995).

Ambient Intelligence (AmI) is another important concept and is best understood as a pervasive and unobtrusive intelligence in the surrounding environment supporting the activities and interactions of the users. Increasingly AmI is used in combination with augmented reality in which scenes also have computer generated objects e.g. sound, graphics etc to enhance the user experience (Riva, Loreti, Lunghi, Vatalaro, and Davide, 2003).

System smartness is defined as the possession of functions and attributes by a system that would be judged to be intelligent in the case of a human operator. One example is such a system being able to pass a modern, cognitive version of the Turing Test. The term smart, as used here, does not necessarily imply true intelligence, merely a simulation or appearance of it (Adams & Russell, 2006; Adams & Granić, 2007).

Of course, significant interactions between these important factors are of growing interest too. For example, are ambient intelligent applications universally accessible? (Adams, Granić & Keates, 2008). These authors evaluated six AmI systems and found an analysis of the accessibility of such systems to be surprisingly more complex than they expected. Thus, whilst the systems were rated highly overall for accessibility and usability, there were a number of complications. All six were rated well for accessibility, all six were significantly less so for system smartness and user satisfaction. Usability was also rated higher than user satisfaction and system smartness. Clearly, there is much more work to do in this area.

COGNITIVE LEARNING APPROACHES TO THE DESIGN OF ACCESSIBLE E-LEARNING SYSTEMS: ISSUES, CONTROVERSIES, PROBLEMS

It is clear from the background information presented earlier in this chapter that there are a number of issues, controversies and problems that relate strongly to our theme of cognitive learning approaches to the design of accessible e-learning systems. They include:

a. a better appreciation of the pedagogical principles underlying e-learning,

b. the psychology of human learning,

c. the development of better learning environments, including e-learning, virtual realities and augmented realities,

d. design for accessible and usable e-learning systems,

e. the development of ambient intelligence and smarter systems as well as

f. the appreciation of the synergy between cognitive and emotive factors in human learning.

A Better Appreciation of the Pedagogical Principles Underlying E-Learning

Pedagogic principles point to the sound and effective development of human learning environments based on well established guidelines. For example, consistency between learning objectives, learning and assessment methods might be helpful for effective human learning (Biggs 2001). Additionally, it is important to take into account individual differences between different learners.

Current research in this field is beginning to acknowledge that understanding users' needs is at the core of successful designs for Information Society Technologies (IST) products and services.

This naturally leads to *user-centered design* approaches, a philosophy which places the users at the centre of design (Norman & Draper, 1986) and a process that focuses on cognitive factors (such as perception, memory, learning, problem-solving, and alike) as they come into play during users' interactions with applications (Zaharias, 2005; Adams, 2007a). However, we are far from achieving the goal of user-centered design for systems that support effective human e-learning.

In order to "make people more effective learners", i.e. to take into account the unique needs of users as learners, a shift from user-centered to *learner-centered design* is needed (Soloway, Guzdial & Hay, 1994). It can range from attempts to design with the needs of the learner at the forefront, towards involving the learner at various stages of the design process (Good & Robertson, 2006). Such an approach entails understanding and considering who is the user, what are her/his needs, what we want her/him to learn, how is (s) he going to learn it and how are we going to support her/him in achieving the learning objectives. Accordingly, a variety of learners' types must be considered due to characteristics revealing user individual differences such as personal learning styles and strategies, diverse experience in the learning domain, as well as previously acquired knowledge and abilities. Many authors have attempted to provide comprehensive lists of additional needs for specific educational domains, but (Soloway, Jackson, Klein, Quintana, Reed, Spitulnik, Stratford, Studer & Jul, 1996) concisely summarize them under broad categories of universal applicability. This work begins to provide a foundation for matching the nature of the learning experience to the differentiated requirements of diverse learners. Such a foundation will be increasingly useful when meeting learner diversity. The role of an intuitive user interface and a flexible interaction suited to different needs, preferences and interests becomes even more important for the users' success, as users with a wide variety of background, skills, interests, expertise, goals and learning styles *cf.* (Benyon, Crerar & Wilkinson, 2001; Egan, 1988) are using computers for quite diverse purposes, including for learning purposes. If so, this points to the need for effective learning tools with which practitioners can develop and deliver their own learning environments.

The Psychology of Human Learning

The field of *human learning in psychology* is developing fast. This presents a significant problem for practitioners who wish to apply the best and most relevant findings to improve e-teaching and e-learning. Psychological theories are intended to capture and integrate such findings into coherent bodies of knowledge. However, current theories are often too complex for the practitioner to deploy, though they can offer potential benefits for those who are willing to climb a steep learning close.

Complex and powerful theories of human learning and cognition include ACT-R (Adaptive Control of thought–Rational; Anderson & Lebiere, 1998), SOAR (not an acronym; Newell, 1990), COGENT (not an acronym; Fox, 1980; Fox & Cooper, 1997) and ICS (Interacting Cognitive Subsystems; Barnard, 1999; Barnard, May, Duke & Duce, 2000). A full review of such models is beyond the scope of this chapter or any one chapter, but these models all appear to share a number of important qualities and they deserve attention within the context of the psychology of human learning.

Consider ACT-R briefly (Anderson, 1983). It has a long and distinguished career in psychology and provides a powerful architecture of human cognition. The aim is to help us better understand and simulate human cognitive processes. The long term goal is to develop a fully grown system that can explain the full range of human cognitive activities, including working with interactive systems and, of course, human learning. Further information is available from the ACT-R web site (see URL in references list). ACT-R based research has generated over five hundred publications (as shown in the above web-site) and this count does not include publications about earlier versions of ACT-R and predecessor models. Clearly ACT-R is a powerful and complex theoretical framework but can present difficulties when being applied to practical problems because of that complexity.

Another approach to applying modern psychology to practical problems such as e-learning is to develop "simplistic theories" (Adams, 2007a). Such theories are deliberately designed both to capture relevant and current findings but also to be simple enough to guide practitioners. In the words of Einstein (1934) "Everything should be made as simple as possible, but no simpler." The Model Human Processor (MHP) is an alternative to complex cognitive theories and can be seen as a cut-down psychological theory, one that can be used by designers and other computer scientists, but without the over-powering complexities of a fully-fledged theory. The Model Human Processor (Card, Moran & Newell, 1983) is one outstanding theory that deliberately takes this tactic. MHP has the dual advantages of being simple enough to be applicable and also being developed directly to solve IT design problems. Over the years, the status of MHP as a psychological process has been strongly criticized. Such criticisms have been due, in part, to a failure to appreciate that MHP was never intended as a full psychological theory, but rather an application of then current cognitive psychology to act as a guide to system design and evaluation.

Some subsequent research has attempted, with some success, to develop MHP further (Liu, Feyen & Tsimhoni, 2006). They developed the Queuing Network-Model Human Processor (QN-MHP) in an attempt to integrate the queuing network and the symbolic approaches as a basis for cognitive modeling. The overall aim was unify theoretical and methodological aspects of cognitive modeling and the development of usable, HCI simulation methods. This theory was never intended as a full theory of human cognition but as a tractable guide for system designers and evaluators, providing a simple but coherent model of the intended users. Whilst this approach has been criticized for its incompleteness, it was never intended to be complete, merely to capture and apply the main relevant points of then current theories in cognition (Dix, Finlay, Abowd & Beale, 2004). MHP is clearly useful for personal computer based interfaces but may not be so applicable to the emerging, new types of technology (Byrne, 2001). A number of major paradigm shifts have occurred in system design and in the issues considered important in this field. So MHP perhaps is best seen as a brilliant trail blazer which should encourage us to develop new ways of dealing with interactive technology in all its forms, with user supportive architectures and with adaptable and self-adaptive new systems. However, it has considerable value as both a teaching aid and to inspire new approaches. For example, consider the inclusive design approach (Keates & Clarkson, 2003) that draws explicitly on MHP to construct the inclusion cube.

Broadbent's Maltese cross provided a further, conceptual advance, affording a well defined executive function and the two-way flow of information. This memory-store model has been based upon a considerable volume of high quality research and presented in a seminal paper (Broadbent, 1984). There are four memory stores and a well delineated executive function, i.e. input memory, output memory, working memory, long-term memory and a linking executive function and was presented as a simplistic model of human memory. However, it has the potential to be a cohesive architecture of human cognition. It has been compared with a powerful von Neumann machine.

The concept of the simplistic theory is now relatively well established, the search is now on for such a theory that captures more recent advances in the psychology of human learning that will guide the development of the next generation of e-learning applications.

The Development of Better Learning Environments

Here we include a range of *environments for e-learning*, including the MUD (Multi-User Dimension), the MOO, (MUD Object Oriented or Multi-user Object Oriented), WOO (WEB Object Oriented or 'W3 + MOO'), virtual reality (VR) applications and augmented reality applications. MUDs and MOOS are different from other virtual reality systems since they are primarily text-based virtual realities intended for multi-use and accessible by the Internet. MUDs started as multi-user interactive role-playing games on the Internet but soon developed into communication and collaboration environments where diverse groups of people can meet online. The MOO provides a powerful programming language to support create entirely new objects, building the MOO virtual-world. It is, of course possible to add a graphical front end such as a 3D VR environment; one such example is "Diversity University". However, the potential of the MOO support individual and group learning has yet to been fully appreciated by e-teachers (Fanderclai, 1995).

Turning to more recent developments in VR, current computer technology allows us to create a striking range of imagery, displays, real-time computer graphics multi-sensory environment and virtual worlds that have the potential for a new generation of e-learning. The technology can vary from simple screens and keyboards to head-mounted audio-visual display, position sensors and tactile interface devices. In this way, learners can enter computer-generated environments that are limited only by the imagination of the designers and end-users. For example, Sloodle combines "Second Life", a VR application, with Moodle, a course management system. It promises to open up new opportunities for a social, immersive, e-learning experience, though it is still at an early stage of development (Kemp & Livingstone, 2006). At this stage it is clear that, exciting though these developments may be, they still have to pass several crucial tests. They include; how best to develop such systems without recreating old mistakes, how to keep costs to acceptable levels, accessibility, usability, personalization, adaptability, adaptivity and acceptability (Adams and Granić, 2007; Adams, 2007b; Granić and Ćukušić, 2007; Adams, Granić & Keates, 2008).

Design for Accessible and Usable E-Learning Systems

In the deservedly exciting developments in new and immersive learning environments, it is clear that they tend to be technology-driven rather than learner-driven. If so, there are at least three serious risks. First, their potential may not be realized or realizable given state-or-the-art current technologies and budgets. Second, they may fail to capture the requirements of their intended students and third, they may so easily be functionally exciting but fail to be either usable or accessible. This third point will be developed in more depth later on, but for now it is sufficient to say that technology-driven system solutions can often fail to be relevant, *accessible* or *usable* (Adams and Granić, 2007; Adams, 2007b; Granić and Ćukušić, 2007; Adams, Granić & Keates 2008). Earlier sections of this chapter show how accessibility comprises both a complex and a vital issue for designers of e-learning systems to tackle, if their offerings are to be acceptable to their intended users.

The Development of Ambient Intelligence and Smarter Systems

As discussed above, current work that conducted expert evaluations of six *ambient intelligence* (AmI) systems found that the chosen measures of accessibility, system smartness, user satisfaction and usability were not related to each other in simple ways. We found that ambient intelligence was not always appreciated by users. It was almost as if it acted as a background resource that is not always brought to the foreground and, if so, not always appreciated as much as it should. In addition, we also found that, whatever the explanation, user satisfaction could not be assumed to automatically accompany high levels of accessibility and usability and so cannot be taken for granted by developers and other practitioners (Adams, Granić & Keates, 2008). Riva, Vatalaro, Davide and Alcañiz (2001) set out the basic requirements for ambiently intelligent systems as follows. They argue that it should seamless connectivity, efficient network support and effectively accessible and usable interfaces. As they put it, AmI systems should "not involve a steep learning curve". Thus it should act as if it were aware of (a) the presence of the users, (b) their requirements and preferences, (c) be responsive in apparently intelligent ways to our attempts at communication and to our behaviour, (d) capable of intelligent dialogue, (e) be unobtrusive, even invisible when appropriate and (f) enjoyable.

Synergy between Cognitive and Emotive Factors in Human Learning

Stanford-Smith (2002) has concluded that much current e-learning is dull and boring. He calls it "little more than electronic page turning" or "Click & Yawn"! Yet virtual reality application and other modern solutions offer a learning environment that respects both cognitive and affective learning, providing a student learning experience that is logical and emotive, practical and quirky, organized and spontaneous. Traditionally, research on human cognition has been held at a distance from research on human emotions. For example, recent theories such as ACT-R (Anderson, 1983) and Simplex-One (Adams, Langdon & Clarkson, 2002) focus very much on cognitive processes that contribute to human information processing. However, more recent findings show how *cognitive* (information processing) and *emotive processes* interact. For example, Adams and Russell (2006) compared user performance on two, functionally equivalent websites. However, one of the websites was designed to be more irritating than the other website which, hopefully, was less irritating (one website required repeated log-ins, so the irritation level was quite mild). It turned out that performance on the less irritating website was significantly better than the more irritating website, all else being equal. Therefore more recent theories allow for the interaction between cognition and emotion (e.g. Simplex Two; Adams 2007a), though this forwards step has yet to be reflected in mainstream textbooks.

SOLUTIONS, RECOMMENDATIONS AND FUTURE TRENDS

In the context of the emerging knowledge society for all, the focus of research in this area has been set on applications of technologies for user-centered learning, building on the concept of learning and on sound pedagogical principle. The main objective is to increase the efficiency of learning contributing to a deeper understanding of the learning process by exploring links between human learning, cognition and technologies. What is becoming more evident as we explore advanced learning technologies is that holistic and systemic views of learners and their environments are necessary if we wish to make progress (Spector & Anderson, 2000).

In order to support the improvement of both, the learners' subject matter knowledge and learning strategy application, the e-learning environments should be designed to address learners' diversity in terms of learning styles, prior knowledge, culture and self-regulation skills (Vovides, 2007).

Compatibility of cognitive styles and technology directly impact perceptions of learning effectiveness, motivation and performance. When cognitive styles and technology are compatible, individuals are better equipped to attend to and interpret relevant information, which are important to learning and learning outcomes (Workman, 2004).

Individualized learning and reflective learning are two important ingredients that can enhance an e-learning system that supports learning and instruction offering the necessary scaffolds for the development of meta-cognitive and self-regulatory skills. In essence, the scaffolds within an e-learning system need to be adaptive in order to foster student self-regulation in these open-ended learning environments, *cf.* (Azevedo, 2005).

To achieve a better understanding of cognitive learning approaches for the design of accessible and efficient e-learning systems requires us to declare the systematic framework of learners and their environments that underpins our work. This will enable the well-informed reader to judge if it is adequate or if a better framework is necessary. Our framework is based upon the following, relevant six dimensions of accessible e-learning: profiles of the intended users, the context of use, the tasks to be undertaken, the technological platforms, cultural environment and principles of human learning (see Figure 1).

An essential starting point in effective and accessible e-learning design includes a clear understanding of the intended pedagogical aims and a determination of the pedagogical model or strategy underlying what is being attempted. The selection of technologies will be performed within the context of these pedagogical choices. Hence "pedagogy first, technology second" approach to e-learning is the key to understand both the potential of learning and the development of successful e-learning resources.

Requirements of an Effective E-Learning System

This section proposes that an effective e-learning system must be based upon the cognitive skills of the intended users in general and in the learning skills and preferences of the users in particular. However, such a system must also be accessible, adaptable, adaptive and acceptable, keeping in step with current trends in mobile computing and

Figure 1. Framework for accessible and efficient e-learning

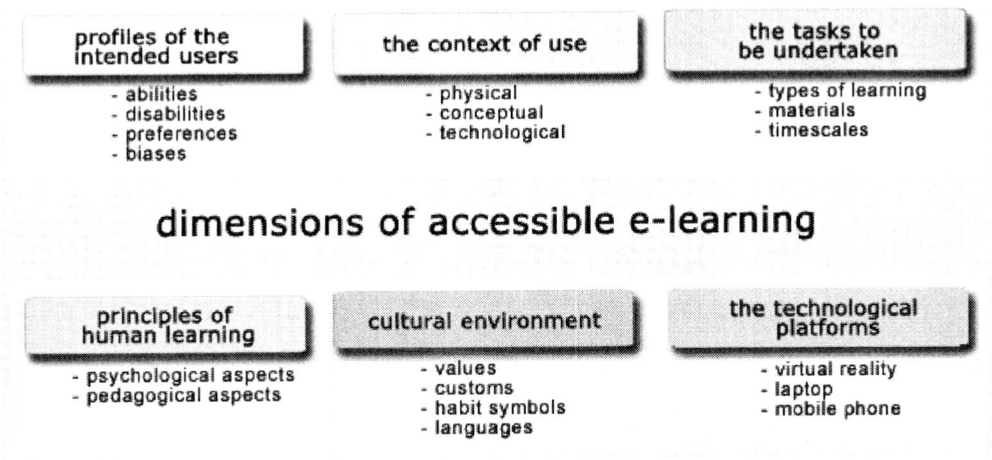

profiles of the intended users	the context of use	the tasks to be undertaken
- abilities - disabilities - preferences - biases	- physical - conceptual - technological	- types of learning - materials - timescales

dimensions of accessible e-learning

principles of human learning	cultural environment	the technological platforms
- psychological aspects - pedagogical aspects	- values - customs - habit symbols - languages	- virtual reality - laptop - mobile phone

ambient intelligence. If so, then it is important to consider the key issues that include, inter alia, user sensitive design, individualized approaches, adaptability and adaptivity (see Figure 2).

User Sensitive Design

User sensitive design can be advocated as one of the most appropriate methodologies developed out of user centered design for the creation of effective e-learning (Gregor, Newell & Zajicek, 2002; Newell & Gregor, 2000). User sensitive design is a natural development from user-centered design. The central concept of user sensitive design is an equal focus on user requirements and the diversity of such requirements in the population of intended users. If so, it follows that it may be beneficial to consider not only typical users but also "outliers" i.e. those users whose needs are more significant than the average user. Designing for these users may provide design insights that benefit all. Why should the average user have to make do with a minimalist solution, when others receive a more customized product or service?

We bring together the *user sensitive approach* with learner-centered design to create a robust approach to learner inclusion in the design process,

learner performance and to the learner experience of twenty-first century e-learning. It is aiming to explore the creation of successful e-learning systems able to increase users' learning outcomes and advance their personal learning experience. First, the hypothesis that the solution is to be found in systems that comply with nine specific factors was explored (Adams, 2007a). Accessibility and learner modeling turned out to be the weakest points. Second, an empirical study was conducted, aiming to investigate the influences of user individual characteristics on users' learning outcomes in e-learning environment (Granić and Nakić, 2007). The experiment indicated that motivation to learn, in addition to expectations about e-learning significantly impacts on users' learning achievements. Third, an enhancement of the designed methodology with user sensitive research issues enabled us to outline improved experimental procedures. Moreover, further experiment results will provide us better insight into arguments needed to carefully assess benefits of developing and involving a user model into an e-learning system.

Figure 2. Effective e-learning

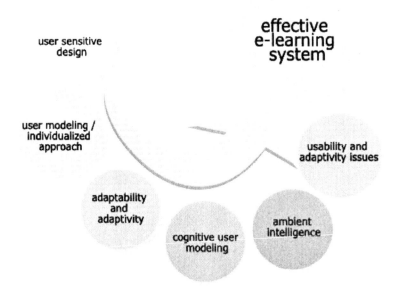

Individualized Approaches

Progress in the field of e-learning has been surprisingly sluggish and "... although technology is often touted as the great salvation of education – an easy way to customize learning to individual needs – it rarely lives up to this broad expectation" (Healey, 1999). It seems that too much of the research may be driven by technical possibilities, while paying inadequate attention to the area of application. Huge resources were spent for e.g. courseware development and not enough was left to improve the actual quality of learning (Nielsen, 1993; Nielsen, 2001).

Additionally, *user modeling* has not yet succeeded in addressing the variety and richness of the educational environment, even in the terms of individual user profiles or characteristics. Learners are diverse and have different requirements such as their individual learning style, their actual level of learning in the learning process and their individual background knowledge. For quite a long

time these issues were out of the focus of research in the hope that new technology will somehow resolve the lack of real progress. However, experience has proved so far that these issues can not be avoided as they determine the type and scope of e-learning systems that are likely to succeed. In this context, a satisfactory framework for taking into account users' heterogeneity have provided adaptable systems, by allowing the user to control the interface customization and adaptive systems, by adapting the interface behaviour to user's individual characteristics (Schneider-Hufschmidt, Kühme & Malinowski, 1993).

Adaptability and Adaptivity

Adaptability refers to changes made to a system or its interface before run-time to accommodate the requirements and preferences of its learners. Clearly, adaptability is a potentially very useful approach to custom e-learning, but it does presuppose the existence of a well validated user profile or model. A simple profile may contain a brief list of learner preferences and past learning experiences. A learner model may capture a more complex account of an individual's strengths and weaknesses. Whilst it is usually the case that the more reliable information the better, there will always be a trade off between information obtained and the costs required to gather it. There are, of course, ethical and practical issues raised by disclosure of information to a system and on the Internet (Adams & Russell, 2006; Adams & Granić 2007).

Adaptivity is a more subtle concept, referring to the ability of a system or website to change to adapt to meet user needs whilst running. For example, if an individual consistently fails to click properly on a series of small icons, the system may diagnose this as an error due to icon size and increase the size of the icons whilst running. Another individual may always select auditory feedback over visual feedback, so the system may ask if they want auditory feedback to be the default mode. As above, adaptivity raises significant ethical and practical problems of information disclosure, perhaps even raising problems of which the individual is unaware. It is also clear that machine learning and intelligence is an important component of an adaptive e-learning system (Adams & Russell, 2006; Adams & Granić, 2007; Granić & Nakić, 2007).

Cognitive User Modeling

The central importance of the concept of *cognitive user modeling* (Adams, 2008) is introduced, defined and refined. If it is easier to work with someone we know, then it may be the case that an e-learning system would be more effective if it also possessed the equivalent of such knowledge. The concept of cognitive user modeling is very important here, taking a cognitive approach to an understanding of the skills and knowledge of the learner. But how can the complexity of human thinking and performance be captured in a coher-

ent way that can be applied by users? As introduced above, complex theories such as ACT (Anderson, Bothell, Byrne, Douglass, Lebiere & Qin, 2004)) and SOAR (Jones, Lebiere & Crossman, 2007) require a considerable learning curve before they can be applied. Simpler theories such as the Model Human Processor (MHP) (Card, Moran & Newell, 1983) and Broadbent's (1984) Maltese cross theory provide a parsimonious capture of then current state-of-the-art theories of human performance. Consequently, then such theories can be created to capture current knowledge and allow it to be applied by practitioners to user modeling and interactive e-learning system design.

To distinguish between these two types of theories, we refer to the former as full theories, whilst the latter are entitled simplistic theories. A full theory is defined as a theory that aims to provide a full account of human cognition. A simplistic theory is defined as a theory that seeks to capture current findings in such a way as to allow practitioners to apply the theory to solve practical problems.

A consideration of all possible simplistic theories is beyond the scope of this chapter; here we use one representative theory to demonstrate current knowledge. Simplex Two (Adams, 2007a) is derived from Broadbent's Maltese cross. He started with four types of memory store (input, output, working memory and long term memory) controlled by an executive function that processes information and transports that information. The separation of memory and processing is a key feature of this theory. Novel features (compared with MHP) are the introduction of the flow of information in all directions and the provision of an executive function to control the memory stores. Simplex Two is introduced and its dual role as a user model and a theory of human cognition is explained with examples.

Usability and Accessibility Issues

The deployment of user sensitive design within the e-learning context promotes individualization and end-user acceptability, ensuring that usability and accessibility should be design concerns, thus avoiding the need for post-hoc adaptations. Unfortunately, studies have regularly shown that the *accessibility* of web-based applications in general falls short of an acceptable level (Sloan, Kelly, Heath, Petrie, Fraser & Phipps, 2006) and most of existing efforts related to accessible e-learning ones propose guidelines that primarily address technical accessibility issues (De Marsico, Kimani, Mirabella, Norman & Catarci, 2006)

Furthermore, when considering e-learning applications it has been claimed that *usability* assessment needs further consideration of learning perspective e.g. Squires and Preece (1999), although some authors propose applying heuristics without further adjustment to the e-learning context e.g. (Parlangeli, Marchigiani & Bagnara, 1999). In the line with the first approach are the results of the study reported in (Granić, 2008). The experience indicated that useful usability assessments with a significant identification of interface limitations can be performed quite easily and quickly. On the other hand, it raised a series of questions that require further comprehensive research, the more so if the employment of universal design within e-learning context is considered. Consequently, when designing an accessible and easy to use e-learning system, system which attempts to address the needs of all potential users, it is important to consider the key issues that include learner-centered design paradigm, context of use approach, individualized approach, pedagogical framework as well as guideline framework. If so, then such an approach will be in accordance with the claim that in e-learning we do not need user interfaces that support "doing tasks", but interfaces that support "learning while doing tasks", *cf.* (Hsi & Soloway, 1998).

While some authors consider accessibility as one of usability's components, e.g. (Zaharias, 2005; Adams 2007a), others point out potential conflicts in including accessibility guidelines alongside usability ones, e.g. (Phipps and Kelly, 2006). This may be due, in part, for a focus of accessibility concerns on the lowest level of design, namely standards for coding in a programming language on in a mark-up language such as HTML or XHTML. One solution offered here is to develop the concept of accessibility into a taxonomy of different types of accessibility. Defining inaccessibility as the presence of barriers to stop or impede user exploitation of a learning system, Adams (2007a) identified different types of accessibility problems. Any of these problems can place the intended user on the wrong side of a digital divide or "haves" and "have-nots". The barriers identified are:

a. hardware barriers i.e. having inadequate or inappropriate hardware,

b. communications barriers i.e. being unable to make reliable contact with system for reasons such as poor signal strength,

c. sensory / perceptual problems such as poor visibility or sound relative to the population of intended users,

d. cognitive barriers, where the cognitive demands made on the user are excessive, given their known cognitive skills levels, particularly in navigational demands and comprehension of contents and

e. barriers to objectives and aims, such that the user cannot achieve their objectives.

A sixth barrier can be created with respect to the learner's abilities to respond appropriately. For example, a touch pad may be too sensitive or a system may require a speed of response that is barely attainable. This simple framework enables accessibility and usability issues to be considered together in a constructive and complementary manner. Whilst Adams (2007b) referred to the "user" this reference should be read as the "learner" in the present context, as it allows for the inclusion of the user's learning objectives.

Brain Computer Interfaces

So far, in our discussion we have focused on relatively familiar methods by which the learner can interact with the system. However, technologies, such as psycho-physiological measurements in general and electroencephalograms (EEG) in particular, are emerging and improving. Future generations of technologies indicate a revolution in the emerging Information Society through the development of *brain-computer interfaces* (BCI) and *augmented cognition solutions*. Ideally, such systems would make e-learning environments more accessible to a range of users, including those with psychomotor disabilities and anyone who cannot use a keyboard or mouse dependent system with facility. Adams, Bahr and Moreno (2008) reviewed some critical psychological and pragmatic factors are to be understood before these technologies can deliver their full potential. They examined a sample (n = 105) BCI papers and found that the most studies provided communication and control resources to people with disabilities or with extreme task demands. Surprisingly, they found that issues of usability and accessibility were rarely considered. They concluded that there is a need for an increased appreciation of these issues and the related large research literatures, if BCI are to contribute significantly to the development of accessible and usable learning environments.

Ambient Intelligence

The role of the concept of *ambient intelligence* (AmI) is introduced, defined and refined above. We are all familiar with the relatively unintelligent systems on most personal computers and laptops. Some of us may also be aware of the increasing "smart" or apparently intelligent systems that are emerging (examples). They are probably best seen as not truly intelligent, thinking systems, but they offer the possibility of sensible responses to learner needs. If intelligence or at least "smart"

systems are emerging in the office or home, there is also the emergence of systems that are located more widely in the environment. For example, when you observe a bus stop or airport display, the system may detect your e-ticket and display information that is relevant to you, in your own language. Such systems are captured by the descriptive title "ambient intelligence" (ISTAG, 2001). Again, there is a trade-off between functionality and convenience on the one hand and information disclosure, willingly or unwillingly of the other.

Relating Human Learning Requirements and E-Learning Solutions

Based upon the work reported above, it is now possible to present a relatively simple taxonomy of types of human learning and a range of e-learning solutions. The relationship between cognitive learning factors and e-learning is developed below. Consider the following table that attempts to set out types of human learning, based on the Simplex Two theory (Adams, 2007a) and related forms of e-learning (see Table 1). The different components of the Simplex theory (column one) are related to different types of human knowledge acquisition (column two) and the different types of related skills attainment (column three). This approach makes the following, testable predictions. For each type knowledge (column two) or skills (column three), there is a corresponding form of e-learning environment, as shown in column four (knowledge acquisition) and column five (skills attainment).

Relating Cognitive User Modeling to E-Learning

Current evidence from cognitive user modeling supports the development of accessible e-learning solutions. In addition to the six levels of accessibility discussed above (hardware barriers,

Table 1. Linking types of human learning to e-learning solutions

Aspects of human learning	Types of knowledge	Types of process skills	e-Learning knowledge	e-Learning skills
Input (I)	Learn New Patterns	Perceptual Skills	Multimedia	Multimedia / VR
Feedback (F)	New Feedback	Manage Feedback	Multimedia	Multimedia / VR
Working Memory (WM)	Add New Items to WM	Improve WM Skills	Mainly Text	Mainly Text
Long Term Memory (LTM)	Add New Items to LTM	Improve LTM Skills	Mainly Text	Mainly Text
Executive Functions (ExF)	Add New Task Structures To ExF	Improve ExF Skills	Task Simulation	Task Simulation / VR
Emotional Evaluation (EE)	Learn New Evaluations	Improve EE Skills	Virtual Reality (VR)	VR
Mental Models (MM)	Learn New Mental Models	Learn New Modeling Skills	Virtual Reality (VR)	VR
Output (O)	Learn New Responses	Learn New Response Skills	Response Learning	Task Learning / VR
Complex Output Sequences (COS)	Learn New Output Sequences	Learn To Create Better Output Sequences	Task Simulation	Varied Task Learning / VR
Episodic Memory (EM) (In WS)	Add New Items To EM	Learn Better EM Skills	Biographical Information	Biographical Tasks / VR
Social Context	New Social Knowledge	Learn New Social Skills	VR	VR

communications barriers, sensory/perceptual problems, cognitive barriers, barriers to learning and performance objectives as well as unrealistic response requirements), the Simplex Two framework identifies those locations within human cognition where accessibility problems can hit. There are two types of accessibility problem, namely problems with memory capacity and second problems with processing capacity.

Changing the Ways E-Learning Environments are Constructed

We have given a general description of the new requirements for the design of effective e-Learning systems. But how will the presented cognitive theories have a significant effect on the presentation of information, the learner navigation, the structure of an e-learning lesson and the complexity of the environment? The key to the answer is that these cognitive theories will enable e-educators to get to know their students better, more objectively and more systematically. The theory Simplex Two has been designed to provide e-educators with an accessible and usable way to profile their students in terms of only nine aspects of human cognition (see above). These nine components have all been validated in a recent, major study. So, we are confident that they capture the bigger picture of the strengths and weaknesses of our students. E-educators can readily familiarise themselves with the simple structure and contents of Simple Two. (It does not require the substantial learning overhead of more complex theories such as ACT-R.). E-educators can then address questions about their students' abilities and disabilities. This can be done in several ways. One method is to judge the strengths and weaknesses of each student. Simply, is this a strong area or not for the student? Then look critically at the e-learning materials. Will the materials overload the student's known weaknesses or stimulate their known strengths? Other ways to collect useful evidence would be for you to evaluate each student's strengths and weaknesses yourself on ten point scales and use these profiles indicate that they will be able to use your e-learning materials well. Or, you could ask the students to evaluate their own strengths and weaknesses. Finally, you could use psychometric tests to evaluate your students' requirements. This is a much more objective approach. All of these approaches enable you to look at the overall e-learning requirements of your students and also you can identify their differing needs and adapt your system to reflect individual differences. Once you have student profiles, you can use them to evaluate the suitability of your systems. For example, if you are concerned about the best ways to present information, your student profiles should contain valuable information about their sensory and perceptual requirements. Effective learner navigation requires the student to have adequate skills in working memory, attention and concentration. The appreciation of the structure of an e-learning lesson reflects the student's abilities to create mental models. The complexity of the environment should support the student's executive skills, not being too complex as that will cause overload, not too simple as they might be boring. The complexity of the environment should also match the learning skills of the student. It should be neither too difficult not too easy. In each case, the demands of the e-learning systems can be matched against the strengths, weaknesses and requirements of your students. If you wish to apply Simplex Two to an evaluation of your students' requirements and the design of your e-learning systems, the present authors would be willing to answer any questions that you might have.

Simplex Two can also explain how different technological innovations can impact e-learning, by relating their features to the different factors of human cognition, as follows. A brain computer interface (BCI) will revolutionise e-learning. A BCI can enable students with limited physical movement to engage with an e-learning system without the requirement for gross physical movements such as required by using a mouse or a keyboard. Signals from the electroencephalogram of the student (due to cognitive events in their brain or due to their slight psychomotor movements e.g. finger flexion) can be relayed as signals with which to communicate and control an external system such as an e-learning system. But this approach will be the cure, par excellence, for the accessibility problems faced by any students who are unable or unwilling to interact with physically demanding systems because of physical or cognitive disabilities (Simplex: psychomotor and cognitive responses). Virtual reality (VR) applications will also revolutionise e-learning. Virtual worlds can now be created relatively easily. In such virtual worlds, students can enter much richer learning environments than ever before and learn new skills in realistic settings that can be repeated or modified on demand (Simplex: executive and memory functions). If BCI and VR can be combined one day, students with accessibility problems could also benefit from richer and more realistic learning environments. In contrast, a MOO (*MUD, object oriented*) system is a text-based, online and virtual reality system to which multiple users (learners) connect at the same time. Such systems can bring e-learning to widespread or technologically limited communities, where more advanced options are not accessible. Blind users can also use screen readers to interact with such a system. Finally, ambient intelligence (AmI) technologies are those technologies that can detect the presence of people and respond smartly to significant aspects of them (perhaps with use of an RFID tag). For example, a student can enter a room or a study space and be identified by an e-learning system that can adapt to her requirements, for example changing the language, mode of presentation or choice of lesson. If so, this opens the possibility of e-learning that is portable or is adaptive.

DISCUSSION AND CONCLUSION

In this chapter, we have been able to address the research issues and practical questions associated with the design of accessible e-learning systems by taking a cognitive learning approach. Whilst this is a complex and developing field, we have identified some of the key issues that support the development of theory and practice. Such issues include; a better appreciation of the pedagogical principles that underlie e-learning, the development of a more advanced psychology of human learning, the development of better learning environments, the design of accessible and usable e-learning systems, the development of ambient intelligence and smarter systems, a greater appreciation of the potential synergy between cognitive and emotive factors in human learning. Our solution to the problems associated with these issues is based upon: setting requirements for effective e-learning, adopting a user-sensitive design approach, building in both adaptability and adaptivity, basing user requirements on cognitive user modeling, taking usability and accessibility factors into account and making better use of ambient intelligence in e-learning environments. On this basis, we have been able to show how human learning requirements can be used to identify the most appropriate e-learning solutions. Lastly, we have been able to use a cognitive user modeling perspective to support the creation of e-learning applications that are both usable and accessible. In this way, we have shown how evidence and insights from diverse subjects such as cognitive science, computing science and social sciences can be integrated to provide a robust platform for the next generations of pedagogically sound e-learning systems.

Finally, looking to the future, exciting new systems like Second Life and Sloodle learning systems for virtual environments (Kemp & Livingstone, 2006) are emerging to offer new technological platforms upon which to build accessible, new learning environments. However, it is also clear that technology alone is necessary but not sufficient for functional systems to be smart, usable and accessible. That will depend upon system designers being able to call upon expertise in such areas as user modeling, cognitive science, computing science and social sciences to do so. It will be the biggest challenge to technology enhanced e-learning in the future.

ACKNOWLEDGMENT

The research has been supported within the project 177-0361994-1998 Usability and Adaptivity of Interfaces for Intelligent Authoring Shells funded by the Ministry of Science, Education and Sports of the Republic of Croatia and also with the financial support of the School of Engineering and Information Sciences, Middlesex University, United Kingdom.

REFERENCES

ACT-R. (2002). *Welcome to ACT-R*. Retrieved October 12, 2003, from http://act-r.psy.cmu.edu/

Adams, R. (2007a). Decision and stress: Cognition and e-accessibility in the information workplace. *Universal Access in the Information Society, 5*, 363-379.

Adams, R. (2007b). User modeling for intelligent interfaces in e-learning. In *Universal access in human-computer interaction, application and services* (LNCS 4556).

Adams, R. (2008). User modeling & monitoring: A universal access perspective. In C. Stephanidis

(Ed.), *Universal access handbook*. Mahwah, NJ: Lawrence Erlbaum Associates Inc.

Adams, R., Bahr, G. S., & Moreno, B. (2008). Brain computer interfaces: Psychology and pragmatic perspectives for the future. In *AISB Proceedings*, Aberdeen.

Adams, R., & Granić, A. (2007). Creating smart and accessible ubiquitous knowledge environments. In C. Stephanidis (Ed.), *Universal access in HCI, part II, Proceedings of HCII 2007* (LNCS 4555, 3-12). Berlin, Germany: Springer-Verlag Berlin Heidelberg.

Adams, R., Granić, A., & Keates, L. S. (2008). Are ambient intelligent applications universally accessible? In *Universal Access to Novel Interaction Environments: Challenges and Opportunities, Proceedings of the 2nd International Conference on Applied Ergonomics AE International 2008) with the 11th International Conference on Human Aspects of Advanced Manufacturing (HAAMAHA)*, Las Vegas, NV, USA.

Adams, R., Langdon, P., & Clarkson, P. J. (2002). A systematic basis for developing cognitive assessment methods for assistive technology. In *Universal Access and Assistive Technology, Proceedings of the CWUAAT, Cambridge Workshop for Universal Access and Assistive Technology*.

Adams, R., & Russell, C. (2006). Lessons from ambient intelligence prototypes for universal access and the user experience. In *Universal access in ambient intelligence environments* (LNCS 4397, pp. 229-243). Berlin, Germany: Springer.

Anderson, J. R. (1983). *The architecture of cognition*. Cambridge, MA: Harvard University Press.

Anderson, J. R., & Lebiere, C. (1998). *The atomic components of thought*. Mahwah, NJ: Lawrence Erlbaum Associates.

Anderson, J. R., Bothell, D., Byrne, M. D., Douglass, S., Lebiere, C., & Qin, Y. (2004). An integrated theory of the mind. *Psychological Review, 111*(4), 1036-1060.

Azevedo, R. (2005). Using hypermedia as a meta-cognitive tool for enhancing student learning? The role of self-regulated learning. *Educational Psychologist, 40*(4), 199-209.

Barnard, P. J. (1999). Interacting cognitive subsystems: Modelling working memory phenomena with a multi-processor architecture. In A. Myake & P. Shah (Eds.), *Models of working memory*. Cambridge, UK: Cambridge University Press.

Barnard, P. J., May, J., Duke, D., & Duce, D. (2000). Systems interactions and macrotheory. *Transactions on Computer Human interface, 7*, 222-262.

Benyon, D., Crerar, A., & Wilkinson, S. (2001). Individual differences and inclusive design. In C. Stephanidis (Ed.), *User interfaces for all: Concepts, methods, and tools* (pp. 21-47). Mahwah, NJ: Lawrence Erlbaum Assoc.

Biggs, J. B. (2001). *Teaching for quality learning at university: What the learner does*. Open University Press.

Broadbent, D. E. (1971). *Decision and stress*. London: Academic Press.

Broadbent, D. E. (1984). The Maltese cross: A new simplistic model for memory. *Behavior and Brain Sciences, 7*, 55-94.

Byrne, M. D. (2001). ACT-R/PM and menu selection: Applying a cognitive architecture to HCI. *International Journal of Human-Computer Studies, 55*, 41-84.

De Marsico, M., Kimani, S., Mirabella, V., Norman, K. N., & Catarci, T. (2006). A proposal toward the development of accessible e-learning content by human involvement. *Universal Access in Information Society, 5*. 150-169

Dix, A., Finlay, J., Abowd, G., & Beale, R. (2004). *Human-computer interaction* (3rd ed.). London: Prentice Hall.

Egan, D. (1988). Individual differences in human-computer interaction. In M. Helander (Ed.), *Handbook of human-computer interaction* (pp. 543-568). Elsevier Science B.V. Publishers North-Holland.

Einstein, A. (1934). On the method of theoretical physics. *Philosophy of Science, 1*(2) 163-169.

Fanderclai, T. L. (1995). MUDs in education: New environments, new pedagogies. *Computer-Mediated Communication Magazine, 2*(8).

Fox, J. (1980). Making decisions under the influence of memory. *Psychological Review, 87,* 190-211.

Fox, J., & Cooper, R. (1997). Cognitive processing and knowledge representation in decision making under uncertainty. In R. W. Scholz & A. C. Zimmer (Eds.), *Qualitative theories of decision making* (pp. 83-106). Lengerich, Germany: Pabst.

Good, J., & Robertson, J. (2006). CARSS: A framework for learner-centred design with children. *International Journal of Artificial Intelligence in Education,* 16(4), 381-413.

Granić, A. (2008). Experience with usability evaluation of e-learning systems. *Universal Access in the Information Society,* 7, 209-221.

Granić, A., & Nakić, J. (2007). Designing intelligent interfaces for e-learning systems: The role of user individual characteristics. In *Universal access in human-computer interaction. Applications and services* (LNCS 4556, pp. 627-636).

Granić, A., & Ćukušić, M. (2007). Universal design within the context of e-learning. In *Universal access in human-computer interaction. Applications and services* (LNCS 4556, pp. 617-626).

Gregor, P., Newell A. F., & Zajicek, M. (2002). Designing for dynamic diversity - interfaces for older people. In J. A. Jacko (Ed.), *Proceedings of the ASSETS 2002. The Fifth International ACM Conference on Assistive Technologies,* Edinburgh, Scotland (pp. 151-156).

Hannafin, M., Land, S., & Oliver, K. (1999). Open learning environments: Foundations, methods, and models. In C. Reigeluth (Ed.), *Instructional design theories and models* (pp. 115-140). Mahwah, NJ: Lawrence Erlbaum Associates.

Healey, D. (1999). Theory and research: Autonomy in language learning. In J. Egbert, & E. Hanson-Smith (Eds.), *CALL environments: Research, practice, and critical issues* (pp. 391-402). Alexandria, VA: Teachers of English to Speakers of Other Languages, Inc.

His, S., & Soloway, E. (1998). Learner-centred design: Addressing, finally, the unique needs of learners. In *Proceedings of the Computer Human Interaction '98, CHI '98,* Los Angeles, USA (pp. 211-212). ACM Press.

Hook, K. (2000). Steps to take before intelligent user interfaces become real. *Journal of Interaction with Computers, 12*(4), 409-426.

Information Society Technologies Advisory Group (ISTAG). (2001). *Scenarios for ambient intelligence in 2010* (Final Report, EC 2001).

Jones, R. M., Lebiere, C., & Crossman, J. A. (2007). Comparing modeling idioms in ACT-R and Soar. In *Proceedings of the Eighth International Conference on Cognitive Modeling,* Ann Arbor, MI.

Keates, S., & Clarkson, J. (2003). *Countering design exclusion: An introduction to inclusive design.* London: Springer.

Kemp, J., & Livingstone, D. (2006). Putting a second life "Metaverse" skin on learning management systems. In *Proceedings of the Second Life Education Workshop at SLCC,* San Francisco (pp. 13-18).

Kobsa, A. (1995). Supporting user interfaces for all through user modeling. In *Proceedings of the 6th International Conference on Human-Computer Interaction HCI International 1995*, Yokohama, Japan (pp. 155-157). Retrieved from http://www.ics.uci.edu/~kobsa/papers/1995-HCI95-kobsa.pdf

Lieberman, H. (1997). Introduction to intelligent interfaces. Retrieved from http://web.media.mit.edu/~lieber/Teaching/Int-Int/Int-Int-Intro.html

Little, B. (2008). Giving learning a 'second life' chance. *Human Capital Management*, (Jan/Feb).

Liu, Y., Feyen, R., & Tsimhoni, O. (2006). Queuing network-model human processor (QN-MHP): A computational architecture for multitask performance in human-machine systems. *ACM Transactions on Computer-Human Interaction*, *13*, 37-70.

Newell, A. (1990). *Unified theories of cognition*. Cambridge, MA: Harvard University Press.

Newell, A. F., & Gregor, P. (2000). User sensitive inclusive design in search of a new paradigm. J. Scholtz & J. Thomas (Eds.), *Proceedings of the First ACM Conference on Universal Usability*, Washington, DC (pp. 39-44).

Nielsen, J. (1993). *Usability engineering*. London: Academic Press.

Nielsen, J. (2001, January 16). *Jacob Nielsen on e-learning. E-learning post*. Retrieved from http://www.elearningpost.com/features/archives/001015.asp

Norman, D., & Draper, S.W. (1986). *User centred system design*. Hillsdale, NJ: Lawrence Erlbaum Assoc.

Pantazis, C. (2001). *Executive summary: A vision of e-learning for America's workforce* (Report of the Commission on Technology and Adult Learning, ASTD). Retrieved from http://www.learningcircuits.org/2001/aug2001/pantazis.html

Parlangeli, O., Marchigiani, E., & Bagnara, S. (1999). Multimedia systems in distance education: Effects of usability on learning. *Interacting with Computers, 12*, 37-49

Phipps, L., & Kelly, B. (2006). Holistic approaches to e-learning accessibility. *Association for Learning Technology, 14*(1), 69-78.

Piccoli, G., Ahmad, R., & Ives, B. (2001). Web-based virtual learning environments: A research framework and a preliminary assessment of effectiveness in basic IT skills training. *MIS Quarterly, 25*(4), 401-426.

Pimentel, J. R. (1999). Design of net-learning systems based on experiential learning. *Journal of Asynchronous Learning Networks, 3*(2), 64-90.

Pulkinen, J., & Peltonen, A. (1998). Searching for the essential elements of Web-based learning environments. In *Proceedings of the 3rd International Open Learning Conference*, Brisbane, Queensland, Australia.

Riva, G., Vatalaro, F., Davide, F., & Alcañiz, M. (Eds.). (2001). *The evolution of technology, communication and cognition towards the future of human-computer interaction*. Amsterdam, The Netherlands: IOS Press.

Riva, G., Loreti, P., Lunghi, M., Vatalaro, F., & Davide, F. (2003). 4 presence 2010: The emergence of ambient intelligence. In G. Riva, F. Davide, & W. A. IJsselsteijn (Eds.), *Being there: Concepts, effects and measurement of user presence in synthetic environments*. Amsterdam, The Netherlands: IOS Press.

Savidis, A., & Stephanidis, C. (2004). Unified user interface design: Designing universally accessible interactions. *Interacting with Computers, 16*(2), 243-270.

Schneider-Hufschmidt, M., Kühme, T., & Malinowski, U. (Eds.). (1993). *Adaptive user interfaces: Principles and practice.* North-Holland, Elsevier Science Publishers B.V.

Sloan, D., Kelly, B., Heath, A., Petrie, H., Fraser, H., & Phipps, L. (2006). Contextual Web accessibility - maximizing the benefit of accessibility guidelines. In *Proceedings of the WWW 2006,* Edinburgh, Scotland. Retrieved from http://www.ukoln.ac.uk/web-focus/papers/w4a-2006/

Soloway, E., Guzdial, M., & Hay, K. E. (1994). Learner-centred design: The challenge for HCI in the 21st Century. *Interactions, 1,* 36-48

Soloway, E., Jackson, S., Klein, J., Quintana, Ch., Reed, J., Spitulnik, J., Stratford, S., Studer, S., Jul, S., Eng, J., & Scala, N. (1996). Learning theory in practice: Case Studies of Learner-Centred design. In *Proceedings of the Conference on Human Factors in Computing Systems (CHI96),* Vancouver, British Columbia (pp. 189-196). New York: ACM Press.

Spector, J. M., & Anderson, T. M. (Eds.). (2000). *Integrated and holistic perspectives on learning, instruction and technology: Understanding complexity.* Dordrecht, The Netherlands: Kluwer Academic.

Squires, D., & Preece, J. (1999). Predicting quality in educational software: Evaluating for learning, usability and the synergy between them. *Interacting with Computers, 11,* 467-483

Squires, D., & Preece, J. (1996). Usability and learning: Evaluating the potential of educational software. *Computers Education, 27*(1), 15-22.

Stanford-Smith, B. (2002). *Challenges and achievements in e-business and e-work.* Amsterdam: IOS Press.

Vovides, Y., Sanchez-Alonso, S., Mitropoulou, V., & Nickmans, G. (2007). The use of elearning course management systems to support learning strategies and to improve self regulated learning. *Educational Research Review, 2*(1), 64-74.

Web Accessibility Initiative. (2005). *WAI: Strategies, guidelines, resources to make the Web accessible to people with disabilities.* Retrieved May 15, 2008, from http://www.w3.org/WAI/intro/accessibility.php

Workman, M. (2004). Performance and perceived effectiveness in computer-based and computer-aided education: Do cognitive styles make a difference? Computers in Human Behavior, 20(4), 517-534.

Zaharias, P. (2005). E-learning design quality: A holistic conceptual framework. In C. Howard, J. Boettcher, L. Justice, K. Schenk, P. L. Rogers, & G. A. Berg (Eds.), *Encyclopaedia of distance learning* (Vol. II). Hershey, PA: Idea Group Publishing.

Chapter XIII
Intelligent Books:
Combining Reactive Learning Exercises with Extensible and Adaptive Content in an Open-Access Web Application

William Billingsley
University of Cambridge, UK

Peter Robinson
University of Cambridge, UK

ABSTRACT

"Intelligent Books" are Web-based textbooks that combine computer-supported exercises with content that is both adaptive and extensible. They impose very few restrictions on the kind of exercise that can be placed within the book, and they allow students to contribute material that they have written, and to incorporate material from the Web into the book. In this chapter, the authors describe the influences that affect the design of intelligent books. These come from looking at the roles that textbooks and course notes play in education, and economic factors that affect the sustainability of intelligent books – competing for the attention of users, and ensuring that network externalities do not prevent a sufficient quantity of material from being usable within the book.

INTRODUCTION

The book you are reading now is not an Intelligent Book. It uses the same words to say the same thing to every reader regardless of whether or not they can understand it. It cannot help readers to work through problems and it cannot say anything that is not already in the book. In 2003, the University of Cambridge and the Massachusetts Institute of Technology embarked on a joint project to develop the concept of Intelligent Books – textbooks that can model what they teach, that can gather new examples and material from users, and that can make use of existing material from the Web.

The outcomes of the project were not simply to develop a software product (although we did develop software during the project) but also to understand how economic, usability, and role issues affect the useful design of intelligent online learning resources. Particularly, we wanted to identify complementary features and design choices that would be able to take advantage of these factors. As we describe later in the chapter, we expect many of these design choices will come into mainstream practice through existing software gradually moving in a similar direction, rather than through our own product necessarily beating the competition.

The project set out from the beginning to develop "Intelligent Books" rather than tutoring systems, but there are reasons why we believe this is a valuable approach. At some point, any automated system for homework exercises has to be able to correct students about factual errors. This involves describing a piece of content, so it is useful if the exercise can be combined with some kind of content system. The conventional take-home resource that students use as a source of exercises and content is a textbook. So, we believed that if we were to develop intelligent on-line teaching materials, "Intelligent Books" replacing textbooks could be a more appropriate model than "intelligent tutors" replacing human tutors. This might sound like a petty distinction of terminology, but it has implications for the role the technology will fill: a tutor is usually a student's master, whereas a textbook is only ever the student's slave.

A textbook does not send you nagging emails to do your assignments like a Courseware Management System, nor does it mark you down for requiring more assistance than another student. If a textbook were to take on those roles, the way students interact with it would probably change. As a simple example, if a textbook were to grade students for course credit, that could be an incentive for students to take their learning elsewhere and only come to the textbook when they were sure they would make no credit-losing mistakes. A textbook is also not compulsory – there is nothing to prevent a student from reading a page from a different book instead. Indeed, most students use more than just the textbook: they also use Google, Wikipedia, and many other resources. The chal-

lenge, then, is how an Intelligent Book can meet these more varied use cases, without losing the value of the textbook's traditional role.

In this chapter we describe the role, economic, and usability factors that we identified, and how these drove particular design choices for Intelligent Books. Some of the decisions that we made may appear to go against the grain of other recent research projects. For instance, Intelligent Books favour informal modelling in the content, leaving it up to individual exercises to decide what details about the student to model (and usually the exercises model the question in much more detail than they model the student) – a lot of recent research has focussed on modelling users' knowledge and skills in careful ontological detail. However, because of the open and extensible nature of Intelligent Books, there are reasons why a less restrictive model is potentially more usable and more helpful.

BACKGROUND

For many university teachers, if they are going to place content and exercises online, the Courseware Management System (CMS) is where they will place them. Systems such as the commercial Blackboard and the open-source Moodle (Dougiamas & Taylor, 2003) and Sakai (Hardin, 2006) provide common tools for content to be uploaded onto the Web and to enable student interaction with the content and with each other. However, it is rarely the teacher of a course that gets to decide which CMS should be used – they are often institution-wide systems. So, an institution's CMS faces the difficult challenge of supporting many disparate subjects across one institution, where a textbook would support similar subjects across a number of institutions. However, there has also been a growing interest in the use of non-institutional software chosen by individual teachers or even by the students themselves, thanks largely to the rise of social networking sites (Pankhurst & Marsh, 2008). This suggests there might be an opportunity for a return to the textbook model, where content and exercises can be sourced from outside the university.

There is a long history of research in technology-enhanced learning that we drew upon in our project. Almost every university engages in teaching and in computing research, and has at some point combined the two in a research project. Intelligent Books are necessarily wide-reaching applications. Even for fairly narrow courses, there are a wide variety of exercises, diagram forms, and pedagogical techniques that might be useful to include in a textbook. So, a large proportion of the previous research is useful to the design of Intelligent Books. However, this also makes it difficult to provide deep and broad enough coverage of the previous research in the short space of a single chapter's background section. In this section we limit ourselves to introducing projects that particularly informed our work and that provide examples of techniques that we discuss later in the chapter.

Content

One of the earlier attempts to produce an adaptive Web-based textbook was ELM-ART (Brusilovsky, Ritter, & Weber, 1996; Weber & Brusilovsky, 2001), which taught LISP programming. Lessons were derived hierarchically into sections, and a four-layered user model was kept about each section. This recorded whether a student had visited a unit, which test items they had attempted, whether the material could be inferred as being known from the user's knowledge of other units, and whether the student had manually marked the material as being understood. This information was used to make automated recommendations about what a student should study next. Peter Brusilovsky, one of the authors of ELM-ART, also wrote some early papers (Brusilovsky, 1996; Brusilovsky, 2000) investigating and categorising the methods and techniques of "Adaptive Hypermedia". For

instance, whether systems alter the content within their pages or only adapt the navigation, altering the links to take users to the most relevant page for them. More recent work has included examining *social adaptive navigation* (Brusilovsky, Chavan, & Farzan, 2004) – learning from the navigation patterns of previous users.

ActiveMath (Melis *et al*, 2001; Melis & Siekman, 2004), a European project to develop an adaptive interactive textbook platform for mathematics, takes the detailed artificial intelligence based approach a step further. It keeps fine-grained semantic models of the content that it is trying to teach in a format called OMDoc (Kohlhase, 2000). As well as describing the mathematical relationships between concepts, ActiveMath's OMDoc documents also contain pedagogical metadata, for example describing how abstract a particular concept is. The system models each student against a number of competencies for each topic. By drawing on these models, ActiveMath can automatically generate personalised courses that match the learning goals and knowledge levels of individual students.

The Living Book (Baumgartner *et al*, 2004) promoted the idea of slicing an existing source, such as a set of lecture notes, to populate an adaptive learning system. An existing text is divided automatically into topic-sized slices, and the relationships between the slices are inferred from the text. The slices can be reassembled in different levels of detail, depending on the student's level of knowledge and the scenario they wish to use the book for. For example, students can examine all the exercises for a topic to revise for an exam, or can find all the references to further literature.

Questions

A very wide variety of approaches have been taken to guiding students through questions in tutoring systems. At the closest level of detail, Model Tracing Tutors, such as Andes (Gertner & VanLehn, 2000) and Carnegie Mellon University's

Cognitive Tutors (Anderson *et al*, 1995), model the step-by-step process that a student should undertake in order to answer the question. Constraint Based Tutors such as SQL-Tutor (Mitrovic & Ohlsson, 1999) and CAPIT (Mayo & Mitrovic, 2001) examine the rules that students break in their answers, for example CAPIT examines the rules of punctuation. In both cases, a key output of the tutor is a fine-grained model of which steps or rules the student has understood and which they have not. At a much looser level of detail, systems such as rely on the fact that different students often make the same mistakes, so there are often common wrong answers that students will come to. Feedback for these common wrong answers can be handwritten by the teacher, and automatically delivered to the students that enter that answer.

Reactive Learning Environments were first proposed in the 1970s, with the SOPHIE system (Brown, Burton, & Bell, 1975). Students are encouraged to try out their own ideas, and receive detailed feedback based on a machine model of the scenario. In SOPHIE, students were presented with a hypothetical faulty circuit, and were able to measure circuit properties and propose theories as to what the fault might be. A machine model supplied the measurement data, and also verified whether the students' theories were consistent with the measurements they had made so far. If they were not, it could describe the discrepancy. This style of pedagogy is important because it does not assume that the modelling system itself can automatically solve the question, making it suitable for design tasks such as programming or proofs. The act of compiling a student's code and showing a detailed error message is fundamentally a reactive approach.

Many interactive systems have been developed that can provide an educational benefit without marking or correcting the students' work at all. For example, John Billingsley's JOLLIES (Billingsley, 2001) are Web-based simulations that expose the relevant parts of the program to the student. The intention is that by altering this code and observing the results, students gain an understanding not only of the system being modelled but also of how to write simulations. The exercise does not need to examine the student actively for this learning to take place; students learn simply by seeing the results of changes they make to the program. GeoGebra (Hohenwarter & Preiner, 2007) is a geometry component designed to be embedded into Web pages as a "mathlet". It allows teachers to create dynamic geometry constructions with which students can interact. These can be made part of worksheets by surrounding the mathlet with text instructions for the students, or by scripting the component using a JavaScript API. Teachers can share their worksheets at a central community site, the GeoGebra Wiki.

Just as students can learn by assessing the results of their own work, they can also learn by comparing their work with others'. In the unpublished Exegesis system developed by CARET for the University of Cambridge, students are asked to write glosses (footnotes) for sections of Shakespearian text. Once a student has written a gloss, they can then compare it with the glosses that other students have written for the same text. To ensure that students contribute glosses, rather than only comparing others' work, they are prevented from accessing the glosses that others have submitted until they have submitted one themselves.

THE NATURE OF AN INTELLIGENT BOOK

There are some characteristics of a textbook, or of the way students work with textbooks, that we believe it is important for an Intelligent Book to preserve. These are design principles that feed into the discussion later in the chapter.

An Intelligent Book is a Voluntary Resource

As we described in the introduction, we see textbooks as being the servants of students. Even where teaching courses require the use of a particular textbook, or require students to answer particular exercises from the book, those requirements come from the teaching course and are not part of the textbook itself.

An Intelligent Book's Exercises Should be Varied within Subjects

A textbook for a subject usually contains a variety of different kinds of exercise. For example, a book on digital circuits might include exercises working with circuit diagrams, timing diagrams, state charts, and simulations of how individual transistors in the circuit behave. For each of these exercises, a different modelling system might be appropriate, and it might be appropriate to use a different pedagogical technique. It would be a pity if an Intelligent Book restricted the range of techniques and questions that could be used, rather than enabling yet more possibilities.

An Intelligent Book Should Support Multiple Explanations of the Same Content

This might sound like an unusual claim, as traditional textbooks often only explain material once, and indeed many notable systems such as ELM-ART and ActiveMath (described earlier) have had some success keeping a single underlying record of the material. However, in April 2007, the booksellers WHSmith listed thirteen different textbooks for thermodynamics as being in stock, and twelve more as available on order. Most university libraries do not limit themselves to a single text on a subject, and most courses' reading lists include more than one book. Many students do not limit themselves to textbooks but also use Wikis and Web-based tutorials. So we would suggest that students do not, presently, work in an environment where there is a single canonical explanation of a piece of material, nor even an adapted explanation that is "best for them". Instead, they work in an environment where there is a competing marketplace of explanations. We believe that allowing these competing explanations to be "brought into the book" would more closely match the way students work than trying to automatically adapt a single explanation of our own and excluding all others.

An Intelligent Book Should be Varied between Subjects

Anecdotal experience from the textbook publishing industry is that different subjects centre around very different styles of interaction (A. Black, personal communication, 2007). For example, for physics students the centre of activity might be working through example problems, while language students find community-based interaction much more important as they need to practice speaking to each other. This suggests that if a textbook infrastructure is to be useful for different subjects, then some care needs to be taken to ensure assumptions about the way students work in one subject are not so ingrained into the architecture that it cannot be adapted for the way students work in another subject.

An Intelligent Book Should be Affordable

Anecdotally, a number of computerised tutoring systems have been abandoned by the universities they were developed within simply because it was cheaper to offer additional human tutoring than to maintain and support the tutoring system. So if teaching systems are to be successful, they should consider the economic influences that will affect whether they become sustainable or not.

SOME ECONOMIC FACTORS INFLUENCING THE DESIGN OF INTELLIGENT BOOKS

Content Availability and Network Effects

A network effect, sometimes called a network externality, is where the value of a product depends upon the number of people using it (Katz & Shapiro, 1985). The classic example is the telephone: if only one person in the world owns a telephone it is useless, but as more and more people come to own telephones so each one becomes progressively more useful. As well as propelling the growth of popular products, it is also a barrier to entry for new products that have no established network.

Extensible and adaptive learning platforms can face network effects in a number of ways. For example, the first user could face a platform with no content and that has learned from no previous users. In that situation its unique selling point – the collaborative and adaptive nature of the platform – is essentially useless. So, it is important to make it easy to "seed" the platform with content at very little cost to overcome this barrier to entry. A second challenge is that platforms can find themselves competing with a larger network. For example, ActiveMath is based on high quality semantic content in the OMDoc format. Not only does OMDoc take a high level of expertise to write, but also there are also comparatively many more producers writing less formal Wiki and HTML materials as well as many more consumers reading them. So, as Claus Zinn (2006) noted, the amount of informal Wiki materials for mathematics on the Web is growing much more quickly than the content within ActiveMath. This is not to say that ActiveMath will not succeed, but it is an economic barrier that ActiveMath is working to overcome.

Price of Entry and the Market for Lemons

If a textbook is a voluntary resource, that is if the student can as easily choose to look material up in a different resource such as Wikipedia, then it is in competition. Just as the value of the content to the student is important, so is the outlay of effort the student must make in order to receive that content. Here, the situation is similar to what Akerlof (1970) describes in economics as the "market for lemons". In our scenario, a student finds it difficult to judge how useful a piece of content material will be to them – both whether they will understand it and whether it fits their purpose – until after they have read it. So, if they have a choice between a source that is costly to access and a source that is cheap to access, they will often choose the cheap source even if the costlier one would have been more valuable. So, cheap low quality resources theoretically may out-compete expensive high quality resources.

Particularly, this affects the use of pre-tests. These are questionnaires or miniature tests that some adaptive systems ask students to complete when they first use the system, in order to collect enough information about the student to adapt the content appropriately. However, a pre-test significantly raises the initial cost of access, in terms of the effort students must invest. If students are unable to judge in advance that the material within the book is significantly more valuable than other information on the Web, then this will tend to drive students away to other sources.

This seems to be borne out if we look at adaptive systems in e-commerce, such as the recommendation system used by Amazon.com (Linden, Smith, & York, 2003). They do not require users to enter significant quantities of data about themselves before they can first use the site, but instead use algorithms that are tailored for the fact that they have a very limited amount of information on new customers.

Spreading the Technical Cost

Some of the costs involved with intelligent teaching systems are technical. The software needs to be improved and maintained, as does the hardware it runs upon. An obvious way to mitigate this cost is to spread it over several courses, or across several universities. In commercial software, there has recently been an increased acceptance of "Software as a Service" (SIIA, 2000), where Web software is hosted by the vendor so that the customer does not need to have the capacity to support the software, nor the hardware capacity to run it. This is an attractive approach for Web-based education, because it allows the early cost to be spread between similar courses at different universities, rather than different courses at the same university (which would have more diverse needs in terms of the content, appropriate interaction styles, and modelling systems required).

There are convenient advantages here that the "Intelligent Book" approach has over intelligent tutoring. While universities might be reluctant to outsource their teaching or tutoring to an external provider, they already source most of their textbooks from external publishers. Also, as Intelligent Books are voluntary by nature and not used for summative assessment, some of the privacy issues of student interaction data being stored off-site are mitigated. Finally, as textbooks are usually recommended by the faculty but bought by students, externally hosted collaborative textbooks can potentially avoid lengthy university technology purchasing processes in a way that locally installed collaborative teaching software cannot.

Spreading the Content Cost

Traditional paper textbooks are expensive to produce. The writing and reviewing process can take two to four years. It is unrealistic to expect textbook authors to make this kind of investment in developing material for a new technology platform until it has not only had previous deployments, but has proven itself commercially successful. So, new technologies like Intelligent Books face a bootstrapping problem that they must prove their worth cheaply before content authors will be willing to invest the cost and effort required to produce material to the same standard as published paper books.

BASIC CONTENT MODELLING

A design goal for the Intelligent Book's content model (Billingsley & Robinson, 2005; Billingsley, 2007) was to allow each book to contain more than one explanation of the same material. Particularly, this was to allow users to contribute their own material, and so that resources and explanations that are available on the Web can be brought into the book. Effectively, we decided that rather than trying to compete with the network of low cost materials that are available on the wider Web, we wanted to make use of it. This has implications for how an Intelligent Book should model its content.

For example, it suggests that an Intelligent Book's content model should use page-level adaptation, selecting different pages to show to different users, rather than altering content within a page. It would be very difficult to alter external Web pages, and it could be confusing to users if the book had very different models for internal and external pages. So, the content model effectively becomes a Semantic Web database of metadata about pages.

It also suggests that the content model should not be a strict and detailed ontology. External pages might not fit easily into a very fine-grained ontology, and a very detailed ontology would also be a barrier to students contributing to the book – they would need to know the ontology in detail in order to fit their material within it. We were also aware that many metadata schemes for educational materials, such as LOM (IEEE,

2002), are so extensive that they are very tedious for authors to understand and complete.

The approach we took is that the content model should only expect the minimum amount of metadata that is required for the user to be able to interact with the book, but that it should accept any additional metadata that it is given. There are two fundamental pieces of metadata about a page URI that we require the user to enter when a page is added to the database:

- Students need to be able to look up content, and the machine model for a question might need to refer to content that the student appears not to have understood. So, pages require a *topic*.
- Students should be able to navigate between different kinds of content for the same topic – for example, once a student has read an *introduction*, they might wish to see an *example*, and then attempt an *exercise*. So, we also require a *type* for each page in the system. Types differ from topics in that while a book can contain an open ended number of topics, it is useful if the number of types is limited – if readers could create new types of entry at whim, then the list of entry types available for a given topic could quickly become so large that it would be unnavigable by other readers.

Some additional metadata is collected automatically. When an external page is added, the book extracts the host name from the URI so that students can navigate based on the provider of the information – *"what does Wolfram Mathworld have to say on the subject?"* Titles and excerpts are extracted from the page, and the user ID of the person who added the material is recorded. Figure 1 shows a screenshot of a user looking up a topic within the book, and indicates the actions they can take.

Because the content model is open-ended, in that additional metadata can be added, this al-

lows for some flexibility in the way that different books work. We said earlier that as a technology, the Intelligent Book should support variability in the way students interact in different subjects. For example, in some subjects material might not only describe a topic, but might represent a particular *view* on that topic, or might be a response to another view. For example, in economics, there might be a Keynesian view of inflation, and there might also be a monetarist response to those Keynesian arguments. It might, therefore, be important for students to be able easily to navigate between different views and responses, or even to add their own responses. Because the core metadata of the Intelligent Book is so small, and because the metadata model (represented in RDF) is flat and extensible, it takes very little code to specialise a book to support subject-specific interactions. In addition, the user model collects data on the way each user responds to each page – from rating, to commenting, to rejecting the page and choosing another one. The selection scripts, that choose appropriate pages to show to individual students, can make use of any of this data and any metadata about the page in making their choice.

EDITING STRUCTURE AS WELL AS CONTENT

Textbooks are not just directories of material for particular topics. They also impose a structure and an order on those topics – the chapters, subchapters, and sections. This is what allows students to turn to page one and start reading, rather than looking up every topic from the alphabetical index at the back.

Just as it can be helpful to edit pages and add alternative pages to an Intelligent Book, it can also be helpful to be able to edit chapter structures and add alternative chapter structures – alternative routes to lead students through the material. The way we achieve this is by requiring each chapter to have a contents page, which is the first page of

Figure 1. Two toolbars help users to work with content. The chapter toolbar navigates in an ordered way through the topics in chapters and subchapters. The content toolbar helps users to work with content for a particular topic. The user can see the topic and the type of this page, and navigation links both for the other types of page for this topic, and for pages from external sites. They can reject pages and select alternatives, write their own pages or add content they have found on the Web. They can also rate pages and comment on the topic or the individual page. Books for particular subjects might also introduce subject-specific navigation mechanisms.

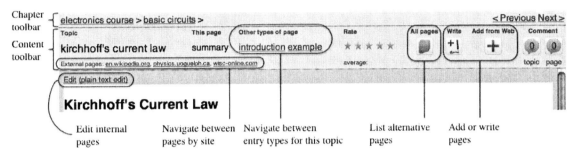

the chapter the student will visit. This contents page has the structure of the chapter embedded within it. This means that chapters can be stored in the content model simply as another content entry – there may be a summary of a topic and there may be a chapter listed next to it. They can also be edited in the same manner as any other internal page within the book.

When we first developed the Intelligent Book, pages were edited using Wiki mark-up. More recently, we have moved to WYSIWYG editing, using the open source TinyMCE editor. In either case, authors of pages can easily insert links to other topics within the book. These links can be constrained on any piece of metadata – so, a link could be inserted to lookup an *example* of *Kirchhoff's Current Law*. If links in a page are marked as "subtopics", then the page becomes a chapter, and the marked links are interpreted as the structure of the chapter. When the user visits the page, and follows any of the links, the structure of the chapter will be remembered. The chapter toolbar, shown in Figure 1, appears and the user can progress through the topics using "next topic" and "previous topic" links without having to revisit the contents page. Of course one of those

links might lead to another chapter, in which case the structure becomes hierarchical – subchapters and sections are simply chapters that are within other chapters. In Figure 1, "basic circuits" is a subchapter of the "electronics course".

It is fairly easy for authors also to insert components into the page, such as diagram components for exercises, and videos from YouTube or stored within the book's content database.

ARTIFICIAL SEPARATION, SLICING, AND NARRATIVE CONTINUITY

An Intelligent Book is a collaborative learning environment. However, the interaction between thirty students studying the same course at the same university would be quite different from the interaction between a million users sharing a textbook. Shared experiences, such as studying for the same exam at the end of the course, would be lost in a completely open textbook. There seems to be some value in artificially separating the community so that it appears as though each course has its own textbook.

We mentioned earlier that it is important to be able to prime an Intelligent Book with material quickly and easily, so that the first users are not faced with an empty book. One solution, inspired by the Living Book (Baumgartner *et al*, 2004), is to slice an existing resource such as the course's lecture notes automatically. Considering the role that lecture notes play in a course, this is very valuable practically. In a traditional course, lecture notes are not only a source of content, they also help to set expectations. From the lecturer's perspective, the course notes are designed to cover exactly the course that is being taught. Our anecdotal evidence from tutoring students is that they do look at what material is covered in the lecture notes and to what depth, in order to judge what they are expected to know on the exam. The Intelligent Book allows lecturers or other tutors to mark pages in the book as "*show first*" – that is, they will be shown to students in preference to any other page in the book on the same topic, regardless of what the adaptive selection algorithm might say. We expect that the main use for this will be lecturers or teachers who have sliced their notes and want to ensure they are shown first. They can also set a "*no additions*" flag on the topic if they wish, in order to prevent users from contributing pages at all.

Slicing the lecture notes can also help to alleviate two other issues with collaboratively written books. Firstly, there is the matter of confidence in the material. For example, a lecturer might be happy for students to be given easy access to a former student's casual but easily understood explanation of the material, but be unwilling for the system to give that casual explanation primacy over his precisely written notes. The second issue is narrative continuity. Imagine if a student was reading a topic from Site A, and when they moved on to the next topic, the book showed them content from Site B. There are likely to be some differences between those sites. Most obviously, the visual styling of the pages might look very different, and the writing styles of the authors might differ too. However, there might also be dangling threads in the narrative. For example,

phrases like "continuing our example from the previous section" can be problematic if the previous section that the student saw came from a different site and used a different example.

Finally, separating the book per course allows a "rinse and repeat" step to be introduced. Rather than have each year's cohort use the same book, with forums filling up with pages upon pages of comments, a "rinsed" book can be created. This gives an opportunity for the less useful pages to be dropped, for successful pages from other books on the same subject to be automatically transferred in, and for the lecturer to understand feedback from the way that students have been working with the book, to see whether the course itself needs restructuring. In some cases it might even be worth dropping some of the useful pages – so that the following years' cohort can also engage in the exercise of finding, discussing, and developing good explanations for the material they are learning.

EXERCISES

Even textbooks for narrow subjects normally contain a wide variety of different kinds of exercises. These can require working with different diagrams or notations, and need very different modelling systems at the back end – both in the way they model the subject and in the way they model the student. For some questions, it is practical to "debug the student's thinking" at a very fine level, such as is done in Model Tracing tutors. For many kinds of questions it is neither possible nor appropriate to do so. We have found that there are generally four occasions where this is the case:

1. *The steps cognitive steps to solve the question might not be known, or might be beyond the model.* For many higher order questions, and design tasks, this can be the case because the search-space of possible actions is too

broad. For example, consider programming exercises: while compilers and analysis tools can check students' code, they are generally not capable of writing programs themselves.

2. *The mistakes the student makes might be difficult to relate to the model of their understanding.* An exercise we developed (Billingsley *et al*, 2004) asked students to choose appropriate circuit properties and component values for a transistor amplifier. While the student worked, a constraint propagator followed their work, using the rules of electronics to deduce what other values needed to be from the ones the student had already set. Sometimes, the model would identify an inconsistency in the student's work that involved a chain of six or more deductions, each of them on simple rules. It seems unreasonable to mark the student down on each of the six rules involved, just as it would be unreasonable to mark a student down on "understanding multiplication" because they cannot calculate 593,421 × 647,823 quickly in their head.

3. In higher-order questions, the student has not been taught the process to answer the question, but is expected to discover a way to the solution by exploring. While it might be possible to model the final solution, modelling the exploration process is an open question.

4. An Intelligent Book should be able to incorporate existing exercises that have proven effective. These might not have been designed with a detailed student model in mind, and potentially might not mark students' work at all.

We have also found that there can be a trade-off between usability and level-of-detail in exercises. For example, in earlier work, we developed two kinds of question that asked users to write proofs in number theory. One kind of question (Billingsley & Robinson, Student proof exercises, 2007) was backed by a formal model: a research-grade automated proof assistant. Although the exercises reduced the learning barrier to the use of formal proof systems, these questions were very labour intensive to develop, and there remained some usability issues. If the proof assistant gave an intermediate result (it could not verify a step but could not invalidate it either), it was hard for students to understand why. Also, some concepts about the way that proof assistant does its reasoning were difficult to communicate to students, for example what steps it would consider trivial. The second set of exercises (Billingsley & Robinson, Searching questions, 2007) asked students to construct their proofs from pre-written English language statements, hidden behind a "search and select" mechanic so that students would find it harder to guess the answer based on what statements were available. These questions were modelled using much simpler predicate logic. They were an order of magnitude quicker to develop, could support a wider range of questions from the course, and could not give an intermediate result.

Because different teaching situations call for different kinds of exercise, the Intelligent Book attempts to make it possible to write any exercise using bespoke pedagogies, but also makes it very easy to include simple questions.

At the lowest level of complexity, support is provided for multiple choice, short answer and "massively multiple choice" (Billingsley & Robinson, Searching questions, 2007) items.

It is also easy to slightly more complex components, such as GeoGebra or JOLLIES, into editable pages. These components perform their modelling in the browser, which keeps the processing load away from the server, improving scalability. The components can read from and write to the book's student model using a simple REST API, to save the state of the students' work, and to write their findings about the student.

Some questions, however, require server-side processing – a research-grade proof assistant would be difficult to provide in JavaScript. So, the Intelligent Book also provides a detailed infrastructure (Billingsley, 2007) that allows questions to contain different diagram components, different models, and different teaching scripts. Although it requires some technical skill to write an entirely new kind of question, it is much simpler to write new instances of that question – questions that use the existing diagrams and models, but with different data, and that perhaps provide a little bit of extra analytical advice. The detailed design of this infrastructure is beyond the scope of this paper, but one general observation is worth mentioning. We observed that students often find the output of machine reasoning systems difficult to follow, as they work at a different level of detail to most students. We found (Billingsley *et al*, 2004) that specifying the diagram the student works with separately from the computer model, and automatically translating between them, was a successful approach to solving this problem.

The diagram presents the mental model that the teacher wants the student to have of the problem. By pruning the output of the computer model, using the diagram as context, the machine explanation is therefore translated to the student's model of the question.

Figure 2 shows the electronics exercise we described earlier. The system is in the process of explaining a problem in the student's work that involves a chain of deductions – these are animated step by step on the diagram. If the student were to click on the rule (Kirchhoff's Current Law) in the step, that would look up the law within the book.

STUDENT MODELLING AND ADAPTATION

When we were developing the Intelligent Book, we came to the conclusion that the student modelling

Figure 2. An electronics exercise, backed by a constraint propagation engine. The system is explaining an inconsistency it has found in the student's circuit – the steps of the reasoning engine's deductions are played back on the diagram, with each rule (Kirchhoff's Current Rule in the picture) linking automatically into the book's content.

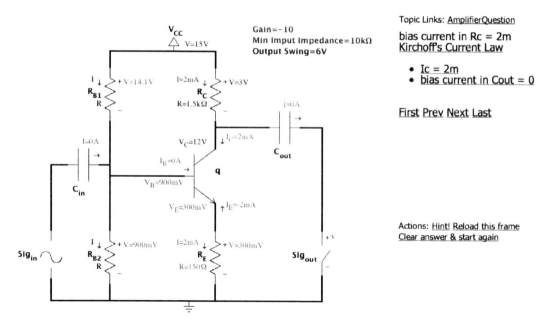

needed to be open-ended and *ad hoc*. Because the exercises vary so much in what they decide to model, we did not want to force a particular student modelling scheme upon them.

As we described earlier, we did not believe that it would be sensible to include a pre-test because it become an incentive to use a different resource instead – students do not need to take a pre-test to search in Google. It would also raise the effort of extending the book, as new content topics would require new pre-test questions.

We also realised that the student model would spend most of its time being out-of-date. Because the Intelligent Book is a voluntary resource, it cannot assume that it is the only teaching resource being used. We developed the system in Cambridge, where students receive regular small group human-led supervisions, in an approximation to what Bloom (1984) described as the ideal learning situation. So, far from being able to assume that students' knowledge levels remain fairly constant unless they are interacting with the Intelligent Book, we found ourselves actively hoping that they would change dramatically from use to use.

Even if we had an up-to-date student model, it would still have limited usefulness when it comes to recommending content. This is because recommending an entry is a one-shot activity. When a student first asks for a page for a particular topic, the system has the opportunity to choose the page that it believes is the most appropriate. But when the same student revisits the topic, it is important that the system shows exactly the same page again, even if new data suggests that a different page would be more useful. Otherwise, the book would become a shifting sand, constantly changing while the student's attention is elsewhere. So, recommendations have to be "sticky" in that once a student has seen a page, it must remain in that student's book until the student explicitly asks for it to be removed. Of course, because the choice happens when the student *first* looks up the topic, it is being made just when the book knows the *least*

about the student in regard to that topic. In fact, we realised that often the system will not even get to choose the page the first time. If an Intelligent Book is primed with a sliced set of lecture notes, it is quite likely that the lecturer will choose to set those lecture notes as "*show first*".

Instead, as with the content model, the book requires very little data, but collects as much as it is given. Firstly, the book records internally the interactions with each page – the rating the student gave the page, which pages they seen, which they have rejected (seen and then picked an alternative page instead), and which they have commented on. We suspect that page rejections will prove to be more useful for adaptation than page ratings – students might not rate a page, but if they do not understand one they will need to find another that they do – but we have not yet tested this theory. This collected data can then be used by the page selection scripts.

Additionally, we provide a simple REST API for recording data about students. This allows exercises that do make inferences about students' knowledge to record that data in a way that other exercises (as well as the page selection scripts) can use. However, we expect that the most beneficial use of this data will be as a reflective tool for students – what Kay (2001) refers to as scrutable student modelling. Simple reporting gadgets can be written against the student model API and embedded into "performance" pages for the topic, in a similar manner to the mash-ups that have become popular on Web 2.0 sites. These would show students how they have performed in the exercises and any areas that exercises have identified they consistently make mistakes.

FUTURE TRENDS

In this chapter, we have described economic, usability, and role factors that affect the useful design of "intelligent" educational textbooks. However, there is no reason why these factors would only apply to the Intelligent Book software, where the developers have carefully examined these particular issues. Quite the opposite is true – we believe that the same factors also apply to the learning systems that universities are already using, and that over time they will push existing software in a similar direction. For instance, there is currently development work on the Sakai open source CMS to introduce a simpler way of editing content that can include adding rich "gadgets" to pages, and to add social networking tools. It is easy to imagine these efforts adding social book-marking, student-editable content, and embeddable exercises in a way that might allow students to contribute alternative explanations, link to third-party explanations of material, and use rich exercises that can refer to that content. It is also easy to imagine enterprising companies offering future versions of Sakai (or other systems) with specialised content as hosted applications – allowing university teachers to sign their classes up in the same way that they might choose a textbook for the class to use.

Intelligent Books were originally developed as a research project, but we have started to make the system available as a constantly improving prototype at *www.theintelligentbook.com*, and we would welcome approaches from teachers who wish to use the system with their classes. However, we currently do not have a marketing budget, and development occurs in conjunction with a research interest. So, we would hesitate to claim that our software would out-compete well-funded existing products. However, the design factors we have described are ones we would expect to see in educational software of the future.

CONCLUSION

As we have described in this chapter, an Intelligent Book needs to be quite flexible in the way that it models students, content, and exercises. Particularly it needs to support shallow and easy

modelling – so that it can take advantage of eighty-twenty rules and the large amount of simple but successful material – while being possible to add more complex modelling for specialised cases.

From looking at the ways that teachers and students use textbooks and course notes, it seems there are practical limits to how adaptive an Intelligent Book can be while still serving all the needs and expectations. Instead, Intelligent Books add value in four different ways. They allow students to work through different kinds of exercise from those that they could before, they integrate the exercises with the content in a practically useful way, they allow materials from the Web to be brought into the book, and by being collaboratively developed they reduce the cost of writing textbooks. Traditionally, writing a textbook was something only a subset of lecturers would attempt, it would take a large amount of time, and then the finished would finally be released as a fixed item for sale at a profit. Intelligent Books, however, are intended to be used before they are finished – from automatically sliced course notes, or from content from other Intelligent Books on the same topic – and are then collaboratively developed by the teachers and the readers.

We have been developing Intelligent Books since 2003. We have developed exercises from fields as diverse as number theory, electronics, and high school biology. Many of these could not be supported in more traditional or fixed ontological systems. A public prototype of the system is available, at *www.theintelligentbook.com*, and we would welcome interest from teachers and universities wishing to use it, as the proof of any flexible collaborative system is when it is used by many people, not just a few.

ACKNOWLEDGMENT

We gratefully acknowledge the help of our collaborators during the Intelligent Book project: Hal Abelson, Gerald Sussman, and Chris Hanson at the Massachusetts Institute of Technology, and Mark Ashdown, Kasim Rehman, and Sparsh Gupta in Cambridge. Our work was supported by the Cambridge-MIT Institute, and recent development has been carried out within the Centre for Applied Research in Educational Technology (CARET).

REFERENCES

Akerlof, G. A. (1970). The market for "lemons": Quality uncertainty and the market mechanism. *Quarterly Journal of Economics, 84*, 488-500.

Baumgartner, P., Furbach, U., Groß-Hardt, M., & Sinner, A. (2004). Living book: Deduction, slicing, and interaction. *Journal of Automated Reasoning, 32*(3), 259-286.

Anderson, J. R., Corbett, A. T., Koedinger, K. R., & Pelletier, R. (1995). Cognitive tutors: Lessons learned. *The Journal of the Learning Sciences, 4*(2),167-207.

Billingsley, J. (2001). Javascript jollies can bring simulations to life. In *Proceedings of the 12ᵗʰ Australasian Conference on Engineering Education*, Queensland University of Technology, Brisbane, Australia (pp. 63-67).

Billingsley, W., Robinson, P., Ashdown, M., & Hanson, C. (2004). Intelligent tutoring and supervised problem solving in the browser. In *Proceedings of the IADIS International Conference WWW/Internet 2004*, Madrid, Spain (pp. 806-811).

Billingsley, W., & Robinson, P. (2005). Towards an intelligent online textbook for discrete mathematics. In *Proceedings of the 2005 International Conference on Active Media Technology*, Takamatsu, Japan (pp. 291-296).

Billingsley, W., & Robinson, P. (2007). Searching questions, informal modelling, and massively multiple choice. In *Proceedings of the Interna-*

tional Conference of the Association for Learning Technology (ALT-C 2007), Nottingham, UK.

Billingsley, W., & Robinson, P. (2007). Student proof exercises using MathsTiles and Isabelle/HOL in an intelligent book. *Journal of Automated Reasoning, 39*(2), 181-218.

Billingsley, W. (2007). *The intelligent book: Technologies for intelligent and adaptive textbooks focussing on discrete mathematics*. Unpublished doctoral dissertation, University of Cambridge, Cambridge, UK.

Bloom, B. (1984). The two sigma problem: The search for methods of group instruction as effective as one-to-one tutoring. *Educational Researcher, 13*, 4-15.

Brown, J. S., Burton, R. R., & Bell, A. G. (1975). SOPHIE: A step towards a reactive learning environment. *International Journal of Man-Machine Studies, 7*, 675-696.

Brusilovsky, P. (1996). Methods and techniques of adaptive hypermedia. *User Modeling and User-Adapted Interaction, 6*(2-3), 87-129.

Brusilovsky, P., Ritter, S., & Weber, G. (1996). ELM-ART: An intelligent tutoring system on the World Wide Web. In *Intelligent Tutoring Systems* (LNCS 1086, pp. 261-269). Springer-Verlag.

Brusilovsky, P. (2000). Adaptive hypermedia: From intelligent tutoring systems to Web-based education. In *Proceedings of ITS2000* (LNCS 1839, pp. 1-7). Springer-Verlag.

Brusilovsky, P., Chavan, G., & Farzan, R. (2004). Social adaptive navigation support for open corpus electronic textbooks. In *Proceedings of Adaptive Hypermedia 2004* (LNCS 3137, pp. 24-33). Springer.

Dougiamas, M., & Taylor, P. (2003). Moodle: Using learning communities to create an open source course management system. In D. Lassner & C. McNaught (Eds.), *Proceedings of the*

World Conference on Educational Multimedia, Hypermedia and Telecommunications 2003 (pp. 171-178). Chesapeake, VA: AACE.

Gertner, A. S., & VanLehn, K. (2000). Andes: A coached problem solving environment for physics. In *Intelligent Tutoring Systems* (LNCS 1839, pp. 133-142). Springer.

Hohenwarter, M., & Preiner, J. (2007). Dynamic mathematics with GeoGebra. *Journal of Online Mathematics and its Applications, 7.*

Hardin, J. (2006). *The Sakai Project final report to the Mellon Foundation.* University of Michigan.

IEEE. (2002). *Standard for learning object metadata* (IEEE Standard 1484.12.1-2002). IEEE.

Katz, M. L., & Shapiro, C. (1985). Network externalities, competition, and compatibility. *The American Economic Review, 75*(3), 424-440.

Kay, J. (2001). Learner control. *User Modeling and User-Adapted Interaction, 11*(1-2), 111-127.

Linden, G., Smith, B., & York, J. (2003). Amazon. com recommendations: Item-to-item collaborative filtering. *IEEE Internet Computing, 7*(1), 76-80.

Mayo, M., & Mitrovic, A. (2001). Optimising ITS behavior with Bayesian networks and decision theory. *International Journal of Artificial Intelligence in Education, 12*, 124-153.

Melis, E., Andrès, E., Büdenbender, J., Frischauf, A., Goguadze, G., Libbrecht, P., Pollet, M., & Ullrich, C. (2001). ActiveMath: A generic and adaptive Web-based learning environment. *International Journal of Artificial Intelligence in Education, 12*, 385-407

Melis, E., & Siekman, J. (2004). ActiveMath: An intelligent tutoring system for mathematics. In *Proceedings of the Seventh International Conference 'Artificial Intelligence and Soft Computing' (ICAISC)* (LNAI 3070, pp. 91-101). Springer-Verlag.

Mitrovic, A., & Ohlsson, S. (1999). Evaluation of a constraint-based tutor for a database language. *International Journal of Artificial Intelligence in Education, 10*, 238-256.

Pankhurst, R., & Marsh, D. (2008). Communities of practice: Using the open Web as a collaborative learning platform. In *Proceedings of the iLearning Forum 2008*, Paris, France.

SIIA. (2000). Software as a service: Software on and off like a light. In *Building the Net: Trends report 2000 – trends shaping the digital economy.* Software and Information Industry Association.

Weber, G., & Brusilovsky, P. (2001). ELM-ART: An adaptive versatile system for Web-based instruction. *International Journal of Artificial Intelligence in Education, 12*(4), 351-384.

Zinn, C. (2006). Bootstrapping a semantic wiki application for learning mathematics. In S. Schaffert & Y. Sure (Eds.), *Semantic systems: From visions to applications. Proc. of the Semantics 2006 conference.* ACS.

Chapter XIV

Enhancing Individuals' Cognition, Intelligence and Sharing Digital/Web–Based Knowledge Using Virtual Reality and Information Visualization Techniques and Tools within K–12 Education and its Impact on Democratizing the Society

Jorge Ferreira Franco
Universidade de São Paulo (NATE –LSI/USP), Brazil

Irene Karaguilla Ficheman
Universidade de São Paulo (NATE –LSI/USP), Brazil

Marcelo Knörich Zuffo
Universidade de São Paulo (NATE –LSI/USP), Brazil

Valkiria Venâncio
Universidade de São Paulo (NATE –LSI/USP), Brazil

Roseli de Deus Lopes
Universidade de São Paulo (NATE –LSI/USP), Brazil

Marlene Moreno
Secretaria Municipal de Educação de São Paulo - SME, Brazil

Marlene Gonçalves da Silva Freitas
Secretaria Municipal de Educação de São Paulo - SME, Brazil

Ana Luiza Bertelli Furtado Leite
Secretaria Municipal de Educação de São Paulo - SME, Brazil

Gláucia Almeida
Secretaria Municipal de Educação de São Paulo - SME, Brazil

Sandra Regina Rodrigues da Cruz
Secretaria Municipal de Educação de São Paulo - SME, Brazil

Marcos AntonioMatias
Universidade Bandeirante, Brazil

Nilton Ferreira Franco
Universidade Presbiteriana Mackenzie, Brazil

ABSTRACT

This chapter addresses an ongoing work strategy for developing and sharing knowledge related to digital/Web-based technology and multimedia tools, information visualization, computer graphics, desktop virtual reality techniques in combination with art/education. It includes a large body of research about advanced and contemporary technologies and their use for stimulating individuals' education. These interactive processes of researching, developing and sharing knowledge have been carried out through interdisciplinary and collaborative learning and teaching experiences in the context of k-12 education in a primary public school and its surrounding community. The learning and direct manipulation of advanced and contemporary technologies have improved individuals' technical skills, stimulated cooperative and collaborative work and innovations in the way of developing school's curriculum content as well as supported ones' independent learning. Furthermore, there have been changes on individuals' mental models, behavior and cultural changes related to reflecting about diverse possibilities of using information and communication technology within collaborative formal and informal sustainable lifelong learning and teaching actions.

INTRODUCTION

This chapter addresses an ongoing educational experience of sharing digital/web-based knowledge (Franco & Lopes, 2005b; Franco, Stori, Lopes & Franco, 2005) related to disseminate and use a combination of contemporary and advanced technologies (Barbosa, 2006), culture, science and arts in the context of a primary education school for supporting individuals' collaborative, interdisciplinary, dynamic, interactive, sustainable, high quality and lifelong learning (Burdea & Coiffet, 2003; Cunningham, 2008; Estação Ciência, 2009; Franco, 2000; Franco, 2001; Franco, Ficheman, Assis, Zuffo, Lopes, Moreno & Freitas, 2008; Grasset, Woods & Billinghurst, 2007; IINN-ELS, 2009; Kaufmann & Meyer, 2008; Projeto Clicar, 2009; Sherman & Craig, 2003; Tan, Lewis, Avis & Withers, 2008).

The educational experience has been developed through using a wide variety of technologies such as web-based technology, desktop virtual reality -VR, information visualization and computer graphics techniques, and low cost multimedia tools and files, which in this text, we call contemporary and advanced technologies. The contemporary technologies have been applied in the context of a public primary municipal school that is situated in the Parada de Taipas neighborhood, in the suburb of the city of Sao Paulo. Many students that live

on this area are from low-income families, are under socio-economic disadvantage and at risk situation (Franco, Cruz & Lopes, 2006; Projeto Clicar, 2009; Estação Ciência, 2009).

On the other hand, within the goal of contributing to improve this uncomfortable social situation, through learning and using information and communication technology in combination with other multimedia, advanced and contemporary technologies for stimulating individuals' education, students and educators have developed technical skills, as well as engaged in cooperative and collaborative and independent learning attitudes (Franco, Ficheman, Venâncio, Moreno, Freitas, Leite, Franco, Matias & Lopes, 2008c; Franco & Lopes, 2008).

According to Singer (2002) individuals' will and attitudes to learn and experiment are key points for developing a solidarity economy able to support under socio economic communities improvements. Furthermore, the learning situations and activities based on contemporary and advanced technologies have encouraged a community that by its own initiative has improved its life condition, renewed its cultural tradition and rebuilt individuals' human dignity.

We believe and our observations related to individuals' learning attitudes when they are dealing with the learning situations proposed for problem solving have highlighted that using contemporary and advanced technologies, including information systems knowledge in combination with human mediation can stimulate individuals' will to learn. For instance, through exploratory learning, bringing about more possibilities for supporting human's dignity enhancements, stimulating lifelong learning (Wikipedia Lifelong Learning, 2009) and impacting on democratizing society.

The design of information systems requires the application of techniques from experimental psychology like exploratory learning, which is the combination of problem solving and learning behavior, covering trail and error and instruction taking activities (Reiman, Young & Howes, 1996). The use of these techniques in combination with diverse learning paradigms plus contemporary and advanced technologies in formal and informal educational environments can stimulate individuals' will to learn, as well as inspire and reinforce collective intelligence (Levy, 1993) development for understanding the relevance of ones' dominating and using digital/web-based and other contemporary and advanced technologies for supporting individuals' education enhancements.

In this work ones' education enhancements has been supported by the application of the combination of ICT and techniques from experimental psychology in synergy with well known learning theories and methodologies such as constructivism and constructionism (Piaget, 1987; Papert, 2008), experiential learning (in Maier & Warren, 2000), the concept of zone of proximal development – ZPD (in Fonseca, 1998; Vygotsky, 2007), the theories of Mediated Learning Experience - MLE and of Structural Cognitive Modifiability - SCM that are related to Feuerstein's work (in Wikipedia, 2008; Fonseca, 1998) and the Theory of Multiple Types of Intelligence (Gardner, 1991; Kassin, 1995).

Other contemporary learning concepts, projects and scientific investigation that support this work are: 'ambient intelligence' – AmI in (Ambient Intelligence Org, 2008; Ducatel, Bogdanowicz, Scapolo, Leijten, & Burgelman, 2001; ISTAG,

2003; ISTAG, 2004); Computational Thinking (Wing, 2006); Systems Dynamics (Forrester, 1992; Forrester, 1994; Forrester, 1996); projects such as the New Media Consortium (NMC)'s Horizon Project (2008); International Institute of Neuroscience of Natal Edmond and Lily Safra - IINN-ELS (2009) and the "Campus of the Brain" project (Nicolelis, 2008) related to the use neuroscience and neurotechnology for social and scientific development; and Alice programming project (Alice org., 2008) that investigates tendencies and suggests practices related to the use of emerging and contemporary technologies on education and their influence to develop, for instance, individuals' technical skills, having as a consequence ones' collective intelligence and perception improvements (Lévy, 1993) to apply these tools effectively, as well as approximating people from computer science, technology, arts and culture such as (Colson, 2007; Franco and Lopes, 2008; Gardner, 1994; Popper, 2007; Wands, 2006).

The use of advanced technologies has also influenced students and educators' engagement in active learning and teaching mediated practices that have brought about individuals' psychological empowerment (Mrech, 1999) for increasing their intellectual attitudes of learning and sharing contemporary digital technologies and related knowledge inside and outside the school environment (Franco, 2005a; Franco & Lopes, 2005b; Franco, Cruz & Lopes, 2006; Franco, Mariz, Lopes, Cruz, Franco & Delacroix, 2007).

Such individuals' practices and attitudes have brought about opportunities for the school community participating in innovative educational collaborative projects such as the one-to-one learning model from the ONG - One Laptop Per Child - OLPC and Feira Brasileira de Ciências e Engenharia - FEBRACE (Febrace, 2009; Franco, Ficheman, Assis, Zuffo, Lopes, Moreno & Freitas, 2008; Portal Aprendiz, 2009; OLPC, 2008).

Fonseca (1998) states that the computing revolution, which has been run within the called 'cognitive society' has implicated in stimulating individuals' knowledge creativity and innovation, *'which are cognitive attributes by excellence, and of excellence'* and individuals can not develop them by passive perception and massive information. For instance, according to Glasser (2009) and his investigations on how we learn, an interactive learning process and active ones' knowledge, creativity, innovation and perception development can be the result of:

10% of what we READ; 20% of what we HEAR; 30% of what we SEE; 50% of what we SEE and HEAR; 70% of what is DISCUSSED with OTHERS; 80% of what is EXPERIENCED PERSONALLY; 95% of what we TEACH TO SOMEONE ELSE. (William Glasser, 2009)

Glasser's investigation supports the logic of using digital/web-based knowledge, contemporary and advanced technology, including information visualization tools on students' learning and educators' training to stimulate ones' interactive learning and knowledge based sensorial perception (visual, auditory, mental, tactile) development (in Reilly & Munakata, 2000).

The application of this logic can also support to reverse the idea of a "black box" that many non-technical individuals have about possibilities of producing two-dimensional 2D and tri-dimensional 3D virtual environments VE by using computers graphics principles (Foley, Dam, Feiner & Hughes, 1993), Virtual Reality VR (Burdea & Coiffet, 2003; Sherman & Craig, 2003) and related technologies. For example, Brutzman & Daly (2007) state that 3D graphics is best known from movies or computer games. It is something "special" created by others, and viewed only in movie theaters, by DVD playback, or by locally installed computer-game programs.

On the other hand, due to the decreasing costs of hardware and software and the evolutionary work that has been carried out related to web-based technologies, individuals under socio-economic disadvantage have had an increase in their access to information systems devices and technologies. Furthermore, they have had their mental models and perception stimulated by playing and sharing video games at home and LAN houses.

These facts have brought about ones' mental models and knowledge development for understanding explanations about how to create simple and complex 2D and/or 3D VE using computers graphics principles (Foley, Dam, Feiner & Hughes, 1993) and related technologies at school and at home (Franco & Lopes, 2005b; Franco, Cruz, S. R. R., Aquino, Teles, Gianevechio, Franco, Ficheman, & Lopes, 2007b).

We believe that increasing individuals' fluency to deal with contemporary and advanced technologies can bring about benefits to them and impact on democratizing the society. For instance, relevant benefits can be opportunities for improving ones' *"capabilities of more efficiently utilizing geographically distributed technological assets and skilled labor forces"* through understanding and dominating *"innovative knowledge and technology creation, arguably the most unique by-products of the human brain, are likely to become the most valuable commodities fueling the global economy"* (Nicolelis, 2008). And developing individuals' technical skills to create digital content and turn the activity to an income, which is an important social and learning work achievement that have been carried out in the projects such as (Computer Clubhouse, 2008; Meninos do Morumbi, 2008).

Within the belief that it is possible to provide similar work through a primary school learning environment, since 2002, in Parada de Taipas district, inside a primary school, here called Ernani Silva Bruno - ESB, this digital/web-based knowledge and technology work has been carried out. We have attempted to introduce contemporary and advanced technologies to individuals from the school and surrounding community and supporting possibilities of stimulating and improving ones' knowledge and lifelong learning attitudes.

The development of the learning and teaching experiences based on contemporary and advanced technologies have supported individuals' cognition, perception, attention and intelligence enhancements under supervised, unsupervised and reinforcement learning actions (Luger, 2002; Russell & Norvig, 2003). It includes ones' knowledge development on how to meaningfully organize and visualize information, through stimulating *human's primary sensory apparatus, vision, as well as the processing power of the human brain* (Schroeder, Martin & Loresen, 1998). Vision is the most studied of our senses and our somewhat unitary and transparent *"subjective visual experience is constructed from a wide array of processing areas, each specialized to some extent to a particular aspect of the visual world (eg. shape, color, texture, motion, depth, location and so on"* (Reilly & Munakata, 2000).

Due to the growth influence of visual information on citizens' lives, this work has also attempted to stimulate ones' use of information visualization techniques and tools as a support for their traditional (verbal), digital and visual alphabetization and literacy processes (Demo, 2008; Donis, 2007; Franco, Cruz & Lopes, 2006; Gombrich; 2007). By involving school and surround community in a collaborative, interdisciplinary and sustainable work (Barber & Fullan, 2005; Franco, Ficheman, Assis, Zuffo, Lopes, Moreno & Freitas, 2008; OLPC, 2008; Fullan, 2005; Fullan 2008).

Within a long term process, through applying such techniques and tools, it has been achieved an increase on the level of individuals' conscience about the relevance of developing their skills for reading, writing, researching, communicating, producing digital content and sharing knowledge.

Individuals' knowledge, creativity, innovative and technical skills development have been achieved under the strategy of providing students and educators learning situations in which they

can direct-manipulate web-based technologies such as (Hypertext Markup Language – HTML (Zakour, Foust & Kerven, 1997), Virtual Reality Modeling Language – VRML (Ames, Nadeu & Moreland, 1997) and Blogs and reflect about technology application. It includes the named technologies integration and interoperation with web-based knowledge and standard multimedia files such as MPEG, JPEG, and WAV (Brutzman & Daly 2007; Web3D consortium, 2008).

Through learning how to manipulate contemporary technologies and tools and reflect about their uses, individuals have adopted independent learning attitudes (Maier & Warren, 2000) for producing digital content, sharing the developed knowledge with the surrounding community and using diverse technologies as problem solving tools.

By applying their technical knowledge, individuals have achieved innovative ways of improving and developing school curriculum and human interactions within a cooperative and collaborative construction of more dynamic, innovative, effective, high quality and interactive learning environments inside and outside school (Cook, 1998; Dede, Salzman, Loftin & Ash, 1997; Franco, 2001; Franco, Cruz & Lopes, 2006; Franco, Ficheman, Assis, Zuffo, Lopes, Moreno & Freitas, 2008; Gardner, 2001; Johnson, 2006; Osberg, 1995, Osberg 1997a; Osberg 1997b).

Across cooperating and collaborating, individuals have learned and contributed to diffuse the art of stimulating cultural and educational changes at local community and beyond. These actions have formed a cognitive and digital learning ecosystem (in Ficheman & Lopes, 2008; Levy, 1993) supported by cross media approach (Miller, 2004) in synergy with cross-disciplinary orientation, which has been fundamental to role of innovation in economic and social change (Fagerberg, 2006). According to Lam (2006) inspired in (Weick 1979, 1995; Walsh, 1995) *""cognition" or "cognitive" refer to the idea of individuals develop mental models, belief systems, and knowledge structures that they use to perceive, construct, and make sense of their worlds and to make decisions about what actions to take".*

Following this introduction reflection and logic, this chapter focuses on the formal and informal use of digital and web-based knowledge through virtual reality, information visualization and computer graphics techniques on individuals' learning and cognitive development. It also addresses how the use of these technologies has brought about innovative learning opportunities for the school and surrounding community.

For achieving such goals, paraphrasing Resnick's ideas (2006) this chapter presents an alternate vision of how children might use computers. In this vision children use computers more like paintbrushes and less like televisions, opening new opportunities for children to playfully explore, experiment, design, and invent.

Hence, the combination between the theoretical and practical examples that will be showed on this chapter highlight how children, young students and adults have become protagonists by using computers as paintbrushes. By supporting individuals' knowledge and capabilities improvements we have applied the concept of stimulating ones' development as freedom (Sen, 2000).

This way, we have contributed for reducing the problem of digital divide within a sustainable mood. And also for decreasing the problem that computers are stifling children's learning and creativity, engaging children in mindless interaction and passive consumption, which is a problem that a growing number of educators and psychologists have expressed according to Cordes & Miller (2000) and Oppenheimer (2003) (in Resnick, 2006). For instance, we have seem this kind of situation related to children's preference for games that require 'mechanic like actions' instead of reflective thinking at ESB's School computers lab (Franco, Cruz and Lopes, 2006).

According to Sancho (2006) and Istance's (2006) investigation, this chapter development can also contribute to the reflection about how to

decrease education problems such as to provide protagonist opportunities to a learning community in a way that a community can act as an agent of transformation, bringing about school development; to offer alternatives that can support to overcome the limitations that have caused difficulties to improve learning environments such as the necessity of reducing the number of students per class (currently about 35- 40) for (15-20). The reduction can impact on the educators and students' communication and scaffolding quality in a very positive way (Ficheman, Saul, Assis, Correa, Franco, Tori & Lopes, 2008b; Franco, Cruz and Lopes, 2006); and improving educators' training opportunities lifelong in quality and quantity (Demo, 2009b).

Sancho and Istance's investigation also includes the necessity of providing a school scenario of high level of research and development, individuals' lifelong training, group activities, professional networks and mobility inside and outside educators' carrier, equality of learning opportunities for all, respecting the diversity of ones' learning capabilities but within good human and technical support, enhancing the economic resources available to develop schools' quality.

According to our observations and practical work, in this kind of school scenario, contemporary and advanced technologies can be used for constructing knowledge such as in universities and scientific communities (Durlach & Mavor, 1994; Istance, 2006; IINN-ELS, 2009).

We have applied contemporary and advanced technologies to mediate learning situations (Franco, Cruz & Lopes, 2006; Franco, Ficheman, Assis, Zuffo, Lopes, Moreno & Freitas, 2008). This is a fact that has stimulated *'face-to-face knowledge exchanges'* and human computer interactions enhancements (Te'eni, Carey & Zang, 2007, p. 393), as well as influenced changes on individuals' mental models. Ones' mental models transformations have led them to the culture of using better the informational resources related to the *internet culture,* which has been built based on the *"techno-meritocracy of science and technological excellence that comes from the big science and the academic world"* (Castells, 2003, p. 53).

This ongoing cultural change in the learning environment object of this chapter has brought about ones' lifelong learning attitudes, which have implicated on improving individuals' wisdom for using contemporary and advanced technology attempting to reach and demonstrate knowledge of excellence. As Nicolelis (2008) states, it is the use of *"Science as an agent of social transformation"*.

From here, during the chapter's development we will present the initial motivation for developing this work, the background highlighting technical tools, learning and economic concepts including related work, methodology for keeping this work sustainable, case study, evaluation and conclusion.

MOTIVATION

The initial support for developing this work comes from author1's motivation for offering better education quality to the students. The initial desire and vision were to increase students' motivation for learning English within practical and real world applications by using better school's computers lab and other multimedia digital resources available (Franco, 2000; Franco, 2001a).

Through researching and learning how to develop web-based standalone applications, author1 shared knowledge with his high school students on how to directly manipulate web-based technologies and how to construct web pages developing HTML files and using its templates, in 1999. It was a period that the school did not have Internet connection. The work was carried out using a text editor such as a notepad, and installing a browser such as Internet Explorer™ in the Window 95™ operating system and using an image editor such as the Paint™ software.

Educator and students improved and shared reading, writing, researching and communication skills. They developed curriculum content related to the English language and produced digital material with support of the digital/web-based technology standalone features. Students worked in teams sharing their common interests and knowledge for achieving their group goals. For example, students designed and prototyped their web pages related to their subjects of interest such as cartoons, fashion shop, online car sales, marketing, and artifact projects (Franco, 2001a).

At that period, one of the students who worked on a cartoon project related to airplanes and had good drawing skills, suggested that he could learn how to develop the project in 3D using a computer. After that, by investigating new tools, author1 bought and shared a computer magazine with him, showing a picture of a 3D VRML model of an airplane (in Internet Guianet, 1999). Although, the magazine brought a VRML code on it, there was no browser available to test the sample. Either author1 had enough knowledge for solving that problem.

On the other hand, that interactive, dialogic (Freire, 2004), collaborative and mediated learning experience has led to author1's lifelong and independent learning attitudes based on open learning possibilities (Peters, 2001, p.179). By synchronism of actions related to ones' attitudes and lifetime opportunities, in the year of 1999, author1 got a scholarship for doing a master course through the program (British Council Chevening, 2008).

The active mediated multimedia learning experience that occurred at school inspired author1 to chose a Master Science Course in Virtual Environments (NICVE, 2008), at the University of Salford, United Kingdom, where he begun to deepen his knowledge, among others, on 3D graphics and on the Internet technologies (Franco, 2001b). After coming back to Brazil, at the end of 2000, autor1 returned to teaching English and two years late started working as an ICT facilitator.

Since the middle of 2002, he has worked as an ICT facilitator at ESB School (Franco & Lopes 2005; Franco, Cruz & Lopes, 2006). He has shared with other educators, students and researchers the digital/web-based knowledge developed through learning and teaching actions such as the ones described on this chapter. For instance, the first learning action related to using web-based technology at ESB School was a collaborative and interdisciplinary learning experience among him and a 4th grade primary educator and her 40 students for creating a chess board 3DVE.

The small scale interactive learning experience was mediated through presenting an author1's VRML 3DVE to the educator and her students. The chess board 3DVE designed using VRML had as reference author1's Musiquarium 2000 project, which was modeled in proprietary software during his master course (Franco, 2001b). After that, author1 and students created a small scale 3DVE applying low cost tools for representing the game culture and Brazilian carnival, which students were investigating. They also simulated a prototype home page using HTML scripts.

Both the chess board and the home page were developed using a text editor (Notepad™) in a computer (Compaq™) 133MHz and 16RAM and visualized in a VRML viewer such as Cortona™ and Cosmo Player™ Figure 1.

Again, there was not Internet connection available in the school's computers lab, but author1's technical skills acquired during the master course and his lifelong learning attitudes supported to learn how to install a 3D web browser (Cosmo Player™) suitable to run the experiment and visualize the chess board simulation and develop a learning situation of sharing web-based knowledge with the 4th grade educator and her students.

An interesting result of this collaborative learning experience is that six months later when asked about the importance of it for the class development, the 4th grade educator said that she observed that the development of the web-based learning experience brought about increasing students' confidence, collaborative work and engagement on learning attitudes (in Franco & Lopes, 2004).

After this informal talk, in 2003, the school computers lab configuration was upgraded. Twen-

Figure 1. On the left, author1's interactive 3DVE used for presenting web-based technologies to a 4th grade educator and her students. On the right, a sample of the chess board prototype developed during the learning experience.

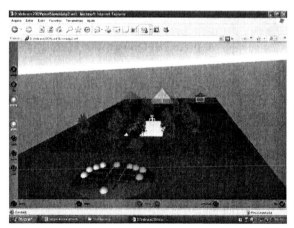 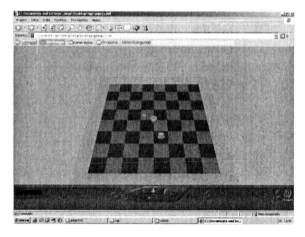

ty-one Computers Pentium III, 900MHz and 128 RAM with Internet connection were installed. So, since the first semester of 2003, autor1 has invited and shared the developed knowledge with students and educators, bringing about to build the work that has been carried out and results described on this chapter (Franco, Cruz & Lopes, 2006; Franco, Cruz & Lopes, 2006; Franco, Mariz, Lopes, Cruz, Franco & Delacroix, 2007a; Franco, Ficheman, Venâncio, Moreno, Freitas, Leite, Franco, Matias & Lopes, 2008c).

BACKGROUND

In this section we will describe some technical tools and projects that have supported researches and initiatives of creating and using advanced technologies in education.

Over the last three decades there have been several research and initiatives of creating and using interactive contemporary and advanced technology on individuals' education as a way of inspiring and improving learning and teaching practices. It includes a tendency of using 3D advanced technologies.

With the growth and expansion of web-based technologies such as HTML (Zakour, Foust, & Kerven, 1997), VRML (Ames, Nadeu, & Moreland, 1997) and (Java and Java3d API™, 2008) and their interoperations (Roehl, Couch, Reed-Ballereich, Rohaly, & Brown, 1997), diverse collaborative, interdisciplinary, creative work and references have been developed and shared on the Internet ((Franco, Ficheman, Venâncio, Moreno, Freitas, Leite, Franco, Matias & Lopes 2008c; Mitchell, 1999; Perlin, 2008; Virtual Dundee, 2008; VRML sourcebook 2.0 on-line, 2008; Web3D consortium, 2008).

For instance, these and other related technologies have allowed using the state-of-the-art of 3D graphics and computer modeling to produce interactive museums exhibitions for introducing visitors to relevant ideas related to sciences, art,

culture and technology (Colson, 2007; Wands, 2006) that help to explain complex ecosystems but also economic markets, immune systems, and even traffic jams (Ficheman & Lopes, 2008; Resnick, Strimpel & Galyean, 2008; Tan, Lewis, Avis & Withers, 2008).

TECHNICAL TOOLS DEFINITIONS

The main technical tools we have used to carry out this work are web-based and low cost ones. Most web documents are structured based on a markup language. According to Stanek (1996), these documents can be simple and/or complex structures described in terms of plain text. It ensures the widest distribution to any type of computer and presents the formatting in a human-readable form called markup. As demonstrated in the motivation section, *"because the markup contains standard characters, this also means anyone can create documents in a markup language without needing special software"* (Stanek, 1996, p. 17).

Having the school curriculum development in mind, by using a digital/web-based platform for supporting it, individuals have acquired and developed technical knowledge to create electronic documents similar to some traditional publications such as comics and comic books, magazines, books, newsletters, newspapers. Individuals' technical knowledge acquired has also been applied for producing their own 2D and 3D simulations beyond the school (Franco, Ficheman, Venâncio, Moreno, Freitas, Leite, Franco, Matias & Lopes 2008c).

This way, through using scripts related to web-based standard markup languages we have contributed for developing individuals' reading, writing, researching and communicating skills, as well as reducing the problem of digital divide.

Hypertext Markup Language – HTML is the predominant markup language for Web pages. It provides a means to describe the structure of text-based information in a document — by denoting certain text as links, headings, paragraphs, lists, and so on — and to supplement that text with interactive forms, embedded images, and other objects such as video and audio (HTML Wikipedia definition, 2008; Murugesan, 2008: Rossi, Pastor, Schwabe & Olsina, 2008; Zakour, Foust & Kerven, 1997).

Virtual Reality Modeling Language- VRML is a standard file format for representing 3-dimensional (3D) interactive vector graphics, designed particularly with the World Wide Web in mind. It is a text file format where, e.g., vertices and edges for a 3D polygon can be specified along with the surface color, UV mapped textures, shininess, transparency, and so on. URLs can be associated with graphical components so that a web browser might fetch a web-page or a new VRML file from the Internet when the user clicks on the specific graphical component. Animations, sounds, lighting, and other aspects of the virtual world can interact with the user or may be triggered by external events such as timers (Ames, Nadeu & Moreland, 1997; VRML Wikipedia definition, 2008).

Virtual reality (VR) is a technology, which allows a user to interact with a computer-simulated environment, be it a real or imaginary one. Most current virtual reality environments are primarily visual experiences, displayed either on a computer screen or through special or stereoscopic displays, but some simulations include additional sensory information, such as sound through speakers or headphones. Some advanced, haptic systems now include tactile information, generally known as force feedback, in medical and gaming applications. Users can interact with a virtual environment or a virtual artifact (VA) either through the use of standard input devices such as a keyboard and mouse, or through multimodal devices such as a wired glove, the Polhemus boom arm, and omnidirectional treadmill. The simulated environment can be similar to the real world, for example, simulations for pilot or combat training, or it can

differ significantly from reality, as in VR games (Wikipedia Virtual Reality definition, 2008).

According to Ronald Azuma's definition, Augmented Reality – AR is an environment that includes both virtual reality and real-world elements. For instance, an AR user might wear translucent goggles; through these, he could see the real world, as well as computer-generated images projected on top of that world. Azuma defines an augmented reality system as one that combines real and virtual, is interactive in real-time, is registered in three dimensions (in Wikipedia Augmented Reality definition, 2008). Azuma's definition is a classical view of AR that is focused on "grafting" 3D virtual objects onto the real world (in Bowman, Kruijff, LaViola & Poupyrev, 2005). Augmented reality (AR) is a relatively mature technology, but so far it remains largely undiscovered by schools as a means of enhancing traditional lesson delivery. The advantage of AR is its ability to overlay information on real physical objects as viewed on a LCD projector or interactive white board (Lewis, Avis & Withers, 2008).

Blog is another tool that is applied, attempting to stimulate individuals for using digital and web based technologies. The term blog (a contraction of the term "Web log") is a Web site, usually maintained by an individual, with regular entries of commentary, descriptions of events, or other material such as graphics or video (in Blog Wikipedia definition, 2008).

TECHNICAL TOOLS FOR SUPPORTING THE WORK

The tools we have used for running this work are low cost third-party and free software such as Paint™, Notepad™ and GIMP™ (2008), Blender™ (2008) as well as accessible standard languages from WEB such as (Hypertext Markup Language – HTML, Virtual Reality Modeling Language – VRML, JavaScript) and their templates (Zakour, Foust, & Kerven, 1997; Ames,

Nadeu, & Moreland, 1997). Recently, we have also applied blog as a platform for supporting students to publish their work and develop the culture of using better digital/web resources.

Individuals have used the school computers lab Intranet and the Internet for researching and developing off-line and on-line projects. The Internet browsers htat ones have applied to visualize information and interact with are Cortona VRML client™, and Internet Explorer™ (Franco, Ficheman, Venâncio, Moreno, Freitas, Leite, Franco, Matias & Lopes 2008c).

Other multimedia resources employed for researching as well as creating content have been the school's library and computers labs, as well as multimedia instruments such as video cameras, webcams, TV capture card - PlayTVMPG-2™, tape recorder, microphones and the XO Laptop version B2 and B4 related to one to one learning model (Ficheman, Saul, Assis, Correa, Franco, Tori & Lopes, 2008b; Franco, Ficheman, Lopes, Ferreira, Santos, Ferreira, Araújo & Moreno 2008).

Some students have reported that at home they use Windows ™ operating system for practicing with HTML and VRML, but some of them have asked about the possibility of using Linux™. It would be excellent that non-technical individuals could install easier a browser able to read wrl. files in a Linux™ system. We did tests with Linux Ubuntu™ operation system in combination with FreeWRL™ (2008) browser and the combination worked well with native wrl. files without movie textures. So, individuals would benefit from the XO B4 laptops which run under Linux, Fedora™ operating system to develop 3D computer graphics skills and curriculum content.

UNDERSTANDING SOME LEARNING AND ECONOMIC CONCEPTS AND APPROACHES

Here learning as well as economic concepts and approaches that have supported educational and economic systems development and can serve for guiding this work improvement and sustainability are described.

The solidarity economy is often considered part of the social economy, forming what might be termed the "social and solidarity economy" (from the French "économie sociale et solidaire"). The concepts are still under development and the difference between the two terms is gradually being clarified. An organization seeing itself as part of the solidarity economy generally goes beyond achieving purely social aims: it aims to put right an injustice by expressing solidarity. For example, a local sports club has a social aim and so can be considered part of the social economy, but would not normally be considered part of the solidarity economy except in special circumstances (e.g. a township sports club in South Africa in the days of apartheid (in Wikipedia solidarity economy, 2008). For some theorists of the movement, solidarity economy begins with a redefinition of economic space itself. The dominant neoclassical story paints the economy as a singular space in which market actors (firms or individuals) seek to maximize their gain in a context of scarce resources. These actors play out their profit-seeking dramas on a stage wholly defined by the dynamics of the market and the state. Countering this narrow approach, solidarity economics embraces a plural and cultural view of the economy as a complex space of social relationship in which individuals, communities, and organizations generate livelihoods through many different means and with many different motivations and aspirations -- not just the maximization of individual gain. The economic activity validated by neoclassical economists represents, in this view, only a tiny fraction of human efforts to meet needs and fulfill desires (in Miller, 2006).

According to Wing (2006) the concept of computational thinking represents a universally applicable attitude and skill set everyone, not just computer scientists, would be eager to learn and use. To reading, writing, and arithmetic, we should add computational thinking to every child's analytical ability. Computational thinking involves solving problems, designing systems, and understanding human behavior, by drawing on the concepts fundamental to computer science. Computational thinking includes a range of mental tools that reflect the breadth of the field of computer science. Some computational thinking characteristics are conceptualizing, not programming; fundamental, not rote skill; a way that humans, not computers, think; complements and combines mathematical and engineering thinking; ideas, not artifacts; and for everyone, everywhere.

System dynamics is a powerful methodology and computer simulation modeling technique for framing, understanding, and discussing complex issues and problems. It deals with internal feedback loops and time delays that affect the behavior of the entire system. What makes using system dynamics different from other approaches to studying complex systems is the use of feedback loops and stocks and flows. These elements help describe how even seemingly simple systems display baffling nonlinearity. The basis of the method is the recognition that the structure of any system — the many circular, interlocking, sometimes time-delayed relationships among its components — is often just as important in determining its behavior as the individual components themselves. Examples are chaos theory and social dynamics (Wikipedia System dynamics, 2008).

According to Forrester (1992) system dynamics can provide that dynamic framework to give meaning to detailed facts. Such a dynamic framework provides a common foundation beneath mathematics, physical science, social studies, biology, history, and even literature:

In spite of the potential power of system dynamics, it could well be ineffective if introduced alone into a traditional educational setting in which students passively receive lectures. System dynamics can not be acquired as a spectator sport any more than

one can become a good basketball player by merely watching games. Active participation instills the dynamic paradigm. Hands-on involvement is essential to internalizing the ideas and establishing them in one's own mental models. But traditional class rooms lack the intense involvement so essential for deep learning. (Forrester, 1992)

Ambient Intelligence - AmI is "a set of properties of an environment that IST Advisory Group is in the process of creating". It is not necessary to more tightly define the term Ambient Intelligence. Most importantly, AmI remains a principal focus for information and communication technology. But it is important to appreciate that AmI remains an 'emerging property' and that future scenario building and iterations of the vision should treat AmI as an 'imagined concept' and not as a set of specified requirements. While AmI should not be promoted as a panacea for social problems, it does represent a new paradigm for how people can work and live together. AmI enables and facilitates participation by the individual - in society, in a multiplicity of social and business communities, and in the administration and management of all aspects of their lives, from entertainment to governance. Radical social transformations are likely to result from the implementation of the AmI vision (ISTAG Working Group, 2003; ISTAG Working Group, 2004)

According to Ficheman & Lopes (2008a) the concept of Digital Learning Ecosystems - DLE has its development inspired on nature ecosystems, consisting of species, populations and communities interacting with each other and with the environment. As in nature ecosystems, a DLE is the set of all relationships between biotic factors and between biotic and abiotic factors. Biotic factors are two major communities: the community of actors and the community of content. Actors are individuals that interact with digital technologies. Actors can be learners, teachers, parents, tutors, content creators, engineers or support technicians. Content is any kind of digital educational content i.e. learning tools, authoring tools, educational games, browsers, simulators and educational information. Actors and content can be viewed as two communities of biotic factors. They consider hardware technologies, software technologies and network technologies abiotic factors that compose the environment. In nature, a group of communities interacting with each other and acting on or suffering the action of abiotic factors constitute an ecosystem. A Digital Learning Ecosystem consists of communities of actors and content (biotic) interacting with each other and supported by their environment: hardware, software and network technologies (abiotic).

RELATED WORK EDUCATIONAL PROJECTS BASED ON CONTEMPORARY TECHNOLOGIES

In this section we keep developing the background showing related work that has involved the use of the contemporary and advanced technologies presented on the section of technical tools definition and can be used in combination with the learning as well as economic concepts and approaches named on this chapter.

The NICE (Narrative Immersive Constructionist /Collaborative Virtual Environment) project focus is on informal and formal education, social content domains, embracing a constructivist approach, collaboration, plus narrative development. It uses virtual reality main power: a combination of immersion, tele-presence, immediate visual feedback, and interactivity. Software development is based on open standard languages such as HTML, JAVA, VRML and C++. The virtual reality environment is designed for both multi-projection CAVE™ and PC systems (Johnson, Roussos, Leigh, Vasilakis, Barnes & Moher, 1999). The goal of NICE project is to construct a testbed for the exploration of virtual realty as a learning medium within the context of the primary educational reform themes of the past three de-

cades. The project's focus is on informal education and domains with social content, embracing the constructivist approach to learning, collaboration, and narrative development. The project has been extended to non-immersive users through on line connection. It has been used an interface based on VRML allowing participation of children using their personal computers. Children have access to the garden and also can write stories associating text and characters of NICE 's garden. Although the project was designing for children, adults have also experienced the garden environment (Roussos, Johnson, Leigh, Vasilakis, Barnes & Moher, 1997).

Following the world tendency for developing applications that can improve children education, the NIMIS project also applies the state of the art of computer graphics, artificial intelligence and intelligent agent technologies to reach its pedagogical and technological objectives. The NIMIS project is a distributed collaborative project evolving universities from several countries such as England, Portugal and Germany. The researches use intelligent agents as base for interactive learning in the project. For example, using agents as active components in virtual game-oriented environments that support school-beginners learning to read and write, particularly for reading through writing, and applications for revising and publishing kids' own stories with integrated multimedia features, including writing conferences. By using these tools children gain notions of how to develop a narrative. The project structure also takes care about the right size of the equipment in terms of ergonomics, providing robust hardware, simple software and multimedia interfaces suitable for young children, balancing this way the use of best that technology can offer. Respecting grown pedagogical traditions and class-room procedures, the project has put into practice a specific classroom environment for early learning with general tools and specific applications supporting literacy-related activities. Based on an integrated desktop environment for young children, three applications have been developed in the NIMIS project: "T'rrific Tales" (CBLU, Leeds) aims at supporting collaborative story telling in a cartoon format. A second application, "Teatrix" (INESC, Lisbon), aims at promoting collaborative acting in 3D scenarios. The third application, "Today's Talking Typewriter" (T³) provides a phonics-based learning environment for the acquisition of initial reading and writing skills by enabling children to freely and flexibly compose their own words. All NIMIS applications are embedded in distributed classroom activities, i.e. they are Not designed as stand-alone tools but as customisable and user-adaptive tools in a collaborative setting (NIMIS, 2008).

Project LISTEN (Literacy Innovation that Speech Technology ENables) is an inter-disciplinary research project at Carnegie Mellon University to develop a novel tool to improve literacy -- an automated Reading Tutor that displays stories on a computer screen, and listens to children read aloud to provide a pleasant, authentic experience in assisted reading. The Reading Tutor lets the child choose from a menu of high-interest stories from Weekly Reader and other sources -- including user-authored stories. The Reading Tutor adapts Carnegie Mellon's Sphinx-II speech recognizer to analyze the student's oral reading. The Reading Tutor intervenes when the reader makes mistakes, gets stuck, clicks for help, or is likely to encounter difficulty. The Reading Tutor responds with assistance modeled in part after expert reading teachers, but adapted to the capabilities and limitations of the technology. The current version runs under Windows(TM) 2000 or XP on an ordinary personal computer. Though not (yet) a commercial product, the Reading Tutor has been used daily by hundreds of children, as part of studies to test its effectiveness. Thousands of hours of usage logged at multiple levels of detail, including millions of words read aloud, provide unique opportunities for educational data mining (Project Listen, 2008; Wikipedia Data mining, 2008). The Reading Tutor aims for the zone of

proximal development - ZPD. It has a system for scaffolding children reading. By explaining unfamiliar words and concepts in context, it can remediate deficits in vocabulary and background knowledge. It provides spoken and graphical assistance when it notices the student click for help, hesitate, get stuck, skip a word, make a mistake, or encounter a word likely to be misread. Its "visual speech" uses talking-mouth videoclips of phonemes to scaffold phonemic awareness (Mostow, 2006) and supports knowledge transfer's investigation, for instance, if a certain practice on one skill improves another skill (Zhang, Mostow, & Beck, 2007).

At James Cook University the investigation carried out involves students from primary school who directly manipulate virtual reality (VR) software on a Pentium 90MHz computer with 8 MB RAM. The school is officially recognized as a socio-economically disadvantage school. Although, results are not conclusive the use of VR in the classroom seems to be effective for the students' cognitive development, as well as providing active learning even beyond a short-term novelty period (Cook, 1998).

The rehabilitation of aesthetics in the context of teaching computer science and digital media in schools is on the ArtDeCom. It is a creative, collaborative learning project, which involves all human senses, even when the process is digital media-supported and computer science teaching-oriented. The project shows how interdisciplinary, digitally extended learning environments can be created with the help of free or low cost applications. Such learning environments focus especially on the idea that sensorial perception and co-construction of knowledge should be an integrated part of a creative learning process (Winkler, Reimann, Herczeg, & Hopel, 2003).

The project Rapunzel, (Flanagan, M. & Perlin, 2008) develops a software environment for real time, applied programming for underrepresented students' early literacy (RAPUNZEL). The project addresses the critical shortage of women in technology related careers and degree programs by empowering them to create with computer programming. For the researchers children who can learn how to program computers will have more opportunities for authorship and creativity afforded them, as well as more options in schooling and career paths.

The X3D Earth Working Group (Web3D working group, 2008) uses the Web architecture, XML languages, and open protocols to build a standards-based X3D Earth specification usable by governments, industry, scientists, academia, and the general public. The Group project supports individuals' know, understand, use, and disseminate Web3D technology anywhere, anytime.

The Computer Clubhouses is a collaborative project that provides young people with the opportunity to become digitally fluent. The Massachusetts Institute of Technology (MIT) Media Lab and the Boston Museum of Science have established a network of learning centres in economically disadvantaged communities. At these centres, young people become designers and creators with new digital technologies. Clubhouse members use leading-edge software to create their own artwork, animations, simulations, multimedia presentations, musical compositions, websites, and robotic constructions (Computer Clubhouse, 2008; Resnick, 2002, Resnick, 2006).

According to Billinghurst (2008) the Human Interface Technology Laboratory New Zealand (HIT Lab NZ) conducts research with new emerging technologies such as augmented reality, next generation video conferencing, immersive visualization and perceptual user interfaces. Interaction design techniques are used to adapt these technologies to the needs of end users and solve real world problems. At HilLabNZ several augmented reality evolutionary projects have been developed following hardware and software improvements and accessibility to general public. The end goal is to improve the user experience with technology. The HIT Lab NZ's projects go through designing of a mixed-reality book (Grasset, D"unser,

& Billinghurst, 2008); supporting low ability readers with interactive augmented reality book (Dünser, 2008); blending art and mixed reality for merging between virtual and real, as well as investigating Maori's cultural heritage (Grasset, Woods & Billinghurst, 2007); and researching and adapting contemporary interfaces for table top and mobile devices including their usability related to human factors and architectural design (Na, Billinghurst, & Woo, 2008; Schnabel, Wang, Seichter & Kvan, 2008).

At Associação Meninos do Morumbi – AMM, a project called "Meninos do Linux", which covers digital and social inclusion for a community of children under socio-economic disadvantage is carried out. AMM promotes interdisciplinary work focused on supporting children's growth in positive learning environment where children have contact with both theoretical and practical concepts related to music, English language, photography, and information and communication technology. In the digital area the project Meninos do Linux offers to children opportunities for learning computer graphics and digital animation concepts, JAVA programming (using freeware environments such as Netbeans™ from SUN and JavaBuilder™ from Borland), including teaching digital audio, which involves music theory, audio digital theory, as well as production and mixing. The incorporation of Knowledge development related to digital content, including the use of Web standards and 3D information visualization comes from 2002. At that time author1 shared knowledge with individuals involved in AMM project who were experimenting with HTML and VRML. This sharing of knowledge occurred during an AMM project called "Garagem Digital", in which it was used proprietary software platforms for digital productions (Franco & Lopes, 2002; Meninos do Morumbi, 2008).

The Virtual Harlem is a collaborative VR tour of Harlem in which participants can travel back 80 years to see historical figures, and hear speeches and music from that period. The Virtual Harlem project is an effort to create a learning environment that can enrich students understanding of the Harlem Renaissance, bringing about individuals' approximation from Afro-American cultural heritage. The VR prototype enables students to become more than passive receptors of information, which is so common in many literature courses. The project goal is to develop rich, interactive, and narrative learning experiences to augment classroom activities (Park, Leigh, Johnson, Carter, Brody & Sosnoski, 2001).

The Human Interface Technology Laboratory's (HIT Lab) Learning Center has been providing students with the opportunity to construct their own virtual environments since 1990, by working through special programs such as the Pacific Science Center's Technology Camp, and through other educational environments. Starting in 1995, the Learning Center created the Virtual Reality Roving Vehicle (VRRV) program, which allowed students to take a more active role in the entire virtual development process by taking the technology directly into the classroom (Osberg, Winn, Rose, Hollander, Hoffman, & Char, 1997c). For instance, in her work Virtual Reality and Education Osberg (1993) analyses the advantages and disadvantages of using VR on children's education based on empirical seven weeks camp experience with children aged 8 to 18 in the Pacific Science Center (PSC) Creative Technology Camp held in Seattle. Osberg's investigation (1997d) compares the educational value of constructivist pedagogy as applied through the design, development and experience of 3-D interactive virtual learning environments to a traditional classroom approach and to a no instruction control. The constructivist treatment provided students with access to their choice of source content, 3-D modeling tools and instruction in virtual world development to assist in developing visual, auditory and interactive signs and symbols in the virtual environment. Traditional instruction included a biology textbook, worksheets and teacher-led discussions. The work is expand to educators' training

Mario Schenberg Spaceship is a collaborative interactive installation at Parque CienTec (2008) that aims to reach out young visitors and awaken their interest for science, physics and astronomy: through a space trip simulation. The Spaceship is designed to offer learning and entertaining environment, so a group of young learners can experience an adventure in space within an interactive and educational environment and game simulator. The environment design and construction is conducted by researchers from the Laboratory of Integrated Systems of the University of São Paulo (Globo Video, 2009; Fichemann & Lopes, 2008a; FEBRACE, 2008).

The Virtual Fishtank is an innovative new museum exhibit, developed by a collaborative work among the Boston Museum of Science, the MIT Media Lab, and NearLife Inc., with generous support from the National Science Foundation. Museum visitors can: create their own artificial fish; design behaviors for their fish; play with their fish in the giant fishtank; observe their fish interact with other fish analyze the ecological patterns that emerge (Resnick, Strimpel & Galyean, 2008).

Alice is an evolutionary (Conway, 1997) and innovative 3D programming environment that makes it easy to create an animation for telling a story, playing an interactive game, or a video to share on the web. Alice is a freely available teaching tool designed to be a student's first exposure to object-oriented programming. It allows students to learn fundamental programming concepts in the context of creating animated movies and simple video games. In Alice, 3-D objects (e.g., people, animals, and vehicles) populate a virtual world and students create a program to animate the objects. In Alice's interactive interface, students drag and drop graphic tiles to create a program, where the instructions correspond to standard statements in a production oriented programming language, such as Java, C++, and C#. Alice allows students to immediately see how their animation programs run, enabling them to easily understand the relationship between the programming statements and the behavior of objects in their animation. By manipulating the objects in their virtual world, students gain experience with all the programming constructs typically taught in an introductory programming course (Alice org, 2008). The evolutionary 3D programming environment has supported student's at risk (Moskal, B., Lurie, D., Cooper, S., n.d.) developing computer science skills by reducing the complexity of details that the novice programmer must overcome; providing a design first approach to objects and visualizing objects in a meaningful context. And according to Kelleher (2006) storytelling for engaging woman in computer science through motivating middle school girls to learn computer programming and choose to pursue computer science.

Tan (2008) presents a study related to the effects of using blogs for stimulating high education students to create content. The research attempts to understand students' perceptions of learning and sharing based on investigating their blog using experience. Although, they are referent to a small group sample of a more general population, his conclusions highlight potential students' ICT skills development, a well as reading, writing, communication abilities improvements. The conclusions also indicate a tendency of improving students' personal conduct, stimulating knowledge sharing and promoting active informal learning and lifelong learning.

METHODOLOGY

We have presented to individuals digital and web-based knowledge through providing to them diverse learning situations and activities for direct manipulating virtual reality, information visualization techniques and other contemporary and advanced technologies (Franco & Lopes, 2005a; Franco, Cruz & Lopes, 2006; Franco, Ficheman, Assis, Zuffo, Lopes, Moreno & Freitas, 2008; Franco & Lopes, 2008).

The interactive experiential learning and teaching actions have been related to ones' exposure and experience the named technologies similar to the work (in Osberg, 1993). The learning and teaching actions have happened inside a municipal public school, as described in the introduction section. However, the learning actions that have been carried out are non restrictive to the municipal school learning environment.

Over the time, the learning/teaching strategies have benefited the surrounding community and beyond not just related to exposure and experience. We have achieved individuals' cognition improvements, bringing about ones' technical and practical skills enhancements to support knowledge transfer that is "clearly central to innovation process" (Powell & Grodal, 2006).

The approach have consisted in mediating ones' education, by offering to students, educators and other people formal and informal learning/teaching situations, in which they can know, direct manipulate and understand the diverse technologies suggested for increasing ones' knowledge building process, with support of spiral and incremental work (Pressman, 2006).

There has been a combination of theory and practice, for instance, of diverse and well known learning theories and methodologies such as Piaget's constructivism and Papert's constructionism. Such approaches can enhance individuals' understanding about how people learn and grow, providing better support for designing teaching and learning materials and environments (Ackerman, n.d.; Papert & Harel, 1991).

We have also integrated the concept of scaffolding and/or software scaffolding use in education, which is a process that requires direct teaching and monitoring by an adult. It should be noted that one of the distinguishing feature of scaffolding is the role of dialogue between teacher and student. In addition, we have used from Vygotsky's theory, which is of great interest to educators, the zone of proximal development – ZPD concept. The ZPD is the difference between the child's capacity to solve problems on his own, and his/her capacity to solve them with assistance (Henry, 2002; Johnson, Roussos, Leigh, Vasilakis, Barnes & Moher, 1999; Luckin, Boulay, Yuill, Kerawalla, Pearce & Harris, 2003; Vigotski, 2007).

In addition, we have employed in our project development the Experiential Learning concept that has supported school community's inside and outside learning interactions (Maier & Warren, 2000; ELT, 2008). Affective aspects have also been relevant to the student's learning experience success. Our consideration on affective aspects has been inspirited by Paulo Freire and Ivan Illich's thoughts about the necessity of revolutionizing the curriculum content and the pedagogy of the present-day schools. In particular, transforming them in order they have become more practical and inclusive based on a horizontal relationship among educators and pupils, as well as supported by love, humility, hope, faith, confidence and respect for the freedom of expression (Freire, 2004; Gadotti, 1994). We include in this list the word "empathy" that can define successful communication in human relationship as suggested (in Peters, 2001).

Te'eni, Carey & Zhang (2007, p. 111) state that new psychological basis of Human Computer Interaction - HCI that balances and integrates affective and cognition aspects is rapidly gaining popularity. These researchers highlight that there is a necessity of *"models that explain how feelings affect function, what limitations on feelings are, and how feelings impact behavior and performance in order to design HCI that considers the affective, including the cognitive aspects of human behavior"*.

For instance:

in today's competitive market of computer systems and the Internet, attitudes towards the systems determine whether costumers will use and re-visit systems, because many instances of use are discretionary. Understanding discretionary use, especially when the user is a client rather than an *employee of the organization, is rapidly becoming one of the most important issues in HCI.* (Te'eni, Carey & Zhang, 2007, p. 111).

Our learning/teaching experiences have showed that the logic stated above is applicable to support educators and students' awareness about the relevance of using contemporary technologies on citizens' everyday life. Individuals' understanding the importance of applying computers, information systems and the Internet in synergy with human's scaffolding as media learning resources inside and outside the school environment, and as communication facilitators has encompassed the integration between affective and cognitive aspects in HCI.

Schramm's field of experience model, and model of communication feedback (1954) in (Tannenbaum, 1998) reinforce the importance of the communication process for both the sender and the receiver. Then, whether interpersonal or mass, the sender and the receiver decode, interpret, and encode messages. The message received is decoded and passed to the brain in form of "sign," and the interpretation process is initiated:

If the receiver has learned the sign previously, then the receiver has learned that certain responses to it are possible. The responses are the meaning that the sign has to the receiver. The sign is always interpreted on the basis of both prior experience and the present context. (Tannenbaum, 1998, p. 263-264)

Tannenbaum (1998) states that communicators are constantly decoding signs, interpreting them, and encoding responses and he highlights such statement with a Schramm's thought. *"We can think of communication as passing through us – changed to be sure, by our interpretations, our habits, our abilities, and capabilities, but the input still being reflected in the output"* (Schramm, 19954, p.8) (in Tannenbaum, 1998, p.264. For Schramm without an overlap in their field of experience, two people could not communicate.

For example, paraphrasing Tannenbaum (1998) two people who have a common language can communicate because both have overlapping fields of experience. Hence, a student who is new to a discipline, say computer science, mass communication or computer graphics, may have a difficult time understanding the concepts commonly used in that subject, because the students' field of experience does not overlap extensively with those already in the discipline.

When the student attempts to communicate with a professor, the communication may be difficult because of the differences in the experience and the technical language that the student has yet to master. If the professor is to communicate successfully, he or she will have to work within only the symbol system and the experiences that both have in common. The professor may need to use examples or analogies for further explanation. That is, the professor must use a "sign system" that is shared with the student. (Tannenbaum, 1998, p.264)

In the case study section development we will identify the concept of overlap of the fields of experience for helping the communication among students and educators and as an excellent guide that supports the application of multimedia and contemporary technologies in the communication process, as well as its affective influence for the success of the interactive learning and teaching actions.

For example, Doman (2009) demonstrates the power of the process of communication and its affective influence on individuals' learning/teaching attitudes in Facilitated Communication that is a method, in which the parent provides the physical and emotional support that enables the child to express himself.

While the result of facilitated communication is profound, the technique itself is simple. The parent merely supports the child's hand so the child can point to letters on a board, typewriter, or computer in order to spell out words, sentences, and paragraphs. The parent stabilizes the child's movement so the child can effectively point, and through the experience of trial and error the parent learns the exact support the child needs to "write" his message. (Doman, Janet, 2009)

Relevant theoretical and practical works that have reinforced the idea of more horizontal relationship related to supporting individuals' knowledge construction and interactive learning and teaching for improving education using low cost interactive and advanced contemporary technologies are Doman and Doman (2007) with the book How to Multiply Your Baby's Intelligence and their work at (The Institutes for the Achievement of Human Potential, 2009) through stimulating children's vision, auditory and tactile competence (Doman, 2009).

This kind of teaching/learning action has supported increasing the development of the competence of the brain of children who have sustained a brain injury and accelerated neurological development of normal children (Wikipedia Institutes for Achievement of Human Potential, 2009) by using Doman's *bit of intelligence* BOI concept (Encyclopedic Knowledge, 2009). Gardner (2001) also does reference to the work of Glenn Doman at The Institutes for the Achievement of Human Potential. In addition, Gardner (2001) describes the educational artwork developed at the projects Zero (2009) and Spectrum (2009) for improving individuals' intelligence by using a methodology similar to Doman's BOI in combination with interactive contemporary technologies.

Paraphrasing, Osberg (1993), through the work that has been carried out, the idea is empowering individuals' cognition and skills by maximizing the opportunity for learning, creating environments, materials, and processes to make learning fun and effective for everyone and in everywhere.

So, supervised, unsupervised and reinforcement learning actions are applicable to this work development (Luger, 2002; Russell & Norvig, 2003). This strategy has tended to contribute for scaling individuals' knowledge on how to use information, and information systems effectively by supporting individuals' ability to apply all their perceptual senses, yet be able to discriminate what is necessary and what is not, essentially through higher-level thinking skills as states Dede:

In a world where data increases exponentially each year, a major challenge for schools is to prepare students to access and use information effectively...This requires a refocusing of current uses of multimedia in the curriculum, from engines for transmitting massive amounts of data to tools for structured inquiry based on higher-order thinking (...) Reconceptualizing multi-media now is important because, over the next decade, the fusion of computers and telecommunications will lead to the development of highly realistic virtual environments that are collaborative and interactive. The evolution of this "meta-medium" will enable artificial realities that immerse students in information-laden virtual worlds. Such learning environments risk overwhelming their users unless they incorporate tools that help students and teachers to master the cognitive skills essential to synthesizing knowledge from data. (Dede, 1992, p. 54, in Osberg, 1993)

This work strategy has been supported by practicing how to model a 3D object and develop VRML worlds using a common text editor and other trademark software as much as we can, having in mind to foment and support individuals' collaborative and interdisciplinary work based on computer graphics principles, accessible and low cost multimedia and ICT.

Paraphrasing Cunningham (2007, p.xxiii), the use of computer graphics and multimedia in the problem-solving process has been based on the development cycle of identifying the problem;

addressing the problem by building a model that represents it and allows it to be considered more abstractly; finding a way to represent the problem geometrically; creating an image from that geometry so that the problem can be seem; using the image to understand the problem or the model and try to grasp a possible solution.

Hence, in recent research Lajoie & Nakamura (2006) highlight the necessity of increasing the degree of educational interactivity with more varied types of media. Teaching and learning using computer graphics and multimedia tools requires more scaffolding of learners, more attention to assisting learners self-regulation, and perhaps media that serves in a pedagogical manner through coaching, pedagogical agents, mobile devices, and realistic and imaginary environments that include virtual reality and even augmented reality dimensions (Ficheman, Saul, Assis, Correa, Franco, Tori & Lopes, 2008b; Lajoie & Nakamura, 2006; Na, Billinghurst, & Woo, 2008).

Our learning experiences inside and outside school have showed that this work strategy of using computer graphics, virtual reality and multimedia tools and techniques in several learning situations in context (Cunningham, 2008) as problem solving tools can be an exciting undertaking and can be one to be widely shared. Yet, as Osberg (1993) states, *it is important to give yourself a break if things don't go exactly according to the plan. Enjoy yourself and your students during this creative process!*

According to Osberg (1997d) it is important make sure that everyone in your near vicinity knows what you are up to, and what it is going to take to be successful. This can include peers, administrative individuals, school boards, partners and your own children. And can be a key point in achieving environment scaffolding support.

There is evidence that school community's awareness relate to the work that has been carried out is a key point, and has been relevant for this work to become sustainable. At ESB School, principal, pedagogic coordinators, educators and students' awareness about contemporary technology relevance for the educational environment has been a key point for developing a digital/web-based interdisciplinary and collaborative work inside school and expand it to individuals' home.

For instance, the community's awareness about technology existence allowed ICT facilitators' to undertake collaborative work during 2003 to 2005. This collaborative work also supported some flexibility in classes schedule in order to develop an interdisciplinary work related to the learning and teaching of measuring systems and cartography in the first semester of 2005 (Franco, Cruz & Lopes 2006).

This work was extended to the surrounding community via community public library's coordinator awareness and involvement about what was carried out in terms of pedagogic and technology work at ESB School. This kind of partnership work was collaboratively designed attempting to improve students' reading, writing, researching and communication knowledge within active practice, as well as empowering community library's services to individuals. For instance, students created a prototype of the community library home page with HTML scripts and using their VRML knowledge they modeled in 3D some spaces of the community's library (in Franco, Cruz & Lopes 2006).

This kind of work methodology has brought about individuals' awareness enhancements related to technology existence and its applications for promoting innovation's sustainability in the learning environment. It includes stimulating individuals' lifelong learning attitudes through spiral, incremental and evolutionary work, in which individuals have as their technical and development companion tools, among others, web-based and other contemporary and advanced technologies as will be showed in the case study section that follows (Brutzman & Daly 2007; Franco & Lopes, 2005b; Franco & Lopes, 2005c; Franco, Cruz & Lopes, 2006; Pressman, 2006;

Franco, Ficheman, Lopes, Ferreira, Santos, Ferreira, Araújo & Moreno 2008).

CASE STUDY

In this section we provide examples of interactive formal and informal learning situations we have carried out with diverse individuals. These learning situations have been based on providing individuals' experience with contemporary and advanced technologies, bringing about stimulating ones' lifelong learning attitudes through spiral, incremental and evolutionary work.

Case Study 1: Working with Educators

Following a previous interdisciplinary and collaborative work presented on the SIGGRAPH 2006 conference (in Franco, Cruz & Lopes 2006), on September 2006, during an educators training time at ESB school, it was carried out a brainstorm about the work presented on the conference for educators that did not followed the interactive digital and web-based work carried out during 2005 (Franco & Lopes, 2005b).

A school pedagogic coordinator, four 5th to 8th grade level educators (2 Math, 1 Portuguese, 1 ICT facilitator) and a primary educator were in the workshop. After the brainstorm, we shared with them how to develop an application for teaching a curriculum subject through using some web-based technologies described on the background section. We discussed possibilities of improving individuals' English language, writing, reading, researching, communicating and digital skills within an interdisciplinary vision involving arts and culture.

Author1 constructed an hybrid interface based on the combination and interoperation of 2D HTML and 3D VRML including to that MPEG, WAV and JPG as a dynamic and interactive way of teaching English attempting to improve educators' understanding how to use technology in real time to improve their students reading, writing, listening, communicating and researching skills. The context of the work development was thought for using both electronic media if on-line or/and diverse traditional materials such as books and dictionaries from individuals and school library.

The hybrid 2D and 3D virtual interface was constructed using the following features:

- **Menu:** Initial Page, Introduction, Reading, Writing, Listening, Vocabulary, Grammar, Gallery, Practicing, Bibliography;
- **Objectives:** Improving socio-cultural interactions - via web-based technology (e-mail, Okurt, voice, video, letters (also more traditional ways and so on); supporting individuals' developing programming skills, which can make students increase other sciences, arts and communication abilities; stimulating creative writing through storytelling for constructing digital visual media content; understanding cultural trends and perspectives - related to diverse societies, cultures, genres; increasing individuals' research possibilities related to the global on-line database - (the Web) such as in the related work (Flanagan & Perlin, 2008) and in (Colson, 2007; Chun, 2006).
- **Culture and Art:** We chose as a culture, art, science and technology support the theme 'peace and society' and developed it by using, reusing and constructing multimedia files related to pictures researched on the Internet and audio and visual material from authorsl's personal collection. The theme inspiration came from the book Visual Arts and Communication – Unit 1 (Rueda & D'Angelo, 1999), which is designed to support English teaching, however, within an interdisciplinary vision.
- **Information Visualization:** Following the book suggestion for comparing im-

ages such as ("The Meninas", Velazquez; "Metamorphosis of Narcissus" Dali, "The sunflowers" Van Gogh, "Guernica" Picasso, and "Marlyn" Warhol) a 3D interface was designed for providing individuals navigating and reflecting about human's problems such as war and lifestyle over the time.

The interactive workshop went on through direct manipulating the HTML code and page components (video, audio and text) and their use in context. For instance, the video and text were related to Marvin Gaye's artwork – 'What is going on'. The meaning of Gaye's lyric seems to complete the pictures of the virtual gallery (in Franco, Ficheman, Alves, Venâncio, Lopes, Cruz, Santiago, Teles, & Aquino, 2007).

This workshop was a good opportunity to produce and presenting material related to teach English language and active learning and teaching possibilities referent to improve individuals' digital literacy. The workshop also served as way of reflecting about general technology knowledge development, within enough flexibility to be adapted to the learning and teaching of other subjects such as Geography, History, Arts, Sciences, Mathematics, Physical Education and Portuguese.

The web-based and low cost technology application visualized and directed manipulated on a desktop personal computer, brought about individuals' awareness on how to built a virtual reality environment and have the possibility of modifying it according to his/her ideas based on the procedural literacy concept as follows:

By procedural literacy I mean the ability to read and write processes, to engage procedural representation and aesthetics, to understand the interplay between the culturally-embedded practices of human meaning-making and technically-mediated processes. With appropriate programming, a computer can embody any conceivable process; code is the most versatile, general process language ever created. Hence, the craft skill of programming is a fundamental component of procedural literacy, though it is not the details of any particular programming language that matters, but rather the more general tropes and structures that cut across all languages. Without an understanding of how code operates as an expressive medium, new media scholars are forced to treat the operation of the media artifacts they study as a black box, losing the crucial relationship between authorship, code, and audience reception. Code is a kind of writing; just as literary scholars wouldn't dream of reading translated glosses of work instead of reading the full work in its original language, so new media scholars must read code, not just at the simple level of primitive operations and control flow, but at the level of the procedural rhetoric, aesthetics and poetics encoded in a work. (Mateas, 2005)

Similar 90 minutes workshop was carried out with international educators during the (ICEL, 2008) 11th International Conference on Experiential Learning through hands on experience of dealing with web-based technologies (Franco & Lopes, 2008), proceeding interactive learning and sharing knowledge actions from the code to the information visualization under author1's supervision.

Educators constructed a small scale 3D digital environment evolving WRL, WAV, JEPG and MPEG files. Although educators were not used to deal with 3D technologies, at the end of that section they were satisfied with the interactions and technologies possibilities for improving individuals' intelligence and communication through lifelong learning. Due to children natural tendency of being attracted and dominating contemporary technology (Miller, 2004), educators' evaluation, related to using such technologies for improving children's digital, math, spatial, imaginary and creative thinking skills, was considered effective.

An Australian educator from The Foundation for Young Australians (FYA, 2009) suggested for author1 using a software called (Scratch, 2009) with less literate children and educators for starting the technical work. She also indicated (Kahootz, 2009) a 3D modeling and digital audio software designed for supporting primary and secondary school students' learning through active actions during curriculum development related to arts, math, language, environmental and social studies. Her words sent to authors1 e-mail:

(...) take a look at scratch - http://scratch.mit. edu/. > This is a free animation software that is brilliant to use > with students using a simple programming language. I > really do believe it is easier to start with a simple > program like this with your staff compared to the one you > showed us. The one you showed us is brilliant for more > experienced ICT users but is complicated for most teachers. > I have worked in the area of ICT in Education for many years > and have found working with any programming language a > challenge for many teachers. If you begin with something > more achievable for them then you will have more of them > using it with their students. They can then progress to the > one you are using" (...) GP. December 13, 2008

Author1 replayed to her keeping the knowledge sharing after the workshop.

(...) I think as a researcher it may interest you http://www.processing.org/learning/3d/texture1. html. And following the VRML stuff there is an evolution called X3D format that is Java Based and is free http://www.web3d.org/x3d/. And may be for native English speakers can be easier for using. (Author1, December, 2008)

Another educator from the Faculty of Mechanical and Manufacturing Engineering, of The University Tun Hussein Onn Malaysia (UTHM,

2009) said that the web-based technology would a great way of attempting to stimulate his 12 years son to become a digital content developer instead of just a video game consumer. The educator kept talking with author1 about one hour more after the schedule time of the workshop doing hands on exercises, taking notes, visiting VRML sites and tutorials on the Internet.

Case Study 2: Individuals' Technical Skills Development and Lifelong Learning

Our approach of providing individuals' exposure and experience with 2D and 3d graphics through developing small scale VE under supervised learning has been effective to attracting students' attention. It has brought about students' lifelong and independent learning attitudes with support of web-based technology as companion.

For instance, after observing a previous interdisciplinary and collaborative work involving Geography, Math, Geometry, English language and ICT for supporting students learn scale, metric measure system and cartography concepts, including how to research, read, write and communicate using ICT (Franco & Lopes, 2005b; Franco, Cruz & Lopes, 2006) a student that was in the 3rd grade level in 2005 asked the author1 to teach how to develop a 3D model using the same techniques that other students from 7th and 8th grade level had applied to build their virtual worlds.

The learner was oriented within an interactive workshop experience of 30 minutes. The student created a red box by developing a VRML file. He direct manipulated Notepad text editor to produce the virtual and visualize it by using a browser called Cosmo player 2.1™, what brought about learning bits of computer graphics principles and stimulating him to keep investigating further the production of 3D worlds.

At the end of interactions the learner seemed to be satisfied. He was smiling and telling his mother he had understood the experience while he was also holding a piece of paper with his notes highlighting the references of X, Y and Z axes related to the computer monitor in order he could comprehend and use that (Franco & Lopes, 2005c).

According to his mother (author9), he carried out exercises at home, and the red box was transformed in a room with other objects. Further than that, the family and social interactions were improved through digital/web-based knowledge shared with his father, mother and brother who was at the 2nd grade at the same school.

Although, the student's mother was one of the ESB School ICT facilitators and worked in the school computers lab till the end of 2005, it is relevant to highlight that the student's independent learning attitude for developing programming and information and communication technology skills was his initiative.

His learning attitudes and creative knowledge development are relevant evidences that indicate the added value of using web-based and information visualisation technologies on individuals' education as lifelong learning companion tools. He has improved his technical skills, designed and produced work, which was shared with us through his mother. She sent an e-mail to author1 in April 2007 with a 3D VRML model that was designed having as a reference his home 2D blueprint (in Franco, Cruz, Aquino, Teles, Gianevechio, Franco, Ficheman, & Lopes, 2007b).

Her e-mail demonstrates that the technical domain of contemporary tools such as web-based technology can be very useful in terms of supporting individuals' cognitive skills improvements and lifelong learning attitudes.

During these three years even without much contact with new Cosmo tools (we used the browser Cosmo player™ for supporting the work at school from 2002 to 2005. It means VRML tools) L (her sun) keeps working at home. For instance, with the construction of my house, he took the 2D blueprint and transformed it in 3D. My husband works in the construction market, due to that L has contact with some blueprints of his father's clients. As he did with my house blueprint, he has developed similar 3D work with these clients' blueprints. These clients have observed and appreciated my sun's work. Now my sun's objective is to introduce his work to an engineering that draws the blueprints of the houses in the region where I live (The city of Caieras). He wants she gave him an opportunity of working through using his 3D technical skills. But, he has not got to demonstrate the work to her yet. I believe that her great difficult in accepting it is that he is only twelve years old. (Author1's translation)

Case Study 3: Sustaining the Use of Contemporary Technology at School

Our collaborative and interdisciplinary web-based work had good results in 2005 (in Franco, Cruz & Lopes, 2006) and these have been reverberating inside and outside school environment and on individuals' collective intelligence, bringing about dynamic and high quality knowledge based on academic and social interactions as demonstrated in the case study 1 and 2 and will be discussed in the evaluation section.

On the other hand, the changes that policy makers did in law that rules the school computers lab in the beginning of 2006, when the text of 'Portaria 303/98' was changed to 'Portaria n° 103' on January 2006, and later on to 'Portaria n° 3669' on August 2006, decreased the times, spaces and human interactivity for the collaborative and interdisciplinary support for individuals' learning and dominating digital technologies it was developed in the learning environment (Franco, Ficheman, Alves, Venâncio, Cruz, Gianevechio, Teles, Aquino & Lopes, 2007; SINPEEM, 2007).

As said before, due to the changes in law, one of the ICT facilitators (author9) had to leave the ESB School in the beginning of 2006. Also, the computers lab class schedule was changed for activities before or after students' regular classes.

This action dramatic decreased the possibility of developing collaborative and interdisciplinary work among educators and students. It also brought about great entropy in the school lab environment. The entropy came from having one ICT facilitator to thinking and acting to support 35 to 40 students, and manage 20 computer machines at once. For instance, you can imagine an educator and 40 first year primary students, age 6 and 7, in the school computers lab at once!

When the Portaria 303/98 was created the rule was that the ICT facilitator should work supporting other educators and students and curricular disciplines development. At the end of 2006, the Portaria n°3669 determined that the computers lab classes should be back to the regular classes' schedule. But, the ICT facilitator should keep working isolated in the school computers lab not as a facilitator but as a teacher. This situation has not happened at ESB School, yet, because the school has a schedule of five classes in the period of 4 hours. But in the schools where there are six classes in 4 hours and 45 minutes it has occurred.

So, during 2006, it was difficult period of adaptation. We had some moments with educators as described in the case study 1. And the work with students and contemporary technologies was almost isolated. However, some students that saw and participated on the web-based project in 2005 and new students kept this work sustainable.

Due to the work with contemporary technologies and the good results in the diverse contextualized learning experiences, even without technical appropriation of the tools used for producing curriculum content, educators became aware about technology possibilities for supporting curriculum content improvements.

However, to be aware of technology by observing others doing projects was not enough to individuals to gain lifelong learning autonomy to create digital content. For instance, an arts teacher Glaucia (author8) and a math teacher

Marlene (author6) asked how to create content using VRML because they were directly involved in the development of the diverse web-based technologies and interdisciplinary projects. So, we did some small scale workshops.

On the other hand, even with educators demonstrating will to develop technical skills, the school dynamics as well as educators' busy time and space schedule created difficulties for educators researching and dominating with autonomy how to create content direct manipulating web-based technology and multimedia tools.

Nevertheless, contemporary technologies applications generated students' interest in keep researching and producing content inside and beyond the school computers lab activities.

Based on the previous work developed in 2005 when he was in the 7th grade, a student kept developing his VRML world at home. Through his lifelong learning attitudes, he got enough expertise for supporting his and other students' creative design and productive processes. For instance, from supervised learning in the previous year, he got an unsupervised stage of knowledge development by deconstructing a hybrid 2D HTML and 3D VRML interface related to the Cosmo Player™ fish tank example. He reused the fish's VRML code into the building of his 3D VE outside living room. In his living room environment the student created diverse virtual objects based on his real home furniture.

An example of new student's engagement on developing knowledge related to digital/web technology and computer graphics principles due to the accessibility to the tools provided in the school computers lab comes from a student that was in 5th grade adult education in 2006. The adult education classes used to happen in the evenings from 7 to 11 pm until the end of 2007.

The student was 53 years old at that time and had a good knowledge on hardware. He visited the school computers' lab seeking for improving his computers technical skills related to software and digital content production. Author1 offered and

reflected with him about learning VRML stuff for developing his cognitive abilities such as memory, attention, perception, planning (in Benyon, Turner & Turner, 2005; Preece, Sharp & Rogers, 2007). He was introduced to the 8th grade student and his artwork in Figure 5a we referred in the above example and they exchanged some ideas.

After that, he was told to install the necessary software at home, and after some installing troubles and three weeks for breaking his initial learning curve he started producing VRML files with autonomy. In general, at that time autor1 was used to meet the students twice a week, 1 hour and 30 minutes on Mondays and Tuesdays. The 5th grade student went seven times to the lab between September and November, 2006.

When he was asked about his feelings related to the 3D programming experience, the 5th grade student, Sir Germal said that at the beginning he was having problems for concentrating because the younger students' noise in the school computers lab. On the other hand, at home he had Internet access and could follow the VRML Sourcebook V2.0 on-line examples (2008) and VRML Portuguese tutorials (Manssour, 2008; Barros, 2004). Sir Germal reported that he developed a 3D environment at home using his grandchild picture to training VRML texture mapping features. These facts brought about to him confidence to have unsupervised learning attitudes to do transformations in the VRML code, including adding animation to an object, playing with background colors, changing the transform and material parameters, developing textures with Paint ™ program.

On the middle of the second semester 2006, students and educators' technology awareness and appropriation led us to designing a prototype game project called 'Uma Aventura no Espaço'/'An Adventure in Space'. The idea was to share their 3D knowledge with other students and educators at school and surrounding community and participate in the projects selection of FEBRACE 2007. It included to stimulating other students to engage further in their learning process through using interactive technologies as support for developing the diverse curriculum content subjects.

Although, it was not possible to pass on FEBRACE selection, students and educators' improved their research, communication, traditional and digital literacy, and other cognitive skills such as writing and reading.

The initial game designing was based on the game 'Jogo do Dinossauro do Spectrum' – 'Dinosaur Game from Spectrum' project that is related to math curriculum development and supported by Gardner's multiple types of intelligence theory (in Chen, Isberg & Krechevesky, 2001; Franco, Cruz & Lopes, 2006).

The project development idea was to construct a game for supporting teaching and learning the concept of positive and negative numbers in math, by creating both virtual and real versions of the game. The real prototype was not so difficult to design and implement. For the virtual version the plan was using VRML and HTML features related to hyperlinks and interoperation of multimedia files and modeling 2D and 3D VE.

Students designed the interface in several ways and learned how much work is necessary for producing digital content of quality. The work addressed the problem of learning to design simple and complex 3D interfaces by applying theory and practice. Ones used desktop virtual reality features to simulate, or adapt from the real physical world as investigated (in Bowman, Kruijff, LaViola & Poupyrev, 2005).

The work development supported the concept of problem solving as a form of learning to think, assuming that thinking is the primary mechanism for human understanding and improving the world. It includes expanding this idea for interactive forms of problem solving that depend on the behavior of the world rather than on a priori human beliefs (Wenger & Goldin, 2006).

Based on such concept, we attempted to carry out interdisciplinary and collaborative work by inviting math and arts educators (authors 6 and

8), including a former school's student, who left school at the end of 2005, but kept researching with us and participating on other school projects development in 2006 to contribute with the school development.

Due to our lack of programming skills, we could not complete the project 'An Adventure in Space' with the quality and usability that we wished.

On the other hand, during our game prototype experience with advanced technology resources we got support outside the school environment for solving an interface design problem that was to produce a virtual dice for compounding the virtual game interface. The support came during the project implementation through the arts' educator (author 8). She asked her brother in law, who had programming skills deeper than us to develop a virtual dice interface in a way we could use the virtual dice to complete the game interface.

He developed the dice interface quickly using the Visual Basic language. Unfortunately, because of languages incompatibility and our lack of programming abilities, we could not integrate the virtual dice in the HTML and VRML game interface. Nevertheless, due to JavaScript language compatibility with HTML and VRML, we asked him to develop the dice interface using JavaScript, but it was not possible for him to achieve that.

However, across the development of this interactive learning and teaching process, author8 reported that her brother in law said that he had not seem a kind of work like this before applying virtual reality technology inside a primary school, and that this type of learning/teaching methodology should be continued.

Case Study 4: Intensifying the Use of Contemporary Technology at School

In 2007, after adapting to the scholar system changes as described in the case study 3, we got an increase in the quantity and quality of interactive, collaborative and interdisciplinary work supported by contemporary technology, what brought about to energize students and educators' interactions, as well as lifelong learning and education quality and opportunities as attempted in the work described (in Fullan, 2008).

The increment in the use of digital/web based tools in combination with curriculum content development approximated individuals from the diverse sciences, art, culture and technology as investigated and demonstrated (in Colson, 2007; Wands, 2006), impacting in democratizing digital/web based and general knowledge inside the school. It also improved ones' communication skills in terms of dominating and using techniques and concepts related to information visualization, computer graphics, web-based technology and multimedia low cost resources to design and produce content, with support of the concept of overlap of fields of experience (in Tannenbaum, 1998) .

Individuals direct manipulated these technologies to produce digital content at school and expanded the knowledge developed to informal home meetings and other learning environments in diverse communities (Franco, Cruz & Lopes, 2006; Franco, Ficheman, Assis, Zuffo, Lopes, Moreno & Freitas, 2008), contributing for forming diverse, interoperable, high quality, dynamic and interactive digital learning ecosystems (Ficheman & Lopes, 2008; Forrester, 1992).

We believe that a great support for keeping this work sustainable over the past six years has come from the local community engagement in the interactive learning process. Students and educators' interactive work and outcomes have gained visibility and served as a reference inside and outside the learning environment ecosystem. For some reason, perhaps the collective intelligence (Lévy, 1993), the community's work has been extended to individuals the challenge of keeping the learning environment in continuous development for pushing the next generation of students. From this kind of work, the new generation of students has kept involved psychologically in improving

their knowledge and confidence for enhancing the learning ecosystem, within a never ending spiral and incremental learning cycle.

For instance, through a middle term virtual reality technology appropriation, an 8th grade student (M1) in 2007 developed an interesting research work and web-based 3D presentation related to Charles Chaplin' artwork.

M1's technology background is related to his visit to the school computers lab when he asked to author1 to teach him how to develop a 3DVE in 2006. M1 had heard about the creation of 3DVE at home across (M2) his brother's comments about the 2D and 3D web-based learning actions in 2003 and 2004. M2 studied at ESB School until the end of 2004. Other relevant reference that influenced M1 curiosity is that he observed other students' work using VRML at school computers lab in 2005.

Franco, Mariz, Lopes, Cruz, Franco & Delacroix (2007a) state that M2 was one of the ESB School's former students that supported the initial author1's informal investigation (2003) related to the use of contemporary and advanced technologies on primary education for stimulating students' knowledge development. This interactive and dynamic educational process has brought about a collaborative knowledge based partnership with the Laboratory of Integrated Systems from The University of São Paulo, in which educators and students have been achieved protagonist participation during the Feira Brasileira de Ciências e Engenharia – (Brazilian Fair of Sciences and Engineering) - FEBRACE 2004 and 2009 (in Franco, 2005; Franco, Cruz & Lopes, 2006; Imprensa Jovem, 2009; Portal Aprendiz, 2009).

Under supervision of author1, M1 developed an interactive 3D virtual museum environment about Charles Chaplin's artwork based on VRML features such as video and still bitmap texture. The 3DVE was composed by content that he researched on the Internet. The work presentation was watched by his Portuguese teacher and student's classmates.

The work was considered excellent by the Portuguese language teacher who had asked a research about Chaplin's life. She also congratulated the student at the moment she knew that the 3DVE was developed by him.

It was a collaborative and interactive work, in which author11 provided the film Morden Times to be edited according to the student's research on the site (YouTube, 2009). After that, similar to the combination of advanced technologies to support artistic and cultural heritage work developed (in Park, Leigh, Johnson, Carter, Brody & Sosnoski, 2001; Roussos, Johnson, Leigh, Vasilakis, Barnes & Moher, 1997), M1's 3D VRML model was reused by autor1 and 11 for supporting information visualization of author11's investigation related to Afro Brazilian cultural heritage and the visibility of Negroes' artists.

The work happened through combining in the 8th grade student's virtual museum gallery a research related to negroes Brazilian musicians' record cover illustrations. The record covers' illustrations were referent to Pixinguinha, Paulinho da Viola, João Nogueira, Trio Mocotó and Clementina de Jesus artwork. The gallery was completed with a recent video related to Tony Tornado's artistic life showed on channel Globo in the program 'Estrelas' (in YouTube Estrelas, 2009).

In the beginning of August, 2007, M1 saw and said that he enjoyed seeing the artwork he did, adapted and reused by the authors1 and 11. In sequence, M1 was asked to share his work with Professor Marcelo Zuffo (author 2) from the LSI. The Professor was visiting the ESB School computers lab. Professor Zuffo is an expert in web-based technology, virtual reality, scientific visualization, computer graphics and digital TV technology (Zuffo, 2001; in Globo Videos, 2009).

Supported by the common knowledge on information visualization and virtual reality techniques that M1developed they talked 15 minutes about the student's artwork development with minor interventions from author1. Through this and other examples showed through this chapter development, we infer that contemporary technologies can be used as 'common ground' or 'common language' for enhancing students and educators' communication as highlighted (in Laurel, 1993), as well as impacting the development of knowledge of individuals under risk situation lifelong.

In the second semester of 2007, from September to November M1 contributed for modelling a 3DVE related to a scientific research that was presented to the school audience in November 2007. The scientific research was referent to the problem of water pollution and was developed with support of school educators and students' interdisciplinary work. Under the school ICT facilitator and a Science educator (author5)'s collaboration and supervision, and using contemporary technologies as a common ground, fifth and sixth grade students investigated, formatted and presented the work through using digital/web-based 2D and 3D information visualization and low cost multimedia tools.

M1 shared his 3D knowledge with 5th and 6th grade students designing with their research support a 3DVE. The virtual environment was constructed by integrating GIF, JPG and MPEG files as textures, and WAV files for auditory enhancements through using Virtual Reality Modeling Language – VRML (in Franco, Ficheman, Assis, Zuffo, Lopes, Moreno & Freitas, 2008a).

Case Study 5: 2008, More Possibilities of Sharing Web-Based Knowledge

At the beginning of 2008, inspired on the water pollution museum project and based on Brazilian national curriculum parameter (PCN Matemática 5ª A 8ª series, 1998) related to math teaching we attempted to support one hundred and fifty 6th grade level students' understanding how measure systems function and influence everyday life. This educational process also involved approximating educators and students from visual the culture (Barbosa, 2006; Hernández, 2000; Projetc Zero, 2008), visual arts as suggested (in PCN 5ª a 8ª Séries Arte, 1998), and digital technologies in a way that individuals could dominate and use web-based ICT as companion and with autonomy within a lifelong learning process.

We carried out the work through doing small scale workshops during educators' training time once a week. With students, the process was developed during their classroom time once a week and three research classes divided in three different sections of forty-five minutes each (Wednesday, Thursday and Friday) inside the school computers lab.

The idea of using web-based 3D technologies for understanding measuring concepts came from an informal talk between author1 and 10, at the beginning of 2008. During the talk they reflected about how to improve the way of teaching math in a more active mood and also associate it with the domains of 2D and 3D web-based technology, information visualization and computer graphics principles and tools.

Through informal way, author10 has followed author1's research since 2005. Author10 was doing his third year undergraduate course on math. Author10 has background in drawing and CAD systems.

This collaborative learning experience proposal was a way of investigating the validity of providing to a undergraduate student experience with digital/web-based standard languages and technology and the real world school environment within its everyday learning and teaching challenges as described in (Franco, 2001; Franco, Cruz & Lopes, 2006).

The idea of the measuring project was shared with math and science educators at school. Both had experienced web-based 3DVE projects before during 2005, 2006 and 2007. They read the proposal, considered that interesting and started applying it on March 2008.

The actions of developing and sharing knowledge involved a mass collaboration process that Tapscott & Williams (2006) call collaborative science, which is based on the Web features related to increase individuals' abilities of self-organize into large-scale networks, bringing about rapid diffusion of best scientific practices, stimulating new technological hybrids and recombination, availability of just in time expertise and increasingly powerful tools for conducting research with innovation within horizontal and distributed models, including greater openness of scientific knowledge, tools and networks.

The measuring learning project proposal was related to decrease the problem that students showed for understanding measure systems. The idea was to challenge the students to create their own measuring systems using as reference, for example, an eraser, a pen, or any other object they wish. From that the next step was to measure a wall.

In this case, it was measuring a classroom wall using the measure system that the group of students created. After that, students were asked to simulate the wall through creating a 3D virtual environment using a combination of web-based and desktop virtual reality technologies. The wall's simulation also involved creating a design for wall tile and setting tiles in the wall. At the end of the process it was expected that students would be able to grasp measuring systems (in Brazil, the most used measuring system is the metric one) and improve their contemporary technology knowledge.

Math educators started working with students presenting the project proposal of developing work in collaboration with the ICT facilitator. The actions for achieving the proposal goal were carried out and redirect according to students' needs, educators' reflections about the teaching and learning experiences, and school's schedule related to classes time and space.

During the learning process development and educators' reflections, through informal and formal meetings, math educators reported that the idea was well accepted by students. This means that the hands-on workshop with educators demonstrating and reflecting about the usability of digital technologies for supporting their work was effective.

Although, it is difficult for educators to have time for dominating and using technology with autonomy, the fact of direct manipulating it helped them understanding its value. Educators' lack of time for dominating technology comes from too many classes per week, going to two up to four different schools during the week. Hence, for ones' self investing in learning contemporary and advanced technologies is expensive. The average cost of advanced technology courses is higher than 30% of educators' remuneration.

In the pre-work preparation workshop we also involved more two math and arts educators, both were introduced to VRML scripts and 3D technology. The educators initially said that students would have to type VRML code and this action could difficult students focus on understanding how a measure system works. But, in sequence, they were told about copy and paste techniques, contextualized through the VRML graphic pieces' transformations such as (translation, diffuseColor, imageTexture).

The techniques used to share knowledge with the arts' educator were researching one of the pictures "Aquarelas" painted by Lasar Segal (in Museu Segal, 2008) and apply it as texture on a Cylinder in real time. We also demonstrated to and reflected with them about concepts such as how to reuse the content created and to integrate diverse interdisciplinary content through applying copy and paste techniques on a 3DVE file's construction and transformations Figure 2.

At the beginning of the experience the math educator who had programmed in Fortran language before, by mentally comparing Fortran (in Miller, 2002) and VRML code said that it would be difficult to students using VRML to produce their work. On the other hand, after experiencing

how to save and visualize a file employing VRML 'code' or 'scripts', she agreed that it would be possible to apply VRML language for supporting individuals' computational thinking and learning math's concepts Figure 2.

We did further reflections at the end of the workshop. For instance, that this kind of interactive teaching and learning experience allows educators' approximating from and reflecting with students about the importance of reading and writing words in a correct way. For example, because VRML is case sensitive, with reference to upper and lower cases. This makes *'geometry Box'* different form *'Geometry Box'*. And it is a way of working individuals' cognitive abilities related to attention and perception (Benyon, Turner & Turner, 2005; Preece, Sharp & Rogers, 2007).

Hence, we can make an analogy with real life in which ones' writing and reading with effectiveness as well as developing skills for dealing with contemporary technology can bring about to them better communication skills and lifetime opportunities for self development. For instance, such as the opportunity that author1 had when he conquered the scholarship for doing his master course as described in the motivation section.

So, through these ones' interactive horizontal proximity within learning and teaching processes, it is possible to achieve the necessary awareness about the whys, what for and how we should read, write, research and communicate with effectiveness. For example, for producing simple and /or complex content and organize it adequately in order to storytelling in a virtual environment it is necessary to research, read, think, understand, plan and write how the diverse narrative agents will interact with each other (Franco, 2001b, Laurel, 1993).

Paraphrasing Juul (2005p.15), this interactive learning process development uses the concept of *"narrative as the primary way in which we make sense of and structure the world"*. Across this interactive learning process we constructed a narrative structure that enabled us to support

Figure 2. First, on the left, author's 1 visual representation of the VRML script that follows below the image and on the right. The reader can experience with this piece of code and visualize the figure above. For achieving that, download and install a VRML viewer (for instance Cortona™). After that, open a text editor (notepad) and write the code. Save the file as "bookexample.wrl" /(Type – Text document). The (.wrl) is important to visualize the 3D world above. Then go to the folder where you saved the file and double click on it.

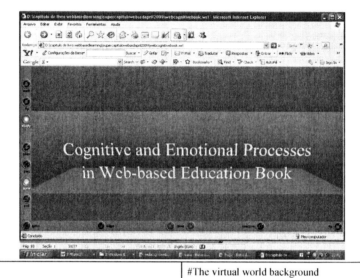

```
#VRML V2.0 utf8
#Created by Jorge Ferreira Franco in April/06/2009
#Here we start the shape in form of text
Shape{
        appearance Appearance{
        material Material{ diffuseColor 1.0 1.0 0.0}
        }
        geometry Text {
        string ["Cognitive and Emotional Processes",
        "in Web-based Education Book"]
        fontStyle FontStyle{
        size 8.5
        justify "MIDDLE"
        spacing 1.2

                }
        }
},
#Here we present the initial view point
Viewpoint {

     position 0.0 5.0 80.0
        description "Abertura"
        orientation 0.0 0.0 0.0 0.0
     },
```

```
#The virtual world background
Background{
        skyColor[
        0.0 0.2 0.7
        0.0 0.5 1.0
        0.2 0.4 0.6
        ]
        skyAngle[1.309, 1.571]
        groundColor[
        0.5 1.0 0.4,
        0.4 0.25 0.2,
        0.6 0.60 0.6,
        ]
        groundAngle [1.309, 1.571]
}

#virtual world base
Transform {
                translation 0.0 -10.4 0.0
                scale 2.0 1.0 1.0
                children Shape {
            appearance Appearance {
            material Material {diffuseColor 1.0 0.0 0.0 }
                        texture ImageTexture {
                        url "mt.jpg" }
                        }
            geometry Box {size 60.0 0.1 30.0 }
                }
},
#Lighting the world
PointLight {
        location 0.0 50.0 0.0
        radius 150.0
        intensity 1.0 }
```

students' grasping math measuring systems and its relations with real world, including preparing educators and students to deal with advanced and contemporary technologies.

Laurel (1993, pp.32, 33) states that *"designing human computer experience isn't about building a better desktop. It is about creating imaginary worlds that have special relationship with reality-worlds in which they can extend, amplify, and enrich our own capacities to feel, think, and act".*

While individuals write VRML scripts and concentrate on the action of visualizing the scripts, they can improve their higher order thinking, mental models and spatial literacy skills (Mc-Cullough, 2004), as well as organize themselves in order to understand the complexity that an enlargeable work in development such as this one can become.

The building of an enlargeable work like this implicates in developing diverse individuals' cognitive and technical skills such as:

- Individuals' technical skills development in computer literacy
- Review and learn math's operations such as fraction and decimal number concepts
- How to calculate a wall area, simulate and setting tiles on it
- Dominating a measure system concept
- Learning to work cooperatively and collaboratively
- Improving students and educators' visual arts domain
- Learning how to manipulate image processing programs
- Imagining and designing new products such as wall tiles textures
- Learning how to research
- Stimulating the learning of a second language (English), due to in Brazil the first one is Portuguese
- Improving spatial literacy

- Using, comparing and transforming the diverse existing measure units
- Developing Portuguese language reading, writing and communication skills

Real world examples of using Portuguese language related to learning math were students' reports, in which they describe the initial process of creating their own measuring parameter and comparing it with the metric system. One of the math educators asked to her 70 students from the 6th grade level reports about the measuring activity they did. Author1 also read some of these reports.

During an informal talk between the ESB School ICT facilitator and one of the math educators, the math educator said that she was satisfied with the initial results of the project because students' reports showed that they understood the proceedings they did and the math operations they executed.

After that, educators also discussed about the digital implementation of the project, which was carried out with good students acceptance according to the math educator observations and oral survey developed with students.

Despite of students' engagement on the work carried out in the classroom, there were difficulties for educators supporting students' technical skills development for finishing the digital work. Such problems happened because of difficulties related to the great average of number of students for one School ICT facilitator and due to school dynamics. Then, it was not possible to support students with deepen VRML technical foundations and regular frequency to the school computers lab.

On the other hand, the initial plan that was related to improve math teaching and learning became a collaborative, incremental and interdisciplinary research. During one of the meetings in the computers lab, the students were told to designing their own wall tile textures. This action approximated students from arts and history knowledge. In order to gaining more reference to designing wall tiles, they were asked to research on the Internet diverse images of wall tiles. They also had access to a cultural and historic video that tells a story about Portuguese's wall tile influence in Brazilian Culture (Jornal da Gazeta, 2008).

Similar to the case study 1, the interactive project development brought about educators' hands-on experience on contemporary technologies and as consequence a math educator (author 6) changed her way of teaching and proposing learning activities. Based on the interactive skills developed during the measuring project, she guided her students for creating real world interactive games for understanding math concepts such as fraction Figure 3.

We think that by observing and supporting previous collaborative and interdisciplinary learning projects based on contemporary and advanced technology (Franco, Mariz, Lopes, Cruz, Franco & Delacroix, 2007a) as in the case study 3, author7's interactive attitudes used for teaching math demonstrate that is possible to developed a feeling of understanding a problem within a certain situation (for instance, students' learning needs) and transfer knowledge to solve it.

She applied her developed knowledge for solving problems with advanced and contemporary technology in appropriate way by transferring it

Figure 3. Author7 sharing results of her work with students to teach fraction

to the use of more traditional materials to solve the problem of students grasping the concept of fraction. It seems that her understanding related to a problem solving and attitudes to reduce it go beyond the cognitive reasoning. It goes deeper to the state of developed wisdom. And the state of developed wisdom comes from processes of learning and experiencing through the time and space.

Senge, Scharmer, Jaworski & Flowers (2007, pp. 87) state that this kind of wisdom comes from ones internal feelings in combination with logical reasoning. For instance, as a good race driver a person does not act by deduction. She/he uses internal feelings while is going through the pitch lane.

Inspired on the math project with 6th grade level students, the ESB School ICT facilitator talked with and introduced the advanced and contemporary technologies that have been discussed during this chapter to 7th and 8th grade students.

We reflected that individuals' domain on technology could bring about autonomy to use it lifelong to support the learning of diverse subjects such as Math, Portuguese, Arts, as well as individuals' entrepreneurship and that there is no magic for achieving such performance. The key for improving performance is hard work.

It is necessary to study, learn to be patient to deal with problems that come with the intensive use of technology, to be persistent to learn technologies' complexity and create complex 3DVE. It is a process that can support students and educators' understanding the bottom-up culture where, for example, *gamers use sharing and open-source techniques to existing products of the mainstream practices of the cultural industries* (Raessens, 2006, pp. 382).

One of the problems of an educator attempting to do such action alone at the school computers lab is that with 35 up to 40 students inside, it is a great challenge for the educator to support physically and mentally students' assistance needs to understand and do the technical exercises.

Then, one approach that has been used to decrease this problem is to ask the students who understand the process of creating, saving and visualizing VRML files to collaborate with the other students for achieving the goal established. Indeed, some of the goals of this work have been learning how to raise individuals' spirit of collaboration and sharing knowledge.

Fortunately, these goals have been achieved through a long term and persistent work. Collaborative work and sharing knowledge have become common practices and part of the learning environment's collective intelligence with support of digital/web-based and advanced technologies. It includes stimulating the excellence of human resources that have been developed over the past years inside the school environment.

The combination among collective intelligence, technical skills and individuals' confidence and excellence has been a key point for recalling and sustaining the 3D web-based work. Furthermore, some students have developed their own web-based work and inviting other ones to joining in their learning process. In particular, one of them has investigated, shared and used deepen contemporary and advanced technology and his artwork has served as a relevant local reference to other ones inside and outside the school environment as we will describe in the evaluation section (Reportagem 1, 2008; Wellington, 2009).

We introduced 3D web-based principles through developing a small scale 3D environment using VRML nodes such as illumination, viewpoint, texture and transform, at the end of April 2008. Hence, in November 2008 we observed that the principles of that work were still on students' mind.

During September and October we carried out a work in which students from 7th and 8th grade levels were asked to designing a 2D blueprint of a house with eight environments and calculating the individual area of each environment and the total house area *(Area Wikipedia, 2008)*. So, after the blueprint design to be ready, the ICT facilitator proposed that they developed a 3D representation of the blueprint by coding it using VRML.

At the beginning the students were a bit resistant to do that task, and asked how to do that. But when the ICT facilitator explained and demonstrated how to do that, recalling students' memory to the previous 3D web-based technology experience in the first semester of 2008, they understood that they were able to do the task and started to work, and some students achieved the objective.

Because the work novelty related to improve individuals' technical skills domain, in terms of stimulating students' production, the best results came from doing practical work for about 80 minutes. It was the time for them *observing, discovering, inventing and producing* their digital content following Dewey's learning cycle proposal (in Senge, Scharmer, Jaworski & Flowers, 2007).

This learning/teaching experience was another real world example of using this work methodology to developed classroom content through learning and practicing math concepts, stimulating individuals' communication, digital technical skills and spatial abilities improvements, by applying computer graphics and multimedia tools in context for solving problems and enhancing individuals' cognition (Cunningham, 2008; Franco, Ficheman, Venâncio, Moreno, Freitas, Leite, Franco, Matias & Lopes, 2008c; Franco & Lopes, 2008; Kaufmann, 2004; Kaufmann & Meyer, 2008; Miller, 2004).

Paraphrasing, Miller, (2004) we have carried out work, in which interactive, advanced and contemporary technologies have been vehicles to teach, and the packing of educational content that is both entertaining and interactive. *"Furthermore, this unique hybrid is an effective way of engage adult learners as well children. It has been put to work for everything from teaching basic math and reading skills to training sophisticated leadership techniques to business professionals".* (Miller, 2004, p. 137)

EVALUATION

Computers and emerging, interactive, advanced and contemporary technologies such as VR and video games have had a psychological appeal on individuals' mind as well as behavior (Dede, Salzman, Loftin & Ash, 1997; Franco, 2001; Merch, 1999; Miller, 2004). Due to that, we believe that these technologies can serve as problem solving tools related to improve Brazilian individuals' low level of alphabetization that is a fact, which direct influences the low level of literacy related to ones' reading, writing, math and science skills. Due to these structural problems, individuals lack of quality of knowledge to access and use arts, technology and culture with effectiveness according to recent surveys (in INAF, 2005; PISA, 2006).

Obviously, if people can not read and write well, probably they will have problems for accessing, understanding and benefiting from the technical, artistic and cultural artifacts that contemporary society has offered to citizens.

On the other hand, we believe that it is possible to enhance individuals' digital and traditional literacy, including science, cultural, artistic and technology silks since the primary education with support of advanced and contemporary technology. Our work described through this chapter, mainly in the case study section, has showed the effectiveness of such proposal in practice via applying low cost tools for achieving that.

Within the related work section we presented many more experiences that demonstrate evidence that children have benefited from the support of the combination of teachers, their peers, the specific hardware and the use of both side by side, including networked collaboration to write electronic stories. For example, with the T'rrific Tales software within the NIMIS project (Brna & Cooper, 2003). The design and implementation of the NIMIS classroom is reasonably successful but this is due to a complex mix of factors that mainly complement each other (Brna & Cooper, 2003).

Similar to NIMIS project, our work has achieved reasonably successful and its effectiveness has been increased, mainly, due to educators and students' awareness of technology existence and the raising on their understanding of what for, and how to use it for solving problems. This individuals' comprehension has also supported the development of their technical skills.

Individuals direct manipulating digital, advanced and contemporary technologies has conducted ones to human computer interactions HCI, collaborative and interdisciplinary work and to the training of the human's cognitive abilities (Dede, 2000; Franco, Cruz & Lopes, 2005a; Rusk, Resnick, Berg & Pezalla-Granlund, 2008).

Through the development of a long term work, this educational experience has attempted to support individuals' cognition abilities improvements related to attention; perception and recognition; memory, learning, reading, speaking and listening; problem-solving, planning, reasoning, decision making and language by using contemporary technologies as demonstrated in the case studies one to five and investigated (in Benyon, Turner & Turner, 2005; Preece, Sharp & Rogers, 2007).

This educational experience has benefited individuals with the convergence among interactive technologies, education and human knowledge of excellence. This convergence has brought about individuals to access and develop content that engages humans' multiple senses and offers several ways of ones acquire information and develop new skills – via hearing, reading, viewing moving and still images, and by manipulating and producing digital content and communicating in a variety of ways (Miller, 2004).

Across ones' *direct manipulating* (Preece, Rogers, Sharp, Benyon, Holland, & Carey, 1994) digital/web-based technologies and low cost multimedia tools synergy we have addressed the problem of using "*computers not simply as information machines, but also as a new medium for creative design and expression"* as states Resnick (2006) through actions that can stimulate a culture of classrooms focusing on supporting students' cognitive abilities development as creative thinkers (Resnick, 2007).

CONNECTING BIOLOGY, LEARNING AND TECHNOLOGY

These students' cognitive abilities can be encapsulated within a simplified model, which represents the human information processing HIP paradigm to be visualized and that support ones' better understanding the process of brain function and that direct affects ones' thinking and acting for building intelligence. According to Benyon, Turner & Turner (2005), this HIP model is composed by *" 'blocks' or subsystems: (a) a sensory input subsystem, (b) a central information processing subsystem, and (c) a motor output subsystem "* (p.101).

It is not the scope of this chapter to do a detailed investigation about brain function. However, the biological influence of brain function has gained, among others, neuroscience, artificial intelligence and educators researchers' attention for grasping how the human brain learns and develops knowledge (Churchland, 2004; Del Nero, 1997, Doman e Doman, 2007; Reilly & Munakata, 2000; Outras Palavras, 2009).

The human beings' biologic nature provides to them equal possibilities of brain development if the brain is stimulated within an appropriate way. So, to be conscious that the brain grows dramatic through its use during the first six years of children's lives and that we can do the brain grow if we want, it is a *'key information'* for parents and educators (Doman e Doman, 2007, p.129; Child brain development, 2009).

Due to children's brain development openness util the age of six, providing them quality and quantity information within a systemic and flex-

ible way across **precise** 'with adequate details'; **discrete** 'only one item'; and **not ambiguous** 'with a name that can be interpreted only in one way' **'bit of intelligence'** as said (in Doman and Doman, 2007, 244 - 245) is relevant. For example, the quality and quantity of visual stimulation changes the neural networks of the brain and changes the quality of output from the left brain as it develops (Accelerated Learning Methods, 2009).

According to Yamamoto (2009) in a recent research published in the Neurological Research magazine, auditory and tactile stimulation developed by learning how to play piano influenced and supported better learning outcomes, since music-making nurtures the intellect and produces long-term improvements. For instance, the children who were learning piano once a week scored 34% higher than the other groups on tests designed to measure spatial-temporal reasoning skills - those required for mathematics, chess, science and engineering.

Interestingly, the computer kids scored no higher than the group who received no special instruction. (…) *"The high proportion of children who evidenced dramatic improvement in spatial-temporal reasoning as a result of music training should be of great interest to parents, scientists and educators,"* added Dr. Shaw.

Paraphrasing Yamamoto (2009) this study shows that interactive and high quality learning experiences early in life can determine which brain cells (neurons) will connect with other brain cells, and which ones will die away. Because neural connections are responsible for all types of intelligence, a child's brain develops to its full potential only with exposure to the necessary enriching experiences in early childhood:

What Drs. Rauscher and Shaw have emphasized has been the causal relationship between early music training and the development of the neural circuitry that governs spatial intelligence. Their studies indicate that music training generates the neural connections used for abstract reason-

ing including those necessary for understanding mathematical concepts. (Yamamoto, 2009)

The neural connections are related to the biologic processes called synapses. Synapses are functional connections between neurons, or between neurons and other types of cells. The synapse is the junction between the sending neuron's axon and the receive neuron's dendrite. The end of the axon that enters into the synapse is called the axon terminal or button (Reilly & Munakata, 2000, p. 30; Churchland, 2004, p. 209):

A typical neuron gives rise to several thousand synapses, although there are some types that make far fewer. Most synapses connect axons to dendrites, but there are also other types of connections, including axon-to-cell-body, axon-to-axon, and dendrite-to-dendrite. Synapses are generally too small to be recognizable using a light microscope except as points where the membranes of two cells appear to touch, but their cellular elements can be visualized clearly using an electron microscope. Chemical synapses pass information directionally from a presynaptic cell to a postsynaptic cell and are therefore asymmetric in structure and function. The presynaptic terminal, or synaptic button, is a specialized area within the axon of the presynaptic cell that contains neurotransmitters enclosed in small membrane-bound spheres called synaptic vesicles. Synaptic vesicles are docked at the presynaptic plasma membrane at regions called active zones (AZ). (Wikipedia Synapse, 2009)

Back to the case of piano classes (in Yamamoto, 2009), even without having to much detail about the learning process, it seems that good learning experience's achievements are related to the way that the piano lessons and practices were developed and supported by human expertise, meaning also good emotional influence on students' knowledge development.

We do not know what kind of tasks were developed using computers in that experience.

Although, that interactive technologies and computers attract children's attention (Miller, 2004), obviously, nobody can guarantee that they will support individuals' intelligence improvements without adequate learning situations and activities able to stimulate ones' learning attitudes and engagement for knowledge development. There has been the necessity of combining human's excellence, hardware and software scaffolding in order to achieve individuals' good knowledge development (Franco, Cruz & Lopes, 2006; Harrison & Hood, 2008; IINN-ELS, 2009; Luckin, Boulay, Yuill, Kerawalla, Pearce & Harris, 2003; Warner-Rogers & Reed, 2008).

On the other hand, paraphrasing Del Nero (1997), it seems that the piano experience achieved the objective of stimulating individuals' mental operations through developing language and manual sensory-motor competence without overloading the brain, since there was only one piano's class per week.

According to Del Nero (2007) it is necessary to preserve the brain from cognitive overload in a way it can operate within a good flow and with effectiveness. The nature, across biologic pressure or influence has conducted the human evolution to decrease the cognitive overload not necessary to the brain function. For him, one of the learning functions related to the invention of the writing and reading culture is to decrease brain's functions that can be done by other means/media. For instance, let's think about the writing function. On the one hand, we were born without dominating the writing skill and we can survive without learning to do it.

On the other hand, we have means/media of learning and automating the writing skill in a way it can be transformed in a concrete brain's department (or virtually concrete). The mind allows establishing relations between the brain and the world. From these relations can result concrete departments and even virtual ones outside the body that are allocated in the culture, in the science and in the technology.

Due to that, it is not necessary to have all the information recorded in the brain. The information can be transmitted in diverse ways, abolishing the direct experience. However, as a condition for all these processes happen, it is necessary to separate volunteer and non-volunteer will or automatic. It is necessary that individuals act within attitudes of *will*. (Del Nero, 1997, p. 120).

So, the idea of representing based on mental operations is fundamental. In a certain way, more than symbols, representations are scenarios on which individuals set up diverse degrees of uncertainty. The manipulation of these representations-scenarios through logical rules or other related models is one of the mental life's centers that formatted by the language in adequate way, formulates heuristics (proximity of general solutions) on scenarios with several degrees of uncertainty. Del Nero (1997, p. 121) illustrates the thoughts above by stating that *"the mind could be a result of interactions among language, will, thinking and emotion. All of them are running on the conscience stage. The language is able to establish a link with the natural and cultural world. The mental operations would be the ones that results from the neural groups' synchronization and they would serve as a base for constituting 'atoms' of conscience".*

MENTAL OPERATIONS, CONTEMPORARY TECHNOLOGY, HUMAN DEVELOPMENT

We have carried out work for influencing individuals' cognition abilities improvements and stimulating ones' learning attitudes for using and reusing the contemporary technologies. This influence and positive results have brought about to consider the effectiveness of this kind of flexible, dynamic and exploratory work for stimulating individuals' mental operations and developing human's intelligence.

It is important to have in mind that human's intelligence improvements seems to be linked with good learning opportunities supported by adequate human and technical infrastructure in an educational environment, such as in the concept of ambient intelligence (ISTAG, 2003) within the logic of inspiring individuals' achieving the highest level of cognitive progress that is enhanced wisdom (Flynn, 2007). According to Flynn (2007 p. 159), *"Wisdom is knowledge of how to live a good life and, if one is fortunate enough to understand other peoples and their histories as well, it is knowledge of how to make a better world".*

At some extent to make a better world depends on developing everyone's knowledge and capabilities as key factors for achieving individuals' freedom. Sen (2000) explains *freedom* as a primordial resource for individuals' development. It is a social state in which individuals develop capabilities that make them able to avoid, for example, bad life situations such as starving. Further than that, individuals are able to live freedom associated with acquired capabilities of knowing how to read, write, calculate, and participate on policy decisions with freedom of expression.

This vision of *freedom* is based on enhancing human's life. In this kind of scenario an individual is always conscious about his/her social and political rights and is prepared for using them or not according to his/her will. It is the possibility of ones being able to participate in the socio-technical decisions as investigates and suggests (Levy, 1993) and is discussed later in this section.

We believe and our practical learning/teaching experiences have showed that a vision such as The Moving Picture Experts Group's one - MPEG-21 of enabling individuals' access to any multimedia content supports the idea of improving ones' development as *freedom*. The idea of providing individuals' access to any multimedia content can be expanded further and effectively within the information society (Burnett, Pereira, Walle, & Koenen, 2006) since the primary education.

The MPEG-21's vision has been transformed into action by inspiring common citizens to access and produce content through knowing and direct manipulating *'digital objects'* of diverse multimedia formats such as (MPEG, JEPG, HTML, WRL, XML, WAV, MP3). This kind of practice when is carried out within collaborative learning actions and reflections can lead individuals to enhanced wisdom and participation on society's socio-technical decisions.

Fortunately, due to the *internet culture,* which has been built based on the *"techno-meritocracy of science and technological excellence that comes from the big science and the academic world"* (Castells, 2003), the MPEG-21's vision and related learning/teaching practices are among the reasons why it is so relevant to influence individuals to develop technical skills lifelong learning.

So, based on Lévy's investigations and reflections (1993), to support individuals' knowing, understanding, dominating and using digital technologies addresses the problem of allowing citizens to be aware and to take part of the socio-technical decisions, which despite we have lived in a democracy, in everyday life, rarely, have been taken with collective reflection. Lévy (1993) states that is necessary individuals retake mental appropriation of the technical phenomenon related to the human development before the industrial revolution.

This reflection is based on his concerns about the contemporary media influence in everyday life. *"There is no more socio-technical ground, but the scene of media. The foundations of social behavior and cognitive activities have been transformed in great speed that everyone can notice immediately"* Lévy (1993, p. 8). He presents a historical and cultural reflection about the relevance of information and communication technologies ICT (digital and emerging technologies) for the building of communities' culture and intelligence. Also, Lévy highlights the relevance of using ICT for supporting ones' knowledge

construction process and a progressive building of a sustainable techno-democracy.

An important reason for these thoughts is that ICT encompass through advanced informational devices and emerging technologies such as computers, hypertext and simulation techniques diverse possibilities of stimulating human's knowledge and cognitive abilities related to writing, reading, communicating, researching, vision, hearing, creativity, and learning (Dede & Palumbo, 1991; Lévi, 1993; Osberg, 1995; Franco, Cruz & Lopes, 2006). In the related work within the background section we showed diverse examples of projects that apply contemporary, emerging and advanced technologies for building educational applications, attempting to improve individuals' knowledge acquisition and cognitive abilities.

This ongoing work have contributed to create and transform individuals' habit, mental models and culture of using digital, contemporary and emerging technologies for ones' researching and learning to think based on developing programming skills, using procedural literacy and computer graphics techniques since the primary education as demonstrated, investigated and recommend in (Flanagan & Perlin, 2008; Franco, 2000; Franco, Cruz and Lopes, 2006; Franco, Mariz, Lopes, Cruz, Franco & Delacroix, 2007a; Mateas, 2005; Osberg, 1995; Siggraph Education Report, 2007).

Empirical investigations and practices such as the ones in the case study section have showed that even non-technical individuals can develop programming skills through direct manipulating scripting languages (Franco & Lopes, 2005d). These possibilities of developing individuals' computer skills have improved the way that ones think influencing better and constant mental activity, bringing about brain's neuronal connections development. According to Piazzi's investigation (2007) some of the current good professionals in the computing area had their intelligence stimulated while they were learning how to program, which is an activity that influences brain's neuronal connections development. This kind of learning process has support of the logic that an individual that is intelligent is also curious, so, he/she will have constant interest in learning and accepting challenges and so forth (Piazzi, 2007).

Satinover's investigation (2007) related to increasing fractal dimensions in the human's brain cortex when it is stimulated in adequate way reinforces the logic of exposing individuals to complex information such as classical music and other forms of complex music. However, as stated before, learning how to program is also a complex task and can influence brain development. So, we believe that it is relevant to stimulate brain through active learning processes related to developing ones' programming skills supported by contemporary and advanced technologies since the early school days such as in the project (IINN-ELS, 2009; Nicolelis, 2008) and suggested (in Mateas, 2005).

We illustrate the above statement through describing an informal and prototyping learning/teaching experience, in which author1 produced and used an web–based hybrid interactive 3D virtual environment VE developed and visualized with digital resources using a combination of VRML, still JPEG. and moving MPEG. textures, including audio and text files (Franco, 2005). During the experience, the code of the 3D digital environment was direct manipulated first by an educator who has worked in the alphabetization process, and after that by a 1st grade level student. Under author1 scaffolding the 1st year student modified the code to input his video related to a 'parlenda' in the 3D VE for understanding the importance of writing and reading well, including accessing to innovative digital knowledge (in Franco J., Mariz, Lopes, Cruz, Franco N. & Delacroix, 2007a).

Although it was a prototype learning experience, the 1st year primary educator considered that it was interesting due to the possibility of building and experiencing learning and teaching within

a VRML adaptive hybrid interface (in Franco, 2005). Through the 3DVE adaptive hybrid interface it was possible to combine natural, cultural, and virtual worlds with learning situations within a way that connected sensory-motor experience (auditory, vision, tactile) with conscious brain operations ruled by thinking, emotion and will as (in Del Nero, 1997).

It was possible to apply Doman and Doman's (2007) 'bit of intelligence' concept by learning how to virtually interoperate on mind diverse 'bits of intelligence' across real world physical operations such as recording audio and video files, modifying text files, spatial navigation in a 3DVE, including human to human communication and human computer interactions. It seems that these learning/teaching actions brought about ones' brain neural network simple and complex operations and learning through stimulating several synaptic activities.

We used 'parlenda' that is a type of children's game genre that combine text, speech and body expression as a base to support the learning experiment because educators are used to apply this genre to develop children's reading and writing skills related to their alphabetization process. The logic of using 'parlenda' in the teaching and learning processes is alphabetizing children through stimulating them to associate the sounds of the words that they already know and memorize when they pronounce while they are playing with the written representation.

Hence, it was a way of connecting indoor (video games) and outdoor games as tools for personal and group developing with primary school adequacy in terms of improving children's cognitive reasoning abilities and physical skills (Bartunk, Martin & Martinová, 2007).

This kind of learning practice involved stimulating individuals' perceptual and cognitive development. It seems to be a good strategy that can be used for improving educators, students and surround community's traditional and digital alphabetization, including literacy skills related to arts, technology and culture in a collaborative mood by adapting and using the synergy between the real world content and the digital one in a mixed reality experience as explains (Milgram & Colquhoun, 1999) and shows the interactive work carried out (in Franco, 2005; Franco J., Mariz, Lopes, Cruz, Franco N. & Delacroix, 2007a).

The use of digital tools in combination with curriculum content and human development has approximated individuals from the diverse sciences and technology. It has also improved ones' communication skills in terms of dominating, using and sharing techniques and concepts related to information visualization, computer graphics, web-based technology and low cost multimedia resources (Franco & Lopes 2005; Franco & Lopes, 2008). Individuals have direct manipulated these technologies to produce digital content at school and expanded the knowledge developed to informal home meetings and other learning environments in diverse communities such as demonstrated in case study 2 .

Here, we show more two examples that highlight how this work has been expanded to other learning communities.

First, the ICT facilitator (author 9) who left Ernani School at the beginning of 2006, because of the law changes as explained before, used her VRML knowledge for supporting her math teaching with secondary education students. In 2007, her knowledge referent to VRML supported her math's teaching in a state public school in the city of Caieras, which is located in the surrounding of São Paulo city.

As results of her work, author9 reported that even with the school computers lab environment under low level of technical conditions and great number of students per computer (about eight computers for forty students), by introducing to high school students of the city of Caieras VRML examples of the work she did at Ernani School. She got students' interest in learning math concepts by challenging them to deal with computer graphics

principles, desktop virtual reality, and information visualization tools and techniques.

She also reported that students enjoyed the interactive learning and teaching actions and shared knowledge to develop the tasks. They also asked her if that kind of digital tool would allow them to produce their own games. The fact that 7th and 8th grade level students from ESB created 3D virtual worlds also served as challenge for her students in Caieras to keep developing their math learning and 3D work. Unfortunately, she could not finish all the technical and visual work planed because she was pregnant and had a medical license before the end of the year (in Franco, Cruz, Franco & Lopes, 2007c). Recently, March of 2009, due to this chapter development process that she shared with her colleagues at school, she reported by e-mail to author1 that there have been from other high school educators and the principal of the school interest in doing a workshop and developing knowledge in VRML.

Second, the collaborative knowledge sharing and constant exposure and reflection about digital technologies has improved author11's digital skills through direct manipulating contemporary technologies and producing digital content. For example, authors 1 and 11 as attempted to improve their digital knowledge exchanging interdisciplinary knowledge related to use the art/education concept in combination with advanced and contemporary technologies (Barbosa, 2006; Mitchell, 1999) by experiencing with the fusion among photography, art and computer graphics such as the work carried out (in Parrish, 2002).

They developed a 3D web-based application for investigating cultural heritage related to the City of Carapicuiba, an action that stimulated individuals' traditional and digital literacy skills through researching in books and on the Internet, and mixing real and virtual realities in practice. The walkthrough 3DVE artwork developed by authors1 and 11 served as their self-training for exploring and understanding how to integrate diverse digital technologies to produce content related to school curriculum development. The authors1 and 11's artwork also showed the possibility of developing qualitative 3DVE with low cost tools. It is a mixed reality environment showing a composition of real pictures from the city of Carapicuiba, a Historical City, with little flags textured on the floor with inspiration on Alfredo Volpi's artwork. The VE is a simulation that demonstrates how Carapicuiba could be if the houses of the central village were designed with inspiration on Volpi's artwork (in Franco, Stori, Lopes & Franco, 2005; Franco, Cruz, Franco & Lopes, 2007c).

Author11 used further his digital skills at home to support his daughter, who was in the 6th grade level in 2007. He scaffold his daughter develop content related to produce a film of 8 minutes about Rita Lee's life using low cost multimedia tools. In this film it was also included artistic, cultural and political facts from the sixties. Later on, author1 presented the film as an example to students inside the school computers lab inside the ESB School aiming to inspire them to do their own productions. This expectative was transformed into reality during the development of the science project related to the 'water pollution' in case study 4 and in (Franco, Ficheman, Assis, Zuffo, Lopes, Moreno & Freitas, 2008a).

Author11 has also applied his digital knowledge and skills to prepare classroom material and conduct his History teaching at a public school in the city of Carapicuíba that is in the east of São Paulo metropolitan area. Step by step he has influenced his students to develop their digital skills through guiding students how to use better the Internet and computer resources to understand History by investigating and accessing to arts and culture. Author11 has used low cost software and capture card (TV capture card - PlayTVMPEG-2™) for capturing and editing movies through compounding collages that illustrate his speech during the classes and also improve students' knowledge in art and culture. Author11 has said that students use to look after him to get information about the

film productions beyond the collages they saw in the classroom and many of the students have watched the films at home.

Author11 has thought that for using digital and emerging technologies with effectiveness, it is necessary that educators keep studying and researching lifelong. His conclusion is because to select the images that are used to produce the learning material need to be researched and previous contextualized on educators' mind. His argument has been that when an individual is working with information visualization, computer graphics, the Internet, and multimedia tools, he/she is opening the material and subject researched to interdisciplinary and transdisciplinary work that can involve concepts such as ethics, values, and inference and interference from other diverse disciplines.

The diverse examples in the related work, through the case study section and implications in the evaluation section are according to the logic that supports the use of digital/web-based and advanced information visualization tools on students' learning and educators' training to stimulate ones' interactive learning and knowledge based on sensorial and perception (visual, auditory, tactile, mental) development (Reilly & Munakata, 2000).

The learning/teaching actions have contributed to reverse the idea of "black box" that many non-technical individuals have about possibilities of producing two-dimensional 2D and tri-dimensional 3D virtual environments VE by using computers graphics principles (Foley, Dam, Feiner & Hughes, 1993) and related technologies as problem solving tools through several learning situations.

According to Del Nero's investigations (1997), during the learning experiences and lifelong, it is important for understanding and using with effectiveness the combination among technology, sciences, culture and arts to take in consideration forms and media to be linked with individuals' education. It is also relevant to consider collaborative, dialogic, interdisciplinary and lifelong learning education as key-point to society development. Del Nero (1997) recommends developing students' knowledge and capabilities with diverse learning experiences that goes from math to drama, from language studies to reading daily journals, from sports to the intensive use of computers. Computers should be used in practical aspects via individuals' direct manipulating software programs and programming languages, and related to theory ones should learn about languages, logic and electronic fundamentals.

Churchland (1998) demonstrates the importance of applying high level programming languages through scripts that allows ones' dominate and control information processing in computers. For instance, scripting languages such as HTML, DHTML, VRML, and Java Script enable designers' programming to create hypertext (Dabbagh, 2008; Wikipedia Scripting languages, 2008).

This can be a powerful way of stimulating and improving individuals' with low literacy abilities (functional analphabetism) through integrating and interoperating several technologies related to drawing, modeling, writing, programming, researching, reading and communicating. Furthermore, paraphrasing Pietraß (2007) researchers on cognitive psychology state that the combination of text and picture induces to increase students' mental representation and operation than mere text according to (Blömeke 2003, Issing 1997) in (Pietraß, 2007).

Del Nero states that *"education is the great tool to execute corrections in the brain-mind"* (Del Nero, 1997, p. 439). He reflects about form and media and their relation with world's transformations and the education field. The reflection is that besides the traditional disciplines, there are new areas emerging that have blended with the old ones and beyond. Another reflection is that computers have taken human's place in tasks where the rules are well defined. His inference related to these reflections highlights the necessity of changing

the old traditional way of expositive classes and classical schooling subjects.

According to Del Nero (1997) it is time for new ways of teaching and learning that develop rapidly an interface among the disciplines (opacity zones of intersection, which will take long to be executed by computers). Furthermore, it is necessary to stimulate individuals' desire (will) to develop knew knowledge and persistence to study lifelong. Hence, school environments should have well trained educators, as well as no more than 20 students per class at k-12 education.

A better average of students per educator seems to be essential to stimulate sustainable interactivity and better individuals' communication inside the classroom under applying *the concept of overlap of fields of experience,* which is considered an excellent guide for supporting the use of multimedia and contemporary technology within a critical way (in Tannenbaum, 1998).

Using the modular features of web-based technology has enabled individuals to understand and practice how to construct simulations with support of the synergy among web-based 2D and 3D technology, desktop VR techniques and information visualization tools for visual communication (Cunningham, 2007), within simple and complex operations. Due to the features of modularity of these technologies, one can use these contemporary technologies as *'bits of intelligence'* as (in Doman and Doman, 2007) for supporting brain neural development with respect to the biological processes related to the synapses; reducing brain overload due to the existing on-line/off-line libraries and templates and the ones to be created referent to the mentioned technologies.

Despite of ICT complexity when it is viewed as a whole for non-technical people, ICT, in this case, referent to web-based technology, is composed by many modular features which have brought about support from electrical engineering processes for building web-based learning environments (Pressman, 2006). The web-based modular features have allowed the construction of flexible, knowledgeable and rich media learning environments with great potential for supporting collective intelligence's technical development. This support has come from the development of individuals' cognitive and technical abilities, as well as intelligence related to the concept of modularity and its uses within the different disciplinary contexts 'of modular thinking'. Callebaut and Gutman, (2005) state that modularity:

(...) the attempt to understand systems as integrations partially independent and interacting units – is today a dominant theme in the life science, cognitive science, and computer science. The concept goes back at least implicitly to the Scientific (or Copernican) Revolution, and can be found behind later theories of phrenology, physiology, and genetics; moreover, art, engineering, and mathematics relay on modular design principles(...) (Callebaut & Gutman, 2005, back cover).

Then, it is relevant individuals' understanding, learning, dominating, using and producing simple and complex systems applying the concept of modularity to support brain-mind development.

We believe that the concept of modularity is compatible with the synergy between "modular thinking" and the HIP model described within the connecting biology, learning and technology on this evaluation section. This compatibility can bring about modularity to be a useful support for knowledge transferring between diverse fields and impact as a useful consequence of this knowledge transfer, on the development of individuals' cognitive abilities.

Using web-based technology as communication tool, knowledge development and digital content production instrument supported by the developmental psychology (Kassin, 1995; Miller, 2004) in combination with the concept of modularity and its relation with a developmental process that involves transformation and self-organized hierarchical systems reinforce the base for this work technical implementation in diverse contexts. Self-organization is supported by a mass of interactions between the smallest entities (subsystems), which basically consists of either collaborative or competitive relations with a wide range of nonlinear interactions, spatiotemporal scales, recurring commonly in natural systems as studied in biology, physics, and economics (Buscalioni, Iglesia, Buscalioni & Dejoan, 2005).

We have achieved the described results in this chapter, by learning to develop research and simulations using contemporary and advanced technology. As Dede states:

Simulation and visualisation tools help students recognise patterns, reason qualitatively about physical processes, translate among frames of reference, and envision dynamic models. These curricular approaches improve success for all types of learners and may differentially enhance the performance of at-risk students. (Dede, 1999)

Dede's statement (Dede, Salzman, Loftin & Ash, 1997) supports Teixeira's investigations and reflections (1977) about democracy and universal k-12 education. Teixeira's reflections address the necessity of providing excellence of learning and teaching in k-12 education for forming students' knowledge, mind and capabilities within high quality. The argument we sustain to claiming for an excellent technical and pedagogical infrastructure in learning environments is that educators and students, in particular the individuals at risk situation, are already at schools and can benefit from high quality and dynamic education (in Forrester, 1992; Franco, 2001; Franco, Cruz and Lopes, 2006; Wikipedia System dynamics, 2008).

Providing excellence on education in terms of combining adequate learning environments and or ecosystems (Ficheman and Lopes, 2008a), high quality tools and good human expertise may promote individuals' active preparation and participation within a solidarity and democratic economy. Adequate learning ecosystems can contribute to improve the current bad situation of too many citizens who are under economic and social vulnerability, bringing about lifetime opportunities to these individuals and enhancing society commonwealth (IINN-ELS, 2009; Miller, 2006; Nicolelis, 2008; Sen, 2000, Singer, 2002a).

Learning ecosystems and schools which have planned to work within good work quality and stimulate individuals' development of excellence in a ethical way (Gardner, Csikszentmihalyi & Damon, 2004), should inspire individuals learning in practice the importance of lifelong education in the current time of constant changes in economy and technology (Senge, 2002b).

One school's paradigm for achieving such goal is what has been called 'democratic school'. The hypothesis that has been worked in the 'democratic schools' is that human beings are naturally curious and desire to learn all the time without someone else force these attitudes.

Paraphrasing Senge (2002c) in these schools students learn, play, interact with mates and adults and also develop a great sense of responsibility and conscience. When they left these schools they know more than the ones who went to conventional schools. Hence, students have left democratic schools with their spirit and intellect prepared to be critical and conduct these individuals with more autonomy through life.

We believe that this kind of citizens' preparation has been adequate to the type of society that the concept and practice of solidarity economy has attempted to reinvent all the time within the little opportunities that the capitalism has opened to it.

TECHNOLOGY SUPPORTING DEMOCRATIC INTERACTIONS INSIDE AND OUTSIDE SCHOOL

Due to the collaborative and interactive work inside and outside ESB school environment, as we said before, we have achieved good work quality results even when students have left school. It is

thought that through using scripting languages and exposing students to diverse 3D environments as well as supporting students dominate contemporary technology, we have sustained students' curiosity to learn how to use more sophisticated digital tools. This way they have improved their computational thinking within systemic, flexible, spiral, incremental and experiential learning actions.

For instance, in 2007, the 8th grade student who supported the 'water pollution' project in case study 4 has benefit from the 2D and 3D computer graphics technical skills he started developing at ESB School (Garrido, 2009). During his visits to the school computers lab, accordingly to the development of his evolutionary web design skills and curiosity to create more realistic 2D and 3D digital content he was introduced to tools such as GIMP™ and Blender™.

Although, the 8th grade student finished his studies at Ernani School in the end of 2007, due to the good quality of the human to human and human computer interactions he has shared his knowledge in computer graphics with other individuals and developed a Blog since 2007 showing his drawing artwork (Garrido, 2009).

Hence, the horizontal dialog between him and the ESB ICT facilitator has been developed based on digital/web-based technology knowledge, which has been applied as a 'common ground'- (language/medium) (in Laurel, 1993), including as a form of overlapping the student and educator fields of experience (in Tannenbaum, 1998). For example, in February 2008, at the gate of the school, during an informal talk, the student expressed to the ICT facilitator that he had difficulties for installing a VRML browser (Cortona™) in his computer at home. He described the diverse proceedings he had carried out for installing the browser, but it did not work.

Then, both went to the student's home where they installed the VRML browser. In student's home they carried out one and half hour of interactive VRML workshop discussing and practicing how to develop animation, understanding English terms and 3D modeling possibilities. In sequence, they developed more fifty minutes of interactive workshop for understanding how to do animations in Photoshop™, comparing those proceedings with the ones necessary to develop animations in the Gimp™ software.

During the informal talk at student's home, his brother a former student from Ernani School and his mother also participated. The 8th grade student's brother was one of the first students to participate in the interactive digital and emerging technologies investigation during the beginning of this work development from 2003 to 2004 (Franco & Lopes, 2004; Franco, Mariz, Lopes, Cruz, Franco & Delacroix, 2007a).

According to the informal talks and formal lessons, we observed that the work carried out has influenced the student's cognition and intelligence leading him to enhanced knowledge, which can be related to wisdom as described in (Flynn, 2007). This thought is because, the student has shared his web-based knowledge with other mates at his current technical course, in which he has learned how to fix the hardware of computers and web design. He also is doing a secondary education course.

His autonomy for dealing with web-based technology as lifelong learning companion has been improved. A proof of that it is the interactive 3DVE he designed after that meeting at his home and on March 02/ 08 he sent by mail to the ICT facilitator. The student developed a nice house and a beautiful garden. The 3DVE was compounded by diverse still images as textures, VRML animation features for opening and closing the door at the entrance of the house. He worked with VRML material proprieties using transparency and coloring the 3DVE within a balanced way.

Later on during May 2008, he sent more examples of his artwork in design that reflected his deepen efforts in learning and using Blender™ software.

In another human computer interaction including human to human interaction based on contemporary technology knowledge, at the end of April 2008, during the students' research time within the school computers lab, one of the 7th grade level students reported that he talked with his father that he was learning HTML and VRML at school. He said that his father approved the idea of students' access to advanced technology at school. At the beginning his father was afraid about installing a VRML browser in the family machine. But after two weeks, in May 2008, the student got enough knowledge to manipulate VRML files and installed a browser.

He reported to the ICT facilitator that he installed a browser in the computer at home and he was sharing knowledge with another colleague from the 7th grade level that had also developed VRML abilities in the school computers lab. This situation is evidence that the individuals' digital knowledge acquired and developed at school computers lab has been a common ground that has influenced communication between individuals from the school environment and the surround community, as well as inspirited students' collaborative and independent learning attitudes (Franco, 2001).

At the end of 2008, the student said he had difficulties for keeping developing 3D worlds because he had not understood some VRML syntax rules. On the other hand, he asked information about how to develop drawings using (Gimp™, 2008) because his friends from the Okurt™ were processing images using Gimp™ software. So, we did a workshop. His latest interest was to design a web page, so he was guided to do some HTML exercises through using a tutorial.

After sometime, in March 2009, when informally asked about how was the development of his digital skills, the student reported that he had stopped training because his colleagues also stopped, and that he was a bit lazy to think about how to develop 2D and 3DVE interfaces. However, the student did not point or link the difficulties in direct manipulating the contemporary technologies that we presented to him as the main reasons to his decision of stopping the practical learning process.

Although, we think it is necessary further investigation for understanding the whys, we have observed similar problem related to other students' lack of will and consequent attitudes to think for solving problems in other school curriculum subjects. Our observations have been confirmed through informal talks with other educators from the ESB School.

We are aware that has been difficult to transform the current school environment in a learning space that can include all the forms of interest-based activities and/or experiential learning opportunities that people voluntary participate in, often with great personal engagement and use of time when they are in leisure time (Illeris, 2007).

On the other hand, through carrying out this work supported by digital/web-based technology, low cost information visualization tools, and free software, students and educators have engaged and improved their digital knowledge and technical skills. It includes that they have applied knowledge and technical skills in practice with great personal engagement in school and beyond, anytime and anywhere, as it has been demonstrated in this chapter. So, as Illeris (2007, p.233) states *"e-learning can constitute an appropriate supplement in many contexts, but it presupposes that the relevant multi-aspect programs are available and – to an even greater extent than other learning – that the participants have considerable motivation."*

An example that reinforces the relevance of developing multi-aspects programs and individuals' digital knowledge and supports our arguments and actions for using web-based technology, low cost and free software tools in ones' education process beyond the proprietary ones comes from Professor Brutzman's speech during his presentation related to the X3D standard and The Extensible

3D (X3D) Earth project (in Forum X3D, 2008) at Polytechnic school, University of São Paulo.

The example that happened in a developed country is referent to a student from secondary education. The professor said that a young student from the region of the Naval Postgraduate School, USA, got an opportunity for studying modeling in a University in Stanford. He learned modeling using Maya™ software. But when the student came back home, he could not afford to buy the tool. The student asked support for solving that problem and keeping his modeling practices. It was offered a free X3D software environment that is an XML based format and extends VRML functionalities (WEB3D consortium, 2008; X3D Earth Implementation Workshop, 2008).

Due to situations like that, it is fundamental that educational systems can provide to educators from primary to higher education technical fluency and pedagogical skills to present and support students new possibilities of using high quality and low cost contemporary technologies to develop individuals' cognition abilities and intelligence far beyond industry 'office' packages, and 'mechanic like games' on the Internet (Franco, Cruz & Lopes, 2005; Resnick, 2002; Resnick, 2007).

It seems that educational systems have kept *'failing or lacking'* in providing educators' technical skills improvements to use contemporary technology to support students' learning and curriculum content development. Then due to this bad situation only a small number of students will have the opportunity of deciding with awareness how they will use digital and emerging technologies effectively after the school days:

When people are introduced to computers today, they are typically taught how to look up information on the Web, how to use a word processor, how to send e-mail. But they don't become fluent with the technology. (Resnick, 2002)

For ameliorating this problem, it is thought that in every educational space designed for children, youth children and adults' education development around the world, policy makers should support the creation of pedagogical and technical infrastructure suitable for forming dynamic and high quality digital learning scenario. That is why having a graduate student such as author10 participation in the development of a learning math project like in the case study 5 is relevant. Author10 participation is an opportunity of approximating a graduate student from the dynamics of real world learning environments and feel how innovative ideas in combination with contemporary technology can scaffold individuals' learning.

The learning environments ecosystems could be based on investigations, concepts and learning paradigms such as the 'ambient intelligence' – AmI in (Ambient Intelligence Org, 2008) and projects such as the New Media Consortium (NMC)'s Horizon Project (2008) that investigates and suggests pedagogical tendencies related to the use of emerging technologies in education and their influence to develop, for instance, collective intelligence. According to (NMC, 2008), due to hardware and software improvements and decreasing costs, it has been increased the tendency of using virtual and augmented reality as learning tools.

An example of this tendency related to the ESB School is the experimental work carried out by LSI researches. They used virtual and augmented reality techniques in combination with low cost mobile computers to create an interactive, interdisciplinary learning and teaching experience. "Religions of the world" was the main theme that involved subjects like history, geography, Portuguese, math and art in individual and collaborative activities. The application was developed using the ARToolkit for fast prototyping and its purpose was to prove the concept of using different mobile tools and technologies to verify how learners transition and alternate from one tool to another (Ficheman, Saul, Assis, Correa, Franco, Tori & Lopes, 2008b).

In times of constant society and technological changes, this work initial motivation has increased and encompassed the perception that is necessary that we as educators learn and use contemporary and advanced technologies as a 'common ground' (language/medium) to support educators and students overlapping their learning fields of experience and interactions with effectiveness.

Achieving a common ground or communication state based on the concept of overlap of fields of experience can bring about individuals' commitment, confidence, and psychological empowerment to engage themselves and keep attracting other ones (students, educators and community) in a persistent citizens' knowledge and intelligence development work that involves diverse combinations such as pedagogy, technology and management, theory and practice, traditional and open learning.

PSYCHOLOGICAL, PEDAGOGIC, TECHNICAL AND HUMAN SUSTAINABILITY

The psychological, pedagogic, technical and human sustainability of this digital/web-based knowledge work has also been supported by learning theories concepts such as Piaget's constructivism and Papert's constructionism in (Cavallo, 2000; Johnson, Roussos, Leigh, Vasilakis, Barnes & Moher, 1999), including the motivation that people have got as a result of the "agency" concept, which is the pleasure of taking meaningful actions and seeing the results of our decisions (Murray, 2003). For example, accessible web-based standard languages such as HTML and VRML combined with 2D and 3D interactive computer graphics and virtual reality techniques, as well as multimedia tools and files can bring about "agency" when individuals can see the tangible results of their programming such as the example in Figure 2.

These actions, techniques, psychological and pedagogic combination address the grasping and the designing of human-centered interactive systems involving people, activities, contexts and technologies (Benyon, Turner & Turner 2005), including sensory perceptions (vision, audition, touch) and their implications for designing, as well as how to apply the combined knowledge of cognitive psychology and information technology to the design of artifacts (Te'eni, Carey & Zhang, 2007).

The thought is in constant dialogic relation with the external world. By the perception phenomenon, the external world talks with individuals through their feelings. After that a message arrives in our psycho where each individual will do a personal reading. This reading can be constituted of a current content or the current content can take individuals to a parallel reading (Revista Mente, Cérebro & Filosofia, 2007).

For example, it is possible to imagine a tree that was born in the ground of the Estação Primeira de Mangueira Samba School. For the ones that will visit the School by the first time, it will be a simple fruit tree. On the other hand, for the individuals who know deeper the history of Estação Primeira de Mangueira, the tree is a symbol of the Samba School. The reflection is the phenomenon of this parallel reading, when the perceptions of ones' living with the object transcend the perception of the object that was seen (Revista Mente, Cérebro & Filosofia, 2007).

It is thought that it is through an interactive exercise of perception and reflection as in the example related to Mangueira Samba School that we have found affective, engaging and effective ways of conducting the digital/web-based learning and teaching experiences, as well as stimulating individuals' computational thinking skills and attitudes.

Some alternatives to conduct the learning experiences are: to make a previous view of the content to be seen by asking a research on the Internet; developing curriculum content in

combination with interactive and digital tools, including technologies from the Internet such as using web browsers as Internet Explorer™, FireFox™, Cortona ™ and Cosmo Player™, as well as a low cost text editor for content creation and visualization in 3D.

There is coherence of the examples that were described in the case study section and the use of contemporary technology as a 'common ground or language' in combination with 'the concept of overlap of fields of experience' to support psycho studies related to children' behavior that have been based on Wallon and Lacan's theories in (Bastos, 2003). According to Bastos' investigation (2003) both authors grasp the individual as an individual social inserted in the culture and in the language.

We believe and have showed through this chapter several examples that the use of web-based and digital technology as a 'common ground or language' to support individuals learning process, it is something that children understand very well and can be a relevant mean/media of scaffolding and approximating educators and students, children and parents, and friends in the contexts of school and home in everyday life.

Through interactive actions supported by digital/web-based knowledge individuals can become aware of the changes in art, science, technology and cultural practices, including social values encompassed in the contemporary technologies and digital/virtual environments that influence citizens' everyday lives (Coslson, 2007; Paul, 2008; Pietraß, 2007; Popper, 2007). For instance, through the creation of simple and complex digital environment content that has involved diverse proceedings, knowledge, and languages to compound it, such as the animated documentary Waltz with Bashir (in Wikipedia Waltz with Bashir, 2009).

According to (Murray, 2003) digital environments are procedural, encyclopedic, participative and spatial. These properties make digital environments powerful tools for simple and complex literary creation. These properties allow constructing flexible learning environments based on the concept of scaffolding and/or software scaffolding use in education such as the Listen Tutor project example in the related work section (in Chang, Beck, Mostow & Corbett, 2006). Scaffolding is a process that requires direct teaching and monitoring by an adult and the distinguishing feature of scaffolding is the role of dialogue between teacher and student (Henry, 2002; Luckin, Boulay, Yuill, Kerawalla, Pearce & Harris, 2003). Scaffolding is related to Vygotsky's theory, which he called the zone of proximal development - ZPD. The ZPD is the difference between the children's capacity to solving problems on his own, and his/her capacity to solve them with assistance (Vigotski, 2007).

COLLABORATIVE WORK REINFORCING INDIVIDUALS' INTERACTIVE TECHNOLOGIES DOMAIN

The collaborative work developed inside the school environment and the surrounding community has also been integrated to the academic educational research related to the – Núcleo de Aprendizagem, Trabalho e Entretenimento - NATE –'Nucleo of Learning Work and Entertainment' from the Laboratory of Integrated Systems LSI from the University of São Paulo since 2004 (Franco & Lopes, 2004; Franco, Mariz, Lopes, Cruz, Franco & Delacroix, 2007a; Franco, Cruz & Lopes, 2006; NATE, 2009).

This collaborative and cooperative work has allowed to school individuals engage in the latest processes of educational researching and using contemporary and advanced technologies in learning and teaching. This collaborative process between primary and higher education has also addressed the necessity of sustain individuals' motivation for developing digital technical knowledge and e-learning skills with support of

multi-aspect programs as proposed (in Illeris, 2007, p. 233).

For instance, researchers from the Laboratory of Integrated Systems - LSI from the University of São Paulo constructed an interactive visual application for supporting a learning and teaching experience which combines diverse tools and devices such as augmented reality and low cost mobile platforms inserted in an educational context.

The interactive visual application was constructed on the top of the ARToolkit software, which is designed for fast prototyping. The learning experience purpose was to investigate the concept of using different mobile tools and technologies to verify how learners adapt and alternate the transition from one tool to another.

The tests were performed at ESB School. The initial application brought about to conclude that even if some mobile platforms have limited computational power, the use of augmented reality combined with other tools can present a new form of representation and interaction and can be an innovative way of using technology in the classroom to improve students' knowledge (Ficheman, Saul, Assis, Correa, Franco, Tori & Lopes, 2008b).

The lifelong learning/teaching collaborative experiences that have been carried out with researchers from LSI have approximated the ESB School and surrounding community from lifetime opportunities such as to participate in a prototype educational experience related to the one-to-one learning model proposal (OLPC Wiki, 2008; Franco, Cruz, Aquino, Teles, Gianevechio, Franco, Ficheman, Camargo & Lopes, 2007; Lopes, 2007; Franco, Ficheman, Lopes, Ferreira, Santos, Ferreira, Araújo & Moreno 2008b). Since April 2007, educators and students from ESB School and researchers from the Laboratory of Integrated Systems have trained with and used the XO laptop related to the one-to-one model in diverse learning/teaching and entertaining contexts.

Due to school community involvement with digital technologies (Franco, Cruz & Lopes, 2006) and its participation in the one-to-one learning model, in 19 April 2007, Nicholas Negroponte and OLPC team visited the school. During their visited they first interacted with primary students from a 2nd grade level class (in Silveira, 2007).

After that, at school computers lab, the OLPC team met other educators and students from 6th to 8th grade levels and talked about the one-to-one learning model project. The common ground for the human to human and human computers interactions was the laptop XO (Yahoo News, 2007).

Later on, August 2007, Professor and researcher Mitchel Resnick visited the school to see the one-to-one learning experience and interacted with students from 7th and 8th grade levels, including author1 at school computers lab. The common ground for this meeting was based on XO laptop and the Squeak (2008) software installed on the machine interface.

The collaborative work between Ernani School and LSI has provided interdisciplinary work references for educators and students, brining about individuals' better understanding on how electronic engineering resources have influenced arts, culture, education and the entertaining industry (Colson, 2007; LSI, 2009; Paul, 2008; Wands, 2006).

The school and university partnership has allowed school community to visit diverse, scientific, cultural and digital art exhibitions such as Mario Schenberg Spaceship, a collaborative interactive installation at park CienTec that aims to reach out young visitors and awaken their interest for science, physics and astronomy: through a space trip simulation. The Spaceship is designed to offer learning and entertaining environment, so a group of young learners can experience an adventure in space within an interactive and educational game simulator. Students from ESB School visited the Mario Schenberg Spaceship project at the end of 2007.

Scientific, artistic, cultural interactions and learning experiences such as this one are always on students' mind. For instance, a 7th grade level student, at the end of 2008, said that she enjoyed her visit to the Parque CienTec, in 2007, and asked to author1 if there would be a new visit to the Mario Schenberg Spaceship (in Parque CienTec, 2008).

Beyond that, she made a lot of questions related to developing real and virtual simulations. During an informal talk she and other classmate proposed to design a school simulation with focus on saving rain water. They said that as public buildings, schools should be the best example for children of how to proceed to save water.

Students were encouraged to do that. However, the idea was not implemented by her and classmate. They talked to another student from the 8th grade level.

The student is the one we cited during the case study 5. He has investigated, shared and used deepen contemporary and advanced technology. His artwork has served as a relevant local reference to other individuals inside and outside the school environment (Reportagem 1, 2008; Wellington, 2009).

One important feature that the student has developed is that he has always invited somebody else to share his technical knowledge developed in computer graphics. For instance, he supported a post graduate student from LSI to learn VRML and build a 3DVE interface related to the Golden Material as we will see later on.

From a basic VRML introduction and reflection about computer graphics applications developed at his classroom, passing by hands-on interactions during his classroom schedule and in the students' research time at school computers lab, as well as carrying out work across using and reusing a 3D virtual world code presented by author1, the 8th grade student improved his knowledge on contemporary technologies and transformed himself in protagonist in several learning/teaching situations. For instance, by merit, his artwork led him to participate with other school students from an international education event called 'I Seminário WEB Curriculum' (2008). During this event the student could improve his writing and communication skills by writing a report about the 3D project he participated at school (Aprende Brasil, 2008). He also talked to the audience, demonstrating the technical skills he developed in real time.

The 8th grade level student shared his web-based knowledge with educational agents from São Paulo Municipal Secretary of Education. They did not know how to use VRML technology. So, the student and author1 developed a workshop of fifteen minutes discussing the technology and its pedagogic potential. At the end of the workshop the educational agents were satisfied with the presentation and congratulated both speakers by the work. Beyond that they asked further information about how to use technology and the possibility of disseminating that for the municipal school network.

During the workshop the student was the main protagonist. He explained to the agents why author1 developed that kind of work with students. Part of the student's work is published (in Aprende Brasil, 2008; Wellington 2009):

Professor Jorge introduced this tool for all my classmates (...) He wishes that this tool can support the diverse curricular disciplines (...) to do the classes more enjoyable (...) a cool way of understanding math, arts, geography, history, Portuguese, English (...) he would like to show a bit of what computers can do (...) due to currently adolescents only want chatting (...). Student (in Aprende Brasil, 2008)

He also reported that he shared knowledge at home with his sister. He was attempting to do that by using pure VRML language but she found difficult. Then, later on, by suggestion of a researcher from the NATE-LSI, we downloaded the Internet Space Builder™ software (ISB,

2009). After that, he reported that she was more interested in developing digital knowledge in computer graphics.

As in the case study 2, with the knowledge sharing example between authors1 and 11 and other real world examples highlighted on this chapter, the computer graphics knowledge shared within the 8th grade student's home environment have engaged the family in diverse interesting ways as the interaction model described in (Franco, 2001a).

Contemporary and advanced technologies have been designed in a way they can integrate easier than few years ago. They also have become affordable for ordinary people. These facts have brought about more possibilities for decreasing the problem of 'digital divide' anytime and anywhere. For instance, in the present days linking computers and TV features and concepts allows amplifying the possibilities of sharing, analyzing and creating visual information of excellent quality at low cost (Figure 4).

Back to the 8th grade level student's work, due to the presence of researchers from the LSI at Ernani School environment, because the one-to-one learning model project, the student's work was shared with them. So, at the end of 2008 author1 asked to the 8th grade student to support the development of one of the post graduate student, (author3)s' knowledge in VRML. She has worked as math educator in primary education and at that moment, she was doing a study for implementing the Golden Material in 3D.

The 8th grade student accepted the challenge. Then, we organize a workshop of 90 minutes within of the interactive style described in the methodology section, with the 8th grade student acting as protagonist to conduct the workshop and minor author1's interventions. After that meeting, she returned once more to ESB School to enhance her VRML knowledge and reinforce her cycle of improving digital and computer graphics knowledge. In sequence we kept scaffolding her by e-mail Figure 5.

Figure 4. Author1 inside LSI Lab demonstrating and using the integration between computers and TVs for visualizing and creating VRML and X3D files

Figure 5. Representing the cycle of development she did to complete her Golden Material work using digital/web-based technology.

The result of the workshops for sharing digital knowledge with her can be considered successful. The collaborative efforts to support technical knowledge transference and her 3DVE Golden Material work developed worth it. A proof of the great value of the work is that her paper describing the work related to the virtual Golden Material and the learning of math concepts will be presented in a conference 2009 (Venâncio, Franco, Correa, Zuffo & Lopes, 2009).

This real world example of sharing and transferring knowledge can support the philosophical thoughts and practical work related to provide horizontal education to individuals (in Freire, 2004), inspire the building of democratic schools (Senge, 2002, b-c), including develop ones' computational thinking skills (in Wing, 2006). These are individuals and society states possible to achieve if everyone will have lifelong opportunities of developing their knowledge and capabilities with respect to the concept of 'development as freedom' (in Sen, 2000) a concept that we discussed before during this section construction.

We are aware that there are much work for doing in terms of scaling to more individuals the achievements of ESB School learning environment and its community. Fortunately, the basic tools for keeping developing the work have been improved and blessed through meritocracy, which has increased the degree of educational interactivity with more varied types of media for teaching and learning (Lajoie & Nakamura, 2006).

That is the case of ESB School and community participation in the one-to-one learning model prototype project. The ESB participation has increased the number of computers at school and Internet access anytime and anywhere across installing wireless connection, bringing about involvement and support from human and technical knowledge of excellence, resulting in access to new projects and devices, and stimulating individuals and institutions collaborative and cooperative work.

Students and educators from the school have learned robotics principles through supporting the interactive experiments of prototypes of new learning devices and influencing their final design, as well as presenting the final industrial product to the public. For instance, students and educators form the ESB tested and showed a new product called "WE DO™" as protagonists on the educational event 'O Brasil que Nós Queremos' from Lego™, in August 2008 and 'I Seminário Web Curriculum', in September 2008. For participating in both events individuals designed an interactive visual narrative in which they were storytelling about some important places related to the city of São Paulo, and compared pictures referent to the Artwork of Tarsila do Amaral and Cândido Portinari with the real ESB School surrounding place Figure 6.

The collaborative work developed for participating in the diverse events resulted in a Lego™'s donation of 39 kits 'WE DO™' that can be shared and support diverse interactive learning situations at ESB School learning ecosystem.

The XO mobile computers have been used by educators and students in order to do research on the Internet (Lopes, 2007). It has also been applied as a common ground that has supported knowledge and empathy development among educators, students and families.

The idea has been to approximate the school actions from the families through students' mediation. The strategy has been allowing students from one or two classes per weekend to take the mobile computers home and share digital knowledge with surrounding community. In general, the educational activities at home are developed using video, text and the diverse software installed on the equipment. It would be very useful if the

Figure 6. A moment of preparation for participating in events outside school

XO capabilities were applied to the development of small scale simulations and scientific visualizations. Still, there is no Internet connection outside school, neither the XO mesh network is functioning. These are the challenges to be solved in a future project.

Some former students have come back to school and through a volunteer work support students from the school that are new monitors to develop their digital skills and organize the laptops logistic Figure 7.

By exchanging ideas with a former student that has kept supporting the laptop logistic organization we investigated and reflected about some solutions for decreasing management problems such as easier access to storage and recover data because of the sharing of the mobile computers has become difficult to find the files. The quantity of laptops available does not allow one-to-one computer paradigm all the time. It is about 900 students for sharing about 160 machines.

On the other hand, having a powerful Internet connection, enough for supporting school network operations can be a solution for using a tool such as Google Docs™. By using Google docs™ we can have access to a spreadsheet not available in the software that originally came

Figure 7. A former student using the XO laptop connected on the Internet. The former student did a workshop to novice (monitors).

in the XO. Google's web solution can provide space for saving the information on-line, so it is possible individuals to store, publish and access information anytime and anywhere through using web/data warehousing (2009) and information visualization resources.

Another solution we have applied referent to use the web to story data since 2007, it is that we have developed the cultural practice of supporting students and educators developing and maintaining their own Blogs, through feeding the Blogs with curricular and entertaining information developed at classroom, school computers lab and home (Beatriz, 2009; Garrido, 2009; Marlene, 2009; Nunes, 2009, Simone, 2009; Wellington, 2009).

CONCLUSION

Through this empirical work supported by mediated learning experience (in Fonseca, 1998), qualitative research (2009) and participant observation (2009) we have addressed how to systematize and stimulate non expert individuals to develop interest by science and technology through integrating and interoperating them with arts, culture, sciences and education.

This work has followed expert researchers' contribution to the understanding of the development and evolution of natural and complex systems using the combination among technology, sciences, culture and arts such as demonstrated in the essays modularity in arts (Jablan, 2005), modularity at boundary between the art and science (Buscalioni, Iglesia, Buscalioni & Dejoan, 2005), and modularity of mind and culture (Callebaut & Gutman, 2005), which is based on Fodor's essay modularity of mind (Fodor wikipedia, 2009; Jerry Fodor on mental architecture, 2009; Modularity on mind, 2009; Visual modularity, 2009).

In order to demystify VR and digital technology "black box" problems to non-technical individuals, to reduce the "digital divide" and to improve individuals' traditional and computers literacy, we have systematized and carried out collaborative, interdisciplinary and transdisciplinary work inside and outside the school environment.

For the context of this work development, contemporary and advanced technologies have been the answer for achieving a 'common ground' (Laurel, 1993). For both, a common ground for enhancing teaching/learning classroom experiences with support of the concept of the overlap of the fields of experience. And common ground for contributing to diffuse the art of stimulating ones' cultural technology appropriation and educational changes within long term educational actions through engaging students, educators and surrounding community (citizens) in persistent spiral and incremental movements of developing and sharing knowledge through lifelong learning experiences (Franco, 2001; Franco & Lopes, 2005; Franco, Cruz & Lopes, 2006; Franco, Ficheman, Lopes, Ferreira, Santos, Ferreira, Santos & Moreno, 2008a; Pressman, 2006).

The school internal and external examples of using contemporary technologies to develop digital content have created relevant local references, including covered how to use e-learning as an appropriate supplement in many contexts, through relevant multi-aspect programs available and – *"to an even greater extent than other learning – that the participants have considerable motivation"* Illeris (2007, p.233). These actions have brought about sustainability to this work development and leading everyone engaged in this process to diverse cognitive and technical abilities enhancements. Among them cognitive abilities for understanding and using new and multiple alphabetization possibilities related to learning how to deal with digital/web-based information, visualization tools, which can contribute for achieving individuals' digital fluency (Demo, 2008b; Demo, 2009; Franco, Cruz & Lopes; 2006).

This kind of work has also brought about creating several references of learning and teaching the diverse curriculum subjects within a balanced support related to the combination of arts, culture, sciences and technology (Franco, Cruz & Lopes, 2006; Popper, 2007) for improving individuals' minds for the future as demonstrates Gardner' investigation and reflections (2007).

His investigation and reflections have covered the interrelation among the disciplined mind that takes information, understands and evaluates it objectively within cognitive and reasoning processes; the synthesizing mind that receives and organizes ideas from diverse resources; the creative mind that acts based on the synthesized knowledge to solve problems and evoke innovative ways of thinking; the respectful mind covers the respect to the diversity among human beings; and the ethic mind address ones' responsibility as workers and citizens beyond their own needs (Gardner, 2007).

We have observed that there are several ways for stimulating and developing writing, reading, researching and communicating skills from children to adults through using digital and interactive graphics tools. This work has provided individuals' access and knowledge acquisition related to contemporary and advanced technologies for building 2D and 3D virtual environments plus improving teaching/learning activities. The strategy adopted has been based on creating learning situations in which individuals can reflect and share knowledge across using interactive technologies tools for enhancing their literacy skills.

We have also focused on improving individuals' awareness about the possibilities of producing digital content of excellent quality making use of open standards, even without high-end machines and/or specific software. The experiments carried out have showed that technical and non-technical educators and students from diverse cultural backgrounds are able to interact with 3D interfaces and construct small-scale examples in real time adapting them to diverse pedagogical and informal contexts (Franco & Lopes, 2005d).

For achieving these goals within an easier way, we believe that educators should not have their cognitive and physical performances overloaded. Hence, such thought is reinforced in Lajoie & Nakamura (2006)'s research, which highlights the necessity of increasing the degree of educational interactivity with more varied types of media. Teaching and learning using computer graphics and multimedia tools requires more scaffolding of learners, more attention to assisting learners self-regulation, and perhaps media that serves in a pedagogical manner through coaching, pedagogical agents, mobile devices, and realistic and imaginary environments that include virtual reality and even augmented reality dimensions (Ficheman, Saul, Assis, Correa, Franco, Tori & Lopes, 2008b; Lajoie & Nakamura, 2006; Na, Billinghurst, & Woo, 2008).

Conversely, educators have worked with too many children at once, as well as long periods of time in order to survive economically. It can be included on these concerns educators' necessity of being up to date with society changes and education transformation needs such as the ones supported by the combination of contemporary advanced technologies and neuroscience (in IINN-ELS, 2009; Nicolelis, 2008).

Within a learning economy that currently points to individuals' lifelong learning attitudes for adapting themselves to world changes such as move away from manufacturing to a services economy, with the emergence of the knowledge economy and the decline of many traditional institutions which has been requiring individuals to become more active in managing their lives as states John Field (2006) (in Wikipedia Lifelong Learning, 2009), policy makers should provide less overwhelming school environmental conditions to educators and students.

Accordingly to the real world examples described during this chapter, it seems that such positive policy makers' action could influence the raising of sustainable and qualitative learning environments, as well as learning and teaching interactions, bringing about improvements on individuals' knowledge and cognition development. These kinds of qualitative learning opportunities could reverse the current logic of more and more quantity of time that individuals have stayed at school. Perhaps, due to the current overwhelming situation to individuals' mind and body, the great amount of time that ones have stayed at schools has not been transformed into ones' knowledge development of quality.

Demo (2009b) reinforces the above criticism, when he reflects that increasing the quantity of individuals' time at a school learning ecosystem has not resulted in better individuals' learning achievements than before. He suggests less guided or passive learning and teaching practices that have been based on learning manuals designed for someone outside the local learning ecosystem. He also recommends that educators have their abilities of learning to learn enhanced in order to improve their minds for thinking deeper about the complexities that involves the act of learning and teaching. Within a scenario of good work conditions, it seems that educators would be able to learn how to use the contemporary and advanced technologies and tools available, and then stimulate and support individuals' lifelong learning with effectiveness.

There is recognition that constant social changes and digital/web-based technologies are elements that have added a rich layer of complexity to learning environments. Then we infer that policy makers' educational initiatives should improve and support intensive, high quality learning opportunities not only in schools, but also at home, parks, community centers, museums, and workplaces (Blikstein & Cavallo, 2002; Blikstein & Zuffo, 2003; Franco, Cruz & Lopes, 2006; Resnick, 2002; Nicolelis, 2008). For instance, the good results of the collaborative and cooperative work carried out between the primary and high education that have been presented on this chapter are other real world evidences that benefiting and improving children and other individuals' knowledge and cognition development lifelong within high quality, interactive, and dynamic learning ecosystems worth it.

Within a cognitive society (Fonseca, 1998) using the synergy among psychology, neuropsychology and technology in schools as support of high quality on individuals' education, in intensive way, keeps a challenge. Although, *"even within the neuroscience understanding how the brain work is still far from complete"* (Harrison & Hood, 2008).

According to recognized learning concepts and projects (in Doman & Doman, 2007; Gardner, 1994) as well as the theory and practice carried out on this work, the synergy between neuroscience and education including its potential to support educators' better educational actions can not be denied. For instance, neuropsychologists could support education through contributing in discussions related to the right type of learning ecosystem structure (best size of school, size of the class, level and type of extra help), modifications in the curriculum taught, thinking ways of using technology and accommodations such as computers, diaries, and so on (Harrison & Hood, 2008).

This chapter development has showed that is relevant to provide an educational policy that enables to broke the paradigm of passive education and transform it in an active learner's centered and knowledge based approach (Bertoline & Laxer, 2006; Freire, 2004; NAC, 2005; Osberg, 1997; Resnick 2007). The research and practical examples have proved that is possible to achieve such goal through applying interactive computer graphics, information and visualization tools and techniques to support educational actions.

The educational actions we have highlighted during this work have supported ordinary users routinely tailor applications to their own use and use this power to invent new applications based on their understanding of their own domains. Users, with their deeper knowledge of their own knowledge domains can increasingly be important sources of new applications at the expense of generic systems programmers (with systems expertise but low domain expertise) (in Wikipedia Human-computer- interaction, 2009).

Due to this work good result, we believe that is relevant to keep learning actions based on dialogic human to human interactions with great influence from human computer interactions. However, with interactions stimulating citizens'

knowledge and cognition development within a scientific rigor (Freire, 2004), and with support of contemporary and advanced technologies. The idea is to sustain teaching and lifelong learning situations as well as the practice of science with the spirit of supporting citizens' cognitive abilities and intelligence improvements, leading them to the state of enhanced wisdom (Flynn, 2007; Senge, Jaworski, Scharmer & Flowers, 2007).

Finally, enhancing individuals' cognition, intelligence and technical skills development through sharing digital/web-based knowledge by using desktop virtual reality and information visualization techniques and tools within K-12 education, has proved to be relevant, and has the potential of supporting individuals' spiral and incremental lifelong learning cycles that can impact on democratizing the society.

ACKNOWLEDGMENT

Thanks to the learning and surrounding community from ESB School, including educators and researchers from LSI that have dreamed and acted in collaboration to keep this work in development lifelong. God Bless you.

REFERENCES

Accelerated Learning Methods. (2009). *Visual stimulation in your accelerated learning environment*. Retrieved January 12, 2009, from http://www.acceleratedlearningmethods.com/visual-stimulation.html

Ackerman, E. (n.d.). *Piaget's constructivism, Papert's constructionism: What is the difference? Massachusetts Institute of Technology*. Retrieved November 16, 2008, from http://learning.media.mit.edu/content/publications/EA.Piaget%20_%20Papert.pdf

Alice Org. (2008). *What is Alice?* Retrieved November 13, 2008, from http://www.alice.org/index.php?page=what_is_alice/what_is_alice

Alice org. (2008). *Alice programming.* Retrieved November 12, 2008, from http://www.alice.org/

Ambiente Intelligence Org. (2008). Retrieved January 12, 2009, from http://www.ambientintelligence.org/

Ames, A. L., Nadeu, D. R., & Moreland, J. L. (1997). *VRML 2.0 sourcebook* (2nd ed.). New York: Wiley and Sons.

Aprende Brasil. (2008). *Sucursal da escola: Alunos da EMEF ernani silva bruno visualizam as matérias em 3D.* Retrieved January 12, 2009, from http://www.aprendebrasil.com.br/alunoreporter/reportagem.asp?idARMateria=531

Area Wikipedia. (2008). *Area.* http://en.wikipedia.org/wiki/Area

Barbosa, A. M. (2006). Dilema da arte/educação como mediação cultural em namoro com as tecnologias contemporâneas. In A. M. Barbosa (Ed.), *Arte/educação contemporânea: Consonâncias internacionais* (pp. 98-112). Brasil:Cortez Editora.

Barros, P. G. (2004). *UFPE, VRML tutorial.* Retrieved November 22, 2008, from http://www.di.ufpe.br/~if124/vrml/vrml.htm

Bartunk, D., Martin, A., & Martinová, L. (2007). *Games in nature: An innovative approach to outdoor and environmental activities for young children.* Czech Republic: IYNF.

Beatriz. (2009). Retrieved February 16, 2009, from http://biaatrevida.blogspot.com/

Benyon, D., Turner, P., & Turner, S. (2005). *Designing interactive systems: People, activities, contexts, technologies,* New York: Addison-Wesley.

Billinghurst, M. (2008). *Hiltlabnz homepage.* Retrieved November 12, 2008, from http://www.hitlabnz.org/wiki/Home

Blender. (2008). Retrieved November 12, 2008, from http://www.blender.org/features-gallery/features/

Blikstein, P., & Cavallo, D., (2002). Technology as a Trojan horse in school environments: The emergence of the learning atmosphere (II). In *Proceedings of the Interactive Computer Aided Learning International Workshop,* Carinthia Technology Institute, Villach, Austria. Retrieved January 13, 2009, from http://www.blikstein.com/paulo/documents/papers/BliksteinCavallo-TrojanHorse-ICL2002.pdf

Blikstein, P., & Zuffo, M. K. (2003). As sereias do ensino eletrônico. In M. Silva (Ed.), *Online education: Theory, practice, legislation and corporate training.* Rio de Janeiro: Ed. Loyola. Retrieved January 13, 2009, from http://www.blikstein.com/paulo/documents/books/BliksteinZuffo-MermaidsOfE-Teaching-OnlineEducation.pdf

Blog definition. (2008). Retrieved November 12, 2008, from http://en.wikipedia.org/wiki/Blog

Bowman, D. A., Kruijff, E., LaViola, J. J., & Poupyrev, I. (2005). *3D user interfaces, theory and practice.* New York: Addison & Wesley.

British Council Chevening. (2008). *Chevening program.* Retrieved November 15, 2008, from http://www.britishcouncil.org/br/brasil-education-chevening.htm

Brna, P., & Cooper, B. (2003). *Lessons from the NIMIS classroom: An overview of progress towards the "classroom of tomorrow" in an English county primary school.* Retrieved November 12, 2008, from http://homepages.inf.ed.ac.uk/pbrna/projects/cblnimis/NIMISbriefing.html

Brutzman, D., & Daly, L. (2007). Preface. In *X3D graphics for Web authors* (pp. xix-xxi). USA: Morgan Kaufmann.

Brutzman, D. (2008). *X3D: Extensible 3D graphics for Web authors, CGEMS educational material.* Retrieved November 20, 2008, from http://cgems.inesc.pt/ListModules.aspx

Burdea, G. C., & Coiffet, P. (2003). *Virtual reality technology* (2nd ed.). New York: Wiley & Sons.

Burnett, I. S., Pereira, F., Walle, R. V., & Koenen, R. (2006). *The MPEG-21 book.* New York: Wiley.

Buscaloni, A. D., de la Iglesia, A., Buscaloni, R. D., & Dejoan, A. (2005). Modularity at the boundary between art and science. In W. Callebaut & D. R. Gutman (Eds.), *Modularity: Understanding the development and evolution of natural complex systems* (pp. 283-204). Cambridge, MA: The MIT Press.

Callebaut, W., & Gutman, D. R. (Eds.). (2005) *Modularity: Understanding the development and evolution of natural complex systems.* Cambridge, MA: The MIT Press.

Cavallo, D. (2000). Emergent designing and learning environments: Building on indigenous knowledge. *IBM Systems Journal, 39*(3/4). Retrieved November 13, 2008, from http://www.research.ibm.com/journal/sj/393/part2/cavallo.html

Castells, M. (2003). *A galáxia da Internet: Reflexões sobre a Internet, os negócios e a sociedade* (M. L. X. de A. Borges, Trans.) Brasil: Jorge Zahar Editor.

Chang, K., Beck, J., Mostow, J., & Corbett, A. (2006, June 26-30). A Bayes Net toolkit for student modeling in intelligent tutoring systems. In *Proceedings of the 8th International Conference on Intelligent Tutoring Systems,* Jhongli, Taiwan. Retrieved November 12, 2008, from http://www.cs.cmu.edu/~listen/pdfs/ChangBeckMostowCorbett.2006.ITS.BNT-SM.pdf

Chen, J. Q., Isberg, E., & Krechevesky, M. (2001). *Projeto spectrum atividades iniciais de aprendizagem* (Vol. 2) (Project Spectrum, early learning activities). Brasil: ARTMED.

Child brain development. (2009). *Make your child smarter.* Retrieved January 12, 2009, from http://www.brainy-child.com/

Chun, W. H. K. (2006). *Control and freedom: Power and paranoia in the age of fiber optics.* Cambridge, MA: MIT Press.

Churchland, P. (2004) *Matéria e consciência: Uma introdução contemporânea à filisofia da mente.* Brasil: Editora Unesp.

Colson, R. (2007). *The fundamentals of digital art.* Singapore: AVA Academia.

Computer Clubhouse. (2008). Retrieved November 12, 2008, from http://www.computerclubhouse.org/

Conway, M. J. (1997) *Alice: Easy-to-learn 3D scripting for novices.* Unpublished doctoral dissertation. Retrieved November 13, 2008, from http://www.alice.org/publications/ConwayDissertation.PDF

Cook, J. U. (1998). Lower achieving primary students' options on virtual reality. *Australian Educational Computing, 12*(2). Retrieved November 12, 2008, from http://www.acce.edu.au/journal/journals/vol12_2.pdf#search='Lower%20achieving%20primary%20students'%20options%20on%20virtual%20reality

Coope, S., Dann, W., & Pausch, R. (2003). Teaching objects-first in introductory computer science. In *Proceedings of the SIGCSE 2003.* Retrieved November 13, 2008, from http://www.alice.org/publications/chialice.pdf

Cunningham, S. (2008). Computer graphics in context: An approach to a first course in computer graphics. In *Educators Paper (abstracts), Proceedings of Siggraph 2008,* Singapura. Retrieved November 12, 2008, from http://www.siggraph.org/asia2008/attendees/edu/3.php

Cuninngham, S. (2007). *Computer graphics: Programming in OpenGL for visual communication*. Upper Saddle River, NJ: Pearson Prentice Hall.

Dabbagh, N. (2008). *Web-based learning framework on mapping instructional strategies to Web features*. Retrieved January 13, 2009, from http://mason.gmu.edu/~ndabbagh/wblg/wblframework.html

Data warehousing. (2009). Retrieved January 17, 2009, from http://kiwitobes.com/wiki/Data_warehouse.html

Dede, C. (1999). *Emerging influences of information technology on school curriculum*. Retrieved January 13, 2009, from http://www.virtual.gmu.edu/ss_pdf/DedeJCS.pdf

Dede, C. (2000). *The role of emerging technologies for knowledge mobilization, dissemination, and use in education - draft report*. Retrieved November 22, 2008, from http://www.virtual.gmu.edu/ss_pdf/knowlmob.pdf

Dede, C., & Palumbo, D. (1991). Implications of hypermedia for cognition and communication. *Impact Assessment Bulletin, 9*(1-2), 15-28. Retrieved November 22, 2008, from http://www.virtual.gmu.edu/ss_pdf/hyper.pdf

Dede, C., Salzman, M., Loftin, R. B., & Ash, K. (1997). Using virtual reality technology to convey abstract scientific concepts. In M. J. Jacobson & R. B. Kozma (Eds.), *Learning the sciences of the 21st century: Research, design, and implementing advanced technology learning environments*. Hillsdale, NJ: Lawrence Erlbaum. Retrieved November 12, 2008, from http://www.virtual.gmu.edu/ss_pdf/jacobson.pdf

Del Nero, H. S. (1997). *O sítio da mente: Pensamento, emoção e vontade no cérebro humano*. Collegium Cognitio, Brasil. Retrieved January 12, 2009, from http://cognitio.incubadora.fapesp.br/portal/producao/livros/sitio%20mente

Demo, P. (2008). *Novas tecnologias: Novas?* Retrieved February 12, 2009, from http://pedrodemo.sites.uol.com.br/textos/novasnovas.html

Demo, P. (2008b). *Novas, multi-alfabetizações*. Retrieved February 13, 2009, from http://pedrodemo.sites.uol.com.br/textos/enilton.html

Demo, P. (2009). *Não vemos as coisas como são, mas como somos*. Retrieved February 13, 2009, from http://pedrodemo.sites.uol.com.br/textos/comosomos.html

Demo, P. (2009b). *Professor: Profissional da aprendizagem*. Retrieved February 13, 2009, from http://pedrodemo.sites.uol.com.br/textos/ppa.html

Dietz, S., Besser, H., Borda, A., Geber, K., & Lévy, P. (2005). *Virtual museum of (Canada) - Canadian virtual museum*. Retrieved November 16, 2008, from http://www.virtualmuseum.ca

Doman, J. (2009). *Facilitated communication*. Retrieved January 9, 2009, from http://www.iahp.org/Facilitated-Communicat.293.0.html

Doman, G., & Doman, J. (2007). *Como multiplicar a inteligência do seu bebê: Mais suave revolução* (5th ed., L. V. Norton, Trans.). Brasil: Artes e Ofícios.

Donis, A. D. (2007). *Sintaxe da linguagem visual* (A primer of visual literacy) (J. L. Camargo, Trans.). Brasil: WMF Martins Fontes.

Ducatel, K., Bogdanowicz, M., Scapolo, F., Leijten, J., & Burgelman, J. C. (Eds.). (2001). *Scenarios for ambient intelligence in 2010: Final report*. IPTS-Seville. Retrieved November 12, 2008, from ftp://ftp.cordis.europa.eu/pub/ist/docs/istagscenarios2010.pdf

Durlach, N., & Mavor, A. S. (Eds.). (1994). *Virtual reality: Scientific and technological challenges*. USA: National Academic Press.

Dünser, A. (2008). Supporting low ability readers with interactive augmented reality. In *Annual* review of cyber therapy and telemedicine: Changing the face of healthcare* (pp. 41-48). San Diego, CA: Interactive Media Institute. Retrieved November 12, 2008, from http://www.hitlabnz.org/publications/2008-SupportingLowAbilityReadersWithInteractiveAugmentedReality.pdf

Estação Ciência. (2009). *Ciência à mão*. Retrieved January 11, 2009, from http://www.eciencia.usp.br/atividades/index.html

ELT. (2008). *CTE introduction experiential learning*. Retrieved November 16, 2008, from www.usoe.k12.ut.us/ate/tlc/cda/experiential.htm

Encyclopedic Knowledge. (2009). *How to give your child encyclopedic knowledge*. Retrieved January 12, 2009, from http://www.brainy-child.com/article/encyclopedic.html

Evaluation methods – Wikipedia. (2008). Retrieved November 12, 2008, from http://en.wikipedia.org/wiki/Evaluation_methods

Fagerberg, J. (2006). Innovation: A guide line to literature. In J. Fagerberg, D. C. Mowery, & R. R. Nelson (Eds.), *The Oxford handbook of innovation* (pp. 2-3). New York: Oxford University Press.

Febrace. (2009). *Feira brasileira de ciências e engenharia criatividade e inovação*. Retrieved April 3, 2009, from http://www.lsi.usp.br/febrace/

Febrace. (2008). *Acontece, spaceship*. Retrieved November 12, 2008, from http://www.lsi.usp.br/febrace/imprensa/acontece/news0008/02sabia.html

Ficheman, I. K., & Lopes, R. D. (2008a). Mobility in digital learning ecosystems. In *Proceedings of the IADIS International Conference Mobile Learning 2008*, Algarve, Portugal (pp. 19-26).

Ficheman, I. K., Saul, J. A., Assis, G. A., Correa, A. G. D., Franco, J. F., Tori, R., & Lopes, R. D. (2008b). Combining augmented reality with mobile technologies to enrich learning experiences. In *Proceedings of the IADIS International*

Conference Mobile Learning 2008, Algarve, Portugal (pp. 191-195).

Flanagan, M., & Perlin, K. (2008). *Rapunzel project*. Retrieved November 12, 2008, from http://www.maryflanagan.com/rapunsel/about.htm

Fodor, J. – Wikipedia. (2009). Retrieved February 13, 2009, from http://en.wikipedia.org/wiki/Jerry_Fodor

Foley, J. D., Dam, A. V., Feiner, S. K., & Hughes, J. (1993). *Computer graphics principles and practice* (2nd ed.). New York: Addison-Wesley.

Forrester, J. W. (1992). *System dynamics and learner-centered-learning in kindergarten through 12th grade education*. Retrieved November 12, 2008, from http://sysdyn.clexchange.org/sdep/Roadmaps/RM1/D-4337.pdf

Forrester, J. W. (1994). *Learning through systems dynamics as a preparation for 21st century*. Retrieved November 12, 2008, from http://sysdyn.clexchange.org/sdep/papers/D-4434-3.pdf

Forrester, J. W. (1996). *Systems dynamics and k-12 teachers*. Retrieved November 12, 2008, from http://sysdyn.clexchange.org/sdep/papers/D-4665-4.pdf

Franco, J. F, Ficheman, I. K., Venâncio, V., Moreno, M., Freitas, M. G. S., Leite, A. L. B. F., Franco, N. F., Matias, M. A., & Lopes, R. D. (2008c). Using virtual reality and Web-based technologies for improving individuals' education. In *Proceedings of the 11th International Conference on Experiential Learning, ICEL 2008, Identity of Experience, Challenges for experiential learning*, Sydney, Australia.

Franco, J. F., Ficheman, I. K., Lopes, R. D., Ferreira, A. L. S., Santos M. E. S. B., Ferreira, G., Araújo, V. R. S., & Moreno, M. (2008b). Empowering an educational community through using multimedia tools in combination with mobile learning actions. In *Proceedings of the IADIS*

International Conference Mobile Learning 2008, Algarve, Portugal (pp. 221–226).

Franco, J. F., & Lopes, R. D. (2005b). Knowledge development through collaborative work supported by interactive technologies. In R. Luckin (Ed.), *Representing and analyzing collaborative interactions: What works? When does is work? To what extent? Proceedings of the 12th International Conference on Artificial Intelligence in Education, AIED Workshop 6,* Holland, Amsterdam (pp. 49-58). Retrieved November 12, 2008, from http://hcs.science.uva.nl/AIED2005/W6proc.pdf

Franco, J. F., & Lopes, R. D. (2005d). Learning to learn from basic to higher education using digital and interactive graphics tools. In *Proceedings of the IPSI – 2005 FRANCE Conference,* Carcassonne, France. Retrieved February 13, 2009, from http://internetconferences.net/france2006/BookOfAbstracts.doc

Franco, J. F., Cruz, S. R. R., Franco, N. F., & Lopes, R. D. (2007c). Experiências de uso de mídias interativas como suporte para autoria e construção colaborativa do conhecimento. In *RENOTE - revista novas tecnologias na educação, ix ciclo de palestras novas tecnologias na educação* (Vol. 5). Retrieved December 4, 2008, from http://www.cinted.ufrgs.br/ciclo9/artigos/2cJorge.pdf

Franco, J. F., & Lopes, R. D. (2002). From children to adults: Improving education through virtual environments technologies. In *Proceedings of the 5th IASTED International Conference Computers and Advanced Technology in Education,* Cancun, Mexico.

Franco, J. F., & Lopes, R. D. (2008). Developing 3D virtual environments supported by Web-based and virtual reality technology as well as low cost multimedia files. In *Proceedings of 11th International Conference on Experiential Learning, ICEL 2008, Identity of Experience, Challenges for experiential learning.*

Franco, J. F., & Lopes, R. D. (2005c). Converging interactive media, arts and culture at basic education as support for enhancing individuals' literacy. In *FILE, Electronic International Language Festival.* Retrieved November 16, 2008, from http://www.file.org.br/file2005/textos/symposium/eng/jorgefrancolopes.doc

Franco, J. F., & Lopes, R. D. (2004). Novas tecnologias em ambientes de aprendizagem: Estimulando o aprender, transformando o curriculum e ações. In *Proceedings of the Revista Renote III Ciclo de Palestras sobre Novas Tecnologias na Educação,* Porto Alegre, Brasil. Retrieved November 12, 2008, from http://www.cinted.ufrgs.br/ciclo3/af/39-novastecnologias.pdf

Franco, J. F. (2005a). *Projeto escrita digital criativa (creative digital scribe project).* Retrieved November 12, 2008, from http://cognitio.incubadora.fapesp.br/portal/atividades/cursos/posgrad/jogos_eletronicos/2005/trabalhos/Jorge/TM_EscritaDigital.pdf

Franco, J. F. (2000). Multimedia in action: Applying 3D environments at school teaching, using VRML for an interactive, dynamic and high quality education. In *GEMISIS conference digest* (UK, ed.). The University of Salford and GEMISIS.

Franco, J. F., Cruz, S. R. R., & Lopes, R. D. (2006). Computer graphics, interactive technologies and collaborative learning synergy supporting individuals' skills development. In *Proceedings of the 33 International Conference And Exhibition on Computer Graphics and Interactive Techniques, SIGGRAPH 2006,* Boston, MA. Retrieved November 12, 2008, from http://delivery.acm.org/10.1145/1180000/1179338/p42-franco.pdf?key1=1179338&key2=0205817711&coll=&dl=ACM&CFID=15151515&CFTOKEN=6184618G

Franco, J. F., Ficheman, I. K., Assis, G. A., Zuffo, M. K., Lopes, R. de D., Moreno, M., & Freitas, M. G. da S. (2008a). Using virtual reality, computer graphics and Web-based technology for developing knowledge and improving k-12 education, In *Proceedings of the IADIS Multi Conference on Computer Science and Information Systems (MCCSIS 2008)*, Amsterdam, The Netherlands (pp. 115-138).

Franco, J. F., Mariz L. R., Lopes, R. D., Cruz, S. R. R., Franco, N. F., & Delacroix, E. (2007a). Developing individuals' cognition, literacy skills and collaborative teaching and learning attitudes through the combination of Web based technology, multimedia tools and files. *Psychology and Scientific Education Magazine, 1*(1), 3-52.

Franco, J. F., Cruz, S. R. R., Aquino, E. M. M., Teles, E. O., Gianevechio, M. M., Franco, N. F., Ficheman, I. K., & Lopes, R. D. (2007b). Using information visualization in the logic of building an interactive knowledge based learning network for social development. In *Proceedings of the Congress of Logic Applied to Technology–LAPTEC'2007*, Santos, São Paulo, Brazil.

Franco, J. F. (2001a). Developing skills teaching and learning using Web standards and interactive 3D virtual environments and multimedia tools. In *Proceedings of the 20th World Conference on Open Learning and Distance Education*, Düsseldorf, Germany. Retrieved November 12, 2008, from http://web.archive.org/web/20050526211138/http://www.educorp.futuro.usp.br/publicacoes/Developing+Skills.doc

Franco, J. F. (2001b). *Lifelike intelligent agents telling me a story in a virtual environment*. Unpublished doctoral dissertation, The University of Salford, UK.

Franco, N. F., Stori, N., Lopes, R. D., & Franco, J. F. (2005). Um caso de construção colaborativa de conhecimento e desenvolvimento educacional interdisciplinar com mediação das tecnologias da informação e da comunicação. In *Proceedings of the Revista RENOTE, Vol.3, Nº2, VI Ciclo de Palestras Novas Tecnologias na Educação.*

Retrieved November 12, 2008, from http://www.cinted.ufrgs.br/renote/nov2005/artigosrenote/a49_cintednovembro.pdf

Franco, J. F. (2005). *Projeto escrita digital criativa*. January 12, 2009, from http://cognitio.incubadora.fapesp.br/portal/atividades/cursos/posgrad/jogos_eletronicos/2005/trabalhos/Jorge/TM_EscritaDigital.pdf/view

Franco, J. F., & Lopes, R. D. (2004). Novas tecnologias em ambientes de aprendizagem: Estimulando o aprender a aprender, transformando o currículo e ações. In *Proceedings of the Cinted Revista Renote, III Ciclo de Palestras sobre Novas Tecnologias na Educação.* Retrieved January 12, 2009, from http://www.cinted.ufrgs.br/ciclo3/af/39-novastecnologias.pdf

Franco, J. F., Ficheman, I. K., Alves, A. C., Venâncio, V., Lopes, R. D., Cruz, S. R. R., Santiago, M., Teles, E. O., & Aquino, E. M. M. (2007c). Desenvolvendo uma experiência educacional interativa usando recursos de visualização de informação e de computação móvel como estímulo à construção colaborativa e continuada de conhecimento. In *Proceedings of the Cinted Revista Renote, Dezembro/2007 - Vol.5 Nº2 - X Ciclo de Palestras Novas Tecnologias na Educação.* Retrieved March 23, 2009, from http://www.cinted.ufrgs.br/renote/dez2007/artigos/5cJorgeFranco.pdf

Freire, P. (2004). *Pedagogia da autonomia: Saberes necessários a prática educativa.* Paz e Terra, Brasil: 29º edição.

Fullan, M. (2008). *Reach every student: Energizing Ontario education.* Retrieved November 12, 2008, from http://www.michaelfullan.ca/Articles_08/EnergizingFull.pdf

Fullan, M. (2005). *Professional learning communities writ large.* Retrieved November 12, 2008, from http://www.michaelfullan.ca/Articles_05/UK_Ireland_preread_final.pdf

FYA. (2009). *The foundation for young Australians (FYA)*. Retrieved January 11, 2009, from http://www.fya.org.au/

Gadotti, M. (1994). *Reading Paulo Freire, his life and work* (J. Milton, Trans.). New York: University of New York Press.

Gardner, H. (1991). *Creating the future: Intelligence in seven steps*. Retrieved January 11, 2009, from http://www.newhorizons.org/future/Creating_the_Future/crfut_gardner.html

Gardner, H. (1994). *A criança pré-escolar: Como pensa e como a escola pode ensiná-la* (C. A. N. Soares, Trans.). Brasil: Artmed.

Gardner, H. (2007). *Cinco mentes para o futuro* (five minds for the future). Brasil: Artmed. January 12, 2009, from http://www.amazon.com/gp/reader/1591399122/ref=sib_dp_pt/102-8485304-6091351#reader-link

Gardner, H., Csikszentmihlyi, M., & Damon, W. (2004). *Trabalho qualificado: Quando a excelência e a ética se encontram*. Brasil: Artmed.

Garrido, M. (2009). *Márcio art & design*. January 12, 2009, from http://marciodesign.blogspot.com/

Glasser, W. (2009). *How we learn*. Retrieved January 11, 2009, from http://members.shaw.ca/priscillatheroux/Glasser.htm

Globo Videos. (2009). *As novas fronteiras do mundo da realidade virtual*. Retrieved March 21, 2009, from http://video.globo.com/Videos/Player/Noticias/0,,GIM984111-7823-AS+NOVAS+FRONTEIRAS+DO+MUNDO+DA+REALIDADE+VIRTUAL,00.html

Gimp. (2008). Retrieved November 12, 2008, from http://www.gimp.org/

Gombrich, E. H. (2007). *Arte e ilusão: Um estudo da psicologia da representação pictórica* (art and illusion – a study in the psychology of pictorial representation) (R. de S. Barbosa, Trans.). Brasil: WMF Martins Fontes.

Grasset, R., D̈unser, A., & Billinghurst, M. (2008). Design of a mixed-reality book: Is it still a real book? In *Proceedings of ISMAR 2008*, Cambridge, UK. Retrieved November 12, 2008, from http://www.hitlabnz.org/publications/2008-TheDesignofaMixed-RealityBookIsItStillaRealBook.pdf

Grasset, R., D̈unser, A., & Billinghurst, M. (2007). Moving between contexts - a user evaluation of a transitional interface. *Image and Vision Computing New Zealand*. Retrieved November 12, 2008, from http://www.hitlabnz.org/publications/2008-MovingBetweenContexts-AUserEvaluationofaTransitionalInterface.pdf

Grasset, R., Woods, E., & Billinghurst, M. (2007). Art and mixed reality: New technology for seamless merging between virtual and real. In *Proceedings of the PERTHDAC 2007*, Perth, Australia. Retrieved November 12, 2008, from http://www.hitlabnz.org/publications/2007-ArtandMixedRealityNewTechnologyforSeamless.pdf

Harrison, S., & Hood, J. (2008). Applications of neuropsychology in schools. In J. Warner-Rogers & J. Reed (Eds.), *Child neuropsychology: Concepts, theory and practice* (pp. 404-419). Singapore: Wiley-Blackwell.

Henry, L. (2002). *Educational concept of scaffolding adolescent learning & development*. Retrieved November 16, 2008, from http://condor.admin.ccny.cuny.edu/~group4/Henry/Henry%20Paper.doc

Hernández, F. (2000). *Cultura visual, mudança educativa e projeto de trabalho*. Brasil: Artmed.

HTML Wikipedia definition. (2008). Retrieved November 12, 2008, from http://en.wikipedia.org/wiki/HTML

ICEL. (2008). *International consortium for experiential learning.* Retrieved January 11, 2009, from http://www.education.uts.edu.au/icel/conference.html

Illeris, K. (2007). *How we learn: Learning and non-learning in school and beyond.* England: Routledge.

Imprensa, J. (2009). *Preparação para o trabalho.* Retrieved March 20, 2009, from http://jovemcomunicavivo.blogspot.com/2009/03/preparacao-para-o-trabalho.html

INAF. (2005). *5º indicador nacional de alfabetismo funcional: Um diagnóstico para inclusão social pela educação.* Retrieved November 22, 2008, from http://www.acaoeducativa.org.br/downloads/inaf05.pdf

IINN-ELS. (2009). *Instituto internacional de neurociências de natal edmond e lily safra (IINN-ELS).* Retrieved February 15, 2009, from http://www.natalneuro.org.br/sobre_iinn/index.asp

Internet Guianet. (1999). Curso de VRML. *Revista Internet Guianet, 1*(2), 10-11.

I Seminário Web Curriculum. (2008). Retrieved January 12, 2009, from http://www.pucsp.br/webcurriculo/

ISTAG Working Group. (2003). *Ambient intelligence: From vision to reality for participation – in society & business.* Retrieved November 12, 2008, from http://74.125.113.104/search?q=cache:-B211_pXgScJ:ftp://ftp.cordis.europa.eu/pub/ist/docs/istag-ist2003_draft_consolidated_report.pdf+ISTAG+Working+Group+draft+report&hl=pt-BR&ct=clnk&cd=2&gl=br

ISTAG Working Group. (2004). *Grand challenges in the evolution of the information society* (DRAFT Report 06 July 2004). Retrieved November 12, 2008, from http://ec.europa.eu/information_society/istevent/2004/cf/document.cfm?doc_id=712

Istance, D. (2006). Os cenários da escola da OCDE, os professores e o papel das tecnologias da informação e da comunicação. In J. M. Sancho & F. Hernández (Eds.), *Colaboradores, tecnologias para transformar a educação* (pp. 177-197) (V. Campos, Trans.). Brasil: Artmed.

ISB. (2009). *Internet space builder.* Retrieved January 13, 2009, from http://www.parallelgraphics.com/products/isb/download/

Jablan, S. V. (2005). Modularity in art. In W. Callebaut & D. R. Gutman (Eds.), *Modualrity: Understanding the development and evolution of natural complex systems* (pp. 259-281). Cambridge, MA: The MIT Press.

Java and Java3d API™. (2008). Retrieved November 12, 2008, from http://java.sun.com/javase/technologies/desktop/java3d/

Jerry Fodor on mental architecture. (2009). February 13, 2008, from http://en.wikipedia.org/wiki/Jerry_Fodor_on_mental_architecture

Johnson, A. (2006). VR as instructional technology: The CAVE as classroom. In J. J. Sosnoski, P. Harkin, & B. Carter (Eds.), *Configuring history: Teaching the Harlem renaissance through virtual reality cityscapes.* Retrieved November 12, 2008, from http://www.evl.uic.edu/aej/papers/harlemchapter.pdf

Johnson, A., Roussos, M., Leigh, J., Vasilakis, C., Barnes, C., & Moher, T. (1999). Learning and building together in an immersive virtual world. *Presence 8*(3), 247-263. Retrieved November 12, 2008, from http://www.evl.uic.edu/aej/vrais98/vrais98.2.html

Jornal da Gazeta. (2008). *A história contada através de azulejos Portugueses.* Retrieved November 27, 2008, from http://www.tvgazeta.com.br/jornaldagazeta/video_destaques/2008/04/15_abr_08_06.php

Juul, J. (2005). *Half-real: Video games between real rules and fictional worlds.* Cambridge, MA: MIT Press.

Kassin, S. (1995). *Psychology*. Boston, MA: Houghton Mifflin.

Kaufmann, M. H. (2004). *Geometry education with augmented reality*. Unpublished doctoral dissertation, Vienna University of Technology. Retrieved January 11, 2008, from https://www.ims.tuwien.ac.at/media/documents/publications/kaufmann_diss.pdf

Kaufmann, H., & Meyer, B. (2008). Simulating educational physical experiments in augmented reality. In *Educators Paper (abstracts), Siggraph 2008,* Singapura. Retrieved November 12, 2008, from http://www.siggraph.org/asia2008/attendees/edu/13.php

Kelleher, C. (2006). *Motivating programming: Using storytelling to make computer programming attractive to middle school girls* Unpublished doctoral dissertation, School of Computer Science, Carnegie Mellon University – CMU. Retrieved November 12, 2008, from http://www.cs.cmu.edu/~caitlin/kelleherThesis_CSD.pdf

Kahootz. (2009). Retrieved January 11, 2008, from www.kahootz.com.au

Lajoie, S. P., & Nakamura, C. (2006). Multimedia learning of cognitive skills. In Mayer (Ed.), *The Cambridge handbook of multimedia learning* (pp. 489-502). New York: Cambridge University Press.

Laurel, B. (1993). *Computers as theatre*. New York: Addison Wesley.

Lévy, P. (1993). *As tecnologias da inteligência: O futuro do pensamento na era da informática* (C. I. da Costa, Trans.). Brasil: Editora 34.

Love to Know Baby. (2009). *Interview with Janet Doman a specialist in infant education and brain development*. Retrieved January 9, 2009, from http://baby.lovetoknow.com/wiki/Interview_With_Janet_Doman-A_Specialist_in_Infant_Education_and_Brain_Development

LSI - Laboratory of Integrated Systems. (2009). *Núcleo de realidade virtual*. Retrieved April 8, 2009, from http://www.lsi.usp.br/interativos/nem/nem.html

Luckin, R., Boulay, B., Yuill, N., Kerawalla, C., Pearce, D., & Harris, A. (2003). *Using software scaffolding to increase metacognitive skills amongst young learners*. Retrieved November 16, 2008, from http://www.cs.usyd.edu.au/~aied/vol2/vol2_Luckin.pdf

Luger, G. F. (2002). *Artificial intelligence: Structure and strategies for complex problem solving*. Reading, MA: Addison Wesley.

Maier, P., & Warren, A. (2000). *Integrating technology in learning and teaching: A practical guide for educators*. UK: Kogan Page.

Manssour, I. H. (2008). *Introdução a linguagem VRML*. Retrieved November 22, 2008, from http://www.inf.pucrs.br/~manssour/VRML/Intro.html

Marlene, F. (2008). *Matmarlenema*. Retrieved February 16, 2009, from http://matprofmarlene.blogspot.com/

Mateas, M. (2005). Procedural literacy: Educating the new media practitioner. *On The Horizon, Special Issue, Future of Games, Simulations and Interactive Media in Learning Contexts, 13*. Retrieved November 18, 2008, from http://www.lcc.gatech.edu/~mateas/publications/MateasOTH2005.pdf

McCullogh, M. (2004). *Digital ground: Architecture, pervasive computing, and environmental knowing*. Cambridge, MA: MIT Press.

Meninos do Morumbi. (2008). Retrieved November 12, 2008, from http://www.meninosdomorumbi.org.br/ingles/frames/principal.html

Milgran, P., & Colquhoun, H., Jr. (1999). A taxonomy of real and virtual world display integration. In Y. Ohta & H. Tamura (Eds.), *Mixed reality: Merging real and virtual worlds* (pp. 5-28). USA: Ohmsha & Springer-Verlag.

Miller, A. J. (2002). *Fortran examples*. Retrieved March 31, 2009, from http://www.esm.psu.edu/~ajm138/fortranexamples.html

Miller, C. H. (2004). *Digital storytelling: A creator's guiding to interactive entertainment*. USA: Focal press.

Miller, E. (2006). *Other economies are possible!* Retrieved November 12, 2008, from http://www.zmag.org/znet/viewArticle/3239

Mitchell, W. L. (1999). *The Egyptian tomb of Menna, Manchester University Metropolitan Area*. Retrieved November 12, 2008, from http://www.doc.mmu.ac.uk/RESEARCH/virtual-museum/Menna/

Modularity on mind. (2009). Retrieved February 13, 2009, from http://en.wikipedia.org/wiki/Modularity_of_mind

Moskal, B., Lurie, D., & Cooper, S. (n.d.). *Evaluating the effectiveness of a new instructional approach*. Retrieved November 13, 2008, from http://www.alice.org/publications/EvaluatingTheEffectivenessOfANewApproach.pdf

Mostow, J. (2006). *Project LISTEN: A reading tutor that listens*. Retrieved November 12, 2008, from http://www.cs.cmu.edu/~listen/research.html

Museu Lasar Segal. (2008). November 27, 2008, from http://www.museusegall.org.br/

Murray, J. H. (2003) *Hamlet no holodeck: O futuro da narrativa no ciberespaço*. Brasil: Editora UNESP.

Mrech, L. M. (1999). *Psicanálise e educação, novos operadores de leitura*. Brasil: Ed. Pioneira.

Murugesan, S. (2008). Web application development: Challenges and the role of Web engineer-ing. In G. Rossi, O. Pastor, D. Schwabe, & L. Olsina (Eds.), *Web engineering: Modeling and implementing Web applications* (pp. 7-32). UK: Springer.

Na, S., Billinghurst, M., & Woo, W. (2008). TMAR: Extension of a tabletop interface using mobile augmented reality. In *Proceedings of Edutainment 2008*, Nanjing, China. Retrieved November 12, 2008, from http://www.hitlabnz.org/publications/2008-TMARExtensionofaTabletopInterfaceUsingMobileAugmentedReality.pdf

NATE. (2009). *NATE – núcleo de aprendizagem, trabalho e entretenimento*. Retrieved January 13, 2009, from http://www.lsitec.org.br/html/aprendizagem_e_entretenimento.html

Nicolelis, M. (2008). Building the knowledge archipelago globalization of a development model. In *Scientific American: Building the Knowledge Archipelago*. Retrieved February 13, 2009, from http://www.nicolelislab.net/Papers/sciam%20dot%20com%20Archipelago+images.pdf

NICVE. (2008). *Master science course in virtual environments*. Retrieved November 12, 2008, from http://www.nicve.salford.ac.uk/

NIMIS - (Networked Interactive Media in Schools) project. (2008). Retrieved November 12, 2008 http://www.stockholmchallenge.se/data/nimis_networked_interacti

NMC. (2008). *The horizon report 2008 edition, a collaboration between The New Media Consortium – NMC and the EDUCAUSE Learning Initiative An EDUCAUSE Program*. Retrieved November 12, 2008, from http://www.nmc.org/pdf/2008-Horizon-Report.pdf

Nunes, M. (2008). Retrieved February 16, 2009 http://sempremichaelnunes.blogspot.com/

OLPC – One Laptop per Child. (2008). Retrieved, October 12, 2008, from http://laptop.org/vision/index.shtml

Osberg, K. (1993). *Virtual reality and education: A look at both sides of the sword* (Tech. Rep.). Seattle: University of Washington, Human Interface Technology Laboratory. Retrieved November 13, 2008, from http://www.hitl.washington.edu/publications/r-93-7/

Osberg, K. (1995). *Virtual reality and education: Where imagination and experience meet, VR in the Schools, 1-2*. Retrieved November 12, 2008, from http://vr.coe.ecu.edu/vrits/1-2osber.htm

Osberg, K. (1997b). *Constructivism in practice: The case for meaning-making in the virtual world*. Unpublished doctoral dissertation, University of Washington. Retrieved November 12, 2008, from http://www.hitl.washington.edu/publications/r-97-47/abstr.html

Osberg, K. (1997d). *A teacher's guide to developing virtual environments: VRRV project support* (Tech. Rep.). Seattle: Human Interface Technology Lab. Retrieved November 13, 2008, from http://www.hitl.washington.edu/publications/r-97-17/

Osberg, K. M. (1997a). *Spatial cognition in the virtual environment* (HITL Technical Publication: R-97-18). Human Interface Technology Laboratory of the Washington Technology Center, University of Washington. Retrieved November 12, 2008, from http://www.hitl.washington.edu/publications/r-97-18/

Osberg, K. M., Winn, W., Rose, H., Hollander, A., Hoffman, H., & Char, P. (1997c). *The effect of having grade seven students construct virtual environments on their comprehension of science*. Retrieved November 13, 2008, from http://www.hitl.washington.edu/publications/r-97-19/

Outras Palavras. (2008). *Prof^a. Lea Fagundes fala sobre como ocorre a aprendizagem e problemáticas do projeto UCA*. January 12, 2009, from http://www.antoniopassos.pro.br/blog/?cat=13&paged=2

PCN 5ª a 8ª Séries matemática. (1998). *Parâmetros curriculares nacionais*. Ministério da Educação – MEC. Retrieved November 27, 2008, from http://portal.mec.gov.br/seb/arquivos/pdf/matematica.pdf

PCN 5ª a 8ª Séries Artes. (1998). *Parâmetros curriculares nacionais*. Ministério da Educação – MEC. Retrieved November 27, 2008, from http://portal.mec.gov.br/seb/arquivos/pdf/arte.pdf

Papert, S., & Harel, I. (1991). Situating constructionism. In *Constructionism*. Ablex Publishing Corporation. Retrieved November 16, 2008, from http://www.papert.org/articles/SituatingConstructionism.html

Papert, S. (2008). *A máquina das crianças: Repensando a escola na era da informática* (S. Costa, Trans.). Brasil: Artmed.

Park, K. S., Leigh, J., Johnson, A. E., Carter, B., Brody, J., & Sosnoski, J. (2001). *Distance learning classroom using virtual Harlem*. Retrieved November 12, 2008, from http://www.evl.uic.edu/park/papers/VSMM01/park_distance.pdf

Parque CienTec. (2008). Retrieved November 12, 2008, from http://www.parquecientec.usp.br/

Participant Observation Wikipedia. (2009). Retrieved February 13, 2009, from http://en.wikipedia.org/wiki/Participant_observation

Parrish, A. D. (2002). *Inspired 3D lighting and composing*. USA: Premier Press.

Paul, C. (2008). *Digital art*. England: Thames & Hudson.

Perlin, K., & Goldberg, A. (1996). Improv: A system for scripting interactive actors in virtual worlds. *Computer Graphics, 29*(3). Retrieved November 12, 2008, from http://mrl.nyu.edu/publications/sig96-improv/sig96-improv.pdf

Perlin, K. (2008). *Perlin home page experiments*. Retrieved November 12, 2008, from http://mrl.nyu.edu/~perlin/

Peter, O. (2001). *Didática do ensino a distância: Experiências e estágio da discussão numa visão internacional* (I. Kayser, Trans.). Brasil: Editora, Unissinos.

Piaget, J. (1987). *O nascimento da inteligência na criança* (4th ed.). Brasil: LTC.

Piazzi, P. (2007). *Aprendendo inteligência.* Brasil: Ed. Vida e Consciência.

Pietraß, M. (2007). *Changes in cultural practices and social values.* Paper presented at the INDIRE-OECD Expert Meeting on the New Millennium Learners/Session 3. Retrieved January 12, 2009, from http://www.oecd.org/dataoecd/0/7/38360803.pdf

PISA – OECD. (2006). *The programme for international student assessment: Science competencies for tomorrow's world, executive summary.* Retrieved November 12, 2008, from http://www.pisa.oecd.org/dataoecd/15/13/39725224.pdf

Popper, F. (2007). *From technological to virtual art.* Cambridge, MA: MIT Press.

Portal Aprendiz. (2009). *Jovens criam soluções para problemas de suas comunidades.* Retrieved March 21, 2009, from http://aprendiz.uol.com.br/content/phiwretuwo.mmp

Powell, W. W., & Grodal, S. (2008). Networks of innovators. In J. Fagerberg, D. C. Mowery, & R. R. Nelson (Eds.), *The Oxford handbook of innovation* (pp. 56-85). New York: Oxford University Press.

Preece, J., Sharp, H., & Rogers, Y. (2007). *Interaction design: Beyond human-computer interaction* (2nd ed.). New York: John Wiley & Sons, Ltd.

Preece, J., Rogers, Y., Sharp, H., Benyon, D., Holland, S., & Carey, T. (1994). *Human computer interaction.* Reading, MA: Addison-Wesley.

Pressman, R. (2006). *Software engineering: A practitioner's approach* (6th ed.). New York: McGraw Hill.

Processing. (2009). *Processing software.* Retrieved January 11, 2009, from http://www.processing.org/learning/3d/texture1.html

Projeto Clicar. (2009). *Dados 'data'.* Retrieved January 11, 2009, from http://www.cepeca.org.br/projetoclicar/pagina.php?id=127

Project Listen. (2008). *Project LISTEN (literacy innovation that speech technology enables).* Retrieved November 12, 2008, from http://www.cs.cmu.edu/~listen/index.html

Project Spectrum. (2009). *Project spectrum.* Retrieved November 12, 2008, from http://www.pz.harvard.edu/Research/Spectrum.htm

Project Zero. (2008). Retrieved January 11, 2008, from http://www.pz.harvard.edu/index.cfm

Qualitative research Wikipedia. (2009). *Qualitative research.* Retrieved February 13, 2009, from http://en.wikipedia.org/wiki/Qualitative_research

Raessens, J. (2005). Computer games as participatory media culture. In J. Raessens & J. Goldstein (Eds.), *Computer games studies* (pp. 373-388). Cambridge, MA: MIT Press.

Reilly, R. C., & Munakata, Y. (2002). *Computational explorations in cognitive neuroscience: Understanding the mind by simulating the brain* (pp. 227-229). Cambridge, MA: MIT Press.

Reiman, J., Young, M., & Howes, A., (1996). A dual-space model of interactively deepening exploratory learning. *Int. J. Human-Computer Studies, 44*, 743-775.

Reportagem 1 (2008). *Alunos da EMEF Ernani Silva Bruno visualizam as matérias em 3D.* Retrieved from http://www.aprendebrasil.com.br/aluno-reporter/reportagem.asp?idARMateria=531

Resnick, M., Strimpel, O., & Galyean, T. (2008). *The Virtual Fishtank.* Retrieved November 12, 2008, from http://llk.media.mit.edu/projects/fishtank

Resnick, M. (2006). Computer as paintbrush: Technology, play, and the creative society. In D. Singer, R. Golikoff, & K. Hirsh-Pasek (Eds.), *Play = Learning: How play motivates and enhances children's cognitive and social-emotional growth.* New York: Oxford University Press. Retrieved November 12, 2008, from http://web.media.mit.edu/~mres/papers/playlearn-handout.pdf

Resnick, M. (2007). *Sowing the seeds for a more creative society. Learning and leading with technology.* Retrieved November 22, 2008, from http://web.media.mit.edu/~mres/papers/Learning-Leading-final.pdf

Resnick, M., (2002). Rethinking learning in the digital age. In G. Kirkman (Ed.), *The global information technology report: Readiness for the networked world.* New York: Oxford University Press. Retrieved January 13, 2009, from http://llk.media.mit.edu/papers/mres-wef.pdf

Revista Mente, Cérebro & Filosofia. (2007). Fundamentos para compreensão contemporânea da psique. In L.H.A de Souza (Ed.), *Dissertação cogito e temporalidade em sartre.* Universidade Federal do Paraná: Edição nº 5.

Riva, G., (2005). The psychology of ambient intelligence: activity, situation and Presence. In G. Riva (Ed.), *Ambient intelligence: The evolution of technology, communication and cognition towards the future of human-computer interaction.* Milan, Italy: IOS Press. Retrieved December 5, 2008, from http://www.emergingcommunication.com/volume6.html

Roehl, B., Couch, J., Reed-Ballereich, C., Rohaly, T., & Brown, A. J. (1997). *Late night with VRML V2.0 with Java.* ZD Press.

Rossi, G., Pastor, O., Schwabe, D., & Olsina, L. (2008). *Introduction.* In G. Rossi, O. Pastor, D. Schwabe, & L. Olsina (Eds.), *Web engineering: Modeling and implementing Web applications* (pp. 3-5). UK: Springer.

Roussos, M., Johnson, A., Leigh, J., Vasilakis, C., Barnes, C., & Moher, T., (1997). The NICE project: Narrative, immersive, constructionist/collaborative environments for learning in virtual reality. *In Proceedings of ED-MEDIA/ED-TELECOM 1997* (pp. 917-922). Retrieved from http://www.evl.uic.edu/tile/NICE/NICE/PAPERS/EDMEDIA/edmedia.paper.html

Rueda, M. de los A. & D'Angelo, D. (1999). *Visual arts and communication* (pp. 10-13). Argentina: Richmond Publishing.

Rusk, N., Resnick, M., Berg, R., & Pezalla-Granlund, M. (2008). New pathways into robotics: Strategies for broadening participation. *Journal of Science Education and Technology.* Retrieved November 12, 2008, from http://web.media.mit.edu/~mres/papers/NewPathwaysRoboticsLLK.pdf

Russell, S. & Norvig, P., (2003). *Artificial intelligence: A modern approach* (pp. 649-711). US: Prentice Hall.

Sancho, J. M. (2006). De tecnologias da informação e comunicação a recursos educativos. In J.M. Sancho, F. Hernández (Eds.), *Tecnologias para transformar a educação* (pp. 15-39). Valério Campos, Brasil: Artmed.

Schnabel, M.A., Wang, X.Y., Seichter, H., & Kvan, T. (2008). Touching the untouchables: Virtual-, augmented- and reality. In *Proceedings of Conference on Computer-Aided Architectural Design Research in Asia.* CAADRIA 2008, Chiang Mai, Thailand. Retrieved November 12, 2008, from http://www.hitlabnz.org/publications/2008-TouchingTheUntouchablesVirtual-Augmented-AndReality.pdf

Schroeder, W., Martin, K. & Loresen, B., (1998). *The visualisation toolkit* (2nd ed., pp. 35-39, 471-494). US: Prentice Hall PTR.

Scratch. (2009). Retrieved January 11, 2009, from http://scratch.mit.edu/

Sen, A. (2000). *Desenvolvimento como liberdade* (L.T. Motta, Trans.). Brasil: Companhia das Letras.

Senge, P., Scharmer, C. O., Jaworski, J., & Flowers, B. S. (2007). *Presença: Propósito humano e o campo do futuro* (G.C.C. de Sousa, Trans.) (pp. 86-104). Brasil: Cultrix.

Silva, L. I. L., Haddad, F. & Nicolelis, M. A. L. (2008). Brazilian *option for science education, Opinion/Forum.* Retrieved February 15, 2009, from http://www.nicolelislab.net/Papers/Editorial_SCIAM_FINAL_Pag34[1].pdf

Silveira, R. M., (2007). Laptop de US$ 100 promete causar uma revolução na educação no Brasil. *Reportagem publicada originalmente nas páginas II e III do Poder Executivo do Diário Oficial do Estado de SP do dia 12/09/2007.* Retrieved January 11, 2009, from http://www.rogeriosilveira.jor.br/reportagem2007_09_12_laptop_100dolares_lsiusp.php

Simone (2009). *Bolg da professora Simone.* Retrieved February 16, 2009, from http://simone-poesia.blogspot.com/

Singer, P., (2002a). *Introdução à economia solidária* (pp. 110-113). Brasil: Fundação Perseu Abramo.

Singer, P. (2002b) *A educação como elemento de transformação econômica, Portal do Sesc.* Retrieved January 11, 2009, from http://www.sescsp.org.br/sesc/conferencias_new/subindex.cfm?Referencia=166&ParamEnd=5

Singer, P. (2002c). *Debate com o professor Paul Singer Perguntas dos participantes após conferência do professor Paul Singer, com coordenação de José Pascoal Vaz.* Retrieved January 11, 2009, from http://www.sescsp.org.br/sesc/conferencias_new/subindex.cfm?Referencia=166&ParamEnd=5

Sherman, W. R., & Craig, A. B., (2003). *Understanding virtual reality: Interface, application and design.* US: Morgan Kaufman.

Soares, C. (2008). *Building a future on science.* Retrieved February 15, 2009, from http://www.nicolelislab.net/Papers/Building%20a%20Future%20on%20Science.pdf

Squeak. (2009). Retrieved January 11, 2009, from http://www.squeak.org/

Stanek, W., (1996). *HTML, JAVA, CGI, VRML, SGML Web publishing unleashed* (pp. 9-144). US: Sams Net.

Tan, J., (2008). Motivations and students' perceptions of learning: an empirical study of blogs. In *Proceedings of the IADIS Multi Conference on Computer Science and Information Systems* (MCCSIS 2008) (pp. 10-17). Amsterdam, The Netherlands.

Tan, K., Lewis, E., Avis, N. & Withers, P., (2008). Understanding of materials science to school children. In *Educators Paper (abstracts), Siggraph 2008.* Retrieved November 12, 2008, from http://www.siggraph.org/asia2008/attendees/edu/11.php

Tannenbaum, R. S. (1998). *Theoretical foundations of multimedia.* US: Computer Science Press.

Te'eni, D., Carey, J., & Zhang, P. (2007). *Human, computer interaction: Developing effective organizational information systems.* US: John Wiley & Sons.

The Institutes for the Achievement of Human Potential (2009). Retrieved January 9, 2009, from http://www.iahp.org/

UTHM. (2009). *Faculty of Mechanical and Manufacturing Engineering.* Retrieved January 11, 2009, from http://fkmp.uthm.edu.my/index.php?option=com_content&task=view&id=179&Itemid=295

Venâncio, V., Franco, J. F., Correa, A. G. D., Zuffo, M. K., & Lopes, R. D. (in press). Golden material 3D: An interactive decimal numerical system for children. In *Proceedings of 9th WCCE · IFIP World Conference on Computers in Education.* Bento Gonçalves, Brazil. Retrieved April 11, 2009, from http://www.wcce2009.org/program.html#program

Vigotski, L. S. (2007). *A formação social da mente* (7th Ed., pp. 87-105). Brasil: Martins Fontes.

Visual modularity. (2009). Retrieved January 13, 2009, from http://en.wikipedia.org/wiki/Visual_modularity

VRML Sourcebook V2.0 on-line examples (2008). Retrieved November 12, 2008, from http://www.wiley.com/legacy/compbooks/vrml2sbk/cover/cover.htm

VRML Wikipedia definition. (2008). Retrieved November 12, 2008, from http://en.wikipedia.org/wiki/VRML

Wands, B. (2006). *Art of the digital age.* UK: Thames & Hudson.

Warner-Rogers, J., & Reed, J., (2008). A clinician's guide to child neuropsychological assessement and formulation. In J. Warner-Rogers & J. Reed (Eds.), *Child neuropsychology: Concepts, theory and practice* (pp. 432-449). Singapore: Wiley-Blackwell.

Web3D consortium. (2008). Retrieved November 12, 2008, from http://www.web3d.org/

Wellington. (2009). Retrieved February 16, 2009, from http://wellingtonlorddemon.blogspot.com/

Wenger, P., & Goldin, D. (2006). Principles of problem solving. *Communications of ACM, 49*(7), 27-29.

Wikipedia solidarity economy, (2008). Retrieved November 12, 2008, from http://en.wikipedia.org/wiki/Solidarity_economy

Wikipedia Augmented Reality definition, (2008). Retrieved November 12, 2008, from http://en.wikipedia.org/wiki/Augmented_reality

Wikipedia Institutes for Achievement of Human Potential (2009). Retrieved January 11, 2009, from http://en.wikipedia.org/wiki/The_Institutes_for_the_Achievement_of_Human_Potential

Wikipedia Data mining. (2008). Retrieved November 12, 2008, from http://en.wikipedia.org/wiki/Data_mining

Wikipedia Feuerstein. (2008). Retrieved November 12, 2008, from http://en.wikipedia.org/wiki/Reuven_Feuerstein

Wikipedia Scripting_languages. (2008). Retrieved January 11, 2009, from http://en.wikipedia.org/wiki/Scripting_languages

Wikipedia Synapse. (2009). Retrieved January 11, 2009, from http://en.wikipedia.org/wiki/Chemical_synapse

Wikipedia Virtual Reality definition. (2008). Retrieved November 12, 2008, from http://en.wikipedia.org/wiki/Virtual_reality

Wikipedia Waltz with Bashir. (2009). Retrieved April 9, 2009, from http://en.wikipedia.org/wiki/Waltz_with_Bashir

Wing, J. M. (2006). Computational thinking. *Communications of the ACM, 49*(3). Retrieved November 12, 2008, from http://www.cs.cmu.edu/afs/cs/usr/wing/www/publications/Wing06.pdf

Winkler, T., Reimann, D., Herczeg, M., & Hopel, I. (2003). Creating digital augmented multisensual learning spaces. In *Mensch & Computer 2003: Interaktion in Bewgung. Stuttigart: B.G. Teubner* (pp. 307-316). Retrieved November 12, 2008, from http://mc.informatik.uni-hamburg.de/konferenzbaende/mc2003/konferenzband/muc2003-30-winkler.pdf

X3D Working Group. (2008) Retrieved November 12, 2008, from http://www.web3d.org/x3d-earth/

X3D Earth Implementation Workshop. (2008). Retrieved January 12, 2009, from http://www.

web3d.org/x3d/publiclists/x3dpublic_list_archives/0802/pdfIlG2Re5un9.pdf

Yamamoto, C. C. (2009). *Does learning a musical instrument help make your child smarter?* Retrieved January 12, 2009, from http://www.honoluluadvertiser.com/article/20090107/GETPUBLISHED/901060366/-1/sportsfront

YouTube, (2009). *Modern times.* Retrieved March 21, 2009, from http://www.youtube.com/results?search_type=&search_query=modern+times&aq=f

YouTube Estrelas. (2009). Retrieved March 21, 2009, from http://www.youtube.com/watch?v=UXOMw_Y1V-4

Zakour, J., Foust, J., & Kerven, D., (1997). *HTML How-To.* US: Waite Group Press.

Zhang, X., Mostow, J., & Beck, J. E. (2007, July 9). All in the (word) family: Using learning decomposition to estimate transfer between skills in a Reading Tutor that listens. In *AIED2007 Educational Data Mining Workshop*, Marina del Rey, CA. Retrieved November 12, 2008, from http://www.cs.cmu.edu/~listen/pdfs/AIED2007_EDM_Zhang_ld_transfer.pdf

Zuffo, M. K., (2001). *A convergência da realidade virtual e internet avançada em novos paradigmas de TV digital interativa.* Tese de Livre Docência. Retrieved November 23, 2008, from http://www.lsi.usp.br/~mkzuffo/repositorio/producao/teses%20e%20dissertacoes/Tese_Livre_Docencia_Marcelo_Zuffo.pdf

Section IV
Collaborative Learning and Pedagogical Approaches in Web-Based Environments

Chapter XV
The Impact of Individual Differences on Social Communication Pattern in Online Learning

Robert Z. Zheng
University of Utah, USA

Jill A. Flygare
University of Utah, USA

Laura B. Dahl
University of Utah, USA

Richard R. Hoffman
University of Utah, USA

ABSTRACT

This chapter describes the college students' online social communication patterns and behavior with a focus on the impact of individual differences on learners' online communication. The study consisted of 27 college students who engaged in an online discussion over a period of fourteen weeks as part of requirements in an undergraduate educational technology course. The findings indicated that cognitive styles such as field dependence and field independence played a critical role in forming learners' online social communication. Based on social compensation theory and Witkin et al.'s theory of individual differences, the authors claimed that effective individual communication in an online community can be fostered through creating learning support, taking into considerations factors like cognitive styles, complementary personality, interest and motivation in the process of design. Suggestions for future online learning are made with an emphasis on creating an effective online community for learning.

INTRODUCTION

As an important aspect in online learning, online social communication has drawn attention of educators and researchers (Willing, 2007; Zheng & Ferris, 2007). With the increasing use of Web course tools (e.g., WebCT, Blackboard, Moodle, etc.), particularly the availability of social communication function in such tools as asynchronous and synchronous communication, educators and researchers have become interested in investigating variables and factors that influence learners' socially engaged activities in online learning (Cook & Smith, 2004; Weller, 2007). Following this line of research, researchers have identified social factors (see Dietz-Uhler & Bishop-Clark, 2005; McKenna, Green, & Gleason, 2002; Peter, Valkenburg, & Schouten, 2006; Sheeks & Birchmeier, 2007; Valkenburg & Peter, 2007) and individual factors (Anolli, Villani & Riva, 2005; Chak & Leung, 2004; Johnson & Johnson, 2006; Madell & Muncer, 2007) that have pronounced impact on learners' social communication and behavior in online learning. While there is a plethora of literature pertinent to the social and individual factors that influence online learning, little research has been done to explore learners' social communication patterns in online learning environment, particularly how individual factors such as cognitive styles affect the way learners communicate in web-based learning.

Research indicates that understanding learners' online social communication and behavior is crucial in successfully implementing effective online instructional strategies such as collaboration, group work, etc. (Johnson & Johnson, 2006; Weller, 2007). Online learning is substantiated through the activities of a virtual learning community. Since individual learners constitute the body of online learning communities, individual factors such as cognitive styles can play an important role in formulating the communication pattern and behavior of that community (Johnson & Johnson, 2006). This chapter offers a discussion on online learners' social communication patterns and behavior by (a) studying the differences between field dependent and field independent learners in online social communication; (b) identifying the correlation between cognitive styles and related factors in online learning including self-confidence, support, interest, motivation and so forth; and (c) analyzing learners' performance in online discussion. Discussion on research in online social communication and behavior will be made with guidelines for future studies.

COGNITIVE STYLES AND LEARNING

In the last half century learners' cognitive styles have been heavily studied; these studies encompass a wide range of topics: from brain hemisphere function (Samples, 1975; Springer & Deutch, 1985), to temperament (Gregorc, 1982), to impulsive/reflective cognitive tempo (Kagan, 1966), to field dependent and field independent theory (Witkin & Goodenough, 1977), just to name a few. In an early study Kirby (1979) provided a comprehensive summary of 19 cognitive styles and concluded that all learners learn differently. According to Chinien and Boutin (1992), cognitive styles refer to "the information processing habits representing the learners' typical mode of perceiving, thinking, problem solving, and remembering" (p. 303). They claimed that cognitive styles constitute important dimensions of individual differences among learners and have important implications for teaching and learning.

Differing from learning styles which describe the conditions (i.e., auditory, visual, haptic, etc.) under which we best learn, cognitive styles are about how we perceive and think (Lever-Duffy, McDonald, & Mizell, 2003). The construct of cognitive style has been considered as a consistent, stable variable in learning. Keefe (1982) stated that cognitive styles are "the cognitive, affective, and physiological traits that serve as relatively stable indicators of how learners perceive, interact with, and respond to the learning environment" (p. 1). This view is shared by Smith and Ragan (2005) who propose a framework of learners' characteristics in which cognitive styles are subsumed under the category of stable-differences. Unlike psychosocial factors and prior knowledge which change during learning, cognitive styles are comparatively stable with little change over time. Whereas sensory capacities bear similarities among humans, cognitive styles are marked by a wide spectrum of differences with respect to how people perceive and respond to their learning environment. Because of their dual nature of stability and difference, cognitive styles are considered to have "the most potential utility to instructional design" (Smith & Ragan, 2005, p. 62). Smith and Ragan point out that understanding cognitive styles is important because it not only provides insight into how individual learners learn but also sheds light on why differing learning occurs.

Riding and Read (1996) investigated the relationship between learners' cognitive styles and learning performance and found that learners' cognitive profiles were consistent with their preferences in learning. For example, wholist-imagers like to use pictures whereas verbalizers were more prone to writing. In social learning context, wholist-imagers displayed a tendency for group work whereas analytics, such as verbalizers, preferred individual work. Russell (1997) conducted a similar study and reported that learners' cognitive styles, along with other variables like age and attitude could significantly influence their performance. Ates and Cataloglu (2007) studied first year undergraduates majoring in mechanics and tried to determine if cognitive styles have an influence on learners' achievements and problem-solving skills. Interestingly, they found no significant correlation between cognitive styles and pre/post achievement scores. However, they noted that learners' problem-solving skills were statistically related to their *cognitive* style. With

the increasing presence of computers in teaching and learning, research on cognitive styles and learning has been extended to areas of computer assisted learning (CAL), hypermedia, and distance learning. Ford (2000) examined learners' information processing *styles* and strategies and their deep (transformational) and surface (reproductive) learning in an online environment. He found that the unique features of online learning such as anonymity, synchronous and asynchronous communication enable learners of various cognitive styles to process information differently, which consequently impact their ability to learn both at deep and surface levels. Chen (2002) evaluated the effects of cognitive styles on student-centered learning in a hypermedia program. The author noticed that differences in cognitive style can affect different learners' learning in hypermedia. For example, the flexibility of hypermedia learning environment, e.g., non-linear learning, facilitates positive learning for field-independent learners and impedes the performance of field-dependent learners who often take a passive approach in learning. Taken together, the above research demonstrates that individuals learn differently and their various cognitive styles may affect the way they learn. In addition, educational technology such as hypermedia and the Internet may mediate learners' cognitive styles which could result in differences among learners in terms of their approaches to learning.

As was discussed elsewhere in the chapter, cognitive styles refer to an individual's preferred and habitual approach to organizing and representing information. Within the area of cognitive styles, field dependence (FD) and field independence (FI) have emerged as one of the most widely studied dimensions with the broadest application to problems in education (Meng & Patty, 1991; Witkin & Goodenough, 1977). The following section will focus on the characteristics and function of FD and FI, followed by a discussion on instructional conditions related to FD and FI learning.

Field Dependence (FD) and Field Independence (FI)

Witkin and Goodenough (1977) defined field dependence and field independence as individuals' "tendencies to rely on self or field as primary referents" (p. 661). The word "field" can be a set of thoughts, ideas, or feelings. According to Witkin and Goodenough, people with field-dependent (FD) or field-independent (FI) cognitive styles are different in their interpersonal behavior, social skills, and information processing. FD people tend to make use of external social referents whereas FI people function with greater autonomy under such conditions. FD people are more attentive to social cues than are FI people. As a result, FD people show more interest in others, prefer to be physically close to people, and are emotionally more open, and gravitate toward social situations. In contrast, FI people are characterized by an impersonal orientation, less interested in others, show physical and psychological distancing from people, and prefer non-social situations (Ikegulu & Ikegulu, 1999; Liu & Reed, 1994; Witkin, Moore, Goodenough, & Cox, 1977). The practical implications of FD and FI research have indicated that different learning styles among individuals bear direct impact upon their achievement performance (Zheng, Yang, Garcia, & McCadden, 2008). Many studies have shown that FI people tend to outperform FD people in various settings. In a study by Griffin and Franklin (1996), one hundred and forty-three subjects were identified as FI or FD based on their performance on the Group Embedded Figures Test (GEFT). The results of their study indicated FI students performed significantly better on course tests. The study also suggested that FI students had higher academic potential than their FD counterparts. This finding was echoed by Richards, Fajen, Sullivan, and Gillespie (1997) who conducted two experiments, one in listening and one in reading, in connection to FD/FI cognitive styles. They examined the relationships among signaling (structural cues), notetaking, and FD/FI styles in college students.

The results of both studies indicated that FI subjects seemed to use a tacit structure strategy, whereas FD subjects displayed structuring skills when notetaking. Along the same line, Danili and Reid (2004) studied 105 Greek pupils aged 15 to 16 and found that FI pupils were more organized and self-initiated than FD pupils in learning.

Instructional Conditions Related to FD and FI Learning

There is a concerted view among researchers and educators that instructional conditions should be identified to match the learning for FD and FI learners (Jonassen & Grabowski, 1993; Schmeck, 1988; Smith & Easterday, 1994). Witkin et al. (1977) point out that field dependence and field independence appear to affect many aspects of daily life including the ability to learn, particularly with regard to types of educational reinforcement needed to enhance learning, amount of structure required in an educational environment, cue salience, interaction between teachers and students, and so forth. One of the questions raised by Witkin et al. was whether teachers can adapt their teaching techniques to accommodate students with different cognitive styles. Related to this question is, what are the instructional conditions needed to support FD and FI learners to learn effectively and efficiently? Jonassen and Grabowski (1993) summarized the research on the implications of the style characteristics and came to the conclusion that the instructional conditions differ between FD learners and FI learners. While some instructional conditions support FD learners, they can become, at the same time, challenges to FI learners. Table 1 is a summary of the conditions that capitalize on the preferences of FD and FI learners and challenges to their respective counterparts.

To effectively utilize the instructional conditions so that FD and FI learners can maximally benefit from such learning, it is important to raise the awareness of cognitive style among learners. Perry (1994) pointed out that if there was

Table 1. Instructional conditions that capitalize on the preferences of and challenges to FD-I learners

Instructional Conditions Capitalized on the Preferences of FD Learners and Challenges to FI Learners	Instructional Conditions Capitalized on the Preferences of FI Learners and Challenges to FD Learners
•*Providing structural support with salient cues* •*Including an advance organizer* •*Including an outline or graphic organizer of the content* •*Giving clear directions and guidance in instruction* •*Giving prototype examples* •*Facilitating a synergetic, social learning environment* •*Providing timely and detailed feedback* •*Embedding questions throughout learning* •*Providing multiple cues including visual, oral, and auditory, etc.* •*Providing detailed steps for deductive or inductive instruction*	•*Providing abundant content resources and reference material to sort through* •*Employing inquiry and discovery methods* •*Including minimal guidance and direction* •*Providing independent, contract-based self-instruction* •*Facilitating an independent learning environment* •*Encouraging learners to self-initiate questions* •*Employing inductive methods for instruction and learning* •*Employing outlines, pattern notes, concept maps as instructional strategies for teaching and learning* •*Using theoretical elaboration sequences*

an understanding of cognitive/learning styles, cooperative arrangements could be made between individuals of different styles to possibly compensate for the deficiencies of one style. He also suggested that an appreciation of the diversities (i.e., different cognitive styles) was important in any educational environment. According to Perry, when we allow learners to understand how they learn, there is greater possibility for efficient and effective learning and teaching. To elaborate on the compensatory role between different cognitive styles, our discussion in the next section will introduce social compensation theory to illuminate how learners with different cognitive styles may interact within a social learning environment and how external conditions may facilitate socially compensatory behavior.

SOCIAL COMPENSATION THEORY

Social compensation theory can be traced back to early works done by Otto Kohler (1926, 1927 cited from Williams & Karau, 1991) who demonstrated with dyads or triads working on a conjunctive work, that group performance de-

pended on the relative individual performance of the group members. Kohler explored the group performance of members who showed moderate discrepancies in ability level and found that weaker members worked harder in groups than individually. Kohler explained that the most probable cause being that the weaker members tried to avoid the embarrassment of lowering the group product. Following Kohler's studies conducted some sixty years ago, Williams and Karau (1991) did several experiments to test the hypotheses that a group member will work harder in a group setting than individually if (a) the production of the public good is very important, (b) the task is addictive, (c) the individual perceives control over the production of the public good, and (d) the other group members are unable or unwilling to contribute to the production of the good. Their studies led to several important conclusions. First, when subjects were led to believe that their coworkers were unable or unwilling to contribute to the group product, subjects produced substantially more ideas when working in a group rather than individually. Second, social compensation was only likely to occur under conditions where a capable group member was able and willing to compensate for the weaker member(s) of the team. Similar findings were obtained by Stroebe, Diehl, & Abakoumkin (1996) who identified a social compensatory relationship between high and low ability members in the group. They argued that discrepancy among individual abilities created optimal conditions for mutual influence and resonance. On the one hand, the stronger member somehow motivated the weaker member to work harder while at the same time increasing his own performance. On the other, the weaker member was galvanized by the member responsibility and the urge to avoid the embarrassment of lowering the group product.

The early work on social compensation (Kohler, 1926, 1927 cited from Stroebe et al., 1996; Williams & Karau, 1991) focuses primarily on the relationship between individual abilities and group performance. For example, Kohler's studies (1926, 1927) explored the group social compensation behavior based on the differences between physical strength of weight lifters. That is, the stronger weight lifter appeared to be more willing to contribute to the group performance as he took upon himself as a social obligation to help improve the scores of his group. The similar pattern was found for the group brainstorm activity where the more able learners became actively involved in brainstorming when they realized that it was they, rather than the less able learners, who could make difference in group brainstorming (Williams & Karau, 1991). However, the early work did not explore the social compensation phenomenon from the perspective of learners' cognitive styles, which are considered by many to be crucial in understanding the dynamics of social compensatory behavior (Peter, Valkenburg, & Schouten, 2005; Valkenburg & Peter, 2007). With the increasing presence of the Internet, this line of research seems to be more important as social compensation and cognitive styles are related and intertwined to form the ground for the study of social online communication and behavior.

Social Compensation, Cognitive Styles and Online Communication

A significant body of work has attempted to describe the relationships between individual differences and adolescent online communication (Anolli et al., 2005; Chak & Leung, 2004; Madell & Muncer, 2007; Sheeks & Birchmeier, 2007). Researchers are particularly interested in finding out how personality traits such as introversion/ extroversion, neuroticism, and psychoticism would affect adolescents' behaviors in online communication (Anolli et al., 2005; Chak & Leung, 2004; Madell & Muncer, 2007). Research on introversion and extroversion is polarized in terms of the impact of each of the above personality traits on adolescent online communication. Some researchers argue that since extroverted people are "social, needing to have people to talk to, and disliking reading or studying by him or herself" (Bianchi & Phillips, 2005, p. 41), the Internet which has no time and geographic limitation thus becomes an ideal place for them to establish their social network. Researchers in this school (e.g., Amichai-Hamburger, 2002; Bianchi and Phillip, 2005; Valkenburg & Peter, 2007) support the rich-get-richer hypothesis that extroverted people may be compensated by online social environments that make them become more socially involved in online communication. They also note that extroverted people could become addicted to online communication due to the flexibility, ease of control, and multiple synchronous connections among participants (Madell & Muncer, 2007).

Contrary to the assumptions that the extroversion causes people to become addicted to the Internet communication, researchers (e.g., Chak & Leung, 2004; Widyanto & McMurran, 2004) who studied the relationship between introversion and online behaviors found that the Internet communication appeals to introverted people and the introversion may be the reason to cause people to become addicted to online chat. They argue that introverted people are usually socially shy and often have difficulty in developing relationships with others in a face-to-face setting, particularly when such relationship development is affected by the "gating features" when the individual perceives a self-defeating social inhibitor such as stuttering. Chak and Leung (2004) contend that because of the perceived control of online communication, introverted people are more likely to go to the Internet to meet their social and intimacy needs. With all the affordances of the Internet, that is, anonymity, flexibility, multiple interaction, and so forth, socially anxious or lonely people can be socially compensated by communicating online with others without being overly conscious about who they are or what they say, and at the same time feel that their self-image is safeguarded. This group supports the stimulation hypothesis, arguing that reduced visual and auditory cues in the Internet can alleviate the social anxiety that introverted people experience and *stimulate* them to develop positive relationships with others (Subrahmanyan, Smahel, & Greenfield, 2006; Tajfel, 1978).

As with the research of introvert and extrovert in online communication, studies on personality traits including psychoticism, neuroticism, and etc. have also drawn the attention of researchers. Psychoticism, according to Eysenck and Eysenck (1964), refers to people who are impulsive, hostile, and creative whereas neuroticism includes those who are shy, anxious, and depressed. Anolli et al. (2005) studied the impacts of neuroticism on individuals' online behavior and found a significant correlation between neuroticism and age in terms of online chatting, with similar findings for psychoticism. Conversely, studies by Bianchi and Phillips (2005) and Madell and Muncer (2007) found that neuroticism was negatively related to web usage such as online chat since neurotic people are often overly sensitive and would resist to sensitive talk posted anonymously (also see McKenna & Bargh, 2000). Both studies excluded neuroticism as a factor for influencing individuals' behaviors in online communication. Obviously,

research on online communication pertaining to cognitive styles is inconclusive. Evidence from recent research indicates that further study is needed to better understand the relationship between learners' online communication behavior and their cognitive styles (Peter et al., 2005).

Peter et al. (2005) studied online social communication and behavior. Drawing from a sample of 412 Dutch adolescents, the authors found that the motives of social compensation, along with entertainment and meeting with people, increased adolescents' online communication with strangers. Interestingly, they found no correlation between introversion and adolescents' tendency to talk, a finding that ran counter to the results obtained by Chak and Leung (2004) and Widyanto and McMurran (2004). So far, research on social compensation and cognitive styles in online communication has been limited to Eysenck and Eysenck's framework that focuses on psychoticism, neuroticism, introversion, and extroversion. Few studies have been conducted to explore the relationship between social compensation and FD/FI cognitive styles in online learning. Since FD/FI represent robust cognitive styles related to learning (Witkin et al., 1977), studies on how FD online learners are socially compensated by their counterparts and vice versa would provide important information about as well as new perspectives on learners' online social communication patterns and behavior, thus enabling instructional designers and educators to design and develop strategies and methods that are effective for online learning.

THE STUDY

To understand how FD/FI cognitive styles and other related variables influence learners' online social communication and behavior, and how FD/FI learners differ in their social communication, a study was conducted with the research questions formulated based on the above literature. The specific research questions pertaining to this study are:

1. Is there a difference in performance between FD and FI learners in online discussion?
2. Is there a correlation between cognitive style and related factors such as self-confidence, support, interest, and motivation?
3. Is there a difference between FD and FI learners in terms of postings?
4. Is there a difference between FD and FI learners in terms of computer skills and online chat experience?

Description of the Study

Twenty seven undergraduate students were recruited from a teaching education program in a research I university in the western part of the United States. Participants registered for non-online courses with an on-online component (WebCT) where the online discussion was part of regular course requirements. Participants were asked to (a) complete a demographic questionnaire that collects information about gender, age, etc. and (b) take the Group Embedded Figures Test (GEFT) which measures field dependent (FD) and field independent (FI) learners (Oltman, Raskin, & Witkin, 2003). They then joined in an online discussion forum and were assigned to seven discussion topics over a period of 14 weeks during which time period they (1) self-posted their own comments and (2) critiqued other participants' comments. At the end of the study participants were asked to take a survey of online discussion.

About 15 percent of the participants ($n = 4$) were males and 85 percent were females. A majority of them ($n = 20$) were under age 25 with two between the age of 26-35, two between 36-45, and one over 45. About 26 percent ($n = 7$) reported having excellent computer skills, 63 percent ($n = 17$) having good computer skills, and 11 percent ($n = 3$) having poor computer skills. With regard to online chat experience, 85 percent ($n = 23$) reported having been involved in online discussion, and 15 percent ($n = 4$) reported having no experience at all. Of 27 participants, 17 reported having home access, 2 having work access, and 8 having campus access.

Instrumentation

Group Embedded Figure Test (GEFT)

The GEFT was developed by Oltman et al. (2003). The test is designed to measure learners' perceptual ability. It consists of three sections with second and third sections being counted as valid GEFT test scores. The first section is not scored but can be used as reference for the final GEFT scores. Participants were provided with a sample form sheet that has eight sample figures. They were required to identify the embedded figure in the test item that matches one of the figures in the sample form. It took about 12 minutes to complete the entire test. The total possible score for the test is 18 points. A moderate-to-high reliability was reported for college students with a Cronbach alpha of .85 and .79 for males and females respectively.

Online Discussion Study Survey (ODSS)

The survey was developed by the first author based on social cognitive theories (Bandura, 1993); motivation (Keller, 1987); and social compensation (Peter et al., 2005; Valkenburg & Peter, 2007). The instrument contain ten items with items 1 and 10 probing into students' motivation, 3 and 9 for values, 5 and 6 for social compensation, 2 for self-confidence, and 4 for social support. The instrument was reviewed by a panel of experts who have used online social communication tools in their instruction. Feedback from the panel members was carefully considered to further revise the survey. The survey uses a 5-point

Figure 1. *Scree plot for factors related to ODSS*

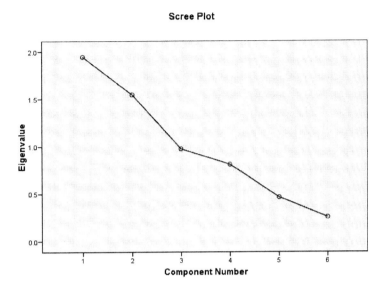

Likert scale with *Strongly disagree/Very low* = 1 and *Strongly agree/Very high* = 5 (Appendix I). The factor analysis was conducted to identify the factors related to ODSS. Figure 1 shows the scree plot of six factors. Three valid factors were extracted based on the criteria of (1) factor loading greater .40 (Hair, Anderson, Tatham, & Black, 1998) and (2) eigenvalue greater than 1. The factors and variances are presented in Table 2. The instrument reports a medium inter-item reliability with Cronbach Alpha = .79.

Methodology

Several methods were employed pertaining to the research questions previously proposed. They include social network analysis (SNA), correlation and t-test analyses.

Social Network Analysis

According to Willging (2007), SNA is widely used to analyze participation, interaction, and learning in asynchronous online discussions. It provided important applications for organizational behavior, inter-organizational relations, social support, and so forth. Although traditional statistical approach has been predominately used to analyze the behavior of online performance and learning, such an approach often emphasizes linear causal relationship while overlooking the structural characteristics of the interactions. SNA has been applied to a variety of problems, and they have been successful in uncovering relationships not seen with any other traditional methods.

As was mentioned above, SNA tried to unveil the patterns of people's behavioral interaction. SNA measures many structural characteristics of the network such as the existence of subgroups, the relative importance of individuals which are called actors or nodes, and the strength of the links between actors or nodes (Wasserman & Faust, 1994; Willging, 2007). While providing a complete treatment of the SNA methodology is out of the reach of this chapter, some basic definitions are needed to conceptualize the SNA. The following discussion focuses on key concepts pertinent to SNA (See Appendix II for a SNA vocabulary list).

Table 2. Factors and variances related to ODSS

	Component					
	1	2	3	4	5	6
Self-confidence	.767	-.468	.205	-.049	-.342	.176
Support	.760	.364	-.443	-.004	-.177	-.249
Motivation	.125	.766	.112	.598	-.060	.154
Interest	.450	-.025	.856	.117	.144	-.173
Complementary Personality	.439	.594	.094	-.634	.160	.133
Value	.710	-.371	-.368	.270	.380	.076
Eigenvalue	1.874	1.464	.965	.784	.492	.421
% of Variance	31.238	24.395	16.090	13.073	8.195	7.009

Components of SNA. The component of SNA consists of a set of nodes and arcs, a sociogram, and a sociomatrix. The nodes which are otherwise called actors can be persons, organizations, or groups. The arcs are the relationships between the nodes. Their strength is measured by the distance between the nodes. The shorter the distance is between the nodes, the stronger the relationship will be. The sociogram is actually a graphic that visually represents the relationships among the nodes. It provides a diagram where researchers can analyze the patterns of group behavior. Finally, the sociomatrix or adjacency matrix delineates the relationship between nodes through a mathematical representation in the form of a matrix (Hanneman & Riddle, 2005). Figure 2 provides an example of SNA in which the relationships between nodes and arcs are presented in a sociogram.

Figure 2 shows two subgroups with dark nodes representing group A and light nodes representing group B. The relationships among the nodes are defined by the arcs (i.e., links). Group B shows a close relationship among the individuals due to the immediate distance among the nodes. In contrast, individuals in group A are less closely connected due to the remote distance among the nodes. Individual A4 plays a mediating role that connects group A and group B.

Density, centrality, and cohesion. In analyzing group social interaction the concepts of density,

centrality, and cohesion are critical in explaining how individuals respond and react to people around them. The density of interaction in a social network means the proportion of all possible ties that are actually present. It is calculated as the sum of ties divided by the number of possible ties. Hanneman and Riddle (2005) noted that density is closely related to the power in a network system. According to Hanneman and Riddle (2005), the power is defined as the number of incoming and outgoing ties of the nodes, which is also known as the communication power among nodes. In a system that has low density, usually not much power can be exerted. Conversely, in high density systems there is a potential for greater power.

The concept of centrality describes how a particular focal node is related to other nodes. This is defined in terms of in- and out-degree of a node. That is, a node that has many ties may have access to (out-degree), and be accessed by other nodes (in-degree) in the network. For example, both A4 and B5 in Figure 1 have high in- and out-degree and are thus considered influential nodes. So, a very simple, but often very effective measure of a node's centrality and power potential is its in- and out-degree (Willging, 2007). Of particular interest to researchers is the betweenness of a node. That is, the intermediatory role that a node plays between groups of points. For example, A4 has a

Figure 2. Sample of sociogram representing nodes and arcs

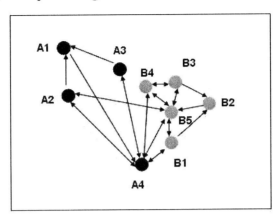

high level of betweenness. If B1 wants to access A2 or A3, it has to go through A4.

The concept of cohesion refers to the homogeneity of the subgroups or network. It is measured by the density, reciprocity, and Geodesic distances among the nodes (Hanneman & Riddle, 2005). The reciprocity ranges from 0 to 1, with 0 indicating minimum reciprocity and 1 maximum reciprocity. In a social network high symmetric reciprocity among the nodes indicates high degree of cohesiveness among the participants. Finally, the Geodesic distance is indexed by a distance-based cohesion ("compactness") which ranges between 0 and 1 with larger values showing greater cohesiveness.

Data Scoring and Encoding

For the purpose of t-test analyses behavioral data were obtained which included learners' performance in both online postings: self-posting and critiquing. They were scored by two researchers using a rubric with numeric values ranging from 1 = *poor performance* to 5 = *excellent performance*. The data were used to analyze participants' performance in online discussion.

Next, the SNA data encoding was performed. The encoding process focused on the presence of critiquing postings. For example, if participant A critiques participants B and C's viewpoints, he/she

gets one point for each. If participant B critiques participant C but not A, he/she gets only one point. Then each participant was matched with his/her cognitive profile based on the results of GEFT test. The data were entered in the UCINET software (Borgatti, Everett, & Freeman, 2002) to create a matrix for social network analysis.

Results and Analysis

Records of online asynchronous discussions which were kept and archived in an online learning system (WebCT) were retrieved by the researchers for data analysis. A total of 541 online discussion messages were retrieved which were generated over a period of 14 weeks. The data were coded with a combination of letters and numbers to protect the anonymity of participants.

Specifically, the researchers were interested in finding out how FD and FI participants differed in online communication. To answer the above question, the SNA was employed to analyze the participants' behavior in online communication.

Results of SNA

The SNA analysis was performed with the UCI-NET software (Borgatti, Everett, & Freeman,

Table 3. Sociomatrix for FD and FI online participants

```
NETWORK BLOCK DENSITIES
-----------------------------------------------------------------------
Method:                     Average
Input dataset:              N:\Cog-emotion-web\revision\online

                        1 1 1 1 1 1 1 1 1 1 2 2 2 2 2 2
              1 2 3 4 5 6 7 8 9 0 1 2 3 4 5 6 7 8 9 0 1 2 3 4 5
              F F F F F F F F F F F F F F F F F F F F F F F F F
          ---------------------------------------------------------
     1 FI1  | 1 1 1 1   1 1   1   1   1 1 1 1   1   1   1     1 |
     2 FI2  | 1 1   1   1 1   1   1   1   1 1           1 1   1 |
     3 FD1  |     1       1     1 1   1     1     1         1 1 |
     4 FI3  |       1 1 1 1             1   1                   |
     5 FD2  | 1 1   1 1 1 1     1 1         1   1               |
     6 FD3  | 1 1   1 1 1 1     1 1         1   1               |
     7 FI4  |       1 1 1 1             1   1                   |
     8 FD4  | 1 1 1             1   1       1     1         1   |
     9 FI5  |     1       1     1   1 1 1 1             1 1   1 |
    10 FI6  |     1       1             1   1                   |
    11 FI7  |   1         1     1 1         1     1         1 1 |
    12 FD5  |   1         1     1 1   1     1     1         1 1 |
    13 FI8  | 1 1     1 1           1   1         1   1 1 1   1 |
    14 FI9  |   1       1   1       1       1     1   1     1 1 |
    15 FI10 |                   1   1       1     1   1 1 1     |
    16 FD6  | 1 1   1 1 1 1     1 1         1   1               |
    17 FD7  | 1 1 1             1   1 1     1     1         1 1 |
    18 FD8  |           1                 1   1                 |
    19 FI11 | 1 1       1 1         1   1     1     1 1 1       |
    20 FI12 |   1         1     1 1   1     1                 1 1 |
    21 FD9  | 1 1             1             1       1 1 1 1     |
    22 FI13 |                 1             1     1 1 1 1       |
    23 FD10 | 1 1             1   1         1       1 1 1 1     |
    24 FD11 |   1         1     1 1         1     1         1 1 |
    25 FI14 |     1 1 1       1       1     1     1         1   |
          ---------------------------------------------------------
```

Reduced BlockMatrix

```
          1
        -----
    1   0.333
```

Use DICHOTOMIZE procedure to get binary image matrix.
Reduced blockmodels saved as dataset Blocked
Actor-by-actor pre-image matrix saved as dataset PreImage

Figure 3. Sociogram for FD and FI online participants

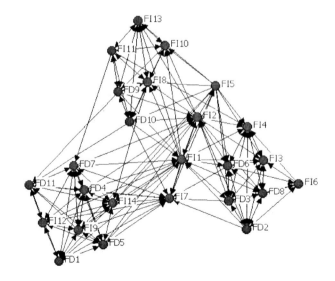

2002). A sociomatrix is presented in Table 3 which delineates the social communication relationships between FD and FI learners in an asynchronous online forum. Based on the above results, a sociogram was created to display the relationship among members in online social community. Three social groups were formed as the result of the SNA analysis. Figure 3 indicates that FD and FI learners were distinctly separated into three groups generated by the UCINET software based on the input data. The sociogram identified focal actors (e.g., FI14, FI9, FI8, FI1, FI2, FI3, FI4, FD4, and FD6) who played a prominent role in organizing the group and implementing the online discussion, which was evidenced by the number of incoming and outgoing ties in the social groups.

Next, analyses on density, centrality, and cohesion of participants' online social communication were performed. Results showed a high degree of density (=.72), which means 72% of all possible ties are present. The analysis of geodesic distance revealed a moderate distance-based cohesion (= .609) which showed moderate-high cohesiveness among the members in the social network. The results showed that FI participants in general played a leading role in online social communication when online discussion involved critiquing and challenging others. In contrast, FD participants seemed to rely on the initiation of FI participants while engaging in online discussion (see Figure 3).

The tests of centrality, reciprocity, closeness (in- and out-closeness) and betweenness were conducted to explore the strength of social communication among the members. The Freeman's degree centrality analysis reported a mean degree of 10.4 (SD = 3.262). Results showed that focal

Table 4. Centrality, reciprocity, closeness, and betweenness of social communication among online participants

	Degree	Symmetric reciprocity	incloseness	outcloseness	betweenness
FI14	21.000	0.890	71.538	57.268	55.252
FI9	18.000	0.778	70.533	50.233	42.743
FI8	15.000	0.801	70.000	51.475	45.998
FI1	14.000	0.752	61.538	59.833	58.817
FI2	14.000	0.821	56.762	66.894	67.046
FI3	13.000	0.700	67.143	50.248	53.550
FI4	13.000	0.831	62.158	40.419	46.368
FI10	12.000	0.652	68.588	42.523	31.010
FI12	11.000	0.750	71.538	41.963	33.978
FD4	11.000	0.735	55.338	34.384	45.143
FD6	10.000	0.883	63.158	51.201	49.548
FI11	10.000	0.581	57.143	61.064	35.856
FI7	10.000	0.864	60.588	60.198	52.547
FI6	10.000	0.542	67.588	40.552	25.230
FI13	10.000	0.521	68.538	42.257	21.176
FD7	9.000	0.768	58.537	37.546	44.598
FD3	9.000	0.654	70.588	35.870	29.548
FD8	9.000	0.734	61.538	41.402	20.303
FI5	8.000	0.544	61.538	58.421	35.912
FD5	8.000	0.765	68.571	37.565	27.250
FD9	8.000	0.687	64.865	35.148	15.300
FD11	8.000	0.641	61.538	40.229	9.336
FD10	7.000	0.648	45.283	38.030	27.001
FD1	7.000	0.458	45.283	41.987	1.987
FD2	6.000	0.434	50.000	46.290	17.241

actors (e.g., FI14, FI9, FI8, FI1, FI2, FI3, FI4, FD4, and FD6) played a central role in organizing and keeping the members together in online discussion (see Table 4). They were prominent actors to whom many other actors sought to direct ties. The finding is further supported by the high reciprocity between the focal actors and their constituent members. As indicated, high reciprocity means high degree of cohesiveness among the participants.

To find out how participants responded to each other in online communication, the test of closeness was run which identified the incoming and outgoing ties of the participants. There was a consistency across the centrality, reciprocity, closeness (in-closeness and out-closeness) for the FI participants. That is, FI participants (e.g., FI14, FI9, FI8, FI1, FI2, and FI3) who scored high on centrality and reciprocity also scored high on closeness. They received more incoming and outgoing ties in social communication than did FD participants (see Table 4). However, FD participants (e.g., FD4 and FD6) who scored high on in-closeness did not score as high on out-closeness. This suggests that FD participants who did well on receiving incoming ties failed to reach out successfully to others. In this study both FD and FI participants received the same support in online discussion. However, due to their heavy reliance on external conditions/support, FD students needed more support than did their counterparts. Thus, it is possible that inadequate support led FD participants to fail to reach out to other participants in online communication. Finally, the results of betweenness indicated that FI participants played a critical role in mediating the group discussions. This is shown in Figure 3 in which FI1, FI2, FI5, and FI7 mediated between the participants from three discussion groups.

Correlation Analysis

To answer research question two, a correlation analysis was performed with SPSS version 14.0.

The following variables were entered for the correlation analysis. They are self-confidence, personal support, motivation, interest, complementary personality, and FDFI type. The results showed that motivation was significantly correlated with personal support ($r = .584, p < .01$), interest was significantly correlated with personal support ($r = .440, p < .05$) and motivation ($r = .530, p < .01$), complementary personality was significantly correlated with interest ($r = .445, p < .05$) and motivation ($r = .592, p < .01$), and value was significantly correlated with personal support ($r = .564, p < .01$), motivation ($r = .793, p < .01$), interest ($r = .487, p < .05$) and complementary personality ($r = .432, p < .05$). The correlations of FDFI with other variables were not significant. However, a marginal significant correlation was observed between FDFI and complementary personality ($r = .361, p = .058$) (Table 5). This suggests that FD and FI learners perceived complementary personality as a contributing factor to the formation of online social community, which is consistent with the social compensation theory that posits people with different personalities and interests tend to draw toward each other as a gesture of social compensation. The finding is supported by the social communication pattern generated by the above SNA analyses where people with opposite cognitive styles worked closely together in online learning environment (see Figure 3).

t-Test Analyses

Research question three asked whether there was a difference in performance between FD and FI learners with regard to online postings. The independent variable which consists of two levels, that is, FD and FI learners was created based on the results of the GEFT test. The dependent variables which included self-posting and critiquing were obtained based on participants' performance scores. A t test was conducted. The means and standard deviations for online postings are reported as follows (see Table 6).

Table 5. Correlation analysis

	1	2	3	4	5	6	7
Self-confidence	-						
Personal Support	-	-					
Motivation	-	**	-				
Interest	-	*	**	-			
Complementary Personality	-	-	*	**	-		
Value	-	**	**	*	*	-	
FD-I	-	-	-	-	-	-	-

** Correlation is significant at 0.01 level (2-tailed)
* Correction is significant at 0.05 level (2-tailed)

Table 6. Descriptive Statistics for FD and FI Learners in self-posting and critiquing messages

	Field Type	Postings						
		1	2	3	4	5	6	7
Self Posting	**FD**	4.45 (1.50)	4.63 (0.67)	4.91 (0.30)	5.00 (0.94)	3.90 (1.04)	4.18 (1.40)	4.09 (1.57)
	FI	4.44 (0.36)	4.06 (0.34)	4.56 (0.26)	4.62 (0.25)	3.62 (0.70)	3.73 (1.83)	4.13 (1.72)
Critiquing	**FD**	2.45 (1.25)	2.68 (1.47)	2.68 (0.78)	2.86 (1.45)	1.95 (1.21)	2.40 (1.60)	2.18 (1.48)
	FI	2.93 (0.26)	2.75 (0.50)	3.31 (0.11)	3.06 (0.27)	2.25 (0.65)	1.70 (1.42)	2.63 (1.67)

Figure 4. FD and FI learners' performance chart

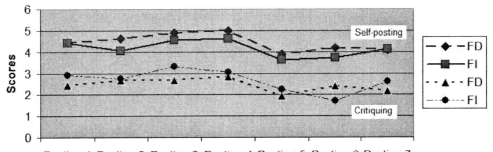

Given the small sample size, the results of *t* test showed no significant difference between FD and FI learners in self-posting ($t(25) = .875$, $p = .441$) and critiquing ($t(25) = -.438$, $p = .666$). However, there was an interesting trend that differentiated FD learners from FI learners in terms of self-posting and critiquing others' messages. Figure 4 demonstrates that FD learners in general outperformed FI learners in self-posting, but didn't perform as well in critiquing. This finding is aligned with the literature that FD learners usually do well in a learning that provides structural support with salient cues. In self-posting, learning is structured around the topics. Therefore, FD learners were able to pick up the cues more easily in their learning. However, in critiquing, learning is dependent on learners' abilities to discern differences in viewpoints, organize relevant resources and develop abstract critical thinking skills. Simply providing a structure with topics will not suffice as FD learners need clear directions and guidance in instruction (Jonassen & Grabowski, 1993; Perry, 1994).

Research question 4 probes into the differences between FD and FI participants in terms of their computer skills and online chat experience. The t-test results revealed a significant difference between FD and FI participants for computer skills (t (25) = 2.714, p = .012) and a marginal significance for online chat experience (t (25) = -2.010, p = .055).

DISCUSSIONS AND CONCLUSION

Different from traditional learning environment, online learning can become quite challenging to both instructors and learners, partly because the learning cues that are observable in traditional classroom become non-existent in online learning, and partly because people often take with them the same traditional teaching and learning paradigms or even the same mentality as they move onto online environment (Zheng, 2006; Zheng & Ferris, 2007). The results of this study indicate that online learning should be designed differently from traditional learning. The following discussion will therefore focus on the important aspects of online instructional design with regard to cognitive styles, learning support, and critical factors related to the success of online learning.

Role of Cognitive Styles in Online Learning

The findings of the study show that cognitive styles can significantly impact learners' social communication and behavior in learning. The SNA revealed a consistent pattern across three online discussion groups where FD and FI learners collaborated in online learning (see Figure 3). According to social compensation theory, discrepancy among individual abilities created optimal conditions for mutual influence and resonance (Stroebe et al., 1996). Research in online communication supports the above conclusion, showing a strong correlation between individual differences and patterns of communication in an online environment (Chak & Leung, 2004; Widyanto & McMurran, 2004).

There is a difference between FD and FI learners with respect to their roles in online community. It appears that FI learners were more active in initiating discussions and had more in- and out-connections among group members. This is especially true when learning involved critiquing others' viewpoints, in which critical thinking skills were demanded. Based on the findings of the study, it is suggested that the design of online instruction should put cognitive styles in perspective, particularly when the design involves developing and promoting high level thinking skills.

Learning Support for FD and FI Learners

When designing instruction to develop learners' critical thinking skills, it is essential that such instruction include adequate support for FD and FI learners. Results from the study showed that FD learners need clear instructional directions and salient cues in learning. This is consistent with the literature pertinent to the instructional conditions for FD learners (Jonassen & Grabowski, 1993). The study found that the FD learners performed less well when they engaged in learning activities that required them to critique others' messages than when they self-posted the messages (see Table 6 and Figure 4). The difference in FD learners' performances for two learning tasks was most likely due to (1) a change in the task demand, i.e., moving from posting messages to critiquing others' messages, and (2) a lack of support to match the task demand. For FD learners, providing support such as giving detailed steps, multiple cues, embedding questions, including an advance organizer, etc. would help them succeed in learning. Likewise, providing abundant content resources, employing inquiry and discovery methods, encouraging self-initiated questions, etc. would give FI learners the kind of support they need to be successful in online learning (Jonassen & Grabowski, 1993; Perry, 1994; Witkin & Goodenough, 1977).

Factors for Successful Online Learning

As discussed above, cognitive styles and learning support are important in online learning. However, based on the findings of the study, other factors like complementary personality, interest, motivation, support and value have shown to be significantly correlated in online learning (see Table 6). Factors like complementary personality, support and value are significantly correlated with interest and motivation – the two most important factors in learning. Additionally, computer skills and online chat experience were seen to influence learners with different cognitive styles. Effective utilization of these factors to leverage online social learning is important for teachers and online trainers.

One of the messages that online instructional designers can probably carry home from this finding is that designers should examine the roles and function of complementary personality, support and value as they design and develop instruction to get learners interested and motivated in online learning. It is thus suggested that online research

should encompass a larger context in which cognitive styles, motivation, interest, learning support, value, and so forth are examined to better understand the factors contributing to the success of online learning.

Limitations of the Study

There are several limitations to the study. Firstly, the small sample size affected the statistical power in t-test analysis which explained the reason why no significance was found for self-posted and critiquing postings. Secondly, the population was limited to one university with primarily educational major students. This could affect the generalizablity of the findings. However, this was a pilot study that would hopefully lead toward a series of more in-depth studies in this area. In fact, the initial findings have already pointed to the need of developing effective instructional intervention to mitigate the difference between FD and FI learners' abilities in critiquing and challenging other people's viewpoints.

In conclusion, this study has provided initial evidence that social compensation is shown to be one of the factors that accounts for the social communication pattern among learners with different cognitive styles. It also shows that other factors such as interest, motivation, support, value as well as learners' computer skills and online chat experience may play important roles in influencing FD and FI learners in online social communication. Results indicate that adequate support is essential for FD learners to obtain positive experience in online learning. It is suggested that future studies should investigate the role of support and its design mechanism so that both FD and FI learners can benefit from this unique form of learning.

AKNOWLEDGMENT

This project was supported in part by a grant from the Utah State Commission on Criminal and Juvenile Justice and the Center for the Advancement of Technology in Education, College of Education, University of Utah.

REFERENCES

Amichai-Hamburger, Y., Wainapel, G., & Fox, S. (2002). "On the Internet no one knows I'm an introvert": Extroversion, neuroticism, and Internet interaction. *CyberPsychology & Behavior, 5*(2), 125-128.

Anolli, L., Villani, D., & Riva, G. (2005). Personality of people using chat: An online research. *CyberPsychology & Behavior, 8*(1), 89-95.

Ates, S., & Cataloglu, E. (2007). The effects of students' *cognitive styles* on conceptual understandings and problem-solving skills in introductory mechanics. *Research in Science & Technological Education, 25*(2), 167-178.

Bandura, A. (1993). Perceived self-efficacy in cognitive development and functioning. *Educational Psychologist, 28*, 117-148.

Bianchi, A., & Phillips, J. G. (2005). Psychological predictors of problem mobile phone use. *CyberPsychology & Behavior, 8*(1), 39-51.

Borgatti, S. P., Everett, M. G., & Freeman, L. C. (2002). *Ucinet for Windows: Software for social network analysis.* Cambridge, MA: Analytic Technologies.

Chak, K., & Leung, L. (2004). Shyness and locus of control as predictors of Internet addiction and Internet use. *CyberPsychology & Behavior, 7*(5), 559-570.

Chen, S. (2002). *A cognitive* model for non-linear *learning* in hypermedia programmes. *British Journal of Educational Technology, 33*(4), 449-60.

Chinien, C. A., & Boutin, F. (1992). Cognitive style FD/I: An important learning characteristic for educational technologies. *Journal of Educational Technology Systems, 21*(4), 303-311.

Cook, J., & Smith, M. (2004). Beyond formal learning: Informal *community* elearning. *Computers and Education, 43*(1-2), 35-47.

Danili, E., & Reid, N. (2004). Some strategies to improve performance in school chemistry, based on two cognitive factors. *Research in Science & Technology Education, 22(2)*, 203-226.

Dietz-Uhler, B., & Bishop-Clark, C. (2005) Formation of and adherence to a self-disclosure norm in an online chat. *CyberPsychology & Behavior, 8*(2), 114-120.

Eysenck, H. Y., & Eysenck, S. B. G. (1964). *Manual of the Eysenck personality inventory.* San Diego: Educational and Industrial Testing Service.

Griffin, R., & Franklin, G. (1996). Can college academic performance be predicted using a measure of cognitive style? *Journal of Educational Technology Systems, 24*(4), 375-379.

Ford, N. (2000). Cognitive styles and virtual environments. *Journal of the American Society for Information Science, 51*(6), 543-57.

Gregorc, A. (1982). *An adult's guide to style.* Columbia, CT: Gregorc Associates.

Hanneman, R. A., & Riddle, M. (2005). *Introduction to social network methods.* Riverside, CA: University of California, Riverside.

Ikegulu, P. R., & Ikegulu, T. N. (1999). The effectiveness of window presentation strategy and cognitive style of field dependence status on learning from mediated instructions. Ruston, LA: Center for Statistical Consulting. (ERIC Document Reproduction Service No. ED428758)

Johnson, G. M., & Johnson, J. A. (2006). *Learning style and preference for online learning support: Individual quizzes versus study groups.* Paper presented at the 18th Annual World Conference on Educational Multimedia, Hypermedia, and Telecommunications, Orlando, FL.

Jonassen, D. H., & Grabowski, B. L. (1993). Handbook of individual differences, learning, and instruction. Mahwah, NJ: *Lawrence Erlbaum.*

Kagan, J. (1966). Reflection-impulsivity: The generality and dynamics of conceptual tempo. *Journal of Abnormal Psychology, 71,* 17-24.

Keefe, J. W. (1982). Assessing student learning styles: An overview. In J. W. Keefe (Ed.), *Student learning styles and brain behavior* (pp. 1-17). Reston, VA: National Association of Secondary School Principals.

Kirby, P. (1979). *Cognitive style, learning style and transfer skill acquisition.* Columus, OH: The National Center for Research in Vocational Education, The Ohio State University.

Lever-Duffy, J., McDonald, J. B., & Mizell, A. P. (2003). *Teaching and learning with technology.* Boston, MA: Allyn & Bacon/Pearson.

Liu, M., & Reed, M. (1994). The relationship between the learning strategies and learning styles in a hypermedia environment. Computers in Human Behavior, 10(4), 419-434.

Madell, D., & Muncer, S. J. (2006). Internet communication: An activity that appeals to shy and socially phobic people? *CyberPsychology & Behavior, 9*(5), 618-622.

McKenna, K., & Bargh, J. (2000). Plan 9 from cyberspace: The implications of the Internet for personality and social psychology. *Personality and Social Psychology Review, 4*(1), 57-75.

McKenna, K., Green, A. S., & Gleason, M. E. (2002). Relationship formation on the Internet: What's the big attraction? *Journal of Social Issues, 58*(1), 9-31.

Meng, K., & Patty, D. (1991). Field dependence and contextual organizers. Journal of Educational Research, 84(3), 183-189.

Oltman, P. K., Raskin, E., & Witkin, H. A. (2003). *Group embedded figures test.* Menlo Park, CA: Mind Garden.

Peter, J., Valenburg, P., & Schouten, A. P. (2005). Developing a model of adolescent friendship formation on the Internet. *CyberPsychology & Behavior, 8*(5), 423-430.

Peter, J., Valkenburg, P., & Schouten, A. P. (2006). Characteristics and motives of adolescents talking with strangers on the Internet. *CyberPsychology & Behavior, 9*(5), 526-530.

Richards, J. P., Fajen, B. R., Sullivan, J. F., & Gillespie, G. (1997). Signaling, notetaking, and field independence-dependence in text comprehension and recall. *Journal of Educational Psychology, 89*(3), 508-517.

Riding, R. J., & Read, G. (1996). *Cognitive* style and pupil *learning* preferences. *Educational Psychology, 16*(1), 81-106.

Russell, A. J. (1997). The effect of learner variables and *cognitive* style on *learning* performance in a vocational training environment. *Educational Psychology, 17*(1-2), 195-208.

Samples, R. E. (1975). Are you teaching online one side of the brain? *Learning, 3*(6), 25-28.

Schmeck, R. R. (1988). Strategies and styles of learning: An integration of varied perspectives. In R. R. Schmeck (Ed.), Learning strategies and learning styles (pp. 317-347). New York: Plenum Press.

Sheeks, M. S., & Birchmeier, Z. P. (2007). Shyness, sociability, and the use of computer-mediated communication in relationship development. *CyberPsychology & Behavior, 10*(1), 64-70.

Smith, T., & Easterday, K. E. (1994). Field dependence-independence and holistic instruction in mathematics. University of Alabama at Birmingham and Auburn University. (ERIC Document Reproduction Service No. ED377072)

Smith, P. L., & Ragan, T. J. (2005). *Instructional design* (3rd ed.). Hoboken, NJ: John Wiley & Sons.

Springer, S., & Deutch, G. (1985). *Right brain, left brain*. San Francisco, CA: W. H. Freeman.

Stroebe, W., Diehl, M., & Abakoumkin, G. (1996). Social compensation and the Kohler effect: Toward a theoretical explanation of motivational gains in group productivity. In E. H. Witte & J. H. Davis (Eds.), *Understanding group behavior: Vol. 2. Small group processes and interpersonal relations* (pp. 37-65). Mahwah, NJ: Lawrence Erlbaum.

Tajfel, H. (1978). Social categorization, social identity, and social comparison. In H. Tajfel (Ed.), *Differentiation between social groups: Studies in the social psychology of inter-group relations* (pp. 61-76). London: Academic Press.

Subrahmanyan, K., Smahel, D., & Greenfield, P. (2006). Connecting developmental constructions to the Internet: Identity presentation and sexual exploration on online teen chat rooms. *Developmental Psychology, 42*(3), 395-406.

Valkenburg, P. M., & Peter, J. (2007). Preadolescents' and adolescents' online communication and their closeness to friends. *Developmental Psychology, 43*(2), 267-277.

Wasserman, S., & Faust, K. (1994). *Social network analysis: Methods and applications*. New York: Cambridge University Press.

Weller, M. (2007). The distance from isolation: Why *communities* are the logical conclusion in e-learning. *Computers & Education, 49*(2), 148-159.

Widyanto, L., & McMurran, M. (2004). The psychological properties of the Internet addiction test. *CyberPsychology & Behavior, 7*(4), 443-450.

Williams, K. D., & Karau, S. J. (1991). Social loafing and social compensation: The effects of expectations of co-worker performance. *Journal of Personality and Social Psychology, 61*, 570-581.

Willging, P. A. (2007). Online interactions: Comparing social network measures with instructors' perspectives. In R. Zheng & S. P. Ferris (Eds.), *Understanding online instructional modeling: Theories and practices* (pp. 150-167). Hershey, PA: Information Science Reference.

Witkin, H. A., & Goodenough, D. R. (1977). Field dependence and interpersonal behavior. *Psychological Bulletin, 84*, 661-689.

Witkin, H. A., Moore, C. A., Goodenough, D. R., & Cox, P. W. (1977). Field dependent and field independent cognitive styles and their educational implications. Review of Educational Research, 47(1), 1-64.

Zheng, R. (2006). From WebQuests to virtual learning: A study on student's perception of factors affecting design and development of online learning. In S. Ferris, & S. Godar (Eds.), *Teaching and learning with virtual teams* (pp. 53-82). Hershey, PA: Information Science Reference.

Zheng, R., & Ferris, S. P. (Eds.). (2007). *Understanding online instructional modeling: Theories and practices*. Hershey, PA: Information Science Reference.

Zheng, R., Yang, W., Garcia, D., & McCadden, E. (2008). Effects of multimedia on schema induced analogical reasoning in science learning. *Journal of Computer Assisted Learning.* doi: 10.1111/j.1365-2729.2008.00282.x

APPENDIX A

Online Discussion Study Survey

Please circle one of the following that mostly reflects your experience of web-based learning.

Items	1	2	3	4	5
1. The online discussion mode can motivate learners to engage in meaningful learning.	Strongly Disagree	Disagree	Don't Know	Agree	Strongly Agree
2. When I was discussing online with other people, my level of self-confidence was	Very low	Low	Don't know	High	Very high
3. The online discussion is an effective tool for social communication	Strongly Disagree	Disagree	Don't Know	Agree	Strongly Agree
4. The online discussion builds up positive support among students	Strongly Disagree	Disagree	Don't Know	Agree	Strongly Agree
5. The rule of complementary personality applies to online discussion as people like to hang around with those of opposite personality	Strongly Disagree	Disagree	Don't Know	Agree	Strongly Agree
6. The rule of congeniality works in online discussion because people like to hang around with those of similar personality	Strongly Disagree	Disagree	Don't Know	Agree	Strongly Agree
7. The rule of complementary personality applies to online discussion as people hang around with those of different interest	Strongly Disagree	Disagree	Don't Know	Agree	Strongly Agree
8. The rule of congeniality works in online discussion as people like to hang around with those of similar interest	Strongly Disagree	Disagree	Don't Know	Agree	Strongly Agree
9. Individuals would be likely to retain in online discussion if they value what they have learned in online	Strongly Disagree	Disagree	Don't Know	Agree	Strongly Agree
10. Individuals would be likely to retain in online discussion if they are motivated by what have learned in online	Strongly Disagree	Disagree	Don't Know	Agree	Strongly Agree

APPENDIX B

Vocabulary list for SNA Analysis

Arcs: Arcs are the relationships between the nodes. Their strength is measured by the distance between the nodes. The shorter the distance is between the nodes, the stronger the relationship will be.

Betweenness: Betweenness of a node refers to the intermediatory role that a node plays between groups of points.

Centrality: Centrality describes how a particular focal node is related to other nodes. This is defined in terms of in- and out-degree of a node. That is, a node that has many ties may have access to (out-degree), and be accessed by other nodes (in-degree) in the network. A very simple, but often very effective measure of a node's centrality and power potential is its in- and out-degree.

Cohesion: Cohesion refers to the homogeneity of the subgroups or network. It is measured by the density, reciprocity, and Geodesic distances among the nodes. Reciprocity ranges from 0 to 1, with 0 indicating minimum reciprocity and 1 maximum reciprocity. In a social network high symmetric reciprocity among the nodes indicates high degree of cohesiveness among the participants. Finally, the Geodesic distance is indexed by a distance-based cohesion ("compactness") which ranges between 0 and 1 with larger values showing greater cohesiveness.

Density: Density of interaction in a social network means the proportion of all possible ties that are actually present. It is calculated as the sum of ties divided by the number of possible ties. Density is closely related to the power in a network system which is defined as the number of incoming and outgoing ties of the nodes, which is also known as the communication power among nodes. In a system that has low density, usually not much power can be exerted. Conversely, in high density systems there is a potential for greater power.

Nodes: Nodes which are otherwise called actors can be persons, organizations, or groups.

Sociogram: Sociogram is actually a graphic that visually represents the relationships among the nodes. It provides a diagram where researchers can analyze the patterns of group behavior.

Sociomatrix: Sociomatrix or adjacency matrix delineates the relationship between nodes through a mathematical representation in the form of a matrix.

Chapter XVI
Collaborative Learning in a Web-Based Environment:
A Comparison Study

Yin Zhang
Kent State University, USA

ABSTRACT

Collaborative learning has long been proven to be an effective approach in the traditional classroom setting. Despite the discussion of the benefits and potential of collaborative learning in a Web-based learning environment, there has been a lack of empirical studies showing whether and how distance learning students may benefit from this learning experience, particularly in comparison to their on-campus peers and from their own perspectives. This chapter reports on a study that uses a comparative approach to evaluate the effectiveness of collaborative learning and related teaching and learning outcomes in both distance learning and on-campus settings. The major findings of this study suggest that distance learning students tend to have more positive perceptions of collaborative learning than their peers in the traditional classroom setting. In addition, distance learning students tend to embrace collaborative learning readily and early compared to their on-campus peers. In terms of student class performance, this study shows that distance learning students can achieve essentially the same learning goals as their on-campus peers. However, there are individual differences in student performance. An analysis of factors contributing to the individual performance differences suggests that engagement is closely correlated to student class performance. This study also shows that, overall, both distance learning and on-campus students provide similar course and instructor evaluations for teaching effectiveness for classes with collaborative learning. Finally, the implications of this study and suggestions for future research are discussed.

INTRODUCTION

Two terms, *collaborative learning* and *cooperative learning*, are used to describe experiences in an educational settings in which students work together to achieve a goal. Kirschner (2001) describes *collaborative learning* as "a personal philosophy, not just a classroom technique" and *cooperative learning* as being "defined by a set of processes which help people interact together in order to accomplish a specific goal or develop an end product which is usually content specific" (p. 4). These two terms have been used interchangeably in the literature. In this chapter, no distinction is made between the two terms. For review and discussion of related research, the original term as presented in the literature will be retained. In other cases, the term *"collaborative learning"* is used throughout for consistency.

Collaborative learning and its impacts on teaching and learning in higher education have been well recognized. Most collaborative learning techniques are developed in the traditional face-to-face educational setting. With the widespread growth of distance education, instructors and researchers have started to explore collaborative learning in a distance learning setting. Despite much discussion regarding the benefits and potential of collaborative learning in this relatively new setting, there has been a lack of related empirical studies focusing on the student perspective and comparing the two distinct learning settings. Filling this gap is part of the calls for research on distance education and is vital to keeping pace with various implementations and practices (e.g., Boling & Robinson, 1999; Gunawardena & McIsaac, 2004; Head, Lockee, & Oliver, 2002; Lock, 2002).

This chapter presents an empirical study that adopts a comparative approach by evaluating collaborative learning in distance education classes in relation to face-to-face classes using a learner-centered approach for assessment and evaluation. Student assessments and evaluations of collaborative learning and overall effectiveness of course and instructor, student class performance, and student participation in class will be the primary source of data for this study. The major questions explored in the study include the following:

1. Do distance learning and on-campus students have different perceptions of collaborative learning activities?
2. Do distance learning and on-campus students' perceptions of collaborative learning activities change over time?
3. Do distance learning and on-campus students perform differently?
4. What factors contribute to individual differences in class performance?
5. Do distance learning and on-campus students perceive the effectiveness of the overall course and instructor performance differently?

BACKGROUND

Collaborative learning has been well covered in the literature. For the purpose of this study, the literature review will focus on collaborative learning primarily in the distance education environment and, particularly, in web-based education. First, the benefits of collaborative learning are enumerated, followed by suggestions for successful implementation of collaborative learning in distance education. Next, the suitability of collaborative learning in different disciplines and education levels is discussed. Finally, methods for evaluating the effectiveness of collaborative learning are examined.

Benefits of Collaborative Learning

The importance and potential of collaborative learning in the online environment have been recognized and confirmed by many researchers. Harasim (2000) suggests, "The principle of collaborative learning may be the single most important concept for online networked learning, since this principle addresses the strong socio-affective and cognitive power of learning on the Web" (p. 53). The notion of group collaboration to produce knowledge is considered essential in the new learning paradigm (Harasim, 2000).

There has been empirical research suggesting that collaborative learning enhances students' problem-solving and critical thinking skills and helps them learn to work in a team and to become more autonomous learners (Neo, 2003). One way in which students benefit from collaborative learning is by an increased exposure to new and different ideas and approaches that may greatly widen an individual's experience and help students tackle larger projects that they could not complete individually (Haythornthwaite, 2001; Watabe, Hamalainen, & Whinston, 1995).

In addition, distance learning students may benefit from cooperative learning activities in both the cognitive and affective domains (Bard, 1996). Particularly, students involved in collaborative learning in distance education report that group participation helps them feel less isolated and more a part of a single integrated class (Bard, 1996). Collaborative learning in a distance learning environment helps students stay focused on the course subject matter. In a distance education course, students may feel alienated due to lack of physical proximity to other students and the instructor. Students working from home at individual computer terminals may experience neither the advantages nor the pressures associated with physically entering a classroom of students at specified times. Working as a group keeps group members on task because of the sense of responsibility to and the positive influence and motivational qualities of the group. Working with a group not only keeps students on-task for their learning experience but also provides them with experience working as a team member. The team-building skills learned in a collaborative educational experience translate into useful work skills (Bard, 1996).

Collaborative learning experiences can be positive for both students and instructors. While some instructors may dread teaching a distance education course, they may find that the as-signment of collaborative projects reduces their workload because some of the student questions are answered during the collaborative learning process (Chang, 2001; Watabe et al., 1995).

Methods for Collaborative Learning in Distance Education

Collaborative learning in distance education courses may require some adjustments in the way the instructor prepares for the course. Several factors contribute to the success of applying collaborative learning in distance education; institutional support, certain teaching methods, activities, strategies, and adequate technology are mentioned in the reviewed literature. In particular, the importance of an instructor's teaching methods and necessary institutional support have been stressed because faculty efforts in the classroom have important influences on student learning. Further, it has been shown that instructors' commitment to teaching is beneficial to student learning (Cabrera, Colbeck, & Terenzini, 2001).

Instructors are advised to explain the responsibilities of both the students and the instructor and to set guidelines in any collaborative learning situation to ensure a successful learning experience (Bard, 1996). Research has also recognized the importance of learners' autonomic behaviors and suggests that instructors clearly state expectations to learners (Chang, 2001). The appropriate size of the group, each student's role within the group, and how the results will be evaluated are important factors to determine in order for instructors to successfully plan collaborative learning activities (Keyser, 2000). Assignments and activities for collaborative learning may include group discussions, group projects, and even group presentations (Bard, 1996; Yakimovicz & Murphy, 1995).

Established and sustained contact among students has been recognized as an important factor for collaborative learning. To begin with, it is important to have structured exercises in which students get to know each other as part of group formation (Watabe et al., 1995). During the learning process, sustained contact is important "for time-limited, distanced, collaborative learners to achieve the strong ties that make it easier to complete their course work" (Haythornthwaite, 2001, p. 224). Some of the suggested ways to maintain the contact include a brief on-campus session during the term of the course, or during the course of the program for students who will proceed as cohorts through the same courses (Haythornthwaite, 2001; Watabe et al., 1995). Such face-to-face contact has proven to be beneficial and positive on student learning and participation (Michinov & Michinov, 2008).

Some researchers have recognized the important role of technology in distance education collaborative learning. For example, Chang (2001) stresses and recommends that an instructor and a web site manager work together to create a web environment that fosters a successful collaborative learning experience for students. Watabe et al. (1995) provide recommendations for the distance learning environment, including a clear, simple, and easy to learn user interface; the ability to use and download/upload various types of information (such as text, graphics, and sound files); and a flexible structure for conferences and permissions. Geyer and Weis (2000) provide similar guidelines about technology for a digital lecture board. Suggestions include the flexibility to utilize various media formats (such as GIF, HTML, MPEG); the functionality to allow users to edit objects with basic functions similar to a word or graphic processing software; and services such as floor control, session control, telepointers, or voting.

In addition, some researchers have explored effective ways of conducting collaborative learning on the Web. Park and Hyun (2006) compare and evaluate seminar-based and project-based models for collaborative learning. Their study shows some differences in learners' activities in terms of interaction level and collaborability under the two models, suggesting new assessment items for evaluating learners as well as proper instructional technique for effective learning. Overbaugh and Casiello (2008) examine student selection and evaluation of various communication tools for collaborative work in a distributed learning environment. Their study surveys student uses of the tools available for various types of instructional activities at varying cognitive levels, and gathers student feedback on the efficacy of the tool for the given tasks.

Applicability to Various Educational Levels and Disciplines

The literature available concerning distance education and collaborative learning covers levels of education from grade school to college courses. Some studies focused on undergraduate courses (Cabrera et al. 2001; Mancuso, 2001; Marbach-Ad & Sokolove, 2002; Neo, 2003) while others examined graduate courses (Bard, 1996; Cronje, 2001; Haythornthwaite, 2001; Yakimovicz & Murphy, 1995). One study (Scadden, 1998) addressed all levels of education but focused on grade school science. Another study (Keyser, 2000) involved library instruction. Other studies did not specify the educational level of the students (Chang, 2001; Geyer & Weis, 2000; Harasim, 2000; Kirschner, 2001; Rovai, 2000; Watabe et al. 1995).

Computers and the Internet tend to be widely used in distance education courses and in web-based distance collaborative learning. In the literature surveyed, the students in the distance courses may have had prior education or experience that rendered them more computer literate than the average student. In addition, the subject nature of the courses may also suggest that these students are more receptive to the idea of distance education and collaborative learning than other students in a technology-intense setting (Bard, 1996; Cronje, 2001; Yakimovicz & Murphy, 1995).

Evaluating the Effectiveness of Collaborative Learning

There are various ways and factors to consider when evaluating whether a collaborative learning distance course, or any course, is effective. The academic performance of the students is considered to be the foremost criterion for such evaluation (Bard, 1996). Other considerations include students' evaluation of their collaborative learning activities and the instructor's observation of group members during such learning activities. The successes and failures of a course can also be documented during the course and evaluated when the course ends. For example, Yakimovicz & Murphy (1995) suggest that students keep journals of their interactions with the technology and with other students during the term. Interviews can be conducted at the conclusion of the term.

Some researchers suggest a comparison approach for effectiveness measures. For example, Marbach-Ad and Sokolove (2002) compare student-instructor communication in a lecture-style class and an active learning class that utilizes collaborative learning groups along with other techniques. They report that the active learning environment stimulates higher rates and quality of student questions. Based on a comparison of seminar-based and project-based learning models for collaborative learning, Park and Hyun (2006) propose new assessment items in three areas: interaction, collaborability, and accountability.

There have been studies examining group interactions in collaborative learning for evaluations of learning effectiveness. In a research study of collaborative learning using group communication to monitor web-based group learning, Chen, Wang, and Ou (2003) develop a method for predicting group performance. They find that group communication patterns significantly affect group performance and, thus, suggest guidelines for teachers to more effectively monitor and direct collaborative learning. In another study, Brewer and Klein (2006) investigate the effect of positive interdependence and affiliation motive in an asynchronous collaborative learning environment. The study shows that participants with higher numbers of interactions attain higher post-test scores and that the type of interdependence and affiliation motive has a significant impact on student attitudes in collaborative learning.

In summary, collaborative learning can benefit both students and instructors in traditional and virtual classrooms through use of careful planning and effective teaching strategies. Learning can take place via distance collaboration at any level, from grade school to grad school. Since most current collaborative learning techniques have been developed in the traditional classroom, it is important to assess their effectiveness in the distance learning environment. The component that has been lacking in current literature and evaluation practices is the inclusion of the learners' perspective and the performance of well-controlled comparative research (Ricketts, Wolfe, Norvelle, & Carpenter, 2000; Sweeney, O'Donoghue, & Whitehead, 2004). Such research will provide valuable insight about whether and which collaborative learning techniques may work well in distance learning settings, which groups of learners are best served, and the reasons why these results occur. Answers to these questions will help teachers develop effective strategies for helping students succeed in the distance learning environment.

METHOD

The distance learning class for this study is a required library and information science course with 78 graduate students from four different physical locations in a state in the Midwestern United States. Students had various undergraduate educational backgrounds. The course was offered through interactive, two-way video conferencing between the central site and three off-site locations. Students in the remote sites could view the instructor on a video screen or monitors, and all students could participate in class discussions. The same instructor taught the same course during the same semester to 64 on-campus students in the same program, providing a well-controlled group for comparison purposes for this study.

The collaborative learning techniques used in this study included group work by individual site followed by a class-wide discussion with all sites involved during class time. Outside of class, study groups were formed with about five students working together on readings and assignments using the WebCT discussion board, chat, and email. Each group included students from different learning sites, and each group had access to its own private discussion board and the class-wide discussion board.

This study collected data for evaluation and comparison using the following multiple sources:

- Student performance: Student performance scores for all assignments and exams for this course were added and used to represent the academic student performance in this class. Both the distance learning and the on-campus classes had the exact same evaluation criteria and score scales. The two classes were different sections of the same course taught by the same instructor during the same semester.
- Student evaluation of collaborative learning activities: Two rounds of student surveys, one administered after the midterm and the other after the final, were used to gather student perceptions of collaborative learning. In addition, an anonymous feedback form was available throughout the semester for gathering student feedback.
- Student evaluation of the course and instructor: Student evaluations of the course and instructor from the two settings were compared using a campus-wide student course evaluation form that contained an overall rating of a course's quality and its instructor's performance.
- Instructor's observation: The instructor's observations of the two classes include activities both in-class and outside of class. Students' outside of class collaborative learning activities were captured by the WebCT courseware automatically through access data, chat room logs, group discussion readings and postings, and group presentations.

RESULTS

The major focus of this study is to compare how traditional and distance learning students perceive collaborative learning activities in their respective settings. In addition, student performance in the two settings is compared to measure the effectiveness of teaching and learning. The findings of this study are summarized to address the research questions as follows:

1. Do distance learning and on-campus students have different perceptions of collaborative learning activities?

The two rounds of student surveys were administered to gather student perceptions of collaborative learning over the duration of the course. The perceptions of the two groups of students regarding collaborative learning activities were analyzed and compared using one-way ANOVA for 13-item measures about the effectiveness of collaborative learning.

In the post-midterm survey, distance learning students were more positive in their perceptions of collaborative learning than their on-campus counterparts. They rated all of the 13 items higher than students who took the class on-campus, including six items (3, 5, 6, 9, 12, and 13) that were rated statistically significantly higher (alpha = 0.05):

1. Higher academic achievement
2. Greater persistence through graduation
3. Better high-level reasoning and critical thinking skills ($F_{1, 136}$=6.73, p=.01)
4. Deeper understanding of learned material
5. More on-task and less disruptive behavior in class ($F_{1, 136}$=5.57, p=.02)
6. Lower levels of anxiety and stress ($F_{1, 136}$=3.81, p=.05)
7. Greater intrinsic motivation to learn and achieve
8. Greater ability to view situations from others' perspectives; more positive and supportive relationships with peers
9. More positive attitudes toward subject areas ($F_{1, 136}$=5.11, p=.03)
10. Higher self-esteem
11. Having group members from other sites help me feel less isolated and more a part of an integrated class (Does not apply to on-campus class in this study)
12. Overall, your assigned study group helps your learning, in particular, during the process of finishing the assignments ($F_{1, 135}$=4.81, p=.03)
13. Overall, you have benefited from class-wide discussion on WebCT ($F_{1, 136}$=11.99, p<.01)

In the post-final survey, distance learning students remained more positive in their perceptions of collaborative learning than their on-campus counterparts. They again rated all of the 13 items higher than students who took the regular, on-campus class except for item 6, which was related to anxiety and stress. However, there is no statistically significant difference between the two groups (alpha = 0.05):

1. Higher academic achievement
2. Greater persistence through graduation
3. Better high-level reasoning and critical thinking skills
4. Deeper understanding of learned material
5. More on-task and less disruptive behavior in class

6. Lower levels of anxiety and stress
7. Greater intrinsic motivation to learn and achieve
8. Greater ability to view situations from others' perspectives, more positive and supportive relationships with peers
9. More positive attitudes toward subject areas
10. Higher self-esteem
11. Having group members from other sites help me feel less isolated and more a part of an integrated class (Does not apply to on-campus class in this study)
12. Overall, your assigned study group helps your learning, in particular, during the process of finishing the assignments
13. Overall, you have benefited from class-wide discussion on WebCT

2. Do distance learning and on-campus students' perceptions of collaborative learning activities change over time?

A one-way ANOVA analysis of the changes in students' perceptions of collaborative learning activities over the two rounds of surveys for each group reveals that as distance learning students engaged in more collaborative learning activities over the duration of the course, their perceptions of collaborative learning progressively became more positive in the following specific areas:

• higher academic achievement, which students appreciated to a statistically significantly degree ($F_{1, 147}$ = 3.84, p=.05);
• deeper understanding of learned material; and
• higher self-esteem.

In contrast, on-campus students' perceptions of collaborative learning progressed more positively across the board over the duration of the course. They rated all of the 13 collaborative learning measure items more positively at the end of the course, except the item regarding greater persistence through graduation (item 2), which remained almost the same. In particular, on-campus students' appreciation of what collaborative learning can offer to higher academic achievement progressed to a statistically significant degree ($F_{1, 112} = 4.43$, p=.04) toward the end of the course.

A multivariate analysis (MANOVA) is also conducted as a follow-up to research question 1 and question 2 to cross-examine how the time progression (*time*) and teaching setting (*setting*) jointly may impact student perceptions of the 13 collaborative learning measures and whether there is any interaction between the two factors. As shown in Table 1, the test result of the interaction effect between the *time* and *setting* factors shows that the F value is not significant (p=.639), indicating there is no interaction effect between the two factors. The F statistics for testing *time* and *setting* are 1.720 and 3.927, respectively. The p value for the *time* factor is 0.057, which is very close to being statistically significant. This result suggests that overall there is a notable change of student perceptions of collaborative learning over time, although such change is not statistically significant. On the other hand, the *setting* factor is statistically significant, indicating that overall there is a significant difference in perceptions on collaborative learning between distance learning students and on-campus students.

3.   Do distance learning and on-campus students perform differently?

Previous related literature suggests that a key criterion for evaluating the effectiveness of collaborative learning is the academic performance of the students. In this study, student performance is also used to compare the two classes engaged in collaborative learning in different settings. The average student performance score is 93.2 and 94.5 for the distance learning class and the on-campus class, respectively. A one-way ANOVA analysis

of student performance shows no statistically significant difference in student performance in the two settings ($F_{1, 140}=1.88$, p=.17). This result suggests that distance learning students performed as well as their on-campus peers as a whole. At the same time, individual differences were observed in student performance in both settings. Such observation led to an inquiry into possible factors that may have contributed to individual performance differences.

4.   What factors contribute to individual differences in class performance?

An examination of students' class performance and participation in collaborative learning activities shows that their engagement in such activities is an important factor for success in class performance. Specifically, based on a one-way ANAOVA analysis, the following factors directly contribute to individual differences in student class performance, all at a statistically significant level (alpha = 0.05):

- The number of times students visited the class WebCT site ($F_{9, 132}=6.54$, p<.01),
- The number of discussion board postings read by students ($F_{8, 133}=5.74$, p<.01), and
- The number of discussion board postings contributed by students ($F_{11, 130}=5.74$, p<.01).

Taking all the above participation variables jointly into consideration, a GLM procedure is conducted to evaluate their impact on student class performance. Together, the three participation variables explain 26.3% of the observed variability in the percentage of student class performance, and their impact is significant to student class performance (see Table 2 and Table 3). Table 4 shows that among the three participation variables, number of postings and number of messages read are statistically significant, while the frequency with which a student visits the class

Table 1. Multivariate tests[b]

Effect		Value	F	Hypothesis df	Error df	Sig.
Intercept	Pillai's Trace	.931	255.665[a]	13.000	246.000	.000
	Wilks' Lambda	.069	255.665[a]	13.000	246.000	.000
	Hotelling's Trace	13.511	255.665[a]	13.000	246.000	.000
	Roy's Largest Root	13.511	255.665[a]	13.000	246.000	.000
Time	Pillai's Trace	.083	1.720[a]	13.000	246.000	.057[c]
	Wilks' Lambda	.917	1.720[a]	13.000	246.000	.057[c]
	Hotelling's Trace	.091	1.720[a]	13.000	246.000	.057[c]
	Roy's Largest Root	.091	1.720[a]	13.000	246.000	.057[c]
Setting	Pillai's Trace	.172	3.927[a]	13.000	246.000	.000[d]
	Wilks' Lambda	.828	3.927[a]	13.000	246.000	.000[d]
	Hotelling's Trace	.208	3.927[a]	13.000	246.000	.000[d]
	Roy's Largest Root	.208	3.927[a]	13.000	246.000	.000[d]
Time * setting	Pillai's Trace	.042	.820[a]	13.000	246.000	.639[c]
	Wilks' Lambda	.958	.820[a]	13.000	246.000	.639[c]
	Hotelling's Trace	.043	.820[a]	13.000	246.000	.639[c]
	Roy's Largest Root	.043	.820[a]	13.000	246.000	.639[c]

a. *Exact statistic*

b. *Design: Intercept+Time+setting+Time * setting*

c. *Not significant at the 0.05 alpha level*

d. *Significant at the 0.05 alpha level.*

website is not. These findings suggest that student participation in collaborative learning activities plays a critical role in student class performance. Particularly, active participation in terms of posting messages and reading messages are critical to student success in class, while visiting class website is a relative passive and less important indicator for participation compared to posting and reading activities.

5. Do distance learning and on-campus students perceive the effectiveness of the overall course and instructor performance differently?

At the end of both classes, students were asked to evaluate the overall effectiveness of the class and the instructor on a 5-point scale. A chi-square analysis of student evaluations of the instructor by the distance learning class and the regular class shows no statistically significant difference (χ^2=5.60, df=5, p=.35). Similarly, there is no difference in student overall course evaluations between the two groups (χ^2=1.25, df=5, p=.94), indicating that the instructor performed similarly in both settings and that the course was delivered at a similarly effective level in both settings.

DISCUSSION AND RECOMMENDATIONS

While this comparative study offers some interesting results, it also raises problems and issues

Table 2. Model summary

Model	R	R Square	Adjusted R Square	Std. Error of the Estimate
1[a]	.513	.263	.247	5.305

a. Predictors: (Constant), posting, visit, reading

Table 3. Participation and its impact on student class performance: analysis-of-variance

Model		Sum of Squares	df	Mean Square	F	Sig.
1[a]	Regression	1388.495	3	462.832	16.447	.000[b]
	Residual	3883.482	138	28.141		
	Total	5271.977	141			

a. Predictors: (Constant), posting, visit, reading
b. Significant at the 0.05 alpha level.

Table 4. Participation and its impact on student class performance: coefficients

Model		Unstandardized Coefficients		Standardized Coefficients	t	Sig.
		B	Std. Error	Beta		
1[a]	(Constant)	19.377	11.803		1.642	.103
	visit	.912	2.414	.043	.378	.706[b]
	reading	6.754	3.272	.245	2.064	.041[c]
	posting	3.827	1.105	.304	3.462	.001[c]

a. Predictors: (Constant), posting, visit, reading
b. Not significant at the 0.05 alpha level
c. Significant at the 0.05 alpha level

related to collaborative learning. First, for instructors, collaborative learning requires timely feedback to students, as well as extra efforts for monitoring, coordinating, facilitating, and in some cases, intervening with dysfunctional groups and addressing misconduct. In a web-based environment, many online courseware applications include monitoring tools that automatically track student activities. However, this transaction log data must be interpreted carefully and in context. For example, frequent login sessions and lengthy courseware use do not always translate to active learning. There is always an issue of quantity vs.

quality when measuring participation of distance learning students.

In this study, suggestions and recommendations collected from the two rounds of student surveys reveal some interesting and helpful insights for effective collaborative learning in the web-based environment that reflect learners' perspectives. These suggestions and recommendations include the following:

- "Right" team dynamics are important for a positive learning experience. Some cited characteristics include cooperative, friendly,

Table 5. Student instructor evaluation chi-square-based measures

	Value	df	Asymp. Sig. (2-sided)
Pearson Chi-Square	5.600[a]	5	.347
Likelihood Ratio	6.858	5	.231
N of Valid Cases	138		

a. 6 cells (50.0%) have an expected count less than 5. The minimum expected count is 1.37.

Table 6. Student course evaluation chi-square-based measures

	Value	df	Asymp. Sig. (2-sided)
Pearson Chi-Square	1.247[a]	5	.940
Likelihood Ratio	1.248	5	.940
N of Valid Cases	138		

a. 4 cells (33.3%) have an expected count less than 5. The minimum expected count is .91.

responsible, supportive, helpful, and eager to contribute to group effort.

- A courseware tool that preserves all collaborative activities is essential for collaborative learning in an asynchronous manner, allowing members to "meet and work together" without coordinating times and schedules.
- A private, group-members only space is very helpful for productive collaborative learning within a group.
- A separate task/assignment-specific space is needed for each collaborative task.
- A public space for the entire class that corresponds to each collaborative group assignment is desirable so that groups can effectively seek outside help. Availability of this space also encourages learning and sharing among groups.
- An effective collaborative learning environment should support various communication tools in order to facilitate expression of thoughts and ideas, as well as the compilation of answers.
- An effective collaborative learning environment should address social and affective

dimensions of collaborative work (e.g., knowing, seeing, supporting, and socializing with other members in the team), which is particularly important for distance learning students.

CONCLUSION AND FUTURE RESEARCH

This chapter presents a comparative study of collaborative learning utilized in two classes with the same course content, taught by the same instructor, offered during the same time frame but in two different settings: via distance learning and in the traditional classroom. The study reveals some interesting findings and suggests more for future research.

First, this study shows that distance learning students tend to view collaborative learning more positively throughout the course than their on-campus peers. In addition, distance learning students tend to embrace collaborative learning from the very beginning, while on-campus students' perceptions of collaborative learning progress positively as they engage in more such activities. Both groups show a strong appreciation for collaborative learning and its contribution to higher academic achievement. It would be interesting for future research to explore why distance learning students tend to more openly embrace collaborative learning than students in a traditional classroom setting and whether different strategies should be implemented for more effective collaborative learning in these two different settings.

Also, it is encouraging that students in this study evaluated the overall course effectiveness and instructor performance similarly for the two different settings, discrediting the common concern of instructors that students tend to evaluate distance courses lower than their counterpart courses offered in a traditional classroom setting. More empirical evidence along this line may help clarify the perception and encourage effective teaching in the online environment.

In terms of student performance, this study shows distance learning students can achieve the same learning goals as their on-campus peers. However, there are individual differences in student performance for the two classes that are related to student engagement variables: the number of times students visit the class site, the number of postings students read on the class discussion boards, and the number of postings students contribute to the class discussion boards. This finding suggests that student engagement is the key to student success in class regardless of course delivery mode. However, this study doesn't answer the question of why some students are more active than others and how to motivate students for active participation. This study and some resent studies may suggest more research in group dynamics and a better understanding of the discourse of student interactions in the online environment (Liu & Tsai, 2008; Michinov & Michinov, 2008). The research will help

instructors develop effective strategies to promote engaged and successful student learning online.

Finally, this study reveals the individual differences in student performance and learning outcomes and their tie to student collaborative learning-related class activities. This finding should be put in a larger context of the array of factors that may contribute to such differences, particularly, factors such as individual characteristics, cognitive and learning styles, and certain situational constraints such as technology and nature of tasks that may also affect collaboration. In addition, some of the student recommendations for better collaborative learning suggest the social and affective dimensions of collaborative work as possible future research topics. Such research would be particularly enlightening as more Web 2.0 technologies and virtual reality tools such as Second Life are being introduced to web-based learning.

REFERENCES

Bard, T. B. (1996). Cooperative activities in interactive distance learning. *Journal of Education for Library and Information Science, 37*(1), 2-10.

Boling, N. C., & Robinson, D. H. (1999). Individual study, interactive multimedia, or cooperative learning: Which activity best supplements lecture-based distance education? *Journal of Education Psychology, 91*(1), 169-174.

Brewer, S., & Klein, J. D. (2006). Type of positive interdependence and affiliation motive in an asynchronous, collaborative learning environment. *Educational Technology Research and Development: ETR&D, 54*(4), 331-354.

Cabrera, A. F., Colbeck, C. L., & Terenzini, P. T. (2001). Developing performance indicators for assessing classroom teaching practices and student learning: The case of engineering. *Research in Higher Education, 42*(3), 327-352.

Chang, C. (2001). Refining collaborative learning strategies for reducing the technical requirements of web-based classroom management. *Innovations in Education and Teaching International, 38*(2), 133-143.

Chen, G. D., Wang, C. Y., & Ou, K. L. (2003). Using group communication to monitor Web-based group learning. *Journal of Computer Assisted Learning, 19*, 401-415.

Cronje, J. C. (2001). Metaphors and models in Internet-based learning. *Computers & Education, 37*, 241-256.

Geyer, W., & Weis, R. (2000). The design and the security concept of a collaborative whiteboard. *Computer Communications, 23*, 233-241.

Gunawardena, C. N., & McIsaac, M. S. (2004). Distance education. In D. H. Jonassen (Ed.), *Handbook of research for educational communications and technology* (2nd ed., pp. 355-396). Mahwah, NJ: Erlbaum.

Harasim, L. (2000). Shift happens: Online education as a new paradigm in learning. *The Internet and Higher Education, 3*, 41-61.

Haythornthwaite, C. (2001). Exploring multiplexity: Social network structures in a computer-supported distance learning class. *The Information Society, 17*, 211-226.

Head, J. T., Lockee, B. B., & Oliver, K. M. (2002). Method, media, and mode: Clarifying the discussion of distance education effectiveness. *Quarterly Review of Distance Education, 3*(3), 261-268.

Keyser, M. W. (2000). Active learning and cooperative learning: Understanding the difference and using both styles effectively. *Research Strategies, 17*, 35-44.

Kirschner, P. A. (2001). Using integrated electronic environments for collaborative teaching/learning. *Research Dialogue in Learning and Instruction, 2*, 1-9.

Liu, C. C., & Tsai, C. C. (2008). An analysis of peer interaction patterns as discoursed by on-line small group problem-solving activity. *Computers & Education, 50*, 627-639.

Lock, J. V. (2002). Laying the groundwork for the development of learning communities within online courses. *Quarterly Review of Distance Education, 3*(4), 395-408.

Mancuso, S. (2001). Adult-centered practices: Benchmarking study in higher education. *Innovative Higher Education, 25*(3), 165-181.

Marbach-Ad, G., & Sokolove, P. G. (2002). The use of e-mail and in-class writing to facilitate student-instructor interaction in large-enrollment traditional and active learning classes. *Journal of Science Education and Technology, 11*(2), 109-119.

Michinov, N., & Michinov, E. (2008). Face-to-face contact at the midpoint of an online collaboration: Its impact on the patterns of participation, interaction, affect, and behavior over time. *Computer & Education, 50*, 1540-1557.

Neo, M. (2003). Developing a collaborative learning environment using a Web-based design. *Journal of Computer Assisted Learning, 19*, 462-473.

Overbaugh, R. C., & Casiello, A. R. (2008). Distributed collaborative problem-based graduate-level learning: Students' perspectives on communication tool selection and efficacy. *Computers in Human Behavior, 24*, 497-515.

Park, C. J., & Hyun, J. S. (2006). Comparison of two learning models for collaborative e-learning. In Z. Pan, et al. (Eds.), *Technologies for e-learning and digital entertainment* (pp. 50-59). Berlin, Germany: Springer-Verlag.

Ricketts, J., Wolfe, F. H., Norvelle, E., & Carpenter, E. H. (2000). Multimedia. *Social Science Computer Review, 18*(2), 132-146.

Rovai, A. P. (2000). Building and sustaining community in asynchronous learning networks. *The Internet and Higher Education, 3*, 285-297.

Scadden, L. A. (1998). The Internet and the education of students with disabilities. *Technology and Disability, 8*, 141-148.

Sweeney, J., O'Donoghue, T., & Whitehead, C. (2004). Traditional face-to-face and Web-based tutorials: A study of university students' perspectives on the roles of tutorial participants. *Teaching in Higher Education, 9*(3), 311-323.

Watabe, K., Hamalainen, M., & Whinston, A. B. (1995). An Internet based collaborative distance learning system: CODILESS. *Computers & Education, 24*(3), 141-155.

Yakimovicz, A. D., & Murphy, K. L. (1995). Constructivism and collaboration on the Internet: Case study of a graduate class experience. *Computers & Education, 24*(3), 203-209.

Chapter XVII
The Effect of Communication Styles on Computer-Supported Collaborative Learning[1]

Hichang Cho
National University of Singapore, Singapore

Geri Gay
Cornell University, USA

ABSTRACT

This chapter investigates the relationships between communication styles, social networks, and learning in a Computer-Supported Collaborative Learning (CSCL) community. Using Social Network Analysis (SNA) and longitudinal survey data, the authors analyzed how 31 distributed learners developed collaborative learning social networks, when they had work together on the design of aerospace systems using online collaboration tools. The results showed that both learner's personality characteristics (communication styles) and structural factors (a pre-existing friendship network) significantly affected the way the learners developed collaborative learning social networks. More specifically, learners who possessed high Willingness to Communicate (WTC) or occupied initially peripheral network positions were more likely to explore new network linkages in a distributed learning environment. The authors propose that the addition of personality theory (operationalized here as communication styles) to structural analysis (SNA) contributes to an enhanced picture of how distributed learners build their social and intellectual capital in the context of CSCL.

INTRODUCTION

A growing body of research has demonstrated that communication and conversation are central elements in collaborative learning environments (Harasim, Hiltz, Teles, & Turoff, 1995; Haythorthwaite, 2002). From the social network perspective, learning is a social and collective outcome achieved through seamless conversations, shared practices, and networks of social connections (Brown & Duguid, 1991). Knowledge, in this sense, is not a static object acquired by an atomic individual but is actively co-constructed through ongoing social exchanges and collaborations among multiple learners embedded in social networks (Cohen & Prusak, 1998; Lave & Wenger, 1991; Nonaka & Konno, 1998). Social networks also play instrumental roles in learning environments as a major conduit of resource and knowledge exchanges (Cho, Stefanone, & Gay, 2002) and as a source of social support and socialization for distributed learners (Haythorthwaite, 2002). Hence, the way individuals create social capital—or the way they are situated in social networks from the structuralist point of view—should significantly influence the acquisition, construction, and exchange of knowledge.

Theoretically, there are abundant discussions emphasizing the value and the impact of social networks in the studies of organizational learning (Nahaphiet & Goshal, 1998), knowledge management (Cohen & Prusak, 1998), and distance learning (Haythorthwaite, 2002). Empirically, however, very few studies have actually examined the "origins" of social networks in actual Computer-Supported Collaborative Learning (CSCL) or Cooperative Work (CSCW) settings (Millen, Fontaine, & Muller, 2002; Woodruff, 2002). In other words, relatively little research has been conducted to explicitly examine what factors influence the creation of different social networks in the context of CSCL, or why some learners occupy structurally advantageous positions than others. This is surprising, as "individual differences" have long been a central variable in educational research (Ellis, 2003; Scalia & Asckmary, 1996; Webb & Palincsar, 1996).

The aim of this study is to identify individual and structural factors that influence the way people develop emergent collaborative social and collaborative structures. In particular, we focus on how learners' personality characteristics (operationalized here as communication styles) interact with social-structural elements of collaborative learning (a pre-existing social network) to influence learning activities in a distributed learning environment. By adding personality theory to structural analysis (SNA), we attempt to contribute to an enhanced picture of how distributed learners build their social and intellectual capital in the context of CSCL.

We conducted a field experiment in which 31 college engineering students from two distant universities collaborated on the design of aerospace systems using online collaboration tools for two academic semesters. First, using social network analysis and longitudinal survey data, we analyzed the development of collaborative learning social networks over time. Second, we identified Communication Styles (CS) and a pre-existing friendship network as the individual- and structural-level factors respectively, and tested the degree to which the two antecedents influenced the structure of collaborative learning social networks. Finally, the paper concludes with a discussion of findings and implications for future research with a special focus on collaborative learning.

LITERATURE REVIEW

Communication and Learning in Online Environments

Growing attention is paid to a perspective of knowledge and learning: *knowledge embedded in a community.* This perspective posits that learning is deeply entwined with social, communicative, and institutional phenomena. It suggests that knowledge is an outcome of actual engagement and participation in communities of practice or networks of practice (Brown & Duguid, 1991; Greeno, 1998; Rogoff, 1990). It also acknowledges that learning is a process of becoming a member of a certain community, which entails the ability to communicate in the language of this community and act according to its particular norms (Sfard, 1998). Cognition and knowing are distributed over both individuals and their environments, and learning is "situated" in these relations and networks of distributed activities of participation (Lave & Wenger, 1991). This view attempts to locate learning within distributed, multi-actor routines rather than individual minds. That is, knowledge is socially constructed and shared by collaboration and communication among multiple actors. Through conversation, shared narratives, and stories, members in a community accumulate such distributed knowledge. Therefore, individual learning is inseparable from collective learning. In other words, learning is not reducible to individuals' cognitive process of acquiring knowledge and skill. From this perspective, learning refers to concerted activity that exists in the form of organizational routines (Nanda, 1996) and shared narratives and stories (Brown & Duguid, 1991). Contrary to traditional notions of knowledge and learning, this perspective sees that the key task in learning design is to create and sustain social and communicative infrastructures that foster seamless conversations and networks of connections among distributed members.

A number of researchers and practitioners have envisioned the possibility of creating online learning environments where distributed learners co-construct knowledge through computer-supported collaborative learning. Computer-mediated communication (CMC) tools such as online discussion boards, instance messaging, video-audio conferencing, and email listservs are regarded as appropriate tools to support such collaborative knowledge sharing and learning practices. Studies have shown that CMC has unique characteristics which affect learning processes and outcomes in both positive and negative ways (Hiltz & Wellman, 1997, Hutchings, 2002). For instance, the limited bandwidth of CMC can cause low social presence and social cues, which make this particular commutation mode inappropriate for learning activities involving social and emotional tasks (Stacey, 2002). Asynchronous CMC makes interactions more convenient but raises new problems such as information overload and electronic normlessness (Hiltz & Wellman, 1997). A number of studies have also demonstrated advantages of CMC-based learning. For instance, Jeong (2007) indicated that CMC tools such instant messaging had the advantage of quick response which can facilitate more effective communication and knowledge transfer between instructor-students or peer-to-peer. Juan (2006) indicated that using CMC in teaching activity will help learners create good learning atmosphere and learning communities. Nicholson (2002) also pointed out that the use of CMC can provide a virtual hallway where instructor-students or peers can communicate with each other or engage in collaborative problem solving more easily. High interactivity afforded by CMC systems can also facilitate community-based learning by enabling active peer interaction, evaluation, and cooperation (Hiltz & Wellman, 1997).

Communication Styles and Willingness to Communicate

Personality plays a significant role in the explanation and prediction of behavior (Tett, Jackson, & Rothstein, 1991). Different learners have different instructional preferences, information processing styles, and cognitive personality styles, which have significant influence on the ways in which learners engage in diverse learning activities (Curry, 1983; Jones, Reichard, & Mokhtari, 2003; Terry, 2001). Jensen (2003) defined learning styles as a preferred way of thinking, processing, and understanding information. It refers to a person's characteristic style of acquiring and using information in learning and solving problems. Studies have shown that such personality type and cognitive styles affect participation in networked learning environment (Ellis, 2003), collaboration method, and instructional media preferences (Sadler-Smith & Riding, 1999).

Among different dimensions of personality, we focus on communication styles since learning in CSCL is inherently mediated by communication actions. Communication scholars have long held the idea that individuals exhibit personality-like differences in their basic communication styles. As a result, researchers have developed a number of communication style/competence indices such as Management Communication Style (MCS) (Richmond, 1979), Willingness To Communicate (WTC) (McCroskey, 1987, 1997), Multivariate Communication Style (MCS) (Norton, 1978), and Interpersonal Communication Competency Scale (ICCS) (Rubin & Martin, 1994). The current study focuses on the WTC and its effects on collaborative learning social networks, given that this particular construct has been validated in various contexts (Richmond & Roach, 1992) and deemed to be most relevant to our study purpose.

WTC is defined as the degree to which an individual is inclined to initiate communication with different people (friends, acquaintances, and strangers) in various social settings (interpersonal, group, and large meetings) (McCroskey 1987, 1997). It is shown that individuals display consistent behavioral tendencies when they communicate with real or anticipated communication partners (McCrosekey, 1987; Richmond & Roach, 1992). A high WTC individual feels more comfortable with initiating, continuing, and strengthening social relationships with new communication partners whereas a low WTC individual tends to be reluctant or less apt to communicate with others (McCroskey, 1987). Conceptualized as the Behavioral Intention (BI) component in the Theory of Reasoned Action (TRA) (Fishbein & Azjen, 1975), WTC has been reported to be a strong indicator of communication behaviors in social life, small groups, and organizations (Richmond & Roach, 1992). For instance, high WTC than low WTC people are more likely to develop heterogeneous relationships in organizations and to explore and initiate new relationships when participating in new social environments. Consequently, high WTC persons tend to occupy more leadership positions or achieve better performance (Richmond & Roach, 1992), whereas low WTC persons tend to be

less successful in organizational positions where much communication is expected of them (Richmond & McCroskey, 1989). It is argued that the WTC concept is similar to introvert and extrovert personality types commonly found in personality measurement schemes such as Myers-Briggs Type Indicator (MBTI) (Myers, 1984). Others also argue that WTC is not conceptually separated from other communication style or personality measures such as communication apprehension, reticence, shyness (Kelly, 1982). Richmond (1979) argues that WTC is different from others since this measure focuses on *behavioral intention* to communicate, which can be caused by many other antecedent factors such as communication apprehension, shyness, trait-based personality, or situational factors.

Communication Styles and Collaborative Learning Social Network

Only a few studies have examined how individuals' characteristics such as communication styles affect the ways in which people create and sustain their social/communication networks. The structural approach to social dynamics in Social Network Analysis (SNA) tends to over-emphasize the structural determination of human behavior, but has neglected the possibility that network positions occupied by individuals might be influenced by their psychology (Kilduff, 1992). As Burt (1986) noted, individual dispositions have often been dismissed as "the spuriously significant attributes of people temporarily occupying particular positions in social structure" (p106).

While there have been investigations of the "origins" of network positions from a cultural or dispositional perspective (e.g., Emirbayer & Goodwin, 1994; Kilduff, 1992), others, however, began to investigate the impacts of individual characteristics on the structure of larger social systems. For instance, previous studies showed that different personality types were associated with distinctive network positions (Burt, Jannotta, & Mahoney, 1998) and influenced the way individuals leveraged their network positions in organizations (Mehra, Kilduff, & Brass, 2001). More specifically, individuals with high entrepreneurial personality occupied more entrepreneurial network positions such as brokerage positions (Burt, Jannotta, & Mahoney, 1998), and those who had high self-monitoring personality were more inclined to leverage their central network positions to perform better in an organization (Mehra, Kilduff, & Brass, 2001).

While increasingly more attention has been paid to examining the micro-foundations of social networks in *organizational* settings, there is little work examining the "origins" or "antecedents" of collaborative learning social networks in *educational* settings. In this study, we identify communication styles (i.e., WTC) as a critical individual factor influencing the way distributed learners develop collaborative learning social networks in a CSCL setting.

As discussed above, learning in a CSCL setting is deeply based on communicative acts such as conversation, collaboration, and social exchanges (Harasim et al., 1995). Further, interactions in such learning environment are often remote, faceless, uncertain, and mediated by newer Computer-Mediated Communication (CMC) systems (Haythorthwaite, 2002). Hence, individuals' disposition toward communication (i.e., willingness to communicate) should significantly affect learners' behaviors, especially how they build new social and learning relationships/networks with distributed, remote learning partners, who are often strangers.

While there is no direct evidence on how communication styles influence the structure of a larger social system, previous studies provide meaningful support for the contentions of this study. For instance, studies on CSCL show that individual learners display varying degrees of inclination toward group work, collaborative technology, and cooperative learning environ-

ments (Hiltz, 1994; Witmer, 1998), which, in turn, significantly influence the way they use instructional technology (Scalia & Sackmary, 1996) and their learning performance (Webb & Palincsar, 1996).

Related to WTC, extrovert/introvert personality types also displayed significant relationships with group collaboration. Because extraverted individuals are sociable, have enhanced social skills and have a high desire to work with others (Thoms, Moore, & Scott, 1996), they are more likely to communicate members within/across the team. In addition, extraversion contains element of positive affectivity (George, 1992), which is an overall sense of well-being and the tendency to experience positive emotional states. Positive affectivity has been shown to promote positive and cooperative interactions with others (Hogan & Holland, 2003; LePine & Van Dyne, 2001), which can lead to better learning outcomes in a networked learning environment.

As noted above, recent SNA studies have observed that personality types affect social network positions and developmental patterns (Burt, Jannotta, & Mahoney, 1998; Mehra, Kilduff, & Brass, 2001). Studies on WTC also demonstrate that communication styles significantly influence various communication behaviors and outcomes including new relationship building, diversity of relational linkages, leadership, and performance (McCroskey, 1987; Richmond & McCroskey, 1989; Richmond & Roach, 1992).

In sum, the aforementioned literature suggests that learners with dissimilar communication styles should act differentially in a networked learning environment, and as a result, build diverse types of social networks. For example, high WTC learners might be more apt or inclined to seek out new relationships in a CSCL setting than low WTC learners. They are more likely to explore new relational opportunities and assets such as information, skills, and knowledge accessible through collaborative learning social networks. On the contrary, faced with high communication uncertainty due to factors such as mediated technology or disposition, low WTC communicators may be more interested in investing in close social relationships in which they and their partners can be trusted, and, thus, create small but cohesive social circles (McCroskey, 1997). Hence, we predict:

Hypothesis 1a*: High WTC learners will be more likely than low WTC learners to explore new social ties and links when they participate in CSCL settings.*

Similarly, we hypothesize that learners with high WTC are more likely to actively build up new connections, create social networks with heterogeneous partners, and thus more actively participate in networked learning activities. As a result, those with high WTC are expected to occupy central positions in a collaborative learning social network.

Hypothesis 1b*: High WTC learners are more likely than low WTC learners to occupy central positions in an emergent collaborative learning social network.*

Pre-Existing Friendship Network

Incorporating the structuralist perspective, we also hold that emergent network social structures are not only determined by individual communication styles and volition, but also influenced by pre-existing social and structural elements of a given social system. As Emirbayer and Goodwin suggested (1994), development of any new social system is dependent upon and constrained by previous social structures, histories, and ties. That is, social networks "exhibit aspects of both *emergence*, being called into existence to accomplish some particular work, and *history*, drawing on known relationships and shared experience" (Nardi, Whittaker, & Schwarz., 2002, p. 207). Consistent with this argument, studies have shown

that a pre-existing network, such as a friendship network, becomes a relational foundation, which provides a base for quick formation of multiple communication and social support networks in various social settings (Jenh & Shah, 1997). A pre-existing social network also has strong effects on the formation of computer-mediated relationships and social networks. Evidence suggests that "electronic links primarily enhance existing interaction patterns rather than creating new ones" (Bikson, Eveland, & Gutek, 1989, p. 102). Child and Loveridge (1990) found that CMC was designed precisely to support ongoing hierarchical relations, while more recently, Wellman, Hass, Witte, and Hampton (2001) observed that people's interaction online supported pre-existing social capital by supplementing face-to-face contacts.

In a typical CSCL setting, students often recruit existing friends and colleagues when they participate in a new learning program. As a result, some take central/peripheral positions from the beginning, and this initial social structure may significantly enable or constrain how distributed learners create and benefit from emerging social networks (Cho, Lee, Stefanone, & Gay, 2005). Accounting for this structural force of a pre-existing social network, we predict:

Hypothesis 2*: Learners' initial positions in a pre-existing friendship network will significantly affect the ways in which distributed learners develop new social ties and move into different social groups in an emerging collaborative learning social network.*

METHOD

Study Site and Sample

The data for this study were collected from a multi-year CSCL research project. The goal of the project was to develop the capability for individuals at distributed geographic locations to interact effectively on development of future aerospace systems. As a part of this larger research project, a distributed CSCL course was co-hosted by two engineering schools at two large eastern universities in the US. Due to requirement for intense collaboration and coordination among remote learners, the class size was set to a small group setting. Sampling of students for this study was conducted on a first come first serve basis during each institution's course enrollment process. Altogether, thirty one senior and graduate-level engineering students enrolled in a year-long design course (14 from University A and 17 from University B). Among the students, 23 were male (Univ. A=9, Univ. B=14) and 8 were female (Univ. A=4, Univ. B=4).

One key feature of this CSCL course was that the distributed virtual teams, consisting of students from two remote locations, had to work closely together in order to design a future aerospace system. The group task focused on the design of the structural sub-system for the next-generation space shuttle, a reusable launch vehicle (RLV), and because of the RLV's complexity, the group task was highly interdependent, cooperative, and multidisciplinary in nature. The teams worked on specific design issues regarding materials and structure, as well as on thermal control and thermal protection. To create effective designs, distributed learners had to be aware of the overall system engineering. However, at the same time, they needed to cooperate and collaborate with others, since each group member had to specialize in one specific area. To create a full multidisciplinary experience, NASA engineers interacted with the class to address such disciplines as propulsion systems, hydraulics, aerodynamics, human factors, and cost analysis. In the first semester, the students considered alternative designs for elements and systems of the RLV. In the second semester, a detailed design was produced, complete with virtual manufacturing, construction and testing. The course ended with a presentation to NASA.

The course emphasized community-level collaboration, cooperation, and socialization among distant learners so that skills, ideas, knowledge, and social support could be exchanged across the boundaries of design teams, classes, and universities. As a means of supporting these collaborative learning activities, a web-based collaboration and communication system, called Advanced Interactive Design Environment (AIDE), was developed. The AIDE is a web-based portal providing a suite of integrated tools including simulation, application sharing, communication, networking, information retrieval, custom information storage, as well as instructor-provided material. The communication tools include real-time audio/video (AV) conferencing, chat and instant messaging (IM), email, and discussion boards. Distributed team members could collaborate on the design project by simultaneously running engineering simulations, sharing applications, exchanging design ideas using digital white boards, etc. (See Figure 1 for a screenshot of the AIDE collaboration system). Additionally, learners could retrieve information and documents by using a natural language search engine. The AIDE also provided public and social knowledge space through which distributed students freely exchanged ideas and suggestions via email, IM, and online discussion boards. Besides information exchange relevant to the group task, students were strongly encouraged to have social interactions with other students to build a sense of belongingness within the class. To enhance a sense of community membership, students also participated in two team building exercise events held in one of the universities in the beginning of the course year. Team level achievements were also frequently posted on the shared web space so that distributed learners could exchange their comments, experiences, ideas, and suggestions for improvements across the boundaries of design groups and universities.

Figure 1. Screenshot of AIDE

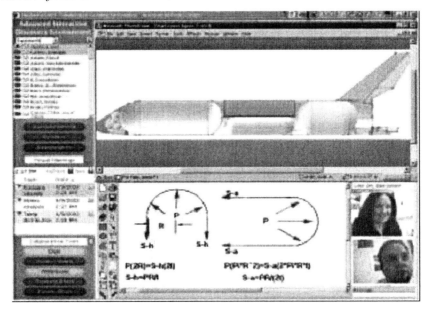

Data Collection

Two separate surveys were administered in the beginning and at the end of the study year, respectively. The first survey was administered in the second week of the first semester to measure any pre-existing networks. Students were asked to look carefully at the class roster and indicate up to five persons whom they most frequently communicated with, and were asked how often they communicated with them during a typical month. Considering these networks were measured before students participated in the group aspects of the design project, and that upper class and graduate students belonged to the same departments or schools for years, it is assumed that the reported relationships were pre-existing friendships rather than any other type of instrumental relation. The first social network survey also contained scale items for communication styles (see below for a description for this measure). In subsequent data collection (at the end of the second semester), students were asked to report names of people they talked to for information exchange. Infor-

mation exchange refers to communication about class, coursework, or design projects. Multi-item self-report Likert type scales ranging from 1 to 7 were used to measure all variables.

Measures

Communication Styles

To measure individuals' communication styles (WTC), a Self-Perception of Communication Competence (SPCC) scale was used (McCroskey & McCroskey, 1988). This measure was selected because it is based on a relatively simple structure, but covers quite comprehensive communication situations. More specifically, a combination of 12 scale items produced different subscales measuring an individual's comfortableness with speaking to acquaintances (Chronbach's alpha=.65) or strangers (alpha =.74) in different contexts. The scale also produced one situation-specific subscale measuring an individual's willingness to communicate with different types of people in a large group meeting (alpha =.72).

Pre-Existing Friendship Network Positions

Individuals' initial network positions in a pre-existing friendship network were measured by two network centrality indices, closeness and betweenness. The two indices were selected according to the assumption that closeness and betweenness were to have the greatest influence on how network distribution creates newer social and collaborative learning networks.[2] *Closeness* centrality measures the degree to which an individual is close to all other members in a given network. Closeness measures can be conceptualized as the "ease of access to others" (Burkhardt & Brass, 1990, p.113). An individual who is maximally close would have direct, unmediated relationships with all other members of the network. *Betweenness* centrality measures the frequency with which an actor falls between other pairs of actors on the shortest or geodesic paths connecting them (Freeman, 1979, p.221). The higher the betweenness score of an actor, the greater the extent to which that actor serves as a structural conduit, connecting others in the network.

Collaborative Learning Social Network

Hypothesis 1 and 2 predict that CS (H1) and pre-existing network positions (H2) will significantly influence the formation of a collaborative social network. The development of collaborative social networks was captured by two measures, *change propensity* and *degree centrality*. Change propensity measures the extent to which an individual explored new social links and circles as the person participated in a CSCL community. Conceptually, change propensity observes how actively an individual has acquired new relational resources and assets in his or her own social circle (i.e., ego network). In other words, it indicates the degree to which an individual renewed his/her social and intellectual capital as the person participates in a new learning environment. Operationally, it is computed by using the following formula in Box 1.

For instance, if person "x" initially reported a, **b, c**, d, e as her/his interaction partners in phase I (pre-existing network) and then reported **b, c**, f, g, t in phase II, then the change propensity for this particular individual in phase II is 0.6 (3/5).

Degree centrality refers to the number of ties (connections) that an actor holds in a given social network. In our study, it conceptualizes the degree to which an individual learner is deeply embedded in an emergent collaborative learning social network (Baldwin, Bedwell, & Johnson, 1997).

RESULTS

As for Hypothesis 1 and 2, multiple regression analyses were conducted in order to examine the degree to which CS and pre-existing network positions influenced the way individuals created new social networks when they participated in a

Box 1.

$$\text{Change Propensity} = \frac{\text{The number of new network ties added in one's social network (Phase II)}}{\text{The total number of network ties in one's pre-existing social network (Phase I)}}$$

networked learning program. In the regression models, the three communication style measures and initial network positions (centrality) were entered as independent variables to predict each of the dependent variables, i.e., change propensity (H1a) and degree centrality (H1b).

Note that we centered both the communication style and centrality variables in order to correct for multicollinearity problems. To check on the severity of the multicollinearity among the independent variables, we examined the conditioning index and variance proportions associated with each independent variable (see Belsley, Kuh, & Welsch, 1980, for a discussion). According to Tabachnik and Fidell (1996), a conditioning index greater than 30 and at least two variance proportions greater than .50 indicate serious multicollinearity. The multicollinearity diagnostics displayed that, even after the measures were centered, the three communication styles had severe multicollinearity problems. Hence, we decided to run three separate regression analyses, by entering each communication style variable at a time to avoid serious threats to the validity of our findings. Since the two social network variables displayed no multicollinearity problem, those two variables were included in the regression model simultaneously.

Table 1 summarizes the results of multiple regression analyses for Hypothesis 1 and 2. Hypothesis 1a was partially supported. Among the three communication style variables, "willingness to communicate with acquaintances" displayed a marginally significant positive relationship with the change propensity (β = .323, p <.06). Given that this analysis was based on a very small sample size, the .06 level results were deemed to be noteworthy.[3] It indicates that those who were more willing to communicate with acquaintances more actively explored new social ties in this particular CSCL community. As a result, they significantly changed their network partners as they participated in the emergent social structure. Other measures for communication styles such as "willingness to communicate with strangers" or "willingness to communicate in a large group," did not display any significant relationships with the dependent variable, i.e., change propensity. It seems that participants in this learning community considered other members in the community as acquaintances, rather than strangers.

Hypothesis 2 was also supported in that students' initial network positions had negative effects on change propensity. As shown in the table, closeness displayed a significant negative association with *change propensity* (β = -.575, p

Table 1. Results of regression analyses predicting an individual's propensity to change social network composition showing standardized beta

	Step I	Step II	Step III
WTC			
Communicate with acquaintances	.323 (p=06)	-	-
Communicate with strangers	-	.180	-
Communicate in a group meeting	-	-	.165
Closeness	-.575**	-.507*	-.539**
Betweenness	-.054	-.069	-.088
R-Square	.450	.376	.374
Adjusted R-square	.368	.282	.280

*p < .05, ** < .01

< 01). The result indicates that those who were maximally close to all other members in the pre-existing network were less likely to form new ties and links in the later periods. In other words, those who were central in the pre-existing network were more likely to stay in their initial social circles, whereas peripheral actors were more likely to alter their network compositions, since they are not bound to pre-existing networks. The results suggest that an actor's centrality in a pre-existing network generally confine people in pre-determined social circles.

Hypothesis 1b was not supported. We ran another set of the regression analyses using the same independent variables to predict degree centrality. Neither the communication style nor the network measures displayed significant associations with the dependent variable, *degree centrality*.

DISCUSSION

It has been argued that in order to foster a CSCL community, it is not enough to implement new instructional technologies or collaboration systems, but an appropriate *social infrastructure*, i.e., social networks and practices that support desired interactions between the participants (Bielaczyc, 2001) should also be put in place. By adding personality theory to structural analysis (SNA), we empirically investigated how individuals' personal characteristics (communication styles) and structural properties (pre-existing social network) interact to influence the ways in which distributed learners build their social and intellectual capital in the context of CSCL.

To summarize, we found that both psychological (individual communication styles) and structural (a pre-existing friendship network) factors significantly influenced the way distributed learners created collaborative learning social networks. As predicted by H1a, we observed that individual differences in communication style resulted in structural differences in ego network

composition. That is, high and low WTC individuals pursued different network strategies, with high WTC learners tending to explore new social worlds and add new relational ties, and low WTC learners tying to more small and trustful social worlds. It suggests that just as people differently manage human and finance capitals, people with different communication styles invest, manage, and utilize their social and learning capital in a different way.

Additionally, a pre-existing friendship network significantly influenced the emergence of collaborative social networks. Students who were holding many strong social relationships in an initial pre-existing social structure were more likely to stay in their initial social circles, whereas initially peripheral actors tended to form more heterogeneous relationships and freely moved into different social circles. Leenders and Gabbay (1999) suggest that pre-existing social ties have both functional and dysfunctional impacts on network-based activities. On one hand, pre-existing social network properties can be social capital, enabling an individual to build up new relational assets by leveraging his/her own existing social ties. On the other hand, pre-existing social ties become a social liability when they restrict one's ability to renew his/her existing capital by confining the social actor to pre-determined social circles (Gargiulo & Benassi, 1999). The negative beta coefficient reported in this study suggests that pre-existing network ties acted as a *social liability* that significantly constrained an actor's ability to explore new social contacts and resources when s/he was making a transition into a new learning environment, or a CSCL community.

As hypothesized in the original research model, we assumed that the two antecedents, communication styles and a pre-existing social network, were independent sources of influences on the development of a collaborative learning social network. However, it can be argued that the two antecedents are rather interrelated factors as communication styles may have influenced the network positions of individuals in a pre-existing network. For instance, high WTC individuals might have occupied central positions in a pre-existing network from the beginning. This alternative reasoning assumes that communication styles would have only *indirect* influence on the social network outcome through the mediation of the pre-existing social network. However, a correlation test checking the association between the two factors displayed that there was no significant relationship, which instead supports our original research model.

With regards to H1b, we failed to support our hypothesis that communication styles would influence final network positions (i.e., centrality) of individual learners. While communication styles (WTC) significantly influenced the way individuals composed their ego network (H1a), it did not affect their final network positions in a larger social system (H1b). The failure to support H1b is not surprising given that this particular result is somewhat consistent with the structuralist arguments made in SNA studies. As noted before, the SNA literature suggests that network position in a larger social structure should not be solely determined by a focal individual's personality or volitions, but influenced by behaviors of multiple network actors and other structural forces (Wasserman & Faust, 1994). Although a social network consists of individual actors and their relationships, the resultant larger social structure is not just a simple sum of many components. In other words, while an individual can decide whom to communicate with or how to compose his or her social capital, the person cannot determine his/her own network position through conscious activity since it is often based on thousands of direct or indirect network linkages. The results suggest that future researchers need to be aware of the multi-faceted nature of the relationship between individual differences and social network formation. As noted above, CS influenced a social network outcome in the ego (individual) level analysis (change propensity) but not in the network level analysis (centrality). It suggests that level of analysis and conceptualizations of network outcomes should be important issues for future researchers focusing on the interrelationship between individual characteristics and the social network.

CONCLUSION, LIMITATIONS, AND DIRECTIONS FOR FUTURE STUDY

Before we conclude our study, we would like to mention some important limitations of the study, together with directions for future research. The CSCL community examined in this study consisted of relatively small, homogeneous learning groups. Studying social phenomena using a small sample size is not unusual in social network research due to the extreme difficulties gathering such rich and complex information (Wasserman & Faust, 1994). Yet, the small sample size restricts the researcher from generalizing findings of the current study to broader social settings, given the complexity of the model to be tested. Similarly, the research site was situated within a special educational context; and all subjects were college engineering students. Caution is advised in attempts to generalize findings to other social settings where social dynamics and structures may be significantly different. Hence, we emphasize that findings and implications of this study are only tentative and preliminary in nature until they are to be further tested and validated by future research employing larger samples in different contexts.

In spite of those limitations, we still believe that the present study has important theoretical, methodological, and practical implications for researchers and practitioners in the field of CSCL. Theoretically, findings of this study render empirical support for the new notions of learning and knowledge revolving around the premise that learning is indeed a social and communication outcome (Brown & Duguid, 1991; Harasim et al.,

1995; Lave & Wenger, 1991; Nonaka & Konno, 1998). The study demonstrated that CS and a pre-existing social network played a significant role in shaping how distributed learners act in a networked learning environment. Given that there is a dearth of empirical research to support many theoretical claims of CSCL (Woodruff, 2002), this study is valuable in demonstrating the possible relationship between communication styles and social network variables to learning in a CSCL learning environment.

The study also proposes that adding personality theory (CS) to structural analysis (SNA) should help forge a useful approach to understanding individual behavior in the context of social structure. Taken together, a combination of these somewhat opposing disciplines contributes to an enhanced picture of how distributed learners with different characteristics build their social and intellectual capitals in a computer-mediated social system. As Mehra and his colleagues suggested (2001), future research may benefit from the further integration of modern social network analysis and the rich traditions of psychology, as opposed to the acceptance of an inevitable duality between those interested in the psychological determinants of individual behavior and those interested in how network structures affect social processes (Emirbayer & Goodwin, 1994).

In a more practical sense, the current study suggests that we should focus both on individual characteristics as well as social/structural elements when designing CSCL activities and environments. Although many have highlighted the importance of "social infrastructures" in CSCL (Bielaczyc, 2001), we often assume that technology will automatically connect remote learners and promote borderless exchange of information, knowledge, and skills among distributed individuals and teams. In order to support seamless participation among network learners, however, one should fully take into account such individual and social factors as communication styles or a pre-existing network in the design of a CSCL com-

munity. For instance, educators may administer a personality/communication style survey and match low WTC individuals with high WTC as peer or team members in order to facilitate more seamless collaboration among all members in a CSCL community. Similarly, the study showed that network centrality significantly influenced students' final learning performance, indicating that some students were structurally advantaged or disadvantaged due to their network positions. Social network analysis can be conducted during the semester to identify central or peripheral members, and this information might be helpful to redesigning social infrastructures in a learning community.

ACKNOWLEDGMENT

The authors gratefully acknowledge the support of NASA Langley Research Center, through Cooperative Agreement No. NCC-1-01004. Additional support was provided by the State of New York and the AT&T Foundation.

REFERENCES

Adler, P. S., & Kwon, S. W. (2002). Social capital: Prospect for a new concept. *Academy of Management Review, 27*(1), 17-40.

Baldwin, T. T., Bedell, M. D., & Johnson, J. L. (1997). The social fabric of a team-based M.B.A. program: Network effects on student satisfaction and performance. *Academy of Management Journal, 40*(6), 1369-1397.

Belsley, D. A., Kuh, E., & Welsch, R. E. (1980). *Regression diagnostics: Identifying influential data and sources of collinearity.* New York: Wiley.

Bielaczyc, K. (2001). Designing social infrastructure: The challenge of building computer-supported learning communities. In P. Dillenbourg, A. Eurelings, & K. Hakkarainen (Eds.), *The Proceedings of the First European Conference on CSCL* (pp.106-114). University of Maastricht.

Bikson, T., Eveland, J. D., & Gutek, B. A. (1989). Flexible interactive technologies for multi-person tasks: Current problems and future prospects. In M. H. Olson (Ed.), *Technological support for work group collaboration* (pp.89-112). Hillsdale, NJ: Erlbaum.

Brown, J. S., & Duguid, P. (1991). Organizational learning and communities-of-practice: Toward a unified view of working, learning, and innovation. *Organization Science, 2*(1), 40-57.

Burkhardt, M. E., & Brass, D. J. (1990). Changing patterns or patterns of change: The effect of a change in technology on social network structure and power. *Administrative Science Quarterly, 35*, 104-127.

Burt, R. S. (1986). Comment. In S. Lindberg, J. S. Coleman, & S. Novak (Eds.), *Approaches to social theory* (pp.105-107). New York: Russell Sage.

Burt, R. S., Jannotta, J. E., & Mahoney, J. T. (1998). Personality correlates of structural holes. *Social Networks, 20*, 63-87.

Child, J., & Loveridge, R. (1990). *Information technology in European services-towards a microelectronic future*. Oxford, UK: Blackwell.

Cho, H., Gay, G., Davidson, B., & Ingraffea, A. (2007). Social networks, communication styles, and learning performance in a CSCL community. *Computers & Education, 49(2)*, 309-329.

Cho, H., Lee, J., Stefanone, M., & Gay, G. (2005). Development of computer-supported collaborative social networks in a distributed learning community. *Behaviour & Information Technology, 24*(6), 435-448.

Cho, H., Stefanone, M., & Gay, G. (2002). Social information sharing in a CSCL community.

In G. Stahl (Ed.), *Computer Support for Collaborative Learning: Foundations for a CSCL Community (Proceedings of the 2002 CSCL conference)* (pp.43-53). Mahway, NJ: Lawrence Erlbaum Associates.

Cohen, D., & Prusak, L. (2001). *In good company: How social capital makes organizations work*. Boston, MA: Harvard Business Press.

Cook, K. S., & Emerson, R. M. (1978). Power, equity and commitment in exchange networks. *American Sociological Review, 43*, 721-739.

Culnan, M. J., & Markus, L. (1987). Information technologies: Electronic media and intraorganizational communication. In E. M. Jablin, L. L. Putnam, K. H. Roberts, & L. W. Porter (Eds.), *Handbook of organizational communication* (pp. 420-444). Beverly Hills, CA: Sage.

Curry, L. (1983). *Learning styles in continuing media education*. Ottawa, Canada: Canadian Medical Association.

Ellis, A. E. (2003). Personality type and participation in networked learning environments. *Education Media International, 40*(1/2), 101-114.

Emirbayer, M., & Goodwin, J. (1994). Network analysis, culture, and the problem of agency. *American Journal of Sociology, 99*, 1411-1454.

Freeman, L. C. (1979). Centrality in social networks, conceptual clarification. *Social Networks, 1*, 215-239.

Fishbein, M., & Azjen, I. (1975). *Belief, attitude, intention, and behavior: An introduction to theory and research*. Reading, MA: Addison-Weasley.

Gargiulo, M., & Benassi, M. (1999). The dark side of social capital. In R. A. J. Leenders & S. M. Gabbay (Eds.), *Corporate social capital and liability* (pp. 298-322). Boston, MA: Kluwer Academic Publishers.

George, J. M. (1992). The role of personality in organizational life: Issues and evidence. *Journal of Management, 18*, 185-213.

Granovetter, M. S. (1973). The strength of weak ties. *American Journal of Sociology, 78,* 1360-1380.

Greeno, J. (1998). The situativity of knowing, learning, and research. *American Psychologist, 53*(1), 5-26.

Harasim, L., Hiltz, S. R., Teles, L., & Turoff, M. (1995). *Learning networks: A field guide to teaching and learning online.* Cambridge, MA: The MIT Press.

Haythornthwaite, C. (2002). Building social networks via computer networks: Creating and sustaining distributed learning communities. In K.A. Renninger & W. Shumar (Eds.), *Building virtual communities: Learning and change in cyberspace* (pp.159-190). Cambridge, UK: Cambridge University Press.

Hiltz, S. R., & Wellman, B. (1997). Asynchronous learning networks as a virtual classroom. *Communications of the ACM, 40*(9), 44-49.

Hiltz, S. R. (1994). *The virtual classroom: Learning without limits via computer networks.* Norwood, NJ: Alex Publishing Corporation.

Hogan, J., & Holland, B. (2003). Using theory to evaluate personality and job-performance relations: A socioanalytic perspective. *Journal of Applied Psychology, 88,* 100-112.

Hutchings, M. (2002). Computer mediated communication: Impact on learning. In S. Fallows & R. Bhanot (Eds.), *Educational development: Through information and communications technology* (pp.87-101). London: Kogan Page.

Jehn, K., & Shah, P. (1997). Interpersonal relationships and task performance: An examination of mediating processes in friendship and acquaintance groups. *Journal of Personality and Social Psychology, 72,* 775-790.

Jensen, G. H. (2003). Learning styles. In J. A. Provost & W. S. Anchors (Eds.), *Using the MBTI instrument in colleges and universities* (pp. 123-155). Gainesville, FL: Center for Applications of Psychological Type.

Jeong, W. (2007). Instant messaging in on-site and online classes in higher education. *Educause Quarterly, 30*(1), 30-36.

Jones, C., Reichard, C., & Mokhtari, K. (2003). Are students' learning styles discipline specific? *Community College Journal of Research and Practice, 27*(5), 363-375.

Juan, C. C., Carmen. P. F., & Jesus, F. (2006). Assessing the use of instant messaging in online learning environments. *Interactive Learning Environments, 14*(3), 205-218.

Kelly, L. (1982). A rose by any other name is still a rose: A comparative analysis of reticence, communication apprehension, unwillingness to communicate, and shyness. *Human Communication Research, 8*(2), 99-113.

Kilduff, M. (1992). The friendship network as a decision-making resource: Dispositional moderators of social influences on organizational choices. *Journal of Personality and Social Psychology, 62*(1), 168-180.

Lave, J., & Wenger, E. (1991). *Situated learning: Legitimate peripheral participation.* Cambridge, UK: Cambridge University Press.

Leenders, R. A. J., & Gabbay, S. M. (1999). *Corporate social capital and liability.* Boston, MA: Kluwer Academic Publishers.

LePine, J. A., & Van Dyne, L. (2001). Voice and cooperative behavior as contrasting forms of contextual performance: Evidence of differential relationships with big five personality characteristics and cognitive ability. *Journal of Applied Psychology, 86,* 326-336.

McCroskey, J. C. (1997). Willingness to communicate, communication apprehension, and self-perceived communication competence: Conceptualizations and perspectives. In J. A. Daly, J. C. McCroskey, J. Ayres, T. Hopf, & D. M. Ayres (Eds.), *Avoiding communication: Shyness, reticence, and communication apprehension* (2nd ed.) (pp.75-108). Cresskill, NJ: Hampton Press Inc.

McCroskey, J. C. (1987). *Personality and interpersonal communication*. Newbury Park, CA: Sage.

McCroskey, J. C., & McCroskey, L. L. (1988). Self report as an approach to measuring communication competence and personality orientations. *Communication Research Reports, 5,* 108-113.

Mehra, A., Kilduff, M., & Brass, D. J. (2001). The social networks of high and low self-monitors: Implications for work place performances. *Administrative Science Quarterly, 46*(1), 121-146.

Millen, D. R., Fontaine, M. A., & Muller, M. A. (2002). Understanding the benefit and costs of communities of practice. *Communications of the ACM, 45*(4), 69-73.

Myers, I. B. (1984). *Myers Briggs type indicator.* Palo Alto, CA: Consulting Psychologists Press.

Nahapiet, J., & Ghoshal, S. (1998). Social capital, intellectual capital, and the organizational advantage. *Academy of Management Review, 23*(2), 242-266.

Nanda, A. (1996). Resources, capabilities and competencies. In B. Moingeon & A. Edmondson (Eds.), *Organizational learning and competitive advantage* (pp. 93-120). Thousand Oaks, CA: Sage.

Nardi, B., Whittaker, S., & Schwarz, H. (2002). NetWORKers and their activity in intensional networks. *Computer Supported Cooperative Work, 11,* 205-242.

Nicholson, S. (2002). Socialization in the 'virtual hallway': Instant messaging in the asynchronous Web-based distance education classroom. *The Internet and Higher Education, 5,* 363-372.

Nonaka, I., & Konno, N. (1998). The concept of "ba": Building a foundation for knowledge creation. *California Management Review, 40*(3), 40-54.

Norton, R. W. (1978). Foundation of a communication style construct. *Human Communication Research,* 4(2), 99-112.

Parker, D. (2001). Inside online learning: Comparing conceptual and technique based learning in place-based and ALN formats. *Journal of Asynchronous Learning Network, 5*(2), 64-74.

Richmond, V. P. (1979). Management communication style, tolerance for disagreement, and innovativeness as predictors of employee satisfaction: A comparison of single-factor, two-factor, and multifactor approaches. *Communication Yearbook, 3,* 359-373.

Richmond, V. P., & Roach, D. K. (1992). Willingness to communicate and employee success in U.S. organizations. *Journal of Applied Communication Research, 31,* 95-115.

Richmond, V. P., & McCroskey, J. C. (1989). Willingness to communicate and dysfunctional communication processes. In C. V. Roberts & K. W. Watson (Eds.), *Interpersonal communication processes* (pp. 292-318). New Orleans, LA: Spectra & Scottsdale.

Rogoff, B. (1990). *Apprenticeship in thinking: Cognitive development in social context.* New York: Oxford University Press.

Rubin, R. B., & Martin, M. M. (1994). Development of a measure of interpersonal communication competence. *Communication Research Reports, 11*(1), 33-44.

Sadler-Smith, E., & Riding, R. (1999). Cognitive style and instructional preferences. *Instructional Science, 27,* 355-371.

Scalia, L. M., & Sackmary, B. (1996). Groupware in the classroom: Applications and guidelines. *Computers in the Schools, 12,* 39-53.

Sfard, A. (1998) On two metaphors for learning and the dangers of choosing just one. *Educational Researcher, 27,* 4-13.

Stacey, E. (2002). Social presence online: Networking learning at a distance. *Education and Information Technologies, 7*(4), 287-294.

Tabachnik, B. G., & Fidell, L. S. (1996). *Using multivariate statistics* (3rd ed.). New York: Harper Collins.

Terry, M. (2001). Translating learning style theory into university teaching practices: An article based on Kolb's experiential learning model. *Journal of College Reading and Learning, 32*(1), 65-68.

Tett, R. P., Jackson, D. N., & Rothstein, M. (1991). Personality measures as predictors of job performance: A meta-analytic review. *Personnel Psychology, 44,* 703-741.

Thoms, P., Moore, K. S., & Scott, K. S. (1996). The relationship between self-efficacy for participating in self-managed work groups and the Big Five personality dimensions. *Journal of Organizational Behavior, 17,* 349-362.

Trevino, L. K., Lengel, R., & Daft, R. L. (1987). Media symbolism, media richness, and media choice in organization: A symbolic interactionist perspective. *Communication Research, 14,* 553-574.

Walther, J. B. (1996). Group and interpersonal effects in international computer-mediated collaboration. *Human Communication Research, 23*(3), 342-369.

Wasserman, S., & Faust, K. (1994). *Social network analysis: Methods and applications.* Cambridge, UK: Cambridge University Press.

Webb, N. M., & Palinscar, A. S. (1996). Group processes in the classroom. In D. C. Berliner & R. Caffee (Eds.), *Handbook of educational psychology* (pp. 841-873). New York: Macmillan.

Wellman, B., Hass, A. Q., Witte, J., & Hampton, K. (2001). Does the Internet increase, decrease, or supplement social capital? Social networks, participation, and community commitment. *The American Behavioral Scientist, 45*(3), 436-455.

Witmer, D. F. (1998). Introduction to computer-mediated communication: A master syllabus for teaching communication technology. *Communication Education, 47,* 162-173.

Woodruff, E. (2002). CSCL communities in post-secondary education and cross-cultural settings. In T. Kochmann, R. Hall, & N. Miyake (Eds.), *CSCL 2: Carrying forward the conversation* (pp. 157-168). Mahwah, NJ: Lawrence Erlbaum Associates.

ENDNOTES

[1] An earlier version of this paper has been published in Computers & Education (Cho, Gay, Davidson, & Ingraffea, 2007).

[2] Originally, we intended to use four centrality indices such as degree centrality, closeness, betweenness, and structural holes. However, multicollinearity diagnostic test showed that degree centrality and structural holes had strong correlations with closeness and betweenness, respectively. In order to avoid the multicollinearity problem and because of the parsimony rule, we used closeness and betweenness for H2. As closeness and betweenness are conceptually similar to degree centrality and structural holes, respectively, we assume that the selected measures can be comprehensive enough to cover various network qualities.

[3] Note that the sample size is reduced to 25 from 31 for this particular analysis, since we excluded six students who were identified as social isolates in a pre-existing network. Since these students had zero or one net-

work partners in the pre-existing network, computing the dependent variable of H1, the degree to which they changed their network composition, would be less meaningful and bias the final results (denominator is zero or 1 in the formula). For all the other analyses, we kept the original 31 student sample size. To test whether the deletion of these people made any significant changes in the results, additional analyses were conducted including those people in the regression model. The results were almost identical except for small changes in coefficient values. Overall, the model fits were lowered and closeness became a less significant predictor (but still significant at .01 level)

Chapter XVIII
Fostering Interactivity through Formative Peer Assessment in (Web–Based) Collaborative Learning Environments

Jan-Willem Strijbos
Leiden University, The Netherlands

Theresa A. Ochoa
Indiana University, USA

Dominique M. A. Sluijsmans
HAN University, The Netherlands, & Open University of the Netherlands, The Netherlands

Mien S. R. Segers
Leiden University, The Netherlands

Harm H. Tillema
Leiden University, The Netherlands

ABSTRACT

Extant literature on collaborative learning shows that this instructional approach is widely used. In this chapter, the authors discuss the lack of alignment between collaborative learning and assessment practices. They will argue that peer assessment is a form of collaborative learning and a mode of assessment that perfectly fits the purpose of collaborative learning. As such, the authors purposefully depart from the more traditional application of assessment as a summative tool and advocate the consideration of formative peer assessment in collaborative learning. This shift towards formative assessment they believe has the potential to enhance learning. Their goal in this chapter is to review both shortcomings of current peer assessment practice as well as its potential for collaborative learning. Interactivity is central to foster the alignment between assessment and collaborative learning and the authors present a set of guidelines derived from research for increasing interactivity through formative peer assessment among peers in collaborative learning contexts.

INTRODUCTION

Most research on collaborative learning has focused on investigating the effectiveness of instructions to support and scaffold learning in small groups, as well as the applicability of web-based technology to foster such collaboration (see Fischer, Kollar, Mandl, & Haake, 2007; Jones, Cook, Jones, & De Laat, 2007; Ochoa, Gottschall, & Stuart, 2004; Strijbos, Kirschner, & Martens, 2004). Interestingly collaborative learning assessment practices have received less attention. Assessment practices tend to be teacher-directed (Chan & van Aalst, 2004; Slavin, 1995) and only few include self- (Barron et al., 1998) and/or peer assessment (Trahasch, 2004). Where peer assessment components are used, they are summative (to determine whether a criterion is met) rather than formative (to determine where a student can improve). Not surprisingly a 'group score' is most often the unit of measure for any given group task, supplemented either with one or multiple individual tasks. Typically, the final score consists of the average with a weighting factor applied. However, as assessment strongly influences learning (Black & Wiliam, 1998; Crooks, 1988; Frederiksen, 1984), we propose in this chapter that any collaborative learning activity should apply an assessment that a) reflects both the collaboration process and product, b) promotes students' collaboration skills as well as cognitive skills, and c) promotes students' self-regulation skills. In fact, we will argue that assessment in collaborative learning does not fully tap the potential benefits of the interactive setting unless it includes a mode of assessment that evokes a high and active responsibility from the learner, a component we hold is a critical aspect in collaborative learning.

As a team of researchers from the education and behavioural science disciplines who share an interest and expertise in collaborative learning, web-based instruction, and peer assessment we first outline the value of peer assessment for collaborative learning settings, illustrated by recent developments in assessment. Subsequently, we present the main shortcomings of current peer assessment practice in light of collaborative learning and provide some reasons why these shortcomings hamper a formative and interactive use of assessment. From the perspective of interactivity, which we define in depth, we present various interactive forms of peer assessment (face-to-face and web-based) and also illustrate how peer assessment can be used to elicit interactivity and subsequently learning (i.e., in terms of collaboration skills, cognitive skills, and self-regulation skills). It should be noted that this chapter predominantly focuses on the pedagogical design issues of peer assessment in collaborative learning (which apply to classroom and web-based settings), and the technology design issues are beyond the scope of this chapter. We close the chapter with a set of guidelines for the application of peer assessment in collaborative learning, and directions for future research and practice of (web-based) peer assessment.

BACKGROUND

Collaborative Learning and Assessment: The Lack of Constructive Alignment

Collaborative learning refers to an instructional approach in which students work together in small groups toward a common goal. The assumption is that learning processes are more effective and productive when students solve problems in collaboration, as compared to when they work alone or only with the teacher (Webb, 1992; Slavin, 1995). In sum, advocates of collaborative learning hold that students learn more in groups than they do in traditional lecture-based instruction (Dochy, Segers, Van den Bossche, & Gijbels, 2003; Ochoa & Robinson, 2005). Research has also shown that collaboration enhances students' motivation, social skills, and self-efficacy (Johnson & Johnson, 1994).

According to Ochoa and Robinson (2005) a cornerstone of collaborative learning is the assumption that negotiating multiple points of view enhances learning. Under this assumption, problem-solving in groups should produce discussion and cognitive dissonance that prompt students to reconsider and revise individual and collective beliefs and opinions. Furthermore, it is assumed that all members of the group will contribute to the group process. Not surprising, reality defies theory and assumptions do not always play out in practice – and simply asking students to interact will not automatically enhance performance.

Further examination of assessment practices used in collaborative learning, reveals that these two are rarely interlinked in research. In general, assessment is the process whereby information on a students' performance is collected and interpreted (Brookhart, 1999). Formal as well as informal procedures, according to Mehrens and Lehman (1991) are used to collect data in order to develop a comprehensive picture of the characteristics of the learner (in terms of knowledge, skills, attitudes or competences). The effectiveness of assessment depends on the quality of assessment and how it is incorporated by students in subsequent performance. In the past two decades educational research and practice has witnessed a rapid development in the area of assessment. Specifically in terms of why, what, when, how and who should (be) assess(ed) (Segers, Dochy, & Cascallar, 2003). These developments are often characterised by the shift from a testing culture to an assessment culture (Birenbaum, 2003).

In a testing culture the main purpose of assessment is to make evaluative decisions for summative purposes. A shortcoming of summative assessment is that it is decontextualised and atomic, isolated from the learning process and takes place only at the end of a course to judge how well a student performed. Summative assessment focuses strongly on the cognitive aspects of learning, often applies a single performance score, and it is designed and conducted by the instructor. In contrast, the features of a formative assessment culture are that assessment does not only serve summative but also (and to a large extent) formative purposes. Formative assessment is contextualised and intends to build a comprehensive picture of the learners' characteristics, it is an integral part of the learning process and it is iterative, takes place at several moments during a course rather than only at the end. Formative assessment focuses on cognitive, social, affective, as well as meta-cognitive aspects of learning, often applies a multi-method approach and therefore leads to a profile instead of a single score. Notably, students are involved in the assessment process. Despite our strong support for formative assessment, we do not deny the important aspects of summative assessment. In fact, we like Shute (2007) promote a unified approach that uses traditional (summative; assessment "of" learning) and progressive (formative; assessment "for" learning) perspectives.

In closing our discussion on the background on assessment practices used in collaborative learning we note that despite the strong attention for the instructional and pedagogical aspects of collaborative learning (e.g., research on collaboration scripts; see Fischer et al., 2007), assessment has only recently received more interest in collaborative learning research (Birenbaum, 2005; Meier, Spada, & Rummel, 2007). Yet, it is striking that the assessment of collaborative learning has hardly evolved beyond summative practices. In most cases, assessment focuses on the final group product and is only conducted by the instructor. Criteria are typically predefined by the instructor and the assessment process is treated as a 'black box' without any involvement of the learners (Sluijsmans, Strijbos, & Van de Watering, 2007; Sluijsmans, 2008). Because the assessment in collaborative learning is typically disconnected from the instructional setting, a lack of 'constructive alignment' exists (Biggs, 1996). The alignment of assessment with the collaborative learning process is therefore crucial (Freeman & McKenzie, 2002). Because an active participation of learners in the assessment process corresponds with active involvement in learning in the collaboration process, this alignment may be achieved through involvement of students using peer assessment (Orsmond, Merry, & Reiling, 2002).

Peer Assessment and Collaborative Learning

According to Topping (1998) peer assessment is an arrangement where equal status students judge a peers' performance with a rating scheme or qualitative report. Under this definition, peer assessment is expected to stimulate students to share responsibility, reflect, discuss and collaborate with peers (Boud, 1990; Orsmond, Merry, & Callaghan, 2004). Peer assessment can be summative or formative, one-way or reciprocal, face-to-face or online, anonymous or non-anonymous, the assessor(s) and assessee(s) may be individuals, pairs or groups, and they may be of the same or different age and/or of the same or different knowledge level (Topping, 2003). Peer assessment is often perceived as a radical change in the assessment process. A primary criticism of peer assessment relates to reliability. Skeptics, question the reliability of peer assessment compared to instructor assessment. Refuting this concern, pivotal research conducted by Falchikov and Goldfinch (2000) investigated forty-eight studies reporting on the agreement between instructor and peer marks in higher education and found an overall correlation of .69 – which is substantial and signifies that peer assessment can be applied as an alternative instructional approach.

Peer assessment incorporates varying features of collaborative learning. Regardless of the educational setting, peer assessment thrives on the interaction among group members. In the case of summative peer assessment this usually consists of peer rating using a predefined set of criteria,

whereas during formative peer assessment students are involved in discussing and negotiating criteria, and providing and receiving feedback. Irrespective of a summative or formative focus, peer assessment is in essence a specific type of collaborative learning. As a consequence individual accountability and positive interdependence – two core mechanisms of any type of collaborative learning (Strijbos, Martens, & Jochems, 2004) – are important aspects for peer assessment as well; and particularly when applied in a collaborative learning context.

Individual accountability refers to the extent to which group members are held individually accountable for tasks or duties, central to group performance or efficiency. Slavin (1980) introduced this mechanism to counter the well-known free-rider effect (a student deliberately does not invest any or limited effort into group performance (see Kerr & Bruun, 1983), and social loafing (a student assumes that his/her work will be carried out by a more motivated group member (see Williams & Karau, 1991). Presence of a free-rider typically often disrupts the collaborative process and compromises the group's dynamics or ability to complete the task (Cohen, 1994; Salomon & Globerson, 1989). The likelihood of the presence of a free-rider increases in large groups. However, the impact of the free-rider will be stronger in a small group if such a group member exists. Thus the need for accountability. Individual accountability necessitates that individual responsibilities for the group task are clearly specified. In collaborative learning, peer assessment can be used to hold students individually accountable for their contribution to the group process and product. In addition, when every group member is required to reach the same learning objective, it is in the interest of all group members to provide assistance and feedback to their peers (Slavin, 1995). Hence, interaction and interdependence are essential.

Positive interdependence refers to the extent that the performance of any group member depends on the performance of all other members. Johnson (1981) implemented it to foster group cohesion and a heightened sense of 'belonging' to a group. Positive interdependence can be achieved through the type of task, resources, goals, rewards, roles or the environment (Brush, 1998) and it has a strong influence on group cohesion. Positive interdependence and cohesion hinge on familiarity and mutual trust. Cohesion becomes important when the contributions made by one (or more) group member (s) are limited or substandard. When positive interdependence and cohesion are limited, students are prone to regard an assessment as the exclusive realm of a teacher (Cheng & Warren, 1997; Sambell, McDowell, & Brown, 1997; Sluijsmans, Brand-Gruwel, Van Merriënboer, & Martens, 2004).

Peer assessment in collaborative learning can be product-oriented (focused on the group product or individual contributions to the product), process-oriented (focused on the group process or individual contributions the group process), or a combination of the two. It should be noted that process-oriented assessment is only feasible at the individual and intra-group level, because assessing the process of another group is strained since the students themselves did not experience that particular group. In general, peer assessment of both the collaborative process and product is recommended (Divaharan & Atputhasamy, 2002; Lopez-Real & Chan, 1999; Macdonald, 2003; Prins, Sluijsmans, Kirschner, & Strijbos, 2005).

Considering how much collaborative learning is used as an instructional arrangement and how long it has been the topic of research inquiry (see for example Rieken, 1958) it is striking that, thus far, peer assessment typologies have not yet explicitly addressed the interactive and formative nature of peer assessment when applied in a collaborative learning context (Gielen, 2007; Topping, 1998; Van den Berg, Admiraal, & Pilot, 2006). Thus, the main question that we address in this chapter is: How can alignment of collaborative

learning and formative peer assessment foster interactivity and enhance learning?

Shortcomings of Current Peer Assessment Practice in Collaborative Learning

In an effort to gain insight in peer assessment practices in collaborative learning Sluijsmans et al. (2007) reviewed fifteen studies on peer assessment in collaborative learning. They found that nearly all studies applied peer assessment as a tool to construct individual grades from group grades. The peer assessment usually involves rating scales and appears especially appealing for the instruction of large numbers of students (when an instructor lectures one hundred plus students handing-in individual assignments to be assessed). This format of peer assessment reflects a narrow perspective on the application and benefits of peer assessment, as well as poor alignment with the interaction taking place during collaborative learning.

However, aligning peer assessment with collaborative learning and utilising its interactive and formative potential, requires that three major shortcomings in current peer assessment practice are addressed: a) the lack of attention for students' ability, b) the lack of attention for the quality of formative feedback, and c) the lack of attention for interpersonal variables.

Students' Ability

In most studies on peer assessment students' proficiency (their level of achievement) is not clarified, which makes it difficult to determine whether high and low ability students equally benefit from peer assessment. In addition, students' ability appears to affect peer assessment: less able students may experience more difficulty to self-assess or assess peers (Webb, 1992). Moreover, ability is not included when assessor-assessee pairs are established (whether these are instructor assigned or self-selected).

Furthermore, ability proved to be related to the learner's self- and peer assessment. Low achievers tend to overestimate the performance by a peer, whereas high achievers tend to underestimate the performance (Davies, 2006; Lejk & Wyvill, 2001; Patri, 2002). These high ability students are also self-critical rather than judgmental, whereas the opposite is observed for low ability students (Orsmond, Merry, & Reiling, 1997). Yet, recent work by Patri (2002) and Orsmond et al. (2002) reveals that students make more accurate judgments – comparable to those by teachers – when assessment criteria are clearly set. Especially the relevance of the criteria appears to be crucial for students' understanding of the assessment process, as well as subsequent application in peer assessment (Freeman & McKenzie, 2002).

Finally, students' are concerned about a potential rating bias (Divaharan & Atputhasamy, 2002). Particularly, naïve assessors may affect peer assessment validity (Langan et al., 2005; Ploegh, Segers, & Tillema, 2007). Students' also doubt their own and theirs peers' knowledge within a given subject area (Hanrahan & Isaacs, 2001) as well as their own and peers' skill to peer assess (Walker, 2001).

Quality of Formative Peer Feedback

Characteristic for formative peer assessment is a strong reliance on the role and importance of feedback. However, feedback does not automatically produce a positive result. Kluger and DeNisi's (1996) review revealed that one-third of the studies reported negative effects. These outcomes could not be solely explained by cognitive processes or the feedback sign (positive or negative). In education, feedback is systematically investigated in the context of 'instructor feedback' and '(computer-assisted) tutoring'. Interestingly, in a recent review by Hattie and Timperley (2007) a peer is mentioned as a feedback source, but peer

feedback and associated implications are not addressed explicitly. Whereas an instructor, book, parent or computer is regarded as an authoritative source, a peer is not readily considered to be a reliable source for feedback by their fellow students (emphasising the role of students' ability). Moreover, since students are not experts in a subject area, peer feedback is susceptible to assessor variation.

Feedback can vary in functional, content-related and formal characteristics. Narciss (2006, 2008) concludes that the nature and quality of an external feedback message (by an instructor, computer or by a peer) is determined by at least three facets: (a) functional aspects related to instructional objectives (e.g. cognitive functions, such as promoting information processing; motivational functions, such as reinforcing correct responses or sustaining persistence), (b) semantic aspects related to the content of the feedback message, and (c) formal and technical aspects related to feedback presentation (e.g., frequency, timing, mode, amount, form). As an example of peer feedback variation we mention the feedback stances (authoritative, interpretative, probing and collaborative) described by Lockhart and Ng (1995). The stances reflect two primary types of feedback: evaluative and informative (Van den Berg, 2003). The widely applied use of rating in peer assessment is typical for evaluative feedback (knowledge of result, e.g. "3 out of 5 are correct"), whereas the qualitative report (hints/suggestions, e.g. "give an example") coincides with informative feedback.

Current research on tutoring focuses on informative feedback, and investigates internal and external feedback loops and the role of persistence and motivation (Narciss & Huth, 2006). In peer assessment, however, the impact of (in)formative feedback on student learning is hardly investigated in relation to student learning (Van Zundert, Sluijsmans, & Van Merriënboer, 2007). Moreover, Van Gennip, Segers and Tillema (2009) could only find fifteen studies, since 1990, which empirically investigated learning effects of peer assessment. Although both quasi-experimental and non-experimental studies do indicate positive effects of peer assessment on learning, their review revealed only one of six quasi-experimental studies controlling for the presence of additional (in)formative peer feedback.

Interpersonal Variables

In current peer assessment practice the term 'reciprocity effects' refers to the bias in peer assessment caused by interpersonal processes. Well-known concepts are: friendship marking (high ratings to friends), collusive marking (high ratings to fellow group members), decibel marking (high ratings to dominant group members) and parasite marking (profiting from the efforts invested by fellow group members) (Cheng & Warren, 1997; Pond, Ul-Haq, & Wade, 1995; Williams, 1992). Reciprocity effects can also influence the social atmosphere in a group (Lejk, Wyvill, & Farrow, 1999) and decrease reliability of peer assessment (Magin, 2001).

Many students also express concerns about the fairness of peer assessment (Dochy, Segers & Sluijsmans, 1999; Sambell et al., 1997; Sluijsmans, Dochy, & Moerkerke, 1999). An increased concern for fairness invokes a central role for the teacher. Zhang (1995) and Sengupta (1998) both found that students' voiced the perspective that evaluation was the role of the teacher. Furthermore, the perceived or actual ability of both assessor and assessee (Kali & Ronen, 2008; Lin, Liu, & Yuan, 2001; Strijbos, Narciss, & Dünnebier, 2007) appears to affect peer ratings and may have an important effect on both acceptance and application of formative peer feedback in relation to performance (e.g., revision induced by comments) and learning benefits.

In essence, reciprocity effects are grounded in interpersonal variables, such as familiarity, trust, psychological safety, dependence on self and other, and the ability of self and other (see Van Gennip,

Segers, & Tillema, 2009). Trust in the self and in peers appears to be especially important for peer assessment and a prerequisite for peer assessment in collaborative learning contexts as most students tend to be hesitant to assess peers, especially when a group member provides a limited or substandard contribution.

Finally, an increasing number of studies indicate that students' emotional state can mediate the impact of feedback on their performance (Shute, 2008). Overall, students express positive attitudes towards peer assessment and state that they benefit from peer assessment (Divaharan & Atputhasamy, 2002; Hanrahan & Isaacs, 2001; Parikh, McReelis, & Hodges, 2001). Those students who gained a better understanding of the assessment process were more productive in terms of reading peers' work, developed empathy, they were more motivated – especially to 'impress peers' (Hanrahan & Isaacs, 2001) and were encouraged to collaborate, as well as to improve their interpersonal skills (Divaharan & Atputhasamy, 2002).

INTERACTIVITY IN FORMATIVE PEER ASSESSMENT

The three shortcomings of current peer assessment practice discussed in the previous section can hamper the alignment between peer assessment and collaborative learning. The extent, to which these shortcomings occur and affect both the alignment of the peer assessment process and collaboration process, appears to depend heavily on the level and intensity of *interactivity* in a specific peer assessment setting.

Thus far, typologies for peer assessment have expressed the relation between assessor and assessee only in terms of the directionality, i.e. who assesses whom: uni-directional (from an assessor to an assessee; not vice versa), reciprocal (two students or groups assess each other) and mutual (more than two students or groups assess each other) (see Gielen, 2007; Topping, 1998; Van den

Berg et al., 2006). However, directionality is but one aspect of interactivity.

To foster interactivity in peer assessment and thus better alignment with collaborative learning, we extend the definition of interactivity by adding two extra dimensions besides directionality: directionality (uni-directional versus bi-directional), frequency (one-off versus iterative) and constellation (one to one versus one to many; student or group level). This leads to four types of interactivity – each of which can vary in terms of directionality, frequency and constellation – one-way, reactive, reciprocal and negotiated (Figure 1).

All illustrations in Figure 1 represent a one-to-one scenario, that is, one student or group assesses a fellow student or group (a one-to-many representation would be too complicated and provides redundant information). Directionality is depicted by a straight arrow, and the broken arrow represents a reply to the received peer assessment. The frequency is depicted by the number of tasks – with negotiated being an exception as here the peer assessment is an ongoing process. The boxed-letters (A, B, C) illustrate the constellation, and may represent either the individual level (a student assesses another student) or the

Figure 1. Four types of interactivity in peer assessment

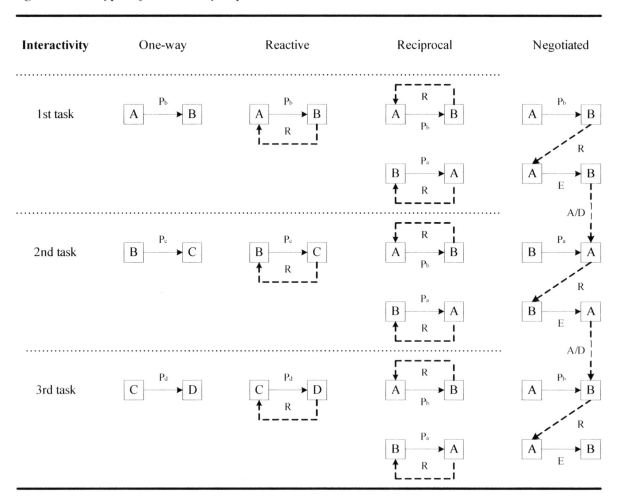

P = peer assessment (subscript indicates who is assessed), R = response, E= elaborate, A/D = agree/disagree

group level. The latter may consist of the intra-group level (each student assess the contribution to a shared product by all other group members) and inter-group level (one or more members of a group assess the performance or the product by another group; Sivan, 2000).

One-way peer assessment is the most commonly applied type of interactivity. One student assesses a fellow student. One-way peer assessment is usually different for consecutive tasks. In Figure 1, student A assesses student B during the first task, and student B assesses student C during the second task. In this case each peer assessment task is a one-off event. That is to say, if student A assesses student B during consecutive tasks, interaction between students A and B would be iterative.

Reactive peer assessment is gaining more attention and allows the assessee to reply to the received assessment. In Figure 1 the reply is depicted by the broken arrow. When people feel threatened, for example when they are judged or an assessment is not in line with a view of self-performance, the fairness of assessment is often questioned. Perceived unfairness induces stronger negative reactions as compared to a non-threatening context (Miedema, 2004), and makes acceptance of peer assessment (irrespective of its accuracy) less likely. In contrast, when offered a reply after an assessment, higher levels of perceived fairness and acceptance are observed (Lind, Kanfer, & Earley, 1990).

Reciprocal peer assessment is also regularly applied. Students' or groups assess each other with respect to their performance on a given task. In essence, this type of interactivity in peer assessment is related to reciprocal teaching (Palincsar & Brown, 1984), scripted cooperation (O'Donnell & Dansereau, 1992) and reciprocal peer tutoring (Fantuzzo, Riggio, Connelly, & Dimeff, 1989). Each student assesses a fellow student and simultaneously s/he is assessed by that fellow student. In Figure 1, student A assesses student B and simultaneously student A is assessed by

student B. In this representation students' also have an opportunity to reply to the assessment. This constitutes the most interactive type of reciprocal peer assessment, although a reply is not prerequisite for an assessment to be reciprocal. The reciprocal nature is further enhanced when students' assess each other during consecutive tasks, as is shown in Figure 1.

Negotiated peer assessment is the least applied type of interactivity. It is also an ongoing process, which is reflected in Figure 1 by the absence of consecutive tasks. Negotiated peer assessment emphasises the role of an assessee (Prins, Sluijsmans, & Kirschner, 2006) in both understanding (i.e., asking for additional clarification) as well as applying the assessment to improve performance. Figure 1 also illustrates the increased interactivity – in contrast to one-way, reactive and reciprocal peer assessment – in terms of elaboration following the reply and subsequent decision by the assessee to agree or disagree with the peer assessment.

Impact of Interactivity in Peer Assessment

Systematically conceptualising interactivity in peer assessment both highlights the interactive nature of peer assessment and provides a framework to foster constructive alignment between peer assessment and collaborative practices.

A reply to an assessment – or ongoing negotiation of an assessment – fosters the alignment because providing assessees with an opportunity to reply to the assessment and/or feedback received, enhances positive interdependence. Furthermore, a reply and negotiation are typical for formative peer assessment. With respect to assumed learning benefits of a peer assessment it is crucial that a peer understands the assessment or feedback, considers it to be fair, correct, and accepts the assessment. Similar to collaborative learning research on giving and receiving help from a peer (Webb & Farivar, 1999), students have to detect inconsistencies between his/her own view and the peers' judgement, understands his/her error(s), and change his/her view accordingly so s/he can meet the criteria in the future (Van de Ridder, Stokking, McGaghie, & Ten Cate, 2008). In sum, a reply may lead recipients to perceive peer assessment as more fair and/or useful, enhance the acceptance of an assessment and subsequently lead to performance improvement (Gielen, 2007; Prins et al., 2005).

An interactivity perspective on peer assessment requires a further specification of what is colluded in the concept of reciprocity effects, namely familiarity and genuine reciprocity. In all types, familiarity – i.e. knowing who you will be assessing and/or who is assessing you – can occur (although it is unlikely to occur in a one-way format). In essence – and as the word 'reciprocity' suggests – genuine reciprocity effects can only occur in the case of reciprocal or negotiated peer assessment. Genuine reciprocity occurs when a favourable peer assessment is provided because of the expectation of receiving a favourable assessment in return. Moreover, interpersonal variables inevitably affect intra-group peer assessment in collaborative learning as students' will need to know the identity of fellow group members in order to judge his/her contribution to the group process and product.

Towards Interactivity During Peer Assessment in (Web-Based) Collaborative Learning

Actual applications of more interactive types of peer assessment in (web-based) collaborative learning contexts are limited. We will briefly discuss three studies to further illustrate the need for and role of interactivity during peer assessment in collaborative learning.

A study by Prins et al. (2005) on formative peer assessment in multidisciplinary groups during a case-based virtual seminar in higher education revealed that students did not apply the predefined criteria for inter-group assessment.

The quality of assessment reports was low, they contained more negative than positive comments, and as a consequence it was difficult for students to accept critical peer feedback. Nevertheless, those students that were actively involved in the peer assessment task expressed positive attitudes towards peer assessment and perceived peer feedback as helpful for revising their report. The results clearly reveal that the alignment of the peer assessment with the collaborative learning context was suboptimal; involving students in defining criteria and providing an opportunity to reply could have increased the quality (and acceptance) of assessment reports.

Sung, Chang, Chiou and Hou (2005) studied the use of web-based peer assessment of multimedia web pages designed by high school students. They investigated the effect of Progressively Focused Self and Peer Assessment (PFSPA) which consists of six steps: self-assessment, peer assessment, discussion in small groups, review the best and poorest work (system selected using criterion set by the instructor), second self-assessment, and discussion among groups. The PFSPA format reduced the number of peer assessments that students had to perform. Results indicated that the quality of web pages improved significantly. Students' selection of the best and poorest work was moderately similar to that of two experts. Overall, their self-rating was closer to expert ratings after PFSPA. Although students worked individually on their web page, the PFSPA format is an expanded, iterative and interactive type of peer assessment. It provides students an opportunity to compare and negotiate the outcome of self- and peer assessment and what characterises high quality work. Unfortunately, this study presents no information on the within-group discussions, which could shed light on students' reviewing approaches.

Finally, Lee, Chan and van Aalst (2006) describe the application of interactive portfolio assessment in secondary education. In contrast to 'traditional' portfolio assessment in which students collect their best work supported by artefacts and evidence, Lee et al. applied the knowledge-building portfolio "for which students are asked to identify collective knowledge advances documenting the community's best work and progress" (p. 283). A portfolio (meta comment) consists of four clusters of messages that provide evidence for knowledge-building principles, e.g. 'working at the cutting edge'. Lee et al. conclude that the exposure to peers' work and diverse conceptual models facilitates learning, application of knowledge-building principles and surpasses merely identifying good answers. The portfolio approach integrates peer assessment of the collectively acquired knowledge and community processes, although the alignment and interactivity could be further enhanced through small group discussion of students' knowledge building portfolios.

These studies clearly illustrate the feasibility and potential of more interactive types of peer assessment in collaborative learning contexts. In the following section we will present a set of guidelines to foster interactivity, as well as deal with the implications of interactivity.

GUIDELINES FOR PEER ASSESSMENT IN (WEB-BASED) COLLABORATIVE LEARNING CONTEXTS

We previously outlined three shortcomings in peer assessment practice with special relevance for web-based collaborative learning. We also described the pivotal role of interactivity with respect to the three shortcomings. In this section we present a set of guidelines compiled from literature on peer assessment, collaborative learning and the lessons learned in studies conducted by the authors. These guidelines will address both general issues, as well issues related to interactivity and how a more intentional focus on

interactivity can help address the shortcomings inherent in peer assessment.

General Guidelines for (Web-Based) Peer Assessment

The nine principles compiled by Kali and Ronen (2005) serve as a sound starting point for peer assessment. They propose: (1) involve students in the development of criteria, (2) make assessment as anonymous as possible, (3) use an overall global score rather than individual dimensions, (4) use scores generated from peer assessment only after validation, (5) minimise instructor workload, (6) enable students to state their personal, non-objective viewpoints about their peers' work, (7) foster discussion about non-objective evaluation criteria, (8) do not grade students according to the results of peer assessment, and (9) evaluate students as evaluators using results from peer assessment.

Assuming that instructors are able to manage time effectively, web-based peer assessment in particular provides a viable way of tracking multiple groups simultaneously. In this sense it becomes an attractive approach to ameliorate the group grade with peer ratings of individuals' contributions. However, a major pitfall for peer assessment during web-based collaborative learning is the apparent 'ease' of application. Instructors should be wary of overly simplistic implementations, i.e. rating is appealing in the large scale web-based courses but the minimal information of rating scores should be carefully balanced against the learning objectives.

Often web-based peer assessment is applied to save instructional time and ease instructor administration. It should be noted that a sole focus on saving instructional time compromises the learning aspects of collaborative learning in general and peer assessment in particular – in practice collaborative learning and peer assessment may not really save time, as it requires considerable amount of up-front time commitment. The use of web-based peer assessment should be determined carefully. We argue in line with Salomon (2000) to "(...) let technology show us what can be done, and let educational considerations determine what will be done" (¶ If it ain't technology, what is it then?) and that the pedagogical design decisions made by the instructor are central to web-based peer assessment. There are several tools available, but first and foremost the instructor should determine whether a web-based format has an added value (for example, students gain access to peer comments outside of classroom time). However, if web-based peer assessment is chosen some examples of available tools include:

- Networked Peer assessment system (Net-Peas; Lin, Liu, & Yuan, 2001);
- Web-based Self and Peer Assessment system (Web-SPA; Sung, Lin, Lee, & Chang, 2003; Sung et al., 2005);
- Self and Peer Assessment Resource Kit (SPARK; Freeman & McKenzie, 2002);
- Online Peer Assessment System (OPAS; Trahasch, 2004);
- Questions Sharing and Interactive Assignments (QSIA; Barak & Rafaeli, 2004);
- Question Posing and Peer Assessment system (QPPA; Yu, Liu, & Chan, 2005);
- Collaborative e-learning Structures (CeLS; Kali & Ronen, 2005; 2008);
- Computerised Assessment by Peers (CAP; Davies, 2006);
- Scaffolded Writing and Rewriting in the Discipline (SWoRD; Cho & Schunn, 2007).

As in the general peer assessment literature, peer rating (marking) is the most common approach in these tools (Web-SPA, QSIA) and usually this is supplemented with open ended comments (NetPeas, QSIA, QPPA, CAP, SWoRD, CeLS). These systems all typically focus on peer assessment of individual student papers or assignments. To our knowledge only CeLS allows the instructor flexibility in the design of peer

assessment (a choice for rating, with or without comments, individuals, groups – in isolation or combination) for alignment with the course and the specific instructional format, for example collaborative learning.

Guidelines to Foster Interactive Peer Assessment During (Web-Based) Collaborative Learning

The application of peer assessment in classroom and web-based collaborative learning is especially suited to implement the more interactive formats, and interactivity is crucial for formative peer assessment. Hence, peer assessment should take interactivity in account as well. We will discuss some guidelines to foster interactivity ordered along directionality, frequency and constellation.

Directionality

- Aim for a mix in directionality types; either through several consecutive tasks during a single course or across multiple courses. Considering peer assessment as an interactive process implies that both research and practice pay more attention to the support of the process of conducting, receiving and replying to peer assessment, as well as processes that are grounded in interaction and may mediate the impact of peer assessment, such as familiarity and genuine reciprocity;
- Of the four interactivity types, reciprocal and negotiated are the most 'constructively aligned' with collaborative learning as students perform the role of both assessor and assessee (and the peer assessment is subject to reflection – either through a reply or a continued dialogue);
- Students often voice that they do not have the ability and/or level of experience to perform an adequate and fair peer assessment. It is

imperative that students are trained in the ability to assess their peers (Sluijsmans et al., 2004) and that their skill as an assessor is included in the overall course assessment (Davies, 2006; Kali & Ronen, 2008). The impact of student ability on peer assessment exists at both the knowledge level as well as their collaboration skills (process) – both of which may affect peer assessment and should be considered when designing or implementing peer assessment.

Frequency

- If possible use multiple tasks: feedback from different peers on different task increases the variation of peer assessment and feedback that students are confronted with, which in turn may lead to performance improvement and enhance learning benefits;
- Peer assessment is most often performed only once – usually on the group product or process – and a combined focus on both the collaborative process and group product is desirable. In addition, iterative or multi-cycle peer assessment (Kali & Ronen, 2008) provides students the opportunity for gradual improvement, exposes them to different assessors, and enables the instructor to determine the intra-rater reliability and assessor consistency.
- Students become comfortable in using peer assessment and value it as contributing to learning as their experiences with it increase (Van den Berg et al., 2006). Make peer assessment an integral aspect of collaborative learning activities in courses and do not present it as an isolated activity.

Constellation

- Aim for a mix in assessor and assessee constellations (individuals, groups, one-to-one, one-to-many). The design of a collaborative

learning setting in itself dictates the type of interactivity best suited for that setting. Negotiated peer assessment is not feasible when there are three hundred students that are all required to assess three peers during one week. Negotiated peer assessment thrives on intensive interaction and a high level of interdependence, and as such it is better suited for small scale courses. It is all about recognising the context and utilising the restrictions placed on peer assessment design by the collaborative setting;

- Variation in constellation may help to better match students based on their ability and as such create pairs or groups whose zone-of-proximal development are in each others reach – ensuring that differences in ability are not too large;
- When peer assessment is applied summatively, it should always include assessment by the instructor. In addition, multiple peer assessments of a students' performance or the contribution to the group process is most effective (Cho & Schunn, 2007).

Purposeful design in peer assessment activities that require students to notice how much each group member contributes, as well as the quality of their own contribution to the groups' process and product, as suggested by Ochoa and Robinson (2005), may yield better peer assessment results. Applying a peer assessment in which each members' contribution is explicitly noted, can help group member to identify a potential free-rider and ingrains in all group members that an important component of collaborative learning is paying attention to both quality and quantity of peers' contributions.

In line with the plea by Gielen (2007) for more systematic description of peer assessment settings (to allow for comparison and aggregation of outcomes), we call for a specification of the type of interactivity (one-way, reactive, reciprocal or negotiated) in terms of directionality, frequency and constellation.

FUTURE TRENDS

In addition to the guidelines to foster peer assessment in general and interactivity in particular, there are several issues we believe are important topics of future research on peer assessment in classroom and web-based settings. The issues revolve around a need to further enhance constructive alignment and interactivity of peer assessment and collaborative learning, and better understand formative peer assessment – both in terms of design and application.

Designing Flexible and Interactive Peer Assessment Formats

At present, peer rating is the dominant peer assessment approach – often in combination with open comments. More variability in the application and design of peer assessment formats is needed. Thus, for research it is important to conceptualise peer assessment also as a design problem, and not merely one of assessment.

Sluijsmans et al. (2007) argue for increased flexibility in peer assessment formats, where peer assessment is used to transform a group mark into individual marks. Current approaches to transformations suffer from five limitations: the type of peer assessment score, using the group mean for calculation, familiarity and genuine reciprocity, scaling down issues, and lack of flexibility. The results reveal that a peer assessment format strongly influences affects the transformation of a group mark into individual marks. Moreover, peer assessment reliability depends on the weight of criteria, the type of scoring scale, the inclusion of self-assessment, and the maximum deviation of an individual mark from the group mark. Finally, the type of peer assessment source, i.e. the peer assessments received by fellow group members

and/or the quality of peer assessments provided to fellow group members (Kali & Ronen, 2008), is an aspect that demands further investigation.

We advocate a use of these formats to foster more interactivity and learning, instead of merely using them to score and calculate. The formats can also be transformed into 'peer assessment scripts' (similar to 'collaboration scripts'), and flexibly applied in web-based collaborative learning contexts (Miao & Koper, 2007) to guide students interactivity, as well as control for some of the shortcomings of current peer assessment practice, for example matching students according to their zone-of-proximal development.

Interpersonal Variables and Anonymity

In response to the familiarity and genuine reciprocity effects, as well as recent indications that students' emotional state (Shute, 2008) and characteristics of the peer assessor (Kali & Ronen, 2008; Strijbos et al., 2007) mediate the impact of peer feedback on performance, anonymous peer assessment is strongly advocated (Cheng & Warren, 1997; Davies, 2006; Freeman & McKenzie, 2002; Kali & Ronen, 2008). Unquestioningly web-based peer assessment systems are very suited to retain anonymity.

We agree that anonymous peer assessment is preferred when the peer assessment outcomes are used summatively or have high-stake implications. However, a formative peer assessment aims to foster reflection and changes in performance and collaborative skills – including skills to cope with feedback received from peers. Furthermore, interpersonal variables inevitably affect intragroup peer assessment in collaborative learning as students' will need to know the identity of fellow group members in order to judge his/her contribution to the group process and product.

Anonymous peer assessment may be less threatening but it simultaneously appears needlessly protective and may even hinder the development of a healthy set of behaviours to provide feedback to fellow students that they are familiar with (or even close friends). We are aware that this position questions the second principle by Kali and Ronen (2005), but familiarity is subject to an intriguing paradox: we are inclined to rate familiar persons more positively and we are more prone to accept feedback from a familiar person than someone unfamiliar.

The call for anonymous peer assessment is predominantly motivated from the perspective of rating bias. When peer assessment is used formatively, the argument for using anonymous assessment should be reconsidered and its benefits weighted against the caveats. The choice for anonymous or non-anonymous assessment is also affected by the perspective of learning how to deal with assessment from persons that students know and learning how to cope with critical feedback, and distil how students can improve and cope with emotions. One approach could be the gradual introduction of personal and performance indicators, or specific instruction as to how students' should deal with peer assessment scores and feedback in particular (e.g., focus on improvements that can be made from the feedback). In case of few comments students can be assigned to contrast their work again in light of the criteria, because there can always be elements that peers failed to notice. Another approach could be a combined anonymous web-based and non-anonymous classroom peer assessment approach, ameliorated with group discussions of the peer assessment outcomes – including students' perceptions of the received peer feedback and their emotions.

CONCLUSION

Towards a Good Marriage between Collaborative Learning and Peer Assessment

In this chapter, our main focus was concerned with the alignment of collaborative learning and interactivity in formative peer assessment. We asked how instructors could enhance learning. Our conclusion, one we elaborated upon, is that interactivity in formative peer assessment (classroom or web-based) is crucial to support the development of students' cognitive skills, collaboration skills and their self-regulation skills. Moreover, we hold that interactivity (e.g., through formative peer assessment) can foster the constructive alignment between assessment and collaborative learning, as such the assessment can be integrated in the collaborative environment instead of a stand-alone feature at the end. This may enhance the perceived relevance, usefulness and fairness of group work assessment.

The overview of shortcomings illustrates that a formative and interactive application of peer assessment to achieve these learning goals is still in its infancy, but that is it also time to reconsider our philosophy on assessment in collaborative learning. We made a first attempt in presenting a perspective on assessment in collaborative learning that warrants for alignment between collaborative learning and assessment, but also addresses the responsibility of the learner. After all, it becomes increasingly important that the learner develops him- or herself as a lifelong learner, who is able to act professionally in each (collaborative learning) context (Boud, 2000).

REFERENCES

Barak, M., & Rafaeli, S. (2004). On-line question-posing and peer-assessment as means for Web-based knowledge sharing in learning. *International Journal of Human-Computer Studies, 61*, 84-103.

Barron, B., Schwartz, D. L., Vye, N. J., Moore, A., Petrosino, A., Zech, L., Bransford, J. D., & The Cognition and Technology Group at Vanderbilt (1998). Doing with understanding: Lessons from research on problem and project-based learning. *The Journal of the Learning Sciences, 7*, 271-311.

Biggs, J. (1996). Enhancing teaching through constructive alignment. *Higher Education, 32*, 347-364.

Birenbaum, M. (2003). New insights into learning and teaching and their implications for assessment. In M. Segers, F. Dochy, & E. Cascallar (Eds.), *Optimising new modes of assessment: In search of qualities and standards* (pp. 13-37). Dordrecht, The Netherlands: Kluwer Academic Publishers.

Birenbaum, M. (2005, October). Multidimensional assessment of computer-supported knowledge building. In *Proceedings of E-Learn 2005* (pp. 1203-1208). Vancouver, Canada: Association for the Advancement of Computing in Education.

Black, P., & Wiliam, D. (1998). Assessment and classroom learning. *Assessment in Education, 5*, 7-74.

Boud, D. (1990). Assessment and promotion of academic values. *Studies in Higher Education, 15*, 101-113.

Boud, D. (2000). Sustainable assessment: Rethinking assessment for the learning society. *Studies in Continuing Education, 22*, 151-167.

Brookhart, S. M. (1999). *The art and science of classroom assessment: The missing part of pedagogy*. ASHE-ERIC Higher Education Report (Vol. 27, No. 1). Washington, DC: The George Washington University, Graduate School of Education and Human Development. (ERIC Document Reproduction Service No. ED432937)

Brush, T. A. (1998). Embedding cooperative learning into the design of integrated learning systems: Rationale and guidelines. *Educational Technology Research and Development, 46*, 5-18.

Chan, C. K. K., & van Aalst, J. (2004). Learning, assessment and collaboration in computer-supported environments. In J. W. Strijbos, P. A.

Kirschner, & R. L. Martens (Eds.), *Computer-supported collaborative learning: Vol 3. What we know about CSCL: And implementing it in higher education* (pp. 87-112). Boston, MA: Kluwer Academic Publishers.

Cheng, W., & Warren, M. (1997). Having second thoughts: Student perceptions before and after a peer assessment exercise. *Studies in Higher Education, 22*, 233-239.

Cho, K., & Schunn, C. D. (2007). Scaffolded writing and rewriting in the discipline: A Web-based reciprocal peer review system. *Computers and Education, 48*, 409-426.

Cohen, E. G. (1994). Restructuring the classroom: Conditions for productive small groups. *Review of Educational Research, 64*, 1-35.

Crooks, T. J. (1988). The impact of classroom evaluation practices on students. *Review of Educational Research, 58*, 438-481.

Davies, P. (2006). Peer assessment: Judging the quality of students' work by comments rather than marks. *Innovations in Education and Teaching International, 43*, 69-82.

Divaharan, S., & Atputhasamy, L. (2002). An attempt to enhance the quality of cooperative learning through peer assessment. *Journal of Educational Enquiry, 3*(2), 72-83.

Dochy, F., Segers, M., & Sluijsmans, D. (1999). The use of self-, peer and co-assessment in higher education: A review. *Studies in Higher Education, 24*, 331-350.

Dochy, F., Segers, M., Van Den Bossche, P., & Gijbels, D. (2003). Effects of problem-based learning: A meta-analysis. *Learning and Instruction, 13*, 533-568.

Falchikov, N., & Goldfinch, J. (2000). Student peer assessment in higher education: A meta-analysis comparing peer and teacher marks. *Review of Educational Research, 70*, 287-322.

Fantuzzo, J. W., Riggio, R. E., Connelly, S., & Dimeff, L. A. (1989). Effects of reciprocal peer tutoring of academic achievement and psychological adjustment: A component analysis. *Journal or Educational Psychology, 81,* 173-177.

Fischer, F., Kollar, I., Mandl, H., & Haake, J. M. (Eds.). (2007). *Scripting computer-supported collaborative learning: Cognitive, computational and educational perspectives.* New York: Springer.

Frederiksen, N. (1984). The real test bias: Influences of testing on teaching and learning. *American Psychologist, 3,* 193-202.

Freeman, M., & McKenzie, J. (2002). SPARK, a confidential Web-based template for self and peer assessment of student team work: Benefits of evaluating across different subjects. *British Journal of Educational Technology, 33,* 551-569.

Gielen, S. (2007). *Peer assessment as a tool for learning.* Unpublished doctoral dissertation, Leuven University, Leuven, Belgium.

Hanrahan, J., & Isaacs, G. (2001). Assessing self- and peer- assessment: The students' views. *Higher Education Research and Development, 20,* 53-70.

Hattie, J., & Timperley, H. (2007). The power of feedback. *Review of Educational Research, 77,* 81-112.

Johnson, D. W. (1981). Student-student interaction: The neglected variable in education. *Educational Research, 10,* 5-10.

Johnson, D. W., & Johnson, R. T. (1994). *Together and alone: Cooperative, competitive, and individualistic learning* (4th ed.). Boston, MA: Allyn & Bacon.

Jones, C., Cook, J., Jones, A., & De Laat, M. F. (2007). Collaboration. In G. Conole & M. Oliver (Eds.), *Contemporary perspectives in e-learning research: Themes, methods, and impact on practice* (pp. 174-189). London: Routledge.

Kali, Y., & Ronen, M. (2005). Design principles for online peer evaluation: Fostering objectivity. In T. Koschmann, D. Suthers, & T. W. Chan (Eds.), *Computer supported collaborative learning 2005: The next 10 years!* (pp. 247-251). Mahwah, NJ: Lawrence Erlbaum Associates.

Kali, Y., & Ronen, M. (2008). Assessing the assessors: Added value in Web-based multi-cyle peer assessment in higher education. *Research and Practice in Technology Enhanced Learning, 3,* 3-32.

Kerr, N., & Bruun, S. (1983). The dispensability of member effort and group motivation losses: Free-rider effects. *Journal of Personality and Social Psychology, 44,* 78-94.

Kluger, A. N., & DeNisi, A. (1996). The effects of feedback interventions on performance: A historical review, a meta-analysis, and a preliminary feedback intervention theory. *Psychological Bulletin, 119,* 254-284.

Langan, A. M., Wheater, C. P., Shaw, E. M., Haines, B. J., Cullen, W. R., Boyle, J. C., Penney, D., Oldekop, J. A., Ashcroft, C., Lockey, L., & Preziosi, R. F. (2005). Peer assessment of oral presentations: Effects of student gender, university affiliation and participation in the development of assessment criteria. *Assessment and Evaluation in Higher Education, 30,* 21-34.

Lee, E. Y. C., Chan, C. K. K., & van Aalst, J. (2006). Students assessing their own collaborative knowledge building. *International Journal of Computer-Supported Collaborative Learning, 1,* 277-307.

Lejk, M., & Wyvill, M. (2001). Peer assessment of contributions to a group project: A comparison of holistic and category-based approaches. *Assessment and Evaluation in Higher Education, 26,* 61-72.

Lejk, M., Wyvill, M., & Farrow, S. (1999). Group assessment in systems analysis and design: A comparison of the performance of streamed and mixed-ability groups. *Assessment & Evaluation in Higher Education, 24*, 5-14.

Lin, S. S. J., Liu, E. Z. F., & Yuan, S. M. (2001). Web-based peer assessment: Feedback for students with various thinking-styles. *Journal of Computer Assisted Learning, 17*, 420-432.

Lind, E. A., Kanfer, R., & Earley, P. C. (1990). Voice, control, and procedural justice: Instrumental and noninstrumental concerns in fairness judgements. *Journal of Personality and Social Psychology, 59*, 952-959.

Lockhart, C., & Ng, P. (1995). Analyzing talk in ESL peer response groups: Stances, functions, and content. *Language Learning, 45*, 605-655.

Lopez-Real, F., & Chan, Y. P. R. (1999). Peer assessment of a group project in a primary mathematics education course. *Assessment and Evaluation in Higher Education, 24*, 67-79.

Macdonald, J. (2003). Assessing online collaborative learning: Process and product. *Computers and Education, 40*, 377-391.

Magin, D. (2001). Reciprocity as a source of bias in multiple peer assessment of group work. *Studies in Higher Education, 26*, 53-63.

Mehrens, W. A., & Lehman, I. J. (1991). *Measurement and evaluation in education and psychology*. New York: Holt, Rinehart and Winston.

Meier, A., Spada, H., & Rummel, N. (2007). A rating scheme for assessing the quality of computer-supported collaboration process. *International Journal of Computer-Supported Collaborative Learning, 2*, 63-86.

Miao, Y., & Koper, R. (2007). An efficient and flexible technical approach to develop and deliver online peer assessment. In C. Chinn, G. Erkens, & S. Puntambekar (Eds.), *Mice, minds and society: The computer supported collaborative learning (CSCL) conference 2007* (pp. 502-510). New Brunswick, NJ: International Society of the Learning Sciences.

Miedema, J. L. (2004). *Fairness and the self* (Kurt Lewin Institute Dissertation Series, 2003-9). Unpublished doctoral dissertation, Leiden University, Leiden, the Netherlands.

Narciss, S. (2006). *Informatives tutorielles feedback* [Informative tutorial feedback]. Münster, Germany: Waxmann Verlag.

Narciss, S. (2008). Feedback strategies for interactive learning tasks. In J. M. Spector, M. D. Merrill, J. J. G. Van Merriënboer, & M. P. Driscoll (Eds.), *Handbook of research on educational communications and technology* (3rd ed.) (pp. 125-143). Mahwah, NJ: Lawrence Erlbaum Associates.

Narciss, S., & Huth, K. (2006). Fostering achievement and motivation with bug-related tutoring feedback in a computer-based training for written subtraction. *Learning and Instruction, 16*, 310-322.

Ochoa, T. A., Gottschall, H., & Stuart S. (2004). Group participation and satisfaction: Results from a PBL computer-supported module. *Journal of Educational Multimedia and Hypermedia, 13*, 73-91.

Ochoa, T. A., & Robinson, J. (2005). Revisiting group consensus: Collaborative learning dynamics during a problem-based learning activity in education. *Teacher Education and Special Education, 28*, 10-20.

O'Donnell, A. M., & Dansereau, D. F. (1992). Scripted cooperation in student dyads: A method for analysing and enhancing academic learning and performance. In R. Hertz-Lazarowitz & N. Miller (Eds.), *Interaction in cooperative groups: The theoretical anatomy of group learning* (pp. 120-144). New York: Cambridge University Press.

Orsmond, P., Merry, S., & Callaghan, A. (2004). Implementation of a formative assessment model incorporating peer and self-assessment. *Innovations in Education and Teaching International, 41*, 273-290.

Orsmond, P., Merry, S., & Reiling, K. (1997). A study in self assessment: Tutor and students' perceptions of performance criteria. *Assessment and Evaluation in Higher Education, 22*, 357–67.

Orsmond, P., Merry, S., & Reiling, K. (2002). The use of exemplars and formative feedback when using student derived marking criteria in peer and self-assessment. *Assessment and Evaluation in Higher Education, 27*, 309-323.

Palincsar, A. S., & Brown, A. L. (1984). Reciprocal teaching of comprehension-fostering and comprehension-monitoring activities. *Cognition and Instruction, 1*, 117-175.

Parikh, A., McReelis, K., & Hodges, B. (2001). Student feedback in problem based learning: A survey of 103 final year students across five Ontario medical schools. *Medical Education, 35*, 632-636.

Patri, M. (2002). The influence of peer feedback on self and peer assessment. *Language Testing, 19*, 109-131.

Ploegh, K., Segers, M., & Tillema, H. (2007, August). *Scrutinizing peer assesment validity: A review of research studies.* Paper presented at the JURE conference, Budapest, Hungary.

Pond, K., Ul-Haq, R., & Wade, W. (1995). Peer review: A precursor to peer assessment. *Innovations in Education and Training International, 32*, 314-323.

Prins, F. J., Sluijsmans, D. M. A., & Kirschner, P. A. (2006). Feedback for general practitioners in training: Quality, styles, and preferences. *Advances in Health Sciences Education, 11*, 289-303.

Prins, F. J., Sluijsmans, D. M. A, Kirschner, P. A., & Strijbos, J. W. (2005). Formative peer assessment in a CSCL environment: A case study. *Assessment and Evaluation in Higher Education, 30*, 417-444.

Rieken, H. W. (1958). The effect of talkativeness on ability to influence group solutions of problems. *Sociometry, 21*, 309-321.

Salomon, G., & Globerson, T. (1989). When teams do not function the way they ought to. *International Journal of Educational Research, 13*, 89-99.

Salomon, G. (2000, June 28). *It's not just the tool, but the educational rationale that counts.* Keynote address at the 2000 ED-MEDIA Meeting, Montreal, Canada. Retrieved February 13, 2009, from http://www.aace.org/conf/edmedia/00/salomonkeynote.htm

Sambell, K., McDowell, L., & Brown, S. (1997). "But is it fair?": An exploratory study of student perceptions of the consequential validity of assessment. *Studies in Educational Evaluation, 23*, 349-371.

Segers, M., Dochy, F., & Cascallar, E. (Eds.). (2003). *Optimising new modes of assessment: In search of qualities and standards.* Dordrecht, The Netherlands: Kluwer Academic Publishers.

Sengupta, S. (1998). Peer evaluation: 'I am not the teacher'. *ELT Journal, 52*, 19-28.

Shute, V. J. (2007). Tensions, trends, tools, and technologies: Time for an educational sea change. In C. A. Dwyer (Ed.), *The future of assessment: Shaping teaching and learning* (pp. 139-187). Mahwah, NJ: Lawrence Erlbaum.

Shute, V. J. (2008). Focus on formative feedback. *Review of Educational Research, 78*, 153-189.

Sivan, A. (2000). The implementation of peer assessment: An action research approach. *As-*

sessment in Education: Principles, Policy and Practice, 7, 193-213.

Slavin, R. E. (1980). Cooperative learning in teams: State of the art. *Educational Psychologist, 15*, 93-111.

Slavin, R. E. (1995). *Cooperative learning: Theory, research and practice* (2nd ed.). Needham Heights, MA: Allyn & Bacon.

Sluijsmans, D. M. A. (2008, June 6). *Betrokken bij beoordelen* [Involved in assessment]. Lectoral address, HAN University, the Netherlands.

Sluijsmans, D. M. A., Brand-Gruwel, S., Van Merriënboer, J., & Martens, R. (2004). Training teachers in peer-assessment skills: Effects on performance and perceptions. *Innovations in Education and Teaching International, 41*, 59-78.

Sluijsmans, D. M. A., Dochy, F., & Moerkerke, G. (1999). Creating a learning environment by using self- peer- and co-assessment. *Learning Environments Research, 1*, 293-319.

Sluijsmans, D. M. A, Strijbos, J. W., & Van de Watering, G. (2007, August). *Designing flexible and fair peer assessment formats to award individual contributions in group-based learning.* Paper presented at the 12th Biennial EARLI Conference, Budapest, Hungary.

Strijbos, J. W., Kirschner, P. A., & Martens, R. L. (Eds.). (2004). *What we know about CSCL: And implementing it in higher education.* Boston, MA: Kluwer/Springer.

Strijbos, J. W., Martens, R. L., & Jochems, W. M. G. (2004). Designing for interaction: Six steps to designing computer-supported group-based learning. *Computers and Education, 42*, 403-424.

Strijbos, J. W., Narciss, S., & Dünnebier, K. (2007, August). *Peer feedback in academic writing: How do feedback content and writing ability-level of the sender affect feedback perception and per-*

formance? Paper presented at the 12th Biennial EARLI Conference, Budapest, Hungary.

Sung, Y. T., Lin, C. S., Lee, C. L., & Chang, K. E. (2003). Evaluating proposals for experiments: An application of web-based self-assessment and peer-assessment. *Teaching of Psychology, 30*, 331-334.

Sung, Y. T., Chang, K. E., Chiou, S. K., & Hou, H. T. (2005). The design and application of a web-based self- and peer-assessment system. *Computers and Education, 45*, 187-202.

Topping, K. J. (1998). Peer assessment between students in colleges and universities. *Review of Educational Research, 68*, 249-276.

Topping, K. J. (2003). Self and peer assessment in school and university: Reliability, validity and utility. In M. Segers, F. Dochy, & E. Cascallar (Eds.), *Optimising new modes of assessment: In search of qualities and standards* (pp. 55-87). Dordrecht, The Netherlands: Kluwer Academic Publishers.

Trahasch, S. (2004, October). *From peer assessment towards collaborative learning.* Paper presented on the 34th ASEE/IEEE Frontiers in Education Conference, Savannah, GA, USA.

Van de Ridder, M., Stokking, K. M., McGaghie, W. C., & Ten Cate, O. Th. J. (2008). What is feedback in clinical education? *Medical Education, 42*, 189-197.

Van den Berg, I. (2003). *Peer assessment in universitair onderwijs: Een onderzoek naar bruikbare ontwerpen* [Peer assessment in higher education: A study on useful designs]. Unpublished doctoral dissertation, Utrecht University, Utrecht, the Netherlands.

Van den Berg, I., Admiraal, W., & Pilot, A. (2006). Peer assessment in university teaching: Evaluating seven course designs. *Assessment and Evaluation in Higher Education, 31*, 9-16.

Van Gennip, N. A. E., Segers, M. S. R., & Tillema, H. H. (2009). Peer assessment from a social perspective: The influence of interpersonal variables and structural features. *Educational Research Review, 4,* 41-54.

Van Zundert, M., Sluijsmans, D. M. A., & Van Merriënboer, J. J. G. (2007, August). *Identifying critical variables to optimise the educational effectiveness and reliability of peer assessment.* Paper presented at the 12th Biennial EARLI Conference, Budapest, Hungary.

Walker, A. (2001). British psychology students' perceptions of group-work and peer assessment. *Psychology Learning and Teaching, 1,* 28-36.

Webb, N. M. (1992). Testing a theoretical model of student interaction and learning in small groups. In R. Hertz-Lazarowitz & N. Miller (Eds.), *Interaction in cooperative group: The theoretical anatomy of group learning* (pp. 102-119). Cambridge, UK: Cambridge University Press.

Webb, N. M., & Farivar, S. (1999). Developing productive group interaction in middle school mathematics. In A. M. O'Donnel & A. King (Eds.), *Cognitive perspectives on peer learning* (pp. 117-149). Mahwah, NJ: Lawrence Erlbaum Associates.

Williams, E. (1992). Student attitudes towards approaches to learning and assessment. *Assessment and Evaluation in Higher Education, 17,* 45-58.

Williams, K. D., & Karau, S. J. (1991). Social loafing and social compensation: The effects of expectations of co-worker performance. *Journal of Personality and Social Psychology, 61,* 570-581.

Yu, F. Y., Liu, Y. H., & Chan, T. W. (2005). A Web-based learning system for question-posing and peer assessment. *Innovations in Education and Teaching International, 42,* 337-348.

Zhang, S. (1995). Reexamining the affective advantage of peer feedback in the ESL writing class. *Journal of Second Language Writing, 4,* 209-222.

Chapter XIX
Supporting Group and Individual Processes in Web–Based Collaborative Learning Environments

F. Pozzi
Istituto Tecnologie Didattiche – CNR, Italy

ABSTRACT

This chapter tackles the issue of how it is possible to integrate individual differences in the learning design of Web-based collaborative learning experiences. In particular, in online collaborative learning environments, it is quite common to adopt techniques to support collaboration and interactions among peers. This contribution proposes to monitor the enactment of the collaborative techniques to make individual and group differences emerge, thus allowing the consequent customization of the learning experience. To this aim, a monitoring model is proposed, whose flexibility allows the tutor to bring different aspects and different levels of the ongoing learning process under control.

INTRODUCTION

One of the main issues in the field of web-based education is how to incorporate individual differences in the learning design (Jonassen & Grabowski, 1993); the problem is currently being addressed from very different perspectives, ranging from the psychological point of view (Anastasi & Foley, 1949; Eysenck & Eysenck, 1985; Merrill, 2001), to more technological perspectives,

aimed at finding new technical solutions to meet individual styles and behaviors (ranging from Intelligent Tutoring Systems (ITS) to Adaptive Hypermedia Systems (AHS)) (Brusilovsky, & Peylo, 2003).

The issue of incorporating individual characteristics in the learning design is strictly related to the two concepts of *individualization* and *personalization*, the former being more focused on the ability of a learning environment to offer an ad hoc learning path to a certain student according to her/his individual characteristics; the latter being devoted to the possibility of the student to personally choose a certain path (Clarke, 2003). Going beyond the differences between the two concepts, there is a common idea underpinning them, that is that web-based education should not coincide with fixed, pre-determined contents to be equally distributed to all learners independently of their individual characteristics, but rather that contents (and the way they are presented) should evolve during the learning experience, on the basis of the learner's styles, attitudes and behaviors (O'Connor, 1999; Henze et al., 2004; Lee, 2004). Even the most common specification in the field of learning design, namely IMS-LD[1], recognizes personalization as a necessary aspect to be addressed (Koper & Olivier, 2004).

But what does this mean in collaborative learning environments? To what extent are individualization and personalization possible in contexts that are primarily based on discussion and negotiation among peers as the way to construct knowledge?

Brusilovsky and Peylo (2003) state that "Intelligent collaborative learning is an interesting group of technologies developed at the crossroads of two fields originally quite distant from each other: computer supported collaborative learning (CSCL) and ITS. The recent stream of work on using AI techniques to support collaborative learning has resulted in an increasing level of interaction between these fields.[...] Currently we can list at least three distinct technologies within the intelligent collaborative learning group: adaptive group formation and peer help, adaptive collaboration support, and virtual students" (p. 161).

This chapter aims to provide a more methodological contribution to the discussion in this field, by focusing on monitoring as a practice able to provide the tutor of an online collaborative learning experience with a run time picture of the participative, the social, the cognitive and the teaching dimensions, as they are developed by

students performing activities, in such a way s/he can individualize the learning path according to the emerging individual and group characteristics. In other words, in this contribution monitoring is considered a valuable, methodological solution to address individualization in web-based collaborative learning processes.

BACKGROUND

In the last decade constructivist approaches have been increasingly appreciated, ranging from "radical constructivism", which states that there is no reality, but only individual speculations and interpretations are possible (Suchman, 1987), to the "situated constructivism" point of view, which assumes that it is by using social patterns that we conceptually interpret events, objects, and perspectives and thus construct knowledge (Jonassen, 1991). According to the mentioned approaches, educational experience has to be as authentic and genuine as possible, so that learners can observe and critically reflect on real situations (Bendar et al., 1992). These methods lead far away from traditional, transmissive paradigms of learning and encourage the adoption of more modern, participative approaches. Partially inspired by these approaches, "social constructivists" definitively stress the importance of the social dimension in the process of developing new knowledge and state that learners develop understanding using language in discussion, collaboration and debate. Language therefore becomes the basic element of an educational experience (Vygotsky, 1962). In other terms, during a learning experience "the process of negotiation is how we construct knowledge and, if the process of negotiation results in agreement, the agreement is reality" (Kanuka & Anderson, 1999).

On this line, *Computer Supported Collaborative Learning* (CSCL) is the research area that focuses on debate-based learning and peer negotiation in online learning environments

(Feenberg, 1989; Harasim, 1989; Kaye, 1991; The Cognition and Technology Group at Vanderbilt, 1991; Rowntree, 1995; Scardamalia & Bereiter, 1994; Berge, 1995; Dillenbourg, 1999; Kanuka & Anderson, 1999). In these contexts, students work online and are subdivided in groups; each group is usually engaged in tasks (discussing a topic, solving a problem, studying a case, etc.) with concrete outputs to produce, which act as catalysts of interaction and collaboration among peers.

In order to facilitate and encourage collaborative dynamics, it is quite common to adopt "techniques" or "strategies" with the aim of providing a structure to activities, so as to foster collaboration and exchange among peers (Kanuka & Anderson, 1999; Dillenbourg 2002; Hernández-Leo et al., 2005; Persico & Sarti, 2005; Jaques & Salmon, 2007; Pozzi, 2007; Persico et al., 2008). Techniques are content-independent procedures, which serve as scaffolds to activities (which on the other hand are content-dependent). Techniques are typically selected by the designer prior to the educational pathway, taking into consideration different variables, such as course objectives and contents, characteristics of target population and – more in general - context constraints. Examples of techniques are: Discussion, Peer Review, Role Play, Jigsaw, Case Study, etc. In particular, a "collaborative technique" is aimed at specifying:

- The *phase repartition and timing of a learning activity*: most of the collaborative techniques adopt a two (or even more)-step model, that is to say that different stages are envisaged in the activity, so that participants contribute at different levels and possibly play different roles. Time availability is an important factor to be considered: some techniques are particularly time consuming; others are less structured and thus require less time.
- The *nature of the task* to be performed and the work distribution: most collaborative

techniques engage learners in concrete tasks, often with very tangible pragmatic outcomes, that can be either the solution to a problem, or the production of an artefact (a document, a concept map, a schema, a hypertext, etc.); this fosters the reciprocal interdependence of participants thus enhancing collaboration.

- The *social structure* of the group(s) (in terms of size, composition, etc.): the numerousness of learners may influence the choice of a collaborative technique (Caspi et al., 2003). Some techniques are more flexible as far as the social structure is concerned and thus they may be applied irrespective of the number of students; on the contrary, other techniques depend very strongly on social organization and thus can be applied only with small or large groups. As already mentioned, very often techniques are carried out into two steps, where one stage may be carried out by small groups (2-6 participants), while the other stage may involve larger groups (typically 20-25 people).
- The *mode of interaction* among participants and groups. In order to carry out collaborative activities, learners usually interact through Computer Mediated Communication systems (CMC), which allow both synchronous and asynchronous textual communication. Such systems can be configured in conferences, forums and/ or thread, so as to support different groups working in parallel and/or in sequence. Each technique is characterized by specific mechanisms of interaction, which may entail one-to-one communication, one-to-many communication or many-to-many communication. The CMC system usually provides group formation tools, so that different levels of permissions allow an easy management of different groups/roles performing different tasks (Dimitracopoulou &. Petrou, 2005).

COLLABORATIVE TECHNIQUES AND STUDENT PROFILES

In the following three examples of collaborative techniques are briefly described, together with the features, which make each of them more or less "theoretically" adequate to certain initial students' characteristics and group profiles.

Discussion

During a Discussion[2], students are subdivided in groups. The technique usually envisages two phases: during the first phase the task consists of individual study of some learning materials. During this phase, the CMC system, which is typically configured in conferences to allow groups to work separately, is used exclusively for asking questions and for expressing personal doubts, ideas or comments to the tutor or to the other members of the group.

The second phase of the technique is much more collaborative, because students are explicitly asked to interact with the peers of their own group to carry out a collaborative task, on the basis of what they have learned from individual study of the first phase. The task at hand may range from information gathering, list-making or problem solving.

As far as the social structure is concerned, since participants have to collaboratively produce an artefact, the technique is most suitable in case of small groups (2-6 people), otherwise interactions may become dispersive.

The choice of Discussion as a collaborative technique within a course should be determined, among the other constraints, by certain students' characteristics. In particular, since Discussion provides an opportunity for learners to share their knowledge, beliefs, values and experiences, it is a proper technique to be adopted when students are characterized by heterogeneity in competences, so that diversity may be exploited at its best.

Moreover, Discussion, by providing a "weak" structure to the learning activity and leaving the interaction process relatively free, will very likely make students with social attitudes (social-oriented leaders), as well as task-oriented leaders emerge. Moreover, by looking at students while interacting, it will be possible to note those students who tend more to individual reasoning, as opposed for example to those with more group-oriented cognitive styles, or even those with reflective attitudes.

This makes this technique particularly indicated in those contexts where the students' profiles are not yet clear; for example, at the beginning of a course, it is very likely that information of this kind is not available to the tutor and this technique may be a good tool to break the ice and allow students to show their natural attitudes and skills at the same time.

Peer Review

Another interesting technique which may turn out to be very useful in online collaborative contexts, is Peer Review. The technique is usually structured in two phases: during the first phase students individually analyse some learning materials and are asked to report their impressions or points of view about what they have read. During the second phase, each student is typically assigned a peer and is required to read his/her analysis, in order to provide comments and/or suggestions. This way, each student receives feedback on the work done in the previous phase.

Structured like this, a Peer Review may be adopted even in the context of large groups (20-25 participants) and this is not particularly disturbing, due to the fact that during the first phase each student simply delivers her/his document, while in the second phase communication occurs mainly in couples.

As a matter of fact, Peer Review is not - per se - associated with a specific social structure and thus it could also be organized in such a way that the reciprocal feedback is provided not only from one individual to another, but from one pair to another , or even between groups. This feature makes the technique suitable also in contexts with large numbers, where the ratio tutor/students is particularly low.

During the Peer Review, a reciprocal teaching approach is stressed, where one's own interpretation of reality is to be faced and compared with those of others (Pozzi & Sugliano, 2006; Pozzi, 2007). In order to exploit the possibility of such reciprocal teaching, this technique is appropriate in those contexts where students have similar competences; another important requirement that students should have in order to effectively adopt this technique, is that they have already developed the ability to receive criticism positively, as well as a strong reciprocal commitment, otherwise they can fail to provide significant suggestions to their colleagues.

Moreover, the adoption of this technique requires a certain knowledge by the designer of the target population, so perhaps Peer Review should not be used at the beginning of a course, but rather as a mid-or late activity, when students' attitudes and groups' behaviours have already emerged. In particular, if groups have already experienced internal conflicts in previous activities, Peer Review should be avoided, due to the risk of flaming. If, on the contrary, students seem to lack the ability to consider others' perspectives and/or comment on them, Peer Review may help.

As far as pair composition is concerned, the tutor should devote special attention to the analysis of students' individual behaviours, in terms of their level of participation on previous activities (for example, very active participants versus lurkers), cognitive styles (for example students who tend to develop individual reasoning, as opposed to those who prefer a group knowledge construction), social behaviors (more open and friendly students, as opposed to shy ones) and teaching attitudes (students who take the responsibility of the learning process more, versus those who

simply carry out the task). If on one hand, a certain heterogeneity of behaviors within a pair may turn out to be fruitful (the student with the more positive attitude may influence the other), on the other hand, the tutor should avoid the opposition of extremely different behaviors: for example pairs composed of students who have shown very different levels of participation, may generate frustration in the more active student, who does not receive any feedback from his/her peer.

Role Play

An interesting technique that can be fruitfully adopted in online collaborative contexts is Role Play. Usually at the beginning of the activity students, subdivided in groups, choose (or are assigned) roles and are asked to individually read some learning materials.

During the second phase of the activity, students are asked to pretend a certain situation and to collaboratively carry out a task (solve a problem, elaborate a shared document, etc.), by playing the assigned roles, in such a way that discussion and negotiation is made richer by the fact that students argument their positions according to their roles.

The adoption of the Role Play technique may be supported in online environments by the fact that in CMC systems it is often possible to assign "aliases" to users: by using an alias, the leaner can act and respond to class mates who will not know her/his "true" identity (Kanuka & Anderson, 1999) and this will make the role play even more "realistic".

As we will see in the following, monitoring collaborative techniques during their enactment is a key element in keeping their effectiveness under control and - at the same time - for making group processes and individual differences emerge, so that the tutor can tune her/his actions and customize the next interventions accordingly.

MONITORING ONLINE COLLABORATIVE LEARNING PROCESSES

Once a collaborative technique has been selected and the learning activity fully designed, it is proposed to students. During the enactment of the collaborative technique, it is very likely that new characteristics of the target population will emerge.

As a matter of fact, some characteristics of the target population are known a priori, such as for example the numerousness of the learning group and the availability of tutors, which determines the ratio tutor/students; thus the designer may take them into due consideration from the very beginning of the learning design. On the contrary, other characteristics may seldom be investigated a priori, and more often emerge *in fieri*, such as for example individual attitudes by students (attitudes towards socialization, learning styles, etc.) and group dynamics. As already mentioned, monitoring can help in capturing the emerging behaviors and attitudes by groups and individual students, so that designers and tutors of the learning experience can customize and tune the subsequent techniques according to individual and group reactions.

As a matter of fact, in order to gain information on the ongoing learning process, CSCL research has been increasingly using interaction analysis techniques, which take advantage of the non-intrusive capability of technology to record events and their effects (from user actions, like logging into the system to the texts of the messages exchanged), therefore replacing or most often complementing more intrusive ways to collect data (questionnaires and interviews with learners and tutors). Interaction analysis techniques may be based on both quantitative and qualitative data, the former being automatically tracked by the CMC system, the latter deriving from content analysis by a human agent of the messages exchanged between participants. In the last few years many approaches have been proposed which rely on both quantitative and qualitative data (Henri, 1992; Hara et al., 2000; Rourke et al., 2001; Lally, 2002; Aviv et al., 2003; Lipponen et al., 2003; Martinez et al., 2003; Daradoumis et al., 2004; Schrire, 2006; Weinberger & Fischer, 2006; ICALTS Kaleidoscope JEIRP[3]).

On this same line, Pozzi et al. (2007) proposed a model for evaluating and monitoring collaborative learning processes, which mainly builds on Henri's model (1992) and Garrison & Anderson's Communities of Inquiry (Garrison & Anderson, 2003). The model has been extensively tested and improved (Persico et al., in press) and its final version encompasses four dimensions as those which mainly characterize the learning processes in collaborative learning environments, namely: the participative, the social, the cognitive and the teaching dimensions.

In order to bridge the gap between the four dimensions and their effective manifestation, suitable indicators have been identified, that is quantitative or qualitative elements that allow the analysis of each dimension according to specific objectives.

Figure 1. The four dimensional model for evaluating and monitoring online collaborative learning processes

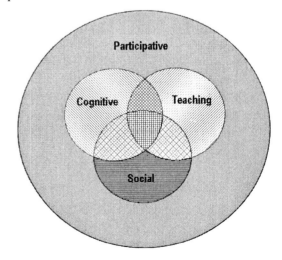

In particular, the participative dimension expresses the quantity of messages exchanged by students in the CMC system to carry out the assigned task and thus indicators of this dimension include: the number of *active actions* by members of the learning community (in terms of sent messages, uploaded documents, etc.), the number of *reactive actions* (e.g. reading messages, downloading documents, etc.), as well as the level of *continuity* in participation across time. As one may note, the participative dimension is based on indicators and data of a quantitative nature, that is to say that procedures to obtain and analyse data of this dimension can be totally automated.

Unlike the participative dimension, the other three dimensions are based on indicators and data of a qualitative nature, that is to say that the evaluator needs to carry out a content analysis of the messages exchanged by participants.

In particular, the social dimension is defined as "the ability of participants… to project themselves socially and emotionally, as 'real' people (i.e., their full personality), through the medium of communication being used" (Garrison et al., 1999); thus indicators of this dimension include clues of *affection* (which is typically revealed by expressions of emotion or intimacy, humour or irony, presentations of personal anecdotes) and *group cohesion* (vocatives, expressions revealing group-self efficacy, references to the group using inclusive pronouns, phatics, salutations).

As far as the cognitive dimension is concerned, this is defined in terms of "the extent to which learners are able to construct and confirm meaning through sustained reflection and discourse…" (Garrison et al., 2001); the model makes a distinction between clues of *individual* and *group knowledge building*, by assuming that a collaborative activity in these contexts requires typically a personal ri-elaboration of contents and the expression of personal points of view, and - at a second stage - discussion and negotiation to collaboratively construct common interpretations of reality. Moreover, according to the model, the

cognitive dimension also encompasses *meta-reflection*, that is to say that monitoring and/or evaluating the process by students is considered an important component of the cognitive process itself.

Lastly, the teaching dimension is defined as "the design, facilitation, and direction of cognitive and social processes for the purpose of realizing personally meaningful and educationally worthwhile learning outcomes" (Anderson et al., 2001). Thus indicators of the teaching dimension include *organizational aspects, facilitating discourse* and *direct instruction*.

Table 1 summarizes the main indicators of the four dimensions.

The innovativeness of this model with respect to the others cited here (see references above) lays in its flexibility, i.e. the fact that its dimensions (both quantitative and qualitative) and the related indicators can be instantiated according to the aim and time of the analysis and the type of the learning experience, in such a way that one can choose on what dimension(s) and indicator(s) to focus, on the basis of the real needs and requirements of the analysis itself. Thus the model can be considered a general framework, able to provide guidance for any analysis, but allowing the evaluator to choose what element to address (e.g. group dynamics, individual behaviors, level and intensity of interactions) and at what level of detail. This makes the model particularly indicated as a means to keep the various aspects of the ongoing learning process under control and consequently to customize the activities according to students' and groups' reactions.

As already mentioned, the model has been extensively used in different online courses all designed and run by the Istituto Tecnologie Didattiche – CNR in the context of the Italian system for teacher training (Delfino & Persico, 2007).

As we will see in the following, in these contexts the model confirmed to be flexible enough to capture and describe the processes deriving from the application of the various techniques by

Table 1. Main indicators of the evaluation model

Participative	Active participation (P1)
	Reactive participation (P2)
	Continuity (P3)
Social	Affection (S1)
	Cohesion (S2)
Cognitive	Individual knowledge building (C1)
	Group knowledge building (C2)
	Meta-reflection (C3)
Teaching	Organizational matters (T1)
	Facilitating discourse (T2)
	Direct instruction (T3)

keeping the participative, the social, the cognitive and the teaching dimensions continuously monitored during the enactment of the activities themselves. Moreover, the flexibility of the model allowed the tutor to capture the performances and behaviors both at group and individual levels, so that s/he could consequently take the most suitable measures to support students, thus guiding them towards the achievement of the learning objectives.

MONITORING GROUPS: CASE STUDIES

In the following, a number of case studies are presented deriving from real experiences, with the aim of demonstrating how the model can be used and what kind of results one may obtain by its application for monitoring groups and single students.

The examples cited derive from the application of the model in the "SSIS", the Italian teacher training institution. In recent years the Istituto Tecnologie Didattiche (ITD) – CNR has designed and run several blended courses for the SSIS of two Italian regions (Liguria and Veneto) on the topic "Educational Technology"

(hereinafter these courses will be referred to as "TD-SSIS"). Although each TD-SSIS course has its own specificities (in terms of learning objectives, contents, activities, schedule, etc.), all of them use a CSCL approach and share a basic aim, namely promoting the development of instructional design competence, with special focus on the evaluation and selection of learning strategies, techniques and tools and on the implementation of educational technology in the school context (Delfino & Persico, 2007). These courses always envisage an alternation between face-to-face lectures and online activities through the use of a CMC system[4]. In particular, face-to-face sessions are devoted to lay the bases for both a better understanding of the subject and an effective participation in online activity, whilst online work is mainly collaborative and asynchronous and is based on techniques such as Discussion, Peer Review and Role Play.

The students of the courses are post-graduate adults with very diversified backgrounds, interests and expectations. Since the size of the audience is usually notable (around one hundred students per year), the students are divided into virtual workgroups each supported and coordinated by a tutor.

The method used to gather data is mixed: as far as the quantitative dimension is concerned (namely the participative one), data were automatically tracked by the CMC system[5]. On the contrary, as already mentioned, information concerning the social, the cognitive and the teaching dimensions relied on data deriving from the content analysis of the messages exchanged among students. This implied one coder to systematically identify significant properties of textual information. The most commonly used property is the frequency of given keywords or patterns or even expressions that are believed to reveal a feature of the communication act. For example, frequent use of emoticons, expressions like "dear X" or informal greetings are regarded as clues of social presence (Delfino & Manca, 2007). The unit of analysis chosen was the "unit of meaning", i.e. each message was split into semantic units[6] and each unit was assigned one indicator.

The coding procedure was carried out by two independent coders, who worked separately after a 40-hour period of training. In order to calculate the inter-rater reliability between the two coders (i.e. the agreement between the two), a sample of messages was selected and coded, corresponding to 10% of the total number of messages in each activity. The selected messages were distributed in time (namely, at the beginning, in the middle and at the end of each activity). The inter-rater reliability was calculated using the Holsti coefficient and considering the agreement on each unit of meaning. This was 0.90 (percent agreement 0.84), which is usually considered a good result. Disagreements were solved through discussion.

As we will see in the following, group behaviors resulting from the monitoring process, guided the tutor's actions and allowed a more customized approach towards groups.

Case Study 1

Figure 2 shows an example of the cognitive dimension as developed by a group of 21 students, during a Discussion (course TD-SSIS Liguria 2007). The technique was chosen a priori by the designers of the course mainly because the students were heterogeneous in competences and this was considered in principle a good factor in view of exchange and sharing of diverse experiences and ideas.

The topic addressed by the activity was the use of blogs in educational contexts. In line with the design principles behind the Discussion, the activity was not particularly structured; nonetheless, two phases were envisaged so to give a pace to the work; besides, an artefact was required from students as output of the whole activity.

In particular, during the first phase of the activity students were required to individually read some materials, navigate a certain number of educational blogs and try to implement a draft of a personal blog. During this phase forums were used exclusively for asking questions and for expressing personal doubts, ideas or comments if any. On the contrary, the second phase of the activity was much more collaborative, because students were in charge of discussing to conceive a common design of an educational blog.

The figure shows the results obtained from the analysis of phase 2 of the Discussion, where there is evidence of a certain richness of indicators, which include: explaining personal points of view (C1.3), agreement (C2.2), suggestions to others (C2.3), offering knowledge to others (C2.4), integrating ideas (C2.5), creation of new meanings (C2.6).

In this case the monitoring model helped in confirming the tutor that the reaction of the group to the proposed activity was positive and that the group composition was satisfying, in that members showed a certain ability to exchange and collaborate, thus leading the group to a positive performance. At the same time, the tutor could observe that the tendency to disagreement (C2.1) and individual reasoning in general (C1) was not so high, so she was able to tune her action accordingly within this group, by fostering individual reflections and expression of personal ideas and by pointing out points of divergence.

Figure 2. Cognitive dimension & Discussion: number of occurrences for each indicator[7]

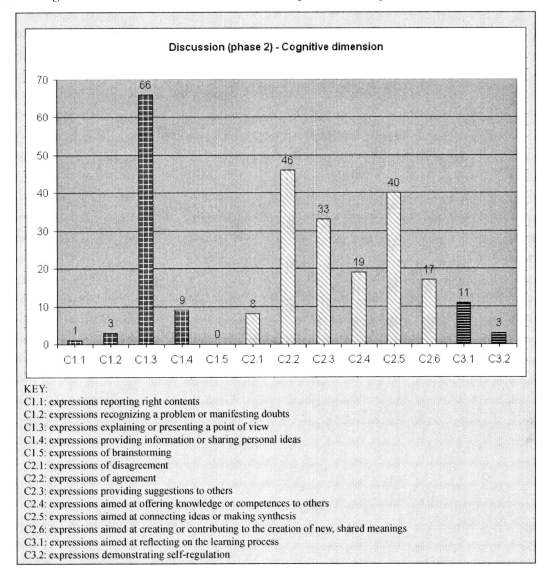

Case Study 2

The second case refers to the results obtained by monitoring a group performing a Peer Review (within TD-SSIS Liguria 2005).

The object of the learning activity was the use of online resources for teaching and learning and the activity was structured in two phases: during the first phase students of the same subject matter individually analysed online resources and were asked to fill in a template with their impressions about the websites they had visited. During the second phase, each student was assigned a peer and was required to read his/her analysis in order to provide comments and/or suggestions. This way each student received feedback on the work done in the previous phase. During the Peer Review interactions occurred among 19 people at a time. Nonetheless, this was not particularly disturbing, due to the fact that during the first phase each

Figure 3. Cognitive dimension & Peer Review: number of occurrences for each indicator in phase 2

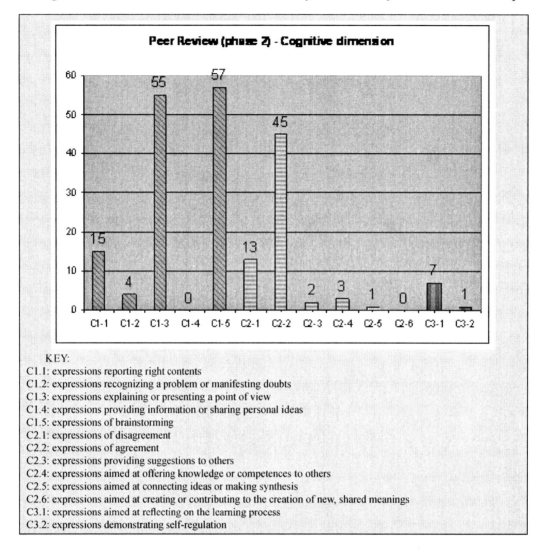

student simply delivered her/his document, while in the second phase communication occurred mainly in couples.

Figure 3 shows that during phase 2 of the activity the group under study is developing a cognitive dimension which is much more characterized by Individual reasoning (C1), rather than Group knowledge building (C2). In this case the model helped in pointing out that the students preferred to state their personal points of view, instead of addressing directly their peers by disagreeing or providing suggestions to them.

The overall low level of exchange and interactions among participants within this group during the Peer Review, was also confirmed by the participative dimension: indicators of *Active participation* (P1) and *Reactive participation* (P2) are not so high, as shown in the Table 2.

Of course, when students receive very poor feedback, or even no feedback at all, the quality of subsequent work is at risk; when the tutor realized this, she started encouraging collaborative and generative feedback, by identifying areas

Table 2. Participative dimension & Peer Review: data of Active and Reactive participation (whole activity)

Number of participants: 19 –Number of messages sent: 91 Number of units of meanings: 654		
Messages sent		**Messages read**
4.05 mean per student	**2.02** mean per student / per week	**0.48** ratio between the mean of messages read by participants and the total number of messages present in the conference

Figure 4. Teaching dimension & Role Play

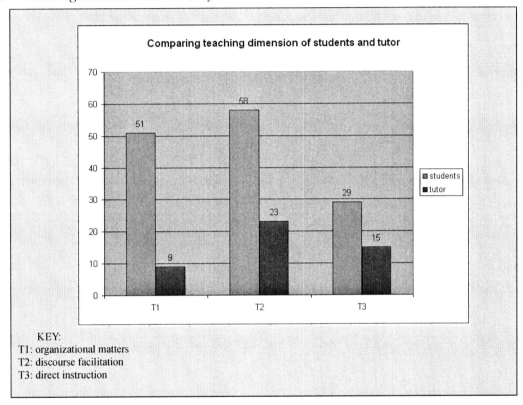

KEY:
T1: organizational matters
T2: discourse facilitation
T3: direct instruction

of agreement/ disagreement, so as to move the process of knowledge construction forward.

Moreover, by isolating data per couple of students, she could even customize her feedback according to the nature of interactions that occurred within each couple.

Case Study 3

Another interesting case emerged from monitoring a Role Play (TD-SSIS Veneto 2007), the topic of which was "Webquests". During this activity, 24 students, organized in 4 sub-groups, were asked to pretend to be groups of teachers in charge of a common analysis and a shared evaluation of a certain number of webquests. The analysis of the webquests was to be carried out from a very particular perspective, i.e. by playing a specific role within the group. At the beginning of the activity, students chose their role, from a list of characters, including the "director" and the "rapperteur" of the group, both in charge

Figure 5. Social dimension & discussion: comparing data of the whole group and of a single student (L.)

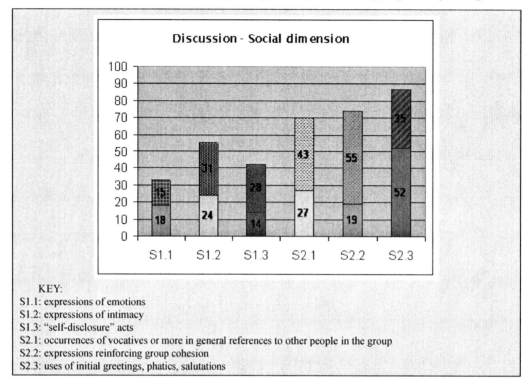

KEY:
S1.1: expressions of emotions
S1.2: expressions of intimacy
S1.3: "self-disclosure" acts
S2.1: occurrences of vocatives or more in general references to other people in the group
S2.2: expressions reinforcing group cohesion
S2.3: uses of initial greetings, phatics, salutations

of facilitating the discourse and organizing the work, and – on the other hand – other roles aiming at soliciting divergent perspectives, such as the "techno-sceptical" teacher, the "techno-loving" teacher, the "bureaucrat", the "defeatist", the "efficient" one, etc.

During the first phase of the activity each student chose a role, while in the second phase s/he was asked to discuss a number of webquests, argument his/her position according to the role and negotiate a common evaluation with others.

By monitoring this activity through the model (results are shown in Figure 4), it emerged that during the Role Play the level of teaching dimension increased and that students were able to take responsibility for the learning process, so that the tutor could react accordingly and limit her action to a few support interventions. At the same time, thanks to the assigned roles, students experimented argumentation and divergence at cognitive level, thus coming out with a very positive performance.

MONITORING INDIVIDUAL STUDENTS: CASE STUDIES

As we have already mentioned, the model also allows one to focus on single students and to understand their personal attitudes, behaviors and weaknesses, by looking at dimensions and indicators each learner develops through time.

For example, looking at the participative dimension of each student, may help the tutor in detecting very active students, lurkers (i.e. people who read messages exchanged by others but rarely participate), or those who are later in accomplishing an activity and need to be reminded of deadlines.

Similarly, by looking at the social dimension each student is developing, the model may help in detecting and bringing to light social-oriented leaders. In Figure 5 the social dimension is described, as developed by a group of 7 students performing the second phase of a Discussion

(TD-SSIS Liguria 2005); values on the bottom represent the social dimension developed by the whole group, excluding that developed by a particular student, whose name is L. (represented at the top of the columns).

In this case the model allowed the tutor to focus on a single student and highlighted that she was particularly active from the social point of view, in that she often told personal anecdotes (S1.3), expressed her feelings (S1.1), used self-irony (S1.2) and this encouraged the others to do the same and contributed to the creation of a friendly climate. Moreover, L. often referred to the group as a whole (S2.1) and used expressions of group self-efficacy (S2.2) thus enhancing group cohesion.

These aspects are determinant for the tutor, whose actions cannot leave these kinds of data out of consideration: starting from them, the tutor increases students' personal involvement, help those who are more peripheral or hard to reach, and thus is able to individualize the proposed activities more, according to students' personal results.

Furthermore, when looking at a single student, especially if s/he is performing a technique that is not particularly pre-structured, the model may highlight his/her cognitive styles, by making reflective attitudes emerge (high levels of *Meta-reflection* (C3)), or a tendency to *Individual* reasoning (C1), or a *Group* oriented attitude (C2).

In the same way, by looking at the indicators of the teaching dimension developed by a student, one may note task-oriented leadership attitudes, such as:

- Organizing the group and coordinating the work, which can make you think of an *organizer* (T1).
- Asking others for contributions, stimulating the group and fostering discussion, which may reflect an *opinion seeker* or an *energizer* (T2).
- Giving additional information which can make you think of an *elaborator* (T3) (Benne & Sheats, 1948).

Such use of the model to capture students' behaviours, may help the tutor to learn more about her/his students, so that s/he can become able - on one hand - of more individualized interventions, and - on the other hand - of better exploiting personal students' attitudes to improve group performances.

DISCUSSION AND CONCLUSION

In this contribution we have focused on online collaborative learning environments and have tackled the issue of how it is possible to make this kind of environment flexible and adaptive to the learners' needs and profiles.

This can be done by monitoring the learning process, so as to keep group and individual reactions to the proposed activities under control; in particular, starting from the collaborative techniques used to enhance collaboration and interactions among students, it is advisable to monitor the participative, the social, the cognitive and the teaching dimensions, as they are developed by single students and groups, so as to take adequate measures when the techniques do not convey the expected results and in order to individualize the next actions.

This chapter mainly assumes a methodological perspective and provides examples of how these dimensions (and the related indicators, as they have been defined in the proposed model) can be used, with the final aim of better customizing the collaborative activities on the basis of what emerges from the enactment of the techniques.

Nonetheless, overall there is a lack of research effort devoted to the integration of individual differences in the learning design of online collaborative learning experiences and further work should be done to bridge this gap. Even the model proposed here suffers from a number of shortcomings, mainly due to the fact that gathering data is not always so easy.

For example, as far as the quantitative data are concerned, it is true that the most recent CMC systems provide functionalities aimed at tracking the learning process and in some cases - where adequately configured – systems can elaborate data and alert tutors and /or students when the actual performance does not match with the expected one. Nonetheless, the possibility to automatically gather and elaborate quantitative data from CMC systems, should not be taken for granted, due to the fact that at the moment there are no standards for these kinds of systems and this causes differences in the kind of data available. Besides, if some sort of automation is possible for quantitative data, it is evident that, as for the content analysis of messages, this cannot be done automatically (at least not completely) and this makes the overall monitoring process strictly dependent on human intervention.

Despite these weaknesses which certainly call for further investigations in the field, the affordances opened by monitoring a web-based collaborative learning process through a mixed and flexible approach and the consequent possibility to adapt at run time the learning process itself according to the emerging individual differences, are worth studying.

Moreover, while in this contribution we have mainly mentioned the affordances provided to the tutor, who may tune her/his actions according to the monitoring results (i.e. in an effort to *individualize* his/her interventions and the following activities), we should not forget the possibilities opened by presenting the same results directly to learners, who may thus increase the level of awareness of their performance, thus improving their ability of self-managing and self-regulating the learning process. This last consideration poses further challenges to the researchers in the field, by highlighting the possibility of bridging the gap between the two fields of *personalization* and *CSCL*, which still seems to be so distant.

REFERENCES

Anastasi, A., & Foley, J. P. (1949). *Differential psychology: Individual and group differences in behavior.* New York: Macmillan Co.

Anderson, T., Rourke, L., Garrison, D. R., & Archer, W. (2001). Assessing teaching presence in a computer conferencing context. *Journal of Asynchronous Learning Networks, 5*(2).

Aviv, R., Erlich, Z., Ravid, G., & Geva, A. (2003). Network analysis of knowledge construction in asynchronous learning networks. *Journal of Asynchronous Learning Networks, 7*(3), 1-23.

Bendar, A. K., Cunningham, D., Duffy, T. M., & Perry, J. D. (1992). Theory into practice: How do we link? In T. M. Duffy & D. H. Jonassen (Eds.), *Constructivism and the technology of instruction: A conversatio*n. Hillsdale, NJ: Lawrence Erlbaum Associates Publishers.

Benne, K. D., & Sheats, P. (1948). Functional roles of group members. *Journal of Social Issues, 4*(2), 41-19.

Berge, Z. (1995). The role of the online instructor/facilitator. *Educational Technology, 35*(1), 22-30.

Brusilovsky, P., & Peylo, C. (2003). Adaptive and intelligent Web-based educational systems. *International Journal of Artificial Intelligence in Education, 13*(2-4), 156-169.

Caspi, A., Gorsky, P., & Chajut, E. (2003). The influence of group size on non-mandatory asynchronous instructional discussion groups. *The Internet and Higher Education, 6*, 227-240.

Clarke, J. (2003). *Changing systems to personalize learning.* The Education Alliance at Brown University. Retrieved April 30, 2008, from http://www.alliance.brown.edu/pubs/changing_systems/introduction/introduction.pdf

Daradoumis, T., Martinez-Monés, A., & Xhafa, F. (2004). An integrated approach for analysing and assessing the performance of virtual learning groups. In *Groupware: Design, implementation and use* (LNCS 3198, pp. 289-304). Springer.

Delfino, M., & Manca, S. (2007). The expression of social presence through the use of figurative language in a Web-based learning environment. *Computers in Human Behavior, 23,* 2190-2211.

Delfino, M., & Persico, D. (2007). Online or face-to-face? Experimenting with different techniques in teacher training. *Journal of Computer Assisted Learning, 23,* 351-365.

Dimitracopoulou, A., & Petrou, A. (2005). Advanced collaborative distance learning systems for young students: Design issues and current trends on new cognitive and meta-cognitive tools. *THEMES in Education International Journal.*

Dillenbourg, P. (Ed.). (1999). *Collaborative learning: Cognitive and computational approaches.* Oxford, UK: Pergamon/Elsevier.

Dillenbourg, P. (2002). Over-scripting CSCL: The risks of blending collaborative learning with instructional design. In P. A. Kirschner (Ed.), *Three worlds of CSCL. Can we support CSCL* (pp. 61-91). Heerlen, The Netherlands: Open University Nederland.

Eysenck, H. J., & Eysenck, M. W. (1985). *Personality and individual differences: A natural science approach.* New York: Plenum.

Feenberg, A. (1989). The written world: On the theory and practice of computer conferencing. In R. Mason & A. R. Kaye (Eds.), *Mindweave: Communication, computers and distance education.* Oxford, UK: Pergamon Press.

Garrison, R., & Anderson, T. (2003). *E-learning in the 21st century. A framework for research and practice.* New York: Routledge Falmer.

Garrison, D. R., Anderson, T., & Archer, W. (1999). Critical inquiry in a text-based environment: Computer conferencing in higher education. *The Internet and Higher Education, 2*(2-3), 87-105.

Garrison, R., Anderson, T., & Archer, W. (2001). Critical thinking, cognitive presence, and computer conferencing in distance education. *The American Journal of Distance Education, 15*(1).

Hara, N., Bonk, C. J., & Angeli, C. (2000). Content analysis of online discussion in an applied educational psychology course. *Instructional Science, 28,* 115-152.

Harasim, L. M. (1989). Online education: A new domain. In R. D. Mason & A. R. Kaye (Eds.), *Mindweave: Communication, computers and distance education.* Oxford, UK: Pergamon Press.

Henri, F. (1992). Computer conferencing and content analysis. In A. R. Kaye (Ed.), *Collaborative learning through computer conferencing: The Najaden papers* (pp. 115-136). New York: Springer.

Henze, N., Dolog, P., & Nejdl, W. (2004). Reasoning and ontologies for personalized e-learning in the Semantic Web. *Educational Technology & Society, 7*(4), 82-97.

Hernández-Leo, D., Asensio-Pérez, J. I., Dimitriadis, Y., Bote-Lorenzo, M. L., Jorrín-Abellán, I. M., & Villasclaras-Fernández, E. D. (2005). Reusing IMS-LD formalized best practices in collaborative learning structuring. *Advanced Technology for Learning, 2*(3), 223-232.

Jaques. D., & Salmon. G. (2007). *Learning in groups: A handbook for face-to-face and online environments.* New York: Routledge.

Jonassen, D. H. (1991). Evaluating constructivist learning. *Educational Technology, 31*(10), 28-33.

Jonassen, D. H., & Grabowski, B. L. (1993). *Handbook of individual difference, learning, and instruction*. Hillsdale, NJ: Lawrence Erlbaum Associates.

Kanuka, H., & Anderson, T. (1999). using constructivism in technology-mediated learning: Constructing order out of the chaos in the literature. *Radical Pedagogy, 1*(2).

Kaye, A. (1991). Learning together apart. In *Proceedings of the NATO Advanced Research Workshop on Collaborative Learning and Computer Conferencing, Series F: Computer and System Sciences, 90*. Berlin, Germany: Springer-Verlag.

Koper, R., & Olivier, B. (2004). Representing the learning design of units of learning. *Educational Technology & Society, 7*(3), 97-111.

Lally, V. (Ed.). (2002). Elaborating collaborative interactions in networked learning: A multi-method approach. In *Proceedings of the Networked Learning Conference 2002*, University of Sheffield.

Lee, Y. (2004), How to consider individual differences in online learning environments. In C. Crawford, et al. (Eds.), *Proceedings of Society for Information Technology and Teacher Education International Conference 2004* (pp. 545-550). Chesapeake, VA: AACE.

Lipponen, L., Rahikainen, M., Lallimo, J., & Hakkarainen, K. (2003). Patterns of participation and discourse in elementary students' computer-supported collaborative learning. *Learning and Instruction, 13*, 487-509.

Martinez, A., Dimitriadis, Y., Rubia, B., Gomez, E., & De La Fuente, P. (2003). Combining qualitative evaluation and social network analysis for the study of classroom social interactions. *Computers and Education, 41*(4), 353-368.

Merrill, M. D. (2002). Instructional goals and learning styles: Which takes precedence? In R. Reiser & J. Dempsey (Eds.), *Trends and issues*

in instructional technology. Upper Saddle River, NJ: Prentice Hall.

O'Connor, T. O. (1999). *Using learning styles to adapt technology for higher education*. Center for Teaching and Learning, Indiana University. Retrieved April 30, 2008, from http://iod.unh.edu/EE/articles/learning-styles.html

Persico, D., Pozzi, F., & Sarti, L. (2008). Fostering collaboration in CSCL. In A. Cartelli & M. Palma (Eds.), *Encyclopedia of information communication technology*. Hershey, PA: Idea Group Reference.

Persico, D., Pozzi, F., & Sarti, L. (in press). A model for monitoring and evaluating CSCL. In A. A. Juan, T. Daradoumis, F. Xhafa, S. Caballe, & J. Faulin (Eds.), *Monitoring and assessment in online collaborative environments: Emergent computational technologies for e-learning support*. Hershey, PA: Information Science Reference.

Persico, D., & Sarti, L. (2005). Social structures for online learning: A design perspective. In G. Chiazzese M. Allegra, A. Chifari, & S. Ottaviano (Eds.), *Methods and technologies for learning, Proceedings of the International Conference on Methods and Technologies for Learning*. Boston, MA: WIT Press.

Pozzi, F. (2007). Fostering collaboration in CSCL: Techniques and system functions. *International Journal on Advanced Technology for Learning, 4*(1).

Pozzi, F., Manca, S., Persico, D., & Sarti, L. (2007). A general framework for tracking and analysing learning processes in CSCL environments. *Innovations in Education & Teaching International (IETI) Journal, 44*(2), 169-180.

Pozzi, F., & Sugliano, A. M. (2006). Using collaborative strategies and techniques in CSCL environments. In A. Méndez-Vilas, et al. (Eds.),

Current developments in technology-assisted education 1 (pp. 703-709). FORMATEX.

Rourke, L., Anderson, T., Garrison, R., & Archer, W. (2001). methodological issues in the content analysis of computer conference transcripts. *International Journal of Artificial Intelligence in Education, 12*, 8-22.

Rowntree, D. (1995). Teaching and learning online: A correspondence education for 21st century. *British Journal of Educational Technology, 26*(3).

Scardamalia, M., & Bereiter, C. (1994). Computer support for knowledge-building communities. *The Journal of the Learning Sciences, 3*(3), 265-283.

Schrire, S. (2006). Knowledge building in asynchronous discussion groups: Going beyond quantitative analysis. *Computers & Education, 46*, 49-70.

Suchman, L. A. (1987). *Plans and situated actions.* New York: Cambridge University Press.

The Cognition and Technology Group at Vanderbilt. (1991). Some thoughts about constructivism and instructional design. *Educational Technology, 31*(10), 16-18.

Vygotsky, L. (1962). *Thought and language* (E. Hanfman & G. Backer, Trans.). Cambridge, MA: M.I.T. Press.

Weinberger, A., & Fischer, F. (2006). A framework to analyze argumentative knowledge construction in computer-supported collaborative learning. *Computers & Education, 46*, 71-95.

ENDNOTES

1   http://www.imsglobal.org/learningdesign/
2   This collaborative technique in literature is also referred to as *Pyramid* (see for example http://gsic.tel.uva.es/~dherleo/clfp/pyramid-en/)
3   ICALTS (Interaction and Collaboration AnaLysis supporting Teachers and Students Self-regulation) is a Jointly Executed Integrated Research Project of the Kaleidoscope Network of Excellence, website at http://www.rhodes.aegean.gr/ltee/kaleidoscope-icalts/
4   In 2005 the system used was FirstClass™ Centrinity, while in 2007 Moodle was adopted.
5   It is worthwhile noting that there are differences as far as the kind of data concerning reactive participation and continuity made available by the two CMC systems (namely First Class and Moodle).
6   For an exhaustive debate on the unit of analysis see (De Wever et al., 2006). "One of the issues under discussion is the choice of the unit of analysis to perform content analysis. Researchers can consider each individual sentence as a single unit of analysis (Fahy et al., 2001). A second option is to identify a consistent "theme" or "idea" (unit of meaning) in a message and to approach this as the unit of analysis (Henri, 1992). A third option is to take the complete message a student posts at a certain moment in the discussion as the unit of analysis (Gunawardena et al., 1997; Rourke et al., 2001)" (De Wever et al., 2006, p. 9).
7   Occurrences are calculated on the basis of the "units of meanings" attributed by the coder to the corresponding indicator. Each unit of meaning could be assigned one indicator only.

Chapter XX
Employing Innovative Learning Strategies Using an E–Learning Platform

Andrina Granić
University of Split, Croatia

Maja Ćukušić
University of Split, Croatia

Aimilia Tzanavari
University of Nicosia, Cyprus

George A. Papadopoulos
University of Cyprus, Cyprus

ABSTRACT

Web-based learning environments have become an integral part of learning. The way that they are employed in the learning process, or in other words the learning strategy followed in that respect, is an important issue that has to be carefully thought of, deciding upon topics such as suitable pedagogical approaches and appropriate assessment techniques for a given context. The chapter deals with this exact issue by visiting the relevant literature on the subject, describing selected learning strategies that have been employed in the use of an innovative eLearning platform in schools in Europe and finally outlining and comparing two real case studies from two European countries.

INTRODUCTION

Informal learning today becomes the dominant form of learning (Tuomi, 2007). Peer-to-peer and problem-based learning in real-world contexts as well as learning through games and entertainment is becoming more and more popular. At the same time, eLearning systems are still being frequently used for teaching (transmissive learning), but noticeably less for autonomous learning, reflection, social and communication skills development, problem solving capacities (expansive learning) and alike (Ulf, 2007). To overcome this, every attempt to design an eLearning experience should begin with the pedagogical strategies that drive it and continue with setting the learning goals and designing learning activities that require the appropriate eLearning content to meet those learning goals, *cf.* (Kelly *et al.*, 2005). The selection of technologies has to be performed then within the context of these pedagogical choices so as to understand both the potential of learning and the development of successful eLearning resources.

Learning often seems to be a natural process; however, the many definitions of and theories on learning confirm that human learning is a complex activity. Literature concerning learning strategies explores different ways of learning. Learning strategies, as defined by Nisbet and Shucksmith (1986), are seen as the processes that underlie performance on thinking tasks, while Mayer (1988) defines learning strategies as behaviors, manners of a learner that are intended to influence a person's cognitive processes during learning. In line with the latter definition, an implementation of theoretical foundations in praxis is illustrated in the chapter. Concerns about the gap between theory and practice, about what instructional designers have learned and experienced in the workplace as well as the lack of a unifying perspective on human learning have raised the question – how an innovative learning strategy can be employed using a Web-based learning environment. Specifically, our objective is to indicate how taken "pedagogical decisions" implicate the selection of suitable pedagogical approaches and assessment techniques to be employed in an innovative eLearning platform.

This chapter first presents a literature review of the area of pedagogy in eLearning, focusing on learning theories and the concept of a learning scenario. It later summarizes the several issues/problems one encounters when it comes to employing an eLearning system and implementing a pedagogical framework for eLearning. A proposal solution for overcoming some of these obstacles is presented in detail, supporting it with the results of two real world case studies. Finally, conclusions are drawn and future research trends are identified.

PEDAGOGY IN eLEARNING

Learning Theories

Teaching and learning activities can be designed and implemented to take principles of learning into account, emphasizing on the fact that learning occurs within certain context and that is active, social as well as reflective (Driscoll, 2002). The spectrum of learning theories consists of a plethora of methodologies and approaches explaining how people learn, with behaviourism, cognitivism and constructivism being well-known categories of these. It is clear that the lack of a unifying theory on human learning gives rise to gaps between the theory and practice of instructional design. Nevertheless, ideas about learning in general fall under two headings – the generic heading of socio-cultural theory, including for example "communities of practice" (Wenger, 1998), and "activity theory" (Engestrom, 1987). Since, from this perspective, the basic unit of analysis is larger than the individual learner (e.g. the "activity system") these theories are able to account for learning in collaborative contexts. The idea of "distributed learning" is important here but it is a term that is not always used consistently. From a socio-cultural point of view learning takes place through the co-construction of meanings, specifically it is distributed across learners (agents/actors). This is a stronger claim than the simple proposition that learning can be distributed, say across a network, in the form of content or other resources. An emphasis on "practice" and "activity" is consistent with constructivist and socio-constructivist theories of learning which place the learner as agent at the heart of the learning process.

Another key idea is that of "situated learning". This is important because it draws attention not only to social context but also to material culture, including technology. A recent and significant development in cognitive science is the emergence of an "embodied-embedded approach", see for example (Wheeler, 2005). Here cognition and, by implication learning, is "outsourced" to the non-neuronal body and the environment, including the social environment. This too is broadly consistent with a socio-cultural approach but, importantly, it also draws attention to the active learner in a material context, where things in the world (texts, artifacts, languages) are not simply tools for learning; they actually do a lot of cognitive work for the learner. Examples of how, hitherto difficult-to-access, concepts and processes are made available to learners through information and communications technology (ICT) are not difficult to find.

Theories about learning such as the ones mentioned above have helped broaden the focus of attention, defining learning in a broad sense as a process that continues from birth to death, in and out of formal environments such as schools.

Figure 1. Livingstone's categories of learning

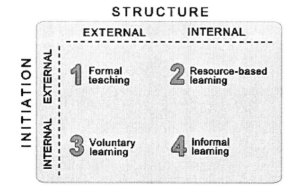

Livingstone (2004), cited in (Taylor and Evans, 2005), defines four categories of learning in terms of the extent to which it is internally or externally structured or initiated, resulting in the matrix depicted in Figure 1.

In resource-based learning learners are encouraged to access resources (including online resources) independently, managing their own learning but towards goals that are set by the curriculum. An example of the third category would be "voluntary learning" in a school setting where students choose to follow certain courses or participate in extracurricular programs. With respect to the formal/informal learning range, examples of eLearning can be found where the roles of teacher and learner are fluid and therefore difficult to define.

Rather than providing an overview of mLearning technologies addressing the specific curriculum areas, Naismith *et al.* (2004) take up an activity-centered viewpoint, considering new practices against existing theories. More specifically, they identify six theory-based categories of learning activities and related examples of the use of mobile technology in each category. mLearning concepts and technology can be considered within the following learning theories:

a. *Behaviourist*: In the course of activities that endorse learning as a change in learners' behavior.

b. *Constructivist*: In the course of activities in which learners construct new ideas or concepts based on their previous and current knowledge.

c. *Situated*: In the course of activities where learning takes place within an authentic context and culture.

d. *Collaborative*: In the course of activities in which learners gain knowledge through social interaction.

e. *Informal and lifelong*: in the course of activities that promote learning outside a formal learning environment and curriculum.

f.   *learning and teaching support*: in the course of activities that support the coordination of learners and resources.

The Learning Scenario Concept

Evans and Taylor (2005) define scenarios as "stories focused on a user or group of users, which would provide information on the nature of the users, the goals they want to achieve and the context in which the activities will take place. They are written in ordinary language, and are therefore understandable to various stakeholders, including users. They may also contain different degrees of detail." As described in (UNITE Public Deliverable 1, 2006) a learning scenario should involve all the methods that need to be applied in planned activities within classrooms, the roles of the actors in the learning process (students, teachers, school headmasters and administrators) and the kind of cooperation among different groups (i.e. classroom as whole, small groups of students in the same classroom or in different classrooms). It should be flexible enough so as to be creatively reusable, to allow teacher's intervention and be adaptable to changes according to the number of students and classes to which is implemented. According to Erskine *et al.* (1997) in scenario-based design the first step is to write down the scenario in a detailed narrative form. Subsequently, claims about the usability and usefulness of particular artifacts envisioned in the scenario are made. These claims are also recorded in a manner that maintains their link to the scenarios they analyze. This process of scenario construction and claims analysis is conducted as an iterative cycle. In the end, the accumulated scenarios and claims constitute the design's description and rationale.

Scenarios support a mutually informing dialogue between technology experts, pedagogues and evaluators (Taylor and Evans, 2005). This is why scenarios call for continuous feedback among them with the view to constantly improving scenarios according to the settled pedagogical objectives, the technical requirements and evaluation offered by all involved agents. Carroll (1999), who also studied the concept of a learning scenario, described it as a sequence of *actions* and *events* that take place in a particular *setting* and are performed by *agents* or *actors* who try to meet certain *goals* or *objectives*.

IMPORTANT ISSUES

New skills – technical, intellectual and social – are becoming essential for living, working and participating actively in a knowledge society and while their scope extends well beyond "digital literacy", they are the basis on which the society depends on (European Commission, 2001). The ability to use ICT is essential in many sectors. A European Reference Framework (European Commission, 2005) sets out the eight key competences: Communication in the mother tongue; Communication in the foreign languages; Mathematical competence and basic competences in science and technology; Digital competence; Learning to learn; Interpersonal, intercultural and social competences and civic competence; Entrepreneurship; and Cultural expression. eLearning platforms can contribute to the development of these competences through specialized courses. Competences like "learning to learn" and "interpersonal, intercultural and social competences" can be developed using new approaches of learning and eLearning functionalities that promote collaboration, group work and communication.

Having outlined the importance of acquiring the key competences and the opportunity of using an eLearning system for that purpose, we will introduce several concerns related to employing innovative learning strategies within the context of using an innovative eLearning platform. eLearning requires certain digital literacy skills in order to offer a beneficial learning experience. The question that emerges is the following one: do we need eLearning systems to help to cope with competence challenges or competencies are needed to cope with eLearning systems? Therefore, the tools for eLearning should not necessarily require a high level of digital literacy before a learner can engage in an eLearning activity (Selinger, 2005).

In order to support the improvement of the learners' subject matter knowledge and the implementation of a learning strategy, eLearning environments should be designed to address learners' diversity in terms of learning styles, prior knowledge, culture and self-regulation skills (Vovides, 2007). Individualized learning and reflective learning are two important ingredients that can enhance an eLearning system that supports learning and instruction offering the necessary scaffolds for the development of meta-cognitive and self-regulatory skills. In essence, the scaffolds within an eLearning system need to be adaptive in order to foster student self-regulation in open-ended learning environments, *cf.* (Azevedo, 2005). The roots of the theory behind software scaffolding lie in Vygotsky's (1978) work on the Zone of Proximal Development (ZPD). In this respect, the software would play the role of the knowledgeable peer who provides the learner with adequately challenging activities and offers the appropriate assistance both in quantity and in quality. As the learner learns that assistance would be gradually withdrawn (Luckin *et al.*, 2003).

Another issue is that of compatibility of cognitive styles and technology which directly impact perceptions of learning effectiveness, motivation and performance. When cognitive styles and technology are compatible, individuals are better equipped to pay attention to and understand relevant information, which are important to learning and learning outcomes (Workman, 2004).

Issues related to the design and implementation of a "pedagogical framework" comprise also learners' diversity in terms of meta-cognitive skills, learning styles, prior knowledge and cultures in addition to the role of the instructor in an eLearning platform. One of the effective ways

of understanding, describing and evaluating the aspects of the design and implementation of an eLearning system that directly affect learning is Reeves' (1994) scale consisting of the fourteen pedagogical dimensions. The pedagogical dimensions refer to the capabilities of an eLearning system to initiate powerful instructional interactions, monitor learner progress, empower effective teachers, accommodate individual differences or promote cooperative learning. As such, dimensions have the potential to provide improved criteria for understanding and comparing eLearning systems. Reeves' methodology will also be used in the chapter to present the findings and to compare the two case studies described.

Among several other problems that inhibit the implementation of innovation strategies in European learning, Dondi (2006) explains the lack of the culture for support in European education and training systems since innovation plans are implemented at a very slow pace and sometimes even abandoned before their final implementation. Another problem he points out is that of low level of effectiveness and efficiency of the accumulation and utilization of available knowledge in the education field (in comparison to health or transport sector for example). Balacheff (2006) states that the academic research community has the responsibility to develop a research domain that is both scientifically robust and productive. He fears the possibility of "reinventing the wheel and developing technologies that are forgotten soon after their development". Also, he is afraid that research needs are not expressed in the same way by all the European nations (since the needs are not the same either). As we firsthand observed while conducting a "national specifics" survey in 14 European countries (Ćukušić *et al.*, 2007), it is difficult to express these "needs" since the educational systems and context in general vary widely between countries. Therefore a common framework could be developed but some issues surely arise in real-life settings upon implementation.

A different issue is that of a competent eLearning team. The team that produces quality eLearning material in a large, complex eLearning project according to Horton (2001) should consist of about sixteen people: one person should manage the whole project, three people should design the course (lead designer, module designers and subject matter experts), six people should build the content (course integrator, writers, graphics specialists, multimedia developers, html/xml coders and programmers), three members should provide the technical infrastructure (network administrators, server/database programmers and technical support specialists) and three members should conduct eLearning (curriculum administrator, course facilitator and online instructor). Downsizing to fit the needs of simpler projects is possible and of course necessary. The actual makeup of the team depends on size and the scope of the project, amount of work outsourced, specific media and technologies required and a like (*ibid.*). Besides, it is possible that the same required skills can be provided by different combinations of team members. The sustainability of an eLearning platform depends on whether there are more than few people involved in the maintenance of the system after its implementation: which structures are in place to support students in their eLearning and which structures are in place to support staff in their implementation of eLearning (support to the pedagogical framework).

Varis (2005) poses other important questions that challenge the implementation of learning in virtual environments: approaches to learning, ways to combine traditional and new ways of learning and the like. How do self-directed, facilitated web-based learning, virtual classrooms and discussion formats perform in practice? What is the present stage of development of experiential and interactive learning models? Are teachers and supporting staff equipped with the right knowledge to apply these approaches? Vuorikari (2004) reflects on use of ICT in learning. According to her study's conclusions, ICT is used but teaching is still "traditional". She offers two possible reasons: teachers are just starting to learn how to use ICT in a more constructive way and eLearning systems hardly support the desired change in the learning and teaching paradigm in school. Tools for new ways of collaborative exercises that support learner-centered pedagogy do not exist; therefore it is easier for a teacher to practice "traditional" teaching. In situation changes special focus is put on pedagogical approaches and ways they could be supported by ICT. To introduce an eLearning system in daily practice, teachers' training in the application of pedagogical models using the system should give them a solid starting point. An ongoing pedagogical support could and should be provided to help teachers with the new practice. The foreknowledge of teachers is not equal and many of them have problems getting enough time to apply the techniques within the school curriculum. Personal motivation is of great importance for those teachers.

This section attempted to pinpoint different eLearning realities affecting pedagogy directly or indirectly. Issues that potentially hinder the successful employment of innovative eLearning platforms, as well as the implementation of a pedagogical framework in that context, were described. For achieving effective and efficient eLearning, that offers learners an optimal learning experience, the issues raised above should be dealt with.

SOLUTIONS AND RECOMMENDATIONS

Designing and Using an Innovative eLearning Platform

Solutions and recommendations to some of the issues presented hereinafter will be based on our firsthand experience from the UNITE (Unified eLearning environment for the school) project. UNITE (2006) is a thirty-month long European research project (February 2006 – July 2008) aiming to provide novel services in education for young Europeans by combining different state-of-the-art (SOTA) technologies in e/mLearning, also taking into consideration innovation in technology and pedagogy. Deployment of UNITE's principles and methods is accomplished through incremental introduction coupled with continuous evaluation. The design and the implementation phase comprised joint work of project partners and partner schools (network of 14 European schools) related to setting up the infrastructure, planning, creation and delivery of new and/or customized learning scenarios as well as validation of performed activities (Ćukušić *et al.*, 2008a).

The UNITE platform is considered an "add-on" to currently used forms of interaction and contributes to developments of interactive learning in the European-wide network of schools (as an illustration see the platform's user interface in Figure 2). It is important to point out that in some participating schools whole-class teaching prevailed before an employment of the new e/mLearning system. Teaching and learning with the UNITE platform implies the use of curriculum material delivered, not only in English, but also in the partners' mother tongue: *eLearning scenario template* along with more than 40 different scenario examples (UNITE Public Deliverable 5.3, 2008), *Content development handbook* (Tzana-

Figure 2. Screenshots of the UNITE platform's user interface

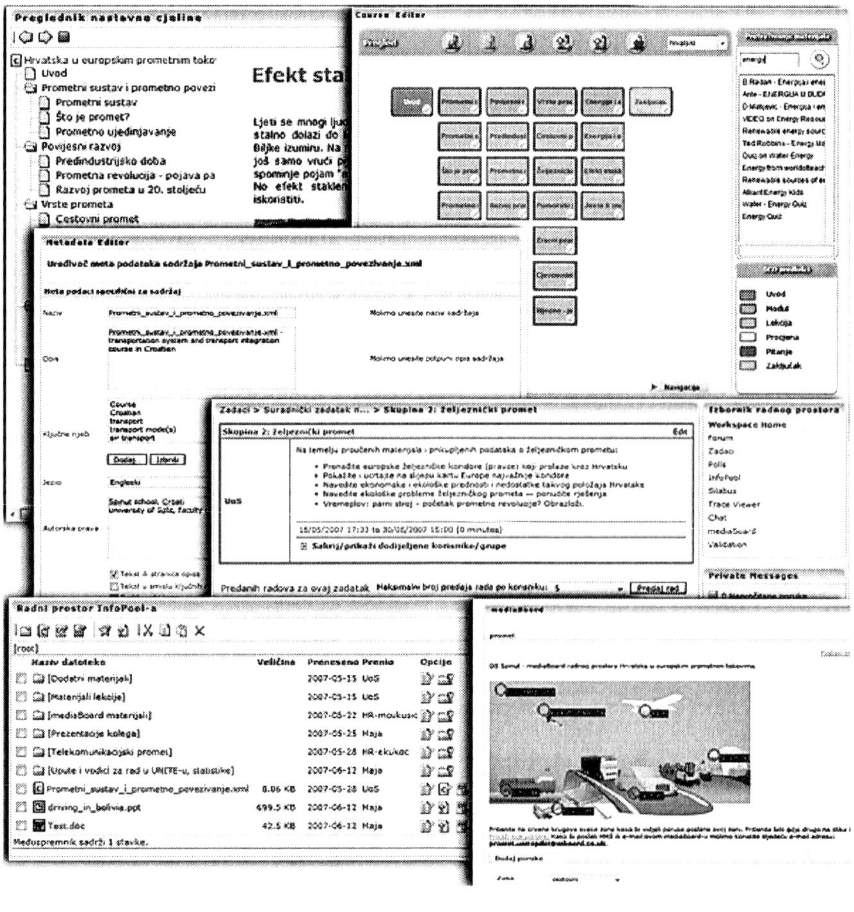

vari, 2007) and *Teachers' handbook* conveying the pedagogical principles (Ćukušić *et al.*, 2007).

While designing the pedagogical framework of the UNITE e/mLearning system, three main aspects were taken into account. First, the existing state-of-the-art models of exploitation of the potential of new technologies in pedagogy along with the list of user requirements related to the pedagogical framework were thoroughly analyzed. Both SOTA models in pedagogy and user requirements are available in (UNITE Public Deliverable 1, 2006). Second, in order to acknowledge local context of the network of schools, national and school specifics regarding educational characteristics and existing pedagogical practices were collected and formulated. Finally, the pedagogical experts analyzed a wider context in order to find out which components should assemble a "best-practice" pedagogical framework (see Figure 3).

Consequently, the following five-component *pedagogical framework* with suitable and beneficial theories and practices was developed (Granić & Ćukušić, 2007):

a. *Pedagogical framework context:* Defines areas that influence the framework itself and

forms the basis for further development of UNITE's theories.

b. *Pedagogical approaches/strategies:* Promotes principles of constructivist theory, along with blended, collaborative and active learning in particular.

c. *Knowledge evaluation techniques/strategies:* Defines and supports diverse types of assessments.

d. *Teacher training:* Enables successful online teaching and thus is introduced as an important part of the pedagogical framework.

e. *Current pedagogical practices and national specifics:* Implementation of pedagogical changes in the schools already has and will have impact on pedagogical process, assessments and pedagogical assumptions in general.

Because the pedagogical and assessment strategies directly influence and inform the learning and teaching process, they are the fundamental part of any pedagogical framework. Namely, pedagogical innovation, if any, should be made clear in pedagogy or assessment applied in or out of everyday teaching classroom environment.

Figure 3. UNITE pedagogical framework (Granić & Ćukušić, 2007)

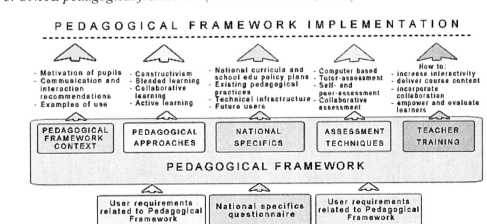

Selected key pedagogical strategies along with employed assessment strategies are briefly described in subsections which follow the subsequent one related to eLearning scenario templates.

As previously mentioned, the list of user requirements related to the pedagogical framework formed the main point of reference for the first learning strategy design phase. Requirements were classified and categorized using a simple matrix (see Figure 4), as one of many possible ways of categorization. On the one hand, matrix rows are associated with autonomous/directed learning and active/passive learning, while on the other hand its columns are related to individualized/collaborative learning.

Learning scenarios are crucial mechanisms for eLearning, holding together pedagogy and technical development through a focus on concrete experience. That is why scenario planning, in which pedagogic and assessment strategies are clearly articulated through detailed descriptions of learning contexts, is very important.

Figure 4. Categorization of user requirements for the pedagogical framework

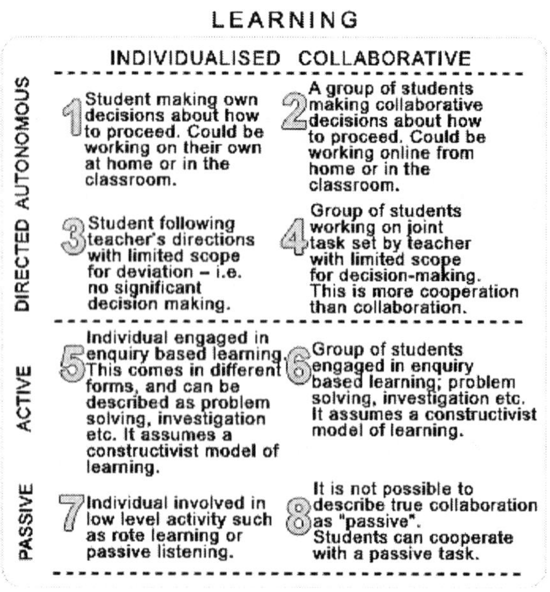

UNITE eLearning Scenario Template

The development process of an eLearning scenario is fundamental because it refers to the codification of the scenario itself, after which it can be implemented in the school environment and potentially or perhaps ideally be reused by others. The quality of this codification, i.e. how well the scenario is described and documented, is directly related to how successful the scenario will be with respect to its reuse by others, its flexibility in implementation and a like (Zoakou *et al.*, 2007).

Within the framework of the UNITE project, an appropriate solution for capturing scenarios was carefully selected based on the state-of-the-art analysis performed. In fact two solutions were identified that qualified as good candidates but would however have to be adapted to the project's particular needs. These were the Kynigos template (Kynigos, 1995) and the JISC template (JISC Template, 2004). The first one follows a narrative format and thus is easier for someone to create, whereas the second is in a structured tabular form with fields to fill-in and so more detailed but also time-consuming. The two of them were studied in relation to UNITE, leading to the creation of a hybrid solution, the *UNITE eLearning scenario template*, which is described in Table 1.

The scenario template was polished and revised, primarily based on the UNITE pedagogical framework, before its final version was developed. The template aims to help teachers organize their eLearning lesson in the most efficient way and have an overall view of the steps they are going to follow. Consequently, it consists of two parts. The first one is related to the curriculum area (see section 1 in Table 1) and the second one is related to the pedagogical activities planned to take place during the scenario implementation (see section 2 in Table 1); each pedagogical activity is matched with a learning objective, the tools/resources the teacher plans to use, how he/she is

Table 1. UNITE elearning scenario template, adapted from (Zoakou et al, 2006)

1. Curriculum area
1.1 Subject/discipline area
1.2 Context/level of study
1.3 Topic/domain
1.4 Pre-requisite skills/ knowledge
1.5 Pedagogical Approach
Brief description of the general pedagogical approach that will inform practice in the scenario outline in section 2. It refers to the theoretical underpinning channeling the modes of delivery and the learning activities that will follow e.g. Constructivist approach with particular focus on problem- based learning or experiential learning, etc.
2. Pedagogic Activities
2.1 Learning Activities
The learning scenario should be outlined as a sequence of activities (i.e. a narrative) including information about what different actors (e.g. students, teachers) are doing at each stage. The way in which activities address learning objectives i.e. the modes of delivery should be clear, and this should be consistent with the overall approach specified in section 1.
2.2 Learning objectives/ outcome(s)
These should be stated in terms of one of the four categories: knowledge (facts), understanding (concepts), skills and attitudes/values. They can be taken directly from prescribed schemes of work where appropriate.
2.3 Tools/ Resources
Any physical/virtual tool (hardware, software) or resource (e.g. textbook) can be specified here. E-/M-learning resources in particular should be described in some detail
2.4 Assessment Strategy (Feedback and/or Evidence)
With an emphasis on formative assessment key activities should be selected. Assessment strategies might include peer-commentary, the use of e-portfolios, self generated success criteria, photographic records
2.5 Time allocated

going to evaluate each learning activity and how long it is going to last.

Pedagogical Strategies

The principles and praxis integrated into eLearning scenarios through the pedagogical framework were addressed in the *Teachers' Handbook* (Ćukušić *et al.*, 2007) and are presented below:

1. **Constructivism:** Constructivism (Alessi & Trollip, 2001) conveys the concept of student as the creator of knowledge and meaning through their interaction with one another, their environment and with teachers. Teachers can be thought of as being coaches, facilitators or even partners with

learners in the learning process. Formalization of the theory of constructivism is commonly credited to Piaget who suggested that through processes of accommodation and assimilation, individuals construct new knowledge from their experiences (for more details see Piaget, 1953). The cognitive or radical constructivism is believed to arise largely from Piaget's work while the social or realist constructivist practice is often held to draw from the work of Vygotsky (Hua Liu & Matthews, 2005). The constructivist approach to teaching and learning forms the theoretical basis upon which the pedagogical model presented here is designed. It was/ will be implemented in various educational contexts in diverse ways (hands-on learning, reflection, interaction, investigation and analysis, *cf.* e.g. (Gray, 2001; Ullrich, 2005)) requiring from teachers to design instruction correspondingly. This emphasizes the fact that in constructivist classroom teacher and student share responsibility and decision making as well as demonstrate mutual respect.

2. **Blended learning:** Teachers used and will use eLearning systems as a technological enhancement to their everyday teaching process. They use the best of both traditional, specifically face-to-face, and online communication according to the principles of blended (hybrid) learning. It has been argued that up to 80% of verbal exchange in the classroom is attributed to the teacher (Grogan, 2006). Conversely, in eLearning courses teachers do not "speak" more than their students (Marcelo, 2006) suggesting that learners, who are too shy to contribute in the classroom, feel more empowered to do so online (Jonassen, 1996). Therefore, blended learning seems as an ideal teaching concept for the future and its employment in UNITE affects and empowers students to considerably contribute online as well.

3. **Collaborative learning:** Collaborative learning (Prince, 2004) is a term used for a variety of educational approaches involving joint intellectual effort by students or students and teachers together. It covers a number of approaches with variability in the amount of in-class or out-of-class time built around groups of students working and mutually searching for understanding, solutions and/or meanings. Some forms of collaborative problem solving include: (i) guided design as a very structured approach to group problem solving where students, working in small groups, practice decision-making in sequenced tasks, with detailed feedback at every step, (ii) cases, stories or real life situations setting up a problem for

students to analyze and resolve in class or in study group session and (iii) peer writing involving students working in small groups at every stage of the writing process, formulating ideas, clarifying their positions, testing an argument or focusing a thesis statement (*ibid.*). One of the key notions in Vygotsky's approach to cognitive development is the Zone of Proximal Development (ZPD), which has significant implications for peer collaboration. Vygotsky (1978, p. 86) defines the ZPD as "the distance between the actual developmental level as determined by independent problem solving and the level of potential development as determined through problem solving under adult guidance or in collaboration with more capable peers". In other words, learners who lack certain skills may learn more effectively in the social context provided by someone with the necessary knowledge (Eysenck & Flanagan, 2001).

4. **Active learning:** Active learning is defined as "any instructional method that engages students in the learning process" (Prince, 2004). It requires from students to think about what they are doing as opposed to passively receiving information from the teacher in traditional teaching methods. There is evidence of importance and effects of active learning to the quality of learning, innovations in education and alike. Some studies find higher class scores and less variably on items presented via active learning (Yoder & Hochevar, 2005) while others as benefits of active learning stress valuable contribution to the development of independent learning skills and ability to apply knowledge, preparing students for future careers (Sivan *et al.*, 2000).

UNITE scenarios engage individuals and/or groups in various forms of active learning like problem solving, case studying and enquiry-based learning, which contributes to the development of qualities like critical thinking and problem solving. Through these activities students are able to discover new information and become self-managed learners. Starting from the late 1980s both cognitive scientists and technologists have suggested that learners might understand the phenomena from the science and technology area better if they could build and manipulate the models of these phenomena (Bransford *et al.*, 2000). This assumption is tested frequently in the classrooms with technology-based modeling tools. Of course, electronic devices and systems can enhance learners' performance but only in the case where they are used as a part of a consistent teaching and learning process consisting of suitable pedagogical and assessment approaches.

Assessment Strategies

Apart from introducing pedagogical principles and approaches, the pedagogical framework also reinforces the use of summative and particularly formative assessments in teaching and learning. Summative assessment is still the predominant way of evaluation of students' achievements. It is usually used at the end of a teaching unit to determine what has been learned by the student. On the other hand, problem solving, stimulations and project work with formative or on-going evaluation, present a step forward in order to acknowledge that assessment is actually part of the learning process. Formative assessment presents "all the activities undertaken by teachers and/or by their students, which provide information to be used as feedback to modify the teaching and learning activities in which they are engaged" (Mödritscher *et al.*, 2006).

How and what is to be assessed depends on the goals and purpose of learning and the types of learning involved. Assessment needs to be embedded in the course design (Laurillard, 2002) to reflect and support the learning processes involved. The assessment of collaborative work is managed whereby individual contributions are recognized on the basis of individual work, with another value to reflect the group effort (Weller, 2002). On the other hand, self-assessment is experienced as promoting autonomy in that the students make their rules and negotiate them with their teachers. Learners are actively involved in decisions about their own criteria for assessment and the process of judging their own and others' work (McConnell, 2000).

There are a number of online assessment techniques (sometimes referred to as "alternative assessments") serving as a tool to support either formative or summative assessment. Tittelboom (2003) introduces Statements of Relevance, Interactive exercises and Peer-assessment of forum activities that support both formative and summative assessment:

- **Formative:** Pupils are presented with a number of questions which they can ask themselves and prepare Statements of Relevance as an exercise in introspection. These statements are not marked but are read and commented by the tutor. Interactive exercises range from reading reference materials and doing multiple choices, matching, gap-filling etc. and receiving programmed feedback messages after each answer (immediate feedback) or at the end of the exercise (delayed feedback). The students assess themselves (based of the feedback and the score indications they receive). They can also be asked to assess and give constructive comments on the contributions made by their group members using forums.
- **Summative:** At the end of the course, students have to submit a final Statement of Relevance summarizing the reflections they have recorded throughout the course (assessed by the tutor). The scores earned by the students in interactive exercises are not tracked or retained. The quality of the comments in forums is not directly marked

but tutor assessment of the students' activities is incorporated in their final score for the course.

Assessment techniques of the pedagogical framework promoted in UNITE learning scenarios are introduced in the following:

1. **Computer-based assessment:** Quizzes are one of computer-based assessment techniques that were introduced in UNITE. Those multiple-choice type tests or quiz type questions were assigned: (i) at the beginning of a course for diagnostic purposes to indicate any areas where prerequisite knowledge may be inadequate, (ii) during a course in order to measure progress in understanding and/or (iii) at the end of a course to assist in revision. Several other assessment techniques mentioned above were employed based on the intended learning objectives, kind of competencies to be mediated to students, extent to which the competencies should be mastered by students, reliability in grading, prevention of cheating, exam construction and a like, *cf.* (Mödritscher, 2006).

2. **Tutor-assessment:** eLearning systems offer students exceptional opportunities for individual communication with their teachers/tutors. Using the platform functionalities and e-mail, teachers were contacted throughout the day and as a result students actually always had a personal tutor available. Since the assessment and the grading were not realized only by computer-based tests, teachers used open-ended questions as well (e.g. writing essays or submitting some project work). In such a case the evaluation process is extremely time-consuming and self-/peer-assessment could ease the teacher's assessment overload.

3. **Self-assessment:** Student involvement in their own assessment is an important part of their preparation for life and future work. Through self-assessment, which is quite opposite to traditional assessment where written tests and oral exams still prevail, students track their personal development and deepen the learning experience. They take more responsibility for their own learning and also become more aware of their own knowledge gaps (if any), since they assess themselves in relation to the course objectives. Using an eLearning platform students accomplish exercises at their own pace and receive private feedback messages. Moreover, they are actively involved in taking decisions about their own assessment criteria as well as in judging their own and others' work, *cf.* (McConnell, 2006).

4. **Peer-assessment:** In peer-assessment students are engaged in helping each other to develop, review and assess other's course work. The UNITE system is well suited for peer-assessment because in forums students can easily share and comment on other students work and contributions. Forum discussions are more "relaxed" and can be used for low-stakes testing only. Exchange of ideas, evaluation and comments on the work of their peers makes peer-assessment part of learning process and valuable resource for mutual learning. In order to overcome and avoid comments like "I don't like his/her work", explicit instructions on what and how to assess, what aspects of the work should be taken into account and similar were provided.

CASE STUDIES

The eLearning Scenarios

UNITE has followed a certain procedure in order to implement its theories and practices in schools. UNITE's implementation process advances through four major phases including (i) scenario planning, (ii) scenario implementation, (iii) validation and (iv) platform and process improvement respectively (Ćukušić *et al.*, 2008a).

The Croatia Case

In the Elementary school Spinut (2008), a state school based in Split, a team of five people was formed, consisting of the school's headmaster, the pedagogue and three subject teachers. Support in terms of organizational and technical assistance was provided by the University of Split (UNITE project partner). After implementing two scenarios with older students (13 and 14 year-old), the third scenario approaches younger students also (from 11 to 15 years) and intends to stimulate their interest in science and technology (S&T). Current trends in the EU are showing that innovative experiments on science teaching are proving benefits for education (Buysse, 2007). An elective course entitled *Wonderful World of Inventions* for talented students was therefore developed in order to encourage students' desire to learn and to give a playful dimension to the knowledge acquisition through the new learning scenario. Within its framework and parallel to the activities performed within the school environment, the activities taking place in more informal contexts like field trips, museums, institute laboratories and a like were undertaken.

According to the diverse areas/stages of the course, different pedagogical approaches are implemented. For example there was project work where students were encouraged to take a more active role, that of researchers, and to come up with their own sketches and designs (of a parachute, a plane or similar). Subsequently, students tried-out their designs in practice and actually learned-by-doing. There were elements of exploratory learning, with cooperative learning in groups, along with some couple-work. Students were also taught how to work/learn alone as individuals. The teacher acted mostly as students' mentor and

not as a "typical" teacher. Field work, numerous visits and workshops were a great value-add to this scenario and an opportunity for students to learn astrology, robotics and science in general in a real-life environment(s). These new methods make science teaching more exciting.

UNITE is used as a repository of the learning material and problem-based tasks (either provided by the mentor or collected by students as a part of their research assignment) as well as an irreplaceable communication platform. Both synchronous and asynchronous communication and collaboration functionalities of UNITE are important for this scenario since the course is attended by a heterogeneous group of students. They attend their regular courses in different times of day; they go to different classes and the like. Furthermore, mobile learning capabilities, notes, journals and similar functionalities of the UNITE system were of great importance since students were able to track their progress, update their portfolio, reflect, explore and discuss. In this way, every student was provided with the opportunity to express her/himself, to experiment and to learn.

The Cyprus Case

In the English School (2008), a prestigious private secondary school based in the capital Nicosia, the team involved in eLearning scenario design, development and implementation consisted of the Head Teacher, a senior teacher of English, a senior teacher of Environmental Studies and a researcher from the University of Cyprus (UNITE project partner). The scenario topics were chosen by the teachers themselves, taking into account what the platform had to offer. One of the eLearning scenarios developed within the Environmental Studies subject was entitled *Traffic Survey* and originated from the real problem that students, teachers and parents faced everyday – traffic around and on campus. The students involved in this project were 16-17 years old.

Students were expected to a have good understanding of how modern cities are increasingly dependant on cars leading to all the associated problems. A group of Environmental Studies students carried out a stratified survey of the entire school student population with a 10 to 15% sample. The survey aimed at finding out how students come to school, how long it takes them, how they view the traffic problem on school grounds. The scenario involved activities that took place in the classroom, outdoors (for data collection), in the Geography computer lab and possibly at home.

The students followed an enquiry based approach whereby they set up a hypothesis and tested it. This involved a stage where a clear aim was set, stating what the objective was, designing methods of collecting data, organizing the logistics and the timing of the data collection. What followed was the collaboration of putting together the data collected, analyzing it, presenting it in

a visually effective manner and finally assessing the successes and validity of the results.

Both UNITE's learning resource repository and its communication facilities were used as well as its mLearning component, for visualization and classification of images even while the field work is under way.

Comparison of the Pedagogical Dimensions of the Two Scenarios

Reeves' (1994) methodology was considered suitable and thus was applied in order to explain how UNITE "enhances the learning experience". Pedagogical dimensions, as aspects of the design and implementation of the system that directly affect learning (see Table 2), have the potential to provide criteria for understanding and comparing scenarios/learning programmes. Consequently, the pedagogical dimensions of the scenarios *Wonderful World of Inventions* and *Traffic Survey*

Table 2. Pedagogical dimensions of computer based education (Reeves, 1994)

Pedagogical dimensions of Computer Based Education			
1. Epistemology	Objectivism	↔	Constructivism
2. Pedagogical philosophy	Instructivist	↔	Constructivist
3. Underlying psychology	Behavioural	↔	Cognitive
4. Goal orientation	Sharply-focused	↔	Unfocused
5. Experiential value	Abstract	↔	Concrete
6. Teacher role	Didactic	↔	Facilitative
7. Program flexibility	Teacher-Proof	↔	Easily Modifiable
8. Value of errors	Errorless Learning	↔	Learning from Experience
9. Motivation	Extrinsic	↔	Intrinsic
10. Accommodation of individual differences	Non-existent	↔	Multi-faceted
11. Learner control	Non-existent	↔	Unrestricted
12. User activity	Mathemagenic	↔	Generative
13. Cooperative learning	Unsupported	↔	Integral
14. Cultural sensitivity	Non-existent	↔	Integral

(among others) were qualitatively and graphically compared.

In February 2008, the project partners with the pedagogical background referred back to the fourteen scenarios and rated their pedagogical dimensions (Ćukušić *et al.*, 2008b). The purpose of the exercise was to provide a qualitative and graphical comparison of the scenarios and to create a "profile" of the particular scenario. Figure 5 illustrates how the scenarios *Wonderful World of Inventions* and *Traffic Survey* performed on Reeves' scale. In order to have an insight and be able to compare the profiles of selected scenarios, the third one is presented as well. The *Creating Databases* scenario was developed and implemented

in the Riga Secondary school No 3, Latvia, within the information and technical science discipline area. A group of pupils of an 11th grade (17 year-olds) developed a school database that could be used in the school library. They learned how to create, plan and modify databases, communicate to each other and work in groups.

Concrete experiences for students, collaborative learning, intrinsic motivation and a generative learning environment are features of all three scenarios. The role of teachers in the scenarios is that of integral facilitators who seeks to meet local and individual needs in the context of a loosely structured programme (*ibid.*). An evaluation of the UNITE scenarios based on Reeves' (1994)

Figure 5. Pedagogical dimensions of the Traffic Survey and Wonderful World of Inventions scenarios compared to the Creating Databases scenario

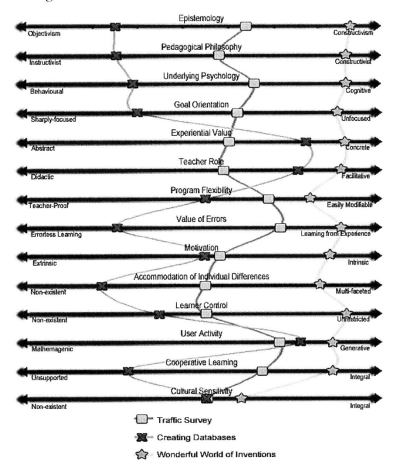

pedagogical dimensions revealed that UNITE is based on constructivist and cognitive foundations. The pedagogical dimensions of UNITE are best represented by the Social Sciences and Student Research Project scenarios (two of which are *Traffic Survey* and *Wonderful World of Inventions*) and are least represented by the ICT scenarios (e.g. *Creating Databases*). Understandably, student research projects like the two presented above, promote learning theories which are more inline with UNITE concepts (presented in the Solutions and Recommendations section). The plotted trend-line shows that the *Traffic Survey* and *Wonderful World of Inventions* scenarios go more towards the right side, more towards the constructivist and cognitive foundations, whereas the *Creating Databases* scenario is very concrete and objective. The majority of the activities were based upon predefined content and scenario workflow whereas the majority of the learning objectives were focused on very specific results. Students could choose among two or three alternatives with respect to learning paths.

FUTURE TRENDS

In the latest biennial joint report of the European Council and Commission (Joint progress report, 2008), education and training are identified as crucial to economic and social change. At the same time lifelong learning is considered highly important since it supports creativity and innovation, enabling full economic and social participation. Early school leavers, upper secondary attainment and key competences are reported as major problem areas where there has not been enough progress since 2000 to reach the EU benchmarks by 2010 (in some countries performance has even worsened between 2000 and 2006). Many young people leave education without the skills necessary for participation in the knowledge society and employment. According to the same report, at the moment 15,3 % people aged 18 to 24 in EU-27

leave school with no more than lower secondary education (*ibid.*). Save for the risk of social exclusion, these people are shut out of lifelong learning early in their lives.

Having outlined the importance of institutional and funded support and the necessity of developments in the EU education area, we will present some more favorable facts and trends in the eLearning field. The Education and Training 2010 work programme (European Commision, 2007) does provide practical support for education and training reforms and significant progress has been achieved since the programme was launched in 2002. Technological innovation is expanding the range of possible solutions that can support teaching and learning processes. The technology that is used for eLearning is as ordinary as a telephone and easy to use, in most cases. The technological challenges of the eLearning process (e.g. providing a usable, stable, universally available technological platform) have essentially been met (Rosenberg, 2001). We have presented UNITE, one of many available eLearning platforms which offers a wide range of capabilities, in both technical and methodological sense.

Challenges for the eLearning area are of the non-technological nature. As we move into the future it is important that we continue to identify successful models, learning strategies for eLearning at the institutional, program, course and activity levels that can be adapted to various contexts (Bonk & Graham, 2006). Only then we will understand and get the most out of the technology. Future research efforts within the eLearning domain will therefore be directed towards building adequate learning and assessment strategies that meet the challenges addressed at the beginning of this chapter. The eLearning environments should be designed to focus on learners' diversity in terms of learning styles, prior knowledge, culture and self-regulation skills (Vovides, 2007). Another important research direction is that of adaptation and self-regulation in the intelligent tutoring systems.

Additionally, the compatibility of cognitive styles and technology which directly impact perceptions of learning effectiveness, motivation and performance is important. In this case, learners are better equipped to pay attention to and understand relevant learning material and achieve learning outcomes (Workman, 2004). Bonk, Kim and Zeng (2006) summarize future trends in the eLearning area focusing on the most usual use of the eLearning systems – the blended learning (see Table 3).

As one may notice, there is only one trend from the Table 3 related to the technological side of the learning – the usage of mobile devices for teaching and learning. The use of mobile and handheld devices can and indeed has created rich and exciting learning opportunities. To a greater extent students bring their computing/mobile devices (e.g. pocket PCs, Smart Phones, notebooks, tablet PCs, graphical calculators, electronic dictionaries and a like) into the classrooms. These devices enable students to access the eLearning content everywhere and anytime, in a variety of situations in and out of school settings. This movement can be referred to as *ubiquitous learning* or *uLearning* (Milrad, 2007). Consequently, in order to identify the driving forces behind innovative learning practices, special focus should be placed on three different learning domains: (i) enhancing teaching practice with ubiquitous technologies in teacher education, (ii) collaborative mobile learning games in corporate settings and (iii) people on the move in a disturbed environment (Sharples, 2007). We find that these domains outstandingly underline three very important spheres of future research efforts of the technology-enhanced learning area. For successful "evolution" from eLearning to mLearning models, it is not enough just to take up mobile devices. Implementations of mLearning should primarily take into consideration several "eLearned" lessons (Wagner, 2005). Wagner also points out the necessity of a rich presentation layer that runs efficiently on a variety of platforms and a variety of form factors (*ibid*, p. 52). The major difference between eLearning and mLearning material is the advancement from more text- and graphics-based lessons to more voice-, graphics- and animation-based ones (Cobcroft, 2006).

Besides the trends caused by rapid development of mobile learning devices, eLearning environments also develop fast. They are becoming individualized; foster greater student responsibility and autonomy, furthermore focusing on real world experiences (using scenarios, simulations, role-play, problem-based learning concepts and a like). The role of an instructor also changes to

Table 3. Trends and predictions related to blended learning (Bonk, Kim & Zeng, 2006)

Trends and predictions related to blended learning linked to the expansion of the online environments usage
Mobile Blended Learning
Greater Visualization, Individualization, and Hands-on Learning
Self-Determined Blended Learning
Increased Connectedness, Community, and Collaboration
Increased Authenticity and On-Demand Learning
Linking Work and Learning
Changed Calendaring
Blended Learning Course Designations
Changed Instructor Roles
The Emergence of Blended Learning Specialists

one of a mentor, coach and counselor. In the years to come, there will no longer be a need to use the prefix "e" in eLearning or "m" in mLearning. The convenience and availability of the learning platforms will be as attractive as they are today and the technology will only be one more resource in the teaching and learning process.

CONCLUSION

This chapter, after visiting the relevant literature on the subject of learning strategies, provided evidence showing the importance of acquiring key competences today and raised some concerns with respect to using eLearning systems for that purpose, which mainly had to do with the appropriate learning and assessment strategies that need to be employed for an optimal learning experience.

Within the framework of a relevant European research project, whose main objective was to provide novel services in education for young Europeans by combining different state-of-the-art technologies in e/mLearning, also taking into consideration innovation in technology and pedagogy, the issue of employment of learning strategies was investigated. An innovative eLearning platform with a great range of functionalities was developed within the course of the project to support these objectives.

Subsequent to carrying out a state-of-the-art analysis, forming a user requirements list and researching into the various parameters that might affect pedagogical decisions, a pedagogical framework consisting of particular learning and assessment strategies was designed and tested in real settings. The chapter described these strategies in detail presenting their background, benefits and implementation possibilities.

The particular strategies were successfully employed in all learning environments involved in the aforementioned research project. Products resulting from this employment included the

design and implementation of forty eLearning scenarios. Two of these scenarios, designed by teachers from two European countries, were presented and compared.

It is important that we continue to identify successful models and learning strategies for eLearning at different levels that can be adapted to various contexts. Addressing learners' diversity in terms of learning styles, prior knowledge, culture, self-regulation, cognitive styles, access to technology and other relevant issues will be the focus of future eLearning research efforts in a world that advances towards mobile learning, visualization, individualization, hands-on learning and similar.

ACKNOWLEDGMENT

This work has been carried out within the project UNITE 026964: Unified eLearning environment for the school, partially supported by the European Community under the Information Society Technologies (IST) priority of the 6th Framework Programme for Research and Development. The research has also been supported within the project 177-0361994-1998 Usability and Adaptivity of Interfaces for Intelligent Authoring Shells funded by the Ministry of Science, Education and Sports of the Republic of Croatia.

REFERENCES

Alessi, S. M., & Trollip, R. S. (2001). *Multimedia for learning: Methods and development.* Boston, MA: Allyn & Bacon.

Azevedo, R. (2005). Using hypermedia as a meta-cognitive tool for enhancing student learning? The role of self-regulated learning. *Educational Psychologist, 40*(4), 199-209.

Balacheff, N. (2006). *There is a growing understanding of the role and needs of teachers and* institutions, of the place of knowledge in the design, and of the implementation and deployment of ICT. Retrieved May 7, 2008, from http://www.elearningeuropa.info

Black, P., & Wiliam, D. (2002). Assessment and classroom learning. In B. Roos (Eds.), *ICT, Assessment and the Learning Society, Proceedings of the European Conference on Educational Research (ECER)*, Lisbon.

Bonk, C. J., Kim, K. J., & Zeng, T. (2006). Future directions of blended learning in higher education and workplace learning settings. In C. J. Bonk & C. R. Graham (Eds.), *Handbook of blended learning: Global Perspectives, local designs*. San Francisco, CA: Pfeiffer Publishing. Retrieved May 07, 2008, from http://bechet.exp.sis.pitt.edu/lis2000/readings/Miscellaneous/c083_bonk_future.pdf

Bransford, J., Brown, A., & Cocking, R. (Eds.). (2000). *How people learn: Brain, mind, experience, and school*. Commission on Behavioral and Social Sciences and Education of the National Research Council, National Academy Press.

Buysse, D. (2007). Giving science a chance. *Research*eu, the magazine of the European research area, Special issue "Reinventing science education", June 2007*, 10.

Carroll, J. M. (1999) Five reasons for scenario-based design. In *Proceedings of the 32nd Hawaii International Conference on System Sciences*. IEEE CS Press.

Cobcroft, R. (2006). *Literature review into mobile learning in the university context*. Retrieved October 3, 2008, from http://eprints.qut.edu.au/archive/00004805/01/4805.pdf

Ćukušić, M., Granić, A., & Maršić, I. (2008a). Launching an e-learning system in a school: Cross-European e-/m-learning platform UNITE: A case study. In J. Cordiero, J. Filipe, & S. Hammoudi (Eds.), *Proceedings of the Fourth International*

Conference on Web Information Systems and Technologies, Volume 1: e-Learning, Internet Technology* (pp. 380-387). Portugal: INSTICC PRESS.

Ćukušić, M., Granić, A., Mifsud, C., & Zammit, M. (2008b). *D 4.3: Pedagogical framework implementation report (final). UNITE report*. Retrieved May 07, 2008, from http://www.unite-ist.org

Ćukušić, M., Granić, A., Mifsud, C., Pagden, A., Walker, R., & Zammit, M. (2007). National and school specifics as a prerequisite for the successful design of an e-learning system: The UNITE approach. In B. Aurer & M. Bača (Eds.), *Proceedings of the 18th International Conference on Information and Intelligent Systems, IIS 2007* (pp. 85-92). Varaždin: FOI.

Ćukušić, M., MacRae, N., Zammit, M., Kellner, A., Pagden, A., Nikolova, N., et al. (2007). *D 4.2: Pedagogical framework implementation report on UNITE-V1; UNITE teachers' handbook. UNITE report*. Retrieved May 07, 2008, from http://www.unite-ist.org

Dondi, C. (2006). *What inhibits the implementation of innovation strategies in European lifelong learning?* Retrieved May 07, 2008, from www.elearningeuropa.info

Driscoll, M. P. (2002). *How people learn (and what technology might have to do with it)* (ERIC Digest). (ERIC Document Reproduction Service No. ED470032). Retrieved May 11, 2008, from http://www.eric.ed.gov/ERICWebPortal/contentdelivery/servlet/ERICServlet?accno=ED470032

Elementary School. (2008). *Elementary school Spinut, Split, Croatia*. Retrieved May 07, 2008, from http://www.os-spinut-st.skole.hr

Engeström, Y. (1987). *Learning by expanding: An activity-theoretical approach to developmental research*. Helsinki, Finland: Orienta-Konsultit Oy.

English School. (2008). *The English school, Nicosia, Cyprus.* Retrieved May 07, 2008, from http://www.englishschool.ac.cy

Erskine, J. A., Leenders M. R., & Maufette-Leenders, L. A. (1997). *Learning with cases.* London: Ivey Publishing.

European Commission. (2001). *Communication from the Commission to the Council and the European Parliament, The elearning action plan - designing tomorrow's education, Brussels, 2001.* Retrieved May 07, 2008, from http://eur-lex.europa.eu

European Commission. (2005). *Proposal for a recommendation of the European Parliament and of the Council on key competences for lifelong learning, Brussels, 2005.* Retrieved May 07, 2008, from http://eur-lex.europa.eu

European Commision. (2007). *Communication from the Commission to the Council, the European Parliament, the European Economic and Social Committee and the Committee of the Regions: Delivering lifelong learning for knowledge, creativity and innovation. Draft 2008 joint progress report of the Council and the Commission on the implementation of the education and training 2010 work programme* (SEC(2007) 1484 /* COM/2007/0703 final */). Retrieved May 07, 2008, from http://eur-lex.europa.eu/LexUriServ/LexUriServ.do?uri=CELEX:52007DC0703:EN:HTML

Evans, D., & Taylor, J. (2005). The role of user scenarios as the central piece of the development jigsaw puzzle. In J. Attewell & C. Savill-Smith (Eds.), *Mobile learning anytime everywhere.* London: Learning and Skills Development Agency.

Eysenck, M., & Flanagan, C. (2001). *Psychology for A2 level.* Psychology Press.

Granić, A., & Ćukušić, M. (2007). An approach to the design of pedagogical framework for e-learning. In *Proceedings of the EUROCON 2007 International Conference on "Computer as a Tool"* (pp. 2415-2422).

Gray, A. (1997). *Contructivist teaching and learning* (SSTA Research Centre Report #97-07).

Grogan, G. (2006). *The design of online discussions to achieve good learning results.* Retrieved May 07, 2008, from www.elearningeuropa.info/directory/index.php?page=doc&doc_id=6713&doclng=6

Horton, W. (2001). *Leading elearning, American Society for Training and Development, Alexandria, USA, 2001.* Retrieved May 07, 2008, from www.astd.org

Hua Liu, C., & Matthews, R. (2005). Vygotsky's philosophy: Constructivism and its criticisms examined. *International Education Journal, 6*(3), 386-399.

Joint Information Systems Committee (JISC) template for describing a unit of (e)learning. (2004). Retrieved from www.jisc.ac.uk/uploaded_documents/Describing%20practice%20v12.doc

Joint progress report of the Council and the Commission on the implementation of the Education and Training 2010 work programme – "Delivering lifelong learning for knowledge, creativity and innovation". (2008). *Official Journal of the European Union, 86,* 1-31

Jonassen, D. (1996). *Computers in the classroom: Mindtools for critical thinking.* Englewood Cliffs, NJ: Merrill, Prentice Hall.

Kelly, B., Phipps, L., & Swift, E. (2005). Developing a holistic approach for e-learning accessibility. *Canadian Journal of Learning and Technology, 30*(3).

Kynigos, C. (1995). We should not miss the chance: Educational technology as a means expression and observation in general education. In A. Kazamias & M. Kasotakis (Eds.), *Greek education, perspectives of reformulation and modernization* (pp. 396-416). Athens. Greece: Seirios.

Laurillard, D. (2002). *Rethinking university teaching.* London: Routeledge.

Luckin, R., Du Boulay, B., Yuill, N., Kerawalla, C., Pearce, D., & Harris, A. (2003). Using software scaffolding to increase metacognitive skills amongst young learners. In *Proceedings of the Eleventh International Conference on Artificial Intelligence in Education*, Sydney, Australia. Retrieved September 17, 2008 from http://www.cs.usyd.edu.au/~aied/vol2/vol2_Luckin.pdf

Marcelo, C. (2006). *Ask whatever you like. Teacher-pupil interaction in new virtual learning environments.* Retrieved May 07, 2008, from http://www.elearningeuropa.info/directory/index.php?page=doc&doc_id=7875&doclng=6

Mayer, R. E. (1988). Learning strategies: An overview. In C. E. Weinstein, E. T. Goetz, & P. Alexander (Eds.), *Learning and study strategies: Issues in assessment, instruction, and evaluation.* New York: Academic Press, Inc.

McConnell, D. (2000). *Implementing computer supported cooperative learning.* London: Kogan Page.

McConnell, D. (2006). *E-learning groups and communities: Imagining learning in the age of the Internet.* OU Press

Milrad, M. (2007). How should learning activities using mobile technologies be designed to support innovative educational practices? In M. Sharples (Ed.), *Big issues in mobile learning: Report of a workshop by the Kaleidoscope Network of Excellence Mobile Learning Initiative* (pp. 28-30). Nottingham: University of Nottingham.

Mödritscher, F., Spiel, S., & Garcia-Barrios, V. (2006). Assessment in e-learning environments: A comparison of three methods. In C. Crawford, et al. (Eds.), *Proceedings of Society for Information Technology and Teacher Education International Conference 2006* (pp. 108-113).

Naismith, L., Lonsdale, P., Vavoula, G., & Sharples, M. (2004). *Report 11: Literature review in mobile technologies and learning.* Futurelab series, Futurelab.

Nikolova, I., & Tzanavari-Smyrilli, A. (2007). *Executive summary of UNITE deliverable 1: State-of-the-art in elearning and user requirements.* Retrieved May 7, 2008, from http://www.unite-ist.org

Nisbet, J., & Shucksmith, J. (1986). *Learning strategies.* London: Routledge.

Piaget, J. (1953). The origins of intelligence in children. London: Routledge and Kegan Paul.

Prince, M. (2004). Does active learning work? A review of the research. *Journal of Engineering Education, 93*(3), 1-10.

Reeves, T. C. (1994). Evaluating what really matters in computer-based education. In M. Wild & D. Kirkpatrick (Eds.) *Computer education: New perspectives* (pp. 219-246). Perth, Australia: MASTEC.

Rosenberg, M. J. (2001). *E-learning: Strategies for delivering knowledge in the digital age.* New York: McGraw-Hill.

Selinger, M. (2005). *Workforce development and access to elearning.* Retrieved May 07, 2008, from www.elearningeuropa.info

Sharples, M. (Ed.). (2007). Big issues in mobile learning. In *Report of a workshop by the Kaleidoscope Network of Excellence Mobile Learning Initiative.* Learning Sciences Research Institute, University of Nottingham. Retrieved September 17, 2008 from http://www.lsri.nottingham.ac.uk/msh/Papers/BIG_ISSUES_REPORT_PUBLISHED.pdf

Sivan, A., Wong Leung, R., & Woon, C. (2000). An implementation of active learning and its effect on the quality of student learning. *Innovations in Education and Training International, 37*(4), 381-389.

Taylor, J., & Evans, D. (2005) Pulling together: Keeping track of pedagogy, design and evaluation through the development of scenarios – a case study. *Learning, Media and Technology, 30*(2).

Tittelboom, S. (2003). Alternative assessment as a tool in support of teaching and learning (some preliminary findings). In *Proceedings of the European Conference for Educational Research*, Hamburg.

Tuomi, I. (2007). *Skills and learning for the knowledge society.* Paper presented at eLearning 2007, Lisbon.

Tzanavari, A. (2007). *D5.2: 1st version of specific UNITE elearning scenarios; PART II: Handbook for content development v.2* (UNITE public deliverable). Retrieved May 7, 2008, from http://www.unite-ist.org

Ulf, D. E. (2007). *Preliminary conclusion (final plenary presentation).* Paper presented at eLearning 2007, Lisbon.

Ullrich, K. (2004). *Constructivism and the 5 E model science lesson.* Retrieved May 07, 2008, from http://cte.jhu.edu/techacademy/fellows/Ullrich/webquest/mkuindex.html

UNITE FP6 IST project. (2006). *Contract No. 026964.* Retrieved May 7, 2008, from http://www.unite-ist.org

UNITE Public Deliverable 1. (2006). *D1: State of the art and requirements list for UNITE.* Retrieved May 7, 2008, from http://www.unite-ist.org

UNITE Public Deliverable 5.3. (2008). D5.3: Final version of the specific UNITE elearning scenarios. Retrieved May 7, 2008, from http://www.unite-ist.org

Varis, T. (2005). *New literacies and elearning competences.* Retrieved May 07, 2008, from http://www.elearningeuropa.info

Vovides, Y., Sanchez-Alonso, S., Mitropoulou, V., & Nickmans, G. (2007). The use of elearning course management systems to support learning strategies and to improve selfregulated learning. *Educational Research Review, 2*(1), 64-74.

Vuorikari, R. (2004). *Results from the OASIS pilot, OASIS project deliverable.* Retrieved May 07, 2008, from http://www.eun.org/insight-pdf/5_5_3_Oasis_Deliverable_final.pdf

Vygotsky, L. S. (1978). *Mind in society: The development of higher psychological processes.* Cambridge, MA: Harvard University Press.

Wagner, E. D. (2005). Enabling mobile learning. *EDUCAUSE Review, 40*(3), 40-53.

Weller, M. (1992). *Delivering learning on the Net: The why, what and how of online education.* London: Kogan Page.

Wenger, E. (1998). *Communities of practice: Learning, identity, and meaning.* Cambridge, UK: Cambridge University Press.

Wheeler, M. (2005). *Reconstructing the cognitive world.* Cambridge, MA: MIT Press.

Workman, M. (2004). Performance and perceived effectiveness in computer-based and computer-aided education: Do cognitive styles make a difference? *Computers in Human Behavior, 20*(4), 517-534.

Yoder, J. D., & Hochevar, C. M. (2005). Encouraging active learning can improve students, performance on examinations. *Teaching of Psychology, 32*(2), 91-95.

Zoakou, A., Tzanavari, A., Papadopoulos, G. A., & Sotiriou, S. (2007). A methodology for elearning scenario development: The UNITE approach. In *Proceedings of the ECEL 2007 - European Conference on e-Learning*, Copenhagen, Denmark (pp. 683-692). ACL publications.

Zoakou, A., Tzanavari, A., Zammit, M., Padgen, A., MacRae, N., & Limanauskiene, V. (2006). *D5.1: Elearning scenario map and generic elearning scenarios* (UNITE public deliverable). Retrieved May 07, 2008, from http://www.unite-ist.org

Chapter XXI
Building a B-Learning Strategy

Paula Peres
Institute of Accounting and Administration of Porto (ISCAP), Portugal

Pedro Pimenta
University of Minho, Portugal

ABSTRACT

The purpose of this chapter is to describe the wide literature review made on computer mediated learning. Online Education system may include models and methodologies based on learning theories that support individual styles and contexts. The use of e-learning environment is limited only by the creativity. If we just decide for providing online contents, even if they are well constructed, at long term it may become uninteresting and based only on theory. We cannot state that e-learning has either more or less quality than traditional learning. E-learning quality depends on the instruction design and on the students engagement. In this review of literature, the authors combine different points of view. A theoretical model that emerged from the inquiry made will be showed and may support the integration of technologies, in order to enhance the learning.

INTRODUCTION

The MIPO model (Model of Integration by Objectives) described in this chapter presents a b-learning instructional design that relates information which is practical, as well as applicable to a number of situations and can also be enriched with practice. It gathers ideas from different authors and gives an approach to the instructional design. As a result, we have incorporated behaviorism, cognitivism, constructivism and socio-constructivism approaches into this model in order to get the benefits of each one.

An effective instructional design model is both flexible and adaptable. There are not two designers approaching a problem in the same way and there are not two problems exactly alike. This model is based on what we know about learning theories, information technology and blended-learning.

The information, concepts and procedures here presented may give support to teachers and instructors, instructional designers and planning teams – anyone who wants to develop effective e-learning instructions.

BACKGROUND

"Learning is an individual, dynamic and interactive process of knowledge construction. In this process, earlier experiences that influence present actions and allow the cognitive re-building are used"(CNS, 2006). The process is personal because adhesion is always optional. It is dynamic because we can see the changes in behaviors. Aguiar Falcão (2006) adds the following features: global, continuous, gradual and cumulative process. Learning is a global process because it demands the interaction among different kinds of knowledge. It is continuous because it is a human and a character-construction feature. It is gradual because it drives from the simplest to the more complex knowledge and skills. At last, it is cumulative because we associate all the knowledge with activities in order to produce new behaviors. In a cognitive point of view, learning demands the use of a set of mental skills, processing information, requires time spent and uses a lot of mechanisms which are associated with memory. Learning is a set of psycho-physiological mechanisms and both cognitive and emotional mental operations that will be visible in further behaviors. We can define Learning as a process of change (Rodrigues & Ferrao, 2006).

Whenever learning is targeted for adult people and is mediated by computer, it is called as a general term - electronic learning or e-learning. E-Learning is a general term used to make reference to computer-enhanced learning. It is commonly associated to the specific field of advanced learning technology, which deals with both the technologies and associated methodologies in learning, using networked and/or multimedia technologies (Wikipedia, 2007). According to

Khan (2005) e-learning is an education environment which uses digital technologies in order to provide a good instruction design, centered on students, interactive and available for everyone at any time.

Hybrid learning or b-learning is the term used to make reference to the combination between traditional and online classroom (Dias, 2004). B-Learning term intends to enhance the best of b-learning but also the traditional classroom (Moran, 2003). In the traditional classroom, it is easier to promote interpersonal and affective relationships, as well as organization of the groups and the teaching-learning process. It is also easier to explain activities sequence, methodologies and schedules. First face-to-face meeting helps tutor to provide start references about subject and present the state of the art. After that, tutors can promote a virtual session using these environment advantages such as: time and space flexibility and the variety of available communication tools. The existence of a new face-to-face meeting might help to summarize process, the deep understanding and the guide towards a new stage of learning (Moran, 2003).

E-Learning Systems

The online environment where we can create, storage and manage the teaching-learning process is named Learning Management System (LMS). A LMS is a web application in which we can manage the teaching process in the perspective of administration/management, pedagogical/Education and also technical, using basic communication tools such as: e-mail, forums, chats, and so on, which support the interaction among participants (Pimenta & Ana, 2004) (Koponen, 2006). For instance, Luvit, Moodle, WebCt, etc.

Technical System

Technical system is the Virtual Learning Environment (VLE). According to the Britain (Britain & Liber, 1999) prototype, we may define two groups of features: the resources and the communication tools.

In the resources area, we may find features such as: the course outline (an overview of the course structure), the model of navigation (allows users to move around the environment), noticeboard (announcements area that appears as soon as a student logs into the system), a class list and students homepages (for them to know the other students or for tutors to collect some ideas about students backgrounds), calendar (a calendar tool), search tools (to provide help when a course structure becomes very large), metadata (a simple information about an object). It is important to categorize and to search objects, bookmarking (may decrease the amount of time spent navigating to frequently used places), multimedia resources (multimedia resources can be accessed and stored within the learning environment) and file upload area (students should be able to upload their own materials) (Britain & Liber, 1999).

In the communication tools area, we may find two kinds of communication tools: asynchronous and synchronous. Asynchronous tools enable communication and collaboration over a period of time through a "different time and different place" mode. People can interact according to their own schedule. To give a good example, we can outline the e-mail (which can be used to email either the tutor or individual students on the course), the conferencing tools (such as forums, blogs and wikis that provide the means for students to engage in collaborative exchange about topics on the course) and assignments (provide a means for students to return completed assignments to the tutor for grading and feedback) (Britain & Liber, 1999). The synchronous tools enable real-time communication and collaboration in a "Same time, different place" mode. People can interact at the same point in time. The relative importance of such tools in a system depends largely on the intended use of the system itself. As an example, we can outline instant messaging, audio-conferences, web-conferences, application sharing, and so on

(Britain & Liber, 1999). The interaction between people without any face-to-face contact allows new kinds of socialization (Santos, 2003). The way as the communication systems come into the screen influences the dialogue and the level of interaction (Vick *et al.*, 2006). However, it is neither the interface, nor the contents that will determine the level of interaction but the dynamic of collaboration promoted (Santos, 2003). Synchronous text communication promotes a social environment and the relationships among participants. Rodrigues (2004) outlines some of the main advantages:

- Allows communication and immediate feedback among participants
- Allows direct communication among students
- Promotes the spontaneous dialogue
- May reproduce the class environment

The same author also outlines some disadvantages of using a synchronous communication:

- Punishes who has not a good written expression and has more difficulties using keyboard
- Demands online presence according to a calendar
- Communication may become chaotic, especially if it involves a large number of students

Synchronous communication must be seen as a complement of asynchronous communication due to the limits of its pedagogical application. In order to be effective, it must be used under a set of conditions, namely the reduced number of participants, a good time management, the identification of participation roles. This kind of communication is useful to the construction of social relationships, but it is not satisfactory to the pedagogical process. On one hand, we may have more adhesion by those who are more acquainted to these technologies and on the other hand we may also get contributions but out of time (Morgado, 2005).

Management System

The learning management system includes administration support of the course, management of tutors and learners and management knowledge systems (Koponen, 2006). Pimenta and Baptista (2004) outline the following management system features:

- Students management
- Contents management
- Profile and views management
- Activities control

Education System

The education system includes models and methodologies based on learning theories that support individual styles and contexts (Koponen, 2006). The use of e-learning environment is limited only by creativity (Souza, 2005). The use of an online environment, with the objective of simply making contents available, even if they are well constructed, in a long-term may become uninteresting and based only in theory. We could not state that e-learning has more or less quality than traditional learning. E-learning quality depends on the instruction design and students engagement (Duffy & Kirkley, 2004).

E-Learning Development Models

A course development model, also named instruction model, intends to be a guide in order to manage, plan, develop and implement a learning process (Kemp *et al.*, 1998).

There are more than 100 learning development instruction models but the main differences among them refer to the number and the names of the steps and the sequence of recommended actions

(Kruse, 2006). Nearly all are based on the ADDIE (Analysis, Design, Development, Implementation, Evaluation) model (McGriff, 2000). Based on ADDIE model, we will explain the main task that may be performed on each stage, in order to develop a blended-learning course.

B-LEARNING STRATEGY

The model showed in this chapter describes a blended-course instruction design, with face-to-face sessions and online sessions. This model joins different points of view and intends to be practical and adjustable according to different contexts. The revision of literature made helps to integrate the different pedagogical approaches. This model is based on information technologies, systematic analysis and learning tools.

The revision of literature added by personal experience resulted in a new conceptual model (MIPO) which may help tutors to integrate web technology on the teaching-learning process. This holistic model aligns on-line strategies with learning objectives.

This alignment seems to be crucial: imagine a teacher who states that it is important to make students understand the main contents and also to make them achieve critical thinking skills on the matter. If we only see the teacher giving information, the learning activities are not aligned with objectives. Students may understand contents but it will be difficult to achieve the ability to develop critical thinking. On the evaluation process, if the teacher asks students to remember and understand contents, he is being honest but if he asks students to have a critical attitude, he is being inconsistent because he did not promote the development of this kind of skills. In this context, there is not a consistence between learning activities and learning objectives.

The investigation process made enhanced the importance of creating learning contexts to guide students in order to reach defined goals. Based on the ADDIE structure, the MIPO model suggests a progress in 5 phases (analysis, design, development, implementation and evaluation) and also adds a dynamic formative evaluation and adaptation, in order to reach defined objectives.

Each phase of the mipo model is set up by some items that were identified as the background of the majority of the authors in the literature review and arranged with personal experience.

In the MIPO model, the first phase of the integration process is the analysis of the system. Teacher acts as an architect who, before starting a project, analyses contextual requirements. Later, the results are reflected on the space organization, that is to say, on the instruction design.

Analysis

The analysis phase is the base for all the other phases of instructional design. During this phase you must define the problem, identify the source of the problem and find possible solutions. This stage may include specific research techniques such as needs analysis, job analysis and task analysis (McGriff, 2000). Kemp, Morrison and Ross (1998) also enumerate within the analysis phase the need for identifying learner features, contents and tasks. During this phase, it is important to consider the context, the pre-requisites, the tools and the skills demand to achieve the objectives. These objectives must be classified according to domain skills such as: intellectual skills, verbal information, psychomotor skills and attitudes (Dick & Carey Lou, 1996).

The holistic context analysis gives us good information about students' preferences. Klein et. al. (2003) give to this stage the general name of "nonrecurring activities".

Context

The context describes the environment where learning will happen, namely by identifying the

unit, the course, school year, class environment, duration, schedule and the number of students enrolled.

Learners' Features

In the process of identifying learners' features Kemp et. al. (1998) outline a few elements: age, motivation, expectation, experiences, special talents, ability to work in certain environments, and others.

Instruction Needs

Kemp et. al (1998) underline the importance of describing instruction needs:

- Means of helping teachers to design instructions, select and organize activities
- An evaluation guide
- Students' guide

Contents

A blended-course may use many learning objects that may be used in different courses in similar contexts. For instance, applets, animations, static images, electronic documents, web pages/web sites (Campbell, 2004).

Prerequisites

The process of prerequisites identification scaffolds student's knowledge.

Tools: (LMS/VLM – technical system)

The identification of available tools, such as LMS, will influence the posterior instruction design. The outputs of this phase will be used as input of the next one (McGriff, 2000).

These elements are summarized in Figure 1.

Figure 1. Main analysis tasks

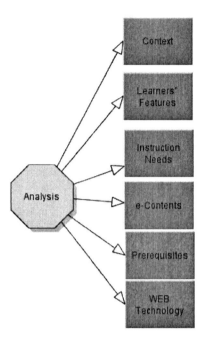

Figure 2. Main tasks of the design phase

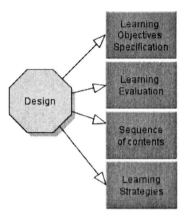

Design

The design phase uses the outputs from the analysis phase to plan the strategy to develop the instruction.

The instruction design is the phase that demands the biggest effort and it is crucial on the learning success. The acknowledgment of the frequency of lecture model used on present classrooms, underlined by the European Comitte (EU, 2004) justifies a deep study in order to clarify and simplify the process and also cause change to happen.

In the instruction design phase of MIPO model, the teacher acts as an architect who organizes the space and its elements. The instruction design phase consists in explanations about learning objectives details, evaluation mode, contents sequences and instruction strategies. This phase includes the specification of objectives, instruction strategy and the sequence of contents (McGriff, 2000) (Kemp *et al.*, 1998). Figure 2 represents the main tasks of the design phase:

Objectives

The instruction design should be directed according to the objectives and to a particular group of students (community) (Dick & Carey Lou, 1996) (Campbell, 2004). These features are identified during the analysis phase and detailed on the design phase. The objectives are what we want students to learn and also both the starting and final point of the learning process (Barreira & Moreira, 2004). The learning objectives specification process conducts the development of an important guide to be used both by teacher and students. The description of the Learning Outcomes as a starting point may help to overcome the difficulties usually felt on this processes. The use of a taxonomy may help the learning objectives specification, regarding cognitive, psicomotor or affective perspectives.

Bloom (1975) suggests the objectives taxonomy in order to organize the learning outcomes. According to Bloom, the concept of taxonomy overcomes the concept of classifier. A classification can be considered valid when it fits some criteria. A taxonomy must be linked to theoretical models (Bloom *et al.*, 1975). Bloom suggests a taxonomy of learning objectives sorted in six levels: Knowledge, Comprehension, Application, Analysis, Synthesis and Evaluation. Although the

Bloom taxonomy of cognitive knowledge has been considered the most well-known, there are many others that we can consider. Rajadell and Serrat (2000) and Barreira and Moreira (2004) outline some of them such as the taxonomy of Guildford, Ebel, Herber, Orlish, and so on.

According to MIPO model, after defining objectives we should design the evaluation process.

Learning Evaluation Process

Making decisions about what to evaluate is useful to understand clearly the learning objectives. Evaluation should be designed in order to provide students a way to demonstrate their knowledge (Morgan & Oreilly, 1999).

To offer an online course without evaluation is nothing more than posting on a static website (Born, 2003).

Evaluation can be classified in two main groups: formative and summative. In the summative way, the evaluation occurs at the end of the instruction. In the formative way, the evaluation occurs during the instruction process and it consists of a continuous collection of learning thoughts. Both these techniques are important in order to get students' evaluations. Formative evaluation includes all activities designed in order to motivate students, enhances understanding and provides students information about their own progress (Born, 2003). Usually, this kind of evaluation does not have assessment. Self-evaluation questionnaires and peers or tutors feedback help students to know about their own knowledge (Morgan & Oreilly, 1999).

The evaluation process may be done either by formative or summative mode and either on face-to-face or online, with or without supervision (Born, 2003).

Sequences of Contents

According to MIPO model, after defining objectives and designing learning objectives, we should establish the sequences of contents.

Sequencing is ordering contents in order to help students to achieve the objectives (Kemp *et al.*, 1998). There are many methods to support the contents sequencing. The most well known suggests a sorting according to the prerequisites and the level of complexity. The learning context, the matter on study and other features may influence this process (Kemp *et al.*, 1998).

The procedures sequence suggested by MIPO model establishes a contents definition after learning specification. This organization avoids the specification of learning objectives based on the contents. This scenario usually results in sentences such as "understand the content A" and in a lowest level of knowledge (first or second Bloom level). Despite the importance of these levels, if the learning objectives consist in achieving a higher critical thinking level, it is important to explicit it on the objectives definition associated with analysis, synthesis and evaluation.

The design of the evaluation process has the objective of making clear the way how students will demonstrate their knowledge. The definition of the evaluation questions nature, the criteria and the standards of evaluation must be based on learning objectives and showed to students. These procedures construct scaffoldings, in order to make students able to evaluate their own assignments. The evaluation may be formative or summative in an online or face-to-face mode, with or without a supervisor.

The specification of learning objectives and the design of the evaluation mode support the identification and the articulation of the contents.

Instruction Strategies

In the MIPO model, the last step of the design phase consists in the instruction strategies description, illustrated on the learning activities, influenced by external factors and aligned with pedagogical models. These prescriptions constitute a guide according to the contents and the objective (Kemp *et al.*, 1998).

Learning is an active process in which students build significances relating old knowledge to new one. A well designed instruction strategy should help them in order to find those relations (Kemp *et al.*, 1998).

The items described below give support to the design of the instruction strategy activity. The reflection based in the literature review is promoted and gives added value to the main topic to be considered.

Influence Features

In the study of the art made we identified some features that may be considered.

Motivation comes up as a crucial element that influences the way as people participate on learning activities and develop self-regulation, time and task management. This motivation may be achieved by linking the class and the individual success (Cotter & Martins, 2006). Motivation scaffolds learning construction because it promotes attention and participation. Give positive feedbacks, promote activities with a balanced complexity, help students finding the importance on the study matter, create an open and positive atmosphere and help students feeling that they are important on the learning community are some of the major features that may be used in order to increase students motivation.

This process may become more sustainable if we add more features such as: frequent contact with students; promotion of students cooperation; use of active learning; give prompt feedback; give correct time to achieve objectives; communicate to students the great expectations; respect differences; use of contextualized activities.

Students' motivation, general principles for the learning success and group organization are, according to many authors, important features to consider on the design strategy phase. Nevertheless, learning something new or developing a deep study on a subject is not a linear process.

The way as we learn, individual learning styles and multiple intelligences characterize the singularity of the learning process. In this sense, we should consider these features when we are designing instructions.

David Kolb (1984) defends that we learn in a circle way. We reflect and interpret an experiment based on previous and present situations. Theoretical concepts help integration and synthesis, in order to allow new tests and applications. Learning is a process in which knowledge is created by changing experiences. This definition enhances some critical learning process features in an experiment way. This point of view enhances knowledge construction opposing contents perspective.

Kolb (1984) suggests an experimental learning cycle divided in four phases: concrete experience, observations and reflection, forming abstract concepts, testing in new situations. The four phases of the experimental learning cycle are not necessarily in sequence. When we are looking for an experience sense, we use previous experiences and theoretical contents or even new experiences. At the beginning, concrete experience enhances curiosity, we look for new ideas and also for old knowledge in order to find a solution. When old knowledge does not match with actual experience, it is reviewed. In this phase, we consider concrete experiences and we try to use real case studies and practical activities in context work. A student learns when he does and writes down observations, as for instance, when he performs some programming experiences. Experiences lead to the reflection. This phase enhances reflection preferences and may integrate discussion. For instance, when a student thinks how to program and sees others programming, he reflects on the best way to program. He analyses the experiences made and the results obtained. The contents read may improve his concepts of reality in order to clarify what he did. Conceptual models are redesigned according to a practical abstraction. In this phase, students preferences go towards reading activities, information analysis and theoretical models study. For instance, when a student tries to understand the concrete experience of reading a programming manual. When we find a practical usefulness, we improve knowledge construction. In this phase, we try to find a new situation to use acquired knowledge. Students prefer to play games, to do practical exercises and simulations as a computer program.

Felder and Brent (2006) show a model similar to Kolb. They defend that teachers and students have a specific learning style to give and receive information. This model has four dimensions: Sensing-intuitive, visual-verbal, active-reflective, sequential-global.

The sensitive dimension is focused on external inputs such as to see, to hear, to taste, to touch or to smell, in a practical perspective. The intuitive dimension is focused on internal inputs such as thoughts, memories or images looking for theories and math models. Everyone is both sensor and intuitive, but everyone has a preference that may be soft, moderate or strong. Most of the undergraduate are sensors. Most professors are sensing learners but they teach intuitively, emphasizing fundamentals, theories and mathematical models. This shows the balance between sensitive and intuitive changes from one field to another and from one situation to another (Felder & Brent, 2006). This duality is related to the concrete experience and abstract concept of the Kolb cycle.

The active-reflective dimension reflects the level of preferences by doing something physical. Dealing with the same kind of material, some people prefer to reflect on it, while others actually prefer to act . All classes have both active and reflective learners. Most classes, except for labs, are passive, the active learners do not act on the material presented and the reflective do not think much during the lectures (Felder & Brent, 2006). This duality is related to observations and testing of Kolb cycle.

In the visual-verbal dimension, visual learners ask for knowledge demonstration, while verbal learners ask for knowledge explanation. Most people are visual learners while 90%-95% of most courses contents are verbal (lectures, readings) except in art and architecture (Felder & Brent, 2006).

The sequential-global dimension shows the differences between preferences for building understandings in logical sequential steps and preferences for absorbing information in order to get a big picture with interrelations and connections to other subjects and personal experiences. Most students, instructors, courses, curricula and textbooks are sequential. Not strictly a mistake, but the global minority is extremely important with multidisciplinary holistic systems thought (Felder & Brent, 2006).

The multiple intelligence theory increases the concepts of learning styles (Gardner, 2000). This theory is generated based on biological skills to solve problems. As a human being, everyone has a skills repertory to solve different kind of problems. According to Wenger, (2002) it is important to develop curriculum strategies that promote the learning among different intellectual profiles. Every year, new technologies that may be used to increase the opportunity to success of learning according to a particular style come up. Intelligences may be developed, but they also demand their own learning strategy using features such as domain skills and age Wenger. Psychologist Gardner (2000) identifies seven distinct intelligences that determine how a person processes external information: Verbal-linguistic, Logical-mathematical, Visual-spatial, Bodily-kinesthetic, Musical-rhythmic, Interpersonal, Intrapersonal.

This classification can be joined with Kolb (1984) and Felder (Felder & Brent, 2006) theories, because each person combines the use of learning styles and different skills to different situations.

Features as culture, motivation, emotional feelings, previous experience, personality are also important. Whenever possible, teachers should give value to diversity, responding to students preferences but never forgetting the learning objectives. We should also consider pedagogical models in order to scaffold interactions (McGriff, 2000) (Kemp *et al.*, 1998).

LEARNING THEORIES

The learning strategies designed may be based on influences features, learning styles, multiple intelligences, but also learning theories. In this context, we do not want a large description about pedagogical models but instead a brief summary enhancing most important aspects. Pedagogical approaches include many theories argued by different authors that many times defend different aspects related to the same idea. Today's theoretical design approaches can be seen as derivatives of behaviorism, cognitivist and constructivist viewpoints (Allen, 2007).

Behaviorist Approach

According to the Behaviorist approach, learning is viewed as a behavior acquisition through mechanical relations between stimulation and answer. Learners can be more or less passive in this process. These theories enhance "know-do". Behaviorism is based on Brandura, Pavlov, Skinner, Thorndike, Watson and other inquiries. They defend contents segmentations in order to be learned in a gradual way. The perspective is focused on the teacher and does not promote information searching. Skinner (1981) psychology is based on action, the repetition leads to the automation. Skinner suggests rewarding answers as a stimulus to new future learning. Knowledge is evaluated by the automatic answer to an external feature in a certain context.

On the WEB the Behaviorist approach may be applied using Practice and Drill applications, where the computer tests and gives feedback immediately.

Cognitive Approach

In the cognitive perspective, learning is viewed as a dynamic codification process and information recognition. Students learn by interacting with environment. Learning is more complex than answer stimulus. It implies students cognitive changing and in a way that they can understand the reality, selecting it and organizing it. In the cognitive perspective, teacher plays the most important role. He should plan activities for moving from a short term memory to a long term. Previous students' knowledge is crucial to get new understandings. Knowledge construction is not stimulated since the teacher is the one who gives all the information and student should construct knowledge by reflecting, peers exchanging, writing, answering questions and practicing.

Constructivist Approach

In the constructivist perspective, we give more importance to students' learning abilities than to professor teaching. The cognitive perspective underlines the importance of students to build their own mental concepts. There are many theorists defending this perspective such as: Bransford & CTGV, Bruner, Dewey, Grabinger, Lave & Wenger, Papert, Spiro and colleagues, Shuman, Vygotsky and so on. Constructivism is based on a theory where everybody constructs their own perspective of world, guided by individual experiences and schemes. This theory is based on the importance of students to solve different kind of problems (Schuman, 1996). Jean Piaget (1974) uses assimilation, accomodation and balance mechanisms that came up from biology in order to explain knowledge construction. Facing a new stimulus, we tend to arrange it in our old structures, but that is not always possible, so it implies a new structure organization and accommodation (Piaget *et al.*, 1974). When we cannot accommodate new external stimulus we lose our internal balance. These principles enhance a multiple knowledge representation, a flexible and continuous mental scheme and student's active engagement.

The open architecture of PC systems helps the implementation of students control in order to construct their own knowledge. The technology evolution provides the notions of hypertext and author tools such as HTML, flash or quicktime. These tools give support to the implementation of educational games and simulations using the constructivist approach (Gillani, 1984).

Socio-Constructivism Approach

In the socio-constructivism theory, knowledge is viewed as a social construction. Learning is a social process and not only a cognitive and individual process. Students build their own knowledge influenced by culture and social interaction. Development is only possible through social interaction. It is important to establish groups in which there is an element with a bigger level of knowledge, Ley Vygotsky (Vygotsky, 1998). In this perspective, collaborative learning plays an important role that initially was used in children education but now is also used in any age groups. Vygotsky identifies two levels in knowledge construction: the real development that is reached after a few learning cycles, and the proximal development zone in which the progress depends on peers' interaction. This concept supports collaborative learning in scholar planning, where cognitive development is done by social activities (Lave & Wenger, 1995). In this perspective, learning is viewed as an activity within a certain context and culture opposing the majority of classes' activities that use abstract knowledge (Lave & Wenger, 1995).

According to Lave and Wenger (1995), contextualized activities promote the sense of community. Social interaction is a critical element to situated learning. Students participate in a knowledge and skill community that demands newcomers, in order to get a movement towards an integral participation. Lave and Wenger suggest

that learning can be viewed as a human historical transformation. This transformation is cyclical and represents the development of a community of practice. The term community of practice was introduced by Lave and Wenger and it refers to a group of people who share a certain interest and improve their knowledge by interaction. Community of practice and learning community are difficult to define due to their own organization, spontaneous and informal nature (Wenger, 2002). Learning community may be viewed as a part of the community of practice because the main objective is to learn through social interaction (Afonso, 2006). A learning community demands a collective participation in classroom or in an online environment in which every group member, including teacher, is involved in a knowledge construction. The community identity is reached by members' engagement towards a common objective. According to Wenger (2002) there are three main features in a community of practice: domain, community and practice. Domain is the topic of interest, of knowledge and debate that identifies the community. The domain legitimates the community existence. Community is related to the relationships established in group in order to share opinions. It does not imply heterogeneous points of view, it is based on the respect by differences. Practice is the knowledge created, shared and maintained by the group using tools, information, works, good practices and ideas. To answer the question "How to create a community of practice" Wenger (2002) suggests the use of social and situated learning and social and identity theories.

The dynamic nature of MIPO suggests the use of enunciated features balanced with objectives and context. If we use workgroup activities, we should consider the group size, the way we make groups and the group cohesion. We should try to maintain the same group from the beginning until the end of the activity. In the literature, we saw many differences in the good group size. We agree, through experience, that we should have groups formed by 3, 4 or maximum 5 elements. Some authors agree that the group size influences the level of knowledge, but we think that we can overcome these barriers using active learning techniques. By using active learning, we try to achieve the highest level of knowledge, such as analysis, synthesis and evaluation. We try to engage students in the act of promoting reading, discussion, writing and reflection on attitudes and values. The difficulties felt on the process of changing avoid the use of this technique. Namely, because subjects may end up not being all covered, more time preparing and performing activities may be spent, difficulties in using it with large classes may appear or finding educational resources may be difficult. The learning strategy design based on network contextual activities may promote learning success.

Based on influences features and pedagogical models selected, the instruction design includes also activities definition in order to reach learning objectives.

The design of learning activities uses the needs analysis for each objective (Laurillard, 2006).

LEARNING ACTIVITIES

Engestrom (2001) groups a set of concepts that are based on an individual and social practical model. Activity concept has participants' domains (subject, object), mediation tools (tools, rules, division of labor) and a particular environment (community). This model represents also the relation between domains. Activity concept has the following interacting components: subject, objectives, community, rules, division of labor, results and tools.

Subjects are individuals or a group of individuals who participate in an activity.

Object or objectives can be the specific direction to an activity sharable materials to be transformed or modified by the participants in an activity or abstract things such as plans or ideas.

According to Engestrom (2001), the objective of the learning activity must be a subset of learning objectives.

Community is a group of people who interacts with the environment to reach objectives. The community element needs cohesion in order to get productivity. This cohesion increases according to the group development (Salmon, 2005): access and motivation, online socialization, exchange information, knowledge construction and development.

Rules are conventions, social relationships or schedules that govern community members' behavior. The rule element of Engestrom activity theory includes norms and schedule, to be followed by all participants.

Division is the distribution of subjects' roles, powers and responsibilities. The tailor model (Schofield *et al.*, 2006) enhances the crucial role of teacher (the tailor) in the educational process. He can provide students Internet resources and allow them to construct their own knowledge (clothes). Tutor is the one who provides the scaffold which students (costumers) may adapt to their own style.

The learning activity design demands the division of labor by participants according to the kind of work, complexity, relation with communication media and also among peers. In the peers relation, it is important to consider the tutor availability to have more or less conversation with the students and the possibility of personalization offered by WEB technology.

In a virtual community, the literature review enhances four main tutor competences: understand online processes, have technical, communication and subject knowledge, and know students features. Tutor action is constructed according to the ability to mediate the process between students and social knowledge, organized in a cultural way and giving students the opportunity to develop personal and social skills (Trindade, 2002). Tutor must help students on matter contextualization, increasing students' universe and helping them in the construction of learning significance (Moran, 2005).

Based on the four dimensions of tutor roles proposed by Berge and Collins (Berge & Collins, 2000) (pedagogical, social, management and technical) it is possible to outline the following main tutors tasks:

- **Pedagogical:**
    - o To use many pedagogical methods in order to keep the discussion on topic and act as a facilitator and guider of learning (Berge & Collins, 1996) (Berge & Collins, 2000) (Garrison & Anderson, 2003);
    - o Design e-learning group activities (Schofield *et al.*, 2006); In the traditional education, the author and the designer of instruction are many times the same person, but on e-learning environment we must make the difference (Schofield *et al.*, 2006). The development of web resource is more expensive than the classic development (Schofield *et al.*, 2006). Tutor may adapt the resources available according to their own requisites (Klein *et al.*, 2003).
- **Social:**
    - o It is important to create a user-friendly environment in order to promote learning throughout a good group feeling;
    - o Moderator acts as a chief of discussion (Berge & Collins, 1996) (Berge & Collins, 2000); interactivity and learning community facilitator (Schofield *et al.*, 2006);
    - o On an online workgroup activities the needs of moderation and the participants skills change according to the stage of group development (Salmon, 2005).

On the theme of community development, Tuckman (1965) identifies four phases: form-

ing, storming, norming and performing. These phases define the level of exchange information. The interaction among students who participate on a learning activity progresses in five stages (Salmon, 2005): Access and motivation, online socialization, information exchange, knowledge construction and development. On the first stage - access and motivation - participants access to the platform individually and become acquainted with technology environment. This is an essential requisite.

On the forming phase, participants tend to be polite without a great confidence on the group (Tuckman, 1965). This phase may be connected to the on-line socialization stage of Salmom model. On the second stage - online socialization - participants interact in order to construct their own individual identity and find their peers.

On the storming phase, participants interact more actively and talk about their own feelings and opinions. Many times, this scenario results on disagreements. This phase may be connected to the information exchange stage of Salmom model. On the third stage - exchange information - the participants give relevant information about the course subject to the colleague.

After this phase, on norming phase, the group achieves a sharable understanding, they also establish norms and group procedures. In this phase, the group is stronger and cooperative, this scenario may be connected to the third stage of Salmom model. On the fourth stage - knowledge construction - the group discusses the course subject and interaction becomes more collaborative. The level of communication depends on the understanding established.

Finally, on the perform phase, the community works more intensively, participants try to get more benefits from the system. This phase may be connected to the development stage of Salmom model. On the last stage - development - participants try to obtain more benefits of the system in order to reach their own personal objectives.

On this stage they reflect on the way they are learning.

According to the "five-step" model, without a help from the moderator, usually the group development stops at the second level - online socialization. Tuckman (1965) agrees that the tutor needs of skills change according to the different level of group development (forming, storming, norming, performing). The accomplishment goes from a motivation orientation towards a work orientation. Tuckman defends that there must be someone with authority, outside the group, to play the role of the activity moderator. During the forming stage, it is important to have a clear leadership in order to help the group to deal with work and simultaneously with interpersonal relationships. At the storming stage, it is important to help the group to solve conflicts and at the norming and performing stage, it is important to guarantee the focus on work development (Tuckman, 1965).

Management

Moderator establishes the schedule and the activity pace, acting as a manager that organizes procedures, administrates and manages messages exchanging (Berge & Collins, 2000)(Berge & Collins, 1996)(Schofield *et al.*, 2006). According to Shea (2004), the tutor has to maintain the learning pace in order to get a significant interaction in an asynchronous environment. In order to make students engage in learning construction, participants need to work together and manage time efficiently. Probably, at the beginning of the course, more face-to-face sessions will be needed. During the progress of the course, the students will be more acquainted and the need of face-to-face session will be lower (Moran, 2003).

Technical

Technical tutor role dimension (Berge & Collins, 1996):

- Tutor should be acquainted with technology in use and promote a good use by students (Berge & Collins, 2000)(Berge & Collins, 1996).
- Tutor must be the chief of learning with technology (Schofield *et al.*, 2006). If tutor or students are not acquainted with technical mechanisms, they will need more time to solve technical problems making them out of discussion. In this way, it is important that all participants have technical orientations.

The "result" element of Engestrom activity theory represents the final product, that is to say, if student learns or not. Usually tutor and course designers make a good value on different kinds of online interactions but rarely get a hoped adhesion (Bento & Schuster, 2003).

The online participation taxonomy is showed by Bento and Shuster (2003) in four quadrants. The quality may be evaluated using a formal, informal or self-evaluation mode.

The quadrants I and II share the low participation feature, represent invisible students who do not participate actively on discussion. Students included on quadrant II, in spite of being also invisible, act as learning witnesses. They are actively engaged on contents (great contents interaction) and ongoing discussion.

As the low visibility (quadrant I and II) is not necessarily bad, the high visibility (quadrant III and IV) is not necessarily good. Quadrant III and IV share the high visibility feature that interacts frequently on on-line discussion.

Students on quadrant IV represent the good participation, what tutor wants. These students are good on social aspects but they are also good on contents interactions. Their online contribution is significant and frequent (Bento & Schuster, 2003).

Beyond online discussion analysis Morgan and Oreilly (1999) outline other ways of online evaluation, namely:

- Peers evaluation and self-evaluation
- Online quizzes
- Digital Portfolio

In activity theory, the "tool" element may be the LMS, the contents or the communication media used to support the activity. Regarding tools element, it is important to consider the constant changing on interactions and contents formats.

There are many ways of interaction Schofield, Sackville e Davey (2006) beyond considering the kind of interactivity proposed by Moore (Moore, 1989) student/contents, student/tutor and student/student adds three ways of interactivity: student/technology, students/tutor and interpersonal interactivity (self-reflection and meta-cognition by the online presence). Hirumi (2006) adds three more ways of interactivity: student/instruction, students/others and students/environment.

The challenge is planning and managing each interaction in a significant way at distance, using communication tools (Hirumi, 2006). Community members should have technical skills, in order to participate on the tasks, should have interpersonal skills, ability to work in groups and to share information (Cotter & Martins, 2006). Students/other interaction allows students to acquire, analyse and apply information from a variety of human resources (Hirumi, 2006).

The relation among the elements of activity theory enhances the importance of considering the ability to achieve the objectives by the community using the available tools (Engestrom, 2001).

To sum up, an instruction strategy's design includes the elements shown in Figure 3.

Development

The development stage is based on previous phases of analysis and design. The purpose of this phase is to generate the lesson plans and lesson materials. During this phase, you will develop instruction lessons and all media and support documentation that will be used. This may include hardware and software (McGriff, 2000). Materials and procedures development must be added to the importance of planning instruction messages and its distribution.

Figure 3. Instruction strategies design

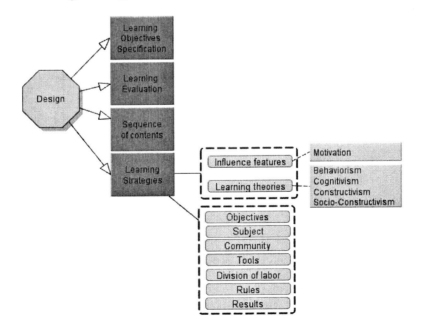

For each lecture, it is important to develop or adapt material, develop presentations, organize lessons, seek for cooperation and represent it on eLearning platform (Klein *et al.*, 2003), Klein et. al. give the general name of "recurring activities" because this fact must be repeated for each lecture.

The following tasks should be performed on the development phase (see Figure 4).

Implementation

The implementation phase refers to the delivery of the course. The purpose of this phase is to promote an effective and efficient delivery of instruction. This phase must encourage learner's understanding on contents. It is important to provide a good support in order to achieve the objectives defined (McGriff, 2000) (Kemp *et al.*, 1998).

The following tasks should be performed on the implementation phase (see Figure 5).

Evaluation

The evaluation phase measures the effectiveness and efficiency of instruction. Evaluation should occur throughout the entire design process, within the phases, between the phases and after implementation. Evaluation may be formative or summative (McGriff, 2000) (Kemp *et al.*, 1998).

The following tasks should be performed on the evaluation phase (see Figure 6).

Formative Evaluation

Formative evaluation occurs during and between the instruction processes. The purpose of this phase is to improve instruction before the implementation phase (McGriff, 2000).

Dick et. al. (Dick & Carey Lou, 1996) outline the tasks of this evaluation phase. They suggest that the description of each phase must include: its purpose, the description of developed contents or selected contents, the summary of tutor presentation and tools used in the formative evaluation.

An idea may seem good, in order to answer the needs but in fact may be useless. This scenario enhances the importance of formative evaluation. Its function is to notice teacher whether the instruction is suitable or not. If an instruction strategy shows weakness, tutor should correct it before it finishes (Kemp *et al.*, 1998).

The formative evaluation intends to check the accuracy of every element of the mipo model. Between the analysis phase and the design phase, it is important to ensure that both global and transversal objectives are covered by the learning activities. For each objective it is possible to have either one or more learning activities. Nevertheless, it is possible for an activity to cover more than only one objective defined in the previous phase.

On the formative evaluation, we should answer questions such as "do the learning strategies cover

Figure 4. Development tasks

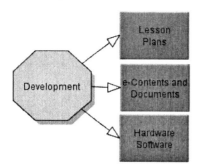

Figure 5. Implementation tasks

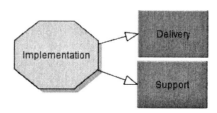

all learning objectives?"; "are there activities that do not cover any objectives?"; "have students all the information?" etc.

Throughout the next phases, we should check if both development and implementation are proceeding according to the analysis and design done.

Summative Evaluation

Summative evaluation usually occurs after the implementation process. This type of evaluation assesses the effectiveness of the instruction. Data from summative evaluation is often used to make decision about instruction (McGriff, 2000). In the redefinition of ADDIE model proposed by Dick et. al. (Dick & Carey Lou, 1996) it is recommended to sum up data from formative evaluation phase in order to identify the weakness on the contents and on the directions followed by tutor. The use of the same contents on a further edition of the course are questioned. Every phase of summative evaluation and the decision made must be described.

In the wide view of the model enunciated by Kemp et. al.(1998) the oval shape suggests a cyclical process which demands a continuous planning that uses the management project techniques. Kemp et. al (1998) add to the enunciated phases the importance of having constant support services and management according to project management.

In order to demonstrate the importance of developing a continuous process, Schofield, Sackville and Davey (2006), suggest the "bespoke tailoring" model. They use a metaphor of a tailor who is designing a suit for his client fitted to his body and during this process he makes a dynamic adjustment.

Schofield, Sackville and Davey (2006) add that technology and tools, model of pedagogy, parameters of interactivity and learning community are the four elements that need design, conceptualization and final product adjustments (Schofield *et al.*, 2006).

In the summative evaluation phase, we should check the learning results and collect all students' perceptions on the learning strategies done, in order to improve further course edition.

There are many instruction models with more or less details, but in general we have three main features: identify learning objectives, develop the instruction and evaluate the effectiveness (Carvalho, 2003).

FUTURE TRENDS

On the next step, we will apply this conceptual model in order to validate it especially on computer science education units in the Portuguese higher education context.

We will use action-research and cases study methodologies in order to find out the benefits

Figure 6. Evaluation tasks

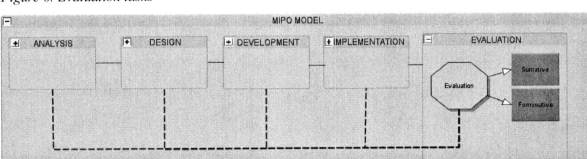

and the weaknesses of this model (Peres & Pimenta, 2008).

CONCLUSION

In this chapter we introduced our point of view on how to construct a well-designed b-learning environment. This model joins research results, experiences and multiple theories.

At the higher education context, besides everything that has been said about the use of e-learning technologies, we attested the idea defended by the European committee (EU, 2004). Our higher institutions continue to use the traditional education schema promoting an environment based on providing information. This scenario is the best for many students, teachers and institutions.

However, in this study we could see many different experiences on the e-learning domain. Many times the changes occur on the technologies and without any methodological or pedagogical support. For instance, whenever printed documents are replaced by digital contents, using the same communication schema (emitter-receiver) but with more sophisticated tools.

If an institution adopts an LMS, it does not ensure the integration of web technologies on the educational process (Parlamento Europeu, 2002).

Acknowledging that Internet increases places and moments of communication and also the access to the information (Parlamento Europeu, 2002) was a study that enhanced the wide unexplored field.

Updated technologies help the construction of a huge set of learning strategies and methods options, as large as our imagination. All technologies should be viewed as work tools and not as an end itself. More important than choosing a tool is the selection of the learning strategy, in order to achieve the defined goals.

We believe that the existence of a model that supports the complex management process of b-learning may promote the systematization, the usefulness and the organization of the web classroom integration. The MIPO model intends to be a dynamic and flexible structure that offers a large set of orientations in order to conduct a combined learning process.

REFERENCES

Afonso, A. (2006). Communities as context providers for Web-based learning. In D. Figueiredo & A. Afonso (Eds.), *Managing learning in virtual settings* (pp. 135-163). Hershey, PA: Information Science Publishing.

Allen, M. (2007). *Designing successful e-learning.* Pfeiffer.

Barreira, A., & Moreira, M. (2004). *Pedagogia das competências. Da teoria a prática.* Edicoes Asa.

Bento, R., & Schuster, C. (2003). Participation: The online challenge. In A. Aggarwal (Ed.), *Web-based education: Learning from experience* (pp. 156-164). Hershey, PA: Information Science Publishing.

Berge, Z., & Collins, M. (1996). *Facilitating interaction in computer mediated online courses.* Retrieved August, 2007 from http://www.emoderators.com/moderators/flcc.html

Berge, Z., & Collins, M. (2000). Perceptions of e-moderators about their roles and functions in moderating electronic mailing lists. *Distance Education: An International Journal, 21*(1), 81-100. Retrieved August, 2007 from http://www.emoderators.com/moderators/modsur97.html

Bloom, B., Engelhart, M., Frust, E., Hill, W., & Krathwohl, D. (1975). *Taxonomia de los objectivos de la educacion: La classificacion de las metas educacionales.* Editorial El Ateneo.

Born, A. (2003). Web-based student assessment. In A. Aggarwal (Ed.), *Web-based education: Learning from experience* (pp. 165-188). Hershey, PA: IRM Press.

Britain, S., & Liber, O. (1999). *A framework for pedagogical evaluation of virtual learning environments.* University of Wales - Bangor.

CNS. (2006). *Teorias, factores e processos de aprendizagem.* Companhia Nacional de Servicos.

Campbell, K. (2004). *E-ffective writing for e-learning environments.* Hershey, PA: Information Science Publishing.

Carvalho, V. (2003). *Conceitos básicos para o desenvolvimento de cursos multimedia.* SPI - sociedade portuguesa de inovacao.

Cotter, M., & Martins, H. (2006). Eficiência na construção de equipas colaborativas online. In A. Rocha (Ed.), *1 Conferência Iberica de Sistemas e Tecnologias da Informação (CISTI06)* (Vol. I, pp. 471-487). Universidade Fernando Pessoa.

Dias, P. (2004). Processos de aprendizagem colaborativa nas comunidades online. In A. Dias & M. J. Gomes (Eds.), *Learning para E-Formadores (2004)* (pp. 19-31). Guimarães: TecMinho.

Dick, W., & Lou, C. (1996). *The systematic design of instruction.* Harper Collins College Publishers.

Duffy, T., & Kirkley, J. (2004). Introduction: Theory and practice in distance education. In T. Duffy & J. Kirkley (Eds.), *Learner-centered: Theory and practice in distance education - cases from higher education.* Mahway, NJ: Lawrence Erlbaum Associates.

EU. (2004). *Distance learning and elearning in European policy and practice: The vision and the reality.* Retrieved April, from http://www.odl-liaison.org/pages.php?PN=policy-paper_2004

Engestrom, Y. (2001). Expansive learning at work: Toward an activity theoretical reconceptualization. *Journal of Education and Work, 14*(1), 133-156.

Falcao, A. (2006). *Teorias, factores e processos de aprendizagem.* ENA (Escola de Negocios e Administracao).

Felder, R., & Brent, R. (2006). *Effective teaching: A workshop.* University of Aveiro.

Gardner, H. (2000). *Inteligências múltiplas: A teoria na prática.* Artmed.

Garrison, D., & Anderson, T. (2003). *E-learning in the 21st century: A framework for research and practice.* Routledge Falmer.

Gillani, B. (1984). *Learning theories and the design of e-learning environments.* University Press of America.

Hirumi, A. (2006). *Analysing and designing e-learning interactions.* Routlege.

Kemp, F., Morrison, G., & Ross, S. (1998). *Designing effective instruction.* Upper Saddle River, NJ: Prentice Hall.

Khan, B. (2005). *Managing e-learning strategies: Design, delivery, implementation and evaluation.* Hershey, PA: Information Science Publishing.

Klein, M., Sommer, D., & Stucky, W. (2003). WeBCEIS - a scenario for integrating web-based education into classical education. In A. Aggarwal (Ed.), *Web-based education: Learning from experience* (pp. 398-414). Hershey, PA: Information Science Publishing.

Kolb, D. (1984). *Experiential learning: Experience as the source of learning and development.* FT Press.

Koponen, E. (2006). Exploring the higher education e-learning in Finland. In V. Carvalho (Ed.), *E-learning e formação avançada: Casos de su-*

cesso no ensino superior da Europa e America Latina (pp. 23-71). Edicoes Politema.

Kruse, K. (2006). *Introduction to instructional design and the ADDIE model, e-learningGuru.* Retrieved April, from http://www.e-learningguru.com/articles/art2_1.htm

Laurillard, D. (2006). *Rethinking university teaching - a framework for the effective use of learnign technologies.* Routledge Falmer.

Lave, J., & Wenger, E. (1995). *Situated learning: Legitimate peripheral participation.* Cambridge University Press.

McGriff, S. (2000). *Instructional system design (ISD): Using the ADDIE model.* State College, PA: Penn State University.

Moore, M. (1989). Three types of interaction. *American Journal of distance Education, 3*(2), 34-54.

Moran, J. (2003). Contribuições para uma pedagogia da educação online. In S. Marco (Ed.), *Educação on-line.* Sao Paulo: Edições Loyola.

Moran, J. (2005). A pedagogia e a didática da educação on-line. In *Educação, aprendizagem e tecnologia. Um paradigma para professores do século XXI.* Edições Sílabo.

Morgado, L. (2005). Novos papéis para o professor/tutor na pedagogia on-line. In R. Silva & A. Silva (Eds.), *Educação, aprendizagem e tecnologia: Um paradigma para professores do século XXI* (pp. 97-120). Edições Sílabo.

Morgan, C., & Oreilly, M. (1999). *Assessing open and distance learners.* Kogan Page.

Parlamento Europeu. (2002). *Decisao do parlamento Europeu e do conselho que adopta um programa plurianual (2004 2006).*

Peres, P., & Pimenta, P. (2008). Uma metodologia para a integração das tecnologias WEB no ensino superior (Tese doutoramento, Universidade do Minho).

Piaget, J., Beth, W., & Mays, M. (1974). *Epistemologia genética e pesquisa psicologica.* Trad. da Livraria Freitas Bastos.

Pimenta, P., & Ana, B. (2004). Das plataformas de e-learning aos objectos de aprendizagem. In A. Dias (Ed.), *E-learning para e-formadores* (pp. 98-109). Tecminho.

Rajadell, N., & Serrat, N. (2000). La interrogacion didatica: Una estrategia para aplicar en el aula. In S. D. L. Torre (Ed.), *Estrategias didaticas innovadoras: Recursos para la formacion y el cambio* (pp. 263-285). Octaedro.

Rodrigues, E. (2004). Competências dos e-formadores. In A. Dias (Ed.), *E-learning para e-formadores* (pp. 72-95). Tecminho.

Rodrigues, M., & Ferrao. (2006). *Formação pedagógica de formadores.* Edições Lídel.

Salmon, G. (2005). *E-moderating: The key to teaching e learning online.* Routledge Falmer.

Santos, E. (2003). Articulação de saberes na EAD online: Por uma rede interdisciplinar e interativa de conhecimentos em ambientes virtuais de aprendizagem. In M. Silva (Ed.), *Educação online* (pp. 217-230). Edições Loyola.

Schofield, M., Sackville, A., & Davey, J. (2006). Designing for unique online learning contexts: The aligment of purpose, audience, and form of interactivity. In F. Dias (Ed.), *Managing learning in virtual settings. The role of context* (pp. 117-134). Hershey, PA: Information Science Publishing.

Schuman, L. (1996). *Perspectives on instruction, SDSU - educational technology.* Retrieved April, 2008, from http://edweb.sdsu.edu/courses/edtec540/perspectives/perspectives.html

Shea, P., Fredericksen, E., Pickett, A., & Pelz, W. (2004). Faculty development, student satisfaction, and reported learning in the SUNY learning network. In T. M. Duffy & J. R. Kirkley (Eds.), *Learner-centered: Theory and practice in distance education* (pp. 343-377). Mahwah, NJ: Lawrence Erlbaum Assoc.

Skinner, B. (1981). *Ciência e comportamento humano*. Livraria Martins Fontes Editora.

Souza, R. (2005). Uma proposta construtivista para a utilização de tecnologias na educacao. In V. Silva & S. Vidigal (Eds.), *Educação, aprendizagem e tecnologia: Um paradigma para professores do século XXI*. Edições Sílabo.

Trindade, R. (2002). *Experiências educativas e situações de aprendizagem*. Asa Editores.

Tuckman, B. W. (1965). Developmental sequence in small groups. *Psichological Bulletin*, *63*, 384-399.

Vick, R., Auernheimer, B., Iding, M., & Crosby, M. (2006). Quality assurance during distributed collaboration: A case study in creating a cross-institutional learning community. In F. Dias (Ed.), *Managing learning in virtual settings* (pp. 274-289). Hershey, PA: Information Science Publishing.

Vygotsky, L. (1998). *A formacao social da mente: O desenvolvimento dos processos psicologicos superiores*. Martins Fontes.

Wenger, E. (2002). *Cultivating communities of practice*. Cambridge, MA: Harvard Business School Press.

Wikipedia. (2007). *Electronic learning*. Retrieved October, from http://en.wikipedia.org/wiki/E-Learning

Compilation of References

Abbott, G., & Bievenue, L. (2007). Gender equity in the use of Educational technology. In Klein (Ed.), *Handbook for achieving gender equity through education* (pp. 191-214). Lawrence Erlbaum Associates.

Abelson, R. P. (1963). Computer simulation of "hot" cognition. In S. Tomkins & S. Messick (Eds.), *Computer simulation of personality* (pp. 277-298). New York: Wiley.

Accelerated Learning Methods. (2009). *Visual stimulation in your accelerated learning environment*. Retrieved January 12, 2009, from http://www.acceleratedlearning-methods.com/visual-stimulation.html

Ackerman, E. (n.d.). *Piaget' s constructivism, Papert's constructionism: What is the difference? Massachusetts Institute of Technology*. Retrieved November 16, 2008, from http://learning.media.mit.edu/content/publications/EA.Piaget%20_%20Papert.pdf

ACT-R. (2002). *Welcome to ACT-R*. Retrieved October 12, 2003, from http://act-r.psy.cmu.edu/

Adams, A.M. & Willis, C. (2001). Language processing and working memory: A developmental perspective. In J. Andrade (Ed.), *Working memory in perspective* (pp. 79-100). Hove: Psychology Press.

Adams, R. (2007). Decision and stress: Cognition and e-accessibility in the information workplace. *Universal Access in the Information Society, 5*, 363-379.

Adams, R. (2007). User modeling for intelligent interfaces in e-learning. In *Universal access in human-computer interaction, application and services* (LNCS 4556).

Adams, R. (2008). User modeling & monitoring: A universal access perspective. In C. Stephanidis (Ed.), *Universal access handbook*. Mahwah, NJ: Lawrence Erlbaum Associates Inc.

Adams, R., & Granić, A. (2007). Creating smart and accessible ubiquitous knowledge environments. In C. Stephanidis (Ed.), *Universal access in HCI, part II, Proceedings of HCII 2007* (LNCS 4555, 3-12). Berlin, Germany: Springer-Verlag Berlin Heidelberg.

Adams, R., & Russell, C. (2006). Lessons from ambient intelligence prototypes for universal access and the user experience. In *Universal access in ambient intelligence environments* (LNCS 4397, pp. 229-243). Berlin, Germany: Springer.

Adams, R., Bahr, G. S., & Moreno, B. (2008). Brain computer interfaces: Psychology and pragmatic perspectives for the future. In *AISB Proceedings*, Aberdeen.

Adams, R., Granić, A., & Keates, L. S. (2008). Are ambient intelligent applications universally accessible? In *Universal Access to Novel Interaction Environments: Challenges and Opportunities, Proceedings of the 2nd International Conference on Applied Ergonomics AE International 2008) with the 11th International Conference on Human Aspects of Advanced Manufacturing (HAAMAHA)*, Las Vegas, NV, USA.

Adams, R., Langdon, P., & Clarkson, P. J. (2002). A systematic basis for developing cognitive assessment methods for assistive technology. In *Universal Access and Assistive Technology, Proceedings of the CWUAAT, Cambridge Workshop for Universal Access and Assistive Technology*.

Adler, P. S., & Kwon, S. W. (2002). Social capital: Prospect for a new concept. *Academy of Management Review, 27*(1), 17-40.

Afonso, A. (2006). Communities as context providers for Web-based learning. In D. Figueiredo & A. Afonso (Eds.), *Managing learning in virtual settings* (pp. 135-163). Hershey, PA: Information Science Publishing.

Akerlof, G. A. (1970). The market for "lemons": Quality uncertainty and the market mechanism. *Quarterly Journal of Economics, 84*, 488-500.

Alani, H., Kim, S., Millard, D. E., Weal, M. J., Hall, W., Lewis, P. H., & Shadbolt, N. (2004). Using Protégé for automatic ontology instantiation. In *Proceedings of the 7th International Protégé Conference*. Bethesda, Maryland, USA

Alessi, S. M., & Trollip, R. S. (2001). *Multimedia for learning: Methods and development.* Boston, MA: Allyn & Bacon.

Alexander, P. A. (1992). Domain knowledge: Evolving themes and emerging concerns. *Educational Psychologist, 27*(1), 33-51.

Alexander, R. J. (2001). Border crossings: Towards a comparative pedagogy. *Comparative Education, 37*(4), 507-523.

Alexander, R. J. (2004). Still no pedagogy? Principle, pragmatism and compliance in primary education. *Cambridge Journal of Education, 34*(1), 7-33.

Alexander, R. J. (2004). *Towards dialogic teaching: Rethinking classroom talk.* York: Dialogos.

Alice org. (2008). *Alice programming.* Retrieved November 12, 2008, from http://www.alice.org/

Alice Org. (2008). *What is Alice?* Retrieved November 13, 2008, from http://www.alice.org/index.php?page=what_is_alice/what_is_alice

Allen, M. (2007). *Designing successful e-learning.* Pfeiffer.

Allessi, S. M., & Trollop, S. R. (2001). *Multimedia for learning: Methods and development.* Boston, Allyn and Bacon.

Allinson, C. W., & Hayes, J. (1996). The cognitive styles index: A measure of intuition-analysis for organisational research. *Journal of Management Studies, 33*(1), 119-135.

Alloway, T. P., Pickering, S. J., & Gathercole, S. E. (2006). Verbal and visuospatial short-term and working memory in children: Are they separable? *Child Development, 77*(6), 1698-1716.

Allport, A., Styles, E. A., & Hsieh, S. (1994). Shifting attentional set: Exploring the dynamic control of tasks. In C. Umilta & M. Moscovitch (Eds.), *Attention and performance XV* (pp. 421-62). Cambridge, MA: MIT Press.

Allport, D. A., Antonis, B., & Reynolds, P. (1972). On the division of attention: A disproof of the single channel hypothesis. *Quarterly Journal of Experimental Psychology, 24*, 225-35.

Ally, M. (2008). Foundations of educational theory for online learning. In T. Anderson (Ed.), *The theory and practice of online learning* (pp. 15-44). AU Press.

Alonso, C. M., Gallego, D. J., & Honey, P. (2002). *The learning styles.* Ediciones Mensajero.

Ambiente Intelligence Org. (2008). Retrieved January 12, 2009, from http://www.ambientintelligence.org/

Ames, A. L., Nadeu, D. R., & Moreland, J. L. (1997). *VRML 2.0 sourcebook* (2nd ed.). New York: Wiley and Sons.

Amichai-Hamburger, Y., Wainapel, G., & Fox, S. (2002). "On the Internet no one knows I'm an introvert": Extroversion, neuroticism, and Internet interaction. *CyberPsychology & Behavior, 5*(2), 125-128.

Anastasi, A., & Foley, J. P. (1949). *Differential psychology: Individual and group differences in behavior.* New York: Macmillan Co.

Anderson, J. R. (1983). *The architecture of cognition.* Cambridge, MA: Harvard University Press.

Anderson, J. R., & Lebiere, C. (1998). *The atomic components of thought.* Mahwah, NJ: Lawrence Erlbaum Associates.

Anderson, J. R., Bothell, D., Byrne, M. D., Douglass, S., Lebiere, C., & Qin, Y. (2004). An integrated theory of the mind. *Psychological Review, 111*(4), 1036-1060.

Anderson, J. R., Corbett, A. T., Koedinger, K. R., & Pelletier, R. (1995). Cognitive tutors: Lessons learned. *The Journal of the Learning Sciences, 4*(2),167-207.

Anderson, J.R. (1983). *The architecture of cognition.* Cambridge, MA: Harvard Univeristy Press.

Anderson, M.D. (2001). Individual characteristics and Web-based courses. In C.R. Wolfe (Ed.), *Learning and teaching on the world wide Web* (pp. 45-72). San Diego, CA: Elsevier.

Anderson, T. (2008). Towards a theory of online learning. In T. Anderson (Ed.), *The theory and practice of online learning* (pp. 45-74). AU Press.

Anderson, T. (Ed.). (2008). *The theory and practice of online learning.* AU Press.

Anderson, T., Rourke, L., Garrison, D. R., & Archer, W. (2001). Assessing teaching presence in a computer conferencing context. *Journal of Asynchronous Learning Networks, 5*(2).

Andrade, J. (2001). *Working memory in perspective.* Hove: Psychology Press.

Andre, E., Klesen, M., Gebhard, P., Allen, S., & Rist T. (1999). Integrating models of personality and emotions into lifelike characters. In *Proceedings International Workshop on Affect in Interactions - Towards a New Generation of Interfaces* (pp. 136-149).

Anolli, L., Villani, D., & Riva, G. (2005). Personality of people using chat: An online research. *CyberPsychology & Behavior, 8*(1), 89-95.

Aprende Brasil. (2008). *Sucursal da escola: Alunos da EMEF ernani silva bruno visualizam as matérias em 3D.* Retrieved January 12, 2009, from http://www.aprendebrasil.com.br/alunoreporter/reportagem.asp?idARMateria=531

Arbaugh, J. B. (2000). Virtual classroom versus physical classroom: An exploratory study of class discussion patterns and student learning in an asynchronous Internet-based MBA course. *Journal of Management Education, 24*, 213-233.

Area Wikipedia. (2008). *Area.* http://en.wikipedia.org/wiki/Area

Ates, S., & Cataloglu, E. (2007). The effects of students' cognitive styles on conceptual understandings and problem-solving skills in introductory mechanics. *Research in Science & Technological Education, 25*(2), 167-178.

Atkinson, R.C. & Shiffrin, R.M. (1968). Human memory: A proposed system and its control processes. In K.W. Spence & J.T. Spence (Eds.), *The psychology of learning and motivation: Advances in research and theory: Vol. 2* (pp. 89-195). New York: Academic Press.

Atkinson, R.C., & Shiffrin, R.M. (1971). The control of short-term memory. *Scientific American, 224*, 82-90.

Aviv, R., Erlich, Z., Ravid, G., & Geva, A. (2003). Network analysis of knowledge construction in asynchronous learning networks. *Journal of Asynchronous Learning Networks, 7*(3), 1-23.

Azari, N. P., Pettigrew, K. D., Pietrini, P., Murphy, D. G., Horwitz, B., & Schapiro, M. B. (1995). Sex differences in patterns of hemispheric cerebral metabolism: A multiple regression/discriminant analysis of positron emission tomographic data. *International Journal of Neuroscience, 81*, 1-20.

Azevedo, R. (2005). Using hypermedia as a metacognitive tool for enhancing student learning? The role of self-regulated learning. *Educational Psychologist, 40*(4), 199-209.

Bablekou, Z. (1989). *Memory processes in children with specific language difficulties.* Unpublished Doctoral Thesis. The University of Leeds, Psychology Department.

Baddeley, A.D. & Hitch G.J. (2000). Development of working memory: Should the Pascual-Leone and the Baddeley and Hitch models be merged? *Journal of Experimental Child Psychology, 77*, 128-37.

Baddeley, A. (1981). The concept of working memory: A view of its current state and probable future development. *Cognition, 10*(1-3), 17-23.

Baddeley, A. (1992). Working memory. *Science, 255,* 556-559.

Baddeley, A. (2000). The episodic buffer: A new component of working memory? *Trends in Cognitive Sciences, 11*(4), 417-423.

Baddeley, A. (2003). Working memory and language: An overview. *Journal of Communication Disorders, 36,* 189-208.

Baddeley, A. D. (2007). *Working memory, thought, and action.* Oxford: Oxford University Press.

Baddeley, A., & Hitch, G. J. (1974). Working memory. In G. Bower (Ed.), *Recent advances in learning and motivation* (Vol. 8) (pp. 47-49). New York: Academic Press.

Baddeley, A.D. & Hitch, G.J. (1974). Working memory. In G.A. Bower (Ed.), *The psychology of learning and motivation: Vol. 8* (pp. 47-90). New York: Academic Press.

Baddeley, A.D. & Wilson, B. (1988). Frontal amnesia and the dysexecutive syndrome. *Brain and Cognition, 7*(2), 212-230.

Baddeley, A.D. (1996). Exploring the central executive. *Quarterly Journal of Experimental Psychology, 49A*(1), 5-28.

Baddeley, A.D. (2000). The episodic buffer: A new component of WM? *Trends in Cognitive Sciences, 4*(11), 417-423.

Baddeley, A.D., Bressi, S., Della Sala, S., Logie, R., & Spinler, H. (1991). The decline of working memory in Alzheimer's disease: A longitudinal study. *Brain, 114,* 2521-42.

Baddeley, A.D., Chincotta, D., & Adlam, A. (2001). Working memory and the control of action: evidence from task switching. *Journal of Experimental Psychology: General, 130,* 641-57.

Baeza-Yates, R., & Ribeiro-Neto, B. (1999). *Modern information retrieval.* ACM Press.

Bagozzi, R. P., Davis, F. D., & Warshaw, P. R. (1992). Development and test of a theory of technology learning and usage. *Human Relations, 45,* 659-686.

Bailey, B.P., & Iqbal. S.T. (2007). Understanding changes in mental workload during execution of goal-directed tasks and its application for interruption management. *ACM Transactions on Computer-Human Interaction, 14*(4), 1-21.

Bajraktarevic, N., Hall, W., & Fullick, P. (2003). Incorporating learning styles in hypermedia environment: Empirical evaluation. In *Proceedings of the International Conference on Adaptive Hypermedia and Adaptive Web-Based Systems (AH2003)* (pp. 41-52).

Balacheff, N. (2006). *There is a growing understanding of the role and needs of teachers and institutions, of the place of knowledge in the design, and of the implementation and deployment of ICT.* Retrieved May 7, 2008, from http://www.elearningeuropa.info

Baldwin, T. T., Bedell, M. D., & Johnson, J. L. (1997). The social fabric of a team-based M.B.A. program: Network effects on student satisfaction and performance. *Academy of Management Journal, 40*(6), 1369-1397.

Bandura, A. (1978). The self-system in reciprocal determinism. *American Psychologist, 33,* 344-358.

Bandura, A. (1993). Perceived self-efficacy in cognitive development and functioning. *Educational Psychologist, 28,* 117-148.

Bangert, A. (2008). The influence of social presence and teaching presence on the quality of online critical inquiry. *Journal of Computing in Higher Education, 20,* 34-61.

Barak, M., & Rafaeli, S. (2004). On-line question-posing and peer-assessment as means for Web-based knowledge sharing in learning. *International Journal of Human-Computer Studies, 61,* 84-103.

Barbosa, A. M. (2006). Dilema da arte/educação como mediação cultural em namoro com as tecnologias contemporâneas. In A. M. Barbosa (Ed.), *Arte/educação contemporânea: Consonâncias internacionais* (pp. 98-112). Brasil:Cortez Editora.

Bard, T. B. (1996). Cooperative activities in interactive distance learning. *Journal of Education for Library and Information Science, 37*(1), 2-10.

Barnard, P. J. (1999). Interacting cognitive subsystems: Modelling working memory phenomena with a multi-processor architecture. In A. Myake & P. Shah (Eds.), *Models of working memory.* Cambridge, UK: Cambridge University Press.

Barnard, P. J., May, J., Duke, D., & Duce, D. (2000). Systems interactions and macrotheory. *Transactions on Computer Human interface, 7,* 222-262.

Baroun, K. A., & Al-Ansari, B. M. (2005). Impact of anxiety and gender on perceiving the Mueller-Lyer illusion. *Social Behaviour and Personality, 33*(1), 33-42.

Barreira, A., & Moreira, M. (2004). *Pedagogia das competências. Da teoria a prática.* Edicoes Asa.

Barron, B., Schwartz, D. L., Vye, N. J., Moore, A., Petrosino, A., Zech, L., Bransford, J. D., & The Cognition and Technology Group at Vanderbilt. (1998). Doing with understanding: Lessons from research on problem and project-based learning. *The Journal of the Learning Sciences, 7,* 271-311.

Barros, P. G. (2004). *UFPE, VRML tutorial.* Retrieved November 22, 2008, from http://www.di.ufpe.br/~if124/vrml/vrml.htm

Bartlett, F. C. (1932). *Remembering: A study in experimental and social psychology.* Cambridge: Cambridge University Press.

Bartunk, D., Martin, A., & Martinová, L. (2007). *Games in nature: An innovative approach to outdoor and environmental activities for young children.* Czech Republic: IYNF.

Bates, J. (1994). The role of emotion in believable agents. *Communications of ACM, 37*(7), 122-125.

Batliner, A., Hacker, C., & Wong, M. (2004). "You stupid tin box" – Children interacting with the AIBO robot: A cross-linguistic emotional speech corpus. In *Proc. Language Resources and Evaluation (LREC '04).* Lisbon.

Batra, S., Bishu, R. R., & Donohue, B. (1993). Effects of hypertext typology on navigational performance. *Advances in Human Factors and Ergonomics, 19,* 175-180.

Baumgartner, P., Furbach, U., Groß-Hardt, M., & Sinner, A. (2004). Living book: Deduction, slicing, and interaction. *Journal of Automated Reasoning, 32*(3), 259-286.

Bayliss, D.M., Jarrold, C., Gunn, D.M., & Baddeley, A.D. (2003). The complexities of complex span: explaining individual differences in working memory in children and adults. *Journal of Experimental Psychology: General, 132*(1), 71-92.

Beatriz. (2009). Retrieved February 16, 2009, from http://biaatrevida.blogspot.com/

Beetham, H. (2005). Personalization in the curriculum: A view from learning theory. In S. De Freitas & C. Yapp (Eds.), *Personalizing learning in the 21ˢᵗ century* (pp. 17-24). Stafford: Network Educational Press.

Belsley, D. A., Kuh, E., & Welsch, R. E. (1980). *Regression diagnostics: Identifying influential data and sources of collinearity.* New York: Wiley.

Bendar, A. K., Cunningham, D., Duffy, T. M., & Perry, J. D. (1992). Theory into practice: How do we link? In T. M. Duffy & D. H. Jonassen (Eds.), *Constructivism and the technology of instruction: A conversation.* Hillsdale, NJ: Lawrence Erlbaum Associates Publishers.

Benne, K. D., & Sheats, P. (1948). Functional roles of group members. *Journal of Social Issues, 4*(2), 41-19.

Bento, R., & Schuster, C. (2003). Participation: The online challenge. In A. Aggarwal (Ed.), *Web-based education: Learning from experience* (pp. 156-164). Hershey, PA: Information Science Publishing.

Benyon, D., Crerar, A., & Wilkinson, S. (2001). Individual differences and inclusive design. In C. Stephanidis (Ed.), *User interfaces for all: Concepts, methods, and tools* (pp. 21-47). Mahwah, NJ: Lawrence Erlbaum Assoc.

Benyon, D., Turner, P., & Turner, S. (2005). *Designing interactive systems: People, activities, contexts, technologies,* New York: Addison-Wesley.

Berge, Z. (1995). The role of the online instructor/facilitator. *Educational Technology, 35*(1), 22-30.

Berge, Z., & Collins, M. (1996). *Facilitating interaction in computer mediated online courses.* Retrieved August, 2007 from http://www.emoderators.com/moderators/flcc.html

Berge, Z., & Collins, M. (2000). Perceptions of e-moderators about their roles and functions in moderating electronic mailing lists. *Distance Education: An International Journal, 21*(1), 81-100. Retrieved August, 2007 from http://www.emoderators.com/moderators/modsur97.html

Betts, G. H. (1909). *The distributions and functions of mental imagery.* New York: New York Teacher's College.

Bianchi, A., & Phillips, J. G. (2005). Psychological predictors of problem mobile phone use. *CyberPsychology & Behavior, 8*(1), 39-51.

Bielaczyc, K. (2001). Designing social infrastructure: The challenge of building computer-supported learning communities. In P. Dillenbourg, A. Eurelings, & K. Hakkarainen (Eds.), *The Proceedings of the First European Conference on CSCL* (pp. 106-114). University of Maastricht.

Biggs, J. (1987). *Student approaches to learning and studying.* Hawthorn, Australia: Australian Council for Educational Research.

Biggs, J. (1996). Enhancing teaching through constructive alignment. *Higher Education, 32,* 347-364.

Biggs, J. B. (2001). *Teaching for quality learning at university: What the learner does.* Open University Press.

Bikson, T., Eveland, J. D., & Gutek, B. A. (1989). Flexible interactive technologies for multi-person tasks: Current problems and future prospects. In M. H. Olson (Ed.), *Technological support for work group collaboration* (pp. 89-112). Hillsdale, NJ: Erlbaum.

Bilda, Z., & Gero, J. S. (2007). The impact of working memory limitations on the design process during conceptualization. *Design Studies, 28*(4), 343-367.

Bilham, T. (2005). Online learning: Can communities of practice deliver personalization in learning? In S. De Freitas & C. Yapp (Eds.), *Personalizing learning in the 21st century* (pp. 73-76). Stafford: Network Educational Press.

Billinghurst, M. (2008). *Hiltlabnz homepage.* Retrieved November 12, 2008, from http://www.hitlabnz.org/wiki/Home

Billingsley, J. (2001). Javascript jollies can bring simulations to life. In *Proceedings of the 12th Australasian Conference on Engineering Education,* Queensland University of Technology, Brisbane, Australia (pp. 63-67).

Billingsley, W. (2007). *The intelligent book: Technologies for intelligent and adaptive textbooks focussing on discrete mathematics.* Unpublished doctoral dissertation, University of Cambridge, Cambridge, UK.

Billingsley, W., & Robinson, P. (2005). Towards an intelligent online textbook for discrete mathematics. In *Proceedings of the 2005 International Conference on Active Media Technology,* Takamatsu, Japan (pp. 291-296).

Billingsley, W., & Robinson, P. (2007). Searching questions, informal modelling, and massively multiple choice. In *Proceedings of the International Conference of the Association for Learning Technology (ALT-C 2007),* Nottingham, UK.

Billingsley, W., & Robinson, P. (2007). Student proof exercises using MathsTiles and Isabelle/HOL in an intelligent book. *Journal of Automated Reasoning, 39*(2), 181-218.

Billingsley, W., Robinson, P., Ashdown, M., & Hanson, C. (2004). Intelligent tutoring and supervised problem solving in the browser. In *Proceedings of the IADIS International Conference WWW/Internet 2004,* Madrid, Spain (pp. 806-811).

Birenbaum, M. (2003). New insights into learning and teaching and their implications for assessment. In M. Segers, F. Dochy, & E. Cascallar (Eds.), *Optimising new modes of assessment: In search of qualities and standards* (pp. 13-37). Dordrecht, The Netherlands: Kluwer Academic Publishers.

Birenbaum, M. (2005, October). Multidimensional assessment of computer-supported knowledge building. In *Proceedings of E-Learn 2005* (pp. 1203-1208). Vancouver, Canada: Association for the Advancement of Computing in Education.

Bjork, R.A. & Whitten, W.B. (1974). Recency-sensitive retrieval processes. *Cognitive Psychology, 6*, 173-89.

Bjorklund, D. F. (2005). *Children's thinking: Cognitive development and individual differences* (4th ed.). Belmont, CA: Wadsworth

Black, P., & Wiliam, D. (1998). Assessment and classroom learning. *Assessment in Education, 5*, 7-74.

Black, P., & Wiliam, D. (2002). Assessment and classroom learning. In B. Roos (Eds.), *ICT, Assessment and the Learning Society, Proceedings of the European Conference on Educational Research (ECER)*, Lisbon.

Black, P., & Wiliams, D. (2001). *Assessment and classroom learning.* London: School of Education, King's College London.

Blackley, J. A., & Curran-Smith, J. (1998). Teaching community health nursing by distance methods: Development, process, and evaluation. *Journal of Continuing Education for Nurses, 29*, 148-153.

Blender. (2008). Retrieved November 12, 2008, from http://www.blender.org/features-gallery/features/

Blikstein, P., & Cavallo, D., (2002). Technology as a Trojan horse in school environments: The emergence of the learning atmosphere (II). In *Proceedings of the Interactive Computer Aided Learning International Workshop*, Carinthia Technology Institute, Villach, Austria. Retrieved January 13, 2009, from http://www.blikstein.com/paulo/documents/papers/BliksteinCavallo-TrojanHorse-ICL2002.pdf

Blikstein, P., & Zuffo, M. K. (2003). As sereias do ensino eletrônico. In M. Silva (Ed.), *Online education: Theory, practice, legislation and corporate training.* Rio de Janeiro: Ed. Loyola. Retrieved January 13, 2009, from http://www.blikstein.com/paulo/documents/books/Blikstein-Zuffo-MermaidsOfE-Teaching-OnlineEducation.pdf

Blochl, M., Rumetshofer, H., & Wob, W. (2003). Individualized e-learning systems enabled by a semantically determined adaptation of learning fragments. In *Proceedings of the 14th International Workshop of Database and Expert Systems Applications* (pp. 640-645).

Blog definition. (2008). Retrieved November 12, 2008, from http://en.wikipedia.org/wiki/Blog

Bloom, B. (1984). The two sigma problem: The search for methods of group instruction as effective as one-to-one tutoring. *Educational Researcher, 13*, 4-15.

Bloom, B. S. (1968). Learning for mastery. *Evaluation Comment, 1*, 1-12.

Bloom, B., Engelhart, M., Frust, E., Hill, W., & Krathwohl, D. (1975). *Taxonomia de los objectivos de la educacion: La classificacion de las metas educacionales.* Editorial El Ateneo.

Boling, N. C., & Robinson, D. H. (1999). Individual study, interactive multimedia, or cooperative learning: Which activity best supplements lecture-based distance education? *Journal of Education Psychology, 91*(1), 169-174.

Bonk, C. J., Kim, K. J., & Zeng, T. (2006). Future directions of blended learning in higher education and workplace learning settings. In C. J. Bonk & C. R. Graham (Eds.), *Handbook of blended learning: Global Perspectives, local designs.* San Francisco, CA: Pfeiffer Publishing. Retrieved May 07, 2008, from http://bechet.exp.sis.pitt.edu/lis2000/readings/Miscellaneous/c083_bonk_future.pdf

Borgatti, S. P., Everett, M. G., & Freeman, L. C. (2002). *Ucinet for Windows: Software for social network analysis.* Cambridge, MA: Analytic Technologies.

Born, A. (2003). Web-based student assessment. In A. Aggarwal (Ed.), *Web-based education: Learning from experience* (pp. 165-188). Hershey, PA: IRM Press.

Boud, D. (1990). Assessment and promotion of academic values. *Studies in Higher Education, 15,* 101-113.

Boud, D. (2000). Sustainable assessment: Rethinking assessment for the learning society. *Studies in Continuing Education, 22,* 151-167.

Bowman, D. A., Kruijff, E., LaViola, J. J., & Poupyrev, I. (2005). *3D user interfaces, theory and practice.* New York: Addison & Wesley.

Bradshaw, J. L., & Nettleton, N. C. (1983). *Human cerebral asymmetry.* New Jersey: Prentice-Hall.

Bransford, J., Brown, A. L., & Cocking, R. R. (1999). *How people learn: Brain, mind, experience, and school.* Washington, D.C.: National Academy Press.

Brewer, S., & Klein, J. D. (2006). Type of positive interdependence and affiliation motive in an asynchronous, collaborative learning environment. *Educational Technology Research and Development: ETR&D, 54*(4), 331-354.

Britain, S., & Liber, O. (1999). *A framework for pedagogical evaluation of virtual learning environments.* University of Wales - Bangor.

British Council Chevening. (2008). *Chevening program.* Retrieved November 15, 2008, from http://www.british-council.org/br/brasil-education-chevening.htm

Brna, P., & Cooper, B. (2003). *Lessons from the NIMIS classroom: An overview of progress towards the "classroom of tomorrow" in an English county primary school.* Retrieved November 12, 2008, from http://homepages.inf.ed.ac.uk/pbrna/projects/cblnimis/NIMISbriefing.html

Broadbent, D. E. (1971). *Decision and stress.* London: Academic Press.

Broadbent, D. E. (1984). The Maltese cross: A new simplistic model for memory. *Behavior and Brain Sciences, 7,* 55-94.

Broadbent, W. H., & Shane, T. R. (2008). Learning and training: They are not the same. *Training and Transfer, 3,* 211-233.

Brookhart, S. M. (1999). *The art and science of classroom assessment: The missing part of pedagogy. ASHE-ERIC Higher Education Report (Vol. 27, No. 1).* Washington, DC: The George Washington University, Graduate School of Education and Human Development. (ERIC Document Reproduction Service No. ED432937)

Brown, J. (1958). Some tests of the decay theory of immediate memory. *Quarterly Journal of Experimental Psychology, 10,* 12-21.

Brown, J. S., & Duguid, P. (1991). Organizational learning and communities-of-practice: Toward a unified view of working, learning, and innovation. *Organization Science, 2*(1), 40-57.

Brown, J. S., Burton, R. R., & Bell, A. G. (1975). SOPHIE: A step towards a reactive learning environment. *International Journal of Man-Machine Studies, 7,* 675-696.

Brown, L. M. (1966). *General philosophy in education.* New York: McGraw Hill.

Brubacher, J. (1962). *Eclectic philosophy of education.* Englewood Cliffs, New Jersey: Prentice Hall.

Brush, T. A. (1998). Embedding cooperative learning into the design of integrated learning systems: Rationale and guidelines. *Educational Technology Research & Development, 46,* 5-18.

Brusilovsky, P., Wade, V. P., & Conlan, O. (2007). From learning objects to adaptive content service for e-learning. In C. Pahl (Ed.), *Architecture solutions for e-learning systems* (pp. 243-261). Hershey, PA: Idea Group Publishing.

Brusilovsky, P. (1996). Methods and techniques of adaptive hypermedia. *User Modeling and User-Adapted Interaction, 6*(2-3), 87-129.

Brusilovsky, P. (2000). Adaptive hypermedia: From intelligent tutoring systems to Web-based education. In *Proceedings of ITS2000* (LNCS 1839, pp. 1-7). Springer-Verlag.

Brusilovsky, P. (2004). Adaptive educational hypermedia: From generation to generation. In *Proceedings of the 4ᵗʰ Hellenic Conference on Information and Com-*

munication Technologies in Education, Athens, Greece (pp. 19-33).

Brusilovsky, P., & Millan, E. (2007). User models for adaptive hypermedia and adaptive educational systems. In P. Brusilovsky, A. Kobsa, & W. Neidl (Eds.), *The adaptive Web: Methods and strategies of Web personalization* (LNCS 4321, pp. 3-53). New York: Springer-Verlag.

Brusilovsky, P., & Nejd, W. (2004). Adaptive hypermedia and adaptive Web. In M. P. Singh (Ed.), *The practical handbook of Internet computing* (pp. 1.1-1.14). USA: Chapman & Hall/CRC.

Brusilovsky, P., & Peylo, C. (2003). Adaptive and intelligent Web-based educational systems. *International Journal of Artificial Intelligence in Education, 13*(2-4), 156-169.

Brusilovsky, P., Chavan, G., & Farzan, R. (2004). Social adaptive navigation support for open corpus electronic textbooks. In *Proceedings of Adaptive Hypermedia 2004* (LNCS 3137, pp. 24-33). Springer.

Brusilovsky, P., Ritter, S., & Weber, G. (1996). ELM-ART: An intelligent tutoring system on the World Wide Web. In *Intelligent Tutoring Systems* (LNCS 1086, pp. 261-269). Springer-Verlag.

Brutzman, D. (2008). *X3D: Extensible 3D graphics for Web authors, CGEMS educational material*. Retrieved November 20, 2008, from http://cgems.inesc.pt/ListModules.aspx

Brutzman, D., & Daly, L. (2007). Preface. In *X3D graphics for Web authors* (pp. xix-xxi). USA: Morgan Kaufmann.

Bryant, P. E. & Bradley, L. (1985). *Children's reading problems*. Oxford: Blackwell.

Bull, R. & Andrews-Espy, K. A. (2006). Working memory, executive functioning, and children's mathematics. In S.J. Pickering (Ed.), *Working memory and education* (pp. 93-123). Burlington, MA: Academic Press.

Bullen, M. (1998). Participation and critical thinking in online university distance education. *The Journal of Distance Education, 13*, 1-32

Burdea, G. C., & Coiffet, P. (2003). *Virtual reality technology* (2nd ed.). New York: Wiley & Sons.

Burger, C. (2007). Gender equity in science, engineering and technology. In Klein (Ed.), *Handbook for achieving gender equity through education* (pp. 255-280). Lawrence Erlbaum Associates.

Burkhardt, M. E., & Brass, D. J. (1990). Changing patterns or patterns of change: The effect of a change in technology on social network structure and power. *Administrative Science Quarterly, 35*, 104-127.

Burnett, I. S., Pereira, F., Walle, R. V., & Koenen, R. (2006). *The MPEG-21 book*. New York: Wiley.

Burt, R. S. (1986). Comment. In S. Lindberg, J. S. Coleman, & S. Novak (Eds.), *Approaches to social theory* (pp.105-107). New York: Russell Sage.

Burt, R. S., Jannotta, J. E., & Mahoney, J. T. (1998). Personality correlates of structural holes. *Social Networks, 20*, 63-87.

Buscaloni, A. D., de la Iglesia, A., Buscaloni, R. D., & Dejoan, A. (2005). Modularity at the boundary between art and science. In W. Callebaut & D. R. Gutman (Eds.), *Modularity: Understanding the development and evolution of natural complex systems* (pp. 283-204). Cambridge, MA: The MIT Press.

Buysse, D. (2007). Giving science a chance. *Research*eu, the magazine of the European research area, Special issue "Reinventing science education", June 2007*, 10.

Byrne, M. D. (2001). ACT-R/PM and menu selection: Applying a cognitive architecture to HCI. *International Journal of Human-Computer Studies, 55*, 41-84.

Cabrera, A. F., Colbeck, C. L., & Terenzini, P. T. (2001). Developing performance indicators for assessing classroom teaching practices and student learning: The case of engineering. *Research in Higher Education, 42*(3), 327-352.

Cacioppo, J. T., Klein, D. J., Berntson, G. G., & Hatfield, E. (1993). The psychophysiology of emotion. In M. Lewis & J. M. Haviland (Eds.), *Handbook of emotions* (pp. 119-142). New York: Guilford Press.

Cain, K. (2006). Children's reading comprehension: The role of working memory in normal and impaired development. In S.J. Pickering (Ed.), *Working memory and education* (pp. 62-91). Burlington, MA: Academic Press.

Cain, K., Oakhill, J., & Bryant, P. (2004). Children's reading comprehension ability: Concurrent prediction by working memory, verbal ability, and component skills. *Journal of Educational Psychology, 96*, 31-42.

Calcaterra, A., Antonietti A., & Underwood, J. (2005). Cognitive style, hypermedia navigation and learning. *Computers & Education, 44*, 441-457.

Callebaut, W., & Gutman, D. R. (Eds.). (2005) *Modularity: Understanding the development and evolution of natural complex systems.* Cambridge, MA: The MIT Press.

Calvo, M. G., & Eysenck, M. W. (1996). Phonological working memory and reading in test anxiety. *Memory, 4*, 289-305.

Campbell, K. (2004). *E-ffective writing for e-learning environments.* Hershey, PA: Information Science Publishing.

Canter, D. Rivers, R., & Storrs, G. (1985). Characterising user navigation through complex data structures. *Behaviour and Information Technology, 4*(2), 93-102.

Cantor, J., & Engle, R. W. (1993). Working memory capacity as a long-term memory activation: An individual differences approach. *Journal of Experimental Psychology: Learning, Memory, and Cognition,* 19, 1101-1114.

Carroll, J. M. (1999) Five reasons for scenario-based design. In *Proceedings of the 32nd Hawaii International Conference on System Sciences.* IEEE CS Press.

Carvalho, V. (2003). *Conceitos básicos para o desenvolvimento de cursos multimedia.* SPI - sociedade portuguesa de inovacao.

Carver, C. A., Jr., Howard, R. A., & Lane, W. D. (1999). Enhancing student learning through hypermedia courseware and incorporation of student learning styles. *IEEE Transactions on Education, 42*(1), 33-38.

Carver, C. S., Scheier, M. F., & Weintraub, J. K. (1989). Assessing coping strategies: A theoretically based approach. *Journal of Personality and Social Psychology, 56*(2), 267-283.

Case, R. (1998). The development of conceptual structures. In D. Kuhn & R. S. Siegler (Eds.), *Handbook of child psychology: Vol. 2. Cognition, perception, and language.* (5th ed., pp. 745-796). New York: Wiley.

Caspi, A., Gorsky, P., & Chajut, E. (2003). The influence of group size on non-mandatory asynchronous instructional discussion groups. *The Internet and Higher Education, 6*, 227-240.

Cassady, J. C. (2004). The influence of cognitive test anxiety across the learning–testing cycle. *Learning and Instruction, 14*(6), 569-592.

Cassady, J. C., & Jonhson, R. E. (2002). Cognitive test anxiety and academic performance. *Contemporary Educational Psychology, 27*(2), 270-295.

Cassidy, S. (2004). Learning styles: An overview of theories, models, and measures. *Educational Psychology, 24*(4), 419-444.

Castells, M. (2000). *The Rise of the Network Society* (2nd ed.): Wiley-Blackwell.

Castells, M. (2003). *A galáxia da Internet: Reflexões sobre a Internet, os negócios e a sociedade* (M. L. X. de A. Borges, Trans.) Brasil: Jorge Zahar Editor.

Cavallo, D. (2000). Emergent designing and learning environments: Building on indigenous knowledge. *IBM Systems Journal, 39*(3/4). Retrieved November 13, 2008, from http://www.research.ibm.com/journal/sj/393/part2/cavallo.html

Cha, H. J., Kim, Y. S., Park, S. H., Yoon, T. B., Jung, Y. M., & Lee J. H. (2006). Learning styles diagnosis based on user interface behaviors for the customization of learning interfaces in an intelligent tutoring system. In *Procs. of the ITS 06.* Springer.

Chak, K., & Leung, L. (2004). Shyness and locus of control as predictors of Internet addiction and Internet use. *CyberPsychology & Behavior, 7*(5), 559-570.

Chan, C. K. K., & van Aalst, J. (2004). Learning, assessment and collaboration in computer-supported environments. In J. W. Strijbos, P. A. Kirschner, & R. L. Martens (Eds.), *Computer-supported collaborative learning: Vol 3. What we know about CSCL: And implementing it in higher education* (pp. 87-112). Boston, MA: Kluwer Academic Publishers.

Chang, C. (2001). Refining collaborative learning strategies for reducing the technical requirements of web-based classroom management. *Innovations in Education and Teaching International, 38*(2), 133-143.

Chang, K., Beck, J., Mostow, J., & Corbett, A. (2006, June 26-30). A Bayes Net toolkit for student modeling in intelligent tutoring systems. In *Proceedings of the 8ᵗʰ International Conference on Intelligent Tutoring Systems*, Jhongli, Taiwan. Retrieved November 12, 2008, from http://www.cs.cmu.edu/~listen/pdfs/ChangBeckMostowCorbett.2006.ITS.BNT-SM.pdf

Chen, G. D., Wang, C. Y., & Ou, K. L. (2003). Using group communication to monitor Web-based group learning. *Journal of Computer Assisted Learning, 19*, 401-415.

Chen, J. Q., Isberg, E., & Krechevesky, M. (2001). *Projeto spectrum atividades iniciais de aprendizagem* (Vol. 2) (Project Spectrum, early learning activities). Brasil: ARTMED.

Chen, L. S., Huang, T. S., Miyasato, T., & Nakatsu, R. (1998). Multimodal human emotion / expression recognition. In *Proceedings of International Conference on Automatic Face and Gesture Recognition*. Nara, Japan: IEEE Computer Society

Chen, S. (2002). A cognitive model for non-linear learning in hypermedia programmes. *British Journal of Educational Technology, 33*(4), 449-60.

Chen, S. Y., & Ford, N. (1998). Modelling user navigation behaviours in a hypermedia-based learning system: An individual differences approach. *Knowledge Organisation, 25* (3), 67-78.

Cheng, W., & Warren, M. (1997). Having second thoughts: Student perceptions before and after a peer assessment exercise. *Studies in Higher Education, 22*, 233-239.

Chi, M. T. H., Glaser, R., & Farr, M. J. (Eds.). (1988). *The nature of expertise*. London: Lawrence Erlbaum Associates.

Chibelushi, C.C., & Bourel, F. (2003). Facial expression recognition: A brief tutorial overview. In *CVonline: Online compendium of computer vision*.

Chieu, V. M., Milgrom, E., & Frenay, M. (2004). Constructivist learning: Operational criteria for cognitive flexibility. In *Proceedings of the IEEE International Conference on Advanced Learning Technologies (ICALT-04)* (pp. 221-225).

Child brain development. (2009). *Make your child smarter*. Retrieved January 12, 2009, from http://www.brainy-child.com/

Child, J., & Loveridge, R. (1990). *Information technology in European services-towards a microelectronic future*. Oxford, UK: Blackwell.

Chinien, C. A., & Boutin, F. (1992). Cognitive style FD/I: An important learning characteristic for educational technologies. *Journal of Educational Technology Systems, 21*(4), 303-311.

Chiu, C-M., Chiu, C-S., & Chang, H-C. (2007). Examining the integrated influence of fairness and quality on learning's satisfaction and Web-based learning continuance intention. *Information Systems Journal, 17*, 271-287.

Cho, H., Gay, G., Davidson, B., & Ingraffea, A. (2007). Social networks, communication styles, and learning performance in a CSCL community. Computers & Education, 49(2), 309-329.

Cho, H., Lee, J., Stefanone, M., & Gay, G. (2005). Development of computer-supported collaborative social networks in a distributed learning community. *Behaviour & Information Technology, 24*(6), 435-448.

Cho, H., Stefanone, M., & Gay, G. (2002). Social information sharing in a CSCL community. In G. Stahl (Ed.), *Computer Support for Collaborative Learning: Foundations for a CSCL Community (Proceedings of the 2002 CSCL conference)* (pp.43-53). Mahway, NJ: Lawrence Erlbaum Associates.

Cho, K., & Schunn, C. D. (2007). Scaffolded writing and rewriting in the discipline: A Web-based reciprocal peer review system. *Computers and Education, 48,* 409-426.

Chrysochoou, E. & Bablekou, Z. (submitted). Phonological loop and central executive contributions to oral comprehension skills of 5.5 to 9.5 years old children.

Chun, W. H. K. (2006). *Control and freedom: Power and paranoia in the age of fiber optics.* Cambridge, MA: MIT Press.

Churchland, P. (2004) *Matéria e consciência: Uma introdução contemporânea à filisofia da mente.* Brasil: Editora Unesp.

Clark, R. E. (1983). Reconsidering research on learning from media. *Review of Educational Research, 53,* 445-459.

Clarke, J. (2003). *Changing systems to personalize learning.* The Education Alliance at Brown University. Retrieved April 30, 2008, from http://www.alliance.brown.edu/pubs/changing_systems/introduction/introduction.pdf

Clore, G. & Ortony, A. (1999). Cognition in emotion: Always, sometimes, or never? In L. Nadel, R. Lane & G.L. Ahern (Eds.), *The cognitive neuroscience of emotion.* New York: Oxford University Press.

CNS. (2006). *Teorias, factores e processos de aprendizagem.* Companhia Nacional de Servicos.

Cobcroft, R. (2006). *Literature review into mobile learning in the university context.* Retrieved October 3, 2008, from http://eprints.qut.edu.au/archive/00004805/01/4805.pdf

Coffield, F. C., Moseley, D. V. M., Hall, E., & Ecclestone, K. (2004). *Learning styles and pedagogy in post-16 Learning: Findings of a systematic and critical review of learning styles models.* London: Learning and Skills Research Centre.

Cohen, D., & Prusak, L. (2001). *In good company: How social capital makes organizations work.* Boston, MA: Harvard Business Press.

Cohen, E. G. (1994). Restructuring the classroom: Conditions for productive small groups. *Review of Educational Research, 64,* 1-35.

Colby, K. M. (1963). Computer simulation of a neurotic process. In S. Tomkins S. & S. Messick (Eds.), *Computer simulation of personality* (pp. 165-179). New York: Wiley.

Collins, A., Brown, J. S., and Newman, S. E. (1989). Cognitive apprenticeship: Teaching the crafts of reading, writing, and mathematics. In L. Resnick (Ed.), *Knowing, learning, and instruction: Essays in honor of Robert Glaser.* (pp. 453-494). Hillsdale, NJ: Lawrence Erlbaum Associates.

Collis J. M., & Messick, S. (Eds.), (2001). *Intelligence and Personality: Bridging the gap in theory and measurement.* Mahwah S., NJ: Lawrence Erlbaum Associates.

Colson, R. (2007). *The fundamentals of digital art.* Singapore: AVA Academia.

Computer Clubhouse. (2008). Retrieved November 12, 2008, from http://www.computerclubhouse.org/

Conati, C., & McLaren, H. (2005). Data-driven refinement of a probabilistic model of user affect. In *Proceedings of the Tenth International Conference on User Modeling* (pp. 40-49). Edinburgh, Scotland

Conati, C., & Zhou., X. (2002). Modeling students' emotions from cognitive appraisal in educational games. In *Proceedings of the 6th International Conference on ITS.* Biarritz, France.

Conlan, C., Dagger, D., & Wade V. (2002). Towards a standards-based approach to e-learning personalization using reusable learning objects. In *Proceedings of E-Learn 2002.*

Conway, A.R.A. & Engle, R.W. (1994). Working memory and retrieval: A resource-dependent inhibition model. *Journal of Experimental Psychology: General, 123,* 354-73.

Conway, M. J. (1997) *Alice: Easy-to-learn 3D scripting for novices.* Unpublished doctoral dissertation. Retrieved

November 13, 2008, from http://www.alice.org/publications/ConwayDissertation.PDF

Cook, J. U. (1998). Lower achieving primary students' options on virtual reality. *Australian Educational Computing, 12*(2). Retrieved November 12, 2008, from http://www.acce.edu.au/journal/journals/vol12_2.pdf#search='Lower%20achieving%20primary%20students'%20options%20on%20virtual%20reality

Cook, J., & Smith, M. (2004). Beyond formal learning: Informal community elearning. *Computers and Education, 43*(1-2), 35-47.

Cook, K. S., & Emerson, R. M. (1978). Power, equity and commitment in exchange networks. *American Sociological Review, 43*, 721-739.

Coope, S., Dann, W., & Pausch, R. (2003). Teaching objects-first in introductory computer science. In *Proceedings of the SIGCSE 2003*. Retrieved November 13, 2008, from http://www.alice.org/publications/chialice.pdf

Cornish, K., Wilding, J., & Grant, C. (2006). Deconstructing working memory in developmental disorders of attention. In S.J. Pickering (Ed.), *Working memory and education* (pp. 157-88). Burlington, MA: Academic Press.

Corsi-Cabrera, M., Arce, C., Ramos, J., & Guevara, M. A. (1997). Effect of spatial ability and sex on inter- and intrahemispheric correlation of EEG activity. *Electroencephalography and Clinical Neurophysiology, 102*, 5-11.

Costa, P. T., & McCrae, R. R. (1992). Four ways five factors are basic. *Personality and Individual Differences, 1*(13), 653-665

Cotter, M., & Martins, H. (2006). Eficiência na construção de equipas colaborativas online. In A. Rocha (Ed.), *1 Conferência Iberica de Sistemas e Tecnologias da Informação (CISTI06)* (Vol. I, pp. 471-487). Universidade Fernando Pessoa.

Cowan, N. (1995). *Attention and memory: An integrated framework.* Oxford Psychology Series 26. New York: Oxford University Press.

Cowan, N. (1999). An embedded-process model of working memory. In A. Miyake & P. Shah (Eds.), *Models of working memory: Mechanisms of active maintenance and executive control* (pp. 62-101). Cambridge, UK: Cambridge University Press.

Cowan, N. (2001). The magical number 4 in short-term memory: A reconsideration of mental storage capacity. *Behavioral and Brain Sciences, 24*, 87-185.

Cowan, N. (2005). *Working memory capacity.* New York: Lawrence Erlbaum.

Cox, M., Webb, M., Abbott, C., Blakeley, B., Beauchamp, T., & Rhodes, V. (2003). ICT and pedagogy: A review of the research literature. *ICT in schools research and evaluation series – No.18.* Nottingham: DfES & BECTA.

Craik, F.I.M. & Lockhart, R.S. (1972). Levels of processing: A framework for memory research. *Journal of Verbal Learning and Verbal Behavior, 11*, 671-684.

Cronje, J. C. (2001). Metaphors and models in Internet-based learning. *Computers & Education, 37*, 241-256.

Crooks, T. J. (1988). The impact of classroom evaluation practices on students. *Review of Educational Research, 58*, 438-481.

Ćukušić, M., Granić, A., & Maršić, I. (2008). Launching an e-learning system in a school: Cross-European e-/m-learning platform UNITE: A case study. In J. Cordiero, J. Filipe, & S. Hammoudi (Eds.), *Proceedings of the Fourth International Conference on Web Information Systems and Technologies, Volume I: e-Learning, Internet Technology* (pp. 380-387). Portugal: INSTICC PRESS.

Ćukušić, M., Granić, A., Mifsud, C., & Zammit, M. (2008). *D 4.3: Pedagogical framework implementation report (final). UNITE report.* Retrieved May 07, 2008, from http://www.unite-ist.org

Ćukušić, M., Granić, A., Mifsud, C., Pagden, A., Walker, R., & Zammit, M. (2007). National and school specifics as a prerequisite for the successful design of an e-learning system: The UNITE approach. In B. Aurer & M. Bača (Eds.), *Proceedings of the 18th International Conference on Information and Intelligent Systems, IIS 2007* (pp. 85-92). Varaždin: FOI.

Ćukušić, M., MacRae, N., Zammit, M., Kellner, A., Pagden, A., Nikolova, N., et al. (2007). *D4.2: Pedagogical framework implementation report on UNITE-V1; UNITE teachers' handbook. UNITE report.* Retrieved May 07, 2008, from http://www.unite-ist.org

Culnan, M. J., & Markus, L. (1987). Information technologies: Electronic media and intraorganizational communication. In E. M. Jablin, L. L. Putnam, K. H. Roberts, & L. W. Porter (Eds.), *Handbook of organizational communication* (pp. 420-444). Beverly Hills, CA: Sage.

Cuninngham, S. (2007). *Computer graphics: Programming in OpenGL for visual communication.* Upper Saddle River, NJ: Pearson Prentice Hall.

Cunningham, S. (2008). Computer graphics in context: An approach to a first course in computer graphics. In *Educators Paper (abstracts), Proceedings of Siggraph 2008,* Singapura. Retrieved November 12, 2008, from http://www.siggraph.org/asia2008/attendees/edu/3.php

Curilem, G. M. J., & De Azevedo, F. M. (2003). Didactic ergonomy for the interface of intelligent tutoring systems. In *Computers and education: Toward a lifelong learning society* (pp. 75-88). Dordrecht: Kluwer Academic Publishers.

Curilem, S. G., Barbosa, A. R., & de Azevedo, F. M. (2007). Intelligent tutoring systems: Formalization as automata and interface design using neural networks. *Computers & Education, 49,* 545-561.

Curry, L. (1983). *An organization of learning styles theory and constructs.* Paper presented at the Annual Meeting of the American Educational Research Association, 67th, Montreal, Quebec.

Curry, L. (1983). *Learning styles in continuing media education.* Ottawa, Canada: Canadian Medical Association.

Dabbagh, N. (2008). *Web-based learning framework on mapping instructional strategies to Web features.* Retrieved January 13, 2009, from http://mason.gmu.edu/~ndabbagh/wblg/wblframework.html

Daft, R. L., & Lengel, R. H. (1986). Organizational information requirements. Media richness and structural design. *Management Science, 32,* 554-570.

Daneman, M. & Carpenter, P.A. (1980). Individual differences in working memory and reading. *Journal of Verbal Learning and Verbal Behavior, 19,* 450-66.

Daneman, M. & Tardif, T. (1987). Working memory and reading skills reexamined. In M. Coltheart (Ed.), *Attention and performance XII: The psychology of reading.* Hillsdale, NJ: Erlbaum.

Danili, E., & Reid, N. (2004). Some strategies to improve performance in school chemistry, based on two cognitive factors. Research in Science & Technology Education, 22(2), 203-226.

Daradoumis, T., Martinez-Monés, A., & Xhafa, F. (2004). An integrated approach for analysing and assessing the performance of virtual learning groups. In *Groupware: Design, implementation and use* (LNCS 3198, pp. 289-304). Springer.

Data warehousing. (2009). Retrieved January 17, 2009, from http://kiwitobes.com/wiki/Data_warehouse.html

Davies, P. (2006). Peer assessment: Judging the quality of students' work by comments rather than marks. *Innovations in Education and Teaching International, 43,* 69-82.

De Bra, P., & Calvi, L. (1998). AHA: A generic adaptive hypermedia system. In *Proceedings of the 2nd Workshop on Adaptive Hypertext and Hypermedia, HYPERTEXT'98,* Pittsburgh, USA.

De Bra, P., Aroyo, L., & Chepegin, V. (2004). The next big thing: Adaptive Web-based systems. *Journal of Digital Information, 5*(1).

De Bra, P., Houben, G.-J., & Wu, H. (1999). AHAM: A dexter-based reference model for adaptive hypermedia. In *Proceedings of the 10th ACM conference on Hypertext and Hypermedia* (pp. 147-156), Darmstadt.

De Freitas, S., & Yapp, C. (Eds.) (2005). *Personalizing learning in the 21st century.* Stafford: Network Educational Press.

De Marsico, M., Kimani, S., Mirabella, V., Norman, K. N., & Catarci, T. (2006). A proposal toward the development of accessible e-learning content by human involvement. *Universal Access in Information Society, 5.* 150-169

De Renzi, E. & Nichelli, P. (1975). Verbal and non-verbal short-term memory impairment following hemispheric damage. *Cortex, 11,* 341-53.

Dede, C. (1999). *Emerging influences of information technology on school curriculum.* Retrieved January 13, 2009, from http://www.virtual.gmu.edu/ss_pdf/DedeJCS.pdf

Dede, C. (2000). *The role of emerging technologies for knowledge mobilization, dissemination, and use in education-draft report.* Retrieved November 22, 2008, from http://www.virtual.gmu.edu/ss_pdf/knowlmob.pdf

Dede, C., & Palumbo, D. (1991). Implications of hypermedia for cognition and communication. *Impact Assessment Bulletin, 9*(1-2), 15-28. Retrieved November 22, 2008, from http://www.virtual.gmu.edu/ss_pdf/hyper.pdf

Dede, C., Salzman, M., Loftin, R. B., & Ash, K. (1997). Using virtual reality technology to convey abstract scientific concepts. In M. J. Jacobson & R. B. Kozma (Eds.), *Learning the sciences of the 21ˢᵗ century: Research, design, and implementing advanced technology learning environments.* Hillsdale, NJ: Lawrence Erlbaum. Retrieved November 12, 2008, from http://www.virtual.gmu.edu/ss_pdf/jacobson.pdf

Dee-Lucas, D., & Larkin, J. H. (1995). Learning from electronic texts: Effects of interactive overviews for information access. *Cognition and instruction, 13,* 431-468.

Dehn, M.J. (2008). *Working memory and academic learning: Assessment and intervention.* Hoboken, NJ: Wiley.

Del Nero, H. S. (1997). *O sítio da mente: Pensamento, emoção e vontade no cérebro humano.* Collegium Cognitio, Brasil. Retrieved January 12, 2009, from http://cognitio.incubadora.fapesp.br/portal/producao/livros/sitio%20mente

Delfino, M., & Manca, S. (2007). The expression of social presence through the use of figurative language in a Web-based learning environment. *Computers in Human Behavior, 23,* 2190-2211.

Delfino, M., & Persico, D. (2007). Online or face-to-face? Experimenting with different techniques in teacher training. *Journal of Computer Assisted Learning, 23,* 351-365.

Della Salla, S. & Logie, R.H. (2002). Neuropsychological impairments of visual and spatial working memory. In A.D. Baddeley, M.D. Kopelman & B.A. Wilson (Eds.), *Handbook of memory disorders* (pp. 271-92). Chichester: Wiley.

Dellaert, F., Polzin, T., & Waibel, A. (1996). Recognizing emotion in speech. In *Proceedings of ICSLP 1996* (pp. 1970-1973). Philadelphia, PA.

Demetriou, A., (2000). Organization and development of self-understanding and self-regulation: Toward a general theory. In M. Boekaerts, P. R. Pintrich, & M. Zeidner (Eds.), *Handbook of self-regulation* (pp. 209-251). Academic Press.

Demetriou, A., Christou, C., Spanoudis, G., & Platsidou, M. (2002). The development of mental processing: Efficiency, working memory, and thinking. *Monographs of the Society for Research in Child Development, 67*(1), 1-155.

Demetriou, A., Efklides, A., & Platsidou, M. (1993). *The architecture and dynamics of developing mind: Experiential structuralism as a frame for unifying cognitive development theories* (Monographs of the Society for Research in Child Development). Chicago, IL: University of Chicago Press.

Demo, P. (2008). *Novas tecnologias: Novas?* Retrieved February 12, 2009, from http://pedrodemo.sites.uol.com.br/textos/novasnovas.html

Demo, P. (2008). *Novas, multi-alfabetizações.* Retrieved February 13, 2009, from http://pedrodemo.sites.uol.com.br/textos/enilton.html

Demo, P. (2009). *Não vemos as coisas como são, mas como somos*. Retrieved February 13, 2009, from http://pedrodemo.sites.uol.com.br/textos/comosomos.html

Demo, P. (2009). *Professor: Profissional da aprendizagem*. Retrieved February 13, 2009, from http://pedrodemo. sites.uol.com.br/textos/ppa.html

DEMOS (2005). About learning: The report of the Working Group. *DEMOS Report*. London: DEMOS. Retrieved May, 13, 2006, from http://www.demos.co.uk.

Dempster, F. N., & Brainerd, C. J. (Eds) (1995). *Interference and inhibition in cognition*. New York: Academic Press.

Derntl, M., & Motschnig-Pitrik, R. (2005). The role of structure, patterns, and people in blended learning. *The Internet and Higher Education, 8*(2), 111-130.

DeStefano, D., & Lefevre, J. (2007). Cognitive load in hypertext reading: A review. *Computers in Human Behavior, 23*(3), 1616-1641.

Dewey, J. (1959). *Dewey on education*. New York: Bureau of Publications, Teachers College, Columbia University Press.

Dewey, J. (1963). *Experience and education*. New York: Collier

Dewey, J. (1966). *Democracy and education*. New York: Free Press.

DfES (2006). 2020 vision. *Report of the Teaching and Learning in 2020 Review Group*. Nottingham: DfES.

Dias, P. (2004). Processos de aprendizagem colaborativa nas comunidades online. In A. Dias & M. J. Gomes (Eds.), *Learning para E-Formadores (2004)* (pp. 19-31). Guimarães: TecMinho.

Dicheva, D., & Aroyo, L. (2002). Concept-based course-ware authoring: An engineering perspective. In *ICALT'2002*.

Dick, W., & Lou, C. (1996). *The systematic design of instruction*. Harper Collins College Publishers.

Dietinger, T., Gütl, C., Maurer, H., Pivec, M., & Schmaranz, K. (1998). Intelligent knowledge gathering and management as new ways of an improved learning process. In *Proceedings of the WebNet 98 - World Conference of the WWW* (pp. 244-249). Charlottesville, USA: AACE.

Dietz, S., Besser, H., Borda, A., Geber, K., & Lévy, P. (2005). *Virtual museum of (Canada) - Canadian virtual museum*. Retrieved November 16, 2008, from http://www.virtualmuseum.ca

Dietz-Uhler, B., & Bishop-Clark, C. (2005) Formation of and adherence to a self-disclosure norm in an online chat. *CyberPsychology & Behavior, 8*(2), 114-120.

Dillenbourg, P. (2002). Over-scripting CSCL: The risks of blending collaborative learning with instructional design. In P. A. Kirschner (Ed.), *Three worlds of CSCL. Can we support CSCL* (pp. 61-91). Heerlen, The Netherlands: Open University Nederland.

Dillenbourg, P. (Ed.). (1999). *Collaborative learning: Cognitive and computational approaches*. Oxford, UK: Pergamon/Elsevier.

Dimitracopoulou, A., & Petrou, A. (2005). Advanced collaborative distance learning systems for young students: Design issues and current trends on new cognitive and meta-cognitive tools. *THEMES in Education International Journal*.

Dipert, R. (1998). *The nature and structure of emotions* (draft). US Military Academy.

diSessa, A. A., Hoyles, C., Noss, R., & Edwards, L. D. (1995). Computers and exploratory learning: Setting the scene. In A. A. diSessa, C. Hoyles, R. Noss, & L. D. Edwards (Eds.), Computers and exploratory learning (pp. 1-12). New York: Springer.

Divaharan, S., & Atputhasamy, L. (2002). An attempt to enhance the quality of cooperative learning through peer assessment. *Journal of Educational Enquiry, 3*(2), 72-83.

Dix, A., Finlay, J., Abowd, G., & Beale, R. (2004). *Human-computer interaction* (3rd ed.). London: Prentice Hall.

Dochy, F., Segers, M., & Sluijsmans, D. (1999). The use of self-, peer and co-assessment in higher education: A review. *Studies in Higher Education, 24*, 331-350.

Dochy, F., Segers, M., Van Den Bossche, P., & Gijbels, D. (2003). Effects of problem-based learning: A meta-analysis. *Learning and Instruction, 13*, 533-568.

Doman, G., & Doman, J. (2007). *Como multiplicar a inteligência do seu bebê: Mais suave revolução* (5th ed., L. V. Norton, Trans.). Brasil: Artes e Ofícios.

Doman, J. (2009). *Facilitated communication.* Retrieved January 9, 2009, from http://www.iahp.org/Facilitated-Communicat.293.0.html

Dondi, C. (2006). *What inhibits the implementation of innovation strategies in European lifelong learning?* Retrieved May 07, 2008, from www.elearningeuropa.info

Donis, A. D. (2007). *Sintaxe da linguagem visual* (A primer of visual literacy) (J. L. Camargo, Trans.). Brasil: WMF Martins Fontes.

Dougiamas, M., & Taylor, P. (2003). Moodle: Using learning communities to create an open source course management system. In D. Lassner & C. McNaught (Eds.), *Proceedings of the World Conference on Educational Multimedia, Hypermedia and Telecommunications 2003* (pp. 171-178). Chesapeake, VA: AACE.

Douglas, G., & Riding, R. J. (1993). The effect of pupil cognitive style and position of prose passage title on recall. *Educational Psychology, 13*, 385-393.

Douglas-Cowie, E., Cowie, R., & Schroder, M. (2000). *A new emotion database Considerations, sources and scope.* Paper presented at the ISCA Workshop on Speech and Emotion: A conceptual framework for research.

Driscoll, M. P. (2002). *How people learn (and what technology might have to do with it)* (ERIC Digest). (ERIC Document Reproduction Service No. ED470032). Retrieved May 11, 2008, from http://www.eric.ed.gov/ERICWebPortal/contentdelivery/servlet/ERICServlet?accno=ED470032

Ducatel, K., Bogdanowicz, M., Scapolo, F., Leijten, J., & Burgelman, J. C. (Eds.). (2001). *Scenarios for ambient intelligence in 2010: Final report.* IPTS-Seville. Retrieved November 12, 2008, from ftp://ftp.cordis.europa.eu/pub/ist/docs/istagscenarios2010.pdf

Duffy, T., & Kirkley, J. (2004). Introduction: Theory and practice in distance education. In T. Duffy & J. Kirkley (Eds.), *Learner-centered: Theory and practice in distance education - cases from higher education.* Mahway, NJ: Lawrence Erlbaum Associates.

Dufva, M., Niemi, P., & Voeten, M. J.M. (2001). The role of phonological memory, word recognition, and comprehension skills in reading development: From preschool to grade 2. *Reading and Writing, 14* (1-2), 91-117.

Dunn, R., & Dunn, K. (1989). *Learning style inventory.* Lawrence, KS: Price Systems.

Dunn, R., & Dunn, K. (1992). *Teaching secondary students through their individual learning styles.* Needham Heights, MA: Allyn and Bacon.

Dunn, R., & Dunn, K. (1999). *The complete guide to the learning styles inservice system.* Boston, MA: Allyn & Bacon.

Dünser, A. (2008). Supporting low ability readers with interactive augmented reality. In *Annual review of cyber therapy and telemedicine: Changing the face of healthcare* (pp. 41-48). San Diego, CA: Interactive Media Institute. Retrieved November 12, 2008, from http://www.hitlabnz.org/publications/2008-SupportingLowAbilityReadersWithInteractiveAugmentedReality.pdf

Durlach, N., & Mavor, A. S. (Eds.). (1994). *Virtual reality: Scientific and technological challenges.* USA: National Academic Press.

Dzbor, M., Stutt, A., Motta, E., & Collins, T. (2007). Representations for semantic learning Webs: Semantic Web technology in learning support. *Journal of Computer Assisted Learning, 23*, 69-82.

Egan, D. (1988). Individual differences in human-computer interaction. In M. Helander (Ed.), *Handbook of human-computer interaction* (pp. 543-568). Elsevier Science B.V. Publishers North-Holland.

Einstein, A. (1934). On the method of theoretical physics. *Philosophy of Science, 1*(2) 163-169.

Eklund, J., & Sinclair, K. (2000). An empirical appraisal of the effectiveness of adaptive interfaces of instructional systems. *Educational Technology and Society, 3*(4), 165-177.

Ekman, P. (1992). An argument for basic emotions. *Cognition and Emotion, 6,* 169-200.

Ekman, P. (1999). Facial expressions. In T. Dalgleish & T. Power (Eds.), *The handbook of cognition and emotion* (pp. 301-320). Sussex, UK: John Wiley & Sons.

Ekman, P., & Rosenberg, E. L. (1997). *What the face reveals: Basic and applied studies of spontaneous expression using the facial action coding system (FACS).* New York: Oxford University Press.

Elementary School. (2008). *Elementary school Spinut, Split, Croatia.* Retrieved May 07, 2008, from http://www.os-spinut-st.skole.hr

Elliman, N. A., Green, M. W., Rogers, P. J., & Finch, G. M. (1997). Processing efficiency theory and the working memory system: Impairments associated with sub-clinical anxiety. *Personality and Individual Differences, 23,* 31-35.

Elliot, C., Rickel, J., & Lester, J. (1999). Lifelike pedagogical agents and affective computing: an exploratory synthesis. In M. Wooldridge & M. Veloso (Eds.) (LNAI 1600, pp. 195-212).

Elliott, C. D. (1992). *The affective reasoner: A process model of emotions in a multiagent system.* PhD thesis, Northwestern University, Evanston, Illinois

Ellis, A. E. (2003). Personality type and participation in networked learning environments. *Education Media International, 40*(1/2), 101-114.

Ellis, D., Ford, N., & Wood, F (1992). Hypertext and learning styles. *Final Report of a Project funded by the Learning Technology Unit.* Sheffield: Employment Department.

ELT. (2008). *CTE introduction experiential learning.* Retrieved November 16, 2008, from www.usoe.k12.ut.us/ate/tlc/cda/experiential.htm

Embretson, S. E. (1998). A cognitive design system approach to generating valid tests: Application to abstract reasoning. *Psychological Methods, 3,* 380-396.

Emirbayer, M., & Goodwin, J. (1994). Network analysis, culture, and the problem of agency. *American Journal of Sociology, 99,* 1411-1454.

Encyclopedic Knowledge. (2009). *How to give your child encyclopedic knowledge.* Retrieved January 12, 2009, from http://www.brainy-child.com/article/encyclopedic.html

Engeström, Y. (1987). *Learning by expanding: An activity-theoretical approach to developmental research.* Helsinki, Finland: Orienta-Konsultit Oy.

Engestrom, Y. (2001). Expansive learning at work: Toward an activity theoretical reconceptualization. *Journal of Education and Work, 14*(1), 133-156.

Engle, R. W., Cantor, J., & Carullo, J. J. (1992). Individual differences in working memory and comprehension: A test of four hypotheses. *Journal of Experimental Psychology: Learning, Memory, and Cognition, 18,* 976-992.

Engle, R.W. (2002). Working memory capacity as executive attention. *Current Directions in Psychological Science, 11*(1), 19-23.

Engle, R.W., Kane, M.J., & Tuholski, S.W. (1999). Individual differences in working memory capacity and what they tell us about controlled attention, general fluid intelligence and functions of the prefrontal cortex. In A. Miyake & P. Shah (Eds.), *Models of working memory: Mechanisms of active maintenance and executive control* (pp. 102-34). Cambridge, UK: Cambridge University Press.

English School. (2008). *The English school, Nicosia, Cyprus.* Retrieved May 07, 2008, from http://www.englishschool.ac.cy

Ericsson, K.A. & Kintsch, W. (1995). Long-term working memory. *Psychological Review, 102,* 211-45.

Erskine, J. A., Leenders M. R., & Maufette-Leenders, L. A. (1997). *Learning with cases*. London: Ivey Publishing.

Essa, I. & Pentland, A. (1997). Coding, analysis, interpretation and recognition of facial expressions. *IEEE Transactions on Pattern Analysis and Machine Intelligence, 19*(7), 757-763.

Estação Ciência. (2009). *Ciência à mão*. Retrieved January 11, 2009, from http://www.eciencia.usp.br/atividades/index.html

EU. (2004). *Distance learning and elearning in European policy and practice: The vision and the reality.* Retrieved April, from http://www.odl-liaison.org/pages.php?PN=policy-paper_2004

European Commision. (2007). *Communication from the Commission to the Council, the European Parliament, the European Economic and Social Committee and the Committee of the Regions: Delivering lifelong learning for knowledge, creativity and innovation. Draft 2008 joint progress report of the Council and the Commission on the implementation of the education and training 2010 work programme* (SEC(2007) 1484 /* COM/2007/0703 final */). Retrieved May 07, 2008, from http://eur-lex.europa.eu/LexUriServ/LexUriServ.do?uri=CELEX:52007DC0703:EN:HTML

European Commission. (2001). *Communication from the Commission to the Council and the European Parliament, The elearning action plan - designing tomorrow's education, Brussels, 2001.* Retrieved May 07, 2008, from http://eur-lex.europa.eu

European Commission. (2005). *Proposal for a recommendation of the European Parliament and of the Council on key competences for lifelong learning, Brussels, 2005.* Retrieved May 07, 2008, from http://eur-lex.europa.eu

Evaluation methods – Wikipedia. (2008). Retrieved November 12, 2008, from http://en.wikipedia.org/wiki/Evaluation_methods

Evans, D., & Taylor, J. (2005). The role of user scenarios as the central piece of the development jigsaw puzzle. In J. Attewell & C. Savill-Smith (Eds.), *Mobile learning anytime everywhere*. London: Learning and Skills Development Agency.

Everson, H.T. & Tobias, S. (1998). The ability to estimate knowledge and performance in college. *Instructional Science, 26*, 65-79.

Eysenck, H. J., & Eysenck, M. W. (1985). *Personality and individual differences: A natural science approach.* New York: Plenum.

Eysenck, H. Y., & Eysenck, S. B. G. (1964). *Manual of the Eysenck personality inventory*. San Diego: Educational and Industrial Testing Service.

Eysenck, M. W. (1992). *Anxiety: The cognitive perspective*. Hove: Lawrence Erlbaum Associates.

Eysenck, M. W., & Keane, M. T. (2005). *Cognitive psychology*. (5th ed.). New York: Psychology Press.

Eysenck, M., & Flanagan, C. (2001). *Psychology for A2 level*. Psychology Press.

Fagerberg, J. (2006). Innovation: A guide line to literature. In J. Fagerberg, D. C. Mowery, & R. R. Nelson (Eds.), *The Oxford handbook of innovation* (pp. 2-3). New York: Oxford University Press.

Faivre, J., Nkambou, R., & Frasson, C. (2002) Integrating adaptive emotional agents in ITS. In *Workshop of Architectures and Methodologies for Building Agent-Based Learning Environments* (In conjunction with ITS 2002 Conference) (pp. 1-7).

Falcao, A. (2006). *Teorias, factores e processos de aprendizagem*. ENA (Escola de Negocios e Administracao).

Falchikov, N., & Goldfinch, J. (2000). Student peer assessment in higher education: A meta-analysis comparing peer and teacher marks. *Review of Educational Research, 70*, 287-322.

Fanderclai, T. L. (1995). MUDs in education: New environments, new pedagogies. *Computer-Mediated Communication Magazine, 2*(8).

Fantuzzo, J. W., Riggio, R. E., Connelly, S., & Dimeff, L. A. (1989). Effects of reciprocal peer tutoring of academic achievement and psychological adjustment:

A component analysis. *Journal or Educational Psychology, 81,* 173-177.

Farrand, P. & Jones, D.M. (1996). Direction of report in spatial and verbal short-term memory. *Quarterly Journal of Experimental Psychology, 49A*, 140-58.

Fasel, B. & Luettin, J. (2003). Automatic facial expression analysis: A survey. *Pattern Recognition, 36,* 259-275.

Febrace. (2008). *Acontece, spaceship.* Retrieved November 12, 2008, from http://www.lsi.usp.br/febrace/imprensa/acontece/news0008/02sabia.html

Febrace. (2009). *Feira brasileira de ciências e engenharia criatividade e inovação.* Retrieved April 3, 2009, from http://www.lsi.usp.br/febrace/

Federico, P. (2000). Learning styles and student attitudes toward various aspects of network-based instruction. *Computers in Human Behavior, 16*(4), 359-379.

Feenberg, A. (1989). The written world: On the theory and practice of computer conferencing. In R. Mason & A. R. Kaye (Eds.), *Mindweave: Communication, computers and distance education.* Oxford, UK: Pergamon Press.

Felder, R. M., & Silverman, L. K. (1988). Learning and teaching styles in engineering education. *Engineering Education, 78*(7). Retrieved from http://www4.ncsu.edu/unity/lockers/users/f/felder/public/Papers/LS-1988.pdf

Felder, R. M., & Silverman, L. K. (1988). Learning and teaching styles in engineering education. *Engineering Education, 78,* 674-681.

Felder, R., & Brent, R. (2006). *Effective teaching: A workshop.* University of Aveiro.

Fernandez, R., & Picard, R. (2003). Modeling drivers' speech under stress. *Speech Comm., 40,* 145-159.

Ferrari, M., & Sternberg, J. J. (1998). The development of mental abilities and styles. In W. Damon, D. Kuhn, & R. S. Siegler (Eds.), *Handbook of child psychology* (Vol. 2) (pp. 899-946). New York: John Wiley & Sons.

Ficheman, I. K., & Lopes, R. D. (2008). Mobility in digital learning ecosystems. In *Proceedings of the IADIS In-ternational Conference Mobile Learning 2008*, Algarve, Portugal (pp. 19-26).

Ficheman, I. K., Saul, J. A., Assis, G. A., Correa, A. G. D., Franco, J. F., Tori, R., & Lopes, R. D. (2008). Combining augmented reality with mobile technologies to enrich learning experiences. In *Proceedings of the IADIS International Conference Mobile Learning 2008,* Algarve, Portugal (pp. 191-195).

Fink, D. (2005). Growing into it. In NCSL (Ed.), *Leading personalised learning in schools* (pp. 13-22). Nottingham: National College of School Leadership.

Fiorina, L., Antonietti, A., Colombo, B., & Bartolomeo A. (2007). Thinking style, browsing primes and hypermedia navigation. *Computers & Education, 49,* 916-941.

Fischer, F., Kollar, I., Mandl, H., & Haake, J. M. (Eds.). (2007). *Scripting computer-supported collaborative learning: Cognitive, computational and educational perspectives.* New York: Springer.

Fischer, G., & Scharff, E. (1998). Learning technologies in support of self-directed learning. *Journal of Interactive Media in Education,* 98(4) Retrieved April 8, 2008, from http://www-jime.open.ac.uk/98/4

Fishbein, M., & Azjen, I. (1975). *Belief, attitude, intention, and behavior: An introduction to theory and research.* Reading, MA: Addison-Weasley.

Flanagan, M., & Perlin, K. (2008). *Rapunzel project.* Retrieved November 12, 2008, from http://www.mary-flanagan.com/rapunsel/about.htm

Flavell, J. H. (1992). Cognitive development: past, present, and future. *Developmental Psychology, 28,* 998-1005.

Flavell, J. H., Miller, P. H., & Miller, S. A. (2004). *Cognitive development.* (4th Ed.). NJ: Prentice Hall.

Flemming, N. D. (1995). I am different; not dumb. Modes of presentation (V.A.R.K.) in the tertiary classroom. In A. Zelmer (Ed.), *Research and development in higher education. Proceedings of the 1995 annual conference of the higher education and research development society of Australia (HERDSA)* (Vol. 18, pp. 308-313).

Flexer, B. K., & Roberge, J. J. (1980). IQ, field-dependence-independence, and the development of formal operational thought. *Journal of General Psychology, 103*, 191-201.

Fodor, J. – Wikipedia. (2009). Retrieved February 13, 2009, from http://en.wikipedia.org/wiki/Jerry_Fodor

Foley, J. D., Dam, A. V., Feiner, S. K., & Hughes, J. (1993). *Computer graphics principles and practice* (2ⁿᵈ ed.). New York: Addison-Wesley.

Ford, N. (2000). Cognitive styles and virtual environments. *Journal of the American Society for Information Science, 51*(6), 543-57.

Forrester, J. W. (1992). *System dynamics and learner-centered-learning in kindergarten through 12ᵗʰ grade education.* Retrieved November 12, 2008, from http://sysdyn.clexchange.org/sdep/Roadmaps/RM1/D-4337.pdf

Forrester, J. W. (1994). *Learning through systems dynamics as a preparation for 21ˢᵗ century.* Retrieved November 12, 2008, from http://sysdyn.clexchange.org/sdep/papers/D-4434-3.pdf

Forrester, J. W. (1996). *Systems dynamics and k-12 teachers.* Retrieved November 12, 2008, from http://sysdyn.clexchange.org/sdep/papers/D-4665-4.pdf

Fox, J. (1980). Making decisions under the influence of memory. *Psychological Review, 87*, 190-211.

Fox, J., & Cooper, R. (1997). Cognitive processing and knowledge representation in decision making under uncertainty. In R. W. Scholz & A. C. Zimmer (Eds.), *Qualitative theories of decision making* (pp. 83-106). Lengerich, Germany: Pabst.

Franco, J. F, Ficheman, I. K., Venâncio, V., Moreno, M., Freitas, M. G. S., Leite, A. L. B. F., Franco, N. F., Matias, M. A., & Lopes, R. D. (2008c). Using virtual reality and Web-based technologies for improving individuals' education. In *Proceedings of the 11ᵗʰ International Conference on Experiential Learning, ICEL 2008, Identity of Experience, Challenges for experiential learning,* Sydney, Australia.

Franco, J. F. (2000). Multimedia in action: Applying 3D environments at school teaching, using VRML for an interactive, dynamic and high quality education. In *GEMISIS conference digest* (UK, ed.). The University of Salford and GEMISIS.

Franco, J. F. (2001). Developing skills teaching and learning using Web standards and interactive 3D virtual environments and multimedia tools. In *Proceedings of the 20ᵗʰ World Conference on Open Learning and Distance Education,* Düsseldorf, Germany. Retrieved November 12, 2008, from http://web.archive.org/web/20050526211138/http://www.educorp.futuro.usp.br/publicacoes/Developing+Skills.doc

Franco, J. F. (2001). *Lifelike intelligent agents telling me a story in a virtual environment.* Unpublished doctoral dissertation, The University of Salford, UK.

Franco, J. F. (2005). *Projeto escrita digital criativa.* January 12, 2009, from http://cognitio.incubadora.fapesp.br/portal/atividades/cursos/posgrad/jogos_eletronicos/2005/trabalhos/Jorge/TM_EscritaDigital.pdf/view

Franco, J. F. (2005). *Projeto escrita digital criativa (creative digital scribe project).* Retrieved November 12, 2008, from http://cognitio.incubadora.fapesp.br/portal/atividades/cursos/posgrad/jogos_eletronicos/2005/trabalhos/Jorge/TM_EscritaDigital.pdf

Franco, J. F., & Lopes, R. D. (2004). Novas tecnologias em ambientes de aprendizagem: Estimulando o aprender a aprender, transformando o currículo e ações. In *Proceedings of the Cinted Revista Renote, III Ciclo de Palestras sobre Novas Tecnologias na Educação.* Retrieved January 12, 2009, from http://www.cinted.ufrgs.br/ciclo3/af/39-novastecnologias.pdf

Franco, J. F., & Lopes, R. D. (2002). From children to adults: Improving education through virtual environments technologies. In *Proceedings of the 5ᵗʰ IASTED International Conference Computers and Advanced Technology in Education,* Cancun, Mexico.

Franco, J. F., & Lopes, R. D. (2005b). Knowledge development through collaborative work supported by interactive technologies. In R. Luckin (Ed.), *Representing and analyzing collaborative interactions: What works? When does is work? To what extent? Proceedings of the 12th International Conference on Artificial Intelligence in Education, AIED Workshop 6,* Holland, Amsterdam (pp. 49-58). Retrieved November 12, 2008, from http://hcs.science.uva.nl/AIED2005/W6proc.pdf

Franco, J. F., & Lopes, R. D. (2005c). Converging interactive media, arts and culture at basic education as support for enhancing individuals' literacy. In *FILE, Electronic International Language Festival.* Retrieved November 16, 2008, from http://www.file.org.br/file2005/textos/symposium/eng/jorgefrancolopes.doc

Franco, J. F., & Lopes, R. D. (2005d). Learning to learn from basic to higher education using digital and interactive graphics tools. In *Proceedings of the IPSI – 2005 FRANCE Conference,* Carcassonne, France. Retrieved February 13, 2009, from http://internetconferences.net/france2006/BookOfAbstracts.doc

Franco, J. F., & Lopes, R. D. (2008). Developing 3D virtual environments supported by Web-based and virtual reality technology as well as low cost multimedia files. In *Proceedings of 11th International Conference on Experiential Learning, ICEL 2008, Identity of Experience, Challenges for experiential learning.*

Franco, J. F., Cruz, S. R. R., & Lopes, R. D. (2006). Computer graphics, interactive technologies and collaborative learning synergy supporting individuals' skills development. In *Proceedings of the 33 International Conference And Exhibition on Computer Graphics and Interactive Techniques, SIGGRAPH 2006,* Boston, MA. Retrieved November 12, 2008, from http://delivery.acm.org/10.1145/1180000/1179338/p42-franco.pdf?key1=1179338&key2=0205817711&coll=&dl=ACM&CFID=15151515&CFTOKEN=6184618G

Franco, J. F., Cruz, S. R. R., Aquino, E. M. M., Teles, E. O., Gianevechio, M. M., Franco, N. F., Ficheman, I. K., & Lopes, R. D. (2007). Using information visualization in the logic of building an interactive knowledge based learning network for social development. In *Proceedings of the Congress of Logic Applied to Technology–LAPTEC'2007,* Santos, São Paulo, Brazil.

Franco, J. F., Cruz, S. R. R., Franco, N. F., & Lopes, R. D. (2007). Experiências de uso de mídias interativas como suporte para autoria e construção colaborativa do conhecimento. In *RENOTE - revista novas tecnologias na educação, ix ciclo de palestras novas tecnologias na educação* (Vol. 5). Retrieved December 4, 2008, from http://www.cinted.ufrgs.br/ciclo9/artigos/2cJorge.pdf

Franco, J. F., Ficheman, I. K., Alves, A. C., Venâncio, V., Lopes, R. D., Cruz, S. R. R., Santiago, M., Teles, E. O., & Aquino, E. M. M. (2007). Desenvolvendo uma experiência educacional interativa usando recursos de visualização de informação e de computação móvel como estímulo à construção colaborativa e continuada de conhecimento. In *Proceedings of the Cinted Revista Renote, Dezembro/2007 - Vol. 5 N°2 - X Ciclo de Palestras Novas Tecnologias na Educação.* Retrieved March 23, 2009, from http://www.cinted.ufrgs.br/renote/dez2007/artigos/5cJorgeFranco.pdf

Franco, J. F., Ficheman, I. K., Assis, G. A., Zuffo, M. K., Lopes, R. de D., Moreno, M., & Freitas, M. G. da S. (2008). Using virtual reality, computer graphics and Web-based technology for developing knowledge and improving k-12 education, In *Proceedings of the IADIS Multi Conference on Computer Science and Information Systems (MCCSIS 2008),* Amsterdam, The Netherlands (pp. 115-138).

Franco, J. F., Ficheman, I. K., Lopes, R. D., Ferreira, A. L. S., Santos M. E. S. B., Ferreira, G., Araújo, V. R. S., & Moreno, M. (2008). Empowering an educational community through using multimedia tools in combination with mobile learning actions. In *Proceedings of the IADIS International Conference Mobile Learning 2008,* Algarve, Portugal (pp. 221–226).

Franco, J. F., Mariz L. R., Lopes, R. D., Cruz, S. R. R., Franco, N. F., & Delacroix, E. (2007). Developing individuals' cognition, literacy skills and collaborative teaching and learning attitudes through the combination of Web based technology, multimedia tools and files. *Psychology and Scientific Education Magazine, 1*(1), 3-52.

Franco, N. F., Stori, N., Lopes, R. D., & Franco, J. F. (2005). Um caso de construção colaborativa de conhecimento e desenvolvimento educacional interdisciplinar com mediação das tecnologias da informação e da comunicação. In *Proceedings of the Revista RENOTE, Vol. 3, Nº2, VI Ciclo de Palestras Novas Tecnologias na Educação.* Retrieved November 12, 2008, from http://www.cinted.ufrgs.br/renote/nov2005/artigosrenote/a49_cintednovembro.pdf

Frederiksen, N. (1984). The real test bias: Influences of testing on teaching and learning. *American Psychologist, 3*, 193-202.

Freeman, L. C. (1979). Centrality in social networks, conceptual clarification. *Social Networks, 1*, 215-239.

Freeman, M. A., & Capper, J. M. (1999). Exploiting the Web for education: An anonymous asynchronous role simulation. *Australian Journal of Educational Technology, 15*, 95-116.

Freeman, M., & McKenzie, J. (2002). SPARK, a confidential Web-based template for self and peer assessment of student team work: Benefits of evaluating across different subjects. *British Journal of Educational Technology, 33*, 551-569.

Freire, P. (2004). *Pedagogia da autonomia: Saberes necessários a prática educativa.* Paz e Terra, Brasil: 29º edição.

Frijda, N. (1994). Varieties of affect: Emotions and episodes, moods, and sentiments. In P. Ekman & R.J. Davidson (Ed.), *The nature of emotion.* New York: Oxford University Press.

Fullan, M. (2005). *Professional learning communities writ large.* Retrieved November 12, 2008, from http://www.michaelfullan.ca/Articles_05/UK_Ireland_preread_final.pdf

Fullan, M. (2008). *Reach every student: Energizing Ontario education.* Retrieved November 12, 2008, from http://www.michaelfullan.ca/Articles_08/EnergizingFull.pdf

Furnham, A. (2001). Test-taking style, personality traits and psychometric validity. In J. M. Collis & S. Messick (Eds.), *Intelligence and personality: Bridging the gap in theory and measurement* (pp. 289-304). Mahwah, NJ: Lawrence Erlbaum Associates.

Fussell, S. R., & Benimoff, I. (1995). Social and cognitive processes in interpersonal communication: Implications for advanced telecommunications technologies. *Human Factors, 37*, 228-250.

FYA. (2009). *The foundation for young Australians (FYA).* Retrieved January 11, 2009, from http://www.fya.org.au/

Gadotti, M. (1994). *Reading Paulo Freire, his life and work* (J. Milton, Trans.). New York: University of New York Press.

Galton, M., Hargreaves, L., Comber, C., Wall, D. & Pell, A. (1999). *Inside the primary classroom: 20 years on.* London: Routledge.

García, P., Amandi, A., Schiaffino, S., & Campo, M. (2007). Evaluating Bayesian networks' precision for detecting students' learning styles. *Computers & Education, 49*(3), 794-808.

García-Barrios, V. M. (2006). A concept-based enhancement of didactical goals and learning needs with a dynamic background library: Semantics vs. pragmatics. In *Proceedings of the IEEE International Conference on Advanced Learning Technologies (ICALT 2006)* (pp. 1-3). IEEE Computer Society Press.

García-Barrios, V. M. (2006). Finding the missing link: Enhancement of semantic representations through a pragmatic model. In K. Tochtermann & H. Maurer (Eds.), *Proceedings of the 6th International Conference on Knowledge Management (I-KNOW 06)* (pp. 296-303), Graz, Austria. Springer.

García-Barrios, V. M. (2007). *Personalisation in adaptive e-learning systems - a service-oriented solution approach for multi-purpose user modelling systems.* Unpublished doctoral dissertation, Institute for Information Systems and Computer Media, Graz University of Technology.

García-Barrios, V. M., Gütl, C., & Mödritscher, F. (2004). EHELP - enhanced e-learning repository: The use of a dynamic background library for a better knowledge transfer process. In M. Auer & U. Auer (Eds.), *Proceedings of the International Conference on Interactive Computer Aided Learning (ICL 2004)*.

García-Barrios, V. M., Gütl, C., & Pivec, M. (2002). Semantic knowledge factory: A new way of cognition improvement for the knowledge management process. In *Proceedings of Society for Information Technology and Teacher Education*, Nashville, USA.

Garcíac-Barrios, V. M., Gütl, C., & Mödritscher, F. (2004). EHELP - enhanced e-learning repository: The use of a dynamic background library for a better knowledge transfer process. In M. Auer & U. Auer (Eds.), *Proceedings of the International Conference on Interactive Computer Aided Learning (ICL 2004)*. Villach, Austria: Carinthia Tech Institute.

Garden, S., Cornoldi, C., & Logie, R.H. (2002). Visuo-spatial working memory in navigation. *Applied Cognitive Psychology, 16*(1), 35-50.

Gärdenfors, P. (2001). Concept learning: A geometrical model. In *Proceedings of the Aristotelian Society* (Vol. 101, pp. 163-183).

Gardner, H. (1991). *Creating the future: Intelligence in seven steps*. Retrieved January 11, 2009, from http://www.newhorizons.org/future/Creating_the_Future/crfut_gardner.html

Gardner, H. (1993). *Multiple intelligences: The theory in practice*. New York: Basic Books.

Gardner, H. (1994). *A criança pré-escolar: Como pensa e como a escola pode ensiná-la* (C. A. N. Soares, Trans.). Brasil: Artmed.

Gardner, H. (2000). *Inteligências múltiplas: A teoria na prática*. Artmed.

Gardner, H. (2007). *Cinco mentes para o futuro* (five minds for the future). Brasil: Artmed. January 12, 2009, from http://www.amazon.com/gp/reader/1591399122/ref=sib_dp_pt/102-8485304-6091351#reader-link

Gardner, H., Csikszentmihlyi, M., & Damon, W. (2004). *Trabalho qualificado: Quando a excelência e a ética se encontram*. Brasil: Artmed.

Gargiulo, M., & Benassi, M. (1999). The dark side of social capital. In R. A. J. Leenders & S. M. Gabbay (Eds.), *Corporate social capital and liability* (pp. 298-322). Boston, MA: Kluwer Academic Publishers.

Garrido, M. (2009). *Márcio art & design*. January 12, 2009, from http://marciodesign.blogspot.com/

Garrison, D. R., Anderson, T., & Archer, W. (1999). Critical inquiry in a text-based environment: Computer conferencing in higher education. *The Internet and Higher Education, 2*(2-3), 87-105.

Garrison, R., & Anderson, T. (2003). *E-learning in the 21st century. A framework for research and practice*. New York: Routledge Falmer.

Garrison, R., Anderson, T., & Archer, W. (2001). Critical thinking, cognitive presence, and computer conferencing in distance education. *The American Journal of Distance Education, 15*(1).

Gathercole, S.E, Hitch, G.J., Service, S., & Martin, A.J. (1997). Phonological short-term memory and new word learning in children. *Developmental Psychology, 33*(6), 966-79.

Gathercole, S.E., & Baddeley, A.D. (1989). Evaluation of the role of phonological STM in the development of vocabulary in children: A longitudinal study. *Journal of Memory and Language, 28*, 200-13.

Gathercole, S.E., & Pickering, S.J. (2000). Working memory deficits in children with low achievements in the national curriculum at 7 years of age. *British Journal of Educational Psychology, 70*, 177-194.

Gathercole, S.E., Pickering, S.J., Knight, C., & Stegmann, Z. (2004). Working memory skills and educational attainment: Evidence from national curriculum assessments at 7 and 14 years of age. *Applied Cognitive Psychology, 18*, 1-16.

Gentile, D. A. & Welsh, D. A. (2002). A normative study of family media habits. *Applied Developmental Psychology, 23*, 157-178.

George, J. M. (1992). The role of personality in organizational life: Issues and evidence. *Journal of Management, 18*, 185-213.

Germanakos, P., Tsianos, N., Lekkas, Z., Mourlas, C., & Samaras, G. (2007). Capturing essential intrinsic user behaviour values for the design of comprehensive Web-based personalized environments. *Computers in Human Behavior (2007).* doi:10.1016/j.chb.2007.07.010

Germanakos, P., Tsianos, N., Lekkas, Z., Mourlas, C., & Samaras. G. (2007). Realizing comprehensive user profile as the core element of adaptive and personalized communication environments and systems. *Oxford Computer Journal,* 1-29.

Germanakos, P., Tsianos, N., Lekkas, Z., Mourlas, C., Belk, M., & Samaras, G. (2007). Embracing cognitive aspects in Web personalization environments – the adaptive Web architecture. In *Proceedings of ICALT 2007.*

Germanakos, P., Tsianos, N., Lekkas, Z., Mourlas, C., Belk, M., & Samaras G. (2007). An adaptive Web system for integrating human factors in personalization of Web content. In *Proceedings of the 11th International Conference on User Modeling (UM 2007)*, Corfu, Greece.

Gertner, A. S., & VanLehn, K. (2000). Andes: A coached problem solving environment for physics. In *Intelligent Tutoring Systems* (LNCS 1839, pp. 133-142). Springer.

Geyer, W., & Weis, R. (2000). The design and the security concept of a collaborative whiteboard. *Computer Communications, 23*, 233-241.

Ghinea, G., & Chen, S. H. (2003). The impact of cognitive styles on perceptual distributed multimedia quality. *British Journal of Educational Technology, 34*(4), 393-406.

Ghinea, G., & Chen, S. Y. (2003). The impact of cognitive styles on perceptual distributed multimedia quality. *British Journal of Educational Technology, 34*(4), 393-406.

Giannakoulopoulos, A., P., & Kodellas, S. N. (2005). The impact of Web information availability in Journalism: The case of Greek journalists. In P. Masip & J. Rom (Eds), *Digital utopia in the media: From discourses to facts. A Balance, Tripodos* (Vol. 2, pp. 547-560). Barcelona, Spain.

Gielen, S. (2007). *Peer assessment as a tool for learning.* Unpublished doctoral dissertation, Leuven University, Leuven, Belgium.

Gilbert, J. E., & Han, C. Y. (1999). Adapting instruction in search of 'a significant difference.' *Journal of Network and Computer Applications, 22.*

Gilbert, J. E., & Han, C. Y. (2002). Arthur: A personalized instructional system. *Journal of Computing in Higher Education, 14*(1), 113-129.

Gillani, B. (1984). *Learning theories and the design of e-learning environments.* University Press of America.

Gilliam, R.B. & van Kleeck, A. (1996). Phonological awareness training and short-term working memory: Clinical Implications. *Topics in Language Disorders, 17*, 72-81.

Gimp. (2008). Retrieved November 12, 2008, from http://www.gimp.org/

Glass, A., & Riding, R. J. (1999). EEG differences and cognitive style. *Biological Psychology, 51*(1), 23-41.

Glasser, W. (2009). *How we learn.* Retrieved January 11, 2009, from http://members.shaw.ca/priscillatheroux/Glasser.htm

Globo Videos. (2009). *As novas fronteiras do mundo da realidade virtual.* Retrieved March 21, 2009, from http://video.globo.com/Videos/Player/Noticias/0,,GIM984111-7823-AS+NOVAS+FRONTEIRAS+DO+MUNDO+DA+REALIDADE+VIRTUAL,00.html

Gobet, F. (2000). Some shortcomings of long-term working memory. *Brisish Journal of Psychology, 91*, 551-570.

Goldberg, E., Harner, R., Lovell, M., Podell, K., & Riggio, S. (1994). Cognitive bias, functional cortical geometry, and the frontal lobes: Laterality, sex, and handedness. *Journal of Cognitive Neuroscience, 6*, 276-296.

Goldman-Rakic, P.S. (1996). The prefrontal landscape: Implications of functional architecture for understanding human mentation and the central executive. *Philosophical Transactions of the Royal Society (Biological Sciences)*, *351*, 1445-53.

Goleman, D. (1995). *Emotional intelligence*. New York: Bantam Books.

Gombrich, E. H. (2007). *Arte e ilusão: Um estudo da psicologia da representação pictórica* (art and illusion – a study in the psychology of pictorial representation) (R. de S. Barbosa, Trans.). Brasil: WMF Martins Fontes.

Good, J., & Robertson, J. (2006). CARSS: A framework for learner-centred design with children. *International Journal of Artificial Intelligence in Education*, 16(4), 381-413.

Graf, S. (2007). *Adaptivity in learning management systems focussing on learning styles*. Unpublished doctoral dissertation, Vienna University of Technology, Austria.

Graf, S., Lin, T., & Kinshuk. (2008). The relationship between learning styles environments with feed-forward neural networks and cognitive traits – Getting additional information for improving student modeling. *Computers in Human Behavior, 24*, 122-137.

Graff, M. (2003). Learning from Web-based instructional systems and cognitive style. *British Journal of Educational Technology, 34*(4), 407-418.

Graff, M. G. (2002). Learning from hypertext and the analyst-intuition dimension of cognitive style. In *Proceedings of E-Learn., Montreal, Canada, 1* (pp. 361-368).

Graff, M. G. (2002). Hypertext navigation and cognitive style. In M. Valcke (Ed.), *Proceedings of the Seventh European Learning Styles Conference* (pp. 185-192). University of Gent, Belgium.

Graff, M. G. (2003). Assessing learning from hypertext: An individual differences perspective. *Journal of Interactive Learning Research, 14*(4), 425-438.

Graff, M. G. (2005). Information recall, concept mapping, hypertext usability and the analyst-intuitive dimension of cognitive style. *Educational Psychology, 25*(4), 409-422.

Graff, M. G. (2005). Individual differences in hypertext browsing strategies. *Behaviour* and Information Technology, 24(2), 93-100.

Granić, A. (2008). Experience with usability evaluation of e-learning systems. *Universal Access in the Information Society.* doi 10.1007/s10209-008-0118-z

Granić, A., & Ćukušić, M. (2007). An approach to the design of pedagogical framework for e-learning. In *Proceedings of the EUROCON 2007 International Conference on "Computer as a Tool"* (pp. 2415-2422).

Granić, A., & Ćukušić, M. (2007). Universal design within the context of e-learning. In *Universal access in human-computer interaction. Applications and services* (LNCS 4556, pp. 617-626).

Granić, A., & Nakić, J. (2007). Designing intelligent interfaces for e-learning systems: The role of user individual characteristics. In *Universal access in human-computer interaction. Applications and services* (LNCS 4556, pp. 627-636).

Granovetter, M. S. (1973). The strength of weak ties. *American Journal of Sociology*, 78, 1360-1380.

Grasset, R., D¨unser, A., & Billinghurst, M. (2007). Moving between contexts - a user evaluation of a transitional interface. *Image and Vision Computing New Zealand.* Retrieved November 12, 2008, from http://www.hitlabnz.org/publications/2008-MovingBetweenContexts-AUserEvaluationofaTransitionalInterface.pdf

Grasset, R., D¨unser, A., & Billinghurst, M. (2008). Design of a mixed-reality book: Is it still a real book? In *Proceedings of ISMAR 2008*, Cambridge, UK. Retrieved November 12, 2008, from http://www.hitlabnz.org/publications/2008-TheDesignofaMixed-RealityBook-IsItStillaRealBook.pdf

Grasset, R., Woods, E., & Billinghurst, M. (2007). Art and mixed reality: New technology for seamless merging between virtual and real. In *Proceedings of the PERTH-DAC 2007*, Perth, Australia. Retrieved November 12, 2008, from http://www.hitlabnz.org/publications/2007-ArtandMixedRealityNewTechnologyforSeamless.pdf

Gray, A. (1997). *Contructivist teaching and learning* (SSTA Research Centre Report #97-07).

Gray, J. A., & McNaughton, N. (2000). *The neuropsychology of anxiety: an enquiry into the functions of the septo-hippocampal system.* (2nd ed.) Oxford: Oxford University Press.

Greeno, J. (1998). The situativity of knowing, learning, and research. *American Psychologist, 53*(1), 5-26.

Greeno, J. G., Collins, A. M., & Resnick, L. (1996). Cognition and learning. In D. B. a. R. Calfee (Ed.), *Handbook of educational psychology* (pp. 15-46). New York: MacMillan.

Gregor, P., Newell A. F., & Zajicek, M. (2002). Designing for dynamic diversity - interfaces for older people. In J. A. Jacko (Ed.), *Proceedings of the ASSETS 2002. The Fifth International ACM Conference on Assistive Technologies*, Edinburgh, Scotland (pp. 151-156).

Gregorc, A. (1982). *An adult's guide to style*. Columbia, CT: Gregorc Associates.

Griffin, R., & Franklin, G. (1996). Can college academic performance be predicted using a measure of cognitive style? *Journal of Educational Technology Systems, 24*(4), 375-379.

Grigorenko, E. L., & Sternberg, R. J. (1995). Thinking styles. In D. H. Saklogske & M. Zeidner (Eds.), *International handbook of personality and intelligence* (pp. 205-229). UK: Plenum Press.

Grimley, M., Dahraei, H., & Riding, R. J. (2008) The relationship between anxiety stability, working memory and cognitive style. Educational Studies, *34*(3) 213-223.

Grogan, G. (2006). *The design of online discussions to achieve good learning results*. Retrieved May 07, 2008, from www.elearningeuropa.info/directory/index.php?page=doc&doc_id=6713&doclng=6

Guildford, J. P. (1959). *Personality*. New York: McGraw-Hill.

Gullahorn, J. T., & Gullahorn J. E. (1963). A computer model of elementary social behavior. In E.A. Feigenbaum & J. Feldman (Eds.), *Computers and thought* (pp. 375-386). New York: McGraw-Hill.

Gunawardena, C. N., & McIsaac, M. S. (2004). Distance education. In D. H. Jonassen (Ed.), *Handbook of research for educational communications and technology* (2nd ed., pp. 355-396). Mahwah, NJ: Erlbaum.

Gütl, C. (2002). *Ansätze zur modernen wissensauffindung im Internet: Eine annäherung an das information gathering and organizing system xFIND (extended framework for information discovery)* (pp. 84-97). Unpublished doctoral dissertation, Graz University of Technology, Austria.

Gütl, C. (2007). Context-sensitive and personalized concept-based access to knowledge for learning and training purposes. In *Proceedings of the ED-MEDIA 2007*, Vancouver, Canada.

Gütl, C. (2007). Moving towards a generic, service-based architecture for flexible teaching and learning activities. In C. Pahl (Ed.), *Architecture solutions for e-learning systems* (pp. 1-24). Hershey, PA: Idea Group Publishing.

Gütl, C., & García-Barrios, V. M. (2005). The application of concepts for learning and teaching. In M. Auer & U. Auer (Eds.), *Proceedings of the International Conference on Interactive Computer Aided Learning (ICL 2005)*. Villach, Austria: Carinthia Tech Institute.

Gütl, C., & Pivec, M. (2003). A multimedia knowledge module virtual tutor fosters interactive learning. *Journal of Interactive Learning Research, 14*(2), 231-258.

Gütl, C., & Safran, C. (2006). Personalized access to meeting recordings for knowledge transfer and learning purposes in companies. In *Proceedings of the 4th International Conference on Multimedia and Information and Communication Technologies in Education (m-ICTE 2006)*, Seville, Spain.

Gütl, C., Dreher, H., & Williams, R. (2005). E-TESTER: A computer-based tool for auto-generated question and answer assessment. In G. Richards (Ed.), *Proceedings of the World Conference on E-Learning in Corporate, Government, Healthcare, and Higher Education (E-Learn 2005)* (pp. 2929-2936). AACE.

Gütl, C., García-Barrios, V. M. (2005). The application of concepts for learning and teaching. In M. Auer (Ed.), *Proceedings of the International Conference of Interactive Computer Aided Learning (ICL) 2004*, Villach, Austria.

Gütl, C., Pivec, M., & García-Barrios, V. M. (2002). Quality metadata scheme xQMS for an improved information discovery process for scholar work within the xFIND environment. In *Proceedings of the Society for Information Technology and Teacher Education*, Nashville, USA.

Hall, J. K. (2000). *Field dependence-independence and computer-based instruction in geography.* Unpublished doctoral dissertation, Faculty of the Virginia Polytechnic Institute and State University. Retrieved Nov 20, 2007, from http://scholar.lib.vt.edu/theses/available/etd-05022000-19260058/unrestricted/JudithHallDissertation.pdf

Halpern, D. F. (1997). Sex differences in intelligence: Implications for education. *American Psychologist, 52*(10), 1091-1102.

Halpern, D., F (1992). *Sex differences in cognitive abilities.* New Jersey: Lawrence Erlbaum Associates.

Hancock, D. R. (2001). Effects of test anxiety and evaluative threat on student's achievement and motivation. *The Journal of Educational Research, 94*(5), 284-290.

Hanley, J.R., Young, A.W., & Pearson, N.A. (1991). Impairment of the visuospatial sketchpad. *Quarterly Journal of Experimental Psychology, 43*(1), 101-25.

Hannafin, M., Land, S., & Oliver, K. (1999). Open learning environments: Foundations, methods, and models. In C. Reigeluth (Ed.), *Instructional design theories and models* (pp. 115-140). Mahwah, NJ: Lawrence Erlbaum Associates.

Hanneman, R. A., & Riddle, M. (2005). *Introduction to social network methods.* Riverside, CA: University of California, Riverside.

Hanrahan, J., & Isaacs, G. (2001). Assessing self- and peer- assessment: The students' views. *Higher Education Research & Development, 20*, 53-70.

Hansen, J., (1999). *Speech under stress.* Paper presented at ICASSP'99. Phoenix, Arizona.

Hara, N., Bonk, C. J., & Angeli, C. (2000). Content analysis of online discussion in an applied educational psychology course. *Instructional Science, 28*, 115-152.

Harasim, L. (2000). Shift happens: Online education as a new paradigm in learning. *The Internet and Higher Education, 3*, 41-61.

Harasim, L. (2006). A History of e-learning: Shift happened. In J. N. Joel Weiss, Jeremy Hunsinger and Peter Trifonas (Ed.), *The international handbook of virtual learning environments* (pp. 59-94). The Netherlands: Springer.

Harasim, L. M. (1989). Online education: A new domain. In R. D. Mason & A. R. Kaye (Eds.), *Mindweave: Communication, computers and distance education.* Oxford, UK: Pergamon Press.

Harasim, L., Hiltz, S. R., Teles, L., & Turoff, M. (1995). *Learning networks: A field guide to teaching and learning online.* Cambridge, MA: The MIT Press.

Harasty, J., Double, K. L., Halliday, G. M., Kril, J. J., & McRitchie, D. A. (1997). Language associated cortical regions are proportionally larger in the female brain. *Archives of Neurology, 54*, 171-175.

Hardin, J. (2006). *The Sakai Project final report to the Mellon Foundation.* University of Michigan.

Harrison, S., & Hood, J. (2008). Applications of neuropsychology in schools. In J. Warner-Rogers & J. Reed (Eds.), *Child neuropsychology: Concepts, theory and practice* (pp. 404-419). Singapore: Wiley-Blackwell.

Harwell, M., Stone, C. A., Hsu, T. & Kirisci, L. (1996). Monte Carlo studies in item response theory. *Applied psychological measurement, 20*(2), 101-125.

Hattie, J., & Timperley, H. (2007). The power of feedback. *Review of Educational Research, 77*, 81-112.

Hayes, J. & Allinson, C. W. (1998). Cognitive style and the theory and practice of individual and collective learning in organizations. *Human Relations, 51*, 847-871.

Haykin, S. (1998). *Neural networks: A comprehensive foundation* (2nd ed.). Upper Saddle River, NJ: Prentice Hall.

Haythornthwaite, C. (2001). Exploring multiplexity: Social network structures in a computer-supported distance learning class. *The Information Society, 17*, 211-226.

Haythornthwaite, C. (2002). Building social networks via computer networks: Creating and sustaining distributed learning communities. In K. A. Renninger & W. Shumar (Eds.), *Building virtual communities: Learning and change in cyberspace* (pp.159-190). Cambridge, UK: Cambridge University Press.

Hazeltine, E., Ruthruff, E. & Remington, R. W. (2006). The role of input and output modality parings in dual-task performance: Evidence for content-dependent central interference. *Cognitive Psychology, 52*, 291-345.

Head, J. (1996). Gender identity and cognitive style. In P. Murphy and C. Gipps (Eds.), *Equity in the classroom:Towards effective pedagogy for girls and boys* (pp. 59-69). London, UNESCO Publishing:.

Head, J. T., Lockee, B. B., & Oliver, K. M. (2002). Method, media, and mode: Clarifying the discussion of distance education effectiveness. *Quarterly Review of Distance Education, 3*(3), 261-268.

Healey, D. (1999). Theory and research: Autonomy in language learning. In J. Egbert, & E. Hanson-Smith (Eds.), *CALL environments: Research, practice, and critical issues* (pp. 391-402). Alexandria, VA: Teachers of English to Speakers of Other Languages, Inc.

Healey, J. (2000). *Wearable and automotive systems for affect recognition from physiology.* PhD thesis, Massachusetts Institute of Technology.

Healy, J. M. (1998). *Failure to connect: How computers affect our children's minds – For better or for worse.* New York: Simon & Schuster.

Hebb, D. O. (1949). *Organization of behaviour.* New York: Wiley.

Hedges, L. V. & Nowell, A. (1995). Sex differences in mental test scores, variability, and numbers of high-scoring individuals. *Science, 269*, 41-45.

Hembree, R. (1988). Correlates, causes, effects and treatment of test anxiety. *Review of Educational Research, 58*(1), 47-77.

Henri, F. (1992). Computer conferencing and content analysis. In A. R. Kaye (Ed.), *Collaborative learning through computer conferencing: The Najaden papers* (pp. 115-136). New York: Springer.

Henry, L. (2002). *Educational concept of scaffolding adolescent learning & development.* Retrieved November 16, 2008, from http://condor.admin.ccny.cuny.edu/~group4/Henry/Henry%20Paper.doc

Henze, N., Dolog, P., & Nejdl, W. (2004). Reasoning and ontologies for personalized e-learning in the Semantic Web. *Educational Technology & Society, 7*(4), 82-97.

Hernández, F. (2000). *Cultura visual, mudança educativa e projeto de trabalho.* Brasil: Artmed.

Hernández-Leo, D., Asensio-Pérez, J. I., Dimitriadis, Y., Bote-Lorenzo, M. L., Jorrín-Abellán, I. M., & Villasclaras-Fernández, E. D. (2005). Reusing IMS-LD formalized best practices in collaborative learning structuring. *Advanced Technology for Learning, 2*(3), 223-232.

Herrmann, N. (1996). *The whole brain business book.* McGraw-Hill.

Hester, R. & Garavan, H. (2005). Working memory and executive function: The influence of content and load on the control of attention. *Memory and Cognition, 33*, 221-233.

Hill, J. R., & Hannafin, M. J. (1997). Cognitive strategies and learning from the World Wide Web. *Educational Technology Research and Development, 45*(4), 37-64.

Hiltz, S. R. (1994). *The virtual classroom: Learning without limits via computer networks.* Norwood, NJ: Alex Publishing Corporation.

Hiltz, S. R., & Wellman, B. (1997). Asynchronous learning networks as a virtual classroom. *Communications of the ACM, 40*(9), 44-49.

Hirumi, A. (2006). *Analysing and designing e-learning interactions*. Routlege.

His, S., & Soloway, E. (1998). Learner-centred design: Addressing, finally, the unique needs of learners. In *Proceedings of the Computer Human Interaction '98, CHI '98*, Los Angeles, USA (pp. 211-212). ACM Press.

Hitch, G. J. (1990). Developmental fractionation of working memory. In G. Vallar & J. Shallice (Eds.), *Neuropsychological impairments of short-term memory* (pp. 221-246). New York: Cambridge University Press.

Hmelo-Silver, C. (2004). Problem-based learning: What and how do students learn? *Educational Psychology Review, 16*(3), 235-266.

Hodges, C. B. (2004). Designing to motivate: Motivational techniques to incorporate in e-learning experiences. *Journal of Interactive Online Learning, 2*(3). Retrieved March 17, 2008, from http://www.vcolr.org/jiol/issues/getfile.cfm?volID=2&IssueID=8&ArticleID=31

Hogan, J., & Holland, B. (2003). Using theory to evaluate personality and job-performance relations: A socioanalytic perspective. *Journal of Applied Psychology, 88*, 100-112.

Hohenwarter, M., & Preiner, J. (2007). Dynamic mathematics with GeoGebra. *Journal of Online Mathematics and its Applications, 7*.

Holzman, P. S., & Klein, G. S. (1954). Cognitive system principles of levelling and sharpening: individual differences in visual time error assimilation effects. *Journal of Psychology, 37*, 105-122.

Honey, P., & Mumford, A. (1986). *A manual of learning styles*. Maidenhead, UK: Peter Honey Publications.

Honey, P., & Mumford, A. (2000). *The learning styles helper's guide*. Maidenhead, UK: Peter Honey Publications Ltd.

Hook, K. (2000). Steps to take before intelligent user interfaces become real. *Journal of Interaction with Computers, 12*(4), 409-426.

Hopko, D. R., Ashcraft, M. H., & Gute, J. (1998). Mathematics anxiety and working memory: Support for the existence of a deficient inhibition mechanism. *Journal of Anxiety Disorders, 12*, 343-355.

Horton, W. (2001). *Leading elearning, American Society for Training and Development, Alexandria, USA, 2001*. Retrieved May 07, 2008, from www.astd.org

Horvitz, E. Breese, J. Heckerman, D. Hovel, D., & Rommelse, K. (1998). The Lumiere Project: Bayesian user modeling for inferring the goals and needs of software users. In *Proceedings of the Fourteenth Conference on Uncertainty in Artificial Intelligence* (pp. 256-265). Madison, WI.

Hsu, Y. & Schwen, T. (2003). The effects of structural cues from multiple metaphors on computer users information search performance. *International Journal of Human Computer Studies, 58*(1), 39-55.

HTML Wikipedia definition. (2008). Retrieved November 12, 2008, from http://en.wikipedia.org/wiki/HTML

Hua Liu, C., & Matthews, R. (2005). Vygotsky's philosophy: Constructivism and its criticisms examined. *International Education Journal, 6*(3), 386-399.

Huffaker, D. A., & Calvert, S. L. (2003). The new science of learning: Active learning, metacognition, and transfer of knowledge in e-learning applications. *Journal of Educational Computing Research, 29*(3), 325-334.

Hutchings, M. (2002). Computer mediated communication: Impact on learning. In S. Fallows & R. Bhanot (Eds.), *Educational development: Through information and communications technology* (pp. 87-101). London: Kogan Page.

Hyde, J. S. (2005). The gender similarities hypothesis. *American Psychologist, 60*(6), 581-592.

Hyde, J. S., & Linn, M. C. (1988). Gender differences in verbal ability: A meta-analysis. *Psychological Bulletin, 104*(1), 53-69.

Hyde, J. S., Fennema, E., & Lamon, S. J. (1990). Gender differences in mathematics performance: A meta-analysis. *Psychological Bulletin, 107*(2), 139-155.

I Seminário Web Curriculum. (2008). Retrieved January 12, 2009, from http://www.pucsp.br/webcurriculo/

ICEL. (2008). *International consortium for experiential learning*. Retrieved January 11, 2009, from http://www.education.uts.edu.au/icel/conference.html

IEEE. (2002). *Standard for learning object metadata* (IEEE Standard 1484.12.1-2002). IEEE.

Iida, A., Campbell, N., Iga, S., Higuchi, F., & Yasumura, M. (2000). A speech synthesis system with emotion for assisting communication. In *Proceedings of the ISCA Workshop on Speech and Emotion* (Vol. 1, pp. 167-172). Belfast.

IINN-ELS. (2009). *Instituto internacional de neurociências de natal edmond e lily safra (IINN-ELS)*. Retrieved February 15, 2009, from http://www.natalneuro.org.br/sobre_iinn/index.asp

Ikegulu, P. R., & Ikegulu, T. N. (1999). The effectiveness of window presentation strategy and cognitive style of field dependence status on learning from mediated instructions. Ruston, LA: Center for Statistical Consulting. (ERIC Document Reproduction Service No. ED428758)

Illeris, K. (2007). *How we learn: Learning and non-learning in school and beyond*. England: Routledge.

Imprensa, J. (2009). *Preparação para o trabalho*. Retrieved March 20, 2009, from http://jovemcomunicavivo.blogspot.com/2009/03/preparacao-para-o-trabalho.html

INAF. (2005). *5° indicador nacional de alfabetismo funcional: Um diagnóstico para inclusão social pela educação*. Retrieved November 22, 2008, from http://www.acaoeducativa.org.br/downloads/inaf05.pdf

Information Society Technologies Advisory Group (ISTAG). (2001). *Scenarios for ambient intelligence in 2010* (Final Report,EC 2001).

Internet Guianet. (1999). Curso de VRML. *Revista Internet Guianet, 1*(2), 10-11.

Irwin, D.E. & Andrews, R.V. (1996). Integration and accumulation of information across saccadic eye movements. In T. Innui & J.L. McClelland (Eds.), *Attention and performance XVI: Information integration in perception and communication* (pp. 125-55). Cambridge, MA: MIT Press.

ISB. (2009). *Internet space builder*. Retrieved January 13, 2009, from http://www.parallelgraphics.com/products/isb/download/

ISTAG Working Group. (2003). *Ambient intelligence: From vision to reality for participation – in society & business*. Retrieved November 12, 2008, from http://74.125.113.104/search?q=cache:-B211_pXgScJ:ftp://ftp.cordis.europa.eu/pub/ist/docs/istag-ist2003_draft_consolidated_report.pdf+ISTAG+Working+Group+draft+report&hl=pt-BR&ct=clnk&cd=2&gl=br

ISTAG Working Group. (2004). *Grand challenges in the evolution of the information society* (DRAFT Report 06 July 2004). Retrieved November 12, 2008, from http://ec.europa.eu/information_society/istevent/2004/cf/document.cfm?doc_id=712

Istance, D. (2006). Os cenários da escola da OCDE, os professores e o papel das tecnologias da informação e da comunicação. In J. M. Sancho & F. Hernández (Eds.), *Colaboradores, tecnologias para transformar a educação* (pp. 177-197) (V. Campos, Trans.). Brasil: Artmed.

Izard, C. E. (1977*). Human emotions*. New York: Plenum Press.

Jablan, S. V. (2005). Modularity in art. In W. Callebaut & D. R. Gutman (Eds.), *Modualrity: Understanding the development and evolution of natural complex systems* (pp. 259-281). Cambridge, MA: The MIT Press.

Jacoby, L. L. (1991). A process discrimination framework: Separating automatic from intentional uses of memory. *Journal of Memory and Language, 30*, 531-541

Jaques. D., & Salmon. G. (2007). *Learning in groups: A handbook for face-to-face and online environments*. New York: Routledge.

Java and Java3d API™. (2008). Retrieved November 12, 2008, from http://java.sun.com/javase/technologies/desktop/java3d/

Jehn, K., & Shah, P. (1997). Interpersonal relationships and task performance: An examination of mediating processes in friendship and acquaintance groups. *Journal of Personality and Social Psychology, 72*, 775-790.

Jensen, G. H. (2003). Learning styles. In J. A. Provost & W. S. Anchors (Eds.), *Using the MBTI instrument in colleges and universities* (pp. 123-155). Gainesville, FL: Center for Applications of Psychological Type.

Jeong, W. (2007). Instant messaging in on-site and on-line classes in higher education. *Educause Quarterly, 30*(1), 30-36.

Jerry Fodor on mental architecture. (2009). February 13, 2008, from http://en.wikipedia.org/wiki/Jerry_Fodor_on_mental_architecture

JISC (2007). Designing for learning. *An update on the pedagogy strand of the JISC e-learning programme*. Retrieved 15 March, 2007, from http://www.jisc.ac.uk/elearning_pedagogy

Johnson, A. (2006). VR as instructional technology: The CAVE as classroom. In J. J. Sosnoski, P. Harkin, & B. Carter (Eds.), *Configuring history: Teaching the Harlem renaissance through virtual reality cityscapes*. Retrieved November 12, 2008, from http://www.evl.uic.edu/aej/papers/harlemchapter.pdf

Johnson, A., Roussos, M., Leigh, J., Vasilakis, C., Barnes, C., & Moher, T. (1999). Learning and building together in an immersive virtual world. *Presence 8*(3), 247-263. Retrieved November 12, 2008, from http://www.evl.uic.edu/aej/vrais98/vrais98.2.html

Johnson, D. W. (1981). Student-student interaction: The neglected variable in education. *Educational Research, 10*, 5-10.

Johnson, D. W., & Johnson, R. T. (1994). *Together and alone: Cooperative, competitive, and individualistic learning* (4th ed.). Boston, MA: Allyn & Bacon.

Johnson, G. M., & Johnson, J. A. (2006). *Learning style and preference for online learning support: Individual quizzes versus study groups*. Paper presented at the 18th Annual World Conference on Educational Multimedia, Hypermedia, and Telecommunications, Orlando, FL.

Johnson, S. D., Aragon, S. R. Shaik, N., & Palma-Rivas, N. (2000). Comparative analysis of learner satisfaction and learning outcomes in online and fact-to-face learning environments. *Journal of Interactive Learning Research, 11*(1) 29-49.

Joint Information Systems Committee (JISC) template for describing a unit of (e)learning. (2004). Retrieved from www.jisc.ac.uk/uploaded_documents/Describing%20practice%20v12.doc

Joint progress report of the Council and the Commission on the implementation of the Education and Training 2010 work programme – "Delivering lifelong learning for knowledge, creativity and innovation". (2008). *Official Journal of the European Union, 86*, 1-31

Jonassen, D. (1996). *Computers in the classroom: Mindtools for critical thinking*. Englewood Cliffs, NJ: Merrill, Prentice Hall.

Jonassen, D. H. (1991). Evaluating constructivist learning. *Educational Technology, 31*(10), 28-33.

Jonassen, D. H., & Grabowski, B. L. (1993). *Handbook of individual difference, learning, and instruction*. Hillsdale, NJ: Lawrence Erlbaum Associates.

Jones, C., Cook, J., Jones, A., & De Laat, M. F. (2007). Collaboration. In G. Conole & M. Oliver (Eds.), *Contemporary perspectives in e-learning research: Themes, methods, and impact on practice* (pp. 174-189). London: Routhledge.

Jones, C., Reichard, C., & Mokhtari, K. (2003). Are students' learning styles discipline specific? *Community College Journal of Research and Practice, 27*(5), 363-375.

Jones, R. M., Lebiere, C., & Crossman, J. A. (2007). Comparing modeling idioms in ACT-R and Soar. In *Proceedings of the Eighth International Conference on Cognitive Modeling*, Ann Arbor, MI.

Jorm A.F., Share D.L., Maclean R., & Matthews, R. (1984). Phonological recoding skills and learning to read: A longitudinal study. *Applied Psycholinguistics, 5,* 201-07.

Jornal da Gazeta. (2008). *A história contada através de azulejos Portugueses.* Retrieved November 27, 2008, from http://www.tvgazeta.com.br/jornaldagazeta/video_destaques/2008/04/15_abr_08_06.php

Juan, C. C., Carmen. P. F., & Jesus, F. (2006). Assessing the use of instant messaging in online learning environments. *Interactive Learning Environments, 14*(3), 205-218.

Juul, J. (2005). *Half-real: Video games between real rules and fictional worlds.* Cambridge, MA: MIT Press.

Kagan, J. (1966). Reflection-impulsivity: The generality and dynamics of conceptual tempo. *Journal of Abnormal Psychology, 71,* 17-24.

Kagan, J., Rosman B., Day, D., Albert, J., & Phillips, W. (1964). Information processing and the child: Significance of analytic and reflective attitudes. *Psychological Monographs,* 78.

Kahootz. (2009). Retrieved January 11, 2008, from www.kahootz.com.au

Kali, Y., & Ronen, M. (2005). Design principles for online peer evaluation: Fostering objectivity. In T. Koschmann, D. Suthers, & T. W. Chan (Eds.), *Computer supported collaborative learning 2005: The next 10 years!* (pp. 247-251). Mahwah, NJ: Lawrence Erlbaum Associates.

Kali, Y., & Ronen, M. (2008). Assessing the assessors: Added value in Web-based multi-cyle peer assessment in higher education. *Research and Practice in Technology Enhanced Learning, 3,* 3-32.

Kalyuga, S., Chandler, P., & Sweller, J. (2000). Incorporating learner experience into the design of multimedia instruction. *Journal of Educational Psychology, 92,* 126-136.

Kane, M.J. & Engle, R.W. (2000). Working memory capacity, proactive interference, and divided attention: Limits on long-term memory retrieval. *Journal of Experimental Psychology: Learning, Memory and Cognition, 26,* 336-358.

Kane, M.J. & Engle, R.W. (2002). The role of prefrontal cortex in working memory capacity, executive attention, and general fluid intelligence: An individual-differences perspective. *Psychonomic Bulletin and Review, 9,* 637-671.

Kane, M.J., Bleckley, M.K., Conway, A.R.A., & Engle, R.W. (2001). A controlled-attention view of working memory capacity. *Journal of Experimental Psychology: General, 130,* 169-83.

Kanuka, H., & Anderson, T. (1999). using constructivism in technology-mediated learning: Constructing order out of the chaos in the literature. *Radical Pedagogy, 1*(2).

Kariya, S. (2003). Online education expands and evolves. *IEEE Spectrum, 40,* 49- 51.

Kassin, S. (1995). *Psychology.* Boston, MA: Houghton Mifflin.

Katz, M. L., & Shapiro, C. (1985). Network externalities, competition, and compatibility. *The American Economic Review, 75*(3), 424-440.

Kaufmann, H., & Meyer, B. (2008). Simulating educational physical experiments in augmented reality. In *Educators Paper (abstracts), Siggraph 2008,* Singapura. Retrieved November 12, 2008, from http://www.siggraph.org/asia2008/attendees/edu/13.php

Kaufmann, M. H. (2004). *Geometry education with augmented reality.* Unpublished doctoral dissertation, Vienna University of Technology. Retrieved January 11, 2008, from https://www.ims.tuwien.ac.at/media/documents/publications/kaufmann_diss.pdf

Kay, J. (2001). Learner control. *User Modeling and User-Adapted Interaction, 11*(1-2), 111-127.

Kaye, A. (1991). Learning together apart. In *Proceedings of the NATO Advanced Research Workshop on Collaborative Learning and Computer Conferencing, Series F: Computer and System Sciences, 90.* Berlin, Germany: Springer-Verlag.

Keates, S., & Clarkson, J. (2003). *Countering design exclusion: An introduction to inclusive design.* London: Springer.

Keefe, J. (1979). Learning style: An overview. In *NASSP's Student Learning Styles: Diagnosing and Prescribing Programs* (pp. 1-17).

Keefe, J. W. (1982). Assessing student learning styles: An overview. In J. W. Keefe (Ed.), *Student learning styles and brain behavior* (pp. 1-17). Reston, VA: National Association of Secondary School Principals.

Kelleher, C. (2006). *Motivating programming: Using storytelling to make computer programming attractive to middle school girls* Unpublished doctoral dissertation, School of Computer Science, Carnegie Mellon University – CMU. Retrieved November 12, 2008, from http://www.cs.cmu.edu/~caitlin/kelleherThesis_CSD.pdf

Keller, J. M. (1999). Using the ARCS motivational process in computer-based instruction and distance education. In M. Theall (Ed.), *Motivation in teaching and learning: New directions for teaching and learning.* San Francisco: Jossey-Bass.

Keller, J. M., & Suzuki, K. (2004). Learner motivation and e-learning design: A multinationally validated process. *Journal of Educational Media, 29*(3), 229-239.

Kelly, B., Phipps, L., & Swift, E. (2005). Developing a holistic approach for e-learning accessibility. *Canadian Journal of Learning and Technology, 30*(3).

Kelly, D., & Tangney, B. (2006). Adapting to intelligence profile in an adaptive educational system. *Journal Interacting with Computers, 18*(3), 385-409.

Kelly, L. (1982). A rose by any other name is still a rose: A comparative analysis of reticence, communication apprehension, unwillingness to communicate, and shyness. *Human Communication Research, 8*(2), 99-113.

Kemp, F., Morrison, G., & Ross, S. (1998). *Designing effective instruction.* Upper Saddle River, NJ: Prentice Hall.

Kemp, J., & Livingstone, D. (2006). Putting a second life "Metaverse" skin on learning management systems. In *Proceedings of the Second Life Education Workshop at SLCC*, San Francisco (pp. 13-18).

Kerr, N., & Bruun, S. (1983). The dispensability of member effort and group motivation losses: Free-rider effects. *Journal of Personality and Social Psychology, 44*, 78-94.

Keyser, M. W. (2000). Active learning and cooperative learning: Understanding the difference and using both styles effectively. *Research Strategies, 17*, 35-44.

Khan, B. (2005). *Managing e-learning strategies: Design, delivery, implementation and evaluation.* Hershey, PA: Information Science Publishing.

Kilduff, M. (1992). The friendship network as a decision-making resource: Dispositional moderators of social influences on organizational choices. *Journal of Personality and Social Psychology, 62*(1), 168-180.

Kimberly, B. W. (2007). Blended learning and online tutoring: A good practice guide - A Book Review. *Internet & Higher Education, 10*(4), 283-286.

Kimbrough, R. & Nunnery, M. (1988). *Educational administration.* New York: Macmillian Publishing.

Kimura, D. (1996). Sex, sexual orientation and sex hormones influence human cognitive function. *Current Opinion in Neurobiology, 6*, 259-263.

Kincheloe, J. L. (1993). *Toward a critical politics of teacher thinking.* Westport CT: Bergin & Garvey.

King, J., Bond, T., & Blandford, S. (2002). An investigation of computer anxiety by gender and grade. *Computers in Human Behavior, 18*, 69-84.

Kinshuk, N.A., & Patel, A. (2001). Adaptive tutoring in business education using fuzzy backpropagation approach. In M. J. Smith, G. Salvendy, D. Harris & R. J. Koubek (Eds.) *Usability evaluation and interface design: Cognitive engineering, intelligent agents and virtual reality: Proceedings of The 9th International Conference on Human-Computer Interaction.* New Orleans, USA.

Kintsch, W., Healy, A.F., Hegarty, M., Pennington, B.F., & Salthouse, T.A. (1999). Models of working memory:

Eight questions and some general issues. In A. Miyake & P. Shah (Eds.), *Models of working memory: Mechanisms of active maintenance and executive control* (pp. 412-41). Cambridge, UK: Cambridge University Press.

Kirby, P. (1979). *Cognitive style, learning style and transfer skill acquisition.* Columus, OH: The National Center for Research in Vocational Education, The Ohio State University.

Kirschner, P. A. (2001). Using integrated electronic environments for collaborative teaching/learning. *Research Dialogue in Learning and Instruction, 2,* 1-9.

Kirschner, P. A. (2002). Cognitive load theory: Implications of cognitive load theory on the design of learning. *Learning and Instruction, 12*(1), 1-10.

Klauer, K.C., & Zhao, Z. (2004). Double dissociations in visual and spatial short-term memory. *Journal of Experimental Psychology: General, 133,* 355-81.

Klein, M., Sommer, D., & Stucky, W. (2003). WeBCEIS - a scenario for integrating web-based education into classical education. In A. Aggarwal (Ed.), *Web-based education: Learning from experience* (pp. 398-414). Hershey, PA: Information Science Publishing.

Kluger, A. N., & DeNisi, A. (1996). The effects of feedback interventions on performance: A historical review, a meta-analysis, and a preliminary feedback intervention theory. *Psychological Bulletin, 119,* 254-284.

Kobayashi, H., & Hara, F. (1992). Recognition of six basic facial expressions and their strength by neural network. In *Proceedings of the Int'l Workshop Robot and Human Comm.* (pp. 381-386).

Kobsa, A. (1995). Supporting user interfaces for all through user modeling. In *Proceedings of the 6th International Conference on Human-Computer Interaction HCI International 1995*, Yokohama, Japan (pp. 155-157). Retrieved from http://www.ics.uci.edu/~kobsa/papers/1995-HCI95-kobsa.pdf

Kocel, K. M. (1980). Age-related changes in cognitive abilities and hemispheric specialization. In J. Herron (Ed.), *Neuropsychology of left-handedness*. London: Academic Press.

Koch, N., & Rossi, G. (2002). Patterns for adaptive Web applications. In *Proceedings of the Seventh European Conference on Pattern Languages of Programs* (pp. 179-194). Universitätsverlag Konstanz.

Koedinger, K. R., Anderson, J. R., Hadley, W. H., & Mark, M. (1997). Intelligent tutoring goes to school in the big city. *International Journal of Artificial Intelligence in Education, 8,* 30-43.

Koenen, R. (2000). Mpeg-4 Project Overview, International Organisation for Standardization, ISO/IEC/JTC1/SC29/WG11, La Baule.

Kohli, W. (1995). *Critical conversations in philosophy of education.* Routledge, New York: Miller Publishing.

Kolb, A. Y., & Kolb, D. A. (2005). *The Kolb learning style inventory – version 3.1 2005 technical specifications.* Boston, MA: Haygroup Experience Based Learning Systems Inc.

Kolb, D. (1984). *Experiential learning: Experience as the source of learning and development.* FT Press.

Konradt, U., & Schmook, R. (1999). Telework: Stress and strain in a longitudinal study. *Zeitschrift Fur Arbeits-Und Organisationspsychologie, 43,* 142-150.

Koper, R., & Olivier, B. (2004). Representing the learning design of units of learning. *Educational Technology & Society, 7*(3), 97-111.

Koponen, E. (2006). Exploring the higher education e-learning in Finland. In V. Carvalho (Ed.), *E-learning e formação avançada: Casos de sucesso no ensino superior da Europa e America Latina* (pp. 23-71). Edicoes Politema.

Kortemeyer, G. (1999) Multimedia collaborative content creation (mc3) - the MSU lectureonline system. *Journal of Engineering Education, 88,* 421.

Korthauer, R. D., & Koubek, R. J. (1994). An empirical evaluation of knowledge, cognitive style and structure upon the performance of a hypertext task. *International Journal of Human Computer Interaction, 6*(4), 373-390.

Kotsia, I., & Pitas, I. (2005). Real time facial expression recognition from image sequences using Support Vector Machines. In *IEEE International Conference on Image Processing (ICIP 2005)* (pp. 11-14).

Kozhevnikov, M. (2007). Cognitive styles in the context of modern psychology: Toward an integrated framework of cognitive style. *Psychological Bulletin, 133*(3), 464-481.

Kozma, R.B. (1991). Learning with media. *Review of Educational Research, 61*, 179-211.

Kraut, R. E., Rice, R. E., Cool, C., & Fish, R. S. (1998). Varieties of social influence: The role of utility and norms in the success of a new communication medium. *Organization Science, 9*, 437-453.

Kruse, K. (2006). *Introduction to instructional design and the ADDIE model, e-learningGuru*. Retrieved April, from http://www.e-learningguru.com/articles/art2_1.htm

Kurtz, B.E., & Weinert, F.E. (1989). Metamemory, metaperformance, and causal attributions in gifted and average childern. *Journal of Experimental Child Psychology, 48*, 45-61.

Kyllonen, P.C. & Christal, R.E. (1990). Reasoning ability is (little more than) working memory capacity. *Intelligence, 14*, 389-433.

Kynigos, C. (1995). We should not miss the chance: Educational technology as a means expression and observation in general education. In A. Kazamias & M. Kasotakis (Eds.), *Greek education, perspectives of reformulation and modernization* (pp. 396-416). Athens. Greece: Seirios.

Kyza, E. (2005.) Supporting data-rich inquiries on the Web. In Zacharia, Z. C. & Constantinou, C. P., (Eds.) *Proceedings of the 7th International Conference on Computer-based learning in Science.* Zilina, Slovakia.

Lajoie, S. P., & Nakamura, C. (2006). Multimedia learning of cognitive skills. In Mayer (Ed.), *The Cambridge handbook of multimedia learning* (pp. 489-502). New York: Cambridge University Press.

Lake, M. (2008). Learning perspectives and pedagogical challenges in distance education. *Phukett Thailand: The 3rd Symposium on Distance and Virtual Learning, 4* (pp.122-143).

Lally, V. (Ed.). (2002). Elaborating collaborative interactions in networked learning: A multi-method approach. In *Proceedings of the Networked Learning Conference 2002*, University of Sheffield.

Langan, A. M., Wheater, C. P., Shaw, E. M., Haines, B. J., Cullen, W. R., Boyle, J. C., Penney, D., Oldekop, J. A., Ashcroft, C., Lockey, L., & Preziosi, R. F. (2005). Peer assessment of oral presentations: Effects of student gender, university affiliation and participation in the development of assessment criteria. *Assessment & Evaluation in Higher Education, 30*, 21-34.

Laurel, B. (1993). *Computers as theatre.* New York: Addison Wesley.

Laurillard, D. (2002). *Rethinking university teaching.* London: Routledge.

Laurillard, D. (2006). *Rethinking university teaching - a framework for the effective use of learnign technologies.* Routledge Falmer.

Laurillard, D., Stratfold, M., Luckin, R., Plowman, L., & Taylor, J. (2000). Affordances for learning in a non-linear narrative medium. *Journal of Interactive Media in Education, 62*.

Laurilliard, D. (2007). Technology, pedagogy and education: Concluding comments. *Technology, Pedagogy and Education, 16*(3), 357-360.

Lave, J., & Wenger, E. (1995). *Situated learning: Legitimate peripheral participation.* Cambridge University Press.

Lazarus, R.S. (1991). *Emotion and adaptation.* New York: Oxford University Press

Lee, C. H. M., Cheng, Y. W., Rai, S., & Depickere, A. (2005). What affect student cognitive style in the development of hypermedia learning system. *Computers & Education, 45*(2005), 1-19.

Lee, C.M., & Narayanan, S.S. (2005). Toward detecting emotions in spoken dialogs. *IEEE Trans. Speech Audio Process. 13*(2), 293-303.

Lee, E. Y. C., Chan, C. K. K., & van Aalst, J. (2006). Students assessing their own collaborative knowledge building. *International Journal of Computer-Supported Collaborative Learning, 1*, 277-307.

Lee, M. J., & Tedder, M. C. (2003). The effects of three different computer texts on readers' recall: Based on working memory capacity. *Computers in Human Behavior, 19*(6), 767-783.

Lee, Y. (2004), How to consider individual differences in online learning environments. In C. Crawford, et al. (Eds.), *Proceedings of Society for Information Technology and Teacher Education International Conference 2004* (pp. 545-550). Chesapeake, VA: AACE.

Leenders, R. A. J., & Gabbay, S. M. (1999). *Corporate social capital and liability*. Boston, MA: Kluwer Academic Publishers.

Lejk, M., & Wyvill, M. (2001). Peer assessment of contributions to a group project: A comparison of holistic and category-based approaches. *Assessment & Evaluation in Higher Education, 26*, 61-72.

Lejk, M., Wyvill, M., & Farrow, S. (1999). Group assessment in systems analysis and design: A comparison of the performance of streamed and mixed-ability groups. *Assessment & Evaluation in Higher Education, 24*, 5-14.

Lennon, J., & Maurer, H. (1994). *Applications and impact of hypermedia systems: An overview. Journal of Universal Computer Science, 0*(0), 54-107.

Leontidis, M., Halatsis, C., & Grigoriadou, M. (2008). E-learning issues under an affective perspective. In F. Li, et al. (Eds.), *ICWL 2008* (LNCS 5145, pp. 27-38).

LePine, J. A., & Van Dyne, L. (2001). Voice and cooperative behavior as contrasting forms of contextual performance: Evidence of differential relationships with big five personality characteristics and cognitive ability. *Journal of Applied Psychology, 86*, 326-336.

Lester, J., Towns, S., & Fitzgerald, P. (1999). Achieving affective impact: Visual emotive communication in lifelike pedagogical agents. *International Journal of Artificial Intelligence in Education, 10*, 278-291.

Lever-Duffy, J., McDonald, J. B., & Mizell, A. P. (2003). *Teaching and learning with technology*. Boston, MA: Allyn & Bacon/Pearson.

Levy, J., & Gur, R. (1980). Individual differences in psychoneurological organization. In J. Herron (Ed.), *Neuropsychology of left-handedness*. London: Academic Press.

Levy, J., & Heller, W. (1987). Diversities in right-handers in left-hemisphere processing. In D. Ottoson (Ed.), *Duality and unity of the brain*. Basingstoke: Macmillan.

Lévy, P. (1993). *As tecnologias da inteligência: O futuro do pensamento na era da informática* (C. I. da Costa, Trans.). Brasil: Editora 34.

Liaw, S. S., Ting, I. H., & Tsai, Y. C. (2003). Developing a conceptual model for designing a Web assisted information retrieval system. In *Proceedings of the 2003 International Conference on Computer-Assisted Instruction (ICCAI2003)*.

Lieberman, H. (1997). Introduction to intelligent interfaces. Retrieved from http://web.media.mit.edu/~lieber/Teaching/Int-Int/Int-Int-Intro.html

Lin, B., & Hsieh, C.-T. (2001). *Web-based teaching and learner control: A research review. Computers & Education, 37*(2001), 377-386.

Lin, C. H., & Davidson-Shivers, G. V. (1996). Effects of linking structure and cognitive style on students' performance and attitude in a computer-based hypertext environment. *Journal of Educational Computing Research, 15*(4), 317-329.

Lin, S. S. J., Liu, E. Z. F., & Yuan, S. M. (2001). Web-based peer assessment: Feedback for students with various thinking-styles. *Journal of Computer Assisted Learning, 17*, 420-432.

Lin, T., Kinshuk, & Patel, A. (2003). Cognitive trait model for persistent student modelling. In D. Lassner &

C. McNaught (Eds.), *EdMedia 2003 Conference Proceedings*, Norfolk, USA.

Linacre, J.M. (2000). Computer-adaptive testing: A methodology whose time has come. In S. Chae, U. Kang, E. Jeon & J. M. Linacre (Eds.), *Development of computerized middle school achievement test*. Seoul, South Korea: Komesa Press.

Lind, E. A., Kanfer, R., & Earley, P. C. (1990). Voice, control, and procedural justice: Instrumental and noninstrumental concerns in fairness judgements. *Journal of Personality and Social Psychology, 59*, 952-959.

Linden, G., Smith, B., & York, J. (2003). Amazon.com recommendations: Item-to-item collaborative filtering. *IEEE Internet Computing, 7*(1), 76-80.

Linn, M. C., & Petersen, A. C. (1986). A meta-analysis of gender differences in spatial ability: Implications for maths and science achievement. In J. S. Hyde and M. C. Linn (Eds). *The psychology of gender: Advances through meta-analysis* (pp. 67-101). Baltimore: The Johns Hopkins University Press.

Lipponen, L., Rahikainen, M., Lallimo, J., & Hakkarainen, K. (2003). Patterns of participation and discourse in elementary students' computer-supported collaborative learning. *Learning and Instruction, 13*, 487-509.

Lisetti, C., & Rumelhart, D. (1998). An environment to acknowledge the interface between affect and cognition. In *Proceedings of AAAI Spring Symposium, Stanford University*. Menlo Park, CA: AAAI Press.

Little, B. (2008). Giving learning a 'second life' chance. *Human Capital Management*, (Jan/Feb).

Liu, C. C., & Tsai, C. C. (2008). An analysis of peer interaction patterns as discoursed by on-line small group problem-solving activity. *Computers & Education, 50*, 627-639.

Liu, M., & Reed, M. (1994). The relationship between the learning strategies and learning styles in a hypermedia environment. Computers in Human Behavior, 10(4), 419-434.

Liu, Y., Feyen, R., & Tsimhoni, O. (2006). Queuing network-model human processor (QN-MHP): A computational architecture for multitask performance in human-machine systems. *ACM Transactions on Computer-Human Interaction, 13*, 37-70.

Lock, J. V. (2002). Laying the groundwork for the development of learning communities within online courses. *Quarterly Review of Distance Education, 3*(4), 395-408.

Lockhart, C., & Ng, P. (1995). Analyzing talk in ESL peer response groups: Stances, functions, and content. *Language Learning, 45*, 605-655.

Loggie, R. H., Zucco, G. N., & Baddeley, A. D. (1990). Interference with visual short-term memory. *Acta Psychologica, 75*(1), 55-74.

Logie, R.H. (1996). The seven ages of working memory. In J.T.A. Richardson, R.W. Engle, L. Hasher, R.H. Logie, E.R. Stoltzfus, & R.T. Zacks (Eds.), *Working memory and human cognition* (pp. 31-65). New York: Oxford University Press.

Lopez-Real, F., & Chan, Y. P. R. (1999). Peer assessment of a group project in a primary mathematics education course. *Assessment & Evaluation in Higher Education, 24*, 67-79.

Love to Know Baby. (2009). *Interview with Janet Doman a specialist in infant education and brain development*. Retrieved January 9, 2009, from http://baby.lovetoknow.com/wiki/Interview_With_Janet_Doman-A_Specialist_in_Infant_Education_and_Brain_Development

Lowe, P. A., Papanastasiou, E. C., DeRuyck, K. A., & Reynolds, C. R. (2005). Test score stability and construct validity of the Adult Manifest Anxiety Scale-College Version (AMAS-C) scores among college students: A brief report. *Measurement and Evaluation in Counseling and Development, 37*(4), 220-227.

Lowe, P. A., Peyton, V., & Reynolds, C. R. (2007). Test score stability and the relationship of Adult Manifest Anxiety Scale-College Version scores to external variables among college students. *Journal of Psychoeducational Assessment, 25*, 69-81.

LSI - Laboratory of Integrated Systems. (2009). *Núcleo de realidade virtual*. Retrieved April 8, 2009, from http://www.lsi.usp.br/interativos/nem/nem.html

Luckin, R., Du Boulay, B., Yuill, N., Kerawalla, C., Pearce, D., & Harris, A. (2003). Using software scaffolding to increase metacognitive skills amongst young learners. In *Proceedings of the Eleventh International Conference on Artificial Intelligence in Education*, Sydney, Australia. Retrieved September 17, 2008 from http://www.cs.usyd.edu.au/~aied/vol2/vol2_Luckin.pdf

Lufkin, M. E. & Wiberg, M. (2007). Gender equity in career and technical education. . In Klein (Ed.), *Handbook for achieving gender equity through education* (pp. 421-444). Lawrence Erlbaum Associates.

Luger, G. F. (2002). *Artificial intelligence: Structure and strategies for complex problem solving*. Reading, MA: Addison Wesley.

Lyons, M., Akamatsu, S., Kamachi, M., & Gyoba, J. (1998). Coding facial expressions with Gabor wavelets. In *Proceedings of the Third IEEE International Conference on Automatic Face and Gesture Recognition, IEEE Computer Society* (pp. 200-205). Nara Japan.

Macdonald, J. (2003). Assessing online collaborative learning: Process and product. *Computers & Education, 40*, 377-391.

MacLeod, C. & Donnellan, A. M. (1993). Individual differences in anxiety and the restriction of working memory capacity. *Personality and Individual Differences, 15*(2), 163-173.

Madell, D., & Muncer, S. J. (2006). Internet communication: An activity that appeals to shy and socially phobic people? *CyberPsychology & Behavior, 9*(5), 618-622.

Magali O., Niewiadomski, R., Pelachaud, C., & Sadek, D. (2005). Intelligent expressions of emotions. In *1st International Conference on Affective Computing and Intelligent Interaction ACII*, China.

Magin, D. (2001). Reciprocity as a source of bias in multiple peer assessment of group work. *Studies in Higher Education, 26*, 53-63.

Maglio, P. P., & Matlock, T. (1999). The conceptual structure of information space. In A. J. Munro, K. Hook & D. Benyon (Eds.), *Social navigation of information space* (pp. 155-173). London: Springer.

Maier, P., & Warren, A. (2000). *Integrating technology in learning and teaching: A practical guide for educators*. UK: Kogan Page.

Maki, R. H., Maki, W. S., Patterson, M., & Whittaker, P. D. (2000). Evaluation of a Web-based introductory psychology course. *Behavior Research Methods, Instruments, & Computers, 32*, 230-239.

Mancuso, S. (2001). Adult-centered practices: Benchmarking study in higher education. *Innovative Higher Education, 25*(3), 165-181.

Mansoorizadeh M., & Charkari. (2008). Bimodal person-dependent emotion recognition comparison of feature level and decision level information fusion. In *PETRA 2008*.

Manssour, I. H. (2008). *Introdução a linguagem VRML*. Retrieved November 22, 2008, from http://www.inf.pucrs.br/~manssour/VRML/Intro.html

Marbach-Ad, G., & Sokolove, P. G. (2002). The use of e-mail and in-class writing to facilitate student-instructor interaction in large-enrollment traditional and active learning classes. *Journal of Science Education and Technology, 11*(2), 109-119.

Marcelo, C. (2006). *Ask whatever you like. Teacher-pupil interaction in new virtual learning environments*. Retrieved May 07, 2008, from http://www.elearningeuropa.info/directory/index.php?page=doc&doc_id=7875&doclng=6

Marlene, F. (2008). *Matmarlenema*. Retrieved February 16, 2009, from http://matprofmarlene.blogspot.com/

Marsella, S., & Gratch, J. (2006). EMA: A computational model of appraisal dynamics. In J. Gratch, S. Marsella, & P. Petta (Eds.), *Agent construction and emotions*, (pp. 601-606). Austrian Society for Cybernetic Studies, Vienna

Martinez, A., Dimitriadis, Y., Rubia, B., Gomez, E., & De La Fuente, P. (2003). Combining qualitative evaluation and social network analysis for the study of classroom social interactions. *Computers and Education, 41*(4), 353-368.

Martinez-Torres, M. R., Marin, S. L. T, Garcia, F. B., Vazquez, S. G., Oliva, M. A., & Torres, T. (2008). A technological acceptance of e-learning tools used in practical and laboratory teaching, according to the European higher education area. *Behaviour & Information Technology, 27*, 495-505.

Martinho, C., Machado, I., & Paiva, A. (2000). A cognitive approach to affective user modeling. In A. Paiva (Ed.), *Affective interactions - Towards a new generation of computer interfaces.* (LNCS 1814, pp. 64-75).

Marton, F., & Booth, S. (1997). *Learning and awareness.* Mahwah, New Jersey: Lawrence Erlbaum Associates.

Mason, R. (2004). Online education using learning objects. *British Journal of Educational Technology, 35*, 752-754

Masoura, E.V., Gathercole, S.E., & Bablekou, Z. (2004). Contributions of phonological short-term memory to vocabulary acquisition. *Psychology, 11*(3), 341-55 [in Greek].

Masoura, E.V., Gathercole, S.E., & Bablekou, Z. (2006). Phonological working memory involvement in new-word learning tasks: An investigation among young children. *Annals of the Psychological Society of Northern Greece, 4*, 43-65 [in Greek].

Mateas, M. (2005). Procedural literacy: Educating the new media practitioner. *On The Horizon, Special Issue, Future of Games, Simulations and Interactive Media in Learning Contexts, 13.* Retrieved November 18, 2008, from http://www.lcc.gatech.edu/~mateas/publications/MateasOTH2005.pdf

May, J. (2001). Specifying the central executive may require complexity. In J. Andrade (Eds.), *Working memory in perspective* (pp. 261-77). Hove: Psychology Press.

Mayer, R. E. (1988). Learning strategies: An overview. In C. E. Weinstein, E. T. Goetz, & P. Alexander (Eds.), *Learning and study strategies: Issues in assessment, instruction, and evaluation.* New York: Academic Press, Inc.

Mayer, R. E. (1999). Research-based principles for the design of instructional messages: The case of multimedia explanations. *Document Design, 2*, 7-20.

Mayer, R. E. (2001). *Multimedia learning.* New York: Cambridge University Press.

Mayer, R.E., Heiser, J., & Lonn, S. (2001): Cognitive constraints on multimedia learning: When presenting more material results in less understanding. *Journal of Educational Psychology, 93*(1),187-198.

Mayo, M., & Mitrovic, A. (2001). Optimising ITS behavior with Bayesian networks and decision theory. *International Journal of Artificial Intelligence in Education, 12*, 124-153.

McCombs, B., & Miller, M. (2006). *Learner-centred classrooms practices and assessments.* Thousand Oaks, CA: Corwin Press.

McConnell, D. (2000). *Implementing computer supported cooperative learning.* London: Kogan Page.

McConnell, D. (2006). *E-learning groups and communities: Imagining learning in the age of the Internet.* OU Press

McCrae, R. R., & John, O. P. (1992). An introduction to the five factor model and its applications. Special Issue: The five factor model: Issues and applications. *Journal of Personality, 60*, 175-215.

McCroskey, J. C. (1987). *Personality and interpersonal communication.* Newbury Park, CA: Sage.

McCroskey, J. C. (1997). Willingness to communicate, communication apprehension, and self-perceived communication competence: Conceptualizations and perspectives. In J. A. Daly, J. C. McCroskey, J. Ayres, T. Hopf, & D. M. Ayres (Eds.), *Avoiding communication: Shyness, reticence, and communication apprehension* (2nd ed.) (pp.75-108). Cresskill, NJ: Hampton Press Inc.

McCroskey, J. C., & McCroskey, L. L. (1988). Self report as an approach to measuring communication competence and personality orientations. *Communication Research Reports, 5*, 108-113.

McCullogh, M. (2004). *Digital ground: Architecture, pervasive computing, and environmental knowing.* Cambridge, MA: MIT Press.

McDonald, S., & Stevenson, R. J. (1998). Effects of text structure and prior knowledge of the learner on navigation in hypertext. *Human Factors, 40*(1), 18-27.

McElree, B. (1998). Attended and non-attended states in working memory: Accessing categorized structures. *Journal of Memory and Language, 38*, 225-252.

McGlone, J. (1980). Sex differences in human brain asymmetry: A critical survey. *Behavioral and Brain Sciences, 3*, 215-263.

McGriff, S. (2000). *Instructional system design (ISD): Using the ADDIE model.* State College, PA: Penn State University.

McInerney, D. M. (2005). Educational psychology – Theory, research, and teaching: A 25-year retrospective. *Educational Psychology, 25*(6), 585-599.

McKay, M. T., Fischler, I., & Dunn, B. R. (2003). Cognitive style and recall of text: An EEG analysis. *Learning and Individual Differences, 14*(1), 1-21.

McKenna, F. P. (1984). Measures of field dependence: Cognitive style or cognitive ability. *Journal of Personality and Social Psychology, 47*(3), 593-603.

McKenna, F. P. (1990). Learning implications of field dependence-independence: cognitive styles versus cognitive ability. *Applied Cognitive Psychology, 4*, 425-437.

McKenna, K., & Bargh, J. (2000). Plan 9 from cyberspace: The implications of the Internet for personality and social psychology. *Personality and Social Psychology Review, 4*(1), 57-75.

McKenna, K., Green, A. S., & Gleason, M. E. (2002). Relationship formation on the Internet: What's the big attraction? *Journal of Social Issues, 58*(1), 9-31.

McLeod, C. M. (1991). Half a century of research on the Stroop effect: An integrative review. *Psychological Bulletin, 109*, 163-203.

McNamara, D. S., & Kintsch, W. (1996). Working memory in text comprehension: Interrupting difficult text. In G. W. Cottrell (Ed.), *Proceedings of the Eighteenth Annual Meeting of the Cognitive Science Society* (pp. 104-109). Hillsdale, NJ: Lawrence Erlbaum.

McNamara, T. P., Hardy, J. K., & Hirtle, S. C. (1989). Subjective hierarchies in spatial memory. *Journal of Experimental Psychology: Learning Memory and Cognition, 15*, 211-227.

Meccawy, M., Brusilovsky, P., Ashman, H., Yudelson, M., & Scherbinina, O. (2007). Integrating interactive learning content into an adaptive e-learning system: Lessons learned. In G. Richards (Ed.), *Proceedings of the World Conference on E-Learning in Corporate, Government, Healthcare, and Higher Education 2007* (pp. 6314-6319). Chesapeake, VA: AACE.

Mehra, A., Kilduff, M., & Brass, D. J. (2001). The social networks of high and low self-monitors: Implications for work place performances. *Administrative Science Quarterly, 46*(1), 121-146.

Mehrens, W. A., & Lehman, I. J. (1991). *Measurement and evaluation in education and psychology.* New York: Holt, Rinehart and Winston.

Meier, A., Spada, H., & Rummel, N. (2007). A rating scheme for assessing the quality of computer-supported collaboration process. *International Journal of Computer-Supported Collaborative Learning, 2*, 63-86.

Melara, G. E. (1996). Investigating learning styles on different hypertext environments: Hierarchical-like and network-like structures. *Journal of Educational Computing Research, 14*(4), 313-328.

Melis, E., & Siekman, J. (2004). ActiveMath: An intelligent tutoring system for mathematics. In *Proceedings of the Seventh International Conference 'Artificial Intelligence and Soft Computing' (ICAISC)* (LNAI 3070, pp. 91-101). Springer-Verlag.

Melis, E., Andrès, E., Büdenbender, J., Frischauf, A., Goguadze, G., Libbrecht, P., Pollet, M., & Ullrich, C. (2001). ActiveMath: A generic and adaptive Web-based learning environment. *International Journal of Artificial Intelligence in Education, 12*, 385-407

Melton, A.W. (1963). Implications of short-term memory for a general theory of memory. *Journal of Verbal Learning and Verbal Behavior, 2*, 1-21.

Meng, K., & Patty, D. (1991). Field dependence and contextual organizers. Journal of Educational Research, 84(3), 183-189.

Meninos do Morumbi. (2008). Retrieved November 12, 2008, from http://www.meninosdomorumbi.org.br/ingles/frames/principal.html

Merrill, M. D. (2002). Instructional goals and learning styles: Which takes precedence? In R. Reiser & J. Dempsey (Eds.), *Trends and issues in instructional technology.* Upper Saddle River, NJ: Prentice Hall.

Messick, S. (1984). The nature of cognitive styles: Problems and promise in educational practice. *Educational Psychologist*, 19, 59-74.

Messick, S. (1994). The matter of style: Manifestations of personality in cognition, learning, and teaching. *Educational Psychologist, 29*(3), 121-136.

Meyer, J. J. (2004). Reasoning about emotional agents. In R. L'opez de M'antaras and L. Saitta (Eds.), *16th European Conf. on Artif. Intell. (ECAI)* (pp. 129-133).

Miao, Y., & Koper, R. (2007). An efficient and flexible technical approach to develop and deliver online peer assessment. In C. Chinn, G. Erkens, & S. Puntambekar (Eds.), *Mice, minds and society: The computer supported collaborative learning (CSCL) conference 2007* (pp. 502-510). New Brunswick, NJ: International Society of the Learning Sciences.

Michas, I.C., & Henry, L.A. (1994). The link between phonological memory and vocabulary acquisition. *British Journal of Developmental Psychology, 12*, 147-63.

Michinov, N., & Michinov, E. (2008). Face-to-face contact at the midpoint of an online collaboration: Its impact on the patterns of participation, interaction, affect, and behavior over time. *Computer & Education, 50*, 1540-1557.

Miedema, J. L. (2004). *Fairness and the self* (Kurt Lewin Institute Dissertation Series, 2003-9). Unpublished doctoral dissertation, Leiden University, Leiden, the Netherlands.

Milgran, P., & Colquhoun, H., Jr. (1999). A taxonomy of real and virtual world display integration. In Y. Ohta & H. Tamura (Eds.), *Mixed reality: Merging real and virtual worlds* (pp. 5-28). USA: Ohmsha & Springer-Verlag.

Millen, D. R., Fontaine, M. A., & Muller, M. A. (2002). Understanding the benefit and costs of communities of practice. *Communications of the ACM, 45*(4), 69-73.

Miller, A. J. (2002). *Fortran examples.* Retrieved March 31, 2009, from http://www.esm.psu.edu/~ajm138/fortranexamples.html

Miller, C. H. (2004). *Digital storytelling: A creator's guiding to interactive entertainment.* USA: Focal press.

Miller, E. (2006). *Other economies are possible!* Retrieved November 12, 2008, from http://www.zmag.org/znet/viewArticle/3239

Miller, H. & Bichsel, J. (2004). Anxiety, working memory, gender, and math performance. *Personality and Individual Differences*, 37, 591-606.

Milner, Z. (2006). *Learning by accident: A report for a personalized learning project for disaffected learners.* Bristol: ViTaL Partnerships.

Milrad, M. (2007). How should learning activities using mobile technologies be designed to support innovative educational practices? In M. Sharples (Ed.), *Big issues in mobile learning: Report of a workshop by the Kaleidoscope Network of Excellence Mobile Learning Initiative* (pp. 28-30). Nottingham: University of Nottingham.

Mitchell, W. L. (1999). *The Egyptian tomb of Menna, Manchester University Metropolitan Area.* Retrieved November 12, 2008, from http://www.doc.mmu.ac.uk/RESEARCH/virtual-museum/Menna/

Mitrovic, A., & Ohlsson, S. (1999). Evaluation of a constraint-based tutor for a database language. *International Journal of Artificial Intelligence in Education, 10*, 238-256.

Miyake, A., & Friedman, N. (2008, September). *How are working memory capacity, updating ability, and general intelligence related? A behavioral genetic analysis.* Paper presented at the Fourth European Working Memory Symposium, Bristol, UK.

Miyake, A., & Shah, P. (1999). Preface. In A. Miyake & P. Shah (Eds.), *Models of working memory: Mechanisms of active maintenance and executive control* (pp. xiii-xvii). Cambridge, UK: Cambridge University Press.

Miyake, A., & Shah, P. (1999). Toward unified theories of working memory: Emerging general consensus, unresolved theoretical issues, and future research directions. In A. Miyake & P. Shah (Eds.), *Models of working memory: Mechanisms of active maintenance and executive control* (pp. 442-81). Cambridge, UK: Cambridge University Press.

Mizoguchi, R., & Bourdeau, J. (2000). Using ontological engineering to overcome common AI-ED Problems. *Int. J. AI in Education, 11*, 1-12.

Mizoguchi, R., Sinitsa, K., & Ikeda, M. (1996). Task ontology design for intelligent educational/ training systems. In *Proc. of Workshop on Architectures and Methods for Designing Cost-Effective and Reusable ITSs* (ITS'96) (pp. 1-21). Montreal.

Mödritscher, F. (2007). *Implementation and evaluation of pedagogical strategies in adaptive e-learning environments.* Unpublished doctoral dissertation, Institute for Information Systems and Computer Media, Graz University of Technology.

Mödritscher, F., García-Barrios, V. M., & Maurer, H. (2005). The use of a dynamic background library within the scope of adaptive e-learning. In G. Richards (Ed.), *Proceedings of the World Conference on E-Learning in Corporate, Government, Healthcare, and Higher Education (E-Learn 2005)* (pp. 3045-3052). Chesapeake, VA, USA: AACE.

Mödritscher, F., Spiel, S., & Garcia-Barrios, V. (2006). Assessment in e-learning environments: A comparison of three methods. In C. Crawford, et al. (Eds.), *Proceedings of Society for Information Technology and Teacher Education International Conference 2006* (pp. 108-113).

Modularity on mind. (2009). Retrieved February 13, 2009, from http://en.wikipedia.org/wiki/Modularity_of_mind

Mohageg, M. F. (1992). The influence of hypertext linking structures on the efficiency of information retrieval. *Human Factors, 34*, 351-367.

Monsell, S. (2005). The chronometrics of task-set control. In J. Duncan, L. Phillips, & P. Mcleod (Eds.), *Measuring the mind: Speed, control and age* (pp. 161-90). Oxford: Oxford University Press.

Montgomery, D. A. (1999). Human sensitivity to variability information in detection decisions. *Human Factors, 41*, 90-105.

Moore, M. (1989). Three types of interaction. *American Journal of distance Education, 3*(2), 34-54.

Moos, D. C., & Azevedo, R. (2008). Monitoring, planning, and self-efficacy learning with hypermedia: The impact of conceptual scaffolds. *Journal of Computers in Human Behavior, 24*, 1686-1706.

Moran, J. (2003). Contribuições para uma pedagogia da educação online. In S. Marco (Ed.), *Educação on-line.* Sao Paulo: Edições Loyola.

Moran, J. (2005). A pedagogia e a didática da educação on-line. In *Educação, aprendizagem e tecnologia. Um paradigma para professores do século XXI.* Edições Sílabo.

Morgado, L. (2005). Novos papéis para o professor/tutor na pedagogia on-line. In R. Silva & A. Silva (Eds.), *Educação, aprendizagem e tecnologia: Um paradigma para professores do século XXI* (pp. 97-120). Edições Sílabo.

Morgan, C., & Oreilly, M. (1999). *Assessing open and distance learners.* Kogan Page.

Mortimore, P (Ed.), (1999). *Understanding pedagogy and its impact on learning*. London: Paul Chapman Pubs.

Mortimore, T. (2003). *Dyslexia and learning style*. London: Whurr Pubs.

Mosely, D., Baumfield, V., Elliot, J., Gregson, M., Higgins, S., Miller, J., & Newton, D. (2005). *Frameworks for thinking: A handbook for teaching and learning*. Cambridge: Cambridge University Press.

Moskal, B., Lurie, D., & Cooper, S. (n.d.). *Evaluating the effectiveness of a new instructional approach*. Retrieved November 13, 2008, from http://www.alice.org/publications/EvaluatingTheEffectivenessOfANewApproach.pdf

Moss, M. (2005). Personalized lLearning: A failure to collaborate. In S. De Freitas, & C. Yapp (Eds.), *Personalizing learning in the 21ˢᵗ century*. Stafford: Network Educational Press.

Mostow, J. (2006). *Project LISTEN: A reading tutor that listens*. Retrieved November 12, 2008, from http://www.cs.cmu.edu/~listen/research.html

Mozziconacci, S.J.L., & Hermes, D.J., (2000). Expression of emotion and attitude through temporal speech variations. In *Proceedings of the Internat. Conf. on Spoken Language Processing (ICSLP '00), Beijing* (Vol. 2, pp. 373-378).

Mrech, L. M. (1999). *Psicanálise e educação, novos operadores de leitura*. Brasil: Ed. Pioneira.

Murray, I. R., & Arnott, J. L. (1993). Toward the simulation of emotion in synthetic speech: A review of the literature on human vocal emotion. *Journal Acoustical Society of America, 93*(2), 1097-1108.

Murray, J. H. (2003) *Hamlet no holodeck: O futuro da narrativa no ciberespaço*. Brasil: Editora UNESP.

Murugesan, S. (2008). Web application development: Challenges and the role of Web engineering. In G. Rossi, O. Pastor, D. Schwabe, & L. Olsina (Eds.), *Web engineering: Modeling and implementing Web applications* (pp. 7-32). UK: Springer.

Museu Lasar Segal. (2008). November 27, 2008, from http://www.museusegall.org.br/

Myers, I. B. (1984). *Myers Briggs type indicator*. Palo Alto, CA: Consulting Psychologists Press.

Na, S., Billinghurst, M., & Woo, W. (2008). TMAR: Extension of a tabletop interface using mobile augmented reality. In *Proceedings of Edutainment 2008*, Nanjing, China. Retrieved November 12, 2008, from http://www.hitlabnz.org/publications/2008-TMARExtensionofaTabletopInterfaceUsingMobileAugmentedReality.pdf

Naeve, A., Lytras, M., Nejdl, W., Balacheff, N., & Hardin, J. (2006). Editorial: Advances of the Semantic Web for e-learning: Expanding learning frontiers. *British Journal of Educational Technology, 37*(3) 321-330.

Nahapiet, J., & Ghoshal, S. (1998). Social capital, intellectual capital, and the organizational advantage. *Academy of Management Review, 23*(2), 242-266.

Nairne, J.S. (2002). Remembering over the short-term: The case against the standard model. *Annual Review of Psychology, 53*, 53-81.

Naismith, E. (2005). Enabling personalization through context awareness. In S. De Freitas & C. Yapp (Eds.), *Personalizing learning in the 21ˢᵗ century* (pp. 103-108). Stafford: Network Educational Press.

Naismith, L., Lonsdale, P., Vavoula, G., & Sharples, M. (2004). *Report 11: Literature review in mobile technologies and learning*. Futurelab series, Futurelab.

Nanda, A. (1996). Resources, capabilities and competencies. In B. Moingeon & A. Edmondson (Eds.), *Organizational learning and competitive advantage* (pp. 93-120). Thousand Oaks, CA: Sage.

Narciss, S. (2006). *Informatives tutorielles feedback* [Informative tutorial feedback]. Münster, Germany: Waxmann Verlag.

Narciss, S. (2008). Feedback strategies for interactive learning tasks. In J. M. Spector, M. D. Merrill, J. J. G. Van Merriënboer, & M. P. Driscoll (Eds.), *Handbook of research on educational communications and technology*

(3rd ed.) (pp. 125-143). Mahwah, NJ: Lawrence Erlbaum Associates.

Narciss, S., & Huth, K. (2006). Fostering achievement and motivation with bug-related tutoring feedback in a computer-based training for written subtraction. *Learning & Instruction, 16*, 310-322.

Nardi, B., Whittaker, S., & Schwarz, H. (2002). Net-WORKers and their activity in intensional networks. *Computer Supported Cooperative Work, 11*, 205-242.

NATE. (2009). *NATE – núcleo de aprendizagem, trabalho e entretenimento.* Retrieved January 13, 2009, from http://www.lsitec.org.br/html/aprendizagem_e_entretenimento.html

Neisser, U., Boodoo, G., Bouchard, Jr., T. J., Boykin, A W., Brody, B., Ceci, S. J., Halpern, D. E., Loehlin, J. C., Perloff, R., Sternberg, R. J., & Urbina, S. (1996). Intelligence: Knowns and unknowns. *American Psychologist, 51*(2), 77-101.

Nelson, C. A., de Haan, M., & Thomas, M. M. (2006). *Neuroscience of cognitive development: The role of experience and the developing brain.* New Jersey, NY. Wiley & Sons.

Neo, M. (2003). Developing a collaborative learning environment using a Web-based design. *Journal of Computer Assisted Learning, 19*, 462-473.

Newell, A. (1990). *Unified theories of cognition.* Cambridge, MA: Harvard University Press.

Newell, A. F., & Gregor, P. (2000). User sensitive inclusive design in search of a new paradigm. J. Scholtz & J. Thomas (Eds.), *Proceedings of the First ACM Conference on Universal Usability*, Washington, DC (pp. 39-44).

Nicholson, S. (2002). Socialization in the 'virtual hallway': Instant messaging in the asynchronous Web-based distance education classroom. *The Internet and Higher Education, 5*, 363-372.

Nicolelis, M. (2008). Building the knowledge archipelago globalization of a development model. In *Scientific American: Building the Knowledge Archipelago.* Retrieved February 13, 2009, from http://www.nicolelislab.net/Papers/sciam%20dot%20com%20Archipelago+images.pdf

NICVE. (2008). *Master science course in virtual environments.* Retrieved November 12, 2008, from http://www.nicve.salford.ac.uk/

Nielsen, J. (1993). *Usability engineering.* London: Academic Press.

Nielsen, J. (2001, January 16). *Jacob Nielsen on e-learning. E-learning post.* Retrieved from http://www.elearningpost.com/features/archives/001015.asp

Nikolova, I., & Tzanavari-Smyrilli, A. (2007). *Executive summary of UNITE deliverable 1: State-of-the-art in elearning and user requirements.* Retrieved May 7, 2008, from http://www.unite-ist.org

NIMIS - (Networked Interactive Media in Schools) project. (2008). Retrieved November 12, 2008 http://www.stockholmchallenge.se/data/nimis_networked_interacti

Nisbet, J., & Shucksmith, J. (1986). *Learning strategies.* London: Routledge.

NMC. (2008). *The horizon report 2008 edition, a collaboration between The New Media Consortium – NMC and the EDUCAUSE Learning Initiative An EDUCAUSE Program.* Retrieved November 12, 2008, from http://www.nmc.org/pdf/2008-Horizon-Report.pdf

Noddings, N. (1995). *Philosophy of education.* Boulder, CO: Westview Press.

Nonaka, I., & Konno, N. (1998). The concept of "ba": Building a foundation for knowledge creation. *California Management Review, 40*(3), 40-54.

Norman, D., & Draper, S.W. (1986). *User centred system design.* Hillsdale, NJ: Lawrence Erlbaum Assoc.

Norton, R. W. (1978). Foundation of a communication style construct. *Human Communication Research*, 4(2), 99-112.

Norwich, B., & Lewis, A. (2001). Mapping a pedagogy for special educational needs. *British Educational Research Journal, 27*(3), 313-329.

Nunes, M. (2008). Retrieved February 16, 2009 http://sempremichaelnunes.blogspot.com/

O'Connor, T. O. (1999). *Using learning styles to adapt technology for higher education.* Center for Teaching and Learning, Indiana University. Retrieved April 30, 2008, from http://iod.unh.edu/EE/articles/learning-styles.html

O'Donnell, A. M. (2006). The role of peers and group learning. In P. Alexander & P. Winne (Eds.), *Handbook of educational psychology* (2nd Ed., pp. 781-802). Mahwah, NJ: Lawrence Erlbaum.

O'Donnell, A. M., & Dansereau, D. F. (1992). Scripted cooperation in student dyads: A method for analysing and enhancing academic learning and performance. In R. Hertz-Lazarowitz & N. Miller (Eds.), *Interaction in cooperative groups: The theoretical anatomy of group learning* (pp. 120-144). New York: Cambridge University Press.

Oberauer, K. (2002). Access to information in working memory: Exploring the focus of attention. *Journal of Experimental Psychology: Learning, Memory and Cognition, 28*, 411-421.

Ochoa, T. A., & Robinson, J. (2005). Revisiting group consensus: Collaborative learning dynamics during a problem-based learning activity in education. *Teacher Education and Special Education, 28*, 10-20.

Ochoa, T. A., Gottschall, H., & Stuart S. (2004). Group participation and satisfaction: Results from a PBL computer-supported module. *Journal of Educational Multimedia and Hypermedia, 13*, 73-91.

Oliver, K., & Moore, J. (2008). Faculty recommendations for Web tools: Implications for course management systems. *Journal of Computing in Higher Education, 19, 3-24.*

OLPC – One Laptop per Child. (2008). Retrieved, October 12, 2008, from http://laptop.org/vision/index.shtml

Oltman, P. K., Raskin, E., & Witkin, H. A. (2003). *Group embedded figures test.* Menlo Park, CA: Mind Garden.

Onwuegbuzie, A. J. (2000). Statistics anxiety and the role of self-perceptions. *Journal of Educational Research, 93*, 323-330.

Onwuegbuzie, A., Bailey, P., & Daley, C. (1999). Factors associated with foreign language anxiety. *Applied Socio Linguistics 20,* 218-239.

Oren T.I., & Ghasem-Aghaee N. (2003). Personality representation processable in fuzzy logic for human behavior simulation. In *Proceedings of the 2003 Summer Computer Simulation Conference, Montreal, PQ, Canada, July 20-24* (pp. 11-18).

Orr, R.J., & Abowd, G.D. (2000). The smart floor: A mechanism for natural user identification and tracking. In *CHI '00: CHI '00 Extended Abstracts on Human Factors in Computing Systems* (pp. 275-276). New York: ACM Press.

Orsmond, P., Merry, S., & Callaghan, A. (2004). Implementation of a formative assessment model incorporating peer and self-assessment. *Innovations in Education and Teaching International, 41*, 273-290.

Orsmond, P., Merry, S., & Reiling, K. (1997). A study in self assessment: Tutor and students' perceptions of performance criteria. *Assessment & Evaluation in Higher Education, 22*, 357–67.

Orsmond, P., Merry, S., & Reiling, K. (2002). The use of exemplars and formative feedback when using student derived marking criteria in peer and self-assessment. *Assessment & Evaluation in Higher Education, 27,* 309-323.

Ortony, A., Clore, G. L., & Collins, A. (1988). *The cognitive structure of emotions.* Cambridge: Cambridge University Press

Osberg, K. (1993). *Virtual reality and education: A look at both sides of the sword* (Tech. Rep.). Seattle: University of Washington, Human Interface Technology Laboratory. Retrieved November 13, 2008, from http://www.hitl.washington.edu/publications/r-93-7/

Osberg, K. (1995). *Virtual reality and education: Where imagination and experience meet, VR in the Schools,*

1-2. Retrieved November 12, 2008, from http://vr.coe. ecu.edu/vrits/1-2osber.htm

Osberg, K. (1997). *Constructivism in practice: The case for meaning-making in the virtual world*. Unpublished doctoral dissertation, University of Washington. Retrieved November 12, 2008, from http://www.hitl. washington.edu/publications/r-97-47/abstr.html

Osberg, K. (1997). *A teacher's guide to developing virtual environments: VRRV project support* (Tech. Rep.). Seattle: Human Interface Technology Lab. Retrieved November 13, 2008, from http://www.hitl.washington. edu/publications/r-97-17/

Osberg, K. M. (1997). *Spatial cognition in the virtual environment* (HITL Technical Publication: R-97-18). Human Interface Technology Laboratory of the Washington Technology Center, University of Washington. Retrieved November 12, 2008, from http://www.hitl.washington. edu/publications/r-97-18/

Osberg, K. M., Winn, W., Rose, H., Hollander, A., Hoffman, H., & Char, P. (1997c). *The effect of having grade seven students construct virtual environments on their comprehension of science.* Retrieved November 13, 2008, from http://www.hitl.washington.edu/ publications/r-97-19/

Outras Palavras. (2008). *Prof^a. Lea Fagundes fala sobre como ocorre a aprendizagem e problemáticas do projeto UCA*. January 12, 2009, from http://www.antoniopassos. pro.br/blog/?cat=13&paged=2

Overbaugh, R. C., & Casiello, A. R. (2008). Distributed collaborative problem-based graduate-level learning: Students' perspectives on communication tool selection and efficacy. *Computers in Human Behavior, 24*, 497-515.

Paiva, A. (2000). Affective interactions: Toward a new generation of computer interfaces? In A. Paiva (Ed.), *Affective interactions - Towards a new generation of computer interfaces.* (LNCS 1814).

Paiva, A., Dias, J., Sobral, D., Aylett, R., Woods, S., Hall, L., & Zoll, C. (2005). Learning by feeling: Evoking empathy with synthetic characters. *Applied Artificial Intelligence 19*, 235-266.

Paivio, A. (1971). *Imagery and verbal processes.* New York: Holt, Rinehart & Winston.

Paivio, A. (1991). Dual coding theory: Retrospect and current status. *Canadian Journal of Psychology, 45*, 255-87.

Palincsar, A. S., & Brown, A. L. (1984). Reciprocal teaching of comprehension-fostering and comprehension-monitoring activities. *Cognition & Instruction, 1*, 117-175.

Pankhurst, R., & Marsh, D. (2008). Communities of practice: Using the open Web as a collaborative learning platform. In *Proceedings of the iLearning Forum 2008*, Paris, France.

Pantazis, C. (2001). *Executive summary: A vision of e-learning for America's workforce* (Report of the Commission on Technology and Adult Learning, ASTD). Retrieved from http://www.learningcircuits.org/2001/ aug2001/pantazis.html

Pantic, M. & Rothkrantz, L. J. M. (2000). Expert system for automatic analysis of facial expressions. In B. Parkinson & A.M. Coleman (Eds.), *Image and vision computing. Emotion and Motivation.* London: Longman.

Papanastasiou, E. C. & Paparistodemou, E. (2007). Examining educational technology and achievement through latent variable modeling. In T. Loveless (Ed.), *Lessons learned. What international assessments tell us about math achievement* (pp. 205-225). Washington D.C.: Brookings Institution Press.

Papanastasiou, E. C. & Reckase, M. D. (2008, June). *Item review as a non-traditional method of item analysis.* Paper presented at the Annual conference of the Psychometric Society, Durham, NH.

Papanastasiou, E. C., Zembylas, M., & Vrasidas, C. (2003). Can computer use hurt science achievement? The USA results from PISA. *Journal of Science Education and Technology, 12*(3), 325-332.

Papanikolaou, K. A., & Grigoriadou, M. (2004). Accommodating learning style characteristics in adaptive educational hypermedia systems. In *Procs. of the Workshop* on *Individual Differences in Adaptive Hypermedia*, The University of Technology, The Netherlands.

Papanikolaou, K. A., Grigoriadou, M., Kornilakis, H., & Magoulas, G. D. (2003). Personalizing the interaction in a Web-based educational hypermedia system: The case of INSPIRE. *User-Modelling and User-Adapted Interaction, 13*(3), 213-267.

Papanikolaou, K. A., Grigoriadou, M., Magoulas, G. D., & Kornilakis, H. (2002). Towards new forms of knowledge communication: The adaptive dimension of a web-based learning environment. *Computers & Education, 39*, 333-360.

Papert, S. (2008). *A máquina das crianças: Repensando a escola na era da informática* (S. Costa, Trans.). Brasil: Artmed.

Papert, S., & Harel, I. (1991). Situating constructionism. In *Constructionism*. Ablex Publishing Corporation. Retrieved November 16, 2008, from http://www.papert.org/articles/SituatingConstructionism.html

Paredes, P., & Rodríguez, P. (2004). A mixed approach to modelling learning styles in adaptive educational hypermedia. *Advanced Technology for Learning, 1*(4), 210-215.

Parikh, A., McReelis, K., & Hodges, B. (2001). Student feedback in problem based learning: A survey of 103 final year students across five Ontario medical schools. *Medical Education, 35*, 632-636.

Park, C. J., & Hyun, J. S. (2006). Comparison of two learning models for collaborative e-learning. In Z. Pan, et al. (Eds.), *Technologies for e-learning and digital entertainment* (pp. 50-59). Berlin, Germany: Springer-Verlag.

Park, K. S., Leigh, J., Johnson, A. E., Carter, B., Brody, J., & Sosnoski, J. (2001). *Distance learning classroom using virtual Harlem*. Retrieved November 12, 2008, from http://www.evl.uic.edu/park/papers/VSMM01/park_distance.pdf

Park, O., & Lee, J. (2003). Adaptive instructional systems. *Educational Technology Research and Development, 2003*(25), 651-684.

Parker, D. (2001). Inside online learning: Comparing conceptual and technique based learning in place-based and ALN formats. *Journal of Asynchronous Learning Network, 5*(2), 64-74.

Parkinson, A., & Redmond, J. A. (2002). Do cognitive styles affect learning performance in different computer media? In *Proceedings of the Annual Joint Conference Integrating Technology into Computer Science Education, Proceedings of the 7th annual conference on Innovation and technology in computer science education*, Aarhus, Denmark (pp. 39-43).

Parlamento Europeu. (2002). *Decisao do parlamento Europeu e do conselho que adopta um programa plurianual (2004 2006)*.

Parlangeli, O., Marchigiani, E., & Bagnara, S. (1999). Multimedia systems in distance education: Effects of usability on learning. *Interacting with Computers, 12*, 37-49

Parque CienTec. (2008). Retrieved November 12, 2008, from http://www.parquecientec.usp.br/

Parrish, A. D. (2002). *Inspired 3D lighting and composing*. USA: Premier Press.

Parshall, C. G., Spray, J. A., Kalohn, J. C. & Davey, T. (2002). *Practical considerations in computer-based testing*. New York: Springer.

Partala, T., & Surakka, V. (2003). Pupil size variation as an indication of affective processing. *Int. J. Human–Comput. Stud. 59*, 185-198.

Participant Observation Wikipedia. (2009). Retrieved February 13, 2009, from http://en.wikipedia.org/wiki/Participant_observation

Pask, G. (1972). A fresh look at cognition and the individual. *International Journal of Man Machine Studies, 4*, 211-216.

Passig, D., & Levin, H. (2000). Gender preferences for multimedia interfaces. *Journal of Computer Assisted Learning, 16*, 64-71.

Patri, M. (2002). The influence of peer feedback on self and peer assessment. *Language Testing, 19*, 109-131.

Paul, C. (2008). *Digital art*. England: Thames & Hudson.

Paule, M. P., Pérez, J. R., & González, M. (2003). Feijoo. net. An approach to personalized e-learning using learning styles. In *Procs. of the ICWE* (pp. 112-115).

PCN 5ª a 8ª Séries matemática. (1998). *Parâmetros curriculares nacionais*. Ministério da Educação – MEC. Retrieved November 27, 2008, from http://portal.mec. gov.br/seb/arquivos/pdf/matematica.pdf

Peres, P., & Pimenta, P. (2008). Uma metodologia para a integração das tecnologias WEB no ensino superior (Tese doutoramento, Universidade do Minho).

Perlin, K. (2008). *Perlin home page experiments*. Retrieved November 12, 2008, from http://mrl.nyu. edu/~perlin/

Perlin, K., & Goldberg, A. (1996). Improv: A system for scripting interactive actors in virtual worlds. *Computer Graphics, 29*(3). Retrieved November 12, 2008, from http://mrl.nyu.edu/publications/sig96-improv/sig96-improv.pdf

Persico, D., & Sarti, L. (2005). Social structures for online learning: A design perspective. In G. Chiazzese M. Allegra, A. Chifari, & S. Ottaviano (Eds.), *Methods and technologies for learning, Proceedings of the International Conference on Methods and Technologies for Learning*. Boston, MA: WIT Press.

Persico, D., Pozzi, F., & Sarti, L. (2008). Fostering collaboration in CSCL. In A. Cartelli & M. Palma (Eds.), *Encyclopedia of information communication technology*. Hershey, PA: Idea Group Reference.

Persico, D., Pozzi, F., & Sarti, L. (in press). A model for monitoring and evaluating CSCL. In A. A. Juan, T. Daradoumis, F. Xhafa, S. Caballe, & J. Faulin (Eds.), *Monitoring and assessment in online collaborative environments: Emergent computational technologies for e-learning support*. Hershey, PA: Information Science Reference.

Persinger, M. A., & Richards, P. M. (1995). Women reconstruct more detail than men for a complex five-minute narrative: Implications for right-hemispheric factors in the serial memory effect. *Perceptual and Motor Skills, 80*, 403-410.

Peter, J., Valenburg, P., & Schouten, A. P. (2005). Developing a model of adolescent friendship formation on the Internet. *CyberPsychology & Behavior, 8*(5), 423-430.

Peter, J., Valkenburg, P., & Schouten, A. P. (2006). Characteristics and motives of adolescents talking with strangers on the Internet. *CyberPsychology & Behavior, 9*(5), 526-530.

Peter, O. (2001). *Didática do ensino a distância: Experiências e estágio da discussão numa visão internacional* (I. Kayser, Trans.). Brasil: Editora, Unissinos.

Peterson, E. R., Deary, I. J., & Austin, E. J. (2003). On the assessment of cognitive style: Four red herrings. *Personality and Individual Differences, 34*(5), 899-904.

Peterson, E. R., Deary, I. J., & Austin, E. J. (2003). The reliability of Riding's cognitive style analysis test. *Personality and Individual Differences, 34*(5), 881-891.

Phillips, L.H., & Hamilton, C. (2001). The working memory model in adult aging research. In J. Andrade, (Ed.). *Working memory in perspective* (pp. 101-25). Hove: Psychology Press.

Phillips, M. (2005). Cognitive style's influence on media preference: Does it matter or do they know? In *Proceedings of the World Conference on Educational Multimedia, Hypermedia & Telecommunications (ED-MEDIA)* (pp. 1023-1028).

Phipps, L., & Kelly, B. (2006). Holistic approaches to e-learning accessibility. *Association for Learning Technology, 14*(1), 69-78.

Piaget, J. (1953). The origins of intelligence in children. London: Routledge and Kegan Paul.

Piaget, J. (1987). *O nascimento da inteligência na criança* (4th ed.). Brasil: LTC.

Piaget, J., Beth, W., & Mays, M. (1974). *Epistemologia genética e pesquisa psicologica*. Trad. da Livraria Freitas Bastos.

Piazzi, P. (2007). *Aprendendo inteligência*. Brasil: Ed. Vida e Consciência.

Picard, R. W. (1997). *Affective computing*. Cambridge, MA: MIT Press.

Picard, R.W. (2003). Affective computing: Challenges. *Int. Journal of Human-Computer Studies, 59*(1-2), 55-64.

Picard, R.W., Vyzas, E., & Healey, J. (2001). Toward machine emotional intelligence: Analysis of affective physiological state. *IEEE Trans. Pattern Anal. Mach. Intell., 23*(10), 1175-1191.

Piccoli, G., Ahmad, R., & Ives, B. (2001). Web-based virtual learning environments: A research framework and a preliminary assessment of effectiveness in basic IT skills training. *MIS Quarterly, 25*(4), 401-426.

Pierre-Yves O. (2003). The production and recognition of emotions in speech: Features and algorithms. *Int. J. Human-Computer Studies, 59*, 157-183.

Pietraß, M. (2007). *Changes in cultural practices and social values*. Paper presented at the INDIRE-OECD Expert Meeting on the New Millennium Learners/Session 3. Retrieved January 12, 2009, from http://www.oecd.org/dataoecd/0/7/38360803.pdf

Pillay, H. (1998). An investigation of the effect of individual cognitive preferences on learning through computer-based instruction. *Educational Psychology, 18*, 171-182.

Pimenta, P., & Ana, B. (2004). Das plataformas de e-learning aos objectos de aprendizagem. In A. Dias (Ed.), *E-learning para e-formadores* (pp. 98-109). Tecminho.

Pimentel, J. R. (1999). Design of net-learning systems based on experiential learning. *Journal of Asynchronous Learning Networks, 3*(2), 64-90.

Pintrich, P. R. (1999). The role of motivation in promoting and sustaining self-regulated learning. *International Journal of Educational Research, 31*, 459-470.

PISA – OECD. (2006). *The programme for international student assessment: Science competencies for tomorrow's world, executive summary*. Retrieved November 12, 2008, from http://www.pisa.oecd.org/dataoecd/15/13/39725224.pdf

Ploegh, K., Segers, M., & Tillema, H. (2007, August). *Scrutinizing peer assesment validity: A review of research studies*. Paper presented at the JURE conference, Budapest, Hungary.

Plutchik, R. (1980). *Emotion: A psychoevolutionary synthesis*. New York: Harper & Row.

Pond, K., Ul-Haq, R., & Wade, W. (1995). Peer review: A precursor to peer assessment. *Innovations in Education and Training International, 32*, 314-323.

Poole, D., Mackworth, A., & Goebel, R. (1998). *Computational intelligence: A logical approach*. Oxford, UK: Oxford University Press.

Pope, A., Bogart, E., & Bartolome, D. (1995). Biocybernetic system evaluates indices of operator engagement in automated task. *Biol. Psychol. 40*, 187-195

Popescu, E. (2008). An artificial intelligence course used to investigate students' learning style. In *Procs. of the ICWL 2008* (LNCS 5145, pp. 122-131). Springer.

Popescu, E. (2008). *Dynamic adaptive hypermedia systems for e-learning*. Unpublished doctoral dissertation, University of Craiova, Romania.

Popescu, E., Badica, C., & Trigano, P. (2008). Learning Objects' architecture and indexing in WELSA adaptive educational system. *Scalable Computing: Practice and Experience, 9*(1), 11-20.

Popescu, E., Badica, C., & Trigano, P. (2008). Analyzing learners' interaction with an educational hypermedia system: A focus on learning styles. In *Procs. of the SAINT2008 (workshop SPeL)* (pp. 321-324). IEEE Computer Society Press.

Popescu, E., Trigano, P., & Badica, C. (2007). Towards a unified learning style model in adaptive educational systems. In *Procs. of the ICALT 2007* (pp. 804-808). IEEE Computer Society Press.

Popper, F. (2007). *From technological to virtual art.* Cambridge, MA: MIT Press.

Portal Aprendiz. (2009). *Jovens criam soluções para problemas de suas comunidades.* Retrieved March 21, 2009, from http://aprendiz.uol.com.br/content/phiwretuwo.mmp

Powell, W. W., & Grodal, S. (2008). Networks of innovators. In J. Fagerberg, D. C. Mowery, & R. R. Nelson (Eds.), *The Oxford handbook of innovation* (pp. 56-85). New York: Oxford University Press.

Powers, D. E. (1999). *Test anxiety and test performance: Comparing paper based and computer-adaptive versions of the GRE general test.* (Research Report 99-15). Princeton, NJ: Educational Testing Service

Powers, D. E. (2001). Test anxiety and test performance: Comparing paper based and computer-adaptive versions of the Graduate Record Examinations (GRE) general test. *Journal of Educational Computing Research, 24*(3), 249-273.

Pozzi, F. (2007). Fostering collaboration in CSCL: Techniques and system functions. *International Journal on Advanced Technology for Learning, 4*(1).

Pozzi, F., & Sugliano, A. M. (2006). Using collaborative strategies and techniques in CSCL environments. In A. Méndez-Vilas, et al. (Eds.), *Current developments in technology-assisted education 1* (pp. 703-709). FORMATEX.

Pozzi, F., Manca, S., Persico, D., & Sarti, L. (2007). A general framework for tracking and analysing learning processes in CSCL environments. *Innovations in Education & Teaching International (IETI) Journal, 44*(2), 169-180.

Prashnig, B. (1998).*The power of diversity: New ways of learning and teaching.* Auckland, NZ: David Bateman.

Preece, J., Rogers, Y., Sharp, H., Benyon, D., Holland, S., & Carey, T. (1994). *Human computer interaction.* Reading, MA: Addison-Wesley.

Preece, J., Sharp, H., & Rogers, Y. (2007). *Interaction design: Beyond human-computer interaction* (2nd ed.). New York: John Wiley & Sons, Ltd.

Prendinger, H., Mori, J., & Ishizuka, M. (2005). Using human physiology to evaluate subtle expressivity of a virtual quizmaster in a mathematical game. *International Journal Human–Computer Studies. 62,* 231-245.

Pressman, R. (2006).*Software engineering: A practitioner's approach* (6th ed.). New York: McGraw Hill.

Prince, M. (2004). Does active learning work? A review of the research. *Journal of Engineering Education, 93*(3), 1-10.

Prins, F. J., Sluijsmans, D. M. A, Kirschner, P. A., & Strijbos, J. W. (2005). Formative peer assessment in a CSCL environment: A case study. *Assessment & Evaluation in Higher Education, 30,* 417-444.

Prins, F. J., Sluijsmans, D. M. A., & Kirschner, P. A. (2006). Feedback for general practitioners in training: Quality, styles, and preferences. *Advances in Health Sciences Education, 11,* 289-303.

Prinsen, F., Volman, M.L.L., & Terwel, J. (2007). The influence of learner characteristics on degree and type of participation in a CSCL environment. *British Journal of Educational Technology, 38*(6), 1037-1055.

Processing. (2009). *Processing software.* Retrieved January 11, 2009, from http://www.processing.org/learning/3d/texture1.html

Project Listen. (2008). *Project LISTEN (literacy innovation that speech technology enables).* Retrieved November 12, 2008, from http://www.cs.cmu.edu/~listen/index.html

Project Spectrum. (2009). *Project spectrum.* Retrieved November 12, 2008, from http://www.pz.harvard.edu/Research/Spectrum.htm

Project Zero. (2008). Retrieved January 11, 2008, from http://www.pz.harvard.edu/index.cfm

Projeto Clicar. (2009). *Dados 'data'*. Retrieved January 11, 2009, from http://www.cepeca.org.br/projetoclicar/pagina.php?id=127

Pulkinen, J., & Peltonen, A. (1998). Searching for the essential elements of Web-based learning environments. In *Proceedings of the 3ʳᵈ International Open Learning Conference*, Brisbane, Queensland, Australia.

Qualitative research Wikipedia. (2009). *Qualitative research*. Retrieved February 13, 2009, from http://en.wikipedia.org/wiki/Qualitative_research

Raessens, J. (2005). Computer games as participatory media culture. In J. Raessens & J. Goldstein (Eds.), *Computer games studies* (pp. 373-388). Cambridge, MA: MIT Press.

Rajadell, N., & Serrat, N. (2000). La interrogacion didatica: Una estrategia para aplicar en el aula. In S. D. L. Torre (Ed.), *Estrategias didaticas innovadoras: Recursos para la formacion y el cambio* (pp. 263-285). Octaedro.

Rao, A., & Georgeff M. (1991). Modeling rational agent within a BDI-architecture. In *Proceedings of the 2nd Int. Conf. on Principle of Knowledge Representation and Reasoning, KR91*. San Mateo, CA.

Rapee, R.M. (1993). The utilisation of working memory by worry. *Behavior Research and Therapy, 31*(6), 617-620.

Ravenscroft, A. (2001). Designing e-learning interactions in the 21st century: Revisiting and rethinking the role of theory. *European Journal of Education, 36*(2), 133-156.

Rayner, S. & Riding, R. (1997). Towards a categorisation of cognitive styles and learning styles. *Educational Psychology, 17*(1/2), 5-27.

Rayner, S. (2001). Cognitive styles and learning styles. In N. J. Smelser & P. B. Baltes (Eds.), *International encyclopedia of social & behavioral Sciences*. UK: Elsevier Science Ltd.

Rayner, S. (2007). *Managing special and inclusive education*. London: Sage.

Rayner, S. (2007). Whither styles? In T. Redmond, A. Parkinson, C. Moore & A. Stenson (Eds.), *Exploring style: Enhancing the capacity to learn. Proceedings of the 11ᵗʰ Annual Conference of the European Learning Styles Information Network* (pp. zx-zx). Dublin: University of Dublin.

Rayner, S. G. (2000). Re-constructing style differences in thinking and learning: Profiling learning performance. In R. J. Riding & S. Rayner (Eds.), *International Perspectives in Individual Differences.* (pp. 115-180). Stamford, CT: Ablex Press.

Rayner, S. G. (2007). A teaching elixir, learning chimera or just fool's gold? Do learning styles matter? *Support for Learning, 22*(1), 24-31.

Rayner, S.G. (1998). Educating pupils with emotional and behavioural difficulties: Pedagogy is the key! *Emotional and Behavioural Difficulties, 3*(2), 39-47.

Rayner, S.G. (2001). Aspects of the self as learner: perception, concept and esteem. In R.J. Riding & S.G. Rayner (Eds.), *International perspectives on individual differences* (pp. 25- 52). Westport, CT: Ablex Pubs.

Reeves, T. C. (1994). Evaluating what really matters in computer-based education. In M. Wild & D. Kirkpatrick (Eds.) *Computer education: New perspectives* (pp. 219-246). Perth, Australia: MASTEC.

Rehder, B, Hoffman, A. B. (2005). Eye tracking and selective attention in category learning. *Cognitive Psychology, 51*, 1-41.

Reid, G. (2005). *Learning styles and inclusion*. London: Sage.

Reilly, R. C., & Munakata, Y. (2002). *Computational explorations in cognitive neuroscience: Understanding the mind by simulating the brain* (pp. 227-229). Cambridge, MA: MIT Press.

Reilly, W. S., & Bates, J. (1992) *Building emotional agents*. Pittsburgh: School of Computer Science, Carnegie Mellon University.

Reiman, J., Young, M., & Howes, A., (1996). A dual-space model of interactively deepening exploratory learning. *Int. J. Human-Computer Studies, 44*, 743-775.

Reiser, R. A. (2001). A history of instructional design and technology: Part II: A history of instructional design. *ETR&D, 49*(2), 57-67.

Reiser, R. A. (2001). A history of instructional design and technology: Part I: A history of instructional design. *ETR&D, 49*(1) 53-64.

Reportagem 1 (2008). *Alunos da EMEF Ernani Silva Bruno visualizam as matérias em 3D*. Retrieved from http://www.aprendebrasil.com.br/alunoreporter/reportagem.asp?idARMateria=531

Resnick, M. (2006). Computer as paintbrush: Technology, play, and the creative society. In D. Singer, R. Golikoff, & K. Hirsh-Pasek (Eds.), *Play = Learning: How play motivates and enhances children's cognitive and social-emotional growth*. New York: Oxford University Press. Retrieved November 12, 2008, from http://web.media.mit.edu/~mres/papers/playlearn-handout.pdf

Resnick, M. (2007). *Sowing the seeds for a more creative society. Learning and leading with technology*. Retrieved November 22, 2008, from http://web.media.mit.edu/~mres/papers/Learning-Leading-final.pdf

Resnick, M., (2002). Rethinking learning in the digital age. In G. Kirkman (Ed.), *The global information technology report: Readiness for the networked world*. New York: Oxford University Press. Retrieved January 13, 2009, from http://llk.media.mit.edu/papers/mres-wef.pdf

Resnick, M., Strimpel, O., & Galyean, T. (2008). *The Virtual Fishtank*. Retrieved November 12, 2008, from http://llk.media.mit.edu/projects/fishtank

Revista Mente, Cérebro & Filosofia. (2007). Fundamentos para compreensão contemporânea da psique. In L.H.A de Souza (Ed.), *Dissertação cogito e temporalidade em sartre*. Universidade Federal do Paraná: Edição nº 5.

Reynolds, C. R., Richmond, B. O., & Lowe, P. A. (200a). *The Adult Manifest Anxiety Scale-College Version*. Los Angeles, CA: Western Psychological Services.

Reynolds, C. R., Richmond, B. O., & Lowe, P. A. (2003). *The Adult Manifest Anxiety Scale Manual*. Los Angeles, CA: Western Psychological Services.

Reynolds, M. (1997). Learning styles: a critique. *Management Learning, 28*(2), 115-133.

Rezaei, A. R., & Katz, R. (2004). Evaluation of the reliability and validity of the cognitive styles analysis. *Personality and Individual Differences, 36*(6), 1317-1327.

Richards, J. P., Fajen, B. R., Sullivan, J. F., & Gillespie, G. (1997). Signaling, notetaking, and field independence-dependence in text comprehension and recall. *Journal of Educational Psychology, 89*(3), 508-517.

Richardson, J.T.E. (1996). Evolving concepts of working memory. In J.T.E. Richardson, R.W. Engle, L. Hasher, R.H. Logie, E.R. Stoltzfus, & R.T. Zacks. *Working memory and human cognition* (pp. 3-30). New York: Oxford University Press.

Richardson, J.T.E. (1996). Evolving issues in working memory. In J.T.E. Richardson, R.W. Engle, L. Hasher, R.H. Logie, E.R. Stoltzfus, & R.T. Zacks. *Working memory and human cognition* (pp. 120-54). New York: Oxford University Press.

Richardson-Klavehn, A., Gardiner, J.M., & Ramponi, C. (2002). Level of processing and the process-dissociation procedure: Elusiveness of null effects on estimates of automatic retrieval. *Memory, 10*, 349-364.

Richmond, V. P. (1979). Management communication style, tolerance for disagreement, and innovativeness as predictors of employee satisfaction: A comparison of single-factor, two-factor, and multifactor approaches. *Communication Yearbook, 3*, 359-373.

Richmond, V. P., & McCroskey, J. C. (1989). Willingness to communicate and dysfunctional communication processes. In C. V. Roberts & K. W. Watson (Eds.), *Interpersonal communication processes* (pp. 292-318). New Orleans, LA: Spectra & Scottsdale.

Richmond, V. P., & Roach, D. K. (1992). Willingness to communicate and employee success in U.S. organizations. *Journal of Applied Communication Research, 31*, 95-115.

Ricketts, J., Wolfe, F. H., Norvelle, E., & Carpenter, E. H. (2000). Multimedia. *Social Science Computer Review, 18*(2), 132-146.

Rideout, V. J., Vandewater, E. A., & Wartella, E. A. (2003). *Zero to six: Electronic media in the lives of infants, toddlers and preschoolers.* Menlo Park: The Henry J. Kaiser Family Foundation. Retrieved July 27, 2008, from http://www.kaisernetwork.org/health_cast/uploaded_files/102803_kff_kids_report.pdf

Riding R. J, & Ashmore, J. (1980). Verbaliser-imager learning style and children's recall of information presented in pictorial versus written form. *Educational Psychology, 6*, 141-145.

Riding, R. J. & Read, G. (1996). Cognitive style and pupil learning preferences. *Educational Psychology, 16*, 81-106.

Riding, R. J. (1991). *Cognitive styles analysis user manual.* Birmingham: Learning and Training Technology.

Riding, R. J. (1998). The nature of cognitive style. *Educational Psychology, 17*(1-2), 29-49.

Riding, R. J. (2000). *Information processing index.* Birmingham: Learning and Training Technology.

Riding, R. J., & Al-Sanabani, S. (1998). The effect of cognitive style, age, gender and structure on recall of prose passages. *International journal of Educational Research, 29*, 173-185.

Riding, R. J., & Armstrong, J. M. (1982). Sex and personality differences in performance on mathematics tests in 11-year-old children. *Educational Studies, 8*, 217-225.

Riding, R. J., & Boardman, D. J. (1983). The relationship between sex and learning style and graphicacy in 14-year old children. *Educational Review, 35*, 69-79.

Riding, R. J., & Borg, M. G. (1987). Sex and personality differences in performance on number computation in 11-year-old children. *Educational Review, 39*(1), 41-46.

Riding, R. J., & Cheema, I. (1991). Cognitive styles - an overview and integration. *Educational Psychology, 11*(3/4), 193-215.

Riding, R. J., & Cowley, J. (1986). Extroversion and sex differences in reading performance in eight-year-old children. *British Journal of Educational Psychology, 56*, 88-94.

Riding, R. J., & Douglas, G. (1993). The effect of cognitive style and mode of presentation on learning performance. *British Journal of Educational Psychology, 63*, 297-307.

Riding, R. J., & Dyer, V. A. (1983). The nature of learning styles and their relationship to cognitive performance in children. *Educational Psychology, 3*, 275-287.

Riding, R. J., & Egelstaff, D. W. (1983). Sex and personality differences in children's detection of changes in prose passages. *Educational Studies, 9*, 159-168.

Riding, R. J., & Grimley, M. (1999). Cognitive style and learning from multi-media materials in 11-year-old children. *British Journal of Educational Technology, 30*, 45-56.

Riding, R. J., & Rayner, S. G. (2000). (Eds.) *International perspectives in individual differences.* Stamford, CT: Ablex Press.

Riding, R. J., & Rigby Smith, E. M. (1984). Reading accuracy as a function of teaching strategy, personality and word complexity in seven-year-old children. *Educational Studies, 3*, 263-272.

Riding, R. J., & Sadler-Smith, E. (1992). Type of instructional material, cognitive style and learning performance. *Educational Studies, 18*, 323-340.

Riding, R. J., & Smith, D. M. (1981). Sex differences in the effects of speech rate and repetition on the recall of prose in children. *Educational Psychology, 3*, 253-260.

Riding, R. J., & Vincent, D. J. T. (1980). Listening comprehension: The effects of sex, age, passage structure and speech rate. *Educational Review, 32*, 259-266.

Riding, R. J., & Watts, M. (1997). The effect of cognitive style on the preferred format of instructional material. *Educational Psychology, 17*(1/2), 179-183.

Riding, R. J., & Wigley, S., (1997). The relationship between cognitive style and personality in further education students. *Personality and Individual Differences, 23*(3), 379-389.

Riding, R. J., & Read, G. (1996). Cognitive style and pupil learning preferences. *Educational Psychology, 16*(1), 81-106.

Riding, R. J., Dahraei, H., Grimley, M., & Banner, G. (2001). Working memory, cognitive style and academic attainment. In R. Nata (Ed.), *Progress in education* (Vol. 5) (pp. 1-19). New York: Nova Science Publishers Inc.

Riding, R. J., Grimley, M., Dahraei, H., & Banner, G. (2003). Cognitive style, working memory and learning behaviour and attainment in school subjects. *British Journal of Educational Psychology, 73*(2), 149-169.

Riding, R., & Rayner, S.G. (1995). The information superhighway and individualised learning. *Educational Psychology, 15*(4), 365-378.

Riding, R.J., & Calvey, I. (1981). The assessment of verbal-imagery learning styles and their effect on the recall of concrete and abstract prose passages by eleven-year-old children. *British Journal of Psychology, 72*, 59-64.

Riding, R.J., & Dyer, V.A. (1980). The relationship between extraversion and verbal-imagery learning styles in 12 year old children. *Personality and Individual Differences, 1*, 273-279.

Riding, R.J., & Rayner, S.G. (1998). *Cognitive styles and learning strategies.* London: David Fulton Pubs.

Rieken, H. W. (1958). The effect of talkativeness on ability to influence group solutions of problems. *Sociometry, 21*, 309-321.

Ritchie, R., & Deakin Crick, R. (2007). *Distributing leadership for personalizing education.* London: Continuum Network Pubs.

Ritter, F. E., & Young, R. M. (2001). Embodied models as simulated users: Introduction to this special issue on using cognitive models to improve interface design. *International Journal of Human-Computer Studies, 55*, 1-14.

Ritter, L. (2007). Unfulfilled promises: How inventories, instruments and institutions subvert discourses of diversity and promote commonality. *Teaching in Higher Education, 12*(5 & 6), 569-579.

Riva, G. (2001). From real to virtual communities: Cognition, knowledge, and intention in the world wide Web. In C.R. Wolfe (Ed.), *Learning and teaching on the world wide Web* (pp. 131-51). San Diego, CA: Elsevier.

Riva, G., (2005). The psychology of ambient intelligence: activity, situation and Presence. In G. Riva (Ed.), *Ambient intelligence: The evolution of technology, communication and cognition towards the future of human-computer interaction.* Milan, Italy: IOS Press. Retrieved December 5, 2008, from http://www.emergingcommunication.com/volume6.html

Riva, G., Loreti, P., Lunghi, M., Vatalaro, F., & Davide, F. (2003). 4 presence 2010: The emergence of ambient intelligence. In G. Riva, F. Davide, & W. A. IJsselsteijn (Eds.), *Being there: Concepts, effects and measurement of user presence in synthetic environments.* Amsterdam, The Netherlands: IOS Press.

Riva, G., Vatalaro, F., Davide, F., & Alcañiz, M. (Eds.). (2001). *The evolution of technology, communication and cognition towards the future of human-computer interaction.* Amsterdam, The Netherlands: IOS Press.

Roberts, M. J., & Newton, E. J. (2001). Understanding strategy selection. *Intl. Journal of Computer Studies, 54*, 137-154.

Roca, J. C., & Gagne, M. (2008). Understanding e-learning continuance intention in the workplace: A self-determination theory perspective. *Journal of Computers in Human Behavior, 24*, 1585-1604.

Rocheleau, B. (1995). Computer use by school-age children: trends, patterns and predictors. *Journal of Educational Computing Research, 1*, 1-17.

Rodgers, R.D. & Monsell, S. (1995). Costs of a predictable shift between simple cognitive tasks. *Journal of Experimental Psychology: General, 124*, 207-31.

Rodrigues, E. (2004). Competências dos e-formadores. In A. Dias (Ed.), *E-learning para e-formadores* (pp. 72-95). Tecminho.

Rodrigues, M., & Ferrao. (2006). *Formação pedagógica de formadores*. Edições Lídel.

Roe, K., & Muijs, D. (1998). Children and computer games: A profile of the heavy user. *European Journal of Communication, 13*, 181-200.

Roehl, B., Couch, J., Reed-Ballereich, C., Rohaly, T., & Brown, A. J. (1997). *Late night with VRML V2.0 with Java*. ZD Press.

Rogoff, B. (1990). *Apprenticeship in thinking: Cognitive development in social context*. New York: Oxford University Press.

Rogoff, B. (1998). Cognition as a collaborative process. In D. Kuhn & R.S. Siegler (Eds.), Cognition, perception and language (pp. 679-744). New York: Wiley.

Romiszowski, A. (2004). How's the e-learning baby? Factors leading to success or failure of an educational technology innovation. *Educational Technology, 44*(1), 5-27.

Rosen, V.M., & Engle, R.W. (1997). The role of working memory capacity in retrieval. *Journal of Experimental Psychology: General, 126*, 211-27.

Rosenberg, M. J. (2001). *E-learning: Strategies for delivering knowledge in the digital age*. New York: McGraw-Hill.

Rossi, G., Pastor, O., Schwabe, D., & Olsina, L. (2008). *Introduction*. In G. Rossi, O. Pastor, D. Schwabe, & L. Olsina (Eds.), *Web engineering: Modeling and implementing Web applications* (pp. 3-5). UK: Springer.

Rourke, L., Anderson, T., Garrison, R., & Archer, W. (2001). methodological issues in the content analysis of computer conference transcripts. *International Journal of Artificial Intelligence in Education, 12*, 8-22.

Roussos, M., Johnson, A., Leigh, J., Vasilakis, C., Barnes, C., & Moher, T., (1997). The NICE project: Narrative, immersive, constructionist/collaborative environments for learning in virtual reality. *In Proceedings of ED-MEDIA/ED-TELECOM 1997* (pp. 917-922). Retrieved from http://www.evl.uic.edu/tile/NICE/NICE/PAPERS/EDMEDIA/edmedia.paper.html

Rovai, A. P. (2000). Building and sustaining community in asynchronous learning networks. *The Internet and Higher Education, 3*, 285-297.

Rovai, A. P., & Barnum, K. T. (2003). On-line course effectiveness: An analysis of student interactions and perceptions of learning. *Journal of Distance Education, 18*(1), 57-73.

Rowntree, D. (1995). Teaching and learning online: A correspondence education for 21ˢᵗ century. *British Journal of Educational Technology, 26*(3).

Rubenstein, J., Meyer, D.E., & Evans, J.E. (2001). Executive control of cognitive processes in task switching. *Journal of Experimental Psychology: Human Perception and Performance, 27*, 763-97.

Rubin, R. B., & Martin, M. M. (1994). Development of a measure of interpersonal communication competence. *Communication Research Reports, 11*(1), 33-44.

Rueda, M. de los A. & D'Angelo, D. (1999). *Visual arts and communication* (pp. 10-13). Argentina: Richmond Publishing.

Rusk, N., Resnick, M., Berg, R., & Pezalla-Granlund, M. (2008). New pathways into robotics: Strategies for broadening participation. *Journal of Science Education and Technology*. Retrieved November 12, 2008, from http://web.media.mit.edu/~mres/papers/NewPathwaysRoboticsLLK.pdf

Russell, A. J. (1997). The effect of learner variables and cognitive style on learning performance in a vocational training environment. *Educational Psychology, 17*(1-2), 195-208.

Russell, J.A. (1997). How shall an emotion be called? In R. Plutchik & H. Conte (Eds.), *Circumplex models of personality and emotions* (pp. 205-220). Washington, DC: APA.

Russell, J.A. (2003). Core affect and the psychological construction of emotion. *Psychological Review, 110,* 145-172.

Russell, S. & Norvig, P., (2003). *Artificial intelligence: A modern approach* (pp. 649-711). US: Prentice Hall.

Sabry, K., & Baldwin, L. (2003). Web-based learning interaction and learning styles. *British Journal of Educational Technology, 34*(4), 443-454.

Sadek, D., Bretier, P., & Panaget, F. (1997). Artimis: Natural dialogue meets rational agency. In *Proceedings of 15th International Joint Conference on Artificial Intelligence (IJCAI'97),* (pp. 1030-1035). Nagoya, Japon.

Sadler-Smith, E. (2001). The relationship between learning style and cognitive style. *Personality and Individual Differences, 30*(4), 609-616.

Sadler-Smith, E., & Riding, R. J. (1999). Cognitive style and instructional preferences. *Instructional Science, 27*(5), 355-371.

Safran, S., García-Barrios, V. M., & Gütl, C. (2006). A concept-based context modelling system for the support of teaching and learning activities. In C. M. Crawford, R. Carlsen, K. McFerrin, J. Price, R. Weber, & D. A. Willis (Eds.), Proceedings of the International Conference on Society for Information Technology and Teacher Education (SITE 2006) (pp. 2395-2402). Chesapeake, VA, USA: AACE.

Salmon, G. (2005). *E-moderating: The key to teaching e learning online.* Routledge Falmer.

Salomon, G. (2000, June 28). *It's not just the tool, but the educational rationale that counts.* Keynote address at the 2000 ED-MEDIA Meeting, Montreal, Canada. Retrieved December 22, 2008, from http://www.aace. org/conf/edmedia/00/salomonkeynote.htm

Salomon, G., & Globerson, T. (1989). When teams do not function the way they ought to. *International Journal of Educational Research, 13,* 89-99.

Salthouse, T. A. (1996). The processing-speed theory of adult age differences in cognition. *Psychological Review, 103,* 403-428.

Sambell, K., McDowell, L., & Brown, S. (1997). "But is it fair?": An exploratory study of student perceptions of the consequential validity of assessment. *Studies in Educational Evaluation, 23,* 349-371.

Samples, R. E. (1975). Are you teaching online one side of the brain? *Learning, 3*(6), 25-28.

Sampson, D., Karagiannidis, C., & Kinshuk. (2002). Personalised learning: Educational, technological and standardisation perspective. *Interactive Educational Multimedia, 4,* 24-39.

Sancho, J. M. (2006). De tecnologias da informação e comunicação a recursos educativos. In J.M. Sancho, F. Hernández (Eds.), *Tecnologias para transformar a educação* (pp. 15-39). Valério Campos, Brasil: Artmed.

Sangineto, E., Capuano, N., Gaeta, M., & Micarelli, A. (2007). Adaptive course generation through learning styles representation. *Journal of Universal Access in the Information Society.* doi 10.1007/s10209-007-0101-0

Santally, M. I., & Senteni, A. (2005). A learning object approach to personalized Web-based instruction. *EURODL.* Retrieved March 18, 2008, from http://www. eurodl.org/materials/contrib/2005/Santally.htm

Santos, E. (2003). Articulação de saberes na EAD online: Por uma rede interdisciplinar e interativa de conhecimentos em ambientes virtuais de aprendizagem. In M. Silva (Ed.), *Educação online* (pp. 217-230). Edições Loyola.

Sasakura, M., & Yamasaki, S. (2007). A framework for adaptive e-learning systems in higher education with information visualization. In *Proceedings of the 11ᵗʰ International Conference of Information Visualization (IV)* (pp. 819-824).Washington, DC: IEEE Computer Society.

Savidis, A., & Stephanidis, C. (2004). Unified user interface design: Designing universally accessible interactions. *Interacting with Computers, 16*(2), 243-270.

Scadden, L. A. (1998). The Internet and the education of students with disabilities. *Technology and Disability, 8,* 141-148.

Scalia, L. M., & Sackmary, B. (1996). Groupware in the classroom: Applications and guidelines. *Computers in the Schools, 12*, 39-53.

Scardamalia, M., & Bereiter, C. (1994). Computer support for knowledge-building communities. *The Journal of the Learning Sciences, 3*(3), 265-283.

Scherer, K. (2000). *Psychological models of emotion.* In J. Borod (Ed.), *The neuropsychology of emotion* (pp. 137-162). Oxford/New York: Oxford University Press.

Scherer, K. R. (1981). Speech and emotional states. In J. K. Darby (Ed.), *Speech evaluation in psychiatry* (pp. 189-220). Grune and Stratton, Inc.

Scherer, K. R. (2005). What are emotions? And how can they be measured? *Social Science Information, 44*(4), 693-727.

Schiel, F., Steininger, S., & Turk, U. (2002). The Smartkom multimodal corpus at BAS. In *Proceedings of Language Resources and Evaluation* (LREC '02).

Schmeck, R. R. (1988). Strategies and styles of learning: An integration of varied perspectives. In R. R. Schmeck (Ed.), Learning strategies and learning styles (pp. 317-347). New York: Plenum Press.

Schnabel, M.A., Wang, X.Y., Seichter, H., & Kvan, T. (2008). Touching the untouchables: Virtual-, augmented- and reality. In *Proceedings of Conference on Computer-Aided Architectural Design Research in Asia.* CAADRIA 2008, Chiang Mai, Thailand. Retrieved November 12, 2008, from http://www.hitlabnz.org/publications/2008-TouchingTheUntouchablesVirtual-Augmented-AndReality.pdf

Schneider-Hufschmidt, M., Kühme, T., & Malinowski, U. (Eds.). (1993). *Adaptive user interfaces: Principles and practice.* North-Holland, Elsevier Science Publishers B.V.

Schofield, M., Sackville, A., & Davey, J. (2006). Designing for unique online learning contexts: The aligment of purpose, audience, and form of interactivity. In F. Dias (Ed.), *Managing learning in virtual settings. The role of context* (pp. 117-134). Hershey, PA: Information Science Publishing.

Schrire, S. (2006). Knowledge building in asynchronous discussion groups: Going beyond quantitative analysis. *Computers & Education, 46*, 49-70.

Schroeder, H., & Grabowsky, B. (1995). Patterns of exploration and learning with hypermedia. *Journal of Educational Computing Research, 13*, 313-35.

Schroeder, W., Martin, K. & Loresen, B., (1998). *The visualisation toolkit* (2nd ed., pp. 35-39, 471-494). US: Prentice Hall PTR.

Schulman, A. H., & Sims, R. L. (1999). Learning in an online format versus an in-class format: An experimental study. *T H E Journal (Technological Horizons in Education), 26*, 63-72.

Schulmeister, R. (1997). *Hypermedia learning systems. Theory – dedactics – design* (2nd ed.) (T.Flügel, Trans.). München: Oldenbourg. Retrieved April 8, 2008, from http://www.izhd.uni-hamburg.de/paginae/Book/Ch5/Control.html

Schulmeister, R. (2006). *eLearning: Einsichten und aussichten.* München: Oldenburg Verlag.

Schuman, L. (1996). *Perspectives on instruction, SDSU - educational technology.* Retrieved April, 2008, from http://edweb.sdsu.edu/courses/edtec540/perspectives/perspectives.html

Scratch. (2009). Retrieved January 11, 2009, from http://scratch.mit.edu/

Segers, M., Dochy, F., & Cascallar, E. (Eds.). (2003). *Optimising new modes of assessment: In search of qualities and standards.* Dordrecht, The Netherlands: Kluwer Academic Publishers.

Selinger, M. (2005). *Workforce development and access to elearning.* Retrieved May 07, 2008, from www.elearningeuropa.info

Sen, A. (2000). *Desenvolvimento como liberdade* (L.T. Motta, Trans.). Brasil: Companhia das Letras.

Senge, P., Scharmer, C. O., Jaworski, J., & Flowers, B. S. (2007). *Presença: Propósito humano e o campo do futuro* (G.C.C. de Sousa, Trans.) (pp. 86-104). Brasil: Cultrix.

Sengupta, S. (1998). Peer evaluation: 'I am not the teacher'. *ELT Journal, 52*, 19-28.

Sfard, A. (1998) On two metaphors for learning and the dangers of choosing just one. *Educational Researcher, 27*, 4-13.

Shah, P., & Miyake, A. (1999). Models of working memory: An introduction. In A. Miyake & P. Shah (Eds.), *Models of Working Memory: Mechanisms of active maintenance and executive control* (pp. 1-27). Cambridge, UK: Cambridge University Press.

Shallice, T., & Warrington, E.K. (1970). Independent functioning of verbal memory stores: A neuropsychological study. *Quarterly Journal of Experimental Psychology, 22*, 261-73.

Shapiro, A. M. (1998). Promoting active learning: The role of system structure in learning from hypertext. *Human Computer Interaction, 13*(1), 1-35.

Shapiro, A., & Niederhauser, D. (2003). Learning from hypertext: Research issues and findings. In D. H. Jonassen (Ed.), *Handbook of research for education communications and technology* (2nd ed.). Mahwah, NJ: Lawrence Erlbaum Associates.

Sharples, M. (Ed.). (2007). Big issues in mobile learning. In *Report of a workshop by the Kaleidoscope Network of Excellence Mobile Learning Initiative*. Learning Sciences Research Institute, University of Nottingham. Retrieved September 17, 2008 from http://www.lsri.nottingham.ac.uk/msh/Papers/BIG_ISSUES_REPORT_PUBLISHED.pdf

Shaywitz, B. A., Shaywitz, S. E., Pugh, K. R., Constable, R. T., Skudlarski, P., Fulbright, R. K., Bronen, R. A., Fletcher, J. M., Shankweiler, D. P., Katz, L., & Gore, J. C. (1995). Sex differences in the functional organization of the brain for language. *Nature 373*(16), 607-609.

Shea, P., Fredericksen, E., Pickett, A., & Pelz, W. (2004). Faculty development, student satisfaction, and reported learning in the SUNY learning network. In T. M. Duffy & J. R. Kirkley (Eds.), *Learner-centered: Theory and practice in distance education* (pp. 343-377). Mahwah, NJ: Lawrence Erlbaum Assoc.

Shearer, B. (1996). *The MIDAS handbook of multiple intelligences in the classroom*. OH: Greyden Press.

Sheeks, M. S., & Birchmeier, Z. P. (2007). Shyness, sociability, and the use of computer-mediated communication in relationship development. *CyberPsychology & Behavior, 10*(1), 64-70.

Sherman, W. R., & Craig, A. B., (2003). *Understanding virtual reality: Interface, application and design*. US: Morgan Kaufman.

Sheth, A., Ramakrishnan, C., & Thomas, C. (2005). Semantics for the Semantic Web: The implicit, the formal and the powerful. *International Journal of Semantic Web and Information Systems, 1*(1), 1-18.

Shi, H., Revithis, S., & Chen, S. (2002). An agent enabling personalized learning in e-learning environments. *International Conference on Autonomous Agents: Proceedings of the first international joint conference on Autonomous agents and multi-agent systems, Part 2* (pp. 847-848).

Shute, V. J. (2007). Tensions, trends, tools, and technologies: Time for an educational sea change. In C. A. Dwyer (Ed.), *The future of assessment: Shaping teaching and learning* (pp. 139-187). Mahwah, NJ: Lawrence Erlbaum.

Shute, V. J. (2008). Focus on formative feedback. *Review of Educational Research, 78*, 153-189.

SIIA. (2000). Software as a service: Software on and off like a light. In *Building the Net: Trends report 2000 – trends shaping the digital economy*. Software and Information Industry Association.

Silva, L. I. L., Haddad, F. & Nicolelis, M. A. L. (2008). Brazilian *option for science education, Opinion/Forum*. Retrieved February 15, 2009, from http://www.nicolelislab.net/Papers/Editorial_SCIAM_FINAL_Pag34[1].pdf

Silveira, R. M., (2007). Laptop de US$ 100 promete causar uma revolução na educação no Brasil. *Reportagem publicada originalmente nas páginas II e III do Poder Executivo do Diário Oficial do Estado de SP do dia 12/09/2007.* Retrieved January 11, 2009, from http://www.rogeriosilveira.jor.br/reportagem2007_09_12_laptop_100dolares_lsiusp.php

Simkins, S. P. (1999). Promoting active-student learning using the World Wide Web in economics courses. *Journal of Economic Education, 30*(3), 278-291.

Simone (2009). *Bolg da professora Simone.* Retrieved February 16, 2009, from http://simone-poesia.blogspot.com/

Sims, R., & Hedberg, J. (1995). Dimensions of learner control. A reappraisal for interactive multimedia instruction. In J. M. Pearce & A. Ellis (Eds.), *Proceedings of the Twelfth Annual Conference of the Australian Society for Computers in Learning in Tertiary Education* (pp. 468-475).

Singer, P. (2002) *A educação como elemento de transformação econômica, Portal do Sesc.* Retrieved January 11, 2009, from http://www.sescsp.org.br/sesc/conferencias_new/subindex.cfm?Referencia=166&ParamEnd=5

Singer, P. (2002). *Debate com o professor Paul Singer Perguntas dos participantes após conferência do professor Paul Singer, com coordenação de José Pascoal Vaz.* Retrieved January 11, 2009, from http://www.sescsp.org.br/sesc/conferencias_new/subindex.cfm?Referencia=166&ParamEnd=5

Singer, P., (2002). *Introdução à economia solidária* (pp. 110-113). Brasil: Fundação Perseu Abramo.

Sivan, A. (2000). The implementation of peer assessment: An action research approach. *Assessment in Education: Principles, Policy & Practice, 7,* 193-213.

Sivan, A., Wong Leung, R., & Woon, C. (2000). An implementation of active learning and its effect on the quality of student learning. *Innovations in Education and Training International, 37*(4), 381-389.

Skinner, B. (1981). *Ciência e comportamento humano.* Livraria Martins Fontes Editora.

Slavin, R. E. (1980). Cooperative learning in teams: State of the art. *Educational Psychologist, 15,* 93-111.

Slavin, R. E. (1995). *Cooperative learning: Theory, research and practice* (2nd ed.). Needham Heights, MA: Allyn & Bacon.

Sloan, D., Kelly, B., Heath, A., Petrie, H., Fraser, H., & Phipps, L. (2006). Contextual Web accessibility - maximizing the benefit of accessibility guidelines. In *Proceedings of the WWW 2006,* Edinburgh, Scotland. Retrieved from http://www.ukoln.ac.uk/web-focus/papers/w4a-2006/

Sluijsmans, D. M. A, Strijbos, J. W., & Van de Watering, G. (2007, August). *Designing flexible and fair peer assessment formats to award individual contributions in group-based learning.* Paper presented at the 12th Biennial EARLI Conference, Budapest, Hungary.

Sluijsmans, D. M. A. (2008, June 6). *Betrokken bij beoordelen* [Involved in assessment]. Lectoral address, HAN University, the Netherlands.

Sluijsmans, D. M. A., Brand-Gruwel, S., Van Merriënboer, J., & Martens, R. (2004). Training teachers in peer-assessment skills: Effects on performance and perceptions. *Innovations in Education and Teaching International, 41,* 59-78.

Sluijsmans, D. M. A., Dochy, F., & Moerkerke, G. (1999). Creating a learning environment by using self- peer- and co-assessment. *Learning Environments Research, 1,* 293-319.

Smeets, E., & Mooij, T. (2001). Pupil-centred learning, ICT, and teacher behaviour: Observations in educational practice. *British Journal of Educational Technology, 32*(4), 403-417.

Smith, P. L., & Ragan, T. J. (2005). *Instructional design* (3rd ed.). Hoboken, NJ: John Wiley & Sons.

Smith, T., & Easterday, K. E. (1994). Field dependence-independence and holistic instruction in mathematics. University of Alabama at Birmingham and Auburn University. (ERIC Document Reproduction Service No. ED377072)

Soares, C. (2008). *Building a future on science.* Retrieved February 15, 2009, from http://www.nicolelislab.net/Papers/Building%20a%20Future%20on%20Science.pdf

Soloman, B., & Felder, R. M. (1998). *Index of learning styles questionnaire*. Retrieved from http://www.engr.ncsu.edu/learningstyles/ilsweb.html

Soloway, E., Guzdial, M., & Hay, K. E. (1994). Learner-centred design: The challenge for HCI in the 21st Century. *Interactions, 1*, 36-48

Soloway, E., Jackson, S., Klein, J., Quintana, Ch., Reed, J., Spitulnik, J., Stratford, S., Studer, S., Jul, S., Eng, J., & Scala, N. (1996). Learning theory in practice: Case Studies of Learner-Centred design. In *Proceedings of the Conference on Human Factors in Computing Systems (CHI96)*, Vancouver, British Columbia (pp. 189-196). New York: ACM Press.

Solso, R. L., MacLin, M. K., & MacLin, O. H. (2005). *Cognitive Psychology* (7th Ed). Upper Saddle River: Prentice Hall.

Somekh, B., & Davies, R. (1991). Towards a pedagogy for information technology. *The Curriculum Journal, 2*(2), 153-170.

Sorg, A. B., & Whitney, P. (1992). The effect of trait anxiety and situational stress on working memory capacity. *Journal of Research in Personality, 26*, 235-241.

Souza, R. (2005). Uma proposta construtivista para a utilização de tecnologias na educacao. In V. Silva & S. Vidigal (Eds.), *Educação, aprendizagem e tecnologia: Um paradigma para professores do século XXI*. Edições Sílabo.

Spector, J. M., & Anderson, T. M. (Eds.). (2000). *Integrated and holistic perspectives on learning, instruction and technology: Understanding complexity*. Dordrecht, The Netherlands: Kluwer Academic.

Spelke, E. S. (2005). Sex differences in intrinsic aptitude for mathematics and science. *American Psychologist, 60*(9), 950-958.

Spielberger, C. D, Ritterband, L. M., Sydeman, S. J., Reheiser, E. C., & Unger, K. K. (1995). Assessment of emotional states and personality traits: Measuring psychological vital signs. In J. N. Butcher (Ed.), *Clinical personality assessment: Practical approaches* (pp42–58). New York: Oxford University Press.

Spielberger, C. D. (1980). *Test Anxiety Inventory (TAI)*. Palo Alto, CA: Consulting Psychologists Press.

Spielberger, C. D. (1980). *Test Anxiety Inventory (TAI): Manual*. Palo Alto, CA: Consulting Psychologists Press.

Spielberger, C. D. (1983). *Manual for the state-trait anxiety inventory (STAI)*. Palo Alto, CA: Consulting Psychologists Press.

Spielberger, C.D., & Rickman, R.L. (1991). Assessment of state and trait anxiety. In *Psychobiological and clinical perspectives* (pp. 69-83). Washington: Hemisphere/Taylor & Francis.

Spielberger, C.D., Gorsuch, R.L., Lushene, R., Vagg, P.R., & Jacobs, G.A. (1977). *State-Trait Anxiety Inventory*. Palo Alto, CA: Consulting Psychologists Press.

Springer, S., & Deutch, G. (1985). *Right brain, left brain*. San Francisco, CA: W. H. Freeman.

Squeak. (2009). Retrieved January 11, 2009, from http://www.squeak.org/

Squires, D., & Preece, J. (1996). Usability and learning: Evaluating the potential of educational software. *Computers Education, 27*(1), 15-22.

Squires, D., & Preece, J. (1999). Predicting quality in educational software: Evaluating for learning, usability and the synergy between them. *Interacting with Computers, 11*, 467-483

Stacey, E. (2002). Social presence online: Networking learning at a distance. *Education and Information Technologies, 7*(4), 287-294.

Stanek, W., (1996). *HTML, JAVA, CGI, VRML, SGML Web publishing unleashed* (pp. 9-144). US: Sams Net.

Stanford-Smith, B. (2002). *Challenges and achievements in e-business and e-work*. Amsterdam: IOS Press.

Stanton, N. A., & Stammers, R. B. (1990). Learning styles in a non-linear training environment. In R. MCaleese &

C. Green (Eds.), *Hypertext: State of the art* (pp. 114-120). Norwood, NJ: Ablex.

Stary, C., & Totter, A. (2006). On learner control in e-learning. In *Proceedings of the 13th European Conference on Cognitive Ergonomics: Trust and Control in Complex Socio-Technical Systems* (pp. 41-48). New York: ACM.

Stash, N. (2007). *Incorporating cognitive/learning styles in a general-purpose adaptive hypermedia system.* Unpublished doctoral dissertation, Eindhoven University of Technology, The Netherlands.

Stathacopoulou, R., Grigoriadou, M., Samarakou, M., & Mitropoulos, D. (2007). Monitoring students' actions and using teachers' expertise in implementing and evaluating the neural network-based fuzzy diagnostic model. *Expert Systems with Applications, 32*, 955-975.

Steinhouse, D. (1985). *Active philosophy in education and science.* Englewood Cliffs, New Jersey: Prentice Hall.

Sternberg, R. J., & Grigorenko, E. L. (1997). Are cognitive styles still in style? *American Psychologist, 52*(7), 700-712.

Sternberg, R.J. (1997). *Thinking styles.* NY: Cambridge University Press.

Stocking, M. L., Steffen, M. S. & Eignor, D. R. (2001). *A method for building a realistic model of test taker behavior for computerized adaptive testing* (RR-01-22). Princeton, NJ: Educational Testing Service.

Straus, S., & McGrath, J. E. (1994). Does the medium matter? The interaction of task type and technology on group performance and member reactions. *Journal of Applied Psychology, 79*, 87-97.

Stricker, L. J. & Wilde, G. Z. (2001). *Examinee's attitudes about the TOEFL-CBT, possible determinants, and relationships with test performance* (Research Report 01-01). Princeton, NJ: Educational Testing Service.

Strijbos, J. W., Kirschner, P. A., & Martens, R. L. (Eds.). (2004). *What we know about CSCL: And implementing it in higher education.* Boston, MA: Kluwer/Springer.

Strijbos, J. W., Martens, R. L., & Jochems, W. M. G. (2004). Designing for interaction: Six steps to designing computer-supported group-based learning. *Computers & Education, 42*, 403-424.

Strijbos, J. W., Narciss, S., & Dünnebier, K. (2007, August). *Peer feedback in academic writing: How do feedback content and writing ability-level of the sender affect feedback perception and performance?* Paper presented at the 12th Biennial EARLI Conference, Budapest, Hungary.

Stroebe, W., Diehl, M., & Abakoumkin, G. (1996). Social compensation and the Kohler effect: Toward a theoretical explanation of motivational gains in group productivity. In E. H. Witte & J. H. Davis (Eds.), *Understanding group behavior: Vol. 2. Small group processes and interpersonal relations* (pp. 37-65). Mahwah, NJ: Lawrence Erlbaum.

Subrahmanyan, K., Smahel, D., & Greenfield, P. (2006). Connecting developmental constructions to the Internet: Identity presentation and sexual exploration on online teen chat rooms. *Developmental Psychology, 42*(3), 395-406.

Suchman, L. A. (1987). *Plans and situated actions.* New York: Cambridge University Press.

Sung, Y. T., Chang, K. E., Chiou, S. K., & Hou, H. T. (2005). The design and application of a web-based self- and peer-assessment system. *Computers & Education, 45*, 187-202.

Sung, Y. T., Lin, C. S., Lee, C. L., & Chang, K. E. (2003). Evaluating proposals for experiments: An application of web-based self-assessment and peer-assessment. *Teaching of Psychology, 30*, 331-334.

Sung, Y-T., Chang, K-E, & Haung, J-S. (2008). Improving children's reading comprehension and use of strategies through computer-based strategy training. *Journal of Computers in Human Behavior, 24*, 1552-1571.

Sweeney, J., O'Donoghue, T., & Whitehead, C. (2004). Traditional face-to-face and Web-based tutorials: A study of university students' perspectives on the roles of tutorial participants. *Teaching in Higher Education, 9*(3), 311-323.

Sweller, J. (1988). Cognitive load during problem solving: Effects on learning. *Cognitive Science, 12*, 257-285.

Sweller, J., & Chandler, P. (1994). Why some material is difficult to learn. *Cognition and Instruction, 12*, 185-233.

Tabachnik, B. G., & Fidell, L. S. (1996). *Using multivariate statistics* (3rd ed.). New York: Harper Collins.

Tajfel, H. (1978). Social categorization, social identity, and social comparison. In H. Tajfel (Ed.), *Differentiation between social groups: Studies in the social psychology of inter-group relations* (pp. 61-76). London: Academic Press.

Tan, J., (2008). Motivations and students' perceptions of learning: an empirical study of blogs. In *Proceedings of the IADIS Multi Conference on Computer Science and Information Systems* (MCCSIS 2008) (pp. 10-17). Amsterdam, The Netherlands.

Tan, K., Lewis, E., Avis, N. & Withers, P., (2008). Understanding of materials science to school children. In *Educators Paper (abstracts), Siggraph 2008.* Retrieved November 12, 2008, from http://www.siggraph.org/asia2008/attendees/edu/11.php

Tannenbaum, R. S. (1998). *Theoretical foundations of multimedia.* US: Computer Science Press.

Taylor, J., & Evans, D. (2005) Pulling together: Keeping track of pedagogy, design and evaluation through the development of scenarios – a case study. *Learning, Media and Technology, 30*(2).

Te'eni, D., Carey, J., & Zhang, P. (2007). *Human, computer interaction: Developing effective organizational information systems.* US: John Wiley & Sons.

Teasdale, J.D., Dritschel, B.H., Taylor, M.J., Proctor, L., Lloyd, C.A., Nimmo-Smith, I., & Baddeley, A.D. (1995). Stimulus-independent thought depends on central executive resources. *Memory & Cognition, 23*, 417-33.

Terry, M. (2001). Translating learning style theory into university teaching practices: An article based on Kolb's experiential learning model. *Journal of College Reading and Learning, 32*(1), 65-68.

Tett, R. P., Jackson, D. N., & Rothstein, M. (1991). Personality measures as predictors of job performance: A meta-analytic review. *Personnel Psychology, 44*, 703-741.

The Cognition and Technology Group at Vanderbilt. (1991). Some thoughts about constructivism and instructional design. *Educational Technology, 31*(10), 16-18.

The College Board. (2000, April). *An overview of computer-based testing.* RN-09.

The Institutes for the Achievement of Human Potential (2009). Retrieved January 9, 2009, from http://www.iahp.org/

Thoms, P., Moore, K. S., & Scott, K. S. (1996). The relationship between self-efficacy for participating in self-managed work groups and the Big Five personality dimensions. *Journal of Organizational Behavior, 17*, 349-362.

Thurstone, L. L. (1944). A factorial study of perception. *Psychometric Monograph, Number 4.* Chicago: Chicago University of Press.

Thyagharajan, K., & Nayak, R. (2007). Adaptive content creation for personalized e-learning using Web service. *Journal of Applied Sciences Research, 3*(9), 828-836.

Tian, Y., Kanade, T., & Cohn, J. F. (2001). Recognising action units for facial expression analysis. *IEEE Trans Pattern Analysis and Machine Intelligence, 23*(2).

Tittelboom, S. (2003). Alternative assessment as a tool in support of teaching and learning (some preliminary findings). In *Proceedings of the European Conference for Educational Research,* Hamburg.

Tomlinson, C. A. (1999). *The differentiated classroom: Responding to the needs of all learners.* Alexandria, VA: ASCD Press.

Topping, K. J. (1998). Peer assessment between students in colleges and universities. *Review of Educational Research, 68*, 249-276.

Topping, K. J. (2003). Self and peer assessment in school and university: Reliability, validity and utility. In M. Segers, F. Dochy, & E. Cascallar (Eds.), *Optimising new modes of assessment: In search of qualities and standards* (pp. 55-87). Dordrecht, The Netherlands: Kluwer Academic Publishers.

Trahasch, S. (2004, October). *From peer assessment towards collaborative learning.* Paper presented on the 34th ASEE/IEEE Frontiers in Education Conference, Savannah, GA, USA.

Trevino, L. K., Lengel, R., & Daft, R. L. (1987). Media symbolism, media richness, and media choice in organization: A symbolic interactionist perspective. *Communication Research, 14*, 553-574.

Triantafillou, E., Pomportsis, A., & Demetriadis, S. (2003). The design and the formative evaluation of an adaptive educational system based on cognitive styles. *Computers & Education, 41*, 87-103.

Triantafillou, E., Pomportsis, A., & Demetriadis, S. (2003). The design and the formative evaluation of an adaptive educational system based on cognitive styles. *Computers & Education, 41*(2003), 87-103.

Trindade, R. (2002). *Experiências educativas e situações de aprendizagem.* Asa Editores.

Tsapatsoulis, N., Karpouzis, K., & Stamou, G. (2000). A fuzzy system for emotion classification based on the MPEG-4 facial definition parameter. In *European Association on Signal Processing EUSIPCO.*

Tuckman, B. W. (1965). Developmental sequence in small groups. *Psichological Bulletin, 63*, 384-399.

Tuomi, I. (2007). *Skills and learning for the knowledge society.* Paper presented at eLearning 2007, Lisbon.

Tzanavari, A. (2007). *D5.2: 1st version of specific UNITE elearning scenarios; PART II: Handbook for content development v.2* (UNITE public deliverable). Retrieved May 7, 2008, from http://www.unite-ist.org

Udry, R. J. (1994). The nature of gender. *Demography, 31*(4), 561-573.

Ulf, D. E. (2007). *Preliminary conclusion (final plenary presentation).* Paper presented at eLearning 2007, Lisbon.

Ullrich, K. (2004). *Constructivism and the 5 E model science lesson.* Retrieved May 07, 2008, from http://cte.jhu.edu/techacademy/fellows/Ullrich/webquest/mkuindex.html

UNITE FP6 IST project. (2006). *Contract No. 026964.* Retrieved May 7, 2008, from http://www.unite-ist.org

UNITE Public Deliverable 1. (2006). *D1: State of the art and requirements list for UNITE.* Retrieved May 7, 2008, from http://www.unite-ist.org

UNITE Public Deliverable 5.3. (2008). D5.3: Final version of the specific UNITE elearning scenarios. Retrieved May 7, 2008, from http://www.unite-ist.org

Unsworth, N., & Engle, R.W. (2007). The nature of individual differences in working memory capacity: Active maintenance in primary memory and controlled search for secondary memory. *Psychological Review, 114*, 104-132.

UTHM. (2009). *Faculty of Mechanical and Manufacturing Engineering.* Retrieved January 11, 2009, from http://fkmp.uthm.edu.my/index.php?option=com_content&task=view&id=179&Itemid=295

Valkenburg, P. M., & Peter, J. (2007). Preadolescents' and adolescents' online communication and their closeness to friends. *Developmental Psychology, 43*(2), 267-277.

Vallar, G. & Papagno, C. (2002). Neuropsychological impairments of verbal short-term memory. In A.D. Baddeley, M.D. Kopelman & B.A. Wilson (Eds.), *Handbook of memory disorders* (pp. 249-70). Chichester: Wiley.

Van de Ridder, M., Stokking, K. M., McGaghie, W. C., & Ten Cate, O. Th. J. (2008). What is feedback in clinical education? *Medical Education, 42*, 189-197.

Van den Berg, I. (2003). *Peer assessment in universitair onderwijs: Een onderzoek naar bruikbare ontwerpen*

[Peer assessment in higher education: A study on useful designs]. Unpublished doctoral dissertation, Utrecht University, Utrecht, the Netherlands.

Van den Berg, I., Admiraal, W., & Pilot, A. (2006). Peer assessment in university teaching: Evaluating seven course designs. *Assessment & Evaluation in Higher Education, 31*, 9-16.

Van Gennip, N. A. E., Segers, M. S. R., & Tillema, H. H. (2005, August). *Peer assessment as a tool for learning: A meta-analysis.* Paper presented at the 11th Biennial EARLI Conference, Nicosia, Cyprus.

Van Gennip, N. A. E., Segers, M. S. R., & Tillema, H. H. (in press). Peer assessment for learning from a team learning perspective: The influence of interpersonal variables and structural features. *Educational Research Review.*

van Merriënboer, J. J. G., & Ayres, P. (2005). Research on cognitive load theory and its design implications for e-learning. *ETR&D, 53*, 5-13.

Van Merriënboer, J. J. G., & Sweller, J. (2005). Cognitive load theory and complex learning: Recent developments and future directions. *Educational Psychology Review, 17*(2), 147-177.

Van Zundert, M., Sluijsmans, D. M. A., & Van Merriënboer, J. J. G. (2007, August). *Identifying critical variables to optimise the educational effectiveness and reliability of peer assessment.* Paper presented at the 12th Biennial EARLI Conference, Budapest, Hungary.

Varis, T. (2005). *New literacies and elearning competences.* Retrieved May 07, 2008, from http://www.elearningeuropa.info

Venâncio, V., Franco, J. F., Correa, A. G. D., Zuffo, M. K., & Lopes, R. D. (in press). Golden material 3D: An interactive decimal numerical system for children. In *Proceedings of 9th WCCE · IFIP World Conference on Computers in Education.* Bento Gonçalves, Brazil. Retrieved April 11, 2009, from http://www.wcce2009.org/program.html#program

Verhaeaghen, P., Cerella, J., & Basak, C. (2004). A working-memory workout: How to expand the focus of serial attention from one to four items, in ten hours or less. *Journal of Experimental Psychology: Learning, Memory & Cognition, 30*, 1322-37.

Verheoj, J., Stoutjesduk, E., & Beishuizen, J. (1996). Search and study strategies in hypertext. *Computers in Human Behaviour, 12*(1), 1-15.

Vermunt J. D. (1996). Metacognitive, cognitive and affective aspects of learning styles and strategies: a phenomenographic analysis. *Higher Education, 31*, 25-50.

Vermunt, J. D. H., & Van Rijswijk, F. A. W. M. (1987). *Inventaris leerstijlen voor het hoger onderwijs* (Inventory of Learning Styles for Higher Education). Tilburg. Netherlands: Katholieke Universiteit Brabant.

Ververidis, D., & Kotropoulos C. (2006). Emotional speech recognition: Resources, features, and methods. *Speech Communication, 48*, 1162-1181.

Verwey, W., Veltman, H. (1996). Detecting short periods of elevated workload: A comparison of nine workload assessment techniques. *Journal of Experimental Psychological Applications 2*(3), 270–285.

Vick, R., Auernheimer, B., Iding, M., & Crosby, M. (2006). Quality assurance during distributed collaboration: A case study in creating a cross-institutional learning community. In F. Dias (Ed.), *Managing learning in virtual settings* (pp. 274-289). Hershey, PA: Information Science Publishing.

Vigotski, L. S. (2007). *A formação social da mente* (7th Ed., pp. 87-105). Brasil: Martins Fontes.

Villaverde, J. E., Godoy, D., & Amandi, A. (2006). Learning styles' recognition in e-learning. *Journal of Computer Assisted Learning, 22*, 197-206.

Visual modularity. (2009). Retrieved January 13, 2009, from http://en.wikipedia.org/wiki/Visual_modularity

Vogel, E.K., Woodman, G.F., & Luck, S.J. (2001). Storage of features, conjunctions and objects in visual working memory. *Journal of Experimental Psychology: Human Perception and Performance, 27*, 92-114.

Vovides, Y., Sanchez-Alonso, S., Mitropoulou, V., & Nickmans, G. (2007). The use of elearning course management systems to support learning strategies and to improve selfregulated learning. *Educational Research Review, 2*(1), 64-74.

VRML Sourcebook V2.0 on-line examples (2008). Retrieved November 12, 2008, from http://www.wiley.com/legacy/compbooks/vrml2sbk/cover/cover.htm

VRML Wikipedia definition. (2008). Retrieved November 12, 2008, from http://en.wikipedia.org/wiki/VRML

Vuorikari, R. (2004). *Results from the OASIS pilot, OASIS project deliverable*. Retrieved May 07, 2008, from http://www.eun.org/insight-pdf/5_5_3_Oasis_Deliverable_final.pdf

Vygotsky, L. (1962). *Thought and language* (E. Hanfman & G. Backer, Trans.). Cambridge, MA: M.I.T. Press.

Vygotsky, L. (1998). *A formacao social da mente: O desenvolvimento dos processos psicologicos superiores.* Martins Fontes.

Vygotsky, L. S. (1978). *Mind in society: The development of higher psychological processes.* Cambridge, MA: Harvard University Press.

Wagner, E. D. (2005). Enabling mobile learning. *EDUCAUSE Review, 40*(3), 40-53.

Wainer, H. (2000). CATs: Whither and whence. *Psicologica, 21*(1-2), 121-133.

Walker, A. (2001). British psychology students' perceptions of group-work and peer assessment. *Psychology Learning and Teaching, 1*, 28-36.

Walther, J. B. (1996). Group and interpersonal effects in international computer-mediated collaboration. *Human Communication Research, 23*(3), 342-369.

Wands, B. (2006). *Art of the digital age.* UK: Thames & Hudson.

Wang, T., Wang, K., & Huang, Y. (2008). Using a style-based ant colony system for adaptive learning. *Expert Systems with Applications, 34*(4), 2449-2464.

Warner-Rogers, J., & Reed, J., (2008). A clinician's guide to child neuropsychological assessement and formulation. In J. Warner-Rogers & J. Reed (Eds.), *Child neuropsychology: Concepts, theory and practice* (pp. 432-449). Singapore: Wiley-Blackwell.

Warwick, K. (1998). *March of the machines. In the mind of the machine: The breakthrough in artificial intelligence.* London: Arrow.

Wasserman, S., & Faust, K. (1994). *Social network analysis: Methods and applications.* Cambridge, UK: Cambridge University Press.

Watabe, K., Hamalainen, M., & Whinston, A. B. (1995). An Internet based collaborative distance learning system: CODILESS. *Computers & Education, 24*(3), 141-155.

Web Accessibility Initiative. (2005). *WAI: Strategies, guidelines, resources to make the Web accessible to people with disabilities.* Retrieved May 15, 2008, from http://www.w3.org/WAI/intro/accessibility.php

Web3D consortium. (2008). Retrieved November 12, 2008, from http://www.web3d.org/

Webb, N. M. (1992). Testing a theoretical model of student interaction and learning in small groups. In R. Hertz-Lazarowitz & N. Miller (Eds.), *Interaction in cooperative group: The theoretical anatomy of group learning* (pp. 102-119). Cambridge, UK: Cambridge University Press.

Webb, N. M., & Farivar, S. (1999). Developing productive group interaction in middle school mathematics. In A. M. O'Donnel & A. King (Eds.), *Cognitive perspectives on peer learning* (pp. 117-149). Mahwah, NJ: Lawrence Erlbaum Associates.

Webb, N. M., & Palinscar, A. S. (1996). Group processes in the classroom. In D. C. Berliner & R. Caffee (Eds.), *Handbook of educational psychology* (pp. 841-873). New York: Macmillan.

Weber, G., & Brusilovsky, P. (2001). ELM-ART: An adaptive versatile system for Web-based instruction. *International Journal of Artificial Intelligence in Education, 12*(4), 351-384.

Weber, K. (1982). *The teacher is the key.* Milton Keynes: The Open University Press.

Wehrle, T., & Kaiser, S. (2000). Emotion and facial expression. In A. Paiva (Ed.), *Affect in interactions: Towards a new generation of interfaces,* (pp. 49-64). Heidelberg: Springer.

Weinberger, A., & Fischer, F. (2006). A framework to analyze argumentative knowledge construction in computer-supported collaborative learning. *Computers & Education, 46,* 71-95.

Weiner, B. (1992). *Human motivation.* Sage Publications, Inc.

Weller, M. (1992). *Delivering learning on the Net: The why, what and how of online education.* London: Kogan Page.

Weller, M. (2007). The distance from isolation: Why communities are the logical conclusion in e-learning. *Computers & Education, 49*(2), 148-159.

Wellington. (2009). Retrieved February 16, 2009, from http://wellingtonlorddemon.blogspot.com/

Wellman, B., Hass, A. Q., Witte, J., & Hampton, K. (2001). Does the Internet increase, decrease, or supplement social capital? Social networks, participation, and community commitment. *The American Behavioral Scientist, 45*(3), 436-455.

Wenger, E. (1998). *Communities of practice: Learning, identity, and meaning.* Cambridge, UK: Cambridge University Press.

Wenger, E. (2002). *Cultivating communities of practice.* Cambridge, MA: Harvard Business School Press.

Wenger, P., & Goldin, D. (2006). Principles of problem solving. *Communications of ACM, 49*(7), 27-29.

West-Burnham, J., & Coates, M. (2005). *Personalizing learning.* Stafford: Network Educational Press.

Wheeler, M. (2005). *Reconstructing the cognitive world.* Cambridge, MA: MIT Press.

Whitby, B. (1996). *Reflections on artificial intelligence. The legal, moral and ethical dimensions.* Exeter, UK: Intellect Books.

Widyanto, L., & McMurran, M. (2004). The psychological properties of the Internet addiction test. *CyberPsychology & Behavior, 7*(4), 443-450.

Wiederhold, B., Jang, D., Kaneda, M., Cabral, I., Lurie, Y., May, T., Wiederhold, M., & Kim, S. (2003). An investigation into physiological responses in virtual environments: An objective measurement of presence. In G. Riva & C. Galimberti (Eds.), *Towards cyberpsychology: Minds, cognitions and society in the Internet age* (pp. 175-184). Amsterdam: IOS Press.

Wieland, R. (1999). Mental workload in VDU-assisted office work: Consequences for the design of telework. *Zeitschrift Fur Arbeits-Und Organisationaspsychologie, 43,* 153-158.

Wikipedia Augmented Reality definition, (2008). Retrieved November 12, 2008, from http://en.wikipedia.org/wiki/Augmented_reality

Wikipedia Data mining. (2008). Retrieved November 12, 2008, from http://en.wikipedia.org/wiki/Data_mining

Wikipedia Feuerstein. (2008). Retrieved November 12, 2008, from http://en.wikipedia.org/wiki/Reuven_Feuerstein

Wikipedia Institutes for Achievement of Human Potential (2009). Retrieved January 11, 2009, from http://en.wikipedia.org/wiki/The_Institutes_for_the_Achievement_of_Human_Potential

Wikipedia Scripting_languages. (2008). Retrieved January 11, 2009, from http://en.wikipedia.org/wiki/Scripting_languages

Wikipedia solidarity economy, (2008). Retrieved November 12, 2008, from http://en.wikipedia.org/wiki/Solidarity_economy

Wikipedia Synapse. (2009). Retrieved January 11, 2009, from http://en.wikipedia.org/wiki/Chemical_synapse

Wikipedia Virtual Reality definition. (2008). Retrieved November 12, 2008, from http://en.wikipedia.org/wiki/Virtual_reality

Wikipedia Waltz with Bashir. (2009). Retrieved April 9, 2009, from http://en.wikipedia.org/wiki/Waltz_with_Bashir

Wikipedia. (2007). *Electronic learning.* Retrieved October, from http://en.wikipedia.org/wiki/E-Learning

Willging, P. A. (2007). Online interactions: Comparing social network measures with instructors' perspectives. In R. Zheng & S. P. Ferris (Eds.), *Understanding online instructional modeling: Theories and practices* (pp. 150-167). Hershey, PA: Information Science Reference.

Williams, E. (1992). Student attitudes towards approaches to learning and assessment. *Assessment & Evaluation in Higher Education, 17,* 45-58.

Williams, K. D., & Karau, S. J. (1991). Social loafing and social compensation: The effects of expectations of co-worker performance. *Journal of Personality and Social Psychology, 61,* 570-581.

Wilson, G., & Sasse, A. (2002). Listen to you heart rate: Counting the cost of media quality. In *Proceedings of the International Conference on Intelligent Tutoring Systems, 6.* Biarritz, France.

Wing, J. M. (2006). Computational thinking. *Communications of the ACM, 49*(3). Retrieved November 12, 2008, from http://www.cs.cmu.edu/afs/cs/usr/wing/www/publications/Wing06.pdf

Wingo, G. M. (1997). *Philosophies of education: An introduction.* Boston, MA: Houghton Mifflin.

Winkler, T., Reimann, D., Herczeg, M., & Hopel, I. (2003). Creating digital augmented multisensual learning spaces. In *Mensch & Computer 2003: Interaktion in Bewgung. Stuttgart: B.G. Teubner* (pp. 307-316). Retrieved November 12, 2008, from http://mc.informatik.uni-hamburg.de/konferenzbaende/mc2003/konferenzband/muc2003-30-winkler.pdf

Wise, S. L., Barnes, L. B., Harvey, A. L. & Plakes, B. S. (1989). Effects of computer anxiety and computer experience on the computer-based achievement test performance of college students. *Applied Measurement in Education, 2*(3), 235-24.

Wise, S. L., Roos, L. R., Plake, B. S., & Nebelsick-Gullett, L. J. (1994). The relationship between examinee anxiety and preference for self-adapted testing. *Applied measurement in education, 7*(1), 81-91.

Witkin, H. A. (1962). *Psychological differentiation: Studies of development.* New York: Wiley.

Witkin, H. A., & Goodenough, D. R. (1977). Field dependence and interpersonal behavior. *Psychological Bulletin, 84,* 661-689.

Witkin, H. A., Moore, C. A., Goodenough, D. R., & Cox, P. W. (1977). Field dependent and field independent cognitive styles and their educational implications. Review of Educational Research, 47(1), 1-64.

Witkin, H. A., Moore, C. A., Goodenough, D. R., & Cox, P. W. (1977). Field-dependent and field-independent cognitive styles and their educational implications. *Review of Education Research, 47,* 1-64.

Witkin, H. A., Oltman, P. K., Raskin, E., & Karp, S. A. (1971). *Group embedded figures test manual.* Palo Alto, CA: Consulting Psychology Press.

Witkin, H. A., Oltman, R., Raskin, E., & Karp, S. (1971). *A manual for embedded figures test.* Palo Alto, CA: Consulting Psychologists Press.

Witmer, D. F. (1998). Introduction to computer-mediated communication: A master syllabus for teaching communication technology. *Communication Education, 47,* 162-173.

Woldridge, M. (1999). Intelligent agents. In G. Weiss (Ed.), *Multi-Agent system* (pp. 27-28). Cambridge, MA: The MIT Press.

Wolf, C. (2002). iWeaver: Towards an interactive Web-based adaptive learning environment to address individual learning styles. In *Procs. of the ICL 2002.*

Wolfe, C.R. (2001). Learning and teaching on the world wide Web. In C.R. Wolfe (Ed.), *Learning and teach-*

ing on the world wide Web (pp. 1-22). San Diego, CA: Elsevier.

Womack, B.D., & Hansen, J.H.L. (1996). Classification of speech under stress using target driven features. *Speech Comm. 20*, 131-150.

Womack, B.D., & Hansen, J.H.L. (1999). N-channel hidden Markov models for combined stressed speech classification and recognition. *IEEE Trans. Speech Audio Processing 7*(6), 668-677.

Wood, F. B., Flowers, D. L., & Naylor, C. E. (1991). Cerebral laterality in functional neuroimaging. In F. L. Kitterle (Ed.), *Cerebral laterality: Theory and research.* New Jersey: Lawrence Erlbaum.

Woodman, G.F., Vogel, E.K., & Luck, S.J. (2001). Visual search remains efficient when visual working memory is full. *Psychological Science, 12*, 219-24.

Woodruff, E. (2002). CSCL communities in post-secondary education and cross-cultural settings. In T. Kochmann, R. Hall, & N. Miyake (Eds.), *CSCL 2: Carrying forward the conversation* (pp. 157-168). Mahwah, NJ: Lawrence Erlbaum Associates.

Wopereis, I. G. J. H., Kirschner, P. A., Paas, F., Stoyanov, S., & Hendriks, M. (2005). Failure and success factors of educational ICT projects: A group concept mapping approach. *British Journal of Educational Technology, 36*, 681-684.

Workman, M. (2004). Performance and perceived effectiveness in computer-based and computer-aided education: Do cognitive styles make a difference? *Computers in Human Behavior, 20*(4), 517-534.

Workman, M. (2005). Virtual team culture and the amplification of team boundary permeability on performance. *Human Resource Development Quarterly, 16*, 435-458.

Workman, M. (2006). Virtual communities and imaginary friends: Affiliation and affection from afar. *Proceedings from the Annual Conference on Technology and Innovation, CTI'06* (pp. 122-131), Stowe, VT.

Workman, M. (2007). Virtual team performance and the proximal-virtual team continuum. *Journal of the American Society for Information Science and Technology, 58*, 794-801.

Workman, M., Kahnweiler, W., & Bommer, W. H. (2003). The effects of cognitive style and technology media on commitment to telework and virtual teams. *Journal of Vocational Behavior, 63*, 199-219.

X3D Earth Implementation Workshop. (2008). Retrieved January 12, 2009, from http://www.web3d.org/x3d/publiclists/x3dpublic_list_archives/0802/pdf1lG2Re5un9.pdf

X3D Working Group. (2008) Retrieved November 12, 2008, from http://www.web3d.org/x3d-earth/

Yacoob, Y., & Davis, L. S. (1996). Recognizing human facial expressions from log image sequences using optical flow. *IEEE Transactions on Pattern Analysis and Machine Intelligence, 18*(6), 636-642.

Yakimovicz, A. D., & Murphy, K. L. (1995). Constructivism and collaboration on the Internet: Case study of a graduate class experience. *Computers & Education, 24*(3), 203-209.

Yamamoto E., Nakamura, S., & Shikano, K. (1998). Lip movement synthesis from speech based on Hidden Markov Models. *Speech Communication, 26*, 105-115.

Yamamoto, C. C. (2009). *Does learning a musical instrument help make your child smarter?* Retrieved January 12, 2009, from http://www.honoluluadvertiser.com/article/20090107/GETPUBLISHED/901060366/-1/sportsfront

Yates, G. C. R. (2000). Applying learning styles research in the classroom: Some cautions and the way ahead. In R. J. Riding & S. G. Rayner (Eds), *International perspectives on individual differences. Cognitive styles* (pp. 347-364). Stamford, CT: Ablex.

Yoder, J. D., & Hochevar, C. M. (2005). Encouraging active learning can improve students, performance on examinations. *Teaching of Psychology, 32*(2), 91-95.

YouTube Estrelas. (2009). Retrieved March 21, 2009, from http://www.youtube.com/watch?v=UXOMw_Y1V-4

YouTube, (2009). *Modern times.* Retrieved March 21, 2009, from http://www.youtube.com/results?search_type=&search_query=modern+times&aq=f

Yu, F. Y., Liu, Y. H., & Chan, T. W. (2005). A Web-based learning system for question-posing and peer assessment. *Innovations in Education and Teaching International, 42,* 337-348.

Zaharias, P. (2005). E-learning design quality: A holistic conceptual framework. In C. Howard, J. Boettcher, L. Justice, K. Schenk, P. L. Rogers, & G. A. Berg (Eds.), *Encyclopaedia of distance learning* (Vol. II). Hershey, PA: Idea Group Publishing.

Zakour, J., Foust, J., & Kerven, D., (1997). *HTML How-To.* US: Waite Group Press.

Zhang, S. (1995). Reexamining the affective advantage of peer feedback in the ESL writing class. *Journal of Second Language Writing, 4,* 209-222.

Zhang, X., Mostow, J., & Beck, J. E. (2007, July 9). All in the (word) family: Using learning decomposition to estimate transfer between skills in a Reading Tutor that listens. In *AIED2007 Educational Data Mining Workshop,* Marina del Rey, CA. Retrieved November 12, 2008, from http://www.cs.cmu.edu/~listen/pdfs/AIED2007_EDM_Zhang_ld_transfer.pdf

Zheng, R. (2006). From WebQuests to virtual learning: A study on student's perception of factors affecting design and development of online learning. In S. Ferris, & S. Godar (Eds.), *Teaching and learning with virtual teams* (pp. 53-82). Hershey, PA: Information Science Reference.

Zheng, R., & Ferris, S. P. (Eds.). (2007). *Understanding online instructional modeling: Theories and practices.* Hershey, PA: Information Science Reference.

Zheng, R., Yang, W., Garcia, D., & McCadden, E. (2008). Effects of multimedia on schema induced analogical reasoning in science learning. *Journal of Computer Assisted Learning.* doi: 10.1111/j.1365-2729.2008.00282.x

Zhou, G., Hansen, J.H.L., & Kaiser, J.F. (2001). Nonlinear feature based classification of speech under stress. *IEEE Trans. Speech Audio Processing, 9*(3), 201-216.

Zimmerman, (2008). Investigating self-regulation and motivation: historical background, methodological developments, and future prospects. *American Educational Research Journal, 45*(1), 166-183.

Zinn, C. (2006). Bootstrapping a semantic wiki application for learning mathematics. In S. Schaffert & Y. Sure (Eds.), *Semantic systems: From visions to applications. Proc. of the Semantics 2006 conference.* ACS.

Zoakou, A., Tzanavari, A., Papadopoulos, G. A., & Sotiriou, S. (2007). A methodology for elearning scenario development: The UNITE approach. In *Proceedings of the ECEL2007 - European Conference on e-Learning,* Copenhagen, Denmark (pp. 683-692). ACL publications.

Zoakou, A., Tzanavari, A., Zammit, M., Padgen, A., MacRae, N., & Limanauskiene, V. (2006). *D5.1: Elearning scenario map and generic elearning scenarios* (UNITE public deliverable). Retrieved May 07, 2008, from http://www.unite-ist.org

Zuffo, M. K., (2001). *A convergência da realidade virtual e internet avançada em novos paradigmas de TV digital interativa.* Tese de Livre Docência. Retrieved November 23, 2008, from http://www.lsi.usp.br/~mkzuffo/repositorio/producao/teses%20e%20dissertacoes/Tese_Livre_Docencia_Marcelo_Zuffo.pdf

About the Contributors

Constantinos Mourlas is Assistant Professor in the National and Kapodistrian University of Athens (Greece), Department of Communication and Media Studies since 2002. He obtained his PhD from the Department of Informatics, University of Athens in 1995 and graduated from the University of Crete in 1988 with a Diploma in Computer Science. In 1998 was an ERCIM fellow for post-doctoral studies through research in STFC, UK. He was employed as Lecturer at the Univeristy of Cyprus, Department of Computer Science from 1999 till 2002. His previous research work focused on distributed multimedia systems with adaptive behaviour, Quality of Service issues, streaming media and the Internet. His current main research interest is in the design and the development of intelligent environments that provide adaptive and personalized context to the users according to their preferences, cognitive characteristics and emotional state. He has several publications including edited books, chapters, articles in journals and conference contributions. Dr. C. Mourlas has taught various undergraduate as well as postgraduate courses in the Dept. of Computer Science of the University of Cyprus and the Dept. of Communication and Media Studies of the University of Athens. Furthermore, he has coordinated and actively participated in numerous national and EU funded projects.

Nikos Tsianos is a research assistant and doctoral candidate at the New Technologies Laboratory of the Faculty of Communication and Media Studies of the University of Athens. He holds an Msc in Political Communication from the University of Athens. His main research area is the incorporation of theories from the Psychology of Individual Differences into Adaptive Educational Hypermedia, the development of corresponding systems and the empirical evaluation of such systems in the context of an experimental psychology methodology. He has published numerous articles in conferences and journals regarding this field of research, while he also participates in a number of national and EU funded projects, including research on locative media and mobile applications.

Panagiotis Germanakos, PhD, is a Research Scientist, in the Laboratory of New Technologies, Faculty of Communication & Media Studies, National & Kapodistrian University of Athens and of the Department of Computer Science, University of Cyprus. He obtained his PhD from the University of Athens in 2008 and his MSc in International Marketing Management from the Leeds University Business School in 1999. His BSc was in Computer Science and also holds a HND Diploma of Technician Engineer in the field of Computer Studies. His research interest is in Web Adaptation and Personalization Environments and Systems based on user profiling/filters encompassing amongst others visual, mental and affective processes, implemented on desktop and mobile / wireless platforms. He has several publications, including co-edited books, chapters, articles in journals, and conference contributions.

Furthermore, he actively participates in numerous national and EU funded projects that mainly focus on the analysis, design and development of open interoperable integrated wireless/mobile and personalized technological infrastructures and systems in the ICT research areas of e-Government, e-Health and e-Learning and has an extensive experience in the provision of consultancy of large-scaled IT solutions and implementations in the business sector.

* * *

Ray Adams is the Founder and Centre Head for CIRCUA (Collaborative International Research Centre for Universal Access) that is based in the School of engineering and Information Sciences at Middlesex University. He is also a member of Churchill College, Cambridge. He is on the conference boards for a number of international conferences. He is also on the editorial board of two journals; Universal Access in the Information Society and Advances in HCI. He has published three books and a significant number of papers. His research interests include: human cognition, user modeling, universal access and research methods.

Gláucia Almeida is an Arts Educator that works for São Paulo Municipal Schools Network. She is graduated in Arts with focus on music at the Mozarteum Faculty of São Paulo.

Zoe Bablekou acquired her first degree in the University of Ioannina, Greece and her P-G Diploma in the Institute of Education of the University of London. She was awarded a PhD on memory processes from the Department of Psychology of the University of Leeds. She currently is an Associate Professor in Developmental and in Cognitive Psychology with the Aristotle University of Thessaloniki, Department of Early Childhood Education. Her research interests focus on memory and language in children, with particular reference on WM structure and operations.

Ana Luiza Bertelli Furtado Leite is a Math Educator that works for the São Paulo Municipal Schools. She is graduated in science with focus on Math, Physics and Chemistry at Faculdade Tereza Martin and Universidade de Arara Professor Edmuldo Ulson - UNAR. She also did two years of Architecture at Faculdade de Belas Artes de São Paulo.

William Billingsley. After four years working in the telecommunications industry, William Billingsley undertook his PhD in the University of Cambridge's Computer Laboratory, where he worked on Intelligent Books. He received his PhD in 2007, and became a research associate with the university's Centre for Applied Research in Educational Technology (CARET). In 2009, he became a senior research engineer with National ICT Australia, a computer science research centre established by the Australian Government. His latest research is part of a project working with Queensland Health to develop a system using video and transcript analysis to improve the communication skills training of clinicians and medical students.

Hichang Cho is an assistant professor of the Communications and New Media Programme, National University of Singapore. His current research focuses on computer-mediated communication (CMC), computer-supported collaborative learning (CSCL), and online privacy.

Maja Ćukušić is a teaching assistant at the Faculty of Economics, University of Split, Croatia. She holds BSc degree in Computer Science from the Faculty of Organization and Informatics, University of Zagreb and has just submitted her master thesis. She had worked as an IT consultant in an international holding company for over 3 years prior to her university employment. She teaches Information Technologies, Electronic Business, ERP Systems and Business Intelligence. Her research interests range from IT management and organization to implementation of complex ICTs, Internet technologies, social software and eLearning systems.

Laura B. Dahl is a faculty member in the College of Continuing Education at the University of Utah. Her research interests are multimedia and cognition, human-computer interaction, and educational technology. Laura worked as a software and web developer, and has spent years designing and teaching technology courses. She frequently conducts workshops on technology integration to faculty at higher education institute.

Marlene Gonçalves da Silva Freitas is a math educator that works for both municipal and state schools in the city of São Paulo. She is also a Pedagogue with focus in management.

Roseli de Deus Lopes is a Professor and researcher of the Department of Engineering of Electronic Systems at the Polytechnic School of the University of São Paulo – USP and director of the Estação Ciência of USP. She is graduated, master and doctor in Electrical Engineering at the Polytechnic School of USP. Her research interests are related to interactive electronic media, including computer graphics, image processing, interaction devices, visualization techniques and virtual reality. She has links with national and international technical organizations such as (Sociedade Brasileira de Computação - SBC), (The Institute of Electrical and Electronics Engineering - IEEE) and (Association for Computing Machinery - ACM). She coordinates researches in the field of collaborative learning supported by interactive electronic media and game development. She also coordinates the (Feira Brasileira de Ciências e Engenharia – FEBRACE 'Brazilian Fair of Sciences and Engineering'). And she contributes with the group of pedagogic consultancy referent to the implementation of the project Um Computador por Aluno – UCA, which is run by Secretaria de Educação à Distância SEED/MEC.

Jorge Ferreira Franco is graduated in Portuguese and English, and is postgraduated in Pedagogy in Brazil. He concluded his master degree in Virtual Environments at the University of Salford, England. He is doing his PhD research in Electrical Engineering at (the Escola Politécnica da USP 'Polytechnic School of the University of São Paulo') with research focus on Interactive Technologies for supporting Education. Currently, he works for the São Paulo Municipal School Network as an Information and Communication Technology Facilitator at the Laboratory of a Primary Municipal School in the city of São Paulo. He is also a researcher at the Laboratório de Sistemas Integráveis da POLI-USP and the NATE (Núcleo de Aprendizagem, Trabalho e Entretenimento), in which he collaborates with the implementation of the project Um Computador por Aluno - UCA.

Nilton Ferreira Franco is graduated in History and Geography. Currently, he is a History educator that works for the São Paulo State Schools. He is post graduated in Psychopedagogy. His Master course was in History of Art and Culture at Universidade Presbiteriana Mackenzie. During his Master course he investigated about the Sarau as a popular movement in the periphery of the city of São Paulo.

Jill A. Flygare is currently a faculty member in the Department of Teaching & Learning. She holds a BA in Secondary Social Sciences and a M. Ed in Instructional Design and Educational Technology. Her research interests are in the area of effective online design and online social communication.

Victor Manuel García-Barrios is key researcher and project manager at the Institute for Information Systems and Computer Media (IICM) at Graz University of Technology as well as lecturer at Graz University of Applied Sciences (Campus02). Since 1999 he has been involved in many IICM projects, such as the research projects AdeLE (adaptive e-learning with eye-tracking), MISTRAL (semantic multimodal information management), and APOSDLE (process-oriented, self-directed, work-integrated learning). In the last years he has published numerous papers in renowned international conferences and journals. At present, his research areas include e-learning, adaptive systems, privacy enhancement technologies.

Geri Gay is the Kenneth J. Bissett Professor and Chair of Communication at Cornell University and a Stephen H. Weiss Presidential Fellow. She is also a member of the Faculty of Computer and Information Science and the director of the Human Computer Interaction Lab at Cornell University. Her research focuses on social and technical issues in the design of interactive communication technologies. Specifically, she is interested in social navigation, affective computing, social networking, mobile computing, and design theory.

Martin Graff is a Reader in Psychology at the University of Glamorgan. He is an Associate Fellow of the British Psychological Society and a Chartered Psychologist. He is also an executive member of ELSIN a European wide research group dedicated to furthering research in the area of cognitive style. His research interests include cognitive style, the psychology of individual differences, learning from hypertext and e-learning, and he has published widely in these areas. He has also carried out several major consultancy projects evaluating the success of e-learning provision in the UK. His latest book entitled 'Cyber behaviour: Psychological Interaction with Online Environments' is due out next year.

Andrina Granić is an Associate Professor at the Department of Computer Science; University of Split, Croatia. She holds the Doctorate and MSc degrees in Computer Science and the Dipl.-Ing. degree in Electrical Engineering, all from the Faculty of Electrical Engineering and Computing, University of Zagreb. Her research interests are currently focused on both theoretical and application-oriented aspects of universal access, inclusive design, usability, accessibility and smartness, intelligent user interfaces and user models, concerning interactive systems in general and eLearning systems in particular. Dr. Granić was and still is active in a number of national and international R&D projects and has authored or co-authored over fifty papers as book chapters or in international journals and conferences in her area of interest.

Michael Grimley is interested in the enhancement of learning, and in particular as it relates to cognition, motivation, interest, interactivity , new technologies and e-learning. These interests have led him into the study of how technology can be leveraged to improve learning. He currently specializes in the utility of new technologies for education and has a keen interest in learning and individual differences.

Christian Guetl is Assistant Professor and Key Researcher at the MediaLab at Graz University of Technology, Austria, and Adjunct Research Professor at the School of Information Systems, Curtin University of Technology, Perth, WA. He holds a doctoral degree in computer science. His active research is in Information Retrieval and Visualization, Cross-media Information Retrieval, Adaptive E-learning and Personalization, Virtual Worlds for Learning and Knowledge Transfer, and Kowledge & Skill Assessment and Feedback and he is involved in national and international research projects on these topics. He is also involved in the organization of conferences and workshops, such as the IEEE EDUCON, IEEE DEST, ViWo and CAF.

Constantin Halatsis was born in Athens, Greece, in 1941. He received his BSc degree in Physics in 1964 and his MSc degree in Electronics in 1966, both from the University of Athens. In 1971 he received his PhD degree in Computer Science from the University of Manchester, UK. From 1971 to 1981 he was a researcher with the Computer Centre of NRC Demokritos in Athens. In 1981 he became Full Professor of Computer Science at the University of Thessaloniki, Greece, and in 1988 he was invited as Full Professor of CS at the Department of Informatics and Telecommunications of the University of Athens, where he is today since then. He has been visiting at CERN and the University of Cyprus. His teaching, research and development interests cover a wide area, including computer architecture, high performance computing and networking, artificial intelligence, e-government, cryptography, and theory of computation. He has supervised many PhD students, some of whom are now university professor in Greek Universities. He has been project leader or manager of many national and EU funded projects, and has served as consultant in several public and private organizations. He is author/co-author of more than 120 technical papers published in refereed international scientific journals and conference proceedings.

Richard R. Hoffman is a graduate student in the Department of Educational Psychology, University of Utah. His research interests are in instructional design, educational technology, and cognitive processes web-based learning.

Eleni A. Kyza is a Learning Scientist interested in the design and research of innovative, computer-based learning environments. She received her BSc (summa cum laude), with specialization in educational technology from Boston University, an Ed.M. degree in Technology in Education from Harvard University and a PhD degree in the Learning Sciences, with a minor in cognitive science, from Northwestern University. Her studies were funded by Fulbright while her post-doctoral study at the University of Cyprus was supported by a fellowship from the Cyprus Research Promotion Foundation and a Marie Curie Grant. She is a Lecturer in Information Society at the Department of Communication and Internet Studies at the Cyprus University of Technology. For the last four years she has been working on the development and empirical investigation of the web-based learning and teaching platform STOCHASMOS, examining the role of different technological features in supporting reflective inquiry in science education.

Zacharias Lekkas is a research assistant and doctoral candidate at the New Technologies Laboratory of the Faculty of Communication and Media Studies of the University of Athens. He holds an Msc in Occupational Psychology from the University of Nottingham. He is interested in the role of emotions in web-based educational systems, and has conducted empirical research on the effect of human factors such as anxiety, emotional moderation, emotional intelligence, self efficacy etc. Additionally, his research interests include the field of decision making support in Adaptive Hypermedia and the design of personalized training systems. His work has been published in conferences, journals and edited books.

Makis Leontidis is currently a Research Scientist, in the Laboratory of Educational and Language Technology in the Department of Informatics and Telecommunications, National & Kapodistrian University of Athens. He earned a MSc degree in Studies in Education from H.O.U. and a BSc degree in Computer Science from the Department of Informatics and Telecommunications, National & Kapodistrian University of Athens. His research interests are in the area of Affective Computing, Artificial Intelligence, Web Adaptation and Personalization Environments and Emotional Processes, implemented on Web Educational Systems. He has published articles in Journals as well as in numerous refereed Conference Proceedings.

Patricia A. Lowe, PhD, is an Associate Professor and Director of Training of the School Psychology Program in the Department of Psychology and Research in Education at the University of Kansas-Lawrence. She is a 2000 graduate of the School Psychology Program at Texas A&M University in College Station, Texas. Dr. Lowe completed an APPIC postdoctoral internship at the Warm Springs Counseling Center and Training Institute in Boise, Idaho before beginning her academic career at the University of Kansas. Dr. Lowe is a licensed psychologist and licensed school psychologist. Her research interests include the examination of anxiety from a developmental perspective, behavioral and personality assessment, measurement, neuropsychology, and prevention.

Marcos Antonio Matias is a graduate student in Math at Bandeirantes University. He did a technical course in Electric. He has worked as electrical designer and has used to support that the software AutoCAD™.

Theresa Ochoa is an Associate Professor of special education at Indiana University. She develops problem-based learning computer-supported modules for teacher preparation and conducts research on collaborative decision-making among undergraduate students. She earned her PhD from the University of California Santa Barbara in 1999.

Marlene de Oliveira Moreno is a Science Educator that works for both municipal and state schools in the city of São Paulo. She is also a Pedagogue with focus in management.

George A. Papadopoulos (PhD) holds the (tenured) rank of Professor in the Department of Computer Science, University of Cyprus. His research interests include component-based systems, mobile computing, e-health, e-learning, open and distance learning, distributed systems, service oriented computing and cooperative systems. He has published over 100 papers as book chapters or in internationally refereed journals and conferences and he serves in the Editorial Board of 5 international journals. Professor Papadopoulos is a recipient of an 1995 ERCIM-HCM scholarship award. He has been involved or is currently participating, as coordinator or partner, in over 40 internationally and nationally funded projects (total budget for his participation more than 5 MEURO). He is the Director of the Software Engineering and Internet Technologies Laboratory (http://www.cs.ucy.ac.cy/seit). More information can be found at his personal web site at: http://www.cs.ucy.ac.cy/~george

Elena C. Papanastasiou, has received her Honors BSc in Elementary Education from The Pennsylvania State University, and her PhD in Measurement and Quantitative Methods from Michigan State University. Since 2001, Dr. Papanastasiou has worked at the University of Kansas the University of Cyprus and the University of Nicosia. Dr. Papanastasiou is mostly interested in quantitative research in the areas of assessment, test development and psychometrics, and computer adaptive testing. So far, she has published one book and more than 30 peer reviewed articles. She has also presented and co-presented more than 70 papers at conference. Dr. Papanastasiou is also the Director and co-founder of E.P.S. European Psychometric Services, a Cyprus based company that specializes in providing innovative and state-of-the-art assessment solutions and services for governmental agencies, organizations, companies, and education worldwide.

Paula Peres has recently concluded her doctoral at University of Minho. Master in computer science and graduate in Math Computer. She is currently teaching on the computer scientific science area in the Higher Institute of Accounting and Administration of Porto, ISCAP. She is developing many research activities concerning the Integration of the Information Technologies and Communication in higher education context. She has already participated in some initiatives and courses in blended learning mode and she uses these technologies as a support and to complement her learning practices. She has some books published in the information system area and she has also cooperated in e-learning editions.

Pedro C. C. Pimenta (Moçambique, 1964) ended his Chemical Engineering 'Licenciatura' degree in 1988, and finished his 'Doutoramento' on industrial control in 1997, both by Faculdade de Engenharia da Universidade do Porto. Currently, he is an invited teacher at the Departamento de Sistemas de Informação da Escola de Engenharia da Universidade do Minho, lecturing courses on introductory algortihmics and programming, both at the 1st and 2nd study Bologna cycles. His research interests on adoption of TIC in teaching and learning in Higher Education (e-learning) started in 1997, when he joined Universidade do Minho, and spawned recently to the broader theme of social computing. He has participated / contributed to several european projects like Galecia/Socrates, WebEdu/LdV, Omnipaper/IST, Hybrid Moulds/Leonardo, WeKnow/Minerva, and has an active collaboration with several Higher Education Institutions (U. Portucalense, U. Católica, U. Coimbra, ISEP) on the orientation of post-graduation students. He is also member of IEEE and secretary of the Editorial Commitee of IEEE-RITA since 2006.

Elvira Popescu received the PhD degree in Information Systems from the University of Craiova, Romania and the University of Technology of Compiègne, France, in 2008. She is currently a member of the Software Engineering Department, University of Craiova. Her research interests include technology enhanced learning, adaptation and personalization in Web-based systems, intelligent and distributed computing. She authored and co-authored more than 30 papers in international journals and conferences. She received several scholarships and participated in several national and international research projects. Dr. Popescu is actively involved in the research community by serving as program committee member and reviewer for numerous conferences, and co-organizing two international workshops in the area of social and personal computing for web-supported learning communities (SPeL 2008, SPeL 2009).

Francesca Pozzi is presently researcher at the Institute for Educational Technology of the Italian National Research Council (CNR) and has got a PhD in Cultures, Languages and ICT (University of

Genoa). Her major research interests include the design and run of online courses in collaborative learning environments (CSCL), the design of strategies and techniques for fostering collaboration within these contexts, the issues related to monitoring and evaluating the learning process in CSCL field. In her work the theoretical study of models and methods has always been supported by application in real contexts as part of collaboration with a number of state schools, local and national training agencies, public bodies, etc.

Steve Rayner is Professor of Leadership and Diversity in the Department of Education at the University of Gloucestershire, UK. Current activities include work on knowledge transfer in cognitive style research, the development of differential pedagogy in practice, developing educationists' professional learning at doctoral level, intellectual leadership amongst the professoriate in the University sector, and investigating leadership policy to provision for an inclusive and special education. He has in the past fifteen years authored more than 90 publications on individual differences and managing educational inclusion and diversity. He also co-founded and currently leads the European Learning Styles Information Network (ELSIN). Recent publications include *Managing Special and Inclusive Education.* London: Sage; Rayner S., & Peterson, E. (2009) Re-affirming Style as an Individual Difference – Global Paradigm or Knowledge Diaspora? In, LF. Zhang, & R. Sternberg (Eds). *Perspectives on the Nature of Intellectual Styles.* New York: Palgrave Pubs.

Richard Riding has had a long-term research interest in individual differences in learning and behaviour and the ways in which they can be assessed. He has been involved in research work using computer technology in education and training since the early days of personal computers. He studied psychology at the Universities of Hull and Birmingham in the UK. He is a Chartered Psychologist and a Fellow of the British Psychological Society. For over twenty years he was Director of the Assessment Research Unit in the School of Education at the University of Birmingham.

Peter Robinson is Professor of Computer Technology and Deputy Head of the Computer Laboratory at the University of Cambridge in England, where he leads the Rainbow Group working on computer graphics and interaction. His research concerns new technologies to enhance communication between computers and their users, and new applications to exploit these technologies. Recent work has included desk-size projected displays and inference of users' mental states from facial expressions, speech, posture and gestures. He is a Chartered Engineer and a Fellow of the British Computer Society.

Sandra Regina Rodrigues da Cruz is graduated in Science, and Math at the (Pontifícia Universidade Católica - PUC). She is also a pedagogue postgraduated at Universidade de Arara Professor Edmuldo Ulson - UNAR. She works for the São Paulo Municipal School Network. Currently, she is an Information and Communication Technology Facilitator at the Laboratory of a Primary Municipal School Network in the city of São Paulo.

Mien Segers (PhD, 1993, Maastricht University) is a Professor of Educational Sciences at the department of Educational Studies of Leiden University (the Netherlands) and at the department of Educational Development and Research of the University of Maastricht (the Netherlands). Her major research interest are the evaluation and optimisation of collaborative learning in learner-centred learning environments and the qualities of new modes of assessment within these environments in school as well as organizational settings. Professor Segers has authored numerous publications in this area, including articles in *Review of Educational Research, Learning and Instruction, European Journal of Psychology of Education and Instructional Science.*

Dominique Sluijsmans studied Educational Sciences at the Radboud University of Nijmegen. In 2002, she finished her thesis on *Student involvement in assessment* at the Centre for Learning Sciences and Technologies (CELSTEC) of the Open University of the Netherlands. For her thesis, she was awarded by the Netherlands Educational Research Association (NERA). Besides her work as a PhD-student, she also advised teacher teams in higher education in the design of various forms of assessment. Since March 2002 she has been working as an educational technologist at CELSTEC. Currently, she combines this position with an associate professorship at HAN University in Nijmegen, which focuses on sustainable assessment. Her main interests include peer assessment, self assessment, and the effects of assessment on long term learning.

George Ch. Spanoudis received his B.S. and an Msc degree in Developmental Psychology from Aristotle University of Thessaloniki and his PhD degree in Cognitive Psychology with emphasis in developmental and educational Psychology from the University of Cyprus. He is a Lecturer of Psychology at the Psychology Department at the University of Cyprus, Cyprus. His academic interests include developmental psychology, memory, research methods, and learning disabilities. His areas of expertise and research interest include topics related to children's cognitive development, intelligence and language learning impairments. Dr. Spanoudis is currently investigating age-related changes in intelligence using behavioral and event-related potential (ERP) techniques.

Jan-Willem Strijbos (postdoctoral research fellow, Leiden University, the Netherlands). He received his PhD on *The effect of roles in computer-supported collaborative learning* (summa cum laude) in 2004 at the Open University of the Netherland. His fields of expertise are collaborative learning, peer assessment, and peer feedback – in face-to-face and computer-supported settings. He has published widely in the area of computer-supported collaborative learning (CSCL), for example, editing the third volume in the Springer computer-supported collaborative learning (CSCL) book series *What we know about CSCL: And implementing it in higher education* (2004) and a Learning Instruction special issue on *Methodological challenges for collaborative learning research* (2007).

Harm Tillema (senior lecturer, Leiden University, the Netherlands). His field of expertise is professional development and learning, with a special focus on teaching and teacher education. His interest in particular is assessment as a tool of professional learning. He studied the role of (student) teacher beliefs as it affects learning for and in the profession. In his consultancy work, he is involved in establishing powerful learning environments which make use of assessment tools for learning.

Aimilia Tzanavari is an Associate Professor at the Department of Design and Multimedia, University of Nicosia, Cyprus. She is a computer scientist and holds a PhD in Human-Computer Interaction from the University of Bristol, UK. Dr. Tzanavari has previously held academic and research positions at the University of Bristol (UK), Miami University, OH (USA) and the University of Cyprus (CY). She has published and is interested in the areas of Human-Computer Interaction, e-Learning and Accessibility in Design.

Valkiria Venâncio is graduated in Math Education and specialist in interactive technologies applied to education. She does her master course in Electrical Engineering at (the Escola Politécnica da USP'). She is a researcher at the Laboratório de Sistemas Integráveis da POLI-USP and the NATE (Núcleo de Aprendizagem, Trabalho e Entretenimento), in which she collaborates with the development of two educational projects Nave Mário Schemberg and UCA – Um Computador por Aluno. She works as a primary education teacher for the São Paulo Municipal School network. In this network she coordinated the work of the school computers lab. She also trained educators teaching the discipline of Technological Resources in Education.

Michael Workman earned his PhD at Georgia State University in organizational development, and is an associate professor of management at the Florida Institute of Technology. Prior to coming into academic life in 2001, Dr. Workman spent nearly 30 years managing "knowledge workers" and virtual teams at companies such as Digital Equipment Corporation, Unisys and France Telecom/Equant. He has published over 30 manuscripts in scholarly research journals, several textbooks, and dozens of conference proceedings. His research interests are in human-computer interactions and those impacts on human behaviors.

Yin Zhang is an Associate Professor at the Kent State University School of Library and Information Science. She received her B.S. and MS degrees in Information Science from Wuhan University in China and her PhD in Library and Information Science from the University of Illinois at Urbana-Champaign in the United States. Dr. Zhang's research and teaching interests include user information-seeking behavior, information uses and services, information organization, and distance learning. She has published over 30 papers. Dr. Zhang's research has been funded by Institute of Museum and Library Services (IMLS) and her work has been recognized by the Association for Library and Information Science Education (ALISE). Dr. Zhang is currently serving on the Editorial Board for *The Journal of the Research Center for Educational Technology* and the Advisory Board for *The American Society for Information Science & Technology Bulletin*.

Robert Z. Zheng is a faculty member in the Department of Educational Psychology at the University of Utah. His research interests include online instructional design, cognition and multimedia learning, and human-computer interaction. He edited and co-edited several volumes including *Cognitive Effects on Multimedia Learning*; *Online Instructional Modeling: Theories and Practices*; and *Adolescent Online Social Communication and Behavior: Relationship Formation on the Internet*. He has published numerous book chapters and research papers in the areas of multimedia, online learning, and cognition. He has presented extensively at national and international conferences.

Marcelo Knörich Zuffo is titular Professor in the Department of Electronic Systems Engineering at Polytechnic School of the University of São Paulo - USP. His master and PhD courses were in Electrical Engineering. He works for the Laboratory of Integrated Systems of the Polytechnic School at USP where he coordinates research and development related to interactive electronic media focusing on digital TV, telemedicine, virtual reality, computer graphics, and scientific visualization. In 2001 he coordinated the development of the first totally immersive virtual reality system in Brazil called CAVERNA Digital™. He has coordinated the telemedicine onconet network.

Index